974.817
Wallace, Anthony F. C..
EASTON AREA PUBLIC LIB.

3 1901 00240 4061

190192000063 3491

W9-BHO-843

974.817
W187s

Wallace.

St. Clair.

1987

EASTON AREA PUBLIC LIBRARY
6th & CHURCH STS.
EASTON, PA 18042

NO LONGER PROPERTY
OF EASTON AREA
PUBLIC LIBRARY

Also by Anthony F. C. Wallace

THE SOCIAL CONTEXT OF INNOVATION (1982)

ROCKDALE: The Growth of an American Village in the
Early Industrial Revolution (1978)

THE DEATH AND REBIRTH OF THE SENECA (1970)

RELIGION: An Anthropological View (1966)

CULTURE AND PERSONALITY (1961, 1970)

KING OF THE DELAWARES: Teedyuscung, 1700–1763 (1949)

ST. CLAIR

ST. CLAIR

A Nineteenth-Century Coal Town's

Experience with a

Disaster-Prone Industry

ANTHONY F. C. WALLACE

With maps and technical
drawings by Robert Howard

Alfred A. Knopf   New York 1987

EASTON AREA PUBLIC LIBRARY
6th & CHURCH STS.
EASTON, PA 18042

974.817
W187s

THIS IS A BORZOI BOOK
PUBLISHED BY ALFRED A. KNOPF, INC.

Copyright © 1981, 1985, 1987 by Anthony F. C. Wallace
All rights reserved under International and Pan-American Copyright Conventions.
Published in the United States by Alfred A. Knopf, Inc., New York, and
simultaneously in Canada by Random House of Canada Limited, Toronto.
Distributed by Random House, Inc., New York.

Portions of this work were originally published in slightly different form in
Educational Studies and *The Pennsylvania Gazette*.

Library of Congress Cataloging-in-Publication Data
Wallace, Anthony F. C., [date]
St. Clair : a nineteenth-century coal town's
experience with a disaster-prone industry.
Bibliography: p.
Includes index.
1. Coal miners—Pennsylvania—Saint Clair
(Schuylkill County)—History—19th century.
2. Coal mines and mining—Pennsylvania—Saint Clair
(Schuylkill County)—History—19th century.
3. Saint Clair (Schuylkill County, Pa.)—Social
conditions.   I. Title.   II. Title: Saint Clair.
HD8039.M62U6699   1987   307.7′66′0974817   86-46120
ISBN 0-394-52867-0

Manufactured in the United States of America
First Edition

OCT 1   1987

To Helen and Robert Scherr,
whose encouragement and help were indispensable

CONTENTS

ILLUSTRATIONS · ix
TABLES · xi
PREFACE · xiii
CHRONOLOGY · xvi

PROLOGUE: THE RISE AND FALL OF AN INDUSTRY · 3

I MINING ANTHRACITE · 7
The Structure and Operation of an Anthracite Colliery · 8
Some Peculiarities of Coal as a Commodity · 26
Progress and Regression in Colliery Technology 1830–1870 · 30

II THE DEVELOPMENT OF ST. CLAIR · 54
The Owner Families · 55
The Colliery Operators · 70
Early Undertakings of the Carey Group · 78
Anthracite Iron · 85
The St. Clair Project · 93
The Collieries at St. Clair · 101

III A WORKINGMAN'S TOWN · 123
Boom-town Growth from 1845 to 1850 · 125
The Census of 1850 · 130
Ethnicity and Occupation · 133
The Mine Patches · 138
Wages and Subsistence · 141
The Extended Family · 148
Other Benevolent Associations · 154
Tabernacles and Taverns · 159
A Place of Song · 167
The Old Country in the New World · 171

IV ILLUSIONS OF THE COAL TRADE · 184
Henry Carey and Protectionism · 184
Geological Fact and Coal-Trade Fantasies · 200
The Mind of Enoch McGinness · 215
Celebrating the Industrialist as Hero · 228

V THE POLITICS OF SAFETY · 249
Death and Disablement in the Mines · 249
Business Failures · 258
Insurance · 261
The "Careless Miner" and the Erosion of Employer's Liability · 265
The Rise of the Miners' Union · 275
The First Mine Safety Law · 293
The Avondale Disaster · 296
The Mine Safety Law of 1870 · 302
The Effectiveness of the Mine Safety Laws · 305

VI JUSTICE AND VIOLENCE · 314
The Murder of John Reese · 315
The Miners' Journal and the Anti-Irish-Catholic Movement · 320
The Militarization of the Coal Fields · 324
The Pinkerton Spy in St. Clair · 331
"McKenna" Penetrates the Ancient Order of Hibernians · 340
The Gomer James Case · 346
The Great Showcase Trial · 350
Who Were the Molly Maguires? · 358
Justice Denied · 361

VII A STATE CALLED ANTHRACITE · 367
St. Clair in 1870: Demography and Culture · 367
Middle-Class Control of Town Affairs · 376
The Rituals of Civic Solidarity · 380
John Siney and Large-Scale Labor Organization · 388
Franklin B. Gowen and the New Industrial Order · 403
The Rise of the Company State · 417
A Common Ruin · 427

EPILOGUE: The Survival of St. Clair · 439

APPENDIX: The Disaster-Prone Organization · 446

NOTES · 459
BIBLIOGRAPHY · 483
INDEX · 501

ILLUSTRATIONS

Page

5   The Anthracite District in southeastern Pennsylvania (Map by Robert Howard)

5   Pottsville District, Southern Coal Field, 1871 (Map by Robert Howard)

9   Methods of entry to veins of coal (Drawing by Robert Howard)

10   Methods of entry to veins of coal (Daddow and Bannan, *Coal, Iron, and Oil*, 1866)

11   Interior plat of a coal slope (Bowen, "Coal, and the Coal Miners of Pennsylvania," 1857)

12   Working in a near-vertical breast (Daddow and Bannan, *Coal, Iron, and Oil*, 1866)

14   Miner with a lamp (Bowen, *Pictorial Sketch Book of Pennsylvania*, 1852)

16   The coal breaker (Drawing by Robert Howard)

19   The driver boy (Courtesy of the Historical Society of Schuylkill County)

21   Mule train and drivers (Courtesy of the Historical Society of Schuylkill County)

25   The coal depot at Port Carbon (*Frank Leslie's Popular Monthly*, 1877)

29   Breasts in the Mammoth Vein (Chance, *Mining Methods and Appliances*, 1883)

34   Early form of a coal breaker (Bowen, *Pictorial Sketch Book of Pennsylvania*, 1852)

35   Intermediate form of a coal breaker (Bowen, "Coal, and the Coal Miners of Pennsylvania,"1857)

35   Mature form of a coal breaker (Daddow and Bannan, *Coal, Iron, and Oil*, 1866)

38   Robert Allison (1827–?) (Munsell, *History of Schuylkill County*, 1881)

46   Beadle fan (Daddow and Bannan, *Coal, Iron, and Oil*, 1866)

47   Patent drawing of the Beadle fan (U.S. Patent, 1865; courtesy of National Archives and Records Service)

51   Cross and front sections of a steeply sloping breast (John Price Wetherill, "How Anthracite Coal is Mined," 1881)

56   Henry C. Carey (1793–1879), portrait by T. Henry Smith (Courtesy of the Historical Society of Pennsylvania)

63   John Macomb Wetherill (1828–?) (Wiley and Ruoff, *Biographical Cyclopedia of Schuylkill County*, 1893)

66   Repplier's Mammoth Colliery (1862) (Courtesy of the Historical Society of Schuylkill County)

67   Benjamin Bannan (1807–1875) (Munsell, *History of Schuylkill County*, 1881)

71   Benjamin Haywood (1804–1878) (Munsell, *History of Schuylkill County*, 1881)

91   The Pioneer Furnace at Pottsville, 1866 (Daddow and Bannan, *Coal, Iron, and Oil*, 1866)

97   The St. Clair Furnace, 1866, showing both furnace and foundry (Daddow and Bannan, *Coal, Iron, and Oil*, 1866)

101   Johns Eagle Colliery (1866) (Daddow and Bannan, *Coal, Iron, and Oil*, 1866)

Illustrations

108 Map of mine workings under the St. Clair Tract in 1877 (*Annual Reports of the Inspectors of Coal Mines*, 1877; courtesy of the Hagley Library and Museum)

113 Pine Forest Shaft (1866) (Daddow and Bannan, *Coal, Iron, and Oil*, 1866)

115 Hickory Colliery (1866) (Daddow and Bannan, *Coal, Iron, and Oil*, 1866)

145 Miner's cottage at Johns Patch (Photograph by Anthony F. C. Wallace)

149 Girard Estate trustees with miners' children (Courtesy of the Historical Society of Schuylkill County)

193 St. Clair in 1873 (Courtesy of the Historical Society of Schuylkill County)

212 Bowen/McGinness conception of the geology of the Pottsville Basin (Bowen, *Coal and the Coal Trade*, 1862)

212 Daddow's conception of the geology of the Pottsville Basin (Daddow and Bannan, *Coal, Iron, and Oil*, 1866)

212 Geology of the Pottsville Basin as revealed in the Second Geological Survey of 1895 (Lesley, *Geological Survey of Pennsylvania*, 1895)

232 Samuel Harris Daddow (1827–1875) (Schalk and Henning, *History of Schuylkill County*, 1907; courtesy of Historical Society of Pennsylvania)

245 The Henry Clay Monument (Elssler, "History of the Henry Clay Monument," 1910)

248 Early photographs of miners, laborers, breaker boys (*Annual Reports of the Inspectors of Coal Mines*, 1885)

267 John Maguire (1845–1912) (Maguire, "Reminiscences," 1912)

277 Unidentified St. Clair miners (Courtesy of the Historical Society of Schuylkill County)

297 Workers and superintendent at the Eagle Colliery (Courtesy of the Historical Society of Schuylkill County)

298 Removing bodies after the Avondale Colliery disaster (*Harper's Weekly*, 1869; courtesy of the Historical Society of Pennsylvania)

300 Street scene in Avondale after the colliery disaster (*Harper's Weekly*, 1869; courtesy of Special Collections, Van Pelt Library, University of Pennsylvania)

322 *The Miners' Journal* Building (Courtesy of the Historical Society of Schuylkill County)

341 James McParlan (a.k.a. James McKenna), the Pinkerton spy (Courtesy of the Historical Society of Schuylkill County)

365 Map of the explosion in the Wadesville Shaft Colliery (*Annual Reports of the Inspectors of Coal Mines*, 1877; courtesy of Hagley Library and Museum)

371 Property map of St. Clair, 1875 (Beers and Cochran, *County Atlas of Schuylkill, Pennsylvania*, 1875; courtesy of Hagley Library and Museum)

377 East side of St. Clair, looking north to Mine Hill (Courtesy of Robert Scherr)

381 Waiting for the Fourth of July parade (Courtesy of Historical Society of Schuylkill County)

389 John Siney (1831-1880) (Courtesy of Historical Society of Schuylkill County)

405 Franklin Benjamin Gowen (1836–1889) (Courtesy of the Historical Society of Schuylkill County)

432 Head frame of the East Shaft at the Pottsville Twin Shafts Colliery (Courtesy of the Historical Society of Schuylkill County)

440 Wadesville Colliery in 1930 (Courtesy of the Historical Society of Schuylkill County)

442 Bird's-eye view of St. Clair, from a postcard circa 1890 (Courtesy of Robert Scherr)

443 Second Street, St. Clair, looking north (Courtesy of the Historical Society of Schuylkill County)

TABLES

Page

127	TABLE 1	St. Clair Population by Age and Sex, 1845
131	TABLE 2	St. Clair Population by Age and Sex, 1850
134	TABLE 3	Miner/Laborer Status and Ethnicity, 1850
134	TABLE 4	Age of Oldest U.S.-born Child and Ethnicity, 1850
140	TABLE 5	Ethnicity in Rural East Norwegian Township, 1850
141	TABLE 6	Ethnicity in Rural New Castle Township, 1850
372	TABLE 7	Ethnicity of Foreign-born, 1870
372	TABLE 8	Birthplace of Fathers of U.S.-born, 1870
374	TABLE 9	Miner/Laborer Status and Ethnicity, 1870
374	TABLE 10	Property Ownership and Ethnicity, 1850 and 1870
375	TABLE 11	Multiple Property Ownership and Ethnicity, 1851 and 1870
437	TABLE 12	Miner/Laborer Status and Ethnicity, 1880
437	TABLE 13	Artisan/Merchant Status and Ethnicity, 1880

PREFACE

Small towns provide the historian with an opportunity to examine important social and cultural processes in detail. In the case of St. Clair, a coal town, as in my earlier study of the cotton-manufacturing town of Rockdale, we observe a new town arising in the early Industrial Revolution in America. Such matters as the formation of social classes, the interplay of technology and society, and the creation of illusions suitable to the needs of a new industrial world may be looked at close at hand in St. Clair. Other towns in the neighborhood—Pottsville, Tamaqua, Shenandoah, Mahanoy City, Girardville, Centralia, Minersville, to name a few—experienced industrialization in similar ways, as new towns created by the coal trade. But St. Clair is especially appealing because its small size (not over 6,000 souls in the period of study, approximately 1835 to 1880) makes the collation of data more manageable, and because several historically interesting people lived in the town or owned and operated its mines and (a qualification indispensable to the student) left records that have survived. St. Clair was the site of the first vertical deep-shaft mine in the Schuylkill anthracite district, sunk by one Enoch McGinness. St. Clair was for the most part owned by the celebrated publisher and political economist Henry Carey, and his correspondence with McGinness and other figures in the coal trade has been preserved. The land around St. Clair was owned by the Wetherill family of Philadelphia, and many of their business records have also become available. John Siney, the founder of the first effective region-wide miners' union, lived at St. Clair and it was St. Clair miners who organized the first local. Samuel H. Daddow, the author of a book of poetry and some short stories, and co-author of an 1866 handbook of colliery engineering, lived in St. Clair, where he ran the Miners' Supply Company. It was in St. Clair and nearby towns and mine patches that the folklorist George Korson collected many of the songs and ballads of the anthracite miner. And, finally, St. Clair was close enough to Pottsville for its local news to be reported in the pages of the southern anthracite district's leading newspaper, the *Miners' Journal.*

Many persons have helped me in the conduct of the research. I want to express in particular my gratitude to a resident of St. Clair, the former curator of the Historical Society of Schuylkill County, Robert J. Scherr, who personally guided me around the town, shared his library of records and photographs, introduced me to townspeople, and escorted me on a walking tour of the old colliery sites. On his knowledge both of historical sources and of the locality I have relied heavily. My thanks go to several other residents of St. Clair who invited me and my wife into their homes and gave us help in various ways: Edward Delker, former Phillies first baseman and now caretaker of the Odd Fellows Cemetery; Robert Gray, an authority on the Odd Fellows lodge in St. Clair; and Joseph and Doris James, occupants of one of the remodeled miners' houses in Johns' Patch. My special appreciation also goes to my wife, Betty, who undertook the arduous task, of several years' duration, of reading on microfilm all the issues of the weekly *Miners' Journal* from 1853 to 1874 and making notes and photocopies of material relevant to St. Clair and to a variety of general topics. My son Anthony carried out research at the Historical Society of Schuylkill County. I was very generously aided by H. Gordon Smyth, the former owner of the St. Clair Coal Company, which operated on the site of the former Eagle Colliery; Mr. Smyth showed me around the town, discussed the strategy of the research, and very kindly lent me an old letterbook of his grandfather's when he was superintendent of the colliery. And a number of graduate students and staff members at the University of Pennsylvania have assisted me and I want to thank them all: Pam Crabtree, Christopher Dore, Genevieve Fisher, Brenda Gray, Kristine Howard, Denise Jones, Sandra King, Linda Lee, Sophie Luzecky, Robert Maxwell, Nancy Minugh, Margaret Morrissey, Lauris Olson, Deborah Peabody, Wendy Pollock, and Mary Weigelt.

I am grateful to a number of institutions that have supported and facilitated the study. It was begun while I held a Guggenheim Fellowship (1978–1979) devoted to research on the mechanicians who made the inventions essential to the Industrial Revolution (see my *Social Context of Innovation,* Princeton University Press, 1982, for a report on that work). The University of Pennsylvania has annually provided funds to pay research assistants and incidental expenses connected with the research. Two great research libraries have made available manuscript collections that have been indispensable. Eleutherian Mills Historical Library (now renamed Hagley Museum and Library), at Wilmington, Delaware, was, as usual, a wonderful place to work and my thanks are extended to an ever helpful and attentive staff, including Richmond D. Williams, Betty Bright-Low, Daniel Muir, Carole Hallman, Marjorie McNinch, Heddy Richter, and Mary Lou Neighbor. The Historical Society of Pennsylvania, at Philadelphia, is always a treasure trove of manuscript collections, formerly presided over by Peter J. Parker, the present director, with the assistance of Carolyn Park and Linda Stanley. The valuable collections at the Historical Society of Schuylkill County, rich on legal and technical information on collieries, were shown me by curators Robert Scherr and John Joy. At the American Philosophical Society, then-librarian Whitfield Bell kindly drew my attention to the papers of Pottsville mining engineer John Warner, and Murphy Smith showed me the manuscript drawings of Sherman Day. At the Butler Library of Columbia University, Librarian Kenneth A. Lohf kindly made available the Charlemagne Tower Papers. N. Claudette John directed my assistants to the appropriate sources in the Archives of the Insurance Company of North America. At the Pennsylvania State Archives in Harrisburg, Mary Jacobs helped me sort through and select maps of Schuylkill County. Peter Gottlieb discovered and showed me the last few remaining copies of the *Anthracite Monitor,* surviving in the Department of Historical Collections and Labor Archives, of which he is director, at the Pennsylvania State University Library. And at the Smithsonian Institution's Museum of American History and Technology, Extractive Industries Section, Francis Gadsen found for me fifteen volumes of early papers of the Philadelphia and Reading Coal and Iron Company.

And, finally, I should like to thank students and colleagues at a number of institutions and conferences, including the University of Pennsylvania, Lafayette College, Bryn Mawr College, Pennsylvania State University, Drexel University, the University of Indiana, Wayne State University, Tufts University, Massachusetts Institute of Technology, the Anthracite Museum at Scranton, the Smithsonian Institution, the American Philosophical Society, the American Educational Studies Association, the Pennsylvania Historical Association, the American Anthropological Association, the Society for Industrial Archeology, and Eleutherian Mills Historical Library for listening to me talk about the St. Clair study and for offering stimulating questions and interpretations.

Anthony F. C. Wallace
Philadelphia, Pennsylvania

CHRONOLOGY

1825   Schuylkill Canal constructed
1828   Wetherill group in possession of coal lands around St. Clair
1829   Mill Creek and Mine Hill Railroad connects St. Clair with Port Carbon
1835   Carey group purchases coal lands at Westwood, Pottsville, and St. Clair; Pinkerton commences mining at St. Clair
1836   First Geological Survey of Pennsylvania begins
1837   Financial panic
1838   Rogers' geological report criticizes coal in Pottsville district
1839   Pioneer Furnace at Pottsville makes anthracite iron
1842   Carey group begins development of St. Clair; Reading Railroad reaches Pottsville; protective tariff passed
1843   Coal breaker patented by Battin
1844   Reading Railroad reaches Port Carbon
1845   Lawton sinks test shaft at St. Clair; Snyder and Haywood sink Pine Forest Slope
1846   St. Clair furnace put in blast; murder of John Reese
1847   Trial of Martin Shay for murder of John Reese
1849   Johns brothers begin Eagle Colliery; Bates Union at St. Clair
1850   St. Clair becomes a borough
1853   The Milnes buy Pinkerton slope and rename it Hickory Colliery
1854   McGinness completes St. Clair Shaft
1855   Dedication of the Henry Clay statue in Pottsville
1857   Beadle invents exhaust fan
1858   "Tamaqua correspondent" publishes 18% casualty estimate in *Miners' Journal*; "Battle of St. Clair"
1859   Testimonial dinner in honor of Carey
1860   Explosion in McGinness' slope
1861   Civil War begins
1862   Irish miners in Cass Township resist conscription
1863   Siney arrives at St. Clair; George K. Smith murdered
1864   Gowen resigns as district attorney in Pottsville and is hired as attorney by Reading Railroad
1865   Civil War ends
1866   Allison pipes live steam over 1,000 feet; Pine Forest Shaft completed
1867   Wadesville Shaft completed; attack on Northall's house; murder of Littlehales
1868   WBA organized
1869   First mine safety law (Schuylkill only); disaster at Avondale

Chronology

1870   Beadle and Daddow patent miner's squib; second mine safety law; Gowen elected president of Reading Railroad

1871   Carey group sells St. Clair Tract to Philadelphia and Reading Coal and Iron Company

1872   Wetherill group sells its coal lands

1873   Detective McParlan arrives in coal region; MNA organized; Gomer James kills Cosgrove

1874   St. Clair Shaft Colliery closed down; detective Cumming in St. Clair; Harriet Baker, the "colored lady evangelist," preaches in Schuylkill; Soldiers' Monument at St. Clair dedicated

1875   The Long Strike and demise of WBA and MNA; coal mined for first time from Twin Shafts; a number of "Molly Maguire" murders (including Gomer James)

1876   Detective "McKenna" flees Shenandoah; trials of Molly Maguires

1877   First of twenty Mollies hanged; explosion in Wadesville Shaft

1878   Last Molly hanged (John Kehoe)

1879   John Siney and Henry Carey die

1880   Reading bankruptcy

1882   Miners' Hospital (state) built at Ashland

1884   Reading bankruptcy

1885   Wadesville Shaft closed down (temporarily); Twin Shafts abandoned

1886   Gowen retires

1888   Gowen commits suicide

ST. CLAIR

PROLOGUE

THE RISE AND FALL OF AN INDUSTRY

South of the Blue Mountain, the farms of the Pennsylvania Dutch country cover a softly rolling countryside in a green-and-brown checkerboard pattern. The Blue Mountain itself runs across the horizon from southwest to northeast, 1,000 feet above the valley, pierced every ten miles or so by a narrow gap. North of this low rampart lies a world of radically different contour. It is a land of narrow ravines and cold streams rushing over tumbled rockfalls, of timbered hills and windswept plateaus and laurel swamps. It is not good farming country, but Indians once hunted here and so too the white men who followed in what the early settlers called "St. Anthony's Wilderness." And since 1825 this has been "the coal region."

The hard coal, or anthracite, beds are not really very extensive, about 484 square miles in all, but they contain—or contained—most of the anthracite in the world. They are located in several narrow bands that run northeasterly between the Blue Mountain and the Susquehannah River. The region is divided into three fields—southern, middle, and northern. The southern field was the first to be developed and its central part, the Pottsville district, with which this book is primarily concerned, was the first to suffer the economic decline that eventually closed down almost all anthracite mining everywhere. In all the fields, the coal lies in dozens of seams, or "veins," as they are called locally, some only a few inches thick and unworkable, some as much as forty feet thick. In the middle and northern fields, the veins lie nearly flat or tilt at moderate angles, but in the southern field the strata have been subjected to more powerful lateral forces in the course of mountain formation, so that they undulate like folds in layers of fabric, sometimes tilting to the vertical. Erosion, especially in the southern field, has sheared off the tops of these folds, so that lines of outcrops of the various veins reach the surface, making the Pottsville district initially attractive to the early miners, who had only to scratch the surface to find and take away coal.

3

The Pottsville Basin, in the northern part of which the town of St. Clair was located, was a coal-rich valley about four miles wide and fifty miles long, running roughly east and west between Sharp Mountain on the south and Broad Mountain on the north. Within the basin, also running east and west, extended several anticlinal axes (long lines of adjacent outcrops). Three of these lines of outcrops, the Delaware Anticlinals, were located half a mile to a mile south of St. Clair, where the Primrose, the Lewis, the Diamond, and other veins surfaced. Several old mine settlements were located along this axis, particularly at Mill Creek, Scalpington, the Delaware Coal Company's East Mines, and Centreville. Another anticlinal axis, the South Mine Hill Anticlinal, ran across the north end of the town, and here outcropped the forty-foot-thick Mammoth Vein. The south dip of the Mammoth lay under the town and the north dip formed a vertical dike as much as seventy feet thick. Between this axis and Mine Hill lay a shallow, short basin of the Mammoth and other veins, with a steeply sloping north side pressed against the flank of Mine Hill, where outcrops emerged again.

The long line of Sharp Mountain just below Pottsville neatly divided the world of the Schuylkill County coal trade into two parts. South, beyond the Blue Mountain, lay most of the markets for anthracite: farms and villages, iron plantations, the major manufacturing towns of Reading and Lancaster, and finally, ninety miles away, over the horizon, the metropolis of Philadelphia. South from the Pottsville Gap, straight down along the banks of the Schuylkill River to Philadelphia, ran the three arteries of transportation: the canal, the railroad, and the turnpike. In Philadelphia, New York, and London lived the men and women who owned the coal lands, owned the railroads and canals, and owned the banks that lent the money to sink the shafts and build the collieries. In and north of Pottsville lived the three main components of the population that was concerned with extracting and shipping the coal: the practical miners and the others who worked at the collieries; the shopkeepers, teachers, doctors, tavern keepers, and artisans who provided goods and services; and the lawyers, engineers, landowners' agents, and government employees who clustered about the county courthouse in Pottsville.

Pottsville was the hub of this system, the point to which most of the coal of Schuylkill County and most of the money from Philadelphia came before being distributed, respectively, south and northward. It was the seat of Schuylkill County, the biggest market and manufacturing center, the center of news and entertainment. In its hinterland, flung out along the

4

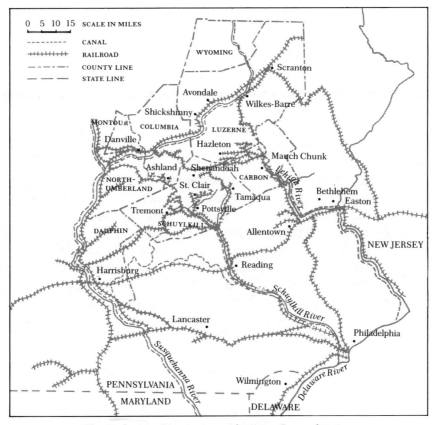

The Anthracite District in southeastern Pennsylvania

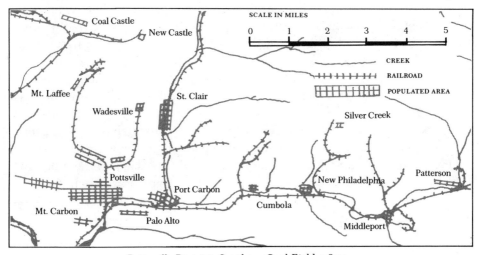

Pottsville District, Southern Coal Field, 1871

streams, railways, and dirt roads that connected Pottsville with the collieries, lay two smaller categories of settlement: the coal towns, with populations of a few thousand and a full complement of stores, schools, tradesmen, doctors, teachers, churches, and taverns, as well as nearby collieries; and mine patches, small outlying hamlets of ramshackle houses nestled at the foot of a coal breaker, providing residence to the families of the miners who worked in a single, more remote colliery. St. Clair was one of the principal coal towns of the Pottsville district.

To businessmen in Philadelphia, Harrisburg and New York, to miners in England and Wales, to poor or landless peasants in Ireland and eastern Europe, the coal regions were—for a time in the nineteenth century—the locus of a dream of wealth and freedom. It seemed to some—for a time— that the 484 square miles of the hard-coal district would become the energy capital of the world. And hard coal did become the fuel that initially made the Pennsylvania iron-and-steel industry the center of the Industrial Revolution in America.

But even as most of America prospered in the mid-nineteenth century, the Pottsville mining district was being blighted. There, the early land-owners and entrepreneurs had invested heavily in what was, for geological reasons, the most difficult part of the entire anthracite region to mine profitably. In the interest of saving money, most colliery operators ignored the best engineering practices of experienced British mine operators and tried to work poorly ventilated, inadequately timbered mines, prone to explosions, roof falls, fires, and floods that killed and crippled hundreds of miners annually and eventually bankrupted almost all colliery operators. But instead of heeding the warnings of geologists, instead of recognizing that the high disaster rate was in large part the cause of the trade's problems, instead of admitting that the high disaster rate was in turn a consequence of unfavorable geology and cheap technology, the owners and operators bemused themselves with illusions. They told themselves and the world that the absence of a high enough tariff on British iron was keeping coal prices too low to make a profit, and that careless miners and Irish revolutionaries were largely responsible for the high rate of disasters. These illusions helped the owners and operators in the Pottsville district, including those at St. Clair, to keep on producing coal to fuel the Industrial Revolution. But the cost, for the miners of St. Clair, was very high.

I

MINING ANTHRACITE

Anthracite or hard coal is the final product of the geological process of coalification. It contains relatively little of the bituminous, volatile hydrocarbons that are present in soft coal and lignite; it is nearly pure carbon, varying (according to nineteenth-century definitions) from about 88 percent to 94 percent carbon by weight. It is very hard and when broken usually produces a shell-shaped (conchoidal) line of fracture. It is heavy: the specific gravity of Schuylkill coal ranges from about 1.5 to 1.6; thus, one cubic yard of solid coal weighs a little over one long ton, and one cubic foot over ninety pounds. Broken coal in the market, however, weighs about half as much per cubic foot. When fully ignited, anthracite burns with a very hot, almost colorless, smokeless flame, retains its structure while burning rather than coalescing in lumps, and yields a small quantity of white or yellowish ("red") ash.[1]

In the ground in Schuylkill, anthracite occurs in a large number of veins, one above the other, separated by thicker or thinner beds of slate and shale. The total thickness of the carboniferous strata, including both coal and slate, must originally have been on the order of three miles, but erosion has reduced the depth in most places to about 2,000 or 3,000 feet. The strata undulate in parallel under the surface like folds in carpeting; along the line of the hills and mountains, the folds have been broken by tectonic forces, tilting the strata backward toward the north. The basins, or lowest folds, are referred to as synclinal axes, and the saddles, or highest folds, as anticlinal axes; both run for miles, roughly east and west, along what is called the thrust or strike of the vein. From each anticline a north dip and a south dip pitch down to separate basins at angles that vary from near 90° to 5°. But erosion has cut across these ancient waves of coal, shaving off mountains to expose outcrops where the top of an ancient anticline has been sliced away, and cutting steep valleys for the south-flowing streams that expose the veins edgewise on either flank.

The methods of mining coal in Schuylkill and the other counties that made up the anthracite region were based on British experience, modified by the unique features of the American situation—the hardness of the mineral, the steeply inclined veins, and the relative scantiness of American capital. By the 1850's the anthracite industry had reached technological maturity; the basic methods of underground mining and of coal processing on the surface have changed little since that time, although underground mining in the twentieth century has been largely replaced by strip mining.

THE STRUCTURE AND OPERATION
OF AN ANTHRACITE COLLIERY[1]

In the first years of the industry, access to the coal was gained by direct quarrying, either cutting a pit down twenty or thirty feet into the coal exposed in an outcrop along a hillside and hauling it up by windlass in large baskets ("corves"), or digging it out of the side of a ravine. But by 1850 the simple quarries had been pretty well exhausted in most places. There were, however, four alternative means of access to coal: drift, tunnel, slope, and shaft. A *drift* was a straight gangway driven directly into the vein along its thrust from its outcrop along the side of a valley or ravine. Tilted slightly upward as it proceeded, the drift drained itself of whatever groundwater might run into the gangway. Outside, the gangway tracks ran over trestles directly to the top of the breaker. A *tunnel mine* was similar to a drift in that access was had via a nearly horizontal entryway that ran into a hillside. But the tunnel was driven into solid rock at right angles to the axis, intercepting the vein deep inside the mountain, where gangways were then run east and west. The *slope* was driven from an outcrop down—generally southward—along the dip of the vein, at whatever pitch the vein took, and at appropriate depths—usually about 100 yards apart—gangways were run east and west. The *shaft* was a vertical hole sunk straight down onto a chosen vein, intercepting it, it was hoped, at the midpoint of a basin, so that not only could gangways be run east and west from the bottom of the shaft, but also coal could be taken from both north and south sides of the gangway.

But, irrespective of the method of entry, the basic plan of colliery operation was the same, for the types of entry were really four different ways of connecting the same underground layout with the same surface layout. The whole colliery was designed to work as a unit so that coal flowed smoothly and continuously from the working face, along the gangways to the entry passage (whether drift, tunnel, slope, or shaft), through

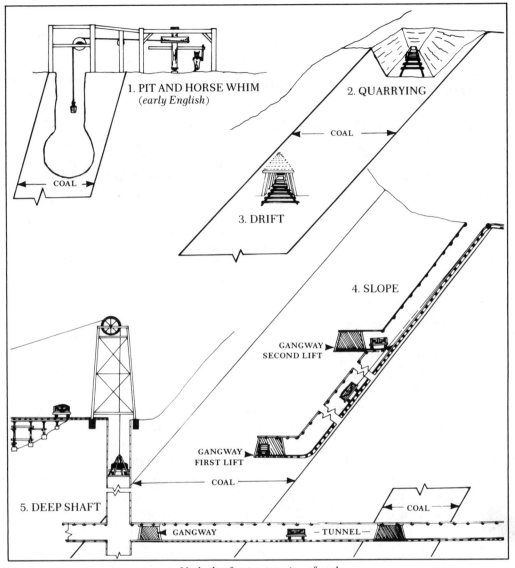

1. PIT AND HORSE WHIM
(early English)

2. QUARRYING

COAL

3. DRIFT

4. SLOPE

GANGWAY
SECOND LIFT

GANGWAY
FIRST LIFT

COAL

5. DEEP SHAFT

COAL

GANGWAY

— TUNNEL —

COAL

Methods of entry to veins of coal

that passage to the breaker, and down into the waiting railroad cars. Mode of entry did have certain important implications, of course. Drifts and tunnels were possible only at those locations above water level where veins were easily accessible along the line of hillside. Slopes and particularly shafts presented difficult problems of drainage and ventilation. But these constraints and risks we shall discuss in detail later. Let us now go on to look more closely at the parts of a colliery as it was designed ideally to operate, above ground and underground.

9

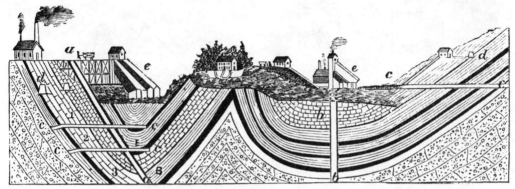

Methods of entry to veins of coal
Key: a–slope   b–shaft   c–tunnel   d–drift   e–breaker 1,2,3–lifts (i.e., levels)
E–Mammoth Vein   B–Buck Mountain Vein

Apart from the entry passage, the underground workings of a Schuylkill County coal mine consisted mainly of two parts: the gangways and the breasts. Two gangways ran east and west from the entry point— i.e., from the end of the tunnel or the bottom of the slope or shaft—toward the boundaries of the operator's lease, a distance on either side that might eventually be two or three miles in length. (The drift by definition was itself a gangway running either east or west.) Gangways were driven straight through the coal, and, if necessary, overlying rock, about seven feet high and nine to ten feet wide. They were graded so as to give a fall of six inches or a foot per 100 feet, to permit drainage water to run in the ditch at one side. Drainage water ran from both gangways to a pit, called a sump, at the bottom of the slope or shaft, where it was pumped out or hauled up in tanks. (Drifts and tunnels drained into the open air.) Here and there a "turnout" was constructed—a section of double width to permit trains to pass—and here the gangway widened to sixteen or more feet. Along the floor of the gangway were laid rails, in the early days wooden, later iron, resting on wooden sills, and on these tracks, pulled by horses or mules, moved the little mine cars, each carrying a load of coal to the entry point, or returning to the breasts for more. Mine cars varied in size and shape from one colliery to the next, depending on the size and condition of the gangway, the power of hoisting equipment, and the dimensions of the entry. In the early 1850's, mine cars held no more than one or two tons, and in some mines even less, the coal being loaded into corves, which one man could hoist, and then placed on small flat cars for hauling. Thirty years later, however, the cars were somewhat larger, on the order of ten feet long, five feet wide, and five and a half feet high from the rail. The content of such a car was about 100 cubic feet and it held, when fully loaded, from two and a half to three long tons of coal. Because cars had to be tailor-made to the needs of each mine, they were built of wood braced with iron in the colliery shops.

The actual passage space in a gangway was reduced by the timbering. Timbering was always needed to support the roof and often also to prevent loose coal and rock from crumbling off the sides and obstructing the track. The size of timber varied and could be massive. The legs and collar used in "heavy" timbering were a foot to a foot and a half in diameter and were set about five feet apart, sometimes with lagging (made from discarded slab wood from sawmills) between ribs to give further protection. Each leg had to be set in a specially cut hole to keep it from slipping, and the collars were forced down on the legs by wedges driven in with sledges. Gangway timbering had to be done with extreme care because the gangway was a permanent construction intended for years of use.

Driving the gangway produced a little marketable coal, but most of the coal was cut out of the seam in separate chambers called "breasts." A breast opened out from the gangway on the uphill side so that, as the miner and his laborer removed coal from the face, the coal would move downhill, with the help of gravity, to the cars in the gangway. A breast varied in width depending on the firmness of the roof; with a good roof, it might be thirty feet or more wide, with a poor one only fifteen. Adjacent

Interior plat of a coal slope showing gangways and breasts, double-track hoisting system, and air hole (at extreme right)

11

breasts were separated by a "pillar" or wall of coal that supported the roof, and pillars too might vary, depending on the roof and the hardness of the coal, from fifteen to thirty or forty feet in width. A breast generally was worked upward eighty to 100 yards, sometimes even to the surface, in a continuing process of extraction that might take a miner and laborer as much as a year and produce on the order of 3,000 tons of coal. In a busy mine, with breasts and pillars thirty feet wide, a gangway a quarter of a mile long would have about twenty breasts in operation.

The actual extraction of the coal was relatively simple: it was blasted out of the face by the miner and loaded onto the cars by his helper. To do

Working in a
near-vertical breast

the blasting, the miner drilled a hole, perhaps a couple of feet long, in the face of the coal with a hand bit and inch-wide auger. (In later years, more elaborate boring machines were employed and, eventually, pneumatic drills.) Black powder was poured into brown paper, which was rolled up and pasted with soap, and the twelve-inch cartridge thus produced was impaled on a long, thin iron needle. The cartridge was pushed into the drill hole, leaving the needle in place, and the opening was tamped with coal dust. Then the needle was withdrawn and a safety fuse was set in the hole and lit. The miner and laborer then scrambled to safety. After the shot, the breast and adjacent gangway were filled with powder smoke, and large chunks of coal were lying on the floor or rolling down the chute. The laborer broke up some of these chunks with his pick and loaded them onto cars, the large pieces by hand and the smaller with a broad, round shovel. The residue was cast aside to form the "gob" or "goaf," a worthless pile of debris lying beside the pillars. A notoriously undependable link in this chain of blasting events was the safety fuse, locally termed a "squib." Because the workings were generally very damp, any fuse was subject to failure on account of moisture acquired during its transport to the work place or in the drill hole, which could not always be kept dry. If a shot failed to fire, it was necessary to replace the fuse, and this was dangerous to do, because a damp fuse might simply be burning slowly, waiting to set off the charge just as the miner stepped up to replace it. The fuses were therefore covered with pitch, tar, or other water-resistant material that would protect against misfiring.

Just where the cars were loaded depended on the pitch of the vein. In flat seams and seams not more than 5° from the horizontal, the cars could be pushed by hand into breasts cut at right angles to the gangway. For seams whose pitch was somewhere between 5° and 25°, the breasts were driven slantwise off the gangway so as to minimize the effective pitch of the road, and the rails were laid in a horizontal bed next to the downhill pillar. Where the pitch was 25° or steeper, breasts were cut at right angles to the gangway, and mining was done "on the run"—i.e., gravity carried the coal down a chute to cars waiting at the gangway. At 25° to 30° the floor of the chute had to be laid with planking or sheet iron, but at steeper pitches it would run freely on the bare slate. In thick seams the coal at the bottom of the chute could be collected behind a wooden door a sufficient distance above the road to empty out directly into the cars as they arrived, but in the thinner seams the cars still had to be loaded by hand. Once the cars were loaded, the mule driver drove his little train down the gangway to the bottom of the slope or shaft, where the cars were hoisted to the breaker.

In deep mines, the area around the bottom of the slope or shaft was a crowded and busy place. In addition to the coming and going of men, cars, and coal, it was the place, or near the place, where the sump and the pumps were located. The sump was a large, deep pit—on the order of ten feet deep and ten feet square—into which all the water in the mine drained from breasts and gangways and the slope or shaft itself. In this sump were located the force pumps (suction pumps would have been useless at these great depths). The pipes that carried the water to the surface, usually in 300-foot "lifts" or stages, were generally laid at the side of the slope or shaft, although sometimes they were placed in a separate upcast airway. The pump rods were connected to a steam engine on the surface. Huge amounts of water had to be lifted from the mine, always as much in weight as the coal that reached the surface, and generally much more, as much as twenty tons of water for every ton of coal brought to the surface. Pumping had to be continuous, night and day, for without the pumps the mine would fill with water to the top of the water table.

Also close to the bottom of the slope or shaft, in the period from about 1835 to 1865, was the furnace. The furnace was needed to ventilate deep mines because the "natural" ventilation, usually resorted to in drifts and tunnels, was inadequate for workings below water level. In the case of drifts and tunnels, the differences in temperature inside and outside the mine, together with pressure differences at the outlet of the airhole, uphill, and at the drift or tunnel mouth, produced a dependable current of air (reversing itself, however, every spring and fall) sufficient to ventilate the mine. But in deep mines, even with the expedient of building a stack over the upcast, natural ventilation was not reliable. In the winter, when the interior of the mine was 54° Fahrenheit or warmer, and the outside temperature was considerably colder, a natural current of warm—and therefore lighter—inside air would rise up the upcast, thus inducing the colder, heavier outside air to fall down the downcast. But in the summer, natural ventilation did not work at all in deep mines, because the cool, heavy inside air simply lay at the bottom of the mine, and the warm, light outside air formed a cap over it. The furnace solved the problem by sending a current of hot air and exhaust gases up the upcast, which served as its chimney, and inducing a current of fresh air to enter the downcast. To ensure continuous, reliable ventilation, the furnace burned year-round, consuming thousands of tons of anthracite.

Air was expected to flow continuously in a single, unbroken stream from the downcast, along gangways, through specially constructed airways along the pillars back from the gangways, across the face of every

Miner with a lamp

working breast, and out through the counter-gangway to the upcast, a distance in a well-developed mine of several miles. It carried out smoke and carbon dioxide from powder charges and miners' lamps, carbon dioxide and other effluvia from men and mules, and the explosive "firedamp" or methane gas that was constantly released from the coal. In a large, complex mine, the routing of the air was controlled by an elaborate system of doors in the gangways, each tended by a young door boy, by headings cut through the pillars between the breasts, and by brattices of wood or cloth nailed to props to channel the air up and down the sides of breasts. It was a system constantly expanding and contracting as gangways and breasts were extended and worked-out areas were abandoned. And it was obviously vulnerable to unexpected interruption should a fall of rock or coal block the passage of the air in some remote or unattended portion of the mine.

The constant presence of firedamp enormously complicated not only the problem of ventilation but also the problem of illumination. Some mines had the reputation of being "gassy" and others were supposed to be relatively safe; but all mines produced some gas, and it was not easy to predict when or where it would be encountered even in safe mines. Miners ordinarily lighted their way and work with small lamps that burned whale oil, which were attached to their caps to leave the hands free. If the concentration of methane in the breast reached 5 percent, or anywhere above that to 13 percent, the naked flame in the lamp would ignite an explosion. So, if the fire boss determined that an area was gassy, he either prohibited entry or required that miners entering extinguish the cap lamp with its naked flame and use instead a safety lamp. There were several varieties of safety lamp, but they were all bulky and heavy, had to be carried by hand, and yielded about half as much light as the ordinary miner's lamp. The safety lamp interposed a fine metal mesh between the atmosphere and the wick, and the mesh prevented gas explosions by absorbing sufficient heat from the flame. But even safety lamps were vulnerable: an excessively rapid flow of air through the mesh, caused by too rapid a current of air or even by swinging the lamp, could produce an explosion. And, obviously, other sources of ignition could occur: striking a match to light a squib or a pipe, a flash of powder during blasting, the flame from the furnace, and (although this was for years denied by practical miners and scientists alike) the spontaneous combustion of waste coal in the gob.

Above ground, the dominant feature of the colliery landscape was the breaker. The breaker was a large wooden structure, in early years fifty to seventy-five and later over 100 feet in height, that contained the machinery used to crush, sort, clean, and deliver the coal by chutes to the hoppers above the railroad track. The breaker was sheathed in wooden siding with numerous windows. Most breakers were designed to dump coal from the mine cars onto a platform at the top, whence it descended by gravity through various machines and past the "breaker boys" who gave it a final cleaning and inspection before it reached the hoppers. In the case of drifts and tunnels, a trestle carried the cars horizontally to the platform at the top of the breaker, whose base rested on the hillside below. But in the case of slopes and shafts, the cars were usually lifted to the top of the breaker by the same ropes or chains that had hoisted them from the bottom of the mine. In the case of slopes, the top of the breaker was reached by an inclined plane that could be a continuation of the slope itself. In the case of shafts, the head house, where the rope from the winding engine passed over pulleys to descend into the mine, was incorporated into the breaker structure so as to deliver the cars directly to the top of the breaker, and the winding engine was similarly embraced by the breaker shell at the base, behind the head frame. Breakers rarely worked up to design capacity be-

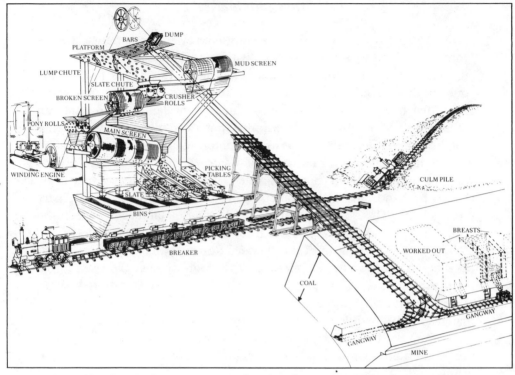

The coal breaker, displaying continuous flow from breast, through breaker, to coal train

cause the mines below them rarely produced coal at the expected rate and because breakers themselves experienced considerable down time.

Breakers contained several different types of moving machinery, connected by gravity chutes, with human hands helping at top and bottom. The first component was the hopper into which the cars dumped their coal at the top of the breaker, and which in turn released coal at a measured rate upon two sets of screen bars, commonly seven inches and five inches apart, respectively, placed one above the other. The screen bars separated the largest pieces of coal from the coal destined to pass through the rolls (the "breakers" proper). The large coal, lump (over seven inches) and steamboat (between seven and five inches), did not pass through the bars, but slid onto a platform, where the two platform men separated it from slate and dirt, shoving the debris into a chute that dropped it down to the rock hopper at the base of the breaker and shoving steamboat and lump coal into other chutes that passed directly to the proper pockets above the railroad loading platform. The part—all small coal—that passed the lower set of screen bars fell into a chute, which carried it to a rotating

16

cylindrical screen, called the mud screen, where fine particles of coal and dirt were separated; the salable coal of small sizes moving out of the screen into its proper chute down to the loading platform, and the "mud," consisting of powdered coal, clay, and bits of slate, dropping down to the culm collector. The remainder of the coal, of intermediate size, moved from the lower bars into a chute that delivered it to the breaker rolls. These were cast-iron cylinders, about three feet in diameter and in length, studded with sharp steel teeth. Rotating inwardly, these teeth drew the coal between the rolls and split it. The broken coal now fell to other screens and sometimes to an additional, smaller pair of rolls, known as pony or monkey rolls. These successive screenings sorted the coal into the various commercial sizes, each of which passed down its proper chute. The last stage in the process was a final chute past the slate pickers. Slate pickers were young boys or older, disabled men, usually four to each side of a chute, who were supposed to remove any remaining slate or other impurities by hand, casting such refuse into still another waste chute. The coal as it passed the slate pickers was wet and glistening from the mine and (after the 1860's) from mechanical washing and from flotation in agitating baths, called jigs, where more slate and impurities were separated from the coal. The entire breaker, in fact, was bathed in highly corrosive sulfuric-acid mine water and at the same time was filled with a haze of coal dust, produced by the crushing and falling of coal, that even the light from the dozens of windows could not fully penetrate. And the din from the rolls and the constant sliding and crashing of coal in the chutes did not stop until the breaker shut down at the end of the day.

The products of the typical Schuylkill County breaker were nine different coal sizes, each delivered from a separate chute into a separate railroad car for delivery to market:

Lump:	does not pass through bars 7 inches apart
Steamboat:	does not pass through bars 5 inches apart
Broken:	passes over 2¾-inch mesh screen
Egg:	passes through 2¾ inches, over 2 inches mesh
Store (large):	passes through 2 inches, over 1½ inches mesh
Store (small):	passes through 1½ inches, over 1 inch mesh
Chestnut:	passes through 1 inch, over ⅝ inch mesh
Pea:	passes through ⅝ inch, over ⅜ inch mesh
Buckwheat:	passes through ⅜ inch, over ¼ inch mesh

Anything smaller than one-quarter inch was waste. Once beyond the breaker, human hands would not touch the coal again until it was, some-day, somewhere down the line, shoveled onto the grate in a stove, firebox, or furnace.

Although the breaker dominated the landscape architecturally, the culm banks overwhelmed it in another way. Rock and slate ended up on a rock bank, and small coal (less than quarter-inch) and dust that fell through the screens ended up on the culm bank, a huge and ever growing black hill of coal dust and mud off to one side of the breaker. Culm was hauled there in coal cars, sometimes on a trestle if it could be dumped down hills, sometimes pulled up a hillside by rope and winding engine. And after washing was introduced, much of the culm had to be deposited in huge settling basins to prevent illegal clogging of streams below the colliery. Culm banks contained a great deal of usable fuel; about 15 to 20 percent of the coal that entered the breaker ended up on the banks. If the fine coal particles could be cemented and compressed into a convenient shape and size, much of this waste could be recovered, and many successful exper-iments had been made, including one by S. H. Daddow at St. Clair. But the cost of these culm brickettes was always higher than the cost of prepared anthracite, and so the culm banks kept growing, sometimes overshadow-ing the breakers themselves.

Any substantial colliery had a number of other surface structures in addition to the breaker. First of all, there were a number of "houses" that contained the several steam engines: the winding engine, already men-tioned, for hauling mine cars up the slope, or cages up the shaft; the pump house, with its own engine, in later years often a copy of the famous Cornish Bull pumping engine from England; again in later years, the engine for the large centrifugal fan that circulated air through the venti-lation system of the mine; and of course the breaker engine that drove the rolls, screens, and jigs in the breaker, usually located in the breaker itself. Boilers were, in later years, concentrated in one long boiler house, above which stood a straight line of smokestacks, and the steam was conducted in insulated pipes to the various engines. There were also a blacksmith shop, a machine shop, a carpenter's shop, a paint shop, and often even a sawmill, for the colliery maintained its own tools, made most of its own repairs, prepared its own timber for props and lagging, and manufactured much of its own equipment, such as mine cars and cages. There were railroad sidings, bridges, and piles of lumber everywhere. There had to be a powder shed, buried in some safe hillside. And, of course, there was a colliery office, where the records were kept and the manager and clerk presided over the entire operation.

The driver boy

To ensure a continuous and profitable flow of coal in this complex organization of men and machines was not an easy task. The typical colliery of the 1850's employed on the order of 100 hands; by the 1870's, collieries were larger and the work force had expanded to 200 men and boys, and often more. There was an elaborate division of labor and a hierarchy of half a dozen levels, roughly corresponding to age. Underground, the lowest and the youngest (ages eight to twelve) were the door boys or "trappers," whose duty it was to open and close the main ventilation doors in gangways and in major headings as men, mules, and equipment passed to and fro. It was a task of extreme importance. Self-closing doors were used at the less crucial points, but they were illegal in main airways because of their liability to failure. The young door boys were subject to much teasing and practical joking from the next level in the hierarchy, the teenage drivers, who drove the mule trains between the breasts and the hoisting platform. The driver boys had an unsavory reputation for being coarse-mouthed with their peers and abusive to their mules. As one old operator put it, "The driver is not the sweetest man or boy in the mines. Most of them are profane, harsh, and rough in manner." The driver might also be expected, in large mines with steeply pitching breasts where mining was done "on the run," to help the loader, who worked at the foot of the chute, draw or heave coal into the wagons. Next in the underground hierarchy were the miners' helpers, usually former drivers, who (in flat seams) pushed the mine cars up to the breast, split large blocks of coal with a pick, loaded the cars, let them down to the gangway, and helped the miner in setting props and such other tasks as were required in the breast. At the top of this labor hierarchy were the miners, who had been trained as helpers. They were either contract miners, who paid their own helpers, or day workers, who were responsible for cutting the coal in their own breasts. The miner analyzed the firmness of the roof, the condition of the air, and the nature of the coal, decided when and where to fire a shot, drilled the hole, placed the powder, and set and lit the fuse. There were also other underground teams of workers with drills and gunpowder who were hired to do specialized jobs whose main purpose was not to extract coal but to drive headings, air holes, and tunnels to other veins, to construct turnouts, to lay track, and to break through faults to find the lost vein. And, finally, there was a host of craftsmen who worked underground: masons and carpenters, sometimes a blacksmith, pump men, and always the hostler or stable boss, who fed and tended the mules, whose entire adult lives were spent underground (until this practice was made illegal). Many mules learned to do their work without direction and even to solve problems. Many were the

Mule train and drivers taking a day off on the surface

pathetic stories told of aged mules being shot when they became infirm or even, according to one tale, climbing up the slope and casting themselves over the edge of the culm bank to die.

In charge of all these underground workers were two men: the fire boss and the mine boss or "inside" boss. The fire boss was an experienced miner whose duty it was every morning at an early hour, before the regular underground workers arrived, to inspect the mine, or his assigned section, for the presence of firedamp. The fire boss walked through all gangways and entered all breasts carrying a safety lamp, whose degree of flaring as he held it up toward the roof indicated the presence and concentration of methane. On his return to the bottom office, he marked his findings on a board or slate, indicating by a combination of X marks whether gas was found in a particular breast, whether a safety lamp was required, or whether a breast should not be entered until the air was cleared and the stoppings, doors, brattices, and airways were repaired. Signs warning against entry were also placed at dangerous breasts or other locations. In general, he was responsible for monitoring the ventilation system, reporting his findings to the mine boss, and issuing orders for immediate repair in case of imminent danger. Theoretically, as one operator expressed it, "The order of a fire boss must be obeyed, it is imperative, and from it there is no appeal."

But actually, and sometimes unfortunately, there was someone to whom the orders of a fire boss could be appealed: the inside boss of the mine. This man had overall responsibility for the productiveness of the mine, and he could change the fire boss's order "in some cases not involving absolute danger, or of trifling consequence," as the old operator expressed it. The inside boss was "the absolute monarch of the interior of a coal mine," responsible for all the employees in all parts of the workings. He carried out the directives of the mine manager and the operator and was to be seen in every part of the mine, often in the most dangerous circumstances, usually accompanied by the fire boss. It is evident that the inside boss had two principal duties, which might be perceived as being always potentially in conflict: first, to maximize the production of coal; and, second, to minimize the likelihood of firedamp explosions and other disasters. In the interest of the first duty, he might be tempted to order, or permit, a miner to enter a dangerous breast or to scant the setting of props or other "dead work." No doubt it was to relieve the mine boss of this conflict of interest that it had become traditional in English coal mines to hire a separate and independent fire boss, and the practice was continued in America. But it should be noted that not all anthracite mines did separate the two roles; in some collieries the inside boss was required to perform the duties of the fire boss himself.

Above ground, a labor hierarchy prevailed similar to that underground. At the bottom of the scale were the slate pickers, who might be as young as four, but the category also included mature men whose injuries or advanced age had made them unfit for more demanding work. Thus a miner's career might begin as slate picker, then progress through all the ranks successively as driver, laborer, and miner, and end up picking slate again. There were relatively unskilled laborers doing a variety of tasks about the breaker—landers at the top of the breaker who unloaded the cars, the platform men who tended the hoppers that loaded the railroad cars, carpenters' helpers, and laborers who dumped the waste onto the culm and rock banks. Outside the breaker, there were a number of highly skilled craftsmen: the engineers who operated and maintained the steam engines, hoisting machinery, and fans, and various machinists, carpenters, masons, blacksmiths, hostlers, sawmill operators, and teamsters. And there were dozens of laborers, from firemen who stoked the steam boilers to ditch diggers, mule drivers, and helpers of all kinds.

Coordinating the surface activities were, as below, not one but two top bosses: the breaker boss, assisted by special foremen who took charge of the slate pickers; and the outside boss. The outside boss, in addition to being chief of operations on the surface, was in many collieries also the superior of the inside boss. And sometimes a general manager or colliery superintendent directed the entire colliery, with the inside boss and outside boss reporting to him.

But the mine manager was not really the final authority. He was, after all, only another salaried employee, or, in some places, one of the day workers at a rate (in 1851) of $1.95 per day (not much more than the top engineer, who got $1.55).[2] The mine operator was the ultimate authority in many cases, but he was not constantly present; he might be simultaneously operating several mines; and "he" might in fact be a corporation, acting through a board of trustees. The operator was ordinarily preoccupied by the exigencies of assembling capital, ordering prop timber, machinery, and other supplies, negotiating with creditors, and traveling and keeping up his correspondence. Furthermore, he usually depended upon the advice of the consulting engineers, who were hired, in some cases (at least in the case of some of the St. Clair mines), not by the operator but by the landowner's agent. These engineers evaluated and reported on the geology of the mine, the design and workmanship below, and the wisest course to take in extending gangways, sinking new lifts, installing more powerful engines and larger pumps, and so on. Thus the operators themselves were ofttimes making decisions on the basis of technical advice provided by outside engineering consultants who represented the interests of the landlord, who always wanted more royalties but who also could afford to calculate on a longer term than the operator.

Evidently there was a serious fragmentation of management, with highly authoritarian procedures at the lower levels and a loose diffusion of decision-making responsibilities at the top. This confusion of administrative functions is reflected in the limitations of the system of records and bookkeeping at most collieries. The colliery records were kept in the manager's office and consisted primarily of payrolls. The operators kept account of orders from suppliers. The railroads recorded tolls and tonnages and the landlord's agent used the railroad tonnage figures to calculate royalties. But nowhere, except for the large corporations, were detailed records kept in such a form as to permit any serious cost accounting. Thus, in answer to the question, How much does it cost to mine and prepare a ton of coal in your colliery? only the narrowest answer was given, based on the day-by-day normal operational costs recorded in the colliery office. As late as 1882, when H. Martin Chance, M.D., state assistant geologist, was collecting data for his comprehensive report on *Mining Methods and Appliances* in the anthracite industry, accounting practice was primitive, even in some of the larger coal companies, and the books were kept "in such a manner" that cost accounting was impossible. In estimating costs of production, some companies did not include royalty costs at all, others did not include depreciation of lands, none included the hiring of consulting engineers, surveyors, and geologists. An effort was made by the four firms who responded to Chance's questions to allocate non-clerical payroll costs to various inside and outside functions, such as "air and gangways," "stable expenses," "breaker," "cars," "timber and props," and to include insurance, legal expenses, taxes, and so forth. Chance's estimates of the cost of mining and preparing one ton of coal, in an industry where intense competition meant standardized market prices for the commodity, varied from $1.56 per ton to $3.16 per ton (and the colliery reporting the latter figure did not include an allowance for royalties). These figures also did not include township taxes on breakers and other surface improvements (in St. Clair they were 1 percent of assessed value, paid by the landowner) and on the underground coal reserves (on the order of $2 per acre, also paid by the landowner), or canal or railroad tolls, or the commission of the agent in Philadelphia who sold the coal to the consumer. And the figures also did not indicate how much of the cost of production was spent in actual mining and preparing and how much while the colliery was just "standing," as a result of mechanical failure, disaster, or a strike by miners (on the average, a colliery's down time was three months out of the year).[3] If the transportation and commission costs were added to the production cost, the cost to the colliery would be much greater: about 25 cents per ton was paid to the dealer, about 1 cent per ton per mile was paid on the six-mile branch railroad from St. Clair to Port Carbon and still more was paid (for most of the coal) for shipping to Philadelphia either by the Philadelphia and Reading Railroad or the Schuylkill Navigation Company's canal. The canal toll was about 60 cents per ton, but the canal was closed from December to March. The railroad toll varied around an average of

The coal depot at Port Carbon, showing trains from collieries delivering coal at canal wharves

about $1.60 per ton from Port Carbon to Philadelphia. Thus the minimum cost of transportation and marketing in Philadelphia of a ton of coal produced at St. Clair would vary from about 91 cents per ton by canal in the summer to about $1.91 per ton by rail in the winter. The cost of mining and preparation was on the order of $2.25 per ton. The actual cost to the operator of the coal he sold was therefore not less than $3.16 by canal and $4.16 by rail.[4] And, finally, none of the cost figures submitted to Chance included an item for depreciation or for interest on loans. Since these loans—mostly for large amounts of money, tens of thousands of dollars— were incurred for the purpose of opening the mine, constructing the breaker and other surface equipment, sinking to deeper levels, and repairing dam ⬥ age after disasters, interest was often a major part of the cost of colliery operation. Not all operators borrowed money, no doubt, but most of those in the St. Clair area did. It seems obvious that under these conditions few operators indeed could have been showing a net profit; but with such disorganized methods of record keeping, it may have taken the typical operator some time to discover that he was losing money.

SOME PECULIARITIES OF COAL AS A COMMODITY[1]

Every commodity is subjected to a series of industrial processes that transform its material from a natural, raw state to the form in which it is presented to the consumer. Ordinarily, in nineteenth-century America, different processes, or groups of related processes, were performed by different firms in different places. Thus, in the case of cotton, the raw material was grown, picked, ginned, and baled on southern plantations; it was unbaled, carded, spun, dyed, and woven into cloth in semi-rural mills in New England and the middle Atlantic states; and the cloth was cut and sewn into garments, upholstery, table linen, curtains, and whatnot, for sale to consumers, in factories in the larger cities and towns. A similar three-tiered structure was characteristic of other industrial commodities, such as lumber and iron, in which the extractive phase, the intermediate processing phase or phases, and the fabrication phase were generally carried out by different companies in different places. Iron ore might be mined at Mount Laffee by a coal operator; transported to Pottsville, smelted, and cast into pigs at the Pioneer Furnace; and then reheated, cast into engine parts, machined, and assembled into a locomotive at Haywood and Snyder's foundry and machine shop. Lumber was cut from one man's forest, rafted to another man's sawmill, where it was cut and planed into standard sizes, and finally assembled into houses by a contractor.

This separation of the various stages in the processing of a commodity by geography and firm was accompanied by another feature—the existence of open-market relationships between stages. Thus the owner of a cotton mill could buy his cotton from any one of a number of different commission merchants, who represented different growers in the South; and the grower could send his cotton to any one of a number of agents. The garment maker could select cloth from a number of different factories. And similarly with iron, lumber, and most other commodities: the industries that processed them were an open network, a reticulate organization, in which the multitude of firms engaging in each phase of processing could in principle buy and sell, through open-market relationships, to each and every one of the participants in the next phase. This open-market organization of commodity processing had two major advantages for the participant: he could, within limits, control his financial fate by picking and choosing the firms he did business with so as to "buy cheap and sell dear"; and he was protected from interruption of his business by the failure of any one supplier or buyer because he could turn to another in the open market.

The coal industry, in stark contrast, was not organized in this way. Coal, like any other commodity, had to be extracted (mined and brought to the surface) and prepared in a breaker for the various classes of consumers (broken, sorted by size, cleaned of foreign matter, and dumped into railroad cars at the foot of the chutes). Once in the car, nothing further was done to it: it was hauled away and sold. What made coal different from other commodities was that *all* the processing was done at one place by one firm, which extracted the material from the ground and performed all the subsequent operations upon it that made it ready for the consumer. Each colliery was a self-contained commodity-processing unit that had virtually no connection with any other colliery (not even with other collieries owned by the same firm). Theoretically, the system might have been designed to work like other commodity systems, by separating the mining company from the breaker company. And, in fact, in the early years a few free-market breakers were built to service the small mines that produced only a dozen or so tons a day, far too little a rate of production to justify the expense of a breaker. An experimental breaker was built at the docks of the Delaware and Hudson Railroad company in New York. The *Miners' Journal* editorialized in 1858:

> We have often wondered why coal breakers were not stationed at the different points of consumption instead of at the mines. The coal if broken in the cities, could be made of requisite size according to order, and the dust made could readily be used in conjunction with bituminous. . . . The advantage of sending Coal from the regions in lump and then breaking it below, will yet be perceived.[2]

But, in practice, the system in Schuylkill County increasingly favored complete-process collieries in which the coal flowed in an uninterrupted stream (theoretically, at least) from the bottom of the mine, up the shaft or slope to the top of the breaker, where it tumbled down through rollers and screens and chutes to the railroad cars waiting below. To have separated mine from breaker would have seemed inefficient, requiring the shipping of waste, the maintenance of large storage areas for coal (and coal does not store very well) and culm, and the intervention of a market mechanism to mediate between mine operators and breaker operators. And so the coal trade, instead of building the three-tiered, reticulate, market-mediated organization characteristic of other commodities, developed what might be called a linear processing structure that emphasized the importance of continuous flow in individual collieries rather than intermittent storage and transport among mine and breaker companies.

The cost to a colliery of maintaining its own breaker was about the

27

same as the cost of shipping to a central breaker (if one disregards the cost of the periodic breaker fires that eventually destroyed most breakers, none insured for more than half the cost of replacement). Shipping to a central breaker, of course, required the operator to pay for shipping a lot of waste (about 16 percent of the coal reaching the breaker ended up on culm banks). But significant amounts of additional waste were created by the jostling of broken coal during the long railway journey to Philadelphia—another argument for centralized breakers. Operating his own breaker cost the operator about 22 cents per ton, about 10 percent of the total cost of production, and if the costs of down time at the breaker, repairs to the breaker, breaker insurance, and depreciation on the breaker are considered, the cost of using a colliery breaker is about the same as the cost of shipping waste and paying a central breaker to prepare the coal.

There were other constraints particular to the coal trade that made the idea of linear processing with continuous flow appealing or even compelling. One was a matter of price and perhaps competitive advantage. If coal from a well-run colliery situated on a vein of good quality was sent to a central breaker for processing, it would either have to be mixed with other run-of-the-mine coal from inferior collieries or else, at added expense, be processed separately and loaded into separate railroad cars. Linear processing at the mine obviated this problem for those who chose to ship coal bearing their own names. Thus Enoch McGinness advised Henry Carey to label his coal for the market as William H. Johns did. "Johns coal is shipped alone and is known. If yours is mixed with everything in the shape or color of coal, it cannot be known or get a reputation."[3]

Further pressure for a continuous flow of coal was exerted by the Philadelphia and Reading Railroad and its subsidiaries, the Schuylkill Navigation Company and the feeder railroads, which held a monopoly of transportation of Schuylkill County coal. The Reading needed a continuous flow of coal because it depended largely on anthracite tolls to keep itself solvent. And the Reading could, and did, attempt to solve its financial problems by varying the tonnage rates in ways that seemed arbitrary and unjustified to the operators. An operator who in normal times could at best expect no more than a profit of 10 cents on each ton of coal he shipped saw his profits cut in half if the Reading raised its tolls from $1.60 to $1.65.

Thus the financial demands of the owner and the transporter forced each colliery operator to strive to increase production by improving the efficiency of his mine and his breaker. And the continuous flow of coal along a track that extended without interruption from the bottom of the mine to the top of the breaker and then down to the waiting cars was a demonstration of that efficiency. But despite the mechanical efficiency of

Breasts in the Mammoth Vein worked to the outcrop on the surface

these collieries, continuous flow was a dream because the individual collieries were, for several reasons, peculiarly vulnerable to interruption of flow.

One of the reasons for this vulnerability was the linear system itself. Any mechanical breakdown, anywhere from the bottom of the shaft up through the breaker, stopped the entire system. If the breaker was out of commission, mining had to stop because there was no central colliery to which to ship the coal. If the pumps failed, or the hoist, mining stopped and the breaker was quickly emptied. If the railroad failed for any reason to send cars, the mine and the breaker both had to cease operation within a day because the chutes were full, waiting for the cars. A colliery was like an electrical system wired in series: if one component failed, everything else became useless.

A second vulnerability was the unpredictability of the region's coal geology. A gangway driven into a perfectly good vein of coal could, within yards, run into a fault—a slippage of the strata—that might require weeks of tunneling blindly through rock to find the coal again. Or the vein could suffer a "pinch," in which a previously thick, productive, easily workable stratum of coal suddenly narrowed to a few feet or even inches. Or the gangway could enter a stretch where the quality of the coal changed into a substance resembling graphite, or was mixed with clay, slate, and shale, both forms useless as fuel. Or the gangway could unexpectedly cut open a large spring that overwhelmed the pumps then in place, requiring replacement with larger pumps and perhaps a stronger steam engine. Any one of these and other unpredictable confrontations with the disturbed condition of the Schuylkill coal bed had the effect of slowing or temporarily terminating the flow of coal while the operator, at his own expense, strove desperately to solve the problem.

The third important reason for the vulnerability of the system was the frequency of major disasters—explosions, fires, and floods—that stopped production for prolonged periods and forced the operator either to spend large amounts of money or to give up the colliery. The most spectacular of these disasters were the explosions of methane gas that wrecked the underground workings, often blew up or set fire to the breaker and other wooden surface structures close to the shaft, and might even set the mine on fire underground. Breakers also were highly prone to catch fire on their own. An underground explosion or a surface fire was apt to damage the pumps, and if this happened, the mine could fill with water before new equipment was in place. And if the mine was on fire underground, it had to be flooded anyway, just to put the fire out.

The system of coal production used in Schuylkill County was consuming itself. Chronic over-production kept prices low, and individual firms, because of the vulnerability to physical breakdown of their linear-processing collieries, were bound to fail sooner or later. The principal historian of the Schuylkill coal trade, Clifton K. Yearley, has estimated that 95 percent of all collieries failed in the period 1820–1875; the median survival time of a coal company was less than one year.[4] One result of the weakness of the individual operators was that they were eventually devoured, in an economic sense, by the Philadelphia and Reading Railroad, which would set an even more linear continuous-flow organization—the Philadelphia and Reading Coal and Iron Company—that merged colliery operation with the transportation and merchandising of coal.

PROGRESS AND REGRESSION IN COLLIERY TECHNOLOGY
1830–1870

The machinery and engineering practice used in the Schuylkill collieries was basically British with American modifications, some of them progressive and others regressive in comparison with the best British practice. Knowledge of basic British methods was brought to the St. Clair area by the earliest Welsh and English immigrant miners, like the Johns from Pembrokeshire and Englishman Benjamin Milnes, who had worked in the coal trade for twenty-one years before coming to the United States. Few if any of these men were trained mining engineers, but some no doubt had worked in supervisory capacities and others as engineers and machinists, building, operating, and maintaining steam engines, pumps, and hoisting apparatus. Information about British mining procedures was also available in printed form in technical handbooks, such as John Hedley's *A Practical Treatise on the Working and Ventilation of Coal Mines; with Suggestions for Improvements in Mining* (1851). Hedley was a "colliery viewer," or underground manager, with twelve years' experience in the Newcastle fields, and wrote for other viewers. Other early manuals were written by Joseph Marlor, Sr, *Coal Mining* (1854), and Ralph Moore, *The Ventilation of Mines* (1859).[1] But it is difficult to judge how many of these works were read by how many people in Schuylkill County or, more particularly, in St. Clair. Certainly Daddow, a St. Clair engineer, displayed familiarity with British writings, and British authorities were frequently cited in the pages of the Pottsville *Miners' Journal*. Copies may have reposed on the shelves of the Pottsville Scientific Association. But these works were not readily accessible to the ordinary colliery employee. John Maguire in his "Reminiscences" recalled how hard it was to obtain technical publications in St. Clair:

> There was practically no mining literature. In the seventies Mr. Maguire got a little book written by an English mine inspector, Atkinson, called "Gases Met With in Coal Mines." He had ordered it from Sam. Holmes, in Saint Clair. It was very hard indeed to get any literature bearing on mining matters until Thomas Foster, of the International Correspondence School began to publish books in that line. Mr. Maguire showed the writer a book published in 1881 by the Fosters, which, he said, was about the first published in that region on mining. I think the title was "The Miner's Hand Book and Pocket companion."[2]

Evidently John Maguire did not read the *Miners' Journal* regularly, for in the 1850's and thereafter it did publish extensively on European mines and mining practice, and even had its own correspondent, the engineer William Jackson Palmer, write a series of technical articles on English mines based on information gained in personal visits while he was making a walking tour of England in the summer of 1855. And the *Journal of the*

Franklin Institute and the *Scientific American* regularly ran articles on methods of coal mining and patents for new machinery.

Englishmen's methods of exploiting their flat veins of soft bituminous coal were not always applicable in Schuylkill County, where the coal was hard, the veins not flat but pitching at angles from 5° to 90° from the horizontal, and the industry organized on what the English regarded as the worst possible basis, the "butty" system, in which undercapitalized entrepreneurs, not wealthy lords, took responsibility for mining coal. Hedley, writing of the Staffordshire field, where the veins as in Schuylkill pitched steeply, was very critical of the system:

> In some mining districts the Proprietor lets the working of his mines to a Contractor (in Staffordshire called a Butty), who provides all labor to raise the coal and to maintain the mine in a workable state. The Contractor again sublets the different branches of labor to the workmen. This way of letting mines operates to a great extent prejudicially to the introduction of good ventilation and discipline; almost every man's object being, under such circumstances, to make the most of his bargain, he attends to such of his duties as bring him a return for his labour, until urgent necessity requires the contrary, and thus, provisions which are necessary for the safety and welfare of the mine are neglected. I admit there may be Contractors who feel the responsibility that rests upon them, and provide not only good ventilation, but conduct the mine under as good regulations as circumstances allow. But the practice being bad, the sooner it is abolished the better, and in its place an approved system of management introduced, whereby the mines may be placed on a footing more secure from accidents, and the produce be raised with greater economy.[3]

The American modifications that can be regarded as adaptive were mostly concerned with the surface structures; those that can be seen as lapses from best British practice were largely underground. But whether above ground or below, the innovations were being made in a region suffused with enthusiastic belief in the possibility of progress through technological improvement. The *Miners' Journal* reported some new invention of significance to the coal trade in every issue. Inventors worked in every community, and nowhere were they more common than in and about St. Clair, Port Carbon, and Pottsville.

The Surface Installation: Breakers, Pumps, and Steam Engines

The surface structure that dominated the colliery landscape from the 1850's on was the coal breaker. The breaker was an American innovation, designed to facilitate the preparation of anthracite. The British, who produced mainly bituminous, did not need the breaker, for the soft coal was pretty well broken up by the time it emerged from the mine.

The method of breaking up anthracite before the invention of the breaker was crude indeed. The raw coal was spread out on iron platforms and pounded with sledgehammers; rock and bony coal were swept aside; and the coal fragments were then pushed over iron screens perforated, section by section, with square holes of different sizes to sort the coal that fell into bins below. It was estimated that one laborer could break eight to ten tons per day at a cost of 10 to 12 cents a ton. To prepare a modest 100 tons a day—about twelve rail cars—would thus require the work of ten men and cost about $10. But other estimates place the cost at 30 to 37 cents a ton for hand breaking and screening. By the 1830's, screening on platforms was being replaced by screening in perforated cylinders five to eight feet long and about two feet in diameter, turned by hand.[4] Also available were separately mounted rotary crushers, inward-turning and fitted with grooves or teeth, and powered by water, by horses or mules, or by steam, that were patterned after crushers long in use by quarry men in the preparation of ores. One such machine, for instance, with fluted rollers, was in use at Beaver Meadows in January 1843 and the subject of a patent application. And an even earlier, if impractical, one was reported in the *Journal of the Franklin Institute* in 1836.[5] In September 1843 a patent was issued to the flamboyant Philadelphia inventor Joseph Battin for a machine that mechanically combined the rollers and the screen in one motion and thus broke and screened the coal simultaneously. Battin's initial patent provided for a single flat inclined screen with progressively larger meshes, agitated by a cam; later versions returned to the conventional rotary screen. He also, in subsequent patents, revised the arrangement of the teeth and incorporated another engineer's idea of fitting one roller with teeth and the other with perforations opposite the teeth. Battin had originally specified that the teeth on one roller be opposite the space between the teeth on the other, to minimize pulverizing the coal, and this design turned out to be popular.

The first fourteen breakers were built in 1844 (including one at the Hickory Colliery at St. Clair) and were relatively small and inexpensive: a shed at the mouth of the drift, with a hopper for the unbroken coal, a pair

33

of rollers about thirty inches long and thirty in diameter, and a single long screen over the chutes that delivered prepared coal into the railroad cars below. Battin owned the breakers he erected and charged the colliery operator one cent for every ton broken. As the annual production of anthracite increased, his royalties went up and he became a rich man. But he experienced great difficulty in collecting royalties, for the operators preferred to erect their own breakers, with or without improvement, and refused the payment of royalties on the ground that Battin's patents were invalid. Although his patent rights were eventually supported by the U.S. Supreme Court, the 1854 decision came only four years before the fifteen-year term of his patent lapsed. After 1858 everyone was free to build his own breaker and Battin agreed to settle his claims for past patent infringement by the operators for $125,000 and half a cent a ton on back royalties.[6]

But improvements in Battin's breaker began well before the 1858 settlement. We have already noticed the patent for an alternative roller design in 1843. Between 1858 and 1862 at least four new roller designs were announced in the *Miners' Journal*. All of the modifications, whether by substituting sharp steel teeth for flat iron, or introducing flat instead of

Early form of a coal breaker (1852)

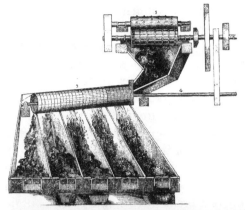

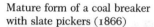

*Intermediate form of a
coal breaker (1857)*

Mature form of a coal breaker
with slate pickers (1866)

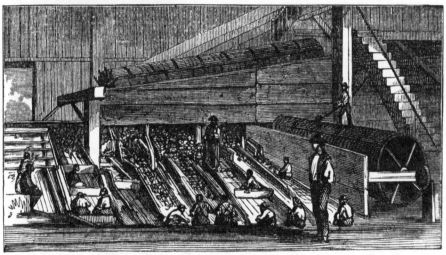

round crushing surfaces, were intended to reduce the great waste of coal by pulverizing, which Battin himself had noticed as a problem, and which even in his breaker amounted to 10 to 20 percent of the coal brought from the mine. By 1866, lump, steamboat, and pea coal were being separated on the dumping platform and at the first screen, to save waste.[7] Heavy wire-mesh screens, made by a newly invented process, were substituted for the original bar-iron screens by 1852.[8] The other major change in breaker design, resulting in a vast increase in the size of the building, was the introduction of washing sprays and additional screens and chutes. Of particular importance was the introduction of a final set of chutes between the screens and the storage bin over the tracks. In Battin's original design, the

35

coal that dropped through a mesh fell upon a platform, from which it was shoveled by hand into the bins, at considerable expense of labor. In 1855, at a drift opened on the Centreville Tract near St. Clair, the mechanician George Martz, who had built the breaker at the St. Clair Shaft the year before, designed a new breaker which included a sheet-iron inclined plane (called a "telegraph") with a curved end that delivered the prepared coal into the bin so evenly that no shoveling was required.[9] Some time after the telegraph chute was designed, places were constructed along it for the slate pickers. The date when slate pickers, or breaker boys, began to work along the telegraph is not easy to fix, but it must have been between 1857 and 1866. Eli Bowen makes no mention of them in his 1857 article in *Harper's,* which has a clear drawing of a breaker with final chutes but no breaker boys, but Daddow and Bannan's 1866 manual on coal mining illustrates final chutes with a small crew of breaker boys picking slate.[10] Washing the coal as it passed through the screens was commonly practiced by 1859.[11] All these improvements in the breaker, together with the hoisting arrangements necessitated by the shift from drifts to slopes and shafts, resulted in the breaker shed assuming the monstrous proportions it acquired in the 1860's.

The increase in the size and complexity of the breaker resulted in an increase in cost. Breakers of the '50's and '60's cost on the order of $40,000 to $50,000 to erect, about a third of the capital investment required for opening a mine. But breakers produced cleaner coal in a variety of sizes for an increasingly discriminating market; and they could readily be adjusted to produce a different mix of sizes by setting the rollers closer or farther apart than the standard three inches. Furthermore, extremely well-prepared coal sold at a premium—and a premium of only 5 cents a ton would mean an increase of 50 percent over the normal profit margin of 10 cents a ton.[12] Without access to an independent breaker industry, the colliery operator simply could not compete in the market without a breaker of his own, even though the cost of preparation by breaker—contemporary estimates ranged from 12 to 37 cents a ton—exceeded the cost of breaking by hand.[13]

Despite the size of its shell, the breaker required only a small ten- to twenty-horsepower steam engine to drive it, for most of the work of moving the coal was performed by gravity. Larger engines were required for pumping water out of the mine and for hoisting coal and men. As we have seen, the weight of water pumped out of a deep mine was very great and generally much more than the coal produced, varying from a low of perhaps two times the weight of the coal to a maximum of about twenty.[14] The water ascended inside a pipe a foot to a foot and a half in diameter and, in the deeper mines, hundreds of feet long, from sump to surface. To pull up such huge columns of water and such lengths of iron pump rod required an engine of hundreds of horsepower, working a four-foot stroke four or five times a minute. In England the "Cornish Bull" type of steam engine of several hundred horsepower was standard, with a walking beam—like the old Newcomen and Watt engines—activating the rod. But the Bull, with its high steam pressure and its cylinders mounted above the beam instead of below it, was rarely used in the anthracite district; instead, a miscellany of engines of all sorts and descriptions were made to order by dozens of fabricators. There was a ceaseless demand for better pumps and pump engines, less liable to break down, more resistant to corrosion from mine water that could eat through inches of cast iron in a few weeks, and strong enough to cope with sudden flooding. Any pump failure quickly brought the entire colliery to a halt and it might take months to drain the mine and make repairs.

The miner-mechanics at and about St. Clair were among the leaders in making improvements in pumping technology. John Holmes, anticipating (incorrectly, as it turned out) the widespread use of Cornish Bull engines, developed a pump especially for use with the Bull engine and installed one at Griffith Jones' colliery at Mill Creek in 1860.[15] But probably the best-known local pump inventor was Robert Allison. Allison had been born in England in 1827, but came to America at the age of two. His father was the mine boss at Charles Lawton's mine at Mill Creek in the 1830's and young Robert worked as a driver boy and laborer. In 1844 Allison was apprenticed in the machine shop of Haywood and Snyder in Pottsville and helped to file the edges of the perforations on Haywood's patent breaker rolls, which were installed at the same old Lawton mine on Mill Creek, now being operated by Haywood and Snyder. There were at that time about fifteen machine shops along the southern edge of the coal field, each of them prepared to make anything mechanical for the coal trade, from hand tools to locomotives. Far from being trained in one traditional artisan's specialty, apprentices in these shops were expected to be versatile. As Allison recalled:

> In those days an apprentice was expected to learn the use of all the tools in the shop, as well as to do all kinds of hand work, and, if apt in learning, would, at the end of his apprenticeship, be able to fit up all parts of an engine, set it up on the foundations, set the valves, and start up in good shape.

After working in several shops, Allison in 1861 with his partner Benjamin Bannan, the editor of the Pottsville *Miners' Journal,* founded the Franklin Iron Works in Port Carbon, Allison providing the expertise and Bannan the capital. The new firm was very successful, "due largely," as Allison put it later, "to the fact that the firm took up new ideas in mining machinery and worked them out to a successful issue." It introduced a number of Allison's patented inventions to the coal trade, including a portable boring mill and rock drills driven by compressed air, but his principal contribution was the Allison Cataract Steam Pump. The cataract pump was based on the idea of piping steam from a surface boiler down to a steam engine and pump underground. The original idea was not Allison's; but he had had the experience, a year or two before, of locating a ventilating fan and engine at the bottom of the St. Clair Shaft and driving it by steam from the surface. At that time many engineers did not believe that steam could be carried such long distances without most of it condensing, but Allison's experiment convinced him that steam could be carried the long distances—1,200 to 1,500 feet— that underground pump installations would require. The Allison Cataract Steam Pump perfected the earlier attempts and, as he put it in his reminiscences, "practically changed the whole system of pumping water from the mines."[16]

Robert Allison (1827-?)

Allison's success in transmitting power in steam lines to underground engines was at least an augury of, if not an important stimulus to, another and more general change in colliery design. The collieries of the 1850's and 1860's bristled with steam engines, usually five or six: the hoisting engine, the pump engine, the fan engine (if there was a fan), the breaker engine, perhaps an engine at the top of the culm bank, and engines at whatever other shops the colliery maintained—sawmill and machine shops, particularly. Each of these engines had its own attached boiler and its own smokestack. As it came to be realized that live steam could be piped hundreds of feet without a critical loss of pressure, the boilers were removed from immediate proximity to the engines they supplied, and concentrated in a row of interconnected boilers that supplied all the engines with steam from a single source. Probably by the end of the century, and certainly early in the twentieth, colliery landscapes typically displayed a line of stacks along the horizon, emerging from the long roofline of the boiler house (cf. plate of the Wadesville Shaft and the contrasting scene at the Mammoth Colliery in 1864).

The enthusiasm with which each new technological triumph was hailed seems almost like a ritual response to the disaster that had prompted the innovation. The starting of George W. Snyder's new Cornish Bull engine, erected at Borda's colliery at Heckscherville in the spring of 1858, was celebrated in the presence of many citizens of Pottsville. Snyder's works were closed for the day and "almost the entire force of workmen" witnessed the event. Borda's colliery had been drowned out for three months the year before and he resolved to replace his inadequate pumping apparatus with an engine and pumps powerful enough "to drain the entire Basin." The description of the new equipment is almost unctuous in its respect for power; praise drips from the pen of the *Miners' Journal's* editor like sacramental wine:

> The engine is probably, the largest in use in this State, and we feel confident a better piece of work, one more creditable in every respect, to all concerned in its construction, could not be turned out by any other machine shop in the country.[17]

Underground: The Problem of Ventilation

British colliers had discovered by the middle of the seventeenth century that in all but open quarries and shallow, bell-shaped pits not more than fifty or sixty feet deep, two openings were required for ventilation. An underground coal mine, as opposed to a simple pit quarry or stripping operation, was conceived for ventilation purposes as a U-shaped tube through which air flows, one of the arms of the tube serving as the intake or downcast, and the other as the exhaust or upcast. The topological transformations of this simple plan were, of course, infinitely various, depending upon the local geology, the method of entry, the depth, and the plan of working the mine. The need to provide fresh air to miners in deep metal mines had been recognized for centuries in Europe. Agricola's classic treatise on mining, *De Re Metallica,* published in Latin and German in 1556 and well known to English entrepreneurs, described and illustrated various devices, including large horse-and-water-powered centrifugal blowers, for introducing fresh air and sucking out poisonous air from the precious metal mines of central Europe.[18] But in addition to the need for fresh air, in coal mines it was important to remove something not ordinarily present in metal mines: the explosive firedamp or methane. In English coal mines, explosions had become frequent enough by the middle of the seventeenth century for the problem of mine ventilation to be repeatedly drawn to the attention of the Royal Society of London for Improving of Natural Knowledge in its first decade. In the context of a series of "subterraneous experiments" on varying barometric pressures in coal pits, Henry Power, a Cambridge-trained physician and a frequent participant in the society's meetings, presented in 1662 a paper on three damps in coal pits and the methods of ventilation then practiced, which he illustrated by a schematic diagram of typical underground workings. He noted that firedamp explosions were known to have killed and mangled men in Newcastle pits. The principal method of ventilation was to dig two pits connected by an airway and to rely on what later came to be called "natural ventilation." He also noted that, in order to increase the current of air, artificial means were sometimes employed:

> Now besides the playing of the vent, they sometimes are necessitated to keep constant fires underground, to purify and ventilate the air; sometimes the running of the scopes, when they begin to work, will set it in motion; sometimes, if the damp draw towards the eye of the pit, they set it into motion, by throwing down of coalsacks: else the heavy vapour will restagnate there, and is not able to rise.

Thus by 1662 the technique of "furnace ventilation" was already in use in English coal mines.[19] One of the selling points of Thomas Savery's fire engine—the first commercially successful steam engine—was, as he forcefully stated in *The Miner's Friend* in 1702, that it improved the ventilation by placing a furnace (i.e., a boiler) in the mine shaft, which served as a chimney.[20] Probably by the mid-eighteenth century it was common practice in English mines to build a furnace (without Savery's engine attached to it) at the bottom of the mine shaft, to carry up through a chimney—in the best-designed mines, a separate shaft, and otherwise a partitioned-off portion of the pit—the dangerous air from the working gangways.

In the north of England, most of the British coal lay in great horizontal sheets and the only practical means of reaching it was by means of vertical pits hundreds or thousands of feet deep. By the beginning of the eighteenth century, depths of 300 feet were common; by the middle of the nineteenth century, some British coal mines reached depths exceeding 2,000 feet. In order to maintain a constant influx of fresh air into the mine and an efflux of foul air out of it, two pits were needed at each colliery, one for the upcast and one for the downcast. The air coursed between them through miles of gangways, gathering the explosive firedamp (methane gas), smoke, carbon dioxide, and other effluvia and exhausting them through an upcast that usually was the chimney for the furnace whose hot ascending gases aided the ventilation. Pumps and pipes were located in the upcast, and the hoisting compartments were in the downcast. The pits were generally round or oval and were lined with two feet of stone or brick, with iron tubbing added to hold back water when passing through aquifers (Scotland was an exception, favoring rectangular pits lined with timber). The two pits might be dozens or even hundreds of yards apart; each had its own steam engine and, in the best mines, a back-up windlass or whim, powered by horses, to provide an emergency hoist if the engine failed. In the best mines, furthermore, arches of brick or masonry were used underground to support the roof at the bottom of the pit and even in the gangways. The essential passageways of a mine so constructed were thus fire resistant and able to withstand both the pressure of the overlying rock and the blast effects of minor methane-gas explosions.[21]

.There were some modifications of this plan, which was best adapted to the relatively level seams of bituminous coal in the north of England, in regions where the coal seams undulated and at times cropped out on the surface. This was particularly the case in the newly developed anthracite districts of South Wales in the 1850's. Here in some cases slopes instead of pits were sunk, starting at the outcrop and slanting down through the coal itself to the bottom. An American traveler in 1856 described a new slope near Swansea that was being driven to a depth of 1,800 feet. It was ten feet wide and eight feet high. The roof was built of small dressed stones in the shape of an arch; no mortar was used. To provide ventilation, this slope was bratticed by a wooden partition in the middle that divided it into upcast and downcast airways, and the upcast at the mouth was diverted into a culvert that ran up the mountainside about 150 feet high. The operators, "should the mine prove to be very fiery," planned to substitute brick for wood in the brattice later on.[22] In the early part of the century, brattices had also been used to save the expense of a second pit in some very deep vertical shafts, but the sides were still constructed of stone or brick. But these single-shaft collieries came under severe criticism as excessively dangerous and were outlawed by Parliament in 1862 after the Hartwell Colliery disaster, in which over 200 men were asphyxiated when the brattices were broken and the ventilation suspended. Thus by the 1850's most new English collieries had two separate pits for upcast and downcast.[23]

Knowledge of the best British ventilation methods were undoubtedly brought to America by the experienced English, Welsh, and Scottish miners who were imported by the hundreds to work the new anthracite collieries from the 1830's on. But best British practice was also communicated in American publications. The *Journal of the Franklin Institute,* for instance, as early as 1841 published an article "On the best method of ventilating Coal Mines" that specified separate upcast and downcast shafts with a furnace at the bottom of the upcast. And the best British standards of practice were also deliberately brought to the attention of American mine operators by the influential newspaper of the coal trade, the Pottsville *Miners' Journal,* which, beginning in 1855, ran several series of letters to the editor from "European Correspondents" like William Jackson Palmer and miscellaneous reprints from English publications.

At the beginning of the anthracite industry, however, these advanced British methods of entry and ventilation were not necessary. As long as drift or tunnel entry to gangways above water level was the norm, natural ventilation could be depended on. Even in the relatively shallow early slopes of the 1830's and 1840's, natural ventilation could be employed in the winter. But for the deeper mines artificial ventilation was required, and this, until the middle of the nineteenth century, took the form of either a furnace or a jet of steam. At first, furnaces were constructed on the surface, at the foot of a stone chimney connected to the upcast by a masonry culvert; later the furnace was generally placed below, at the foot of the upcast, next to a breast that supplied it with coal. Furnaces were obviously dangerous because, if they were fed air from within the mine, they could ignite the methane that had collected as the air passed through the miles of breasts and gangways, and even a dumb drift was no certain protection against a flash-back firedamp explosion. A dumb drift brought fresh air from the surface directly into the furnace through a side tunnel from the downcast airway, while the mine's foul air was diverted into the upcast by a special airway that by-passed the furnace. A safer alternative to the furnace, also developed in England, was to pipe live steam from surface boilers down into the upcast, thus supplying the impetus of lighter-than-air steam to the movement of the air.

Assuming that, whether by natural ventilation or with the assistance of furnace or steam jet, a movement of air through the mine had been established, there were still difficult problems to overcome. The fresh air had to be delivered to all working parts of the mine, while abandoned sections, which of course were still exuding quantities of methane, had to be effectively sealed off. There was no difficulty in taking the air down the slope or pit, running it along a gangway, and up the upcast. But this straight-line movement along the gangway had to be interrupted to pass the air across the working face of the coal in breasts and other chambers off the gangway. In the old days in Europe, and at first in Schuylkill County, side chambers where the miners worked were cleared of methane and stale air in the morning by such primitive techniques as waving blankets, or drawing a pile of brush through the area, or even firing the gas deliberately. But such expedients were inadequate in large mines and soon mine operators had to resort to the careful construction of brattices, headings, and doors. Headings were passages driven through the coal to connect breasts with each other, and to connect the main gangways with counter-gangways that ran parallel to them. Brattices were partitions of boards or cloth stretched over wooden frames to conduct air along the sides of breasts and across the face of the coal, or elsewhere apart from the main-gangway air course. And doors were necessary at various points along the main gangway to force the air into headings and along brattices; hence the need for door boys to open doors for the passage of men and coal cars and to make sure that they stayed shut at other times.[24]

All of this interior complexity obviously slowed down the movement of air; the older and more complex the mine, the slower the movement. Furthermore, if the air moved in one continuous line through all the departments of the mine, its final condition as it neared the upcast was apt to be very poor: low in oxygen and high in methane, carbon dioxide, powder smoke, water vapor, and all the other effluvia of the mine. To solve this problem, British mining engineers had as early as 1813 developed various systems of "splitting the air." To split the air in mines with steeply inclined veins, each working level had to be divided into districts, each composed of three or four (or more) breasts. Fresh air from the gangway was directed up an airway and across the face of the coal in several breasts, then led off into the return airway and so to the upcast. The principles of the method were described in English publications of the 1850's and the

43

practice was attributed to the illustrious Newcastle engineer John Buddle, who concerned himself with improving the ventilation of British mines. With splitting, furnaces, and enlarged airways, Buddle was able by 1850 to increase the volume of air moving through mines under his direction from about 7,000 cubic feet per minute to as much as 190,000 cubic feet per minute without creating a velocity too high for safety. (At high velocity the air could blow out lights and render the safety lamp ineffective by forcing gas through the mesh.[25]) But the practice of splitting the air in imitation of British practice was not even publicly discussed in Pennsylvania until the 1860's. In 1866 Daddow of St. Clair, in his and Bannan's *Coal, Iron, and Oil,* without giving credit to the British system, proposed as a new method of mining in pitching seams what he called "the boundary system," whose main advantage was "dividing or splitting the air." Splitting the air made the mine far safer than the traditional practice of running the air in one long column through the entire length of the mine. And he assumed the need for a flow of about 100,000 cubic feet per minute, far more than standard practice in Schuylkill County.[26] Splitting the air was introduced in the new Wadesville Shaft in 1867. The method of splits was again proposed in an article in the *Miners' Journal* in 1868 by the British mining engineer Thomas H. Walton.[27] But the first operator actually to experiment on a large scale with the method of splits and the boundary system was Colonel David P. Brown of Pottsville, who in about 1870 began to propose what he called the "panel system." Essentially the same as Daddow's "boundary" plan, it was advertised by Brown not because it was safer but because it made it possible to exploit each section in a manner similar to the English longwall method, working back from the airway and allowing the roof to settle as the miner worked toward the main gangway.[28] The standard British system of splitting the air was ostensibly introduced by law in the Pennsylvania Mine Safety Act of 1870, which provided that

> every mine having explosive gas . . . shall be divided into two, four
> or more panels or districts, each ventilated by a separate split or
> current of air, and fifty persons shall be the greatest number that
> shall work in any one panel or district at the same time. . . .[29]

But apparently the rule was laxly enforced. As late as 1883, in Chance's standard work on *Mining Methods and Appliances,* it was observed that in slope mining it was "customary to divide each lift into two splits, one on each side of the slope," and a similar two-split system operated with shafts, except that an additional split was added when a new lift was entered by an interior inclined plane, inside slope, or tunnel to another vein.[30] Inasmuch as most substantial collieries employed 200 or more men underground, it would seem that in many cases 100 or more men would be at work in each split. Indeed, merely to denote the east and west gangways as separate splits is not really an introduction of the English system of splitting the air at all, for the east and west gangways of necessity had always been separate ventilation systems, joined at the foot of the slope or shaft.

An apparent exception to the usual refusal to take advantage of British experience with ventilation was the quickness of the Schuylkill operators to experiment with the exhaust fan. Large, centrifugal blowers to exhaust the foul air from mines had been in use in central European metal mines at least as long ago as the sixteenth century and, as we noted earlier, were illustrated in Agricola's *De Re Metallica;* with steam engines as the source of power, they had been introduced in France and Belgium in the early part of the century. But the first experiments in Britain were not made until 1849, in Wales, and not until 1860 was the first "mechanical ventilator" installed in the great northern coal field. Most of the early British fans were "open" fans, casting out the upcast air from revolving blades at all points of their periphery, but these had the disadvantage of allowing surface air to enter the shaft behind the fan. In 1862 the Guibal fan was patented in Belgium. The Guibal had a spiral case surrounding the blades and a flexible shutter to control the escape velocity, and was so clearly superior to the open-fan design, and to the furnace, that within about a decade hundreds were installed in Great Britain, along with numerous open fans and air pumps.[31]

The Paris exposition of 1856 brought the attention of American engineers to the techniques of mechanical ventilation developed on the continent. French and Belgian progress was reported to readers of the *Miners' Journal* in an extended series of articles in 1856 and 1857. In the issue of March 15, 1856, for example, two ventilators were described and it was noted that 108 of the one and seventy-five of the other were either in operation or on order, including no less than sixty-four at the vast Anzin mines in the north of France. The price for a machine, including engine, capable of producing a current of 25,000 cubic feet per minute—which the *Miners' Journal* declared was the "average ventilation of comparatively extensive mines" in America—was said to be $1,820.

These reports would seem to have had an immediate but limited effect. In the winter of 1857–1858 J. Louden Beadle constructed and in-

*Beadle fan (1866), showing
underground placement
and belt-and-pulley drive*

stalled an enclosed suction fan, of the type reported in the *Miners' Journal*, in George H. Potts' Locustdale Colliery near Ashland. The fan, as described in the published patent specification, was eight feet in diameter and thirty inches wide, and could be run at speeds up to 300 revolutions per minute. No more than ninety rpm were needed at Locustdale, he claimed; at 300 rpm, 60,000 cubic feet of air per minute were discharged from the upcast air shaft, creating "a perfect storm of wind along the air courses." The Locustdale prototype was deemed a success and Beadle then sought and in 1865 obtained a patent, not for the principle of using a fan for force ventilation (already an old method for ventilating mines and large buildings) but for suction or exhaust ventilation.[32] Like Battin, he charged users of the method a fee. Daddow, who had served as a witness to Beadle's patent application, and who was probably related to him by marriage (he married Esther Beadle), in *Coal, Iron, and Oil* gave priority in fan ventilation of mines to Beadle over Guibal and his continental predecessors, and claimed that Beadle's fan was "the most perfect, effective, safe, and economical . . . mode of ventilation, and far superior in every respect to the furnace method."[33] The Beadle fan as commercially developed was a relatively small (usually only four to six feet in diameter), enclosed centrifugal blower placed in the return air course near the surface. It was driven by a pulley-and-belt system, presumably powered by a steam engine, at a high speed—150 to 300 revolutions per minute compared to the much slower (60 rpm), bigger (sixteen-foot to forty-foot diameter) Guibal-type fans that were surface-installed. George W. Snyder was the second operator in the county, after Potts, to try out the new Beadle fan, installing it at Pine Forest in 1863. He was motivated partly by other concerns than ventilating his mine, however, being "anxious to acquire the business of making fans also at his foundry or machine shop," as John Maguire put it.[34] By 1866 a number of large collieries in and around St. Clair had tried out the Beadle, including the Pine Forest, Hickory Slope, the St. Clair Shaft, Wolf Creek, the Mammoth, and the Wadesville Shaft.[35]

But the Beadle fan had serious mechanical disadvantages arising from the length of the belting and the need to run the fan at four times the speed of the engine; and its small size meant that it was unable to operate as more than a supplement to natural ventilation, being located in a return air

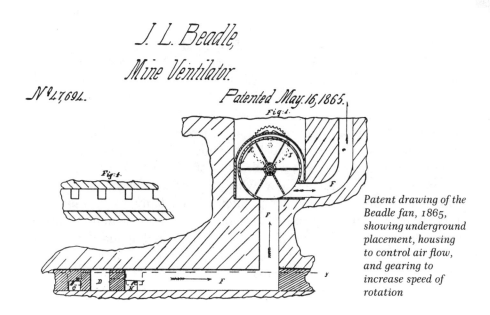

Patent drawing of the Beadle fan, 1865, showing underground placement, housing to control air flow, and gearing to increase speed of rotation

course where it functioned both to pull and to push the column of air. In effect, opting for the Beadle instead of the Guibal was refusing once again to follow best European practice. By 1870 the Beadle fan was being replaced by the much larger, surface-mounted Guibal fans and by large open fans, and the Guibal was virtually universal in the anthracite district by the 1880's.[36] Daddow remained defensive of Beadle and his fan, however. Beadle was attempting to collect royalties on all fans, not just those that copied his in detail, and some operators were refusing to pay him on the ground that there was abundant evidence to show that he was not the first to apply a suction fan to coal mines. Writing to the *Miners' Journal* from St. Clair in 1870, under the title "Honor to Whom Honor is Due," Daddow defended Beadle's claim to priority of invention as well as to being the person who "introduced the suction ventilation into the anthracite regions." Thus Beadle deserved to be paid the patent fee on "all the fans now in use," and Daddow further observed:

> J. Louden Beadle deserves from this community credit and honor, rather than censure and odium. He is modest and retiring.—He never paraded his claims before the public. . . . The inventive spirit, or the spirit of improvement, is not so spontaneous and exuberant in the coal regions, that its pinions need clipping; or its growth stunted by cold treatment and starvation.[37]

Like Battin, with whom he was compared, Beadle was rightly to be lauded as one of the heroes of the coal trade.

There were other aspects of underground mining practice that directly affected, or were affected by, the adequacy of the ventilation, and we must briefly discuss four of them: safety lamps and fuses, props and pillars, brattice work, and disposition of the refuse of the mine. Here the issue was not so much a failure to introduce continental innovations fully and promptly as a reluctance on the part of miners and management alike to slow down the pace of getting coal in the interest of safety and the structural integrity of the mine. It was a matter of mine management.

Safety lamps were not new when the miners began to work in Schuylkill County. The Davy lamp, Stephenson's lamp, the Clanny, and others were all known and for sale in company stores and in miners' supply houses like Bannan's in Pottsville. Because they flared up in the presence of methane, they were effective in warning the fire boss and the miner, and unless the air currents were too strong, or the miner swung his lamp, or a shot or a fall of coal created a blast of air, they protected the miner against setting off explosions of firedamp. But the problem was to persuade the miner to use the lamp. All varieties shed far less light than the naked lamp; furthermore, they were too heavy to be worn on the cap, and had to be carried by hand into the breast and then set down somewhere, necessarily farther from the work than a cap-worn lamp. So miners tended to use them only in presence of the fire boss, or when firedamp was so strong that there was no choice. This meant that the safety lamp was used after the presence of firedamp was detected, not in anticipation of it. John Maguire of St. Clair gave a chilling testimony to the practice in the Pine Forest Shaft:

> A party of men were working at night lowering the track in a gangway. It was necessary to keep open a certain door for quite a while in order to lower the track near it, consequently there was danger of gas having accumulated in the gangway. They had no safety lamps, and one of the men said he would test it with a naked light. He went into the gangway. The others protested, but John Maguire followed the man in order to see the test. He had heard old miners speak about it, but had never seen it done, and he was willing to risk a severe burning in order to learn how it was accomplished. The man took a piece of paper (not a candle), lighted it, and, shading the flame with his hand, watched for the elongation of the flame over his hand. By the elongation he could determine the presence or the absence of gas, if he had raised the naked light but very short distance, from two to four inches, higher, he would have lighted the gas and produced an explosion.[38]

Furthermore, despite the reassuring belief that some mines were fiery and others not, or that particular parts of a mine were safe and others dangerous, firedamp was unpredictable. In some breasts, large quantities accumulated in fissures behind the face, and firing the shot of gun powder could release it suddenly, driving out as much as hundreds of tons of coal with explosive force, killing miners and blasting away props and brattices for as much as twenty yards. Or miners with naked lights might penetrate accidentally into old, gas-filled gangways or breasts that had been sealed off and forgotten years before. Because unexpected confrontations with gas occurred, generally speaking, when the miners were not using safety lamps, miners were apt to produce unanticipated explosions in "safe" districts.

49

Another problem had to do with the firing of shots. Below water level, the mines were usually wet, water dripping from the ceiling, oozing down the walls, lying in pools on the floor. In this soggy environment the fuses that set off the charge were apt to get damp and the fire to run more slowly than the miner calculated. If the shot did not fire in the expected time, the miner faced a dilemma: was the fuse dead or just smoldering? Many a miner, concluding that he would have to set a new fuse, miscalculated and reached the drill hole just as the wall of coal blew down on top of him. To solve this problem, various safety fuses were devised. The most successful of these were invented and patented (in 1871) by Samuel Daddow and his wife's brother, Jesse Beadle, and (in 1872) by John Holmes. The Daddow squib was a fuse with a core of Du Pont powder, wrapped either in varnished paper or in an outer spiral winding of thin brass so as to make it waterproof, with a final coating of "soluble glass." Daddow and Beadle set up the Miners' Supply Company in St. Clair to manufacture a variety of "miners' safety squibs." In the old days, miners made their own squibs of paper or straw down in the mine, and there was some initial prejudice against the new patent devices. But even experienced miners found that the new squibs were more reliable and more economical of time and money (storekeepers paid about a third of a cent per squib at the factory). Daddow's squib was a huge success and within a few years was in widespread use not only around St. Clair but in coal mines all over the country.[39] By the 1880's it was referred to in Appleton's *Encyclopedia of Technology* as the standard squib for coal mining.

Pillars and props were the two methods of supporting the roof. Pillars were the variously shaped sections of coal that were not touched in mining, separating gangways from the breasts, the breasts from each other and from slopes and airways, and one mine from another. Pillars might amount to a quarter of the coal underground, calculating by the rule of thumb that dictated a ten-yard-wide pillar on either side of a thirty-yard-wide breast, and in some mines even larger pillars were left. To the operator, pillars represented a loss of profit, and so there was always a temptation to minimize the thickness of pillars in the opening and development of the mine; furthermore, when the breasts in a section were exhausted (and sometimes even before), the operator usually proceeded to "rob the pillars"—that is, to assign miners to remove the coal in the pillars, working back from the face to the gangway, until the roof crushed down and prevented further extraction. Unfortunately, the crush could be more extensive than anticipated and could interrupt gangways and airways and thus stop the ventilation. It also left a mass of unventilated refuse or "gob"

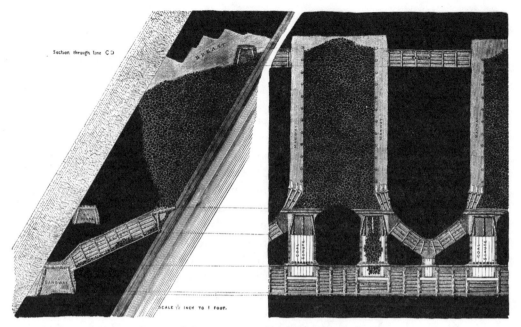

Cross and front sections of a steeply sloping breast

that presented dangers of its own. Thus robbing pillars in a lift near the shaft or slope while workings farther along the gangway were still active posed a threat to the integrity of the whole lift comparable to starting out in the beginning with weak pillars. Yet, at colliery after colliery, premature robbing of pillars and leaving pillars too thin to prevent crushes (or flooding from adjacent abandoned workings) was a practice condoned if not ordered by the operator.

Timbering in the mines of course included the setting of props and collars in all traveling roads in the mine: drifts, slopes, gangways, counter-gangways, tunnels, and headings. The timbering of a passageway generally involved a prop on either side and a collar under the roof, with rough lumber lagging between the sets. In the breasts, however, single props were placed where the miner judged them to be needed to keep the roof from falling, and (in some plans) along the sides of the breasts to partition off airways. Timbering was difficult where pitches were steep and where, as in the Mammoth Vein, the vault eventually reached twenty to forty feet. An enormous amount of round hardwood timber was used in the mines. In the year 1905 (the earliest date for which I have figures) the average

Pennsylvania colliery used nearly 250,000 cubic feet of prop timber. Timber was shipped by rail into the coal regions by hundreds of lumber companies, large and small, from an early date, as the forests around the collieries were stripped away. The cost of timber amounted to about 8.5 cents per ton of coal mined.[40]

The problem with timbering, from the point of view of both the operator and the miner, was that it was a nuisance, costing money that ate into the operator's narrow margin of profit and forcing the contract miner to spend time in unpaid "dead work." And so some operators either deliberately ordered, or silently permitted, the skimping of timbering, allowing the gangway props and collars to be set too far apart, or to be made of logs too narrow for the weight, and letting the miner take chances with his roof by failing to install props where they were needed. Similar carelessness was shown in maintenance. Props rotted in the damp caverns and eventually collapsed, permitting falls of rock and even the crushing of whole sections of a lift.

Similar considerations applied to brattice work. Essential to proper ventilation, brattices of wood or cloth suspended on wooden frames had to be advanced as the gangways and breasts were extended. And they had to be carefully maintained, for each leak of air weakened the current. But brattices too were dead work, costly of time and money, temporarily preventing the operator and the miner from extracting coal. So brattices too were allowed to decay in poorly kept mines: holes were eaten through them by rats, the damp rotted cloth and wood, and flying rocks and coal ripped out sections.

And there was the gob. The gob was the mixture of slate, bony coal, coal dust, and lumps missed in handling that remained on the floor of the breast after the miner and his helper had done the day's work. Eventually this debris, tons of it, remained behind after the breast itself was worked out and abandoned. As the brattices and props decayed and the roof crushed down as the pillars were robbed, the gob became more and more dangerous, a mass of semi-ventilated coal and slate constantly exuding firedamp and gradually heating as it oxidized until a hand could not be laid on it. That spontaneous combustion in the gob could cause mine fires, as well as the ubiquitous fires in culm banks, was reported in a Philadelphia publication, G. Jenkin Phillips' *System of Mining Coal*, as early as 1858, and it must have been common knowledge to miners.[41] But as late as 1883, in his authoritative treatise on *Mining Methods and Appliances*, geologist H. M. Chance of the Second Geological Survey of Pennsylvania denied that it could occur. As usual, the careless miner was blamed for mine fires:

52

The theory of spontaneous combustion has also frequently been advanced as an explanation of the origin of mine fires. . . . The reason why this theory has been so frequently advanced, is attributable to the fact that many mine fires, when first discovered, have been confined to the gob in old workings, but it does not follow that, because the gob is burning and no miner can be found who will acknowledge having any connection with the origin of the fire, that its origin was spontaneous.[42]

In general, one must conclude that with few exceptions the colliery operators of Schuylkill County permitted extremely inefficient and unsafe working practices underground while maintaining relatively advanced engines and breakers on the surface. Failure to insist on the use of safety lamps, failure to replace furnaces with powerful surface fans and to sink double shafts, failure to leave adequate pillars, failure to set and maintain sufficient props and brattices, and failure to ventilate or remove the gob— all these failings were regressions from well-known principles of best practice in European, and particularly British, coal mines of earlier years. The price the operators paid was business failure; the miners paid with their lives.

II

THE DEVELOPMENT OF ST. CLAIR

Three main groups of businessmen were responsible for the development of St. Clair: the owners of the underground mineral rights (the "landowners"); the colliery operators who extracted and processed the coal; and the transportation companies, who carried it to Philadelphia and other markets and there either sold it directly or delivered it to coal merchants and coastal shipping companies. Contract miners, tradesmen, and professional men owned their own hand tools and might consider themselves to be entrepreneurs of a sort, but they were not in the same economic class as the wealthy families and the corporations. Most of the owners were members of two large extended-family partnerships, "the Carey group" and "the Wetherill group." Several of the more remotely related members of the Carey group actually lived in St. Clair, but the senior figures in both groups resided in Philadelphia or in Pottsville, which for financial and legal purposes was at this time a satellite of Philadelphia. The operators too, with the exception of the Johns and Lawton families, lived in Pottsville rather than St. Clair. And the transportation companies—the Schuylkill Navigation Company, the Philadelphia and Reading Railroad, and the Mill Creek and Mine Hill Railroad—were headquartered where most of the stockholders lived, in Philadelphia. Thus most of the major economic decisions that led to the founding and economic progress—and decline—of St. Clair were made by people who lived elsewhere and who were interested in St. Clair only as one of the places where their money was invested. On the other hand, some of the major labor policies that affected the profitability of these investments were being formulated by the workers of St. Clair.

THE OWNER FAMILIES

By English common law (continued in force in Pennsylvania courts after the Revolution), ownership of land ordinarily included ownership not only of the surface but also of whatever stone and minerals lay beneath the surface. But surface and mineral rights could be separated. A landowner could sell off surface rights to other persons, including the right to farm, cut timber, and build houses, roads, and commercial and industrial structures, while he retained ownership of the mineral rights, including the right to lease access to the minerals and the right to make such alterations on the surface as were necessary to the extraction of the said minerals (after, of course, paying just compensation for damages). Both the Wetherills and the Careys initially bought undivided rights to their major tracts and then sold off surface lots while they retained and leased rights to mine and process coal.

The leader of the Carey group was Henry Charles Carey, son of Matthew Carey, the renowned Philadelphia publisher and writer on social issues, and recently the manager of his father's publishing enterprise. In the summer of 1835 Henry quit the book business, invested more than $120,000 of his own and his partners' money in 3,200 acres of coal lands (thus becoming one of the largest landowners in the Pottsville area), and set about the mining of anthracite. He was forty-two years old, wealthy, pugnacious, and determined to help in the economic development of his country. Part of his plan was to formulate and publish a new system of political economy that would guide a developing nation to prosperity, free from British economic imperialism. And part was to make money for himself and his family in the new anthracite industry.[1]

The remainder of the Carey family were Matthew's other surviving children and their spouses.[2] When Matthew died in 1839, he left two sons and four daughters: Henry, Edward, Maria, Eliza, Susan, and Frances. In 1821 Frances had married twenty-nine-year-old Isaac Lea, a merchant and paleontologist who soon became a partner in the Carey publishing business; by 1839 she had two sons of her own. Eliza married an ordnance officer, Thomas Baird, in 1822, and already had six children when he died in 1842. Lea and Baird were helpful scientific and technical advisers to Henry Carey, who, although a man of undoubted brilliance, was largely self-taught and unfamiliar with mechanics' shops and chemists' laboratories. Edward also took part in both the publishing and coal enterprises but deferred to Henry on matters concerning coal.

Lea, the son of a well-to-do Quaker merchant of Wilmington, Delaware, had been sent to Philadelphia in his youth to work in one of the family firms, an import-and-export house. There he had become friends with young Lardner Vanuxem, who later would direct the first New York Geological Survey (which achieved equal fame with Pennsylvania's), and with Vanuxem prowled about southeastern Pennsylvania, visiting geologically interesting localities. He and Vanuxem enlisted in the army during the War of 1812 and thereby lost membership in the Society of Friends. After the war the two continued their geological explorations, including a visit to the new coal mines near Wilkes-Barre. Upon marrying into the family, he

Henry C. Carey (1793–1879),
(portrait by T. Henry Smith)

entered the Carey publishing enterprise. By days he worked as publisher; but in the evenings he devoted himself to chemistry, geology, and paleontology. The study of fossil molluscs would eventually become the center of his life's work and form the subject matter of most of the hundreds of scientific publications that issued from his pen. He is said to have identified about 2,000 new species of *Mollusca*. His most celebrated discovery, however, was a dinosaur footprint preserved in the Red Shale of Sharp Mountain at Pottsville. His first announcement of this remarkable find was published in 1839 and immediately created a stir among geologists both in America and in Europe. It continued to be referred to as "the oldest case of an air-breathing animal on record" as late as 1885. Among his many honors were an LL.D. from Harvard (1852) and the presidency of the American Association for the Advancement of Science.[3]

As the publishing house prospered, so did Isaac Lea. Not content with two careers, he now entered upon a third, that of investor in coal lands. In the early 1830's he became the principal partner in the Dauphin and Susquehanna Coal Company. Lea hired the eminent geologist and mining engineer Richard Cowling Taylor to survey the coal and iron resources of the company's tract, amounting to about 42,000 acres, on the east bank of the Susquehanna River, embracing much of the western end of the southern coal field. He had the coal and iron samples analyzed by his two teenage sons, Henry Charles Lea and Matthew Carey Lea, in the Philadelphia laboratory of geologist James C. Booth. Two of the veins discovered were named Carey and Lea: it was a family enterprise. And it may have been during rambles in the coal region, populated by many recent Irish immigrants, that son Henry Charles Lea acquired some of the aversion to the Irish that he displayed later as a historian. His brother Matthew became an internationally known chemist. Isaac Lea may have provided the initial entrepreneurial impulse to the Carey group.[4]

Baird was probably another of the persons who drew Carey's attention to the desirability of investing in coal lands. Baird was an ex-army officer who had served as an artillerist in the War of 1812 and, before he resigned his commission in 1827, had served as ordnance officer at the Frankford Arsenal in Philadelphia. Carey had also served in the war and probably met Baird then; they were close friends for years before Baird married Carey's sister in 1822.[5] In the summer of 1830, Baird, along with three other engineers, surveyed the 28,460 acres of wilderness in northern Schuylkill County purchased earlier that year by Stephen Girard, a wealthy Philadelphia banker, and this survey revealed—or confirmed—the presence of outcrops of coal on the estate lands. Coal was not seriously mined on the Girard Estate, however, until 1862, thirty-one years after Girard's death.[6] Carey thus had the advice of a man trained in mechanical and civil engineering when he began to purchase property on behalf of the family partnership. Rather than buy remote wilderness tracts, his strategy was to buy land near Pottsville, the county seat, land already proven to produce coal, and provided with mill seats, roads and railroads, and town sites already laid out. Such tracts were much more expensive, of course, than Girard's. Girard had paid only $30,000—a few cents more than $1 per acre—for his 28,460 acres north of Broad Mountain; Carey put down about $40 per acre for his initial estate.[7]

Susan died in 1844, unmarried, and Edward, the youngest, suffering from chronic ill-health and also unmarried, died in 1845 at the age of forty. Thus in 1845 Henry Carey, married in 1818 but still childless, found himself, in effect, the financial guardian of one unmarried sister and one widowed sister with six children; his third surviving sister was married to his business partner. All of Carey's sisters received shares in one or another of the family's coal land investments. Carey also assumed a degree of financial responsibility for his widowed sister's children, who received shares in Carey interests when their mother died. It was, in fact, Eliza's children who continued the line, preserving the Carey family papers through subsequent generations until they were donated to the Historical Society of Pennsylvania in the twentieth century.[8] The eldest of Eliza's daughters, Ellen, married the mine operator Joseph Lawton in 1844 and went to live in the big mansion at St. Clair; when Lawton failed in 1850, he and his family moved west, stopping in various towns where Joseph took positions with the local banks, finally coming to rest in Green Bay, Wisconsin. Throughout this sinking career the Lawtons appealed successfully to their uncle Henry for loans, which were still not repaid when Carey died in 1879 (his will included a provision for forgiving these debts and giving Ellen some shares of railroad stock).[9] Eliza's eldest son, Henry Carey Baird, served as legal agent in Pottsville for the Carey group in various land transactions, and then became part of the family publishing business, issuing a notable line of practical books on various branches of technology and engineering. He also became an enthusiastic convert to his uncle's social philosophy and an ardent pamphleteer and contributor to popular journals promoting the cause of protection and the harmony of interests.[10]

Carey's wife, Patty Leslie, bore him no children in nearly thirty years of marriage and died early, in 1847. She brought Carey into connection, however, with an interesting family who may have contributed something to Carey's lifelong interest in new technology. Her father, Robert Leslie, was a self-taught mathematician and draftsman and a member of the American Philosophical Society in the days of Jefferson and Franklin. Her brother, Charles Robert, emigrated to England, studied with Benjamin West, and eventually became sufficiently celebrated as a historical painter and illustrator to be elected to the Royal Academy. He had been a room-mate in London of Samuel F. B. Morse. And Patty's sister Eliza carried on a long literary career, publishing with Carey and Hart; she was the author of a wonderfully successful cookbook that went into thirty-eight editions in her lifetime (and has just recently been reprinted) and at the time of her death was writing a biography of John Fitch, the steamboat inventor.[11]

As we have seen, Carey and his wife had no children of their own. Carey did, however, have one and perhaps two daughters. One, Virginia, the "adopted daughter" mentioned in his will, married a Philadelphia merchant, Thomas Albert Haven. A large investor in coal lands, Haven owned eighty-one acres within the borough of St. Clair, and bought up much of the property along Mill Creek between the St. Clair Tract and Port Carbon, which thus passed into the hands of the Carey group. Carey also had a natural daughter, according to his second cousin

Elizabeth Sheridan Carey, a poet and feminist who lived in Paris and who claimed that the "Miss McKean" whose name (Kate McKean) stood on the title page of a catechism of Carey's political economy published in 1866 was actually Henry Carey's granddaughter by a woman who eventually married a "drunken Irishman" in Maryland.[12] Carey in his will of 1864 made a bequest of a $200 life annuity to his "cousin" Catherine McKean of Cumberland, Maryland. Elizabeth Sheridan Carey also admitted that she was not "a favorite" of Henry's (although he made her an annuitant in his will). Whether Carey had a natural daughter may never be known.

Also to be included in the roster of the Carey group were two men not related to the Careys by marriage or descent but rather by business connection: Burd Patterson (1788–1867) and Abraham Hart (1810–1885). Burd Patterson was a legendary hero of the coal trade, one of "the enterprising men," as the *Miners' Journal* put it in 1867, "who assisted in building up this Region to its present prominent position." A country boy by birth, he acquired a classical education and as a youth moved to Philadelphia, where he taught Latin and Greek for a time at Mount Airy College. When industry picked up after the War of 1812, he established what was said to be the first factory for spinning wool at Manayunk in Philadelphia (later to become one of the great textile-manufacturing centers in the United States). In 1826, soon after the opening of the coal trade, he moved to Pottsville and promoted the development of the first railroads that sprang up in the late 1820's and early '30's to connect the collieries with the canal landings of the Schuylkill Navigation Company. When Carey met him about 1835 as a partner in coal-land ventures, Patterson had been a resident of Pottsville for nearly ten years. After establishing himself in the Pottsville district, he bought, with partners and borrowed money, remote, inexpensive tracts where he judged coal might later be found and towns established, beyond Broad Mountain at Shamokin, Ashland, and Mahanoy City. Cash flow was maintained by constantly buying and selling town lots and small tracts. He was an aggressive booster of iron and steel, being, as we shall see, the entrepreneur who financed the Pioneer Furnace at Pottsville, a partner in the construction of blast furnaces at Farrandsville, St. Clair, Danville, and Shamokin, a prospector for blackband ore, and at his own expense an early promoter of the Bessemer process for making steel. By the time of his death in 1867, he was worth upward of a million dollars. His ventures with Carey over the years were thus minor parts of Patterson's own strategy for industrial development and personal profit; but his example may have loomed large in Carey's mind, encouraging him to undertake daring technological experiments, like their joint sinking of

the first slope and the building of the furnace at St. Clair. Patterson may
even have encouraged Carey to consider seriously the proposal, by Charles
Lawton and then Enoch McGinness, to sink the county's first vertical
shaft.[13]

Abraham Hart (1810–1885) also had no connection by marriage or
descent: he was a Jewish businessman, the son of a shopkeeper from
Germany, who on the death of his father had been given a job, early in
his teens, by Henry Carey. When the firm was divided in 1829, Hart
joined with Edward Carey as publishers under the title of E. L. Carey and
A. Hart. After Edward Carey died in 1845, his nephew Henry Carey Baird
took his place as partner until 1849, when the firm was dissolved. Baird
went into publishing for himself in the scientific and technical field, and
Hart continued his own firm until 1849, when he retired from publishing
to enter business on his own as a manufacturer of a machine to make
buttonholes automatically. He was prominent in Philadelphia's Jewish
community as president of the congregation of Mickveh Israel, the first in
Philadelphia, and as a promoter of Jewish educational and charitable organizations. In his later years he moved to New York, fell upon difficult
times financially in the 1870's, and was relieved by a subscription from his
friends. Henry Carey felt close enough to Hart to name him as one of the
executors of his will.[14]

The core of the Wetherill group consisted of the children and
grandchildren of the second Samuel Wetherill (1764–1829) of
Philadelphia. Wetherill and his sons operated a lead smelter and
manufactories of dyestuffs and paint pigments (particularly red and
white lead), oil of vitriol, and lead pipe.[15] During the coal-land boom in
the late 1820's, Samuel Wetherill had purchased coal lands amounting to
nearly a square mile in and around Port Carbon and had formed a
partnership with George de B. Keim and Jacob W. Seitzinger, prominent citizens of Pottsville (Seitzinger would become chief burgess of
that town in 1834 and Keim would be a sometime president of the Philadelphia and Reading Railroad), in the purchase of the coal lands north
of Port Carbon, adjacent to Carey's St. Clair Tract. When Samuel died in
1829, his daughter and four sons each inherited an equal share in the
estate, including the coal-land partnership, the Wetherill interest in
which—about 50 percent in the case of the adjoining St. Clair lands—was
held as individual property by the heirs. The Wetherill estate grew,
gradually surrounding the St. Clair Tract on three sides, east, north, and
west, eventually amounting to about 2,000 acres in which the Wetherill
interest added up to about two thirds. For the next forty-two years, until

the sale of the Wetherill estate to the Philadelphia and Reading Coal and Iron Company, the heirs and their children, cousins, and nephews were involved in the administration of these coal lands. In 1850 financial management was being carried on from Philadelphia by John Price Wetherill (1794–1853) and his brother William, as attorneys on behalf of their widowed sister, Rebecca Gumbes, and the widows and children of their brothers Charles and Samuel, who died in 1838 and 1839. These widows had, in keeping with Quaker practice, inherited their husbands' shares in the coal-land estate, partly to keep for their own support and partly as guardians for their children. The children would assume ownership when they came of age.[16] From 1848 on, the estate had as its agent in Pottsville William's son John Macomb Wetherill (1828–1895), who looked after the collection of rents, the buying and selling of lands, the disposition of legal matters, and the proper operation of the collieries that mined the Wetherills' coal. Other members of the family also became involved in the development of the coal trade. Charles Wetherill's son Charles Mayer Wetherill (1825–1871), who studied chemistry and earned his Ph.D. in Germany under Liebig in 1848, traveled around the state investigating iron furnaces on behalf of the Pennsylvania Association of Iron Manufacturers and in 1853, in collaboration with Charles Wilson Peale and his cousin John Macomb, published a *Report on the Iron and Coal of Pennsylvania* to accompany the commonwealth's exhibit at the Crystal Palace Exhibition in New York. And John Price's grandson John Price Wetherill III (1844–1906) became a mining engineer, the author of a standard article on methods of coal mining, and for a time served as superintendent of the collieries of the Philadelphia and Reading Coal and Iron Company. He was to become famous as the inventor of a magnetic separator which revolutionized the dressing of zinc and other ores by vastly increasing the recoverability of metal from pulverized ore.[17] By 1857 there were no less than twelve Wetherills, spanning three generations, who owned part of the coal-land estate.[18]

It would be difficult if not impossible to follow the complexities of the purchase, sale, and division of the Wetherill coal properties from 1829 to 1872. Ownership and administration was complicated by the fact that Samuel P. Wetherill, one of the Wetherill heirs, was married to Anna Seitzinger, daughter of Jacob, and had received some of the coal lands in trust as his wife's dowry. Another Wetherill, William, eventually established a farm in Schuylkill County and in the 1860's became treasurer of the town of Port Carbon. The Wetherill factories and smelters in Philadelphia and later in Bethlehem used anthracite purchased from the coal companies that leased their lands, and they transported it in their own coal barges. But basically the Wetherills treated their mineral lands as an investment, initially regarded as speculative but eventually as income producing, and by judicious additions and partitions acquired a strip of land about three miles long and a mile wide just south of Broad Mountain, where the Mammoth Vein and other rich seams of coal outcropped and could be mined at convenient depths. This estate consisted of seven "tracts," named for the owners at the time the coal trade commenced: the Lee lands, stretching from New Castle on the west nearly to Silver Creek on the east, and including the northern portion of St. Clair where Johns' Eagle Colliery stood; two tracts between St. Clair and Port Carbon, jointly owned with the Repp and Keim estates, of little value as coal land because of the depth and faultiness of the veins; the Saw Mill tract, east and south of St. Clair, containing the Pine Forest Colliery; the Ellmaker Tract, acquired about 1848, adjoining St. Clair on the west, containing a colliery at Wadesville; and the Flowery Field and Oak Hill tracts, just south of Mount Laffee.[19] At one time the Wetherills also owned the vast Valley Furnace Tract, larger than all the rest of their holdings put together, east of the Lee lands, but sold it in 1851.

The goal of the Wetherill administrators was to make money for the heirs, and to this end they wheeled and dealed in coal properties and squeezed every penny they could from their lessees who operated the collieries. They wanted their royalties paid promptly and in full. As "Wetherill and Brother" put it in a stiff letter of instructions to their new attorney in Pottsville in December 1837 regarding some recently acquired mineral lands:

> our part must be worked to the best advantage by operations of some responsibility. We would not let the veins unless to those who can and will pay for the coal they get out[.] our losses in Schuylkill County on business carelessly contracted have already been too great and we will rather keep the coal in the ground untouched than suffer those to operate who unable to pay, open the drifts, carry off a quantity of coal and give up the working, we do not wish to be troubled with such. . . .[20]

The brothers in Philadelphia, John Price and William, occupied as they were with their paint-and-lead business, depended upon conscientious agents in Pottsville to collect royalties, draft and file legal papers, and investigate local situations. They did on occasion visit Schuylkill County, but mostly managed their coal affairs by correspondence. From 1837 to about 1846 their agent was the distinguished lawyer George W. Farquhar. About 1846 John Macomb Wetherill became the family agent, and he remained in place managing the Wetherill interests until the sale to the Philadelphia and Reading Coal and Iron Company in 1872.

John Macomb Wetherill (1828–?)

John Macomb Wetherill took up his duties as resident manager of the Wetherill coal estates at a time of trial in the family. His mother, Dr. William Wetherill's wife of twenty-six years (during which time she had borne fifteen children), had left his father, fearing that his accusations of infidelity and of being a spendthrift were the symptoms of an illness, and had taken refuge with her children in the house of her husband's cousin. When Dr. Wetherill's attorney applied to the legislature for the passage of a bill of divorcement, Isabella took her case to the press. Her impassioned plea to the senators and representatives was published on the front page of the *Miners' Journal* in February 1851.[21] Apparently the breach was healed before divorce, however, and the scandal passed; but John Macomb never married. When he came to Pottsville at the age of eighteen, fresh from two years as an undergraduate at the University of Pennsylvania, he knew nothing of coal mining. But he was immediately plunged into a dispute over the accessibility of the Mammoth Vein and he made his own inquiries into the merits of opposing geological theories. (This dispute will be discussed in detail in Chapter Four.) Perhaps more by accident than design, the Wetherills had acquired lands in the more valuable northern part of the basin, and Wetherill was able to encourage the Johns brothers to proceed in a slow, conservative, and ultimately very successful manner. In his investigation of the geological issues, he was, as his biographer put it, "prominent and indefatigable. . . . In his experimentation he was characterized by enterprise and courage . . . at the cost of much time, labor, and large expenditure of means." Wetherill played a large part in the social life of Pottsville too, as a musician, the author of a play about the anthracite region which we shall discuss later, a leader in Democratic politics, a sportsman, and something of a military hero during the Civil War.[22]

The Carey coal estate, like the Wetherill, at any one time comprised a number of different tracts, each owned by a slightly different group of people; and both the tracts and their ownership changed over time. The St. Clair Tract was originally purchased in 1835 in partnership by Henry Carey and his wife (one-quarter share) and Edward Carey and Abraham Hart (three-quarter share). After Edward Carey's death in 1845, his sisters and Isaac Lea were allotted shares from his holdings. By 1855 the ownership was divided into 240 shares: Isaac Lea, 86; William Blanchard (Lea's partner in the publishing business), 4 (no doubt derived from Lea's portion); Henry Carey, 70; Eliza Baird, 20; Maria Carey, 20; and Abraham Hart, 40. When Maria died in 1863, she left her shares in the tract to Ellen Lawton, Eliza's daughter, the husband of the family's financial invalid, Joseph Lawton.[23]

Before his death in 1845, Edward Carey seems to have been as active as his brother in the management of the coal lands; but although he visited Pottsville regularly, he and Henry mostly worked through their brother-in-law, Thomas Baird. Baird played the same role for the Careys as John Macomb Wetherill did for the Wetherills, acting as general steward for the partnership: preparing leases, collecting rents, remitting payments, keeping the partnership's accounts, supervising the construction and installation of hauling and pumping engines, and inspecting prospective coal lands. He and his wife arrived in Pottsville in the winter of 1835–1836, boarding at first and leaving their daughters with aunts in Philadelphia and their son at Westown, a Quaker boarding school near West Chester. Baird worked hard, spending most of his days on horseback directing "many men . . . in Mining Shipping Coal erecting Steam Engine & c" and his evenings attending to correspondence and business conferences. He quickly became a central social and political figure in the new town, taking charge of the local militia (as Wetherill would do later in his turn), entertaining the governor, contributing (under complaint) to all the charities, attending balls and Masonic functions, and becoming close friends with the important local gentry, including George Snyder, the steam-engine maker (who would name a son after him), George H. Potts, the Careys' colliery lessee, engine-maker Benjamin Haywood, Dr. James Carpenter, and Dr. Andrew Halberstadt, leading physicians, and F. B. Nichols, who had sold Carey the St. Clair Tract. Although Baird sometimes had trouble making ends meet, he and Eliza managed to buy a new house, planted their garden with roses, strawberries, and raspberries, and year after year looked forward to better times. But all this came suddenly to an end when he died in April 1842, after an illness of four days, of an "ulcerated sore throat."[24]

After Baird's death, the Carey group turned to an experienced Pottsville real-estate agent, Andrew Russell, to take care of their financial and legal interests, and thereafter Russell and his son had the property under their charge until it was sold in 1872. Russell was a wealthy, conservative, pious gentleman, especially active in the Temperance Society. He managed an extensive real-estate business and kept the Careys' accounts with the colliery operators. Each month he remitted to Philadelphia a list of the amounts in long tons of coal of different sizes sent to market by each operator, the rent due on each ton, the total rental, and the amount of cash due each partner according to the proportion of his shares. When all was going reasonably well, as, for instance, in October 1855, the five Carey collieries shipped 11,154 tons of regular coal and 1,010 tons of pea coal (the smallest size). The rental on regular coal was 30 cents per ton (except for the smallest mine, where it was 28) and on pea, 10 cents. The total rental was figured by Russell as $3,437.97, of which $55.34 went to William Blanchard, $286.66 each went to Mrs. Baird and Miss Carey, $573.33 to Abraham Hart, $1,232.66 to Isaac Lea, and $1,003.32 to Henry Carey.[25] Even after real-estate taxes, such rentals were sufficient to support comfortable households in both the Carey and Wetherill groups.

But Russell did not have the technological expertise of Baird, so after Baird's death responsibility for local technical supervision had to be exercised by professional mining engineers like Peter W. Sheafer, John Maddison, and George K. Smith, who were from time to time hired by the Careys to survey, inspect, report, and make recommendations. After the deaths of Baird in 1842 and Edward Carey in 1845, however, there can be no doubt that the active manager of the Carey Estate was Henry C. Carey himself. Busy as he was with his economic and political writing, he nevertheless found time to act as the group's managing director. As his voluminous manuscript correspondence shows, Carey kept the reins of the enterprise firmly grasped in his hands, sometimes even bypassing his own agent, Russell, who complained that Carey would draw up and execute leases without consulting him, even though "the property is under my charge." Carey was very aggressive in his management, constantly embroiled in lawsuits against his lessees or brought against him by his neighbors the Wetherills (of whom as businessmen he had a low opinion). And he was relentless in his drive to build up a larger and larger portfolio of coal properties. Starting out in the 1830's with the Westwood, York Farm, Eyre, and Guinea Hill tracts to the west and north of Pottsville, and the St. Clair Tract, he then sought to connect these two properties with a band of tracts spanning Mill Creek. In the 1850's he acquired an eighty-acre tract from his son-in-law, Thomas Haven, between St. Clair and Port Carbon that contained the mines and patch on Mill Creek at Scalpington. With John Tucker, president of the Reading Railroad, he acquired an interest in the Pott and Bannan Tract north of St. Clair, around New Castle, where Joseph Lawton's colliery was located, and, when Lawton failed, entered into the lease of the Mammoth Colliery to George Repplier. He and Isaac Lea bought the 230-acre Duncan Tract and the Hartman Tract, west of St. Clair, in 1855. Between 1858 and the early 1860's, he and Lea held a controlling interest in the largest remaining coal tract between Pottsville and St. Clair, the lands of the languishing North American Coal Company, which in a few years they sold to the Mammoth Vein Consolidated Coal Company.[26]

But Carey's plans went beyond Schuylkill County. Early in the 1850's he bought, on speculation, some coal lands at a place called Shickshinny, south of Wilkes-Barre in Luzerne County. Others thought that Carey had made a mistake, that there was little coal to be found, and that anyway there was no outlet to market for the "small operators" (the large coal companies in Luzerne also owned the railroads). They advised Carey to sell. But Carey hung on, and, with partners from the Carey, Lawton, and other groups, established both a colliery and a company to build a bridge across the Susquehanna. By the summer of 1859, the bridge was complete and a mine opened. In this enterprise, and on occasions when Carey was abroad, Carey's nephew, the hard-driving Henry Carey Baird, served as his personal representative and attorney, keeping him advised on developments and offering his opinion on the best course of action on St. Clair matters.[27]

Repplier's Mammoth Colliery (1862)

Among the landowners, mention must also be made of Benjamin Bannan, publisher and editor of the influential Pottsville *Miners' Journal* and sometime partner in colliery operations on lands owned by both the Carey and the Wetherill groups. Although he dabbled financially in the coal trade, it was through his newspaper and political activities that Bannan played his most important role in the development of the anthracite industry. Bannan, raised

Benjamin Bannan (1807–1875)

as a farm boy and trained as a stereotype printer (a process adapted to the cylindrical presses by which newspapers are printed), in 1829 at the age of twenty-two purchased the nearly defunct *Miners' Journal* and moved to Pottsville. He owned the paper outright for thirty-seven years, and a half-interest thereafter until two years before his death; and even during those last two years he continued to supply the paper with the statistics of coal—its production, price, and transport charges, by colliery and carrier—that made his paper the one essential source for economists and legislators concerned with the coal trade. The paper always carried the imprint of his strongly conservative views. He voted for John Quincy Adams, the last Federalist, in 1828, and it is said that he voted in every presidential election in his lifetime, always for whatever national party was ranged against "The Democracy." He was an early and strong advocate of a protective tariff for American industry, anticipating Henry Carey in this regard, and when Carey was converted to this position, Bannan gave Carey's views liberal space in his columns. For fifteen years he was a director of the Pottsville school and for fourteen years president of the school board. He advocated a national currency long before it was finally adopted by the federal government as a necessity during the Civil War—except for his then radical suggestion that the currency limit be expanded as the wealth of the country increased.

Bannan, in effect, articulated in his newspaper, in miscellaneous separate publications, and in his political and educational activities, the values and policies that seemed to many landowners and operators to be best suited to the expansion of the coal trade.

The Wetherills and the Careys shared the view that as a general rule colliery operators were an untrustworthy lot. As we have observed, the Wetherills were exacting in their requirements of financial responsibility on the part of their lessees; and the Carey group were scarcely less demanding. As Henry Carey Baird remarked to his uncle, Schuylkill County was full of "demoralized and debased" men ready to "pluck" honest land-owners, and the only way to handle the operators was to be always in a position to force them either to pay their rents according to the letter of the contract or to give up the lease.[28] But the most public expression of the condescension and disdain that the owners felt for the operators is to be found in a play entitled *Mars in Mahantango*.[29] It has been attributed to the hand of John Macomb Wetherill, but the title page anonymously de-clares it to be merely "A Play; in Five Acts, Written by Admirers of the Anthracite Drama, and dedicated to its friends in Schuylkill County." It was printed in Pottsville by Benjamin Bannan in 1852 in the hope of stimulating the "legitimate drama" in Schuylkill County and of amusing "the social circle."

The play is a romantic comedy. The hero, Captain Maxwell, is a can-didate for election to the rank of brigadier general of the county militia; the heroine, Caradori, is the daughter of Conglomerate, "a wealthy Coal Op-erator"; the scene is the town of Mahantango, the "New Babylon" of Schuylkill County, founded by Conglomerate near his Digdeep Mines. Conglomerate has borrowed large amounts of money to complete the mine, the miners have just worked through a fault and are now in twelve feet of coal, and "Digdeep Mines are now but just in order." In conversation with his lawyer, Blackstone, his broker, Bond, and his engineer, Tangent, Con-glomerate explains that he now needs money to extend the railroad to his works. When the broker compares the abutments planned for the railroad bridge to those of Babylon, Conglomerate is inspired anew by his vision and reveals his megalomaniac ambition:

> ... Talking of Babylon, reminds me
> Of my new Capital, New Babylon,
> Which, if we get a Tariff, as we Ought,
> (Note that Blackstone) is as sure to be
> More famous than the old one, as the sun
> Is sure to rise, and then, Conglomerate
> Will be another Nebuchadnezzar.

But in private Blackstone reveals that Conglomerate's principal creditors, including "Skruvemmard & Co.," Seizall, and Blackstone himself, are de-manding a million dollars in railroad bonds as additional collateral; failing instant compliance, they will foreclose the mortgage on Digdeep Mines. Unable to meet this new challenge, Conglomerate complains in almost the very words later used by Enoch McGinness:

> Just Heaven! and is it so—and must my days
> Of toil, and sleepless nights enrich another?

But Blackstone is ruthless and Conglomerate, now ruined, plans to depart for "Golden California," leaving his daughter behind to marry Captain (now Brigadier General) Maxwell. Blackstone's soliloquy upon the fate of Conglomerate may be taken to represent Wetherill's judgment upon the likes of the operators he knew:

> And for him; when did he ever consider
> Who was to fall by his stupendous schemes,
> Should they miscarry? or did his former failure
> Teach him a just consideration for the rights
> Of other men? hath he not rather perilled
> Again with sinful recklessness, the fame,
> The fortunes, and the hopes of others, to build
> His own success? What if my plans miscarry
> As well as his—doth that affect him?
> Yes, it affects him that his cursed Tariff
> May or may not be passed—it doth affect him
> In that he may or may not have this scape goat
> To load his sins upon; to fool his creditors
> With hopes of speedy payment, or excuse
> His deep indebtedness and rash speculations
> With faults of other men—then let him go
> And build upon the passage or the failure
> Of his tariff, another precious scheme
> To ruin his confiding friends.

But even if the Careys and the Wetherills agreed that operators were irresponsible and reckless, they disagreed on how to deal with them. The difference came in the way in which "Wetherill and Bro." and Henry C. Carey set the rents and extended allowances and credit. The Wetherills followed the custom of the country, which was to set rents high for a new tenant but also to help him acquire the necessary capital to erect a breaker, sink a slope or shaft, and pay for the initial operating expenses, including wages of miners. This help commonly took the form of an "allowance" of some thousands of dollars on the first year's rental and also of a direct loan, which not only provided money but also encouraged other lenders. Such a proceeding allowed the tenant to be more thorough in the design and construction of a new mine than in the case of lessees who had little operating capital. Carey, however, and his agent, Russell, at the onset of their involvement took the view that it was better to set "low rents and the tenants make all the improvements."[30] This policy squeezed the new colliery operator, or the one whose mine had run into a fault or other difficulty, to work hastily in order to pay coal rents and the interest on loans from banks and other demanding creditors. The consequence, as we shall see, was negative for the technical quality of the mines on the St. Clair Tract.

THE COLLIERY OPERATORS

Many of the collieries in Schuylkill County were small, employing only a dozen or so hands and producing a few thousand tons per year. Their names come and go on the landowners' books or are preserved in terse notices in the county histories (". . . And Samuel Silliman worked a mine at Crow Hollow in the 1840's . . ."). Around St. Clair, like other coal towns, there were literally dozens of little workings that had been opened in the first decades of mining, then abandoned in hard times, and then reopened periodically by under-financed, and sometimes poorly trained, entrepreneurs who hoped to make a quick profit. Some, no doubt, were bootleg mines that yielded the operator a few thousand tons of coal, quickly spirited away and sold, without the promised rent ever being paid to the landowner. And it was probably this kind of here-today-gone-tomorrow operation that aroused the special ire of the Wetherills and the Careys.

The reason for the presence of so many small collieries worked by the lease system was geology. In the lower Schuylkill, and particularly the Pottsville Basin, the steep inclinations and frequent undulations of the strata, and eons of erosion, had produced many outcrops where coal could initially be mined cheaply, on a small scale, through drifts and slopes, without the need for heavy initial investment in deep shafts and heavy machinery. The geological situation around Wilkes-Barre in the Wyoming Valley was different. There the veins lay relatively flat and were in many places accessible only by means of deep shafts. Hence the Wyoming region was dominated by three large railroad corporations with mining privileges written into their charters, while the Pottsville region was a haven for the multitude of anti-monopolistic, individualistic small operators whose trials and tribulations have been so vividly described by the historian Clifton Yearley.[1] The same contrast had developed earlier in England, between the flat seams of the Newcastle coal fields, workable only by wealthy landowners capable of affording the long delays and heavy expense of sinking deep shafts, and the steeply pitching seams of Staffordshire, where the "butty system" prevailed, the landlord leasing to a small operator who could quarry down or sink a slope upon an outcrop with little capital investment.[2]

But the *major* collieries at St. Clair were not, by the late 1840's, operated on a small scale (although not on the scale of major English collieries, to be sure), they persisted at the same site for decades, and their operators were substantial men in the Pottsville district. Most of the major operators came into the coal

Benjamin Haywood (1804–1878)

trade after having achieved financial success in another line of business; coal mining, like investing in coal land, seems to have been a way of investing surplus capital in what was then regarded as a potentially very profitable industry. In the late 1840's and early 1850's there were eight names prominent in St. Clair because of their possessors' success in establishing or maintaining large colliery operations: Haywood, Snyder, Milnes, Lawton, Repplier, Parvin, Johns, and McGinness. All, with the exception of Johns and (temporarily) Lawton, were residents of Pottsville; all but Johns and Milnes had other businesses; all were prominent churchmen. Let us consider them individually.

Perhaps the most flamboyant of the group was Benjamin Haywood (1804–1878).[3] Haywood was born near Nottingham, in England's industrial Midlands; his father and grandfather had been in the hardware-manufacturing trades, and he himself served his time as a blacksmith's apprentice. He emigrated to the United States in 1829, settled briefly in Reading, where he married, and then went on to Pottsville, where he set up shop as a machinist. In 1833 he employed George W. Snyder, another machinist, to install a steam engine in his establishment, the first such engine in the county, and in 1835 the two men joined to form the firm of Haywood and Snyder, for the purpose of manufacturing steam engines and other equipment for the burgeoning collieries of the district. They were very successful and expanded, in 1845 building a large machine shop and foundry at Danville; they made the first set of rolls for the local manufacture of T-rails (for railroad use) and the first apparatus for sawing hot iron. With all the facilities for manufacturing colliery equipment in their hands, they next proceeded to invest their surplus funds and energies in coal operations in various places, including St. Clair, where they sank the

Pine Forest Slope in partnership with an experienced operator, William Milnes. Haywood assumed the principal responsibility for the coal interests of the partnership until 1850, when he decided to join the gold rush to California. He sold all his interests in Schuylkill County, invested the proceeds in a large number of pre-fabricated frame houses, and shipped them to San Francisco, where they failed to sell. Haywood could not even realize the cost of the freight. After building an unsuccessful sawmill, he returned to his roots—blacksmithing and machine work—and in a few years made a small but successful business. This he sold in 1855 and returned to Pottsville, where, it is said, "the old workmen of Haywood & Snyder met him at the depot, and escorted him into the town in triumphal procession." He bought a small rolling mill in Palo Alto and turned it into a large enterprise employing 500 hands and producing 20,000 tons of iron per year.

His later political career we shall have occasion to notice in another chapter; but it is worth observing here his standing in the religious and reform communities of the area. He was an accredited Methodist minister, active in evangelical and temperance work:

> He was ever ready, by word or purse, to advance the cause. His mind being stored with correct information on most subjects, he was competent at a moment's notice to preach an impressive sermon, deliver a powerful temperance lecture, or make a telling stump speech.

Haywood's departure during the gold rush left Snyder and Milnes in charge of the Pine Forest Colliery. George W. Snyder (1805–1887) had received a good secondary education in Philadelphia schools and academies, but he had learned the trade of machinist after his formal schooling. In 1835 he removed to Pottsville and went into the business of manufacturing steam engines and other iron products for collieries, eventually in partnership with Haywood. After Haywood left, Snyder continued to manage the Colliery Iron Works, which eventually became known as the third largest complex of foundry, rolling mill, and machine shops in the state. By 1860 he was worth more than a million dollars.[4] Snyder was a prominent citizen of the town and a leading Episcopal churchman, joining the ranks of Pottsville's elite in the pews of Trinity Church. The list of pew-holders includes many familiar names, including Eliza Baird, Benjamin Bannan (vestryman), Burd Patterson, Andrew Russell (warden and treasurer), John Macomb Wetherill, and other figures in the coal trade whom we shall meet presently. The Episcopal Church was the church of power, not only for

Pottsville but for Schuylkill County as a whole, and it took under its care such fledgling parishes as that at St. Clair, where in 1855 the vestry assigned a "resident missionary."[5] Although Snyder was reputed to be "one of the largest coal operators in Schuylkill County," with collieries at half a dozen places in the vicinity of Pottsville, his basic interests lay in the Colliery Iron Works, which he managed by himself to his seventy-eighth year.

The social connections between the Snyders (and other Pottsville people) and a genteel Philadelphia family help to place the social hierarchy of the coal region in relation to that of the metropolis. In September of 1858, a forty-four-year-old spinster, Clementina Smith, of Philadelphia and Rockdale (a small cotton-manufacturing village near Philadelphia), took the train up to Pottsville to visit her brother Horace, who had recently moved there as an independent broker selling industrial fire insurance. Her letters to her friend Sophie du Pont described the visit and its aftermath.[6]

Clementina was met at the station by an old pupil of hers from the Brandywine Manufacturers' Sunday School, and by Horace's partner, Henry W. Poole, who had worked as a surveyor in the anthracite district for the state geologist, Henry Darwin Rogers, in the summer of 1851. Poole escorted her to the residential hotel where Horace lived, a small establishment but probably the best hotel in town. It was also the home of, among others, John Macomb Wetherill and W. W. Atkins, the ironmaster who now operated the Pioneer Furnace.[7] At the hotel Clementina found Horace and also "Mr. Lincoln and two lovely young daughters, friends of mine whom I see often at St. Lukes" (the fashionable Episcopal church in Philadelphia that the Smiths attended). The Reverend Mr. Washburn, rector of Trinity Episcopal Church, which stood next to the hotel, brought his family to call, and so did George W. Snyder, at whose house Clementina's father had stopped on a recent visit to Pottsville. On Sunday Clementina spent almost the whole day at the church. On Monday morning she "rode all around the coal mines within a few miles immediately about Pottsville," probably including St. Clair in the itinerary, escorted by Mr. Poole, who explained everything to her. And in the afternoon she rode out with Dr. John Carpenter, a young physician who had become a friend and frequent houseguest of the Smith family during his years from 1852 to 1855 as a medical student at the University of Pennsylvania. Clementina liked John:

> I found his heart as warm and his feelings as cordial as ever and
> as I rode with him through the beautiful scenery about his home

we talked over his college days his experience in the interval and his present position with warm interest—Then it was cheering to talk with him and hear him tell those glorious hopes of a better and eternal world where there is no change and separation of friends [and] to find him exercising his profession under a deep sense of its religious responsibility.[8]

After taking her to his home—save one, "the handsomest and most perfectly furnished" house in Pottsville—to meet his wife and child, Carpenter carried her off to what was to be the social high point of her visit to Pottsville—an evening with George W. Snyder and his "delightful family— Father Mother and nine children." She was especially attracted to the two older boys (the eldest was nineteen), who were bright, frank, well instructed, and "(so unusual)" deferential to their parents, but she found the entire family "highly educated and refined and with all having so much kindness of spirit." After tea some of the neighbors came, including Dr. Carpenter with his sister, who was the Reverend Mr. Washburn's wife, and his own "sweet little wife." Then Horace came and they all enjoyed a musical evening.[9]

Clementina left Pottsville the next day for Mauch Chunk on her way back to Philadelphia. She never returned, but Horace stayed on. He became close friends with the Spohn family, owners of some coal lands north of Pottsville, and he spent his evenings regularly with them and may even have been romantically attached to the widow Spohn's daughter Eliza. But Horace died suddenly in February 1865 after a short illness. Dr. Carpenter and Eliza attended him in his room and Eliza visited Philadelphia after his death in order to meet Horace's mother. But Clementina headed her off, seeing her hurriedly the day before the family left for the summer at Rockdale. Eliza was very demonstrative, repeatedly burst into tears, and blamed herself for not having sent the Smiths a telegram before Horace's death. Clementina comforted the "poor child," but closed the door to further communication.[10] After all, the widow Spohn was illiterate, and Eliza's brothers were butchers, and even if they may have been the relics of one of the pioneer operators on the Centreville Tract, where he had given his name to a productive vein, the Smith family were not prepared to enjoy social intercourse with them as they did with the Snyders, the Bairds, and the Careys.

Snyder's partner at Pine Forest from 1850 to 1853 was William Milnes, an English-born miner who had come to the United States about 1827 after twenty-one years of mining experience in England. On his arrival in

Schuylkill County, he had become the agent for the North American Coal Company, which operated mines between Pottsville and St. Clair. He was one of the few men testifying before S. J. Packer's Senate committee in 1834 who spoke in favor of the incorporation of coal companies (not unexpectedly, considering that he was superintendent of mines for one of the two mining corporations in the county) and part of his argument in favor of corporations was that they attracted the steadier miners, "a great majority of those men in the employ of companies, crowding the different churches every Sabbath, which is the greatest honour to any community."[11] With the decline of the North American's fortunes in the general business debacle after 1837, Milnes turned to Haywood and Snyder and managed the Pine Forest Slope. In 1853 he struck out on his own, leaving Snyder and securing the lease to mine coal at an old slope just west of St. Clair. Milnes named this enterprise the Hickory Colliery. After his retirement his sons, Benjamin and William, Jr., continued in the same arrangement with the Wetherills until they in turn were replaced by the Mammoth Vein Coal Company in the 1860's.[12]

Just below the Hickory Colliery was another slope colliery operated by Francis J. Parvin. Parvin was a respected Pottsville miller who ground wheat, rye, and corn flour in a substantial establishment that produced (in 1850) about 13,000 barrels and earned a gross income of about $35,000.[13] He was, like Snyder, a prominent Episcopalian and the female members of his large household taught in the Sunday School. As we shall see, Parvin's Slope began as a prosperous enterprise in the early 1850's, but within a decade had turned into a financial disaster for its owner.

But by all odds the two most prominent operators—but prominent in very different ways—were the Johns family, who owned the Eagle Colliery in the north end of the borough, and Enoch W. McGinness, who sank the St. Clair Slope and Shaft. The Johns family began with two brothers, William and Thomas, who emigrated from Pembrokeshire, in the anthracite district of South Wales, to Schuylkill County in the year 1832. After working for several years as miners, they leased a small drift colliery at Oak Hill, in Norwegian Township. In 1846 they started the Eagle Colliery on the Wetherill lands at St. Clair, again commencing with a drift and then sinking a slope. They developed the Eagle into one of the largest collieries in the county and one of the few profitable ones. Thomas retired in 1854 and William carried on until his death in 1865. At that time he was worth over $2,000,000. The colliery was then carried on by his son, George W. Johns. The architect of this success, William H. Johns, was a cautious and methodical man who designed and constructed his mines in the safest possible fashion and invested his profits not only in additional colliery ventures (eventually the Johns operated "Eagle No. 2" in the middle field) but also in railroad stock and Philadelphia real estate. Like all the other operators, he was a heavy contributor to religious causes, helping to found the Methodist Church in St. Clair and just before his death contributing thousands toward the construction of a new Methodist edifice in Pottsville. And, again fitting the stereotype of the Christian steward, he was charitable to the deserving poor. His obituary in the *Miners' Journal* made the appropriate comment on his character: "To the poor he was benevolent, and many persons have owed to his kindness the money advanced by him to them to enable them to commence business." Unlike the other operators, the Johns family lived in St. Clair, in Johns' Patch along with their miners, within 100 yards of their breaker and only a few feet from the railroad spur that served their colliery. In this noisy mansion in 1850 lived a substantial extended family: Thomas Johns, forty; his wife, Elizabeth, thirty-eight; their three children, Elizabeth, seventeen, George, fourteen, and Mary, twelve; and Thomas's elder brother, William H. Johns, forty-three, and his five children, Caroline, eighteen, Emma, fifteen, George W., fourteen, Clara, twelve, and William, ten. William H. Johns' wife was absent; having become insane some years before, she now lived in the "State Lunatic Asylum," supported there by a trust fund established by her husband. When William H. Johns died of dropsy in 1865, at the age of sixty, all St. Clair mourned his passing and all the businesses in town were closed for four hours.[14]

Not everyone, however, was fond of William H. Johns, and perhaps least of all his unsuccessful business rival Enoch W. McGinness. We shall have to discuss McGinness' likes and dislikes in more detail later, but it is necessary to say something at this point about how he viewed his operator neighbors at St. Clair. William H. Johns, he told Carey, could not be "accused of having an over amount of *brains*." James S. Kirk and John E. Baum, who took over the St. Clair Shaft, were respectively "stubborn" and "pompous." Benjamin Milnes, he said, left the Pine Forest Colliery "in bad condition" and ruined the ventilation in the Hickory workings by trying "to get coal cheap and fast for the time being." Agent Russell he regarded as a conniving rival who foisted "humbug" on Carey and discredited honest operators like himself. And he questioned the competence of Carey's consulting engineer, George K. Smith, to calculate the power of pumps or to draft accurate mine maps.[15]

But McGinness cast these aspersions in the late 1850's and early 1860's, when he was repeatedly in and out of dire financial trouble. At the time of the census in the summer of 1860, McGinness was about fifty years old with an expensive rented residence on fashionable Mahantango Street in Pottsville and a large family to support, including a wife, three sons and three daughters, an aged mother-in-law, and two female servants; a year later he was destitute; and a year later still, he was again a prosperous mine operator and highly touted discoverer of a vein of blackband iron ore near St. Clair. McGinness' whole career was pretty much of a piece. Born in Northampton County, he moved to Schuylkill about 1830 and set up shop as a machinist specializing in the making of colliery equipment. He turned to making steam engines and by 1850 his works had manufactured no less than sixty engines with an estimated total working capacity of 1,755 horsepower. He was the largest manufacturer of steam engines in the county; his nearest competitor, Haywood and Snyder, had produced only forty-seven, and McGinness alone was responsible for about one-third of all the steam engines used in Schuylkill. Nevertheless, McGinness failed in the course of the 1850 depression in the coal trade, which ruined the market for new engines (only four were sold during the entire year). But he was a man of vision (indeed, he regarded himself as a "visionary") and was already touting his celebrated theory of the Schuylkill Coal Formation, which held (mistakenly, as we shall see) that the Mammoth Vein was accessible at modest depths throughout the southern coal field. By 1854, with over $100,000 borrowed from Carey and others, he had sunk the famous St. Clair Shaft; by 1855, unable to ship enough coal to keep up payment of loans and rents, he was forced to sell the colliery. Thereafter he remained in a client relation to his patron Carey, who evidently felt a certain loyalty to a man who had helped him develop the St. Clair Tract. Carey made him his agent in the purchase of the Luzerne lands and in the opening of the abandoned collieries on the North American tracts. Carey also arranged credit for McGinness to open his own collieries along Mill Creek and it was in one of these ventures that McGinness found the vein of blackband ore the exploitation of which in the 1860's was to be his last great project.

McGinness' feverish life ended suddenly in February 1867, at the age of fifty-seven years. As was usual on the death of a man of enterprise, all places of business in the borough of Pottsville were closed during the funeral. And at a public meeting held in his honor, it was resolved:

That the eminent services of the late Enoch W. McGinness in the development of the coal and iron resources of Schuylkill County, rendered as they were under difficulties of no ordinary nature, and in the face of disheartening opposition, merit and receive the gratitude of our people as being not only of great importance to this community, but as giving to the nation a new source of wealth and of enterprise.[16]

EARLY UNDERTAKINGS OF THE CAREY GROUP

From the early 1830's until the temporary collapse of the coal trade in the early 1940's, the Carey group invested in both the iron and the coal businesses. The coal properties that the group developed most aggressively in this period were all located in the southern part of the Pottsville Basin, in and around Pottsville itself; the St. Clair Tract was largely neglected. The administrator of these affairs was Thomas Baird.

Baird entered upon his duties with enthusiasm. One of the properties to be developed was the Westwood Tract west of Pottsville, the largest of the Carey properties, amounting to about 1,700 acres.

The initial plan of development was almost utopian in its vision of economic and social development. A memorandum, prepared by Baird about the time of purchase in 1835, outlined the plans for the town of "Westwood" and its associated coal lands north and west of Pottsville on the Westwood Tract. Located at the junction of the West Branch and the West West Branch of the Schuylkill River, Westwood had already been surveyed and ninety-nine lots laid out (though none was yet sold) and Baird predicted that it would become "a first Town within the Coal Range, and in the midst of a great mining district." In addition to the profits to be taken from royalties on coal, the development of the Westwood Tract would bring additional financial benefits from the sale of town lots, mill seats, and timber, and an extensive "home trade" could be expected from bartering coal for agricultural commodities in the Pennsylvania German towns just south of the mountains. Anthracite was rapidly coming into use among the "Distillers, Limeburners, Hafters, Tavern Keepers, Manufacturers, Smiths, and Inhabitants generally." And since the mining districts could not produce their own food, the "Meal, Grain, horse feed, Straw, Hay, provisions &c." obtained from the German farmers could be sold to the miners and mine operators at a considerable profit (a profit which Pottsville now was monopolizing). And still more profit could be had from constructing houses for the miners who lived in the patches close to the collieries. Baird turned to "the Great Coal Land Proprietors in Great Britain" for his model of how a colliery's community should evolve. It was a rosy vision. "Tis customary," he wrote,

... when Leasing a Colliery to a Contractor or Tenant to put up rows of 20–40 Small Stone houses with garden Ground to each, Charging the Contractor an interest of 4pc. on the Cost–the Contractor rents them to the collieries and others at 8 pc. Nothing can equal the neatness and Comfort of these snug dwellings—the husband sticks regularly, Year in, and Year out, to his daily task— the wife keeps all in order at home, every child at 7 or 8 years gets to work among the Coal, or in the Neighboring Manufactories— Saturday Night collects all the wages and all the family together, and the Sabbath becomes really a Season of rest and of Delight— the Boys and Girls soon take pride in keeping their little Garden and dwelling in Superior order—their industry and saving is shown in their dress—their little parlor gets a Carpet, a Mantel Glass, and often a Sofa &c. An English Gentleman told me, that as neat, and as comfortable a room as he had seen any where, he has occasionally met with in these humble residences of the Collieries.[1]

But the Westwood plan languished and was soon abandoned. Baird turned his attention to the other six properties. During the winter of 1835–1836 he wrote to his father describing his shift in role from gentleman farmer to superintendent of mines:

... there is much more to attract my attention in the bowels of the Earth and [sic] in merely ploughing its surface. My life is a very active one being a great portion of my time either underground or on horseback. My charge consists of about 1500 acres of Coal land distributed around the town in 6 different Tracts the cost of which is considerably over 100,000 dollars of which Carey & Lea & Carey & Hart are the principal Proprietors. I am engaged in putting up 2 steam Engines and expect soon to have a third under way.

The business is one that requires a great deal of capital to get it under way and a great deal of responsibility on my part having the whole control of operations and disbursement of money.

I trust however that I shall be able to make it a profitable concern for them.[2]

In addition to generally supervising the conduct of mining operations by lessees, collecting rents, constructing a railroad through town, shipping coal, and erecting steam engines on properties not yet leased, he assumed personal management of one of the mines himself.

The six tracts actually amounted, according to tax records, to 1,357 acres, and of these the southernmost, just west of the center of Pottsville, were being most actively developed. These were then called the Spohn, York Farm, Eyre, and Duncan tracts.[3] The Carey group purchased these tracts in mid-year of 1835, a strategic moment in the development of mining technology in the region. Up to this point, the coal was taken out only as deep as the level of groundwater, thus obviating the need for pumps to raise the large quantities of water that accumulated in deeper mines. At first, the method had been simply to dig down into the nearly vertical coal outcrops, but it was difficult to haul it up out of these quarries, and it reached the surface "nearly chopped to pieces in the effort to get it out." Then, as Baird described it to his brother-in-law Edward Carey, the English method was introduced of "mining on the run" (i.e., letting broken coal slide down sloping breasts) in above-water-level drifts.

> . . . further observation and enterprise, however, soon led to the More Scientific and Simple mode of seeking out deep ravines which had been cut through or across the coal measures at right angles thus leaving the ends of the different veins exposed to view or slightly covered by an alluvial wash. Excavations are now made at the end, at as low a level as possible and a gangway continued through the longitudinal course of the vein the mining is done by working up the Slope of the vein and the Coal slid down its bottom slots into the drift cars placed on a Railway laid in the gangway. This has consequently led to the mining of coal in the cheapest possible way.[4]

But now, as the second half of the 1830's began, it was clear that the coal available above water level would soon be exhausted.

And so, immediately upon assuming title to the sixty-four-acre Spohn Tract, the Carey group resolved upon an experiment. Some local worthies believed that coal found below water level would be worthless. But Henry Carey contacted Burd Patterson and together they arranged with the operators of the drift mines already opened on the tract to sink a slope below water level. By later standards, the Carey-and-Patterson Slope on the Spohn Tract was a small undertaking. The double gangway, divided in the center by props, went down at an angle of 23°. Rails were laid on either side, one for coal cars, the other for water tubs, both hauled up by a horse gin. The miners walked up and down holding on to boards nailed to the props. By July 1835, according to the *Miners' Journal,* the "enterprising gentleman" who owned the tract had driven the slope 250 feet in length.[5] By February 1836 Baird had replaced the horse gin with a twenty-horsepower steam engine and the slope was 393 feet long and the mine was steadily producing coal.[6] The experiment was a complete success and set the pattern for future operations in the Pottsville district. Within three years at least ten slopes were working coal below the water level; over the next fifteen years, as the superficial coal was exhausted, the slope became the preferred mode of exploitation.[7]

The Carey group encouraged their lessees to develop collieries on the most extensive plan and with the most efficient technology and transport system possible. This meant, at the outset, that the scheme to build a new town at Westwood was abandoned in favor of collieries closer to the canal landings at Mount Carbon, just below Pottsville. Carey money and Baird's supervisory expertise would be expended on two collieries located close enough to the landings for a short mile of railroad to be constructed along Pottsville city streets to deliver coal to the canal boats. Baird contracted with his friends Benjamin Haywood and George W. Snyder, principal machine builders of the locality, for the thirty-horsepower steam engines necessary to drive the pumps. The pumps themselves were of a new double-barreled design invented by one of the lessees and constructed at another local iron works. Two Carey tracts were involved: York Farm, just west of the borough limits, owned jointly by the Careys and Burd Patterson and leased to George H. Potts, a young but experienced collier; and Guinea Hill, a sixty-acre tract east of York Farm in the northern part of the borough, recently acquired by Henry Carey from Thomas Haven, his son-in-law, and leased to Charles Potts, the inventor of the new pump, and Benjamin Bannan, the editor of the *Miners' Journal.*

Both collieries were worked on what was for the time a very extensive scale; and, indeed, a large production of coal was needed to retire the large debt incurred in sinking long slopes and installing heavy machinery. The York Farm Colliery was commenced in the fall of 1836 with a slope on the eight-foot-thick Black Mine or Gate Vein. The slope plunged into "the bowels of the earth" (as the *Miners' Journal* poetically expressed it) on the south dip at an angle of between 30° and 35°. This underground inclined plane was sixteen feet wide and 241 feet long. At the bottom, gangways were driven through the coal, 780 feet to the east, where the work stopped, no good coal having been obtained, and 3,000 feet to the west through good coal after the first 600 feet. In the season of 1837 this vein produced and sent to market 33,000 tons. Then in the fall of 1837 a second slope was sunk 230 feet farther south and another 2,000 feet of gangway was opened. Steam engines drove the pumps and also pulled the loaded mine cars up the tracks laid on one side of the slope (counterbalanced by descending cars on the other side). In the colliery yard there were other structures: platforms with chutes and iron plates where coal was broken with hammers and sized, carpenter and blacksmith shops, a sawmill, a powder magazine, and a stable. A mile of lateral railroad was constructed across Pottsville to deliver the coal to a 500-foot-long private canal landing. The colliery owned eighty drift cars used in the mines, some fifty railroad cars, a locomotive, and thirty or more canal boats. And to work this large double-mine colliery 364 men were employed, half in mining and half in transportation.[8]

The Guinea Hill Colliery was a slightly older colliery, having already been started and abandoned before 1835, and on it the second slope in the county (after Carey and Patterson's experimental slope) was sunk in 1835. It, like York Farm, was extended down the south dip of the Black Mine Vein, at an angle of 40°, fifteen feet wide and eight feet high. The pump and slope cars were run by a twenty-horsepower engine. After gangways were extended to the property lines east and west, underground tunnels through rock five feet wide and seven feet high were driven north to the Lawton Vein and south to the Tunnel Vein, thus requiring that all the coal from three veins be brought to the surface on one slope.[9]

These collieries were built and operated on what for the region was a truly massive scale, more nearly comparable to English workings than the superficial quarries and short drifts with which small operators had been contented hitherto. The capital investment was shared by lessees and landowners; in the case of York Farm, it was estimated by Benjamin Bannan (who was in a position to know) that the Carey group and their lessee, George Potts, together expended $100,000 "before obtaining an ounce of coal."[10] And a similar, perhaps slightly lower, commitment was made at Guinea Hill. A memorandum on the agreement from Thomas J. Baird to Edward L. Carey in 1838 indicates that the Careys, by the summer of 1837, had spent over $35,000 there on steam engines, railroad iron, and other machinery, and that such expenses as the lessee contributed were to be deducted from his future royalty assessment. The royalty was set high, at 60 cents per ton.[11] Furthermore, Baird—anticipating his reward in the form of commissions—spent a great deal of time putting his experience as an ordnance officer to good use, supervising the construction and installation of the engines and in general acting as a consulting engineer. Thus, although George and Charles Potts received most of the public credit, the York Farm and Guinea Hill collieries, between 1837 and 1845 the "most extensive colliery operations in the United States," were technically and financially as much the product of the Carey group as of their lessees.[12]

The York Farm Colliery deserves attention as a center of innovation in other ways than just as the site of the first commercially successful slope. It was also where, according to the *Miners' Journal,* the furnace method of ventilation was first introduced in America. The underground workings, as we have seen, were extensive, the gangways alone running upward of half a mile east and west from the bottom of the slope, and in the Tunnel Vein there accumulated dangerous levels of firedamp (methane gas). Apparently after a number of small, localized explosions created a degree of anxiety among the miners sufficient to discourage work in the mine, the "English method" of ventilation was attempted. "This is," the *Miners' Journal* reported,

> the erection of a cupola between forty and fifty feet high, over an air shaft, driven up about 1500 [*sic*] feet from the bottom of the plane. In the bottom of this [cupola], a furnace is placed, and by heating a current of wind, and causing a vacuum, the foul air of the mines rushes up the shaft, and is consumed in the fire.

The reporter, who observed the roaring flame intensified by a supply of methane, was reminded of Shadrach in the fiery furnace. And he predicted, correctly, that "ere long, its adoption must be general, wherever workings are maintained below water level."[13] And, finally, it was at York Farm or Guinea Hill in 1844 that the second coal-breaker in the anthracite coal fields was erected, a precursor of those dark, towering buildings that were to dominate the horizons, and the imaginations, of men in the anthracite district for the next 100 years.[14]

But notwithstanding the importance of these innovations, the collieries that introduced them were doomed. Part of the problem was the irregularity of demand for coal and the consequent fluctuations in price; poor business conditions, such as those following the panic of 1837, sometimes drove the selling price in Philadelphia below the cost of mining and transportation. In 1839 hundreds of miners from the Pottsville district found themselves without work; many fled as far away as Lonaconing Furnace and its mines in Maryland.[15] Only the best-managed collieries could survive; Baird remarked that even though the winter of 1839–1840 was generally catastrophic, "friend Potts gets along pretty smoothly these hard times." A year later, the inability of some of the Carey lessees to pay coal rents was keeping him "poor as a Rat," and "our working population" was suffering from a "great scarcity of money."[16]

But the basic problem for the mines at York Farm, Guinea Hill, and other localities near Pottsville in the shadow of Sharp Mountain was geology. As the state geologist, Henry Darwin Rogers, had stated in his 1838 interim report of the findings of the First Geological Survey of Pennsylvania, the veins just north of Sharp Mountain had been subjected to crushing overthrust forces, and the result was so much faulting that mining could not be pursued profitably except in the best of times; hard times and the escalation of technological improvement drove even the most competent operators to the wall. And this happened to the collieries at York Farm and Guinea Hill. Matthew Carey Lea's paper in the *American Journal of Science and Arts* in 1841, entitled "On the First, or Southern Coal Field of Pennsylvania," reflected the Carey group's experience, and it again confirmed Rogers' judgment on the inferiority of the coal in the Pottsville Basin. In contrast to the hard, brilliant anthracite from Mauch Chunk and Tamaqua, "Pottsville coal" from the Black Mine Vein had a lower carbon content and did not break in the shell-shaped fractures typical of anthracite because it "contained layers of a darker and softer substance without any splendor, and by these it usually fractured."[17] And even in his early financial memorandum Baird felt it necessary to increase the estimate of the cost by "allowing for faults &c."[18] His estimate in 1838 for the two collieries was that it cost $2.24 to mine a ton of coal and haul it to the landing at Mount Carbon, where it sold for, on the average, $2.50 per ton. He did not add the cost of moving it by canal boat to Philadelphia, but tolls actually ranged from 70 to 92 cents per ton in this period. And the price in Philadelphia was only about $3 per ton! The selling price in Philadelphia had fallen to $2 per ton by 1841; but by then, as a result of faults, production had gone down and costs up. In August he wrote:

> As regards our own particular operations we have not been very fortunate this season having much fault & c in the Mines which causes a deficiency in rents & c.[19]

In the winter of 1841–1842, no more than 2,000 tons were expected to be shipped to Philadelphia.[20] And in 1842 Isaac Lea, by now convinced of the geological problems of the region, called the attention of the American

Philosophical Society to "the disturbed condition of the southern coal field," which had been publicly confirmed by Lyell, and he pointed out that "the conglomerates and coal beds of Sharp Mountain (the southern border of this coal field) are nearly vertical at Tamaqua, Pottsville, Pinegrove, Goldmine Gap, Rauch Gap, Yellow Spring Gap, and Rattling Run Gap. . . ."[21] That year Burd Patterson went bankrupt and his lands were sold by the sheriff, and Carey, Lea, and Hart sold their interest in the unprofitable coal lands in the York Farm and Eyre tracts and at Guinea Hill in Pottsville.[22] By 1848 Potts was bankrupt too.

ANTHRACITE IRON

Most of the anthracite produced in the 1830's was burned in stoves to heat houses, and this domestic use would continue to take the largest share of production until the industry's catastrophic decline a century later. But the leaders of the coal trade sought another use: the smelting of the iron ores of the coal region in furnaces that burned raw, uncoked anthracite. Early efforts to smelt iron with anthracite were not successful because the "stone coal" was difficult to ignite, although chemical analysis revealed that anthracite had so high a carbon content, compared with bituminous, that it should be possible to use it raw. As early as 1825 the newly established Franklin Institute in Philadelphia offered a gold medal to the first person to smelt twenty tons of iron with unmixed anthracite. Experiments began in America, Britain, and France, using either pure anthracite or anthracite mixed with coke or charcoal, but all failed. Even a strong blast was insufficient to heat the ore adequately, and the furnaces clogged.

The basic problem was that all these furnaces used a "cold blast": that is, they blew cold air from outside the furnace (ranging in temperature anywhere from 100° Fahrenheit in summer to, let us say, −10° in winter) under high pressure directly onto the surface of the coal. The effect was to chill the surface below the ignition temperature. The trick was to use the "hot blast" method, newly invented in Scotland by James Neilson in order to increase the efficiency of the coke-iron furnaces of Great Britain, where charcoal had already been replaced by coke in the making and refining of iron. Neilson was granted a patent in 1828. The Neilson hot-blast process doubled the productivity of furnaces using it. The news traveled rapidly. By 1831 the Rev. Dr. Frederick Geissenheimer had already used the hot blast successfully to smelt a small quantity of iron with pure anthracite at his experimental furnace in New York City, and in that year he secured a

United States patent for his method. The *Journal of the Franklin Institute* in 1835 published an enthusiastic account of the English success in smelting the finest coke iron with a blast heated above the temperature for melting lead, 612° Fahrenheit. But the commercial furnace Geissenheimer built in 1836 in Schuylkill County broke down after only two months. In England, furnace owner George Crane had been trying unsuccessfully to smelt iron with anthracite in a cold blast in his Welsh furnaces as early as 1826. In the early 1830's he sent his ironmaster, David Thomas, to Scotland to observe Neilson's apparatus for heating the blast. Returning to Wales with a license from Neilson, Thomas then built a hot-blast furnace and proceeded in February 1837 to smelt iron with anthracite with complete success. Crane then applied for an American patent, but was denied on account of Geissenheimer's priority.

By 1837, therefore, the Pennsylvania coal-and-iron community was eagerly anticipating the perfecting of the hot-blast technique for smelting iron with anthracite. In 1838 Governor Ritner of Pennsylvania (who was himself a member of a family in the business of making iron) declared in his annual address to the legislature: "the successful union of stone coal and iron ore, in the arts, is an event of decidedly greater moment to the prosperity of our state, than any that has occurred since the application of steam in aid of human labor."[1] A law was passed authorizing the incorporation of iron and steel companies, and about the same time a consortium of Philadelphia bankers and industrialists announced a prize of $5,000 to be awarded to the first ironmaster who for three uninterrupted months kept an anthracite furnace in blast.[2]

The Carey and Wetherill connections, like other families of iron and coal, were very much interested in the prospect of their anthracite being used in smelting iron. The economic advantage of expanding the uses of coal was obvious; but owners of coal lands also knew that iron ores were found in thin veins close to the coal strata themselves. Perfecting the anthracite furnace thus promised to expand the market for both the coal and the iron ores that lay beneath the surface of the anthracite district. And both of these extended families could call on the distinguished scientists among their members to serve as technical consultants in the mission to make the commonwealth of Pennsylvania the greatest industrial state in the nation, if not in the world.

In the Carey group there were two men who had a professional interest in iron. Thomas Baird, the retired ordnance officer, was familiar with the necessary qualities of the iron used in the manufacture of those "engines of mortality" with which the military were concerned, and he had made it his business to understand how steam engines and other machinery worked. But the real expert on iron ores and iron-making in the Carey group was Isaac Lea. Lea had a strategic view of the future importance of both iron and coal in national industrialization; and, further, he knew the supreme economic importance for the coal regions of developing the technology for smelting iron with anthracite. He was not alone in this awareness, but his standing as one of America's leading scientists gave his opinion great force. One evening early in the spring of 1838, Lea held a conversation on the subject with Nicholas Biddle, president of the Bank of Pennsylvania (successor to the Second U.S. Bank destroyed by Jackson), and Biddle was so much impressed that he encouraged Lea to publish his views. Lea did so and the resulting public letter to Nicholas Biddle was printed in the Pottsville *Miners' Journal* in April 1838.

Lea's letter was a passionate exhortation to Pennsylvanians—particularly those of the coal regions—to realize their destiny as the great rival of Great Britain. First he outlined the vast extent of the state's bituminous and anthracite beds (the latter being "of greater commercial importance at this time"). Then he reviewed the opinions of British writers on the importance of the coal trade to their own country's power and prosperity; they asserted, in sum, that coal was "the very basis of the wealth of the nation." Next he pointed out how important coal was becoming in Pennsylvania and how fast the coal regions were growing in wealth and population, as evidenced by the fact that the Pottsville post office now handled the third-largest volume of mail in the state, behind only Philadelphia and Pittsburgh. He concluded this section on an almost visionary, and certainly chauvinistic, plane:

> In the coal fields we may naturally expect a very large population. The cheapness of fuel will induce manufacturers to erect their works near to the mines, and we may in time have there as industrious and teeming a population as in the coal fields of England and Wales! . . . there can be no reason why Pennsylvania might not in time nearly equal the present population of that kingdom.

Then he went on to the real meat of the discourse: iron. After noting that Pennsylvania ores were more extensive than those of any other state, he pointed out that America's iron production, even in Pennsylvania, was in its infancy compared with that of Britain. The reason was simple: Americans smelted iron with expensive charcoal and their furnaces produced, on an average, about fifteen tons per week; the British used the far less expensive coke made from bituminous coal and their furnaces averaged about forty-eight tons per week (and rising). He ended by pointing out that Crane in Wales was now smelting a superior iron with raw anthracite and that this development was "likely in a very short time to create a very great change in the manufacturing of iron in Great Britain and in this country."[3]

Lea did not reveal in his public letter that the Carey group were already deeply involved in the race to catch up with British iron-manu-facturing technology. Lea was a stockholder and active member of the board of managers of the ill-fated Danville and Pottsville Railroad, which, in addition to its avowed goal of opening up the coal lands on the Girard Estate, was also intending to provide a southern rail outlet for Danville, already a center for iron manufacture on the upper Susquehanna. Danville, located in the midst of iron, anthracite, and limestone deposits, was a natural site for investment. About 1837, Lea, his partners Carey and Hart, and his brother-in-law Thomas Baird ventured about $30,000 in a furnace at Danville. They very probably intended to experiment with coke or an-thracite smelting, but the remoteness of the location and the consequent difficulty of overseeing operations led them to sell out in 1839.[4] Henry Carey then entered into a partnership with two of the successful pioneers of the coal trade, John White and Burd Patterson, in the ownership of another blast furnace at Karthaus, on the West Branch of the Susquehanna. This furnace had tried unsuccessfully to use coke from the nearby bitu-minous coals. Carey, White, and Patterson now hired a famous English ironmaster, William Firmstone, who introduced the hot blast and made pig iron. But the local ores were of inferior quality and the remote situation of the furnace, buried in the forests of western Pennsylvania 200 miles from Philadelphia, made transportation difficult and expensive. The Karthaus coke-and-hot-blast experiment failed and another at Farrandsville, farther east, failed also about the same time and for the same reasons.[5]

Thus by the time Lea's letter was published in the *Miners' Journal*, the race to perfect the anthracite furnace was on at full tilt. News of Geissenheimer's patent and of Crane's success in Wales had been dissem-inated throughout the anthracite region and every few months another ironmaster was reported by the press to have tried his luck with the proc-ess, always with middling success. Gradually the contest narrowed to two contenders: the Pottsville group and the Lehigh Coal and Navigation Com-pany of Mauch Chunk. The latter, led by the experienced and resourceful Josiah White, had been trying to make anthracite iron since 1826, both in its own furnaces and in those of lessees to whom it offered free coal and water power from its dams. Josiah White learned almost at once of Crane's successful experiment because his nephew, the American engineer Solomon White Roberts, was in Wales inspecting iron rails and visited Crane's works within three months after the trial. In 1838 the Lehigh Company sent an agent to Wales and in November 1838 hired Crane's ironmaster, David Thomas—the actual innovator—to come to America to build a furnace for the new subsidiary company, the Lehigh Crane Iron Company. Thomas began in July 1839 to construct a furnace at Catasauqua, near Bethlehem, using British blowing machinery and fire-brick. Thomas's plan called for a forty-five-foot-high furnace, larger than anything then in use in the United States, and the engine for pumping the hot blast through the tuyeres (tubes through which the blast entered the furnace) into the stack required cylinders five feet in diameter. These, it turned out, were too large to fit into the hatch of the ship intended to carry them over. Eventually the Philadelphia firm of Merrick and Towne agreed to redesign its boring mill to produce the cylinders, but was unable to deliver usable cylinders until May 1840. The Lehigh furnace was finally put in blast in July 1840 and it, and successors designed by Thomas, proved to be an outstanding success.[6]

The delay occasioned by the Lehigh Company's problem with securing the blast-engine cylinders gave the Pottsville group an opportunity to win the $5,000 prize for first keeping an anthracite furnace in blast for three months. The leader in the Pottsville group was Carey's partner in the Karthaus venture and in coal-land holdings near Pottsville, Burd Patterson. By the winter of 1837–1838, Patterson had learned of Crane's success in Wales and begun to plan his own furnace. Patterson owned "the Island" in the Schuylkill River where in 1807 Pottsville's founder, John Pott, had built an early ironworks, and here he determined to establish an anthracite furnace.[7] Borrowing the working capital (about $30,000) from various sources, including merchants and suppliers in Pottsville (and very probably other associates like Carey, Baird, and Lea), in the spring of 1838 he began the building of the Pioneer Furnace. Where he obtained his technical information at first is not clear; the *Miners' Journal* mentioned a Welsh "miner," Richard Jones, who had just returned to Pottsville about April 1838 from a visit to Crane's works, bearing samples of coal, iron ore, and pig from the furnace at Yniscedwyn, and perhaps Patterson obtained advice on construction from him. But it was not until the summer of 1839 that he received the critical input of information, from none other than David Thomas himself, on loan from the halted Lehigh Crane project. Thomas provided the Pottsville group with furnace plans and technical advice.[8] The builder who, with the aid of David Thomas, constructed the Pioneer Furnace was William Lyman from Boston; a local man, Benjamin Pomeroy, was in charge of setting up the machinery. The furnace, built of stone lined with firebrick, was considerably smaller than the one being constructed by Thomas at Catasauqua, thirty-five feet high *vis-à-vis* forty-five feet, and narrower in proportion. After Lyman tried unsuccessfully to blow in the furnace in July (the blast machinery failed), Patterson hired Benjamin Perry, a Welsh furnace manager who had visited Crane's works, and had more recently been the author of a successful experiment at making coke iron at Farrandsville, Pennsylvania. Perry blew in the furnace on the 19th of October 1839. The iron ore came from Mount Laffee, about three miles north of Pottsville on the Wetherill Tract. The blast was heated to 600° Fahrenheit in coal ovens at the base and was blown by a steam engine that drove two blast cylinders fifteen inches in diameter with a six-foot stroke. The blast pressure was raised about a third higher than in Crane's original furnace, but this level apparently depended upon Perry's innovative procedure of partially sealing the lower part of the furnace at the tuyeres and at the hearth. The furnace worked reasonably well, remaining in blast until February 1840 and regularly producing about forty tons a week of good pig iron. The pigs were sent to P. H. Savery's Foundry in Philadelphia, where they were said to have made the finest very thin castings of hollowware he ever did. Through 1840 the furnace produced 390 tons of pig, consumed 960 tons of coal, and employed thirty-five men. But it had been hampered from the first by mechanical problems with the blast machinery and was not able to match the record of sustained production later achieved by the Lehigh Crane Company's furnaces beginning in July 1840.[9]

Nevertheless, the success of the Pioneer Furnace gave a much needed boost to the spirit of those engaged in the coal trade. As Thomas Baird put it:

> We have had one of the most dull and pinching times here this winter that Pottsville has ever seen. . . . The only thing calculated to give us a fresh start is the success of our Anthracite furnace an inspection of which took place about a week since by a Committee from Philadelphia and a favorable report of its Success the Consequence.[10]

But Baird's language does not adequately reflect the enthusiasm with which the event was celebrated. In November, Burd Patterson had already been presented with a "service of plate" cast from the first iron sent to the

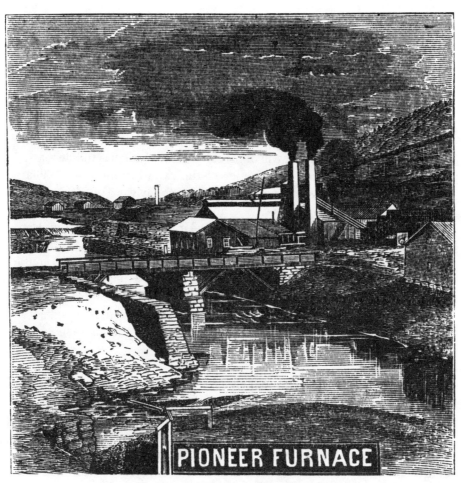

PIONEER FURNACE

The Pioneer Furnace at Pottsville, 1866

Savery Foundry in Philadelphia. In anticipation of final success, the "committee from Philadelphia" arrived on Friday evening in Pottsville; its members included Isaac Lea, of the Carey group, and five others, including Nicholas and Thomas Biddle. On Saturday morning, the 18th of January 1840—the date of completion of the three-month blast—the committee repaired to Mount Laffee to inspect the coal mine that was producing the iron ore. In the meantime the Stars and Stripes were raised over the furnace and a "national salute" was fired from a cannon; the occasion was, in the words of the *Miners' Journal*, "a second Declaration of Independence." After admiring "the neatness and workmanlike appearance" of the colliery, the committee visited other mines, and then at two p.m. assembled at the furnace "to witness the tapping, review the works, and pronounce their judgement on the event." It was favorable, of course.

91

Now the ceremonies moved to the Mount Carbon Hotel, where the testimonial dinner was enjoyed by eighty invited guests, including Henry Carey. It was the first instance of what would become a traditional mode of celebrating the heroes of the coal trade. After the "sumptuous repast," and as the wine began to flow, the toasts began. First, to the governor of Pennsylvania (an iron founder himself). Second, to the iron trade of Pennsylvania—"now an acorn—it will be an oak." Third, Nicholas Biddle toasted the hero of the occasion, the winner of the award, ironmaster William Lyman, pointing out that the distinguished company were here not only to honor Mr. Lyman's "untiring perseverance and public spirit," but also "the advantage to accrue to the community at large" of uniting iron and anthracite. He concluded with a famous toast to "Old Pennsylvania" that, like Commodore Henderson's cannon, gave an ominous military clangor to the occasion:

> OLD PENNSYLVANIA: her sons like her soil—a rough outside, but solid stuff within: plenty of Coal to warm her friends—plenty of Iron to cool her enemies.[11]

The boosters of Pottsville could indeed take pride in the fact that it was their furnace that, using only anthracite for fuel, had first smelted iron continuously for three months. But the important fact was that anthracite furnaces were springing up everywhere and would indeed transform the economy. As the *Miners' Journal* editorialized, under the headline "New Source of National Wealth," even before the Pioneer's success, the hot-blast method for making anthracite iron was

> more important perhaps in its effects on our national resources, than any since the application of the Steam Engine to our rivers. We shall now soon find that all our railroad iron, besides the immense quantity used for other purposes, will be made at home, without a servile dependence on other countries . . . not only Pennsylvania, but our whole Union will feel the relief and advantages.[12]

And on the day when the three-month trial ended, the *Journal* commented:

> The discovery has relieved our political economists from all fears of dangerous dependance on foreign-powers: it has proved that we have the resources within ourselves to supply our foundries,

machine shops, and our military and naval equipment, and we trust it will prove a source not only of individual profit, but of vast national advantage.[13]

The economic impact was in fact felt very quickly. The local landowners at once undertook to explore their properties for iron; Baird, for instance, found himself prevented from traveling to Pittsburgh in the winter of 1839–1840 because he was too busy "exploring the Iron Ore at St. Clair" and on other properties of the Carey group.[14] In February 1840 the *Miners' Journal* reported enthusiastically that its editor had visited the St. Clair Tract to examine the workings of iron ore that were being developed "under the active superintendence" of Captain Baird. The openings had been made in the southwest corner of the tract, on a hillside west of the railroad, where F. B. Nichols had earlier discovered a vein of coal he had named the Hancock. Baird had cut a trench across the hill and exposed no less than twelve veins of iron ore which Bannan conjectured would be "inexhaustible." Bannan suggested that a furnace be built at the mouth of the mine (and a couple of years later Burd Patterson did just that). And veins of ore had also been discovered at a number of other places, including Guinea Hill (a Carey property), Mount Laffee (northwest of St. Clair), the Pott and Bannan Tract on Broad Mountain (in which the Carey group would have a financial interest), and the Gate Vein mine of Charles Lawton in Pottsville.[15] And the local machinery manufacturers, like George W. Snyder, Baird's friend and new owner of the Danville Iron Works, and Enoch McGinness, later the celebrated operator of the St. Clair Shaft, were kept busy winter and summer building and erecting machinery for new furnaces, foundries, and rolling mills. By the end of the year, Danville alone would have five anthracite furnaces, two foundries, and two rolling mills. As the volume of anthracite iron (much of it used for iron rails) rapidly increased during the 1840's, American manufacturers for the first time had available an unlimited supply of cheap, high-quality iron, and Pennsylvania became for a time the center of the American iron industry and thereby the focus of the Industrial Revolution in North America.[16]

THE ST. CLAIR PROJECT

The discovery of iron ore on the St. Clair Tract, coming at the same time as the failure of the Carey collieries in and about Pottsville, dictated a shift of attention of the Carey group to the north, where since 1835 the Carey group had owned 402.75 acres of coal reserves known as the St. Clair Tract.

In 1835, when Carey and his partners took possession of the tract, it contained only the beginnings of a town. The site had already been partly laid out by the former owners, coal merchant Francis B. Nichols and his nephew St. Clair Nichols, on a rectangular grid plan, some of the streets named, and all of the lots numbered (and forty-one already sold, mostly to speculators). There were about 100 inhabitants. One large farm, owned by the Nichols family, stood on the hill west of town, but much of the surveyed part was still undrained swamp, covered with impenetrable thickets of laurel (a wild rhododendron that flourishes in the coal regions), and a forest of oak, spruce, and sweet gum covered the hills flanking the stream. The main street, Second Street, was the road from Port Carbon, and other roads ran south to Pottsville and west to Wadesville, but its central feature was the Mill Creek and Mine Hill Railroad, a ramshackle affair of wooden rails and horse-drawn wagons built six years earlier that ran from the canal docks at Port Carbon northward to an abrupt terminus in the Mine Hill Gap. It was the first of the feeder railways, and at the time of its construction its four-and-one-half-mile length made it the second longest railroad in the United States, exceeded only by the nine-mile line that served the mines at Mauch Chunk. This railroad served the population of St. Clair and also a small rural clientele along the narrow, forested, hill-hemmed valley of Mill Creek, and its spurs ran to the coal workings. In the St. Clair neighborhood, this country clientele included the large Nichols farm, on the hilltop west of, and 300 feet above, the creek; the farm shipped various products to market in Port Carbon and Pottsville, especially cider from the orchards on the hill. The farm had its own cemetery (later to become the town cemetery) and a little building that served the families of the few local English miners both as a Primitive Methodist chapel and as a schoolhouse. On the other side of the creek were located two sawmills and a gristmill. Earlier there had been a number of small coal workings in and around the tract, but virtually all were now abandoned for want of demand for coal. But they had served their function by locating the outcrops of major veins that would soon be explored by a second generation of entrepreneurs. At the crossroads with the road leading west to Wadesville there were two taverns and a number of log and frame houses.[1]

To the north, the Mill Creek and Mine Hill Railroad came close to but was as yet not connected with the new but ill-starred Danville and Pottsville Railroad, which passed just above the town before entering the 800-foot stone-and-brick tunnel that carried the tracks under Mine Hill to the inclined plane that sloped down to Wadesville to the west. The driving of the tunnel in 1834 had brought some work crews to the neighborhood, but in 1835 little was happening except the rolling of twenty-five or thirty cars of coal per day down the plane from Broad Mountain and into the tunnel, bypassing the little crossroads at St. Clair.

The Danville and Pottsville Railroad was, actually, one of the initial coal investments of the Carey group, for Isaac Lea was one of the stockholders and a member of the board of directors. The purpose of the enterprise was to open up the vast coal reserves of the Shenandoah and Mahanoy valleys, north of Broad Mountain, by means of a rail line extending east from a point on the Susquehanna River at Sunbury, near Danville, about sixty miles north of Harrisburg, to the Mill Creek Gap above St. Clair, and thence south to Pottsville. The length would be between forty-five and fifty miles and the cost of construction $1,000,000, to be financed by stock subscriptions. The commonwealth bore the expense of Moncure Robinson's survey in 1828 because Robinson was then employed as an engineer by the commissioners of the state canal system. Robinson was also hired to supervise construction. After the Mount Carbon Railroad, connecting Pottsville with Wadesville by way of the valley of Norwegian Creek, was completed in the spring of 1831 (costing $97,000 for six and three fourths miles), the great project was begun.

The first section of the road traveled eastward from the valley of the Norwegian to the valley of Mill Creek. Between the two valleys, no suitable grade (i.e., a grade of less than 10° from the horizontal) could be found and so a combination of an inclined plane and a tunnel was designed. The inclined plane, sloping up from Wadesville, was 667 feet long and reached 105 feet in elevation. It was planned to lower the loaded cars on an endless chain with a system of brakes and simultaneously to raise empties all without the aid of a horse or steam engine, the weight of the descending cars being sufficient to bring the ascending cars up the incline. The tunnel, which passed eastward through a low ridge south of Mine Hill, entered the Mill Creek Valley just north of the projected town of St. Clair. The tracks then crossed the creek and proceeded up the valley to another plane about a mile farther north. The tunnel was 800 feet long, driven apparently through a vein of coal, arched with brick and the openings faced with stone. This tunnel has been sometimes confused with another "Girard Tunnel" that was driven into Broad Mountain at Bear Ridge some miles north in a search for coal, not as part of the route of the railroad. The tunnel at St. Clair brought a brief season of prosperity in the summers of 1832 and 1833 while construction was in progress. But it also brought legal problems. Mining operations above and below the tunnel threatened to damage it, and the St. Clair operators were required to cease and desist, occasioning suits for damages.

The grand design was never completed. A western section connected some of the interior coal lands with the Susquehanna and the eastern section was finished almost as far as Girardville. But an empty central stretch of thirteen miles still existed in 1838 and the tunnel into Bear Ridge had not reached any large vein of coal. For the three years from 1834 to 1836 during which it was in operation, the railroad carried a total of 18,794 tons of coal, 893,705 board feet of lumber, and 1,300 cross-ties, far too little to meet expenses of further construction, to buy coal wagons, or to complete the mine at Bear Ridge. After that the eastern section of the Danville and Pottsville Railroad lay idle. No horses and wagons moved along the tracks; no maintenance work was done. The iron-shod oaken rails and cross-ties and the machinery at the planes lay rotting and rusting in the rain.[2]

In order to begin coal operations on the St. Clair Tract, in 1835 Carey and his partners initially contracted with an inexperienced local coal prospector, John Pinkerton, to explore and develop the coal mines in the St. Clair Tract.[3] Pinkerton's progress was undoubtedly impeded by the same factors that were hampering coal operators throughout the region: lack of capital; the panic of 1837 and the subsequent depression; and ignorance of the geology of the region. Thus, although he puttered about the tract, driving little tunnels and sinking test pits, he did not commence his major colliery until the 1840's, after the Careys had committed themselves to developing the town.

The initial plan for the residential and commercial development of St. Clair was formed in 1842. In 1844 and 1845, Carey and his partners had the southern and eastern parts of the town resurveyed, dividing it up into blocks, opening streets named for individuals prominent in the coal trade (some of them members of the Carey connection), and breaking down the blocks into numbered individual lots. They began an aggressive plan to sell lots to miners, small businessmen, and industrialists, usually taking a two- or three-year mortgage. The individual lots were generally sixty feet wide by 200 feet deep—about a quarter of an acre—and the average price was $200. One of the first large purchasers was Burd Patterson, who in September 1845 bought sixteen lots on the southern part of Second Street for $2,800. Patterson had already sold the temporarily stilled Pioneer Furnace and now he proceeded to construct a new furnace at St. Clair, which was in blast by 1846, smelting seventy-five tons of anthracite iron per week.[4]

The St. Clair Furnace, 1866, showing both furnace and foundry

Eventually the furnace property expanded to fifteen acres.[5] The sale of lots was successful enough to reduce the Carey holdings of surface rights (they retained the underlying mineral rights) from over 400 acres in 1844 to 253 acres in 1851.[6]

This deliberate development policy and Patterson's decision to move his furnace were undoubtedly correlated with the reconstruction of the Mill Creek railway. After completing its line to Pottsville, the Philadelphia and Reading had by 1844 extended its track to the landings at Port Carbon. This inspired the Mill Creek and Mine Hill Railroad to rebuild its track to accept locomotives and cars of the same gauge as the Reading, enabling coal cars to be loaded at the collieries, run down the Mill Creek, and shunted directly onto the Reading tracks bound for the market in Philadelphia, without the expense and inconvenience of being reloaded at Port Carbon. To facilitate cooperation, the president of the Reading, John Tucker—a friend of Henry Carey's—became the president of the Mill Creek and Mine Hill. The transition was completed and the new system in operation in 1845.[7]

All this activity, of course, was geared to the expectation that coal production would greatly increase as slopes were driven on the south dips of the Mammoth Vein and other outcropping veins at St. Clair and places about Mine Hill Gap. Carey wanted to gain access to the Mammoth Vein from an opening on his own estate, an opening more conveniently located near the railroad than the outcrop at the northern corner. To this end, early in 1845 he commissioned nephew Alfred Lawton to sink a test shaft at St. Clair. Enoch McGinness, who had supplied the engines for the experimental Carey-Patterson slope in 1835, and who had also built a "beautiful engine" for the blast at the Patterson furnace at St. Clair, a shiny sixty-horsepower giant with the boilers installed over the stack to save fuel, now was hired to build the pumping and hoisting engines.[8] A full-size shaft ten and a half by eighteen feet was dropped down seventy-two feet and from there a narrower bore hole continued another fifty feet until it penetrated the Primrose Vein. There Lawton stopped, perhaps because a successful slope already existed in the Primrose, with the opening on the St. Clair Tract a few hundred feet north. The question remained, however, whether the Mammoth Vein, somewhere below, lay at an accessible depth.

The second effort to locate the Mammoth by means of a vertical boring was conducted by the ubiquitous Enoch McGinness in 1850. He was then employed by the Delaware Coal Company, which owned coal lands along Norwegian Creek on the other side of the ridge from St. Clair, to locate the Mammoth Vein at a site somewhat to the south of the Lawton shaft. McGinness sank a shaft to a depth of 170 feet. At 431 feet a further bore hole struck the Mammoth Vein. The third effort was conducted by geologist Peter W. Sheafer, of the State Geological Survey, on behalf of the North American Coal Company at Crow Hollow, just east of St. Clair. Sheafer's boring reached the Mammoth Vein in October 1852 at 405 feet.[9]

Thus bracketed by successful borings east and west, north and south, the distance to the Mammoth at the site of the Lawton shaft could be confidently estimated as in the range of 400 to 500 feet. It now remained only to complete a full-scale shaft, adequate for hoisting coal, the whole way down, and this project McGinness now proposed to Henry Carey. McGinness, at the start, had only $4.50 to his name, having lost his machine shop in some financial scrape, but he had drilled a successful hole, he was an experienced engine builder, and he was enthusiastic about the prospect of opening up access to the Mammoth. So Carey agreed to advance him the money, to be repaid out of royalties, and the credit necessary to capitalize the venture.[10]

Carey's motives in sinking the first deep vertical-shaft mine in the

Schuylkill anthracite district were not merely financial; he had a point to prove. In his economic writings he had vehemently contradicted English economist David Ricardo's thesis that mankind invariably developed the best agricultural lands first, and only extended cultivation to the poorer, marginal lands later, when pressed by poverty. Carey argued that, to the contrary, the poorer lands were the first to be cultivated because they were cheaper to farm; the rich bottom lands, forested and swampy, could only be exploited later, at greater capital expense, but they yielded higher profits. With higher profits, farmers and capitalists would pay labor more, not less. Thus Carey denied Ricardo's pessimistic "iron law of wages," which held that wages always sank to the level of bare subsistence. Considering coal measures in the same light as agricultural land, Carey saw the superficially accessible outcrops as comparable to the inferior soils of initial cultivation: cheap to mine but not very profitable. He wanted to reach the rich veins of coal that must certainly lie in the depths, and was willing to commit considerable capital in the quest. As Enoch McGinness told him a few years later, "This is your favorite mode of doing things, to go deep."[11]

McGinness began in February 1852 by continuing Lawton's bore hole all the way down to the Mammoth Vein, which he reached in April at a depth of 417 feet. The workmen, after pulling out the boring rods and putting planks over the top of the hole, held a celebration in "old country fashion" with "a barrel of Ale, Crackers and Cheese, [and] a few thousand Segars," marching through St. Clair to the tune of a squeaking fiddle. Several days later the town's elite and the shaftsmen joined at a banquet at Buechly's hotel, where speeches and toasts, raised with alcoholic enthusiasm, continued half the night. Jacob Metz, president of the borough council, raised a glass to "St. Clair and its industrious people—it is bound to flourish." Magistrate John Seitzinger saluted "Alfred Lawton, the originator of the St. Clair Shaft, and E. W. McGinness, the undaunted and persevering in establishing his theory." And the toasts went on, praising the heroes of the St. Clair Shaft:

[To] the Laborers and Sinkers—The Iron and Steel of the St. Clair Shaft—May the latter never get blunt or defaced, until the great Mammoth is worked, and a beautiful reward reaped therefrom.

[To] Henry C. Carey, the enlightened and enterprising and financier of the St. Clair Shaft—May there be no obstacles to its immediate completion and successful operation.

99

[To] the men that bored the hole, Through the rock and found the coal.

[To] The Shaftsmen and Miners—From them alone is derived the wealth of Schuylkill County—To their unremitted industry our gratitude is due.

[To] the men who, under the dripping water, in the midst of a severe winter, sunk the St. Clair Shaft—May their names be associated among the great and noble enterprises which distinguish the citizens of old Schuylkill.

[To] Scott Steel, principal superintendent of the St. Clair Shaft—May he be as successful in developing the coal deposits, as he was in sinking the shaft.[12]

Next, in November, after arranging the financing, McGinness proceeded to put down a slope from the Mammoth outcrop in the northeast corner of the tract. This slope would, he argued, from the very start provide both cash income and the coal for powering the engines used in expanding the bore hole into a full-sized shaft. The ten-by-eighteen-foot shaft was sunk down from Lawton's seventy-two-foot level simultaneously with the slope. By the summer of 1853 the slope was down 196 yards, and by the next spring 100 yards farther, reaching a total vertical depth of perhaps 400 feet (exact figures are missing from the engineers' reports).[13] The shaft itself went down fast and by the fall of 1853 had reached the base of the Mammoth Vein at about 450 feet. Nevertheless, the work was expensive: the rock and slate were found to be "exceedingly hard," harder than expected, and there was trouble sealing off the walls of the shaft from deluges of water from the aquifers which the miners penetrated along the way. McGinness had hoped to reach a basin or synclinal axis of the great white-ash vein, but at the point of interception the bed dipped southward at an angle of about 12°.[14] The shaft stood, in fact, on a shelf, a few hundred feet to the south of which the Mammoth Vein dipped steeply downward to depths of thousands of feet; but this fact was not known to McGinness. Through the winter and summer of 1854, McGinness extended his gangways east and west in preparation for mining coal on the north side of the gangway. At the same time, the breaker was being constructed and the elevator and the pumps installed, both housed in structures attached to the breaker, on the slope of a hill 100 feet or so west of

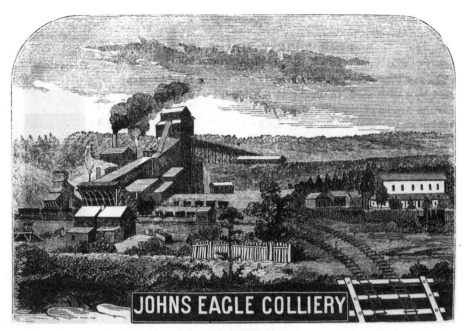

Johns Eagle Colliery (1866)

the railroad tracks, towering over the town as a medieval cathedral might tower over the houses huddled below.

THE COLLIERIES AT ST. CLAIR

Collieries are almost like living beings. They are born, they grow and change, and they finally die as disaster or exhaustion of their coal renders them unproductive. So in describing the collieries at St. Clair we shall adopt a biographical approach, describing the origin, growth, and (in most cases) decline of the collieries that made St. Clair for a time a prominent place in the coal trade. We shall start at the north and work south.

Johns Eagle Colliery

The Johns brothers, William and Thomas, took a lease from Wetherill and Seitzinger in 1846 to mine the coal in what came to be known as the Johns Basin, the small, boat-shaped syncline between Mine Hill and the St. Clair Tract. The Johns had been working the Mammoth at a small colliery at Oak Hill, near Mount Laffee, and they invested their original capital and profits in this new venture. The existing works consisted of a drift that entered the Skidmore Vein from the hillside above Mill Creek. The Johns, however, closed this drift and, over the years, made four new openings. First, in 1849, they drove a tunnel directly into the base of Mine Hill to intercept the thick and closely packed beds of the Four-Foot, Seven-Foot, and Mammoth veins, driving gangways east from this point that eventually extended for miles. Then in 1851 they sank a slope on the Mammoth Vein at a point where it outcropped about 100 yards north of the tunnel.[1] This slope was extended across the basin in two lifts, the gangways running east, with tunnels cutting across to the Four-Foot and Seven-Foot veins. In the 1860's a new tunnel was driven into the mountain from a point a mile or so to the east to intercept the Skidmore, and, about 100 yards in, a slope was sunk on the Mammoth down to water level. All in all, by 1869, when the mine was inspected by the first state mine inspector, there were nearly sixteen miles of interior gangways and hundreds of abandoned breasts separated by pillars twenty feet or more high. By the 1870's the old slope mine was a vast, empty, echoing cavern of a place with no new breasts being opened, and the only work still going on was the robbing of the pillars, which required that only a few men remain inside while section after section of roof collapsed as the supporting coal was taken away.[2]

The Johns built their first breaker in 1849, but in 1857 they replaced it with a new, larger breaker that was the talk of the county (see page 101). In 1858 Kitty Clover, the St. Clair correspondent of the *Miners' Journal,* reported:

> Mr. Wm. Johns' Mammoth breaker is finished, and is quite a curiosity in its way. Persons from different parts of the County visit our town to see it.[3]

The breaker was designed so as to handle conveniently coal both from the tunnel directly behind it and from the slope on the mountainside. The slope coal was carried in mine cars onto a horizontal roadway supported by a wooden trestle that led to the dumping platform at the top of the breaker; the tunnel coal was hoisted by an elevator up a vertical shaft to the same dumping platform. The hoisting machinery, which had to pull up several tons of coal to a height of about 100 feet, was itself massive, weighing sixty tons, and was operated by a ninety-horsepower engine. From year to year, the Eagle Colliery produced 75,000 to 100,000 tons of coal, so the breaker must have been able to prepare up to 500 tons of unbroken coal per day (assuming a six-day work week and a forty-week operating year). This means that it had to dump one coal car with a 2.5-ton load every three minutes of a ten-hour day.

The design and construction of the Eagle Colliery were carried out by professionals. The Johns brothers at first, and their sons later, were no absentee amateur operators: they were themselves experienced miners, originally from the coal district of Wales, and they were seriously interested in making money. Their "mansion" in the patch stood within 100 yards of the breaker and was exposed to all the noise, soot, and mud that afflicted their employees living around them, but they did not move away even when they were worth millions. Their mine bosses were also experienced Welsh miners, earnest Protestants and Republicans like the Johns. The first superintendent was John Reese, who came to America about the same time as the Johns. He served from 1846 to the time of his death in 1856, and his son William, after working as a blacksmith and machinist, served as superintendent from 1871 to 1888.[4] From the beginning to the end of the colliery's life, qualified observers agreed that everything was done in the best way possible to ensure both uninterrupted production ("continuous flow") and the safety of the miners. The first outside observer whose reports have survived was John Maddison, the engineer employed by the Wetherills to inform them as to the manner in which their lessees were developing their collieries. Maddison first reported from 1850 to 1853 and his comments were uniformly favorable:

> The timbering is done in a very creditable and workmanlike manner. . . . Pillar sides well dressed. . . . The slope when all is said and done is a good one: . . . What is done so far, is done in the most strong and substantial manner, besides there is plenty of room for all purposes. . . . This is going to make a splendid Colliery . . . one of the largest as well as one of the most productive Collieries in the Coal Region.[5]

In 1866 Samuel Daddow commented:

> This colliery has always been conducted in the most practical and economical manner, having been developed and improved by two practical and prudent miners, Thomas Johns and the late William H. Johns, who did their work in the most substantial manner, and with the great objects of availability and economy in operation constantly in view. The consequence is, that this has been one of our most successful—if not our most successful—collieries; and has realized for its prudent and fortunate possessors over a million of dollars in net profits.

It is not, and has not been, a better location than many others we might name; nor has the Mammoth here—though uniformly good and productive of splendid coal—been superior in size, or economy of production, to the same magnificent bed in many other places, where it has not been so profitably worked. In mining, as in all other pursuits, practical experience, and a careful, energetic management, is almost always certain of success, and always certain, when the coal exists in comparatively large seams, and is free from fault and impurity.[6]

And in 1869 and 1870 the state mine inspectors still had nothing but praise:

> . . . the pillars are left of sufficient strength to warrant the safety of mines and miners, and the safety roads are very many and the drainage good; with little or no timber used in all the gangways, few collieries are to be met with better managed than the Eagle colliery, and have fewer accidents or complaints.[7]
>
> The mines have been worked on a safe plan, with regard to safety of men. No steam fan ventilation is used, as no fire damp is evolved. The ventilation is produced by a series of air-courses and gangways, which makes coal mining here a safe operation for men. . . .
>
> The character and condition of all the machinery is good. The hoisting and pumping machinery is well secured to avoid accident to men and boys, also the general condition of the miners for safety is satisfactory; such needed improvements as are necessary are pushed forward. The thickness of rock seams is such as will justify the working of the mines with safety to the men. Timber, in proper quantities, is fully supplied to miners to secure their working places. Ventilation is moderate and the air-courses of good size, to conduct a good supply of air. On inquiry on this head no complaints were advanced by the men, and all were evidently satisfied.[8]

In no part of the planning and management of the mine were the Johns and their superintendents more careful than in the matter of ventilation. In the original drift opening, the work at first proceeded slowly, no breasts being opened until airways to the surface were uncovered. The method of working followed that practiced at Kaska William Colliery a few miles to the east. The pillars were marked along the gangway at seven yards wide, but every alternate pillar was nine yards wide, with a two-foot wide manway (a narrow passage for the movement of miners) driven up the center, and every sixth manway was driven all the way to the surface, forming a system of direct ventilation from the gangway up to the surface before any mining was allowed to begin in the breasts between the pillars. Firedamp, being lighter than air, was thus allowed to escape directly to the surface. The manways provided access, through headings at regular intervals, to the breasts which ran up, on a pitch of 70° to 75°, some eighty yards to the outcrop on Mine Hill. Not uncommonly the outcrop caved in, adding to the ventilation. When the slope was sunk, its manways were run up to the drift gangway, so that No. 1 slope and No. 1 drift had a continuous ventilation system, aided in its later years by a furnace and a steam vent in the drift.[9] The doors and brattices were carefully maintained. The result was a mine reputed to be free of gas, with an actual history of few explosions, and twice as much fresh air coursing through as the 1870 mine law required.

As the old drift and slope workings approached exhaustion in the late 1860's, the new drift and slope were opened toward the east end of the Johns Basin, and most of the colliery's 150 or so underground workers were dispatched thence, only a few remaining to rob pillars and maintain ventilation in the old workings. At last in 1878 the old breaker, "composed of timber seasoned by age and saturated with grease," was destroyed by fire.[10] Almost all of the 200 men and boys employed at the colliery were thrown out of work until the new breaker was built later that year. The Johns family gave up their lease on the Eagle Colliery in 1882.

The St. Clair Shaft and Slope

South of the Johns Basin, the southern dip of the next anticlinal outcropped on a long line that crossed the northern edge of the town. Five major collieries were built in or near St. Clair to exploit the Mammoth Vein along that south dip: the St. Clair Slope and the St. Clair Shaft, the Pine Forest Slope and Shaft, and the Hickory Slope and the connecting Wadesville Shaft. In each case the slope was sunk first, and then the vertical shaft to develop coal at depths below which slopes seemed to become impracticable.

The slope-and-shaft colliery built by Enoch McGinness in 1853 and 1854 was the prototype for the Pine Forest and Wadesville shafts in combining a previously sunk slope, which opened the coal in three or four lifts to a vertical depth of several hundred feet, and a vertical shaft that made lower coal accessible. And its fate foreshadowed that of the other two shafts. McGinness first extended an old slope in the northeast corner of the town to provide cash income and coal for the engine sinking the shaft, and then proceeded to sink the shaft itself. The sinking of the "McGinness Shaft" had immense symbolic importance for the coal trade because it purported to prove that the forty-foot-thick white-ash measures of the Mammoth bed underlay, at an easily accessible depth, the whole valley between Broad and Sharp mountains. It appeared that McGinness had opened a vast field of coal in every direction "which will require ages to exhaust." The St. Clair correspondent to the *Miners' Journal* portrayed a vista of endless prosperity:

> As the coal which is now worked near the outcrop of the veins becomes exhausted, other shafts will be sunk to various parts of our coal field, so that shafts will become as numerous as slopes are now, and ages hence, a teeming population will be busily engaged in extracting the rich mineral deposits which a kind Providence has placed beneath our feet. It is true, no doubt, that the centre of the basin lies much deeper than the outcrop and will require a much larger expenditure of the time and money to reach, yet these difficulties will be overcome. The sinking of the first slope was considered a great undertaking and perhaps by some even deemed visionary, but now they are too numerous as to awaken little or no interest. The great body of coal in the region can only be reached by shafting.[11]

And a couple of years later it was estimated that the colliery could produce, with the existing surface equipment, at least 1,000 tons per day, and with a larger breaker, twice that.[12]

The shaft was located on the west side of town, on the hillside just beyond the railroad tracks at the end of Carroll Street. It was a tight ten and a half by eighteen feet in cross-section ("incomplete," it was enlarged some years later to sixteen by twenty-four feet), with three compartments, two for hoisting and one for the pumps, each partitioned by wooden siding. The men were supposed to travel the 450 feet up and down on ladders placed between the pump shafts, but most understandably preferred to ride on the coal cars. Two of the compartments were used as the upcast and downcast airways, and the ventilation furnace at the bottom used the upcast compartment for its chimney. The shift elevator was built into the breaker and brought the loaded cars directly to the top of the fifty-foot-high structure, where they were automatically dumped at a theoretical rate of one per minute. Eli Bowen, in describing the patent hoisting arrangement designed by Pottsville inventor George Martz, clearly, almost rhapsodically, expressed the philosophy of complete-process collieries:

> Now, as the loaded car reaches the head of the Shute, by a certain mechanical movement, one end of it becomes elevated, at the same time that the forward movement of the Coal pushes open the gate of the car (which springs on hinges from the top framework), and the Coal issues out in *one continuous stream into the Shute which supplies it to the Breaker!* No sooner is the Coal discharged, than the car again assumes its original horizontal position in the cage, and descends with rapidity down the Shaft. But while it is going down, another cage is traveling upward, with its load of Coal; and thus the supplies are arriving alternately from each side of the Shaft, and with extraordinary rapidity. In this operation, manual labor is entirely dispensed with.[13]

The breaker, which started up in October 1854, was for its time extremely large and boasted a powerful forty-horsepower engine made by McGinness. The reporter for the *Miners' Journal* was awed to see it looming over the town, "a monstrous mass of timber, which at once strikes the beholder with admiration if not wonder, and conveys a grand idea of the greatness and importance of the coal trade."[14]

The pitch of the vein at the point where the shaft entered the Mammoth was only 12° and McGinness, therefore, thought that the basin lay a few hundred feet to the south; in actuality, he had landed on a narrow shelf that interrupted the vein's general plunge into the depths. But in the initial working of the shaft, this meant that the wagons could be run into the breasts and hand-loaded at the face of the coal, yielding cleaner coal, since the rock and bone (coal mixed with slate) did not "run" down the bottom slate into the cars. But as the breasts were extended to the north, the grade grew steeper, and instead of turning to mining on the run, the breasts were abandoned and the gangways were extended into new coal. A tunnel was driven south from the foot of the shaft to intercept the Seven-Foot Vein and the same procedure was followed there. The shaft colliery thus consisted essentially of one east and one west gangway on the Mammoth and the same on the Seven-Foot Vein, extending eventually all

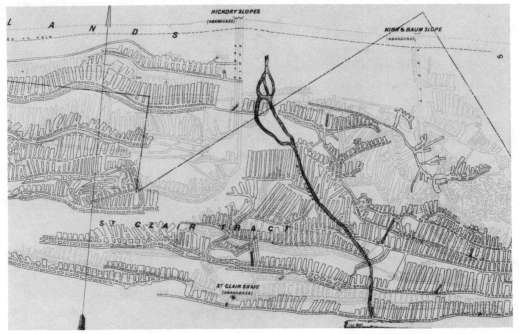

Map of mine workings under the St. Clair Tract in 1877
Key: gray–Mammoth Vein   black–Seven-Foot Vein

the way across the St. Clair Tract, but with short penetration northward into the coal. Late in the history of the mine, a plane was driven at the far eastern side of the tract up through the Seven-Foot Vein to open three lifts. The slope colliery remained confined to the Mammoth at the northeastern corner of the tract. It was a single slope, with its own air-and-pumping shaft running parallel to the slope itself, and eventually four lifts were opened with gangways extending east and west. At the beginning there was no connection between the slope and the shaft gangways; later a tunnel connected the two mines to provide better ventilation. By the 1870's, when they were both closed down, the two collieries together had mined underneath, at varying depths, virtually all of the town of St. Clair north of Lawton Street.[15]

Intimations of future trouble were contained in the confidential reports on the McGinness slope provided in 1853 and 1854 by the same engineer, John Maddison, who was praising the Johns' Eagle Colliery. He was critical of the quality of workmanship: "Timbering is not overtidy. . . ." He was also critical of McGinness' basic design:

West Gangway is stopped . . . but for the want of coal to raise money [it] would have been better to have remained untouched.

A good deal of level has been lost. . . . Pillars are of an irregular thickness and . . . while some are in middling order ["good" crossed out] others are in a distressed condition.

As a result of leaving the pillars too thin, gangways and breasts were being crushed and whole lifts had to be abandoned. As the sinking progressed, under the direction of John Holmes but with design by McGinness, Maddison continued to point out flaws: pillars too narrow, breasts too short, timbering cut short and placed too far apart. And he even cast doubt on McGinness' pet theory. McGinness thought he was sinking to the basin and that the pitch would turn up on the other side, thus making it possible to mine the southern half of the tract. But Maddison said, "Don't think that McGinness is so near to a turnup or Basin as he thinks he is."[16]

Similar problems of quality and design afflicted the shaft colliery. One consequence of McGinness' method of mining was to make it impossible, except eventually at the far end of the east gangway, to drive either breasts or planes beyond the distances mentioned earlier. Probably the whole line of breasts was subject to crushing as a result of narrow, poorly dressed pillars or excessively wide breasts, or both. In any case, whatever the problem, it was impossible for McGinness to gain access to most of the coal in the northern part of the tract; and the coal to the south was impossible to mine because the anticipated basin was not there. These problems had come to Carey's attention by June 1855, when Christian Frantz, another local colliery operator, was commissioned to evaluate both shaft and slope. His report was "not very flattering."[17]

Another major problem was a persistent difficulty in ventilating the mine. At first, the mine was ventilated entirely through the single shaft, with a furnace at the bottom, but this proved to be inadequate to prevent a couple of fatal explosions of methane during McGinness' tenure, and the next tenants, Messrs. Kirk and Baum, made changes. They had a tunnel driven northeasterly from the eastern end of the shaft gangway to intercept the slope at its lowest level. This 1,800-foot-long airway was hailed by the *Miners' Journal* as "a *master piece* in the art of mining" because the miners who drove it used brattices to partition the seven-by-twelve-foot tunnel into an upcast and a downcast to provide themselves with air.[18] Brattices—light wooden frames covered with wooden planks or cloth—had long been employed in England to direct currents of air, but allegedly this was the first time they had been used in Schuylkill County. The slope had its own furnace at the foot of a stone chimney on the surface, so now the slope could be used as the upcast and the shaft as the downcast. This was not an ideal arrangement, however, for the air had to traverse miles of workings before reaching the surface. Furthermore, the badly constructed main gangways and the slope air hole were liable to crushes, which effectively stopped the circulation entirely. This happened at least once in the slope airway, which was closed by a crush, necessitating the driving of a circuitous detour that connected the second- and third-level gangways.[19] And, finally, connecting the two mines meant that in wet weather a great deal of water ran down the slope airway into the tunnel and on to the sump at the bottom of the shaft—by definition the lowest point in the mine. Not infrequently these floods overwhelmed the pumps in the shaft and the water rose. When it rose a few feet, it not only blocked the shaft gangways, but interfered with—and eventually stopped—the ventilation of the slope. A steam fan was installed at the foot of the shaft in the 1860's when the shaft was again separated from the abandoned slope.

As a result of these and other difficulties, coal production at the St. Clair Slope and Shaft Colliery was low and intermittent. From 1854 to 1866, when both shaft and slope were in production, the combined annual tonnage figures were:

1854	41,671	1862	27,574	(August and September figures are estimates)
1855	52,594			
1856	24,897	1863	48,000	(estimate based on returns for June, December)
1857	0			
1858	59,969	1864	67,476	
1859	53,555	1865	37,476	
1860	93,421	1866	38,093	
1861	42,256			

No figures are available for 1867 and 1868; during the final three years, the slope was closed down and the shaft was operated alone:

1869	42,824	1871	92,803
1870	48,633	1872	73,236

No data are available for 1873 and 1874, and the mine was closed in 1874.[20]

The original lease anticipated a production in excess of 200,000 tons per year, on which the unfortunate Enoch McGinness was expected to pay a royalty of 30 cents a ton![21] The total production, during the twenty years of its existence as a pair of collieries, was less than a million tons; the average annual tonnage was about 50,000 tons, or 25,000 tons per colliery. The reason for the poor performance was in part McGinness' flawed design. As his rival for Carey's confidence, agent Andrew Russell, put it, "The mines have never been properly worked. McGinness began wrong and [later operators] have never yet been able to correct that wrong."[22] But the precipitating factor in the series of bankruptcies, sheriff's auctions, and forced sales was an almost endless series of catastrophes. McGinness was forced to sell both collieries to Kirk and Baum in July 1855 after a three-month-long series of accidents and related labor troubles put him hopelessly in debt. In April he was having difficulty hiring men because they were afraid to get into unsafe cages in the elevator. He solved that problem by constructing lighter cages. But at the end of the month, miners "cut a spring in the slope" and the slope was flooded for a month until he could install a larger pump. On the 11th of June there was an explosion in the shaft workings that killed one man and injured four; the miners demanded higher wages and instituted a slowdown. These last accidents resulted in Carey's appointing Christian Frantz superintendent of the slope, while Holmes was transferred to the shaft. But at the end of the month the boilers at the slope blew up, the men had not been paid, and then the slope pump broke down.[23] At this point McGinness gave up and sold all his improvements to Kirk and Baum for $147,000, just sufficient to pay his debts.

Kirk and Baum fared no better and were forced to surrender their lease in 1861, and their personal property was sold by the sheriff. They suffered an even worse series of misfortunes that kept the slope and shaft out of production for months at a time. In August 1856 the breaker and most of the other buildings on the surface burned down and the debris collapsed into the shaft. With the pumps destroyed, the mine filled up with water. Russell's account was graphic:

> The fire has made a clean sweep. There is hardly fragments enough left to make a respectable bonfire. Much rubbish has fallen into the top of the Shaft and having sent to Pottsville for hose they were able to put water in it from a fire plug in St. Clair and have put all the fire out and think little damage has been done the Shaft and nothing below. —they commenced at once to repair damage to the pumps as the important matter now is to keep the water down. The loss is estimated at from $30 to 40,000— Insurance $15,000. . . . It took fire from a lamp set too near tarred rope. The men were at work at the time repairing some slight damage to the pump the fire ran up the roof of the building and could not be stopped—some satisfaction to know how it occurred.[24]

The fire stopped production for the rest of the year 1856 and all of 1857. In 1858 the slope flooded, endangering the shaft, and in the summer of 1860 the slope flooded again, stopping the works until January. In February there was an explosion of firedamp in the shaft, and then in March the pump failed and the shaft filled with water. Kirk and Baum gave up their lease to Carey in December and a third operator, El Hart, took it over. The shaft remained flooded until a new pump was installed in 1862. Then in April 1864 the St. Clair Coal Company of Boston, a group of wealthy investors, took over the lease. But they were even less successful than their predecessors. The breaker at the shaft was again destroyed by fire in July 1865, the pumps stopped, the shaft filled with water to 110 feet, stopping the ventilation of the slope, and then a crush happened in the slope, stopping the slope pumps. The St. Clair Coal Company, to cut its losses, abandoned St. Clair, and the mine remained flooded until 1868, when a new lessee, a partnership of local operators, took over and began to refurbish and enlarge the shaft.[25] Then in 1871 Carey himself gave up, selling the St. Clair Tract to the Philadelphia and Reading Coal and Iron Company, which proceeded to operate the shaft itself with William Kendrick, one of the previous operators, remaining as superintendent. The Coal and Iron Company, evidently persuaded that the mine's problems were irremediable, closed the shaft in 1874.

There can be no doubt that the final common path to financial ruin for the lessees of the St. Clair Slope and Shaft Colliery was physical disaster in the form of crushes, explosions, fires, and floods, some of them resulting from original design flaws and sloppy workmanship in the underground works.

The Pine Forest Colliery

The Pine Forest Slope was sunk in 1845 by Snyder and Haywood, and Crow Hollow Patch grew up around it. The slope itself ran down along the eastern boundary of the St. Clair Tract, leaving a pillar of untouched coal along the property line and opening out gangways on the Mammoth and Seven-Foot veins that extended east for over a mile. All the machinery, of course—engines, pumps, and breaker—was constructed at Snyder and Haywood's machine shop and foundry in Pottsville. By 1850 the colliery was employing sixty hands and producing about 15,000 tons per year; but after Haywood moved to California and Benjamin Milnes left the firm in 1853, Snyder taking charge, a second slope was sunk in 1857 and pro-

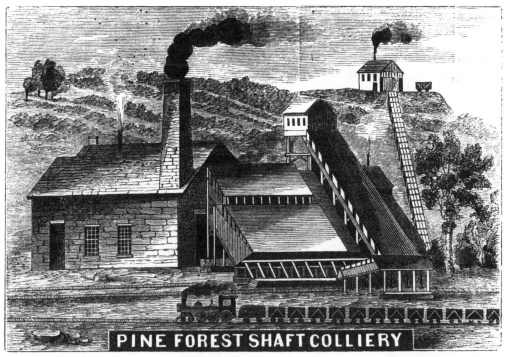

PINE FOREST SHAFT COLLIERY

Pine Forest Shaft (1866)

duction increased rapidly to over 100,000 tons annually from three lifts below water level. By 1860, however, the operators needed to reach lower levels and a vertical shaft was proposed, after the example of McGinness and Carey. The sinking of this shaft began late in 1864, but progress was delayed by water and the work was not completed until November 1866. This twelve-by-twenty-foot shaft struck the Mammoth Vein at 362 feet and a forty-three-foot tunnel south intercepted the Seven-Foot and another, 270 feet north, reached the Skidmore.[26]

Snyder was an aggressive administrator, but did not spend much time on the ground, being primarily concerned with his ironworks. He did, however, insist on the use of the best and most up-to-date machinery. In 1863 he installed a steam fan to aid the ventilation, "the first in the vicinity."[27] The aggregate steam power at the old Pine Forest Slope was 250 horses; at the new shaft it was over 500. As the mine inspector put it in 1869, "The machinery and engines, and the appurtenances of the colliery, cannot be excelled in the county." And again in 1870, "none but competent persons are in charge of engines and machinery." As with the St. Clair Colliery, the breaker stood adjacent to the shaft, so that the cars ran up eighty feet to the top of the breaker and automatically unloaded the coal without leaving the cage; the cage was thoughtfully provided with a cover, some time later, to protect those riding in it.[28]

Nevertheless, despite the mechanical sophistication displayed in the new Pine Forest Shaft Colliery, it turned out to be a failure. Tonnage figures in the mine inspectors' annual reports tell the story. Completed in 1866, it suspended operations in 1884 and was finally abandoned in 1890. During its twenty-four years of existence, it was in condition to ship coal during only twelve years, and during even these twelve years it produced only 628,112 tons, for an average annual production of 52,342—merely half of what the old slope did back in the 1850's, and far below its estimated capacity of 150,000 tons per year.[29]

The problem with the Pine Forest Shaft was the ventilation, which was ill-designed when the shaft was first opened in 1866 and prevented effective working until 1872, when Snyder sold the colliery to the Philadelphia and Reading Coal and Iron Company and a professional operator took over the lease. Snyder chose as the inside boss an Irish immigrant, Thomas Maguire, who had worked for Snyder ever since the sinking of the shaft began. Maguire was a practical miner but illiterate and, as his son put it later in his autobiography, "did not want to be a boss, but they simply made him be one."[30] The elder Maguire depended on his son, then in his twenties, to keep the colliery account books, maintain records of the inside arrangements, and do such calculations as he could on critical matters like air volume and velocity. The result was a poor system that ran the downcast air from the foot of the shaft through the entire mine before returning to the surface at a fan located close to the breaker. The first mine inspector observed, "There is a considerable quantity of gas evolved in the face of the gangway and breasts, so that it is necessary and expedient to use no lamps but the Davy safety-lamps." And he was forced to issue detailed instructions on the use of lamps and other precautions for fire safety. Next year, even after the upcast air shaft and fan were moved to a point 1,000 yards distant from the breaker, the condition was little better: "the accumulation of carburetted hydrogen gas in the mine at present is considerable, and none but the most careful miners should be permitted to work in certain districts with or without safety lamps."[31] At times, all production had to be halted because of rockfalls in the gangways that blocked the flow of air.

In 1872 William Kendrick took charge of the Pine Forest on behalf of the Reading Company, but Thomas Maguire continued as inside boss until his death in 1877. His son John then took his place for a time, before moving on in the employ of the company as superintendent, district superintendent, and finally division superintendent. But, despite the superior

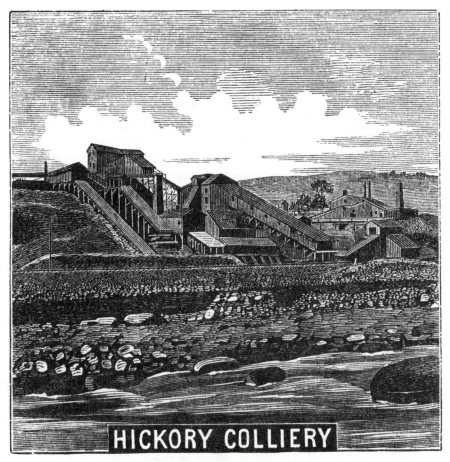

Hickory Colliery (1866)

experience of Kendrick and better technical education of the younger Maguire, the mine never fully lived up to its promise and in 1890 was left to fill up with water.

The Hickory Colliery and the Wadesville Shaft

On the northern edge of St. Clair, on the other side of Mill Creek from Johns' Eagle Colliery and a bit south of it, was another old colliery built on the Mammoth Vein outcrop that dated back to the 1830's. John Pinkerton, an English miner newly arrived in America, leased the coal from the Wetherills in 1835 and drove a tunnel north to an earlier drift gangway, where he drove up an air hole and then continued working west for about half a mile. It was a large establishment for its time and in its heyday shipped as much as 100,000 tons a year. Pinkerton kept a house at St. Clair, a company store, and owned railroad cars and canal boats for transporting his own coal. In the financial debacle of the late 1830's, however, he fell upon hard times and the improvements and personal property were acquired at a sheriff's sale by Thomas Albert Haven, Carey's associate.[32] Pinkerton recovered the colliery in a few years, however, sank a slope, and put up a large breaker. In 1853, Benjamin and William Milnes, father and son, bought out Pinkerton. Benjamin Milnes was an experienced miner who had already been engaged in the coal trade for thirty-seven years, the first twenty-one of them in England, and, as we noted earlier, had in the 1830's served as "Mine agent" for the North American Coal Company. The colliery was now renamed Hickory. Milnes and son sank a new and deeper slope and extended the workings westward, taking coal from the Lee lands owned by the Wetherills and bringing it to the surface through gangways under Carey land (for which they paid an additional royalty). The lower lifts now crossed the boundaries of the St. Clair Tract in its northwest corner, and royalties on this coal also went to the Careys.[33]

In 1860, the Hickory Colliery was the subject of a communication in the *Scientific American* from the Port Carbon mining engineer Robert Allison. The mine was now so extensive that the old furnace ventilation was inadequate, and the Milnes were supplementing the furnace with the so-called "steam-jet" system. Allison's letter described both the old furnace and new steam apparatus:

> . . . Mr. Milnes owns and works a very extensive colliery at St. Clair, in Schuylkill County; and in order to ventilate his works, he has driven an air-way of 30 feet area to the surface, where there is an arched flue, 30 feet in length, containing a grate or furnace on which a very strong fire is constantly kept up. At the end of the flue is a chimney, 6 feet internal diameter and 60 feet high. The air-way is connected with the different parts of the works by means of *brattices* and doors, so that all the workings received their proportionate supply of pure air. This plan of furnace and chimney worked very well until lately, when, the works becoming more extensive, it was found necessary to increase the draft, but it failed to draw off the explosive gases. After fully investigating the matter, Mr. Milnes concluded to introduce what is known in England as the "steam-jet system," and with the cooperation of

Messrs. Pomeroy & Son, machinists, he has done so with the most gratifying results.

At the foot of the chimney he erected two boilers, 30 inches diameter and 20 feet long, from which a steam pipe is carried into the chimney, and so arranged as to distribute 25 jet pipes equally throughout the area of the chimney; these pipes point directly up and have an opening of ⅛ of an inch, through which the steam passes at a pressure of about 75 pounds to the square inch. This plan works admirably, and it was found, by actual measurement, to have nearly doubled the amount of air passing through the air-way. So well pleased was Mr. Milnes with the result, that he has since put up two more boilers and increased the number of jets to 45, with proportionate effects.[34]

But the steam-jet system could not solve problems internal to the mine. By the 1860's the Hickory was becoming an exhausted colliery. Miners had to get to the breasts by trudging a mile underground through old workings filled with gob and supported by rotting props. Crushes destroyed the ventilation in some of the old gangways and forced the closing of whole lifts. According to Enoch McGinness, these crushes were the result of the Milnes' own bad management. In 1861 they were forced to abandon the middle lift entirely because "they lost the air . . . which was brought about by working out a pillar that should have protected the air-way to the surface." And by the end of 1861 they lost most of the air in the lower lift of the Mammoth too because of roof falls and were forced to work almost exclusively in the Seven-Foot Vein. McGinness said that the Milnes had had the same difficulty when they were managing the Pine Forest a decade before. By the end of January 1862 the Milnes were in dire straits, refusing to pay rents and threatening to abandon the works. They struggled on, even sinking a new slope "on the mountain" on the north dip of the Mammoth, but in 1864 they gave up and sold out to the Mammoth Vein Consolidated Coal Company, a large firm that already owned and operated seven other collieries.[35]

In its public announcement, intended to attract investors, the company's consulting engineer, P. W. Sheafer, described the old double-slope colliery in detail. Its "improvements" included thirteen steam engines, three pumps, a $20,000 breaker, a sawmill, carpenter and blacksmith shops, a stable, forty-eight horses and mules, 276 "slope cars," ten blocks of houses (presumably in St. Clair), and hundreds of tons of iron including 500 tons of T-rails for gangway tracks. The Milnes' "new slope" had been turned into the main upcast airway and the furnace and steam-jet system had been replaced by a twenty-five-horsepower exhaust fan twelve feet in diameter. A lithograph accompanying Sheafer's report and an engraving in Daddow and Bannan's book show the arrangement of the surface structures clearly.[36]

The main trouble with the old colliery was the distance of the surface structures from the main body of coal being mined. The miners working in the fourth lift had to descend a slope 1,200 feet long with a dip of 35° and then walk nearly two miles west to get to the breasts; the coal itself had to be hauled back the same distance; and the air, of course, had to move through the same long courses. Milnes reported to the new owners that he had been unable to develop the deeper workings in the west "for want of air." Furthermore, the company had recently acquired favorable leases (the royalty being only 26 cents per ton) from the Wetherills on the coal of Mammoth and Seven-Foot veins at a distance of three-quarters of a mile farther to the west, in the Ellmaker and Flowery Field tracts. The only practical way to develop these new reserves and complete the working out of the old was, in Sheafer's opinion, to sink a vertical shaft on the Mammoth at Wadesville one mile west of St. Clair. By September 1864 the Wadesville Shaft Colliery was under construction, with P. W. Sheafer as directing engineer and his brother W. H. Sheafer as general agent for the company. The new shaft measured fourteen by twenty-two feet and was estimated to strike the Mammoth at a depth of 600 feet. On the 31st of May 1867, nearly three years later, the shaft reached the Mammoth Vein at 663 feet. The top forty feet of the shaft, as it passed through soft ground and unstable rock and gravel, was lined with masonry and the remainder with wood. From top to bottom the shaft was divided into three six-by-twelve-foot compartments by twelve-inch timbers set four feet apart and lined with wooden planking.[37] By November 1867 the men were driving the gangway west into good coal.

The Sheafer brothers wrote an article for the *Miners' Journal*, reprinted in the *Journal of the Franklin Institute*, enthusiastically describing their new shaft and comparing it favorably with the great English coal shafts. The Wadesville Shaft had been made necessary by the dangers of robbing the pillars in the old Hickory workings:

> "Robbing a mine," as it is technically called, is the attempt to remove the pillars of coal left between the chambers to support the top; this is an exceedingly dangerous operation. These columns of coal stand but 10 or 12 yards apart for a mile in length

and a hundred yards in width; they support an enormous pressure of rock, slate and earth. Blasting them away, brings down a mountain and endangers all within its influence, sometimes in detached falls of tons of rock, at other times the whole space gradually settles down with a terrible slow weight and awful groaning, and at other times it comes with a terrific shock and a mighty rush of wind, driven out with the violence of a storm. To avoid this older and catacombed part of the mines, this enterprising company were induced to open into a larger body of coal, one mile to the south-west, by means of their Wadesville shaft, 666 feet deep, to the Mammoth bed.

The Sheafers produced the usual optimistic arithmetic to show the vast amount of valuable coal the new mine could be expected to produce (300,000 tons per year for twenty years). And they congratulated themselves on using "no artificial means of ventilation." All in all, they concluded, the Wadesville Shaft demonstrated the superiority of Pennsylvania mine design over the British. The Americans needed only a single shaft and natural ventilation (aided by an undescribed "simple contrivance"), whereas the British needed furnaces, steam jets, and fans, "and frequently sank an extra shaft for ventilation." And the American mine would yield one third more coal in one sixth the area of the English mine.[38]

That fall, expectations for the Wadesville Shaft were almost utopian in the little town, complete with a chapel and taverns, that now was springing up around it. Costing half a million dollars to complete, the colliery would be the greatest in the world, producing 300,000 tons a year of the best white-ash coal. The shaft and workings were built in the most modern, strong, substantial manner and employed all the newest devices and equipment, even to the powder employed, a newly invented product introduced in Wales that was smokeless and could not be ignited by concussion. The supervising engineer on the site, John C. Northall, was widely respected and was presented with "a memento of their esteem by the Company at the final completion of the shaft."[39] But these sweet hopes were soon to turn to sour disappointment, for the Wadesville Shaft, like the Pine Forest Shaft and the St. Clair, was never able to operate for long without serious interruption. Production figures again reveal the seriousness of the problem. By the end of 1869 the colliery still had not gotten into full production, although no less than twenty gangways on three lifts—a total of six miles of gangways—had been opened up and 350 men and boys were employed above and below ground. No production figures were given for 1869, but from 1870 to 1884, when the Wadesville Shaft was temporarily abandoned, the tonnage figures were extremely variable:

1870	72,500	1878	23,839
1871	4,793	1879	118,326
1872	78,519	1880	106,388
1873	122,033	1881	110,874
1874	0	1882	15,233
1875	0	1883	5,240
1876	34,607	1884	29,554
1877	150,261		

The average for the first fifteen years of its existence as a colliery was 58,144, or about one-fifth of the colliery's estimated capacity.[40] The colliery cost $500,000 to build; at 10 cents a ton, it earned a net profit over operating costs of only $87,216.70, hardly enough to pay the interest on a loan of half a million.

The one, single, over-riding reason for this poor performance was the inadequacy of the ventilation system. Methane accumulation led to a series of disastrous explosions; and spontaneous combustion in the gob in poorly ventilated old workings set off underground fires that could only be extinguished by turning off the pumps and letting the mine fill with water. The ventilation problem was present from the very outset. When the first gangway was being driven from the bottom of the shaft in the fall of 1867, no artificial ventilation was provided, not even a furnace; the upcast and downcast compartments in the shaft, supplemented by the "simple contrivance," were expected to provide proper circulation. But the "contrivance" did not work and an air shaft had to be driven. It was actually a small slope that doubled for an escape road, running from the lower gangway 1,600 yards—nearly a mile—north to the outcrop. At the mouth, an exhaust fan was constructed—the popular Beadle steam fan, eighteen feet in diameter, powered by a twenty-horsepower engine. The fan was in place in 1869. But it was unable to cope with the quantity of air that had to be moved, for air came into the workings not only from the new shaft, but also from the old Hickory Slope, which still served as an escape road. The air was reported by the mine inspector to move "4½ times slow." Also, a great deal of methane was evolved in the old slope workings and was drawn into the general circulation by the negative pressure produced by the fan. And in addition to all this, spontaneous combustion occurred repeatedly in the old workings, where the heat was not carried away by a sufficient flow of air. There were no less than five underground mine fires in the Wadesville Shaft's first fifteen years, resulting in the flooding of the mine and prolonged interruption of production. There were also numerous local explosions of firedamp, despite strict regulations about the use of safety lamps and the closing of check doors. One of these explosions, in 1877, resulted in the death of six men and led to a manslaughter indictment against the mine superintendent by an incensed coroner's jury.[41] We shall examine this disaster in a later chapter.

Other Collieries in and around St. Clair

There were a number of smaller and shorter-lived collieries in St. Clair or close enough to it for residents to take employment there. Most of those south of the borough had been abandoned by the end of the 1850's, as the problems of faults and poor-quality coal drove the operators away. One large slope colliery on Carey's eighty-acre tract, on the west side of the creek between the village of Mill Creek and the borough line, was operated for some years by Wallace and Rothermel, the Philadelphia coal merchants. Their mine, however, caught fire underground in 1855 and the operators abandoned it, being sued by Carey in consequence.[42] It was allowed to fill with water in order to put out the fire and was left unoccupied until 1860, when McGinness attempted to restore it for the North American Coal Company and Carey. Another major slope colliery was the Mammoth Colliery of George Repplier, the St. Clair merchant who replaced the failed Joseph Lawton as principal operator; but Repplier too eventually went under. There were two major slope collieries at Mount Laffee, one of which was operated for a time by Franklin Benjamin Gowen (later president of the Reading) and James Turner. They failed when their mine caught fire underground and filled with water.[43]

In St. Clair itself there was one substantial slope on the Primrose Vein: Parvin's Slope, which slanted south from the outcrop on what was known as Parvin's Hill, just north of the road to Wadesville. It probably made use of the old air hole Pinkerton had sunk to ventilate his drift. It produced on the order of 30,000 tons per year until 1859, when—as the reader may now anticipate—it experienced a large firedamp explosion that set fire to the coal. The mine had to be drowned, and after struggling for a couple of years to get out the water and put the mine in order again, Parvin sold his works to Andrew Russell. They were dismantled and the mine was abandoned in the early 1860's.[44]

There were dozens of other old drafts, small slopes, and test shafts in and around St. Clair, each employing for a few years a dozen or so men. But there is no need to present an encyclopedic list of them here, for our attention must remain focused on the larger collieries that employed most of the miners and incorporated the main lines of innovation—and regression—in technology.

III

A WORKINGMAN'S TOWN

The Carey group sold their first lot in August 1844 to Barton Evans, a Pennsylvania-born butcher, who selected lot number thirteen near the center of St. Clair on the east side of Second Street just south of Hancock. His next-door neighbor was the baker Jacob Gwinner, a German immigrant. Four months later, in partnership with another man, Evans bought the lot next door, and a year later still another on Front Street. The next purchaser was a twenty-six-year-old coal prospector and mine operator, John Holmes, an Irishman who had emigrated to the St. Clair area from Dublin about 1841 and had been working the local drifts ever since. He bought a prime commercial location, the lot on the northwest corner of Second and Franklin just across from the railroad depot, under a bond and mortgage, and would go on to buy other land in the town and nearby. Holmes never committed himself fully to the operator's role; he preferred to contract to do special jobs, like sinking a new slope or driving gangway, with a crew hired for the purpose. But he would play a major role in the development of the coal industry in the area, locating the "Holmes Vein," inventing mine machinery and fuses, and serving as a civic leader. In the latter capacity he conveyed to the Independent Order of Odd Fellows the four acres that later served as a public cemetery, and he built a public hall on Front Street. The third buyer was David Metz, a Pennsylvania German carpenter with an English wife, who set up shop in the same block of tradesmen as Evans and Gwinner, and the fourth was Daniel Slobig, a Pennsylvania-born clerk, who purchased another lot on the tradesmen's block and was to become one of the founders of the local Methodist Episcopal Church. The first miner to buy property was fifty-year-old, English-born Edward Hetherington, who took the southern corner lot in the tradesmen's block and proceeded to build a large house for his family and to take in boarders (two shoemakers and a miner). By 1850 he had also built at least two other houses on the same lot to be rented, one occupied by a widow and her engineer son, and the other by his brother Jacob, Jacob's French wife, and their infant son.

All of the lots fronting on Second Street were sold either by Nichols before 1835 or by the Careys by the end of 1846. The lots on Third Street south of Hancock were less desirable, for they were closer to the noise and dirt of the mines and the railroad, which ran up the middle of Fourth Street at the western edge of town. A number of these lots were purchased in 1846 by immigrant Irish families. The brothers Andrew and Terence McGough, mine laborers aged forty and forty-five, bought a lot together in 1845, built a single and a double house (for rental) apiece, and lived there next door to each other for the rest of their lives; Andrew also invested in another lot down the block. Irish brothers Thomas and Patrick Igo took the lot next door but one, and Evan Evans, a Welsh mine laborer, the lot in between. By the end of 1847 the residential lots on Third Street had all been sold. Most of the remaining lots east of Front Street were sold off between 1847 and 1854.

The lots were not small. The street blocks measured approximately 480 feet in length and 200 in depth (approximately 2.2 acres); each block was divided into six, seven, or eight lots, depending on the value of the location. Thus individual lots were 200 feet deep and from sixty to eighty feet in width, and they fronted on two streets. Lots of this size could be, and were, quickly subdivided by their owners into as many as six smaller lots, and stores or houses were built to occupy the smaller locations and to yield rentals. Some lots and partial lots were soon resold in whole or in part. By 1850, for instance, when the tax assessor came by, Daniel Slobig had already sold half his lot, retaining possession of the other half, on which he had built a house.

By 1850 nearly half the numbered and surveyed blocks in the town— approximately twenty out of forty-four acres—were bought up in this way, lot by lot, by individuals or partners, and about 100 acres of undivided land had also been sold. The Carey group was left with 253 acres to sell, of which only about forty-eight were in numbered lots. Of the divided property, about five blocks had already been sold by Nichols, much of it to Thomas Albert Haven, Carey's business associate and son-in-law. The rest—about seventeen blocks in the town itself—was reserved by Carey for his own use as industrial property or was acquired by large buyers, all of them relatives or business associates of the Careys, and large buyers also took up about 123 undivided acres. Carey's reserve was a couple of blocks between the railroad and Third Street, just opposite the St. Clair Shaft

Colliery, and presumably this land was used to store materials, to erect workshops, and to locate the company office. Alfred Lawton took a large lot on the corner of the block just above Carey's reserve, and half a block on Front Street in the middle of the town, and Charles and John Lawton acquired four lots. But the two next largest buyers after Haven were Carey's nephew Joseph G. Lawton and his former business partner Burd Patterson. Between 1844 and 1847 Joseph Lawton acquired a large tract along Nichols and Morris streets in the northwest corner of town, amounting to about twenty-five acres. In 1845 he built a fancy, well-landscaped mansion. Burd Patterson bought a number of lots fronting on Second Street as a real-estate speculation. But his principal purchase, in 1847, was fifteen acres in the southwest corner of the town, surrounding the St. Clair furnace.[1]

In the sale of these lots, the deeds clearly reserved to the Carey group the underground mineral rights, which were not sold but simply leased to mine operators for a term of years. Carey also asserted that the lots sold by Nichols before 1835 had been subject to a reservation of mineral rights, although this was challenged in a lawsuit brought by Nichols' widow twenty years later. But by that time the seams underneath the town were honeycombed with gangways, breasts, and tunnels, and the Careys continued to collect the royalties on all the coal. The interaction of surface ownership and underground leasehold, of course, also provided endless opportunity for dispute about damaged foundations, leaky cellars, and contaminated wells, and to some degree determined the materials of which the town was built. Although the larger structures, like hotels and warehouses, tended to be built of brick or stone, and stone was used for foundations, most of the residential structures were made of wood, allegedly because the wood withstood better the constant tremors caused by the firing of gunpowder charges in the mines and the occasional subsidence of the ground over an underground "crunch" when the roof collapsed into a breast or gangway.[2]

BOOM-TOWN GROWTH FROM 1845 TO 1850

In the summer of 1845, in one of a series of articles on the renewed growth of mining towns, the *Miners' Journal* praised the rapid progress of St. Clair. "The country around has a sort of half civilized aspect," the editor noted, but he described the town's situation as "beautiful never the less . . . the work of nature in her happiest mood." (Other issues of the *Journal* praised the beautiful hills in the spring, covered by the flowers of mountain laurel and arbutus, and a St. Clair poet even published an ode to the "dear little trailing arbutus.") The completion of a new track by the Mill Creek and Mine Hill Railroad, the rapid progress on Patterson's furnace, and the current sinking of Alfred Lawton's perpendicular shaft (in addition to the five collieries already in operation) had given a stimulus to development. Several "handsome brick buildings, intended for private residences," were under construction, and it was expected that by the end of the year about fifty-five smaller frame houses and other wooden structures would be added. The *Journal* reserved its most earnest compliments for the last paragraph, however, a fulsome celebration of the dedication of the town to Christianity and to education:

> There is but one Church in the Town, a plain building, held in common by all denominations of Christians. There is also a School house, generally among the first buildings erected in all American towns. It is a gratifying reflection that the school house and the teacher seem to be our people's care. "Educate your children." The wise precept which the old Athenian urged daily upon the busy multitude in the thoroughfares of the city, is appreciated by our people; in the newest districts the sturdy settler has hardly lopped the branches of the pine to admit the light of heaven, before he rears a building and dedicates it to knowledge.[1]

The population of the town increased rapidly after 1844, when the Carey group began their development program. During the 1845 season, eighty new buildings were constructed; the plans of one contractor for 1846 called for an additional 130 miners' houses. A private census of Schuylkill County taken in 1845 at the behest of the *Miners' Journal* gave St. Clair a total population of 605, occupying 131 houses; there were three stores and two taverns. The population was heavily weighted by single miners, as the age/sex pyramid indicates (see Table 1):

By 1850, St. Clair had become a town of over 2,000 souls. In April of that year, the legislature established the independent Borough of St. Clair, separating it from New Castle Township. The borough limits embraced most but not all of the St. Clair Tract (the western part of the tract remained in New Castle and Norwegian townships); and a strip of land north and south of the tract boundaries was taken into the borough, including the residence of the Johns family, their Eagle Colliery, and "Johns' Patch," just north of the St. Clair Tract. The borough limits now effectively defined the boundaries of the town of St. Clair. The town was to be a little over one mile square (5,280 feet by 6,600 feet), with the intersection of

TABLE I: *St. Clair Population by Age and Sex, 1845*

	Males	Females	Totals
UNDER 5 YEARS OF AGE	54	62	116
5 TO 10 YEARS OF AGE	34	40	74
11 TO 20 YEARS OF AGE	50	47	97
21 TO 30 YEARS OF AGE	90	44	134
31 TO 40 YEARS OF AGE	66	37	103
41 TO 50 YEARS OF AGE	29	18	47
51 TO 60 YEARS OF AGE	13	6	19
OVER 60 YEARS OF AGE	6	9	15
TOTAL POPULATION	342	263	605

First and Hancock as the geographical center. The voting place was Jonathan Johnson's tavern, a block north of the center, and it was presumably here that the five-member town council met after the first election in May 1850 had selected the town's officials. In addition to the town council, the residents elected a burgess (the equivalent of mayor), a town clerk, a justice of the peace, a high constable (who could be assisted by policemen appointed by the council), three assessors, six school directors, and various election officials. By law the burgess and council were the officers of a corporation having the right to acquire and sell property, to sue and be sued, and the council possessed broad powers to enact laws and make regulations "to promote the peace, good order, and general welfare of the inhabitants." Specifically, the council was responsible for the construction and maintenance of streets and alleys, the regulation of markets, the establishment and enforcement of zoning requirements, public health and sanitation, and the levying of taxes and fines. But there was one restriction upon the council's power that revealed the ultimate governance of coal:

Provided, That no streets, lanes, or alleys shall be laid out or extended in such way as to interfere in any manner with any coal mines or coal operations which may now or hereafter exist within the bounds of said borough.

The first election was held on May 9, 1850. The chief burgess was Charles Lawton, building contractor and brother of Joseph. The council members were Pennsylvania-born Jacob Metz (president of council), a carpenter and one of the original landowners, residing next to Johnson's tavern at the corner of Front and Franklin streets; John Mays, an English miner with a Welsh wife, owner of half a lot and a double house, prosperous enough to hire two servants to help his wife with her two infants; Michael Reilly, an Irish miner, who also owned half a lot and a double house; John R. Williams, Welsh, a miner and landowner; and Jacob Frantz, from Germany, also a miner and landowner; the constable was Joel Metz, brother of the council president and a blacksmith. The town clerk was Lott Evans, from Pennsylvania, a professional clerk. The assessors, all Pennsylvanians, included Benjamin Jackson, teacher and blacksmith; Harry Krebs, butcher; and Daniel Slobig, clerk, whom we have noted as an early landowner. It is a group that varied widely in occupation and ethnic origin but would seem to have been pretty much on a level with respect to wealth—at least, each owned a house and lot.

The council passed six ordinances in the spring and summer of 1850. The first prohibited the encroachment of private property, such as houses, awnings, and piles of building materials, as well as "stables, coal heaps, pig pens, wood piles, dung hills, ash heaps, and fences," onto the regularly laid-out streets, roads, and alleys. Another provided for the arrest and fining of vagrants and disorderly persons. A third required that "all exhibitions" pay a fee. A fourth prohibited the racing of horses in the public streets. A fifth regulated the placing of pumps and awnings between the sidewalk and the curb. And a sixth outlawed the erection or repair of mills for the manufacture of gunpowder or blasting powder anywhere within the borough. After thus providing for clear and safe passage in the streets of the borough, and for the removal of a dangerous powder mill (probably the establishment of John Scharr, a powder miller late from Germany), and (in 1855) for the public water supply, the council passed only two more ordinances in the next seventeen years until a revitalized council issued a flurry of legislation in 1867.[2]

One of the first acts of the council, other than legislation, was to commission a state-mandated map of the town, showing streets, lot numbers, and other major features. It, in conjunction with the list of lot sales from 1844 to 1858 kept by Carey's agent, and with the 1850 census of population and of manufacturers taken in mid-September and the tax assessment of 1851, enables us to obtain a fairly detailed picture of the little town in the summer of 1850. To an outsider riding into St. Clair on the Mill Creek and Mine Hill Railroad and disembarking at the depot at the north end of town, the first impression must have been one of noise. There were at least ten steam engines huffing and puffing at the five major collieries that loomed over the town on all sides, none more than a quarter of a mile from the center; five steam breaker whistles summoned and dismissed employees, morning and evening. There was the sound of coal being smashed in great cast-iron rollers in five breakers, bouncing through wire screens, sliding down chutes, and finally being dumped into coal cars. Iron wheels squealed on iron rails as coal cars negotiated turns on five sidings. When in blast, the Patterson furnace roared night and day. The scream of circular saws rose from two sawmills, and carpenters' hammers resounded from new construction. Half a dozen blacksmiths pounded away on their anvils. And another impression must have been one of dust, as wind blew cinders from steam engines, coal dust from culm banks, and powdered clay from unpaved streets. Now and then the ground vibrated from the firing of gunpowder charges down in the mines. Dogs barked, chickens cackled and roosters crowed, pigs ran in the streets and grunted, and cows mooed (forty-six were kept by householders). But within a few weeks the newcomer would no longer notice these assaults upon the senses and instead would attend with pride to the wide streets, the rows of new houses neatly whitewashed, the taverns and stores and churches along the wide main streets. Virtually every corner had its tavern or store, especially around the intersection of Hancock and Second. The homes of artisans, and their attached shops—carpenters, tailors, butchers, bakers, shoemakers—tended to cluster in the center of town too. The churches were more peripheral in location. At the extreme south end of the borough, outside the St. Clair Tract, was the oldest church, the little chapel of the Welsh Congregationalists. On the east side of town, nearer the center, were the Welsh Calvinist (1846), the Primitive Methodist (1847), and the Methodist Episcopal (1849) churches. The latter two served primarily English-born congregations, as did the Episcopal church built in 1854. The German-speaking immigrants would soon build St. Bonifacius Roman Catholic Church (1852) and, at the south end of town, the German Lutheran church (1855). A separate Catholic church, St. Mary's, was not built for the Irish population until 1864. The borough cemetery was located next to a colliery on the hill just west of town, north of the road to Wadesville; adjacent to it stood the old building that had been variously used as a meeting place for church groups and as a school since 1835.

The houses of the miners ranged along the streets throughout the town, expanding outward as housing was required for the later immigrants. The original "Long Row," housing sixteen miners' families in eight row houses, stood along the west side of Second Street just north of Hancock, and other rows of closely packed frame houses, built for rental to miners, stretched up and down Second and Third streets and those parts of First Street that did not front on Mill Creek, a narrow stream about fifteen feet wide that ran south through the very center of town, between its five-foot banks of earth and stone.

It was, in the summer of 1850, a busy little boom town, mostly managed by tradesmen and miners, prospering with a growing industry in coal and iron, and drawing into itself an industrious population of European miners and artisans.[3]

THE CENSUS OF 1850

The United States census of 1850 for the Borough of St. Clair was conducted in September by the enumerator assigned to New Castle Township. He separated the St. Clair schedules from the rest of the township, and, matching names with lot locations, we can observe how he proceeded. He began at the south end of the principal thoroughfare, Second Street, and walked north on the east side of the street, then south along the west side. After that, he covered the streets east of Second, and he concluded the survey by moving south on Third.[1]

The total population of the borough, housed in 442 dwellings, was 2,217, of whom 1,166 were males and 1,051 females. There were 471 residential family units (but the enumerator counted only 463). The 115 excess males were largely concentrated in the age groups of working miners, as the age-sex table indicates (see Table 2).

The town was overwhelmingly composed of relatively young immigrant families. 1,235 persons—more than half—were foreign-born; of the remainder, 502 were children of foreign-born fathers, most but not all of them born in the United States of American-born mothers; of these, 461 were born in Pennsylvania. The population was entirely white. For the immigrant families, there were four major countries of origin listed in the census: Ireland, England, Wales, and Germany. The Irish were most numerous, amounting to a total of 706 (493 Irish-born, 213 born out of Ireland of Irish-born parents). The English were next with 402 (272 and 130), the Germans with 324 (227 and 97), and, close behind, the Welsh with 315 (227 and 88). There were also 11 Canadian-born, 3 Scots, and 2

TABLE 2: *St. Clair Population by Age and Sex, 1850*

	Males	Females	Totals
0–9	370	351	721
10–19	219	205	424
20–29	220	196	416
30–39	190	153	343
40–49	99	78	177
50–59	44	33	77
60–69	17	22	39
70–79	4	10	14
80–89	1	2	3
NO AGE ENTERED	2	1	3
TOTAL POPULATION	1166	1051	2217

French. As for the "Americans" (children of U.S.-born parents), it would appear from the number of people with German names born in Pennsylvania of Pennsylvania parents that "Pennsylvania Dutch" ethnicity was a noticeable presence, on the order perhaps of 200 persons.

The census recorded the occupation of all males aged sixteen or over; only occasionally did the enumerator record a female occupation, apparently when the rarity of the occupation struck him as worthy of note, such as the one female listed (perhaps in error) as "miner" and one recorded as "governess" in the Johns household. Thus domestic servants, milliners, and female proprietors of candy stores and beer parlors go unrecognized. As one might expect, the categories "miner" and "laborer" were the most numerous, 229 and 254 respectively. The category "miner" here refers to the trade of "contract miner," and "laborer" must usually mean "mine laborer," the contract miner's helper. But no doubt other kinds of manual labor were included under the term "laborer," such as workers on railroad gangs, ditch diggers, and adult breaker boys. Many male children under sixteen worked in and about the mines, particularly as breaker boys, door boys, and mule drivers, but the occupations were not recorded.

The census also recognized a large number of occupations that we can collect under the general rubric of "trades." (Contract miners also considered their calling a skilled trade and a few even paid to be listed in city directories as "miners," along with butchers, stonemasons, physicians, publicans, and shopkeepers.) In St. Clair, in addition to "miner," there were twenty-four other distinct occupations listed that we would recognize as skilled labor; 102 men were thus employed. Two occupations were probably colliery jobs: engineer (12 men), no doubt steam-engine operators, and machinist (2). Of the remaining twenty-two occupations, five were practiced by seven or more men each: carpenter (21), shoemaker (7), blacksmith (13), clerk (12), and teamster (9). The remainder had no more than four practitioners each: mason (3), painter (4), plasterer (4), teacher (2) (i.e., the public-school teacher and the Johns family governess), tailor (4), butcher (3), baker (2), sawyer (2), gardener (2), and one each for the more specialized trades of bottler, hostler, watchmaker, stage driver, stonecutter, cooper, cabinetmaker, and peddler. Although the number of men engaged in the non-mining trades was outweighed five or six to one by miners, laborers, and boys working at the collieries, the town evidently had a wide range of skilled artisans available to supply its own needs and those of the nearby mine patches.

Finally, there was a small group of occupations that may be grouped together as "capitalist and professional." There were 4 men listed as landlords (i.e., hotel keepers), 12 as merchants (including not only storekeepers but also the three principal mine operators), and one each as physician, farmer, and contractor. Of the nineteen persons listed in this group, three were associated by residence or marriage with the Johns family (the Johns brothers and the physician who married a Johns girl) and two were Lawtons; the Johns and the Lawtons were the major colliery operators and Charles Lawton was the principal building contractor in town.

These two extended families were, in 1850, the elite of the town, owning the most land, operating the largest enterprises, residing in the largest houses, employing the most servants, and, at least in the Johns' case, educating their children privately. Next to them, the keepers of the hotels and taverns, the smaller merchants, and the professional men made up the upper-middle class. On the next rung of the occupational status ladder were the contract miners and tradesmen, the respectable working class of St. Clair. At the bottom were the "laborers." In this world of manual work, in 1850, it is not possible to draw a clear status line between the contract miner and the other tradesmen. Some individual miners shifted back and forth between mine and workshop as layoffs, injuries and illness, and financial opportunity dictated; and it was common, as the census schedules show in later years, when children's occupations were listed, for artisans' sons to begin their working lives as breaker boys or mule drivers or laborers, helping to support the family, even if in their later teens they learned a trade or profession and left the mines. There was, however, among the underground miners a clear status distinction between the contract miners and their laborers. Contract miners were paid by the colliery operator, by the ton or wagon load; they furnished their own tools and supplies; and they supervised and paid their own laborers. Miners were more likely to own their own houses (but a sizable number of laborers were home owners too). According to the 1851 tax assessments, 62 miners and 33 laborers owned a house and a lot, while 110 miners and 153 laborers resided with their families or lived in rented quarters. And what made the distinction between miner and laborer peculiarly important was the circumstance that most of the miners were English or Welsh and most of the laborers were Irish.

ETHNICITY AND OCCUPATION

The census figures reveal a pattern of clear occupational disadvantage for the Irish in colliery occupations (see Table 3). This pattern is not repeated in the figures for the other trades, where there appear only 9 Irishmen, but also only 14 English, 9 Welsh, and 12 Germans; the majority of tradesmen were U.S.-born (37 in Pennsylvania, 9 in other states). Among the upper-middle class, only 6 were foreign-born, and 2 of these were Irish.

Clearly, the disadvantage of the Irish is greatest in underground mining, and the most likely reasons are the obvious ones. Ireland had a minuscule coal-mining industry compared to England and Wales, and thus English and Welsh miners on arrival in the United States were technically better qualified to take the more skilled jobs than most Irish countrymen. The English and Welsh were also more apt to arrive in St. Clair with money to invest in the equipment and supplies needed to set up as a

TABLE 3: Miner/Laborer Status and Ethnicity, 1850

	English	Welsh	German	Irish	Other Foreign-born	U.S.-born
MINER	73	73	45	24	2	12
LABORER	10	6	36	167	2	33

TABLE 4: Age of Oldest U.S.-born Child and Ethnicity, 1850

Ethnicity	Total	0–5 Years	6–10 Years	11–15 Years	16–20 Years	21–25 Years	Mean	Range	Standard Deviation
ENGLISH	46	18	9	11	8	0	8.69	18.50	6.04
WELSH	40	22	7	5	6	0	6.57	17.17	5.58
GERMAN	45	29	8	7	1	0	5.23	18.67	4.76
IRISH	100	61	20	14	4	1	5.34	21.67	2.31

contract miner than were Irishmen driven out of Ireland by famine and landlords' evictions. Poverty and inexperience did not characterize all Irish immigrants, of course. Some did qualify as contract miners (some had learned mining during an earlier sojourn in England, some as laborers in American mines); some were well enough endowed financially to buy lots in the town. But in 1850, according to the census, only 10 Irishmen owned real estate, as opposed to 27 English, 21 Welsh, and 13 Germans. The Irish families of St. Clair were not residentially segregated in any obvious pattern; there was an Irish row on Third Street, but there were Irish families scattered all over town. There seems to have been a tendency for ethnic groups to cluster in blocks, to judge by distribution of ethnicity in the enumerator's sequence, but it was probably more out of choice than discriminatory intent by landlords. Another area of possible difference between the Irish immigrants and the others was duration of a family's residence in the United States (which can be roughly measured by the age of the eldest child born in the United States). Comparing the families with American-born children living in the same household, the Irish again stand out (see Table 4). The English and the Welsh families clearly have been in the country longer; the average age of the oldest U.S.-born child is 8.7 and 6.6, respectively. The Germans and the Irish are more recent, on the average, with virtually identical mean ages of oldest U.S.-born child, 5.2 and 5.3, respectively. The Irish profile has, however, an interesting characteristic: there is a core of Irish families long established in the United States, suggesting that the Irish immigration began just as early as the English and Welsh and then underwent a sudden jump in the later part of the 1840's.

All this suggests that the occupational disadvantage of Irish colliery workers may in part have been a consequence of inexperience in mining among the large cohort of young mine laborers recently emigrated from a country without a mining industry. But examination of the relation between length of residence in the U.S. and miner/laborer status shows that experience had not, up to 1850, benefited the Irish as much as other groups. Only one Irish contract miner was older than forty-four; 3 Germans exceeded this age, 17 Welsh, and 19 English. Conversely, no less than 27 Irish laborers were older than forty-four, as compared with 10 Germans, 3 English, and 1 Welshman. Comparing the older German with the older Irish laborers is also illuminating. Using the age of children born in the U.S. or country of origin as an index of length of stay in the U.S., and thus of opportunity to acquire experience in American coal mines, we find that of the five German families with children born in the U.S. living in the same household, in four cases the oldest American-born child was three or younger; the average age was 3.6. Three of the German families had no American-born children, but had young children born in Germany (ages six and seven). Among the Irish laborer families, twelve had U.S.-born children living with them; only one of these children was younger than eight, and the average age was 12.4. It would seem that the Irish mine laborer was less likely to move up in status as he gained experience: only inexperienced older German workers were laborers, while Irish laborers tended to remain laborers all their lives. This did not necessarily mean that they lived in dire poverty: the 1851 tax assessment shows at least eleven Irish laborers as home owners, and, according to the census of 1850, six of the older Irish laborers owned real estate in St. Clair.

But laborer status did carry certain disadvantages probably more galling than the difference in pay. The laborer was sometimes subject to a certain amount of informal abuse by his employing contract miner, such as having dirt kicked into his face as he followed the miner up the ladder into the breast, and being required to do the heavier physical chores, such as carrying timber and loading the coal cars. Furthermore, when the contract miner had fired his shot and was done for the day, he often left his laborer alone in the breast to finish breaking up the coal with pick and hammer, loading it into the cars, and piling the gob out of the way. This additional time implied added risk of accident and a longer period of inhaling coal dust (an effect no doubt enhanced by the deeper breathing entailed by heavier tasks).

As the years went by, the status difference between miners and laborers became increasingly institutionalized. In the late 1860's a Welsh miner wrote back to a Welsh newspaper: "The laborer's work is fairly hard and this is the first work a stranger gets when first coming here and it has become the custom for a man to labor first of all wherever he comes from. Most labor for six to nine months before they get a place of their own. The laborer's wage is one third of that earned by the miner."[1] By the 1870's, laborers were complaining publicly about their condition. A laborer, writing to a newspaper, complained bitterly, "We often hear of the injustice of the coal operators toward the miners. But when have the operators treated the miners so bad as the miners have treated the laborers. . . ."[2] And another Welshman wrote home about

> the unfairness of the system to the laborer who has to fill from six to seven cars a day with coal and he gets but one third of the wages of the miner. There is more water in this works than I ever

saw before in the Old Country. Some here are filling coal in about a foot of water. They wear boots that reach to the top of their knees but the water often comes over the top. The miner and laborer go to work at seven o'clock in the morning and probably the miner will cut enough coal by ten or eleven o'clock. Then he will go out leaving the [laborer to] fill three or four cars with coal after the gentleman had left. He will wash, put on a shirt, and a white collar and will go to dinner boasting that he has cut enough coal for the laborer. After he has had enough, he calls for his cigarbox and enjoys himself for an hour or two and because he is a religious man he says that it is nearly time for him to go to a prayermeeting. Between five and six o'clock the laborer, poor thing, arrives home as wet as a fish and after eating his supper, in spite of his weariness, goes to the prayermeeting and who should be praying at the time but the man he works for. These are the words he uses. "May our peace be like the river our justice like the waves of the sea." Oh! terrible hypocrite![3]

When unions were eventually organized, the miners were careful to create an industrial rather than a craft union, thus preventing their laborers from forming a rival union of their own that might threaten the *status quo*. And in 1885 the miners, after lobbying in Harrisburg, were able to persuade the legislature to include in the Mine Safety Act of that year a requirement that miners be certified. Certification required the applicant to prove that he had worked two years as a miner's laborer and to pass an examination before a board of three miners, answering technical questions about mining. The status of laborer thus was akin to that of apprentice, and the rationalization for the differential in pay and status was the need for experience, which presumably would bring knowledge, skill, and good judgment.[4]

The prolongation of the laborer status of Irish mine workers in the 1840's and '50's thus can hardly have been justified on the grounds of insufficient time; after all, even in 1885 certification could come after two years, and in the 1860's the customary training period was only six to nine months. It would appear more likely that miners and mine operators disliked and distrusted Irish workers on other grounds, such as an alleged propensity for drunkenness, fighting, absenteeism, reckless conduct in the mine, and adherence to Roman Catholicism. Such attitudes were not uncommon among Welsh and English working people, and in 1850 most of the miners, mine bosses, superintendents, and colliery operators were

Welsh or English. Ethnicity and the status difference between contract miners and mine laborers thus formed a single, deepening line of cleavage between Irish and non-Irish workers in St. Clair.

THE MINE PATCHES

Across the hills surrounding St. Clair lay a ring of small hamlets that provided housing, a company store, and little else in the way of amenities, for the mine families associated with various isolated collieries. These patches consisted of a few dozen to a hundred company-owned houses and cabins strung out along the road. To avail themselves of essential services beyond the resources of the company store, the residents had to walk a mile or two to St. Clair, or other nearby towns, to visit tavern, church, shop, post office, or railroad depot; at night they were effectively cut off from the outside world, for walking the paths over the hills was dangerous in the dark, bestrewn as the landscape was with the debris of earlier mining operations and pockmarked with cave-ins and abandoned slopes and air holes. This remoteness gave to these hamlets a rural quality that has appealed to some twentieth-century romantics, who have seen in the life of the mine patch a kind of communal virtue denied the denizens of towns. George Korson, a twentieth-century folklorist, editorialized about the mine patch—"a cluster of squalid hemlock shacks built close to a breaker"—in a fever of nostalgia:

> All classes of mine workers participated in spontaneous communal gatherings which were usually held on the green, part of every mine patch. Under a starry, moonlit sky of a summer evening, against a background of colliery buildings and culm banks, and in an atmosphere infiltrated with coal dust and brimstone smells, the workers and their families sang together, listened to story tellers, played folk games and danced. . . .
> A sheet of iron borrowed from the colliery would be laid on the grass as a sounding board for jigs, reels, hornpipes, and breakdowns as the fiddler scraped out his tunes.[1]

Surrounding St. Clair in 1850 there were a number of such patches: to the east, Crow Hollow and Ravensdale, which served the Pine Forest Colliery; to the south, Mill Creek and Coaquenac; to the north, Johns' Patch (already becoming a part of the town), Dark Water, and New Castle (near Lawton's Mammoth Colliery); to the west, Wadesville, Mount Laffee, and Scalpington (an Irish settlement at the Delaware Coal Company's mines). Mine patches survived only as long as their collieries stayed in business; when the breaker shut down, the patch was deserted, to rot away slowly, eventually to be torn down by strip mining or covered over by railroad yards and highways.

The isolation of the mine patches seems indeed to have nourished a communal spirit that may have had its origin in European working-class communities. In a detailed account of life in Coaquenac in the mid-nineteenth century, based on the recollections of aged survivors in the 1920's and 1930's, the historians of East Norwegian Township described cooperative local institutions that contrasted sharply with those of the towns. Until 1884 relatively acid-free water for washing clothes was obtained from a common well near the race that served the gristmill, and until 1870 bread was baked in an oven "owned in common by all the families in the village." The oven was large enough to bake twenty-four loaves of bread at one time. The women, it was said, had a traditional agreement "whereby the one who fills the oven at night has priority over the others for use of the oven on the next day. . . . If two women want to bake on the same day, they will mutually decide on the previous evening which shall bake first." At night, after a supper of home-grown vegetables, home-butchered pork, home-churned butter, bread baked in the communal oven, and hot black tea, the men congregated on logs in front of their gardens, to smoke their clay pipes and talk over the news of the day. After dark, tales of the supernatural were told, of fairies and vengeful ghosts and melancholy banshees.[2] The patches were not large; few held more than thirty or forty families. East of St. Clair, in all of East Norwegian Township in 1850, not counting the town of Port Carbon, there were only 195 households and 984 white inhabitants, plus one "Col. male," parceled out among five or six distinct patches. The bulk of this population was English and Irish, seventy household family units each, plus a few single boarders (see Table 5). The relationship between occupation and ethnicity emerges as clearly in the patches as in the town. The occupational category "miner" was assigned to 100 males; 62 of them were English, 10 Welsh, and 6 Scottish; 16 were Irish; 4 were Pennsylvania-born; and 2 were German. "Laborers" numbered 92; of these, only 7 were English, none Welsh, and 1 Scottish; 68 were Irish; 13 were Pennsylvania born; and 3 were German. Clearly, with regard to underground mining, there again was a strong relationship between occupational status and ethnicity. And similarly in other trades, a sharp contrast between English and Irish prevailed: there were five English machinists and no Irish, ten English blacksmiths and no Irish, one English iron molder and no Irish. All four farmers were Pennsylvania-born, and so were most practitioners of farm-associated trades, like miller, sawyer, tanner, and teamster. Indeed, only five Irishmen worked in trades other than miner or laborer: there was one Irish "teacher," a watchman, a teamster, a stonemason, and a shoemaker. There was, in effect, an ethnically tripartite occupational structure: Pennsylvania families owned the land and ran the farms, the gristmill and sawmill, and the tannery, and did most of the hauling because they owned the horses and wagons; the English, Welsh, Germans, and Scots were miners and tradesmen; the Irish were laborers.[3]

North and west of St. Clair, a different pattern prevailed in rural New Castle Township (exclusive of the town of New Castle itself). In patches at Wadesville and Mount Laffee, there were fifty-one households containing 280 people (including as one household a boardinghouse run by an Irish couple with seventeen Irish mine-worker residents). There were no Welsh people at all in rural New Castle; only one German family (two persons, the husband a blacksmith) and one German laborer boarding with an Irish family; three English families, including five miners, twenty-three persons in all; and one seven-person U.S.-born family (see Table 6). These patches

TABLE 5: *Ethnicity in Rural East Norwegian Township, 1850*

	No. of Households	Foreign-born	U.S.-born	Total
ENGLISH	70	254	95	349
IRISH	70	197	132	329
WELSH	10	32	17	49
GERMAN	9	15	28	43
SCOTS	8	19	15	34
U.S.-BORN (PA)	17	—	118	118
U.S.-BORN (OTHER)	11	—	62	62
TOTAL POPULATION		517	467	984

TABLE 6: *Ethnicity in Rural New Castle Township, 1850*

	No. of Households	Foreign- born	U.S.- born	Total
IRISH	46	147	100	247
ENGLISH	3	16	7	23
GERMAN	1	3	—	3
U.S.	1	—	7	7
TOTAL POPULATION		166	114	280

were, in effect, Irish ghettoes: 247 Irish, 23 English, 7 U.S.-born of U.S.-born parents, and 3 Germans. But this segregation had its economically beneficial effect for the Irish: of the thirty-five miners, thirty were Irish, one German, and three U.S.-born. The cultural flavor of these western mine patches was undoubtedly Irish as well.[4]

WAGES AND SUBSISTENCE

None of the business records of the St. Clair collieries of this early period have survived except for scraps from the Carey Papers. Nonetheless, a picture of the probable wage rates in the St. Clair area for different categories of work can be obtained from the records of a colliery (Kaska William) located about three and a half miles east of St. Clair. The paybook for Kaska William for a little over two years in 1851, 1852, and 1853 reveals much about how Schuylkill colliery employees were classified and paid.[1] There were basically four categories: management, craftsmen, miners, and laborers. Management included the mine manager, who was paid $1.95 per day, and six foremen, five of whom were paid $1.25 per day and one $1.37. The craftsmen included six "engineers" (presumably the operators of the steam engines, pumps, and hoisting machinery), who received from $1 to $1.55 per day, one machinist at $1.25, two blacksmiths at $1.08 and $1.25, two carpenters at $1.08 and $1.16, three "choppers" at 83 cents and 91 cents and a sawyer (no doubt operating the sawmill) at $1, three teamsters at 99 cents, an hostler at 90 cents, and a storekeeper at 90 cents.

The category "miners" was complex. First of all, the forty-two miners were divided into two groups in the paybook: nine miners paid by the day and thirty-three contract miners. Eight of the day miners received $1.16; if they worked twenty-four days in the four-week pay period, they earned $28 per month. One man received only 91 cents. The contract miners were entered differently from the day workers: the day workers were listed as individuals, by name; the contract miners were recorded in every case as a separate company, thus "Conrad Zimmler Co.," "Dennis David Co.," and so on. The contract miners' accounts listed specific services performed and the rates for each; these rates varied, no doubt on the basis of negotiation about the difficulty of the task. There were two kinds of contract miners: the twenty who worked primarily cutting coal and who were paid by the wagon (which carried a load of about a long ton and a half); and the thirteen who specialized in the more difficult and less productive tasks of driving gangways, digging tunnels, air holes, and headings, and planking chutes. The specialty work was generally paid by the yard or, less frequently, by the day (at $1.16 per day). The wagon workers were generally paid 55 cents per wagon, sometimes less, down to 30 cents, and a wagon "company" on an average loaded four to six wagons per working day. Maximum productivity in May-June 1851 (by "Edward Sheaffer Co.") was 215.5 wagons in four weeks. If this represents one breast worked for twenty-four days, we have Sheaffer and his laborer or laborers cutting and loading nine wagons per day. In Sheaffer's case, this amounted to $99.75 for the month. Other contract miners' gross earnings ranged downward from this to as low as $20 for the same month. But these were gross earnings only. The contract miner had to pay his laborer or laborers, presumably at a rate comparable to what the colliery paid the laborers who worked for the day miner, and he had to pay for lamps, lamp oil and wicks, gunpowder, and tools (shovels, picks, drills, and paper for making squibs). The cost of the items bought from the store averaged about $8. The situation of the specialty miner was even more complex, inasmuch as he had to estimate in advance how much time on the average it would take to advance by one yard the gangway, tunnel, or whatever he was working on, and charge accordingly, the rates ranging from $3 to $6 per yard. Specialty miners also had to buy supplies and pay their workers; because they worked in larger teams, their gross earnings were sometimes higher, but not always, and it would appear that what they cleared after paying their laborers may not have been any greater than what the wagon miners earned.

How much were the contract miner's laborers paid? Unfortunately, the Kaska William books do not tell us because the colliery did not record what the contract miner paid his laborers, although it did sometimes charge the miner with a laborer's expenses, such as rent and grocery-store orders. But the books do, in some months, specify a category "loader," of whom there were anywhere from eleven to twenty-two. Loaders were probably the helpers of the day miners. These helpers were generally paid 91 cents per day, with a few down to 85 cents and two at 95 cents. This would suggest a pay differential between day miners and their helpers of 25 cents per day. It is not likely that the contract miner, whether doing wagon work or working by the yard, could get away with paying his laborer much less. At 91 cents per day, in a twenty-four-day month the laborer would earn $21.84. If the miner's supplies cost him $8 in the same period, he would have to gross better than $50 in the month just to earn for himself as much as he paid his laborer, and this meant producing at least 100 wagons of coal, about four wagons per day. If he averaged five wagons per day, he would earn an extra $12.50 per month; if six wagons, an extra $25. Clearly, the miner had a reason to push his helper to load in the neighborhood of nine or ten tons of coal every day.

Not all of those listed in the paybook, or the census, as "laborers" were miner's helpers, and most were paid considerably less. At Kaska William the lowest-paid worker was the "mail boy," who earned but 14 cents per day. Other day laborers about a colliery included the driver boys, who drove the horses or mules that dragged wagons back and forth between the loading points and the bottom of shaft, and the door boys, who opened and closed the ventilation-control doors as wagons and workers passed to and fro; men who carried prop timber down into the mine, hauled it to where it was needed, and helped to set it up; the men and boys who worked in the breaker; the helpers of the mechanics, carpenters, and other artisans; firemen for the steam engines; and a miscellany of ditch diggers, coal shovelers, culm-bank tenders, and handymen. These laborers in some cases earned as much as miner's helpers, but the less skilled and the youthful earned as little as 30 to 40 cents per day.

These wages if continued throughout the year could generate an income for an individual wage earner well above subsistence level. But demand for coal tended to slacken in the winter because most urban households had filled their bins and because the canal, subject to freezing, closed down for the season, leaving only the more expensive Philadelphia and Reading Railroad to take the coal from Port Carbon to Port Richmond in north Philadelphia. So it is not reasonable to project summer earnings over the twelve months; such projections should perhaps be halved. Thus a laborer at Kaska William earning 91 cents per day for the twenty-four days of work during the four weeks from July 12 to August 9, 1851, would bring home $21.84; the same laborer in the pay period January 24 to

February 21, 1852, worked only eight days on an average, at a rate of 70 cents per day, for a total of $5.60. Furthermore, of the 150 laborers on the payroll in July, fifty-six had been laid off by February. Apparently no miners were laid off, but they too earned less: the day miner's rate went down to $1 per day and he averaged only seven days in the month; the wagon miners filled fewer wagons and were paid at 35 cents per wagon (down from 55 cents); and the miners working by the yard worked less time at lower yardage rates.

In some families, however, there was more than one wage earner: at least fifty-nine family units (about 13 percent of the total) had two or more male wage earners over fifteen years of age, and there must have been some women who earned cash as domestic servants, washerwomen, and seamstresses. Women also added to family income by taking care of male boarders. It is difficult to give an exact number because some apparent "boarders" may have been non-paying cousins or in-laws with a different surname; but approximately thirty families seem to have taken in boarders, to judge from the 1850 census schedules. Thus annual family income must have varied considerably even within the same occupational category. A young laborer with a wife and two young children and no boarders might have depended solely on earnings that varied from $20 per month down to $6 per month from season to season, with a total annual income on the order of $150 to $200. An older laborer with two laborer sons and two boarders might see a family income of $500 to $600 per year. Contract miners' family earnings probably ranged down to $200 and up to $700 or $800 per year.

The cost of living in St. Clair in 1850 was low enough to make permanent residence possible even for laborers' families. Most Kaska William houses rented at $1.25 or $2 per four-week period; for the year, house rental thus might run from $16.25 to $26. A few were somewhat dearer, on the order of $4 to $5 per week, but this figure included coal for the fire. Rentals at St. Clair would not have been much higher. For those who arrived with some savings, a lot could be purchased from Carey for as little as $75, although most of his large lots sold for $200. The cost of a new house was about $200.[2] The houses owned by miners in the town were of various shapes and sizes and not distinguishable from dwellings of the rest of the community, but in the patches, where company housing was the rule, the houses were more standardized. In Johns' Patch, for instance, the colliery rented houses to its employees along North Mill and Carroll streets, where they stood under the watchful eye of the Johns family themselves in their mansion between the patch and the breaker. The patch houses were

*One of the few remaining miners' cottages at Johns' Patch in 1986
(originally a duplex, the house has been converted to single occupancy,
with asbestos shingling and tin roofing added)*

sturdily built (surviving ones are still occupied), of frame construction, resting on stone foundations with no cellar, only a shallow crawl space, and were arranged in pairs with a shared chimney and probably a shared outhouse. There was no front yard, not even a front porch, the door open ing directly onto the street; in back, a garden led down to the creek, or the railroad, or a neighbor's back yard, and here vegetables grew and pigs and chickens and occasionally a cow were kept; the dogs roamed free. The exterior clapboard was painted red; the roofs were wood-shingled. Both the fireplace and the cookstove burned anthracite in chestnut and pea-coal sizes. Each house contained one room upstairs and three down: upstairs, a bedroom, twelve feet by fifteen, with a ceiling that sloped close to the floor front and back; downstairs, a kitchen jutting out to the side, nine by twelve; a front room, twelve by fifteen; and a back room, twelve by twelve. The half-circular staircase ran up the building's center partition at the front: in the middle was the fireplace; and beside the fireplace a closet. There was at least one glass window in every outside wall of every room, and all the floors, walls, and ceilings were laid in tongue-and-groove pan-eling and wainscoting. The use of the downstairs rooms no doubt was flexible and depended on the size and make-up of the family.[3]

Food prices in St. Clair probably were a bit higher than the prices quoted in the *Miners' Journal* for the Pottsville Market, and this means they must have been about on a par with Philadelphia (in Pottsville, for instance, corn sold for 50 cents per bushel, in Philadelphia for 60 cents). Most of the food had to be imported; there were few farms in the coal country. In 1850 there were only seven farms in all of East Norwegian Township and two in New Castle, and only two of these nine farms were larger than eleven acres.[4] On April 27, 1850, at Pottsville, the following prices were quoted:[5]

POTTSVILLE MARKETS
CORRECTED WEEKLY FOR THE JOURNAL

Wheat Flour, bbl.	$5.00	Dr.'d Peaches par'd	$3.00
Rye do do	4.50	do do unpar'd	1.75
Wheat, bush.	1.10	Dr'd Apples, par'd	1.50
Rye, do	.60	Eggs, doz.	.11
Corn, do	.50	Butter, lb.	.18
Oats, do	.35	Bacon,	.07
Potatoes, do	.50	Hams,	.09
Timothy Seed,	2.50	Hay, ton	15.00
Clover do	3.50	Plaster	5.00

Using the reports of the butchers of St. Clair in the 1860 census of manufactures, we find that the preferred meats were beef (from oxen) and mutton; veal (from calves) and pork were eaten sparingly. Meat prices are not evident in the 1850 record, but in 1860 beef was selling in St. Clair at 8 cents per pound and mutton at 5.[6] Commodity prices did not rise much in the decade, so the cost of butchered meat was probably about the same in 1850. Fresh beef and mutton were eaten in large quantities, and about twice as much beef as mutton. The average daily consumption of fresh meat for every man, woman, and child in St. Clair in 1850 was slightly more than a quarter of a pound. Assuming that infants ate little or no meat, and that children and women, being on the average smaller, ate less than men, it would seem likely that a hard-working miner might eat one or two pounds of beef or mutton per day. Although only half as much mutton as beef was eaten over the course of the year, mutton, containing a higher percentage of fat, had much higher caloric value. A pound of beef and a pound of mutton together would yield 2,000 calories or more, close to half a miner's energy requirement. And in addition to fresh meat purchased at the butcher's, people also went to the general store for salt pork products and fish, particularly mackerel. Privately raised chickens, pigs, and some products of the chase—wild fowl, small game, and a few deer—also added to the supply of animal protein. Thus a diet rich in butter and eggs, meats, and breadstuffs was available to the ordinary worker and his family the year round, with green and leafy vegetables and fresh fruits in the summer and dried fruits in the winter. Many householders probably supplemented their store-bought foods with vegetables and fruits grown in back-yard gardens; in the spring, children picked berries on the hillsides nearby, and in the fall the men hunted rabbit, squirrel, turkey, and other small game in the mountains. For a laborer requiring, say, 4,500 to 5,000 calories per day (half expended lifting nine tons of coal four feet into six wagons), a diet rich in meat and dairy products could be had for about 25 cents per day; by cutting proteins and fats, and eating more bread, pancakes, fruit pies, and potatoes, he could eat the same number of calories for about 20 cents per day. Assuming that women and children required far less food than a laborer loading nine tons of coal per day, a family consisting of husband, wife, and two children could get by on about 50 cents per day for food.

Work clothing was probably made in the house from yard goods, but some idea of the cost of store-bought clothes can be had from the 1860 census, which records a tailor as having sold eighty suits consisting of coat, vest, and "pantaloons" for $19.50 apiece ($12.50 for the coat, $3 for the vest, and $4 for the pants).[7]

It would appear that a laborer, with a wife and two children, who earned $20 per month on an average through the year could make ends meet and save some money. More children, or less pay, required supplemental income from other members of the household, from occasional non-colliery jobs, or from boarders. Children usually kept coming, but could be put to work by the time they were eight or nine. But the principal problem was that employment was not steady. In 1850, for example, the mines on Mill Creek suffered three separate, and costly, interruptions of the normal spring and summertime burst of productivity. First, just as the trade was slowly picking up from the winter low of 3,000 tons per week (a low so deep that many left to seek employment elsewhere), the miners and laborers went on strike in May for higher wages. That knocked production—and employment—down nearly to winter levels. After the strike, production began to improve, only to be reduced again late in July by a freshet, the worst in twelve years, that drowned out a number of mines and washed out sections of railroad and canal. And no sooner had the collieries begun to recover from this disaster than another flood, worse than the last, following about eight inches of rain in one twenty-four-hour period, closed everything down again. The dam at Tumbling Run, feeder to the canal, broke and a wall of water plunged into the canal and onto the railroad at Mount Carbon, destroying the iron bridge and washing away the embankments of the canal. The valley below Pottsville was strewn with the wreckage of boats, lumber, furniture, and fragments of buildings. More than fifty people were drowned at Tamaqua and fourteen more along the Schuylkill River below Pottsville.

The damage at St. Clair was not reported but apparently was not so severe as it was along the larger streams, and within a month coal shipments from Mill Creek were back up, although not so high as in May, and there they remained until the winter decline in September. The Schuylkill Canal, however, did not reopen for traffic for the rest of the year. Its closing forced the collieries to ship entirely by railroad and that cost them more money. The added financial pressure on the collieries no doubt was passed on to the colliery employees.[8]

Colliery employment in good times was steady and reasonably well paid. But colliery employment was notoriously subject to reduction or stoppage by seasonal variations in demand, by strikes, by floods, and—as we shall see later—by accidents and disasters. The economic security that the worker sought for himself and his family could not be obtained from the colliery, even with the help of extra jobs, child labor, gardening and berry picking and hunting, and taking in boarders. In the absence of any form of unemployment insurance from public funds, the individual had to go beyond the household family to obtain support when needed. This meant, in effect, the extended family and, beyond this, those metaphorical families, the benevolent associations.

THE EXTENDED FAMILY

St. Clair was a family town. Virtually everyone lived in a house with other members of a nuclear family—husband, wife, father, son, or daughter. Only a handful of widows and widowers occupied a dwelling alone; and only 117 people at most lived as unattached singles in boardinghouses, hotels, or with families. The 1850 census counted 442 residences and 463 families (including some families boarding as units). Eighty-eight families were English as defined by husband's country of birth, 162 Irish, 73 German, 70 Welsh, 61 Pennsylvania-born, and of the nine others 2 were Scottish, 3 New Yorkers, and 4 New Jerseyites.

Whatever differences in economic opportunity, language, or religious

Girard Estate trustees with miners' children,
possibly orphans from collieries on the Girard Estate

persuasion may have been associated with ethnicity in St. Clair, all ethnic groups shared fundamentally the same kinship system in ideology and in practice, and this made possible a small but significant number of inter-ethnic marriages. Such differences as may have existed were slight in comparison with the contrast between these western European forms and the kinship systems of many non-European peoples. Minimally, the system emphasized three things: monogamous marriage; a residence pattern in which a married couple with children ordinarily occupied their own house, with perhaps a few widowed, ailing, or single relatives and paying boarders; and the maintenance over generations of a bilateral extended-family network. The U.S. census has been constructed as a household census and this fact tends to make difficult the recovery of information about extended families from census schedules. But from other sources— letters, diaries, church records, company books, newspapers, and so on— it is clear that for all social classes the bilateral extended family, reckoning marriage and descent through both males and females, was in this period crucially important in providing security for the ill, injured, aged, widowed, orphaned, or impoverished, and served as a network for the mobilization of capital for joint ventures, such as the purchase of real estate or investment in a business. The typical person's kindred included parents, grandparents, brothers and sisters, uncles and aunts, cousins, sons and daughters, nephews and nieces, and grandchildren, and their spouses and *their* children, and a congeries of other in-laws. Such a kindred could include dozens of adult individuals in one or more communities to whom a person could turn for support and assistance of various kinds—money, transportation, temporary housing and food, assistance in obtaining employment, and nursing care, to name a few. For working people, this network of kin was the primary social safety net; for those sick or unemployed who had no kin to help them, there was only an uncertain level of outside relief provided by church congregations, middle-class philanthropies, relief committees, unions, and benevolent associations. When hard times overwhelmed both the kinship network and private charity, there was only the poorhouse.

The census records provide only a partial glimpse of the extended-family system in St. Clair, but it is an illuminating one. If we examine the list of Irish households, for instance, we find that 45 out of the 162 clearly stand in an extended-family relation with another Irish household. The evidence in most cases is the presence of two families with husbands of the same surname living next door to one another (as judged from having adjacent "order of visitation" numbers). For example, family number 2145 was

Michael McCollough	30	Laborer	Ireland (place of birth)
Catherine "	30		"
Mary "	6		"
Patrick "	1		"

and family number 2146 was

Rodger McCollough	33	Laborer	Ireland (place of birth)
Mary "	32		"
Nancy "	10		"
John "	8		"
Patrick "	6		"
Edward "	2		"

It seems reasonable to infer that two brothers McCollough emigrated together from Ireland in 1849 or early 1850, came to St. Clair together, and rented houses side by side.

In some cases, other evidence, from such sources as biographical dictionaries, church records, property maps, or newspaper items, confirms and supplements the inferences from the 1850 census. And if one carries the analysis forward in time to 1880, the evolving picture of the extended families who remained in St. Clair becomes much more complete. Let us look at another Irish extended family, the Igo/Duffy connection, for whom there is more than census data. One of the histories of Schuylkill County contains the biography of a successful businessman named Daniel Duffy, who was born at Crow Hollow in 1853. His father, Martin Duffy, was born in Ireland and came to America in 1838. Along with Martin came his sister Mary and her husband, John Igo. They settled first in Vermont and then moved on to St. Clair in 1840, where the men both "followed the occupation of mining." Martin Duffy married in 1843 one Margaret Lacey, who had come over from Ireland in 1840 with her parents, two brothers, and a sister. The Duffys moved to Crow Hollow; the Igos remained in St. Clair.[1]

Turning to the Igo side, we find that a number of Igos had arrived in St. Clair by 1850; in fact, no less than five Igo families are listed in the 1850 census. John Igo, age thirty-five, miner, and his wife, Mary (Martin Duffy's sister), had five children ranging in age from ten years to five months; the two eldest were born during the stay in Vermont. Next door to John was another Irish-born Igo family: Catherine, age fifty-four, and her two sons, John, twenty-four, and Patrick, twenty-three, both laborers. And two doors away from her lived William Igo, thirty-four, his wife, thirty-five, and two children, age six and three, both born in Pennsylvania, and also one Nancy Holden, sixty, who may have been William Igo's mother-in-law. This group of Igos lived in the eastern part of town. Two other Igo families lived in St. Clair in 1850. Thomas Igo lived on Third Street in the Irish section, where he and Patrick Igo had bought a lot in 1845. Patrick left by 1850, but Thomas prospered and by 1851, although only a laborer, owned a whole lot, three houses, and a cow. He died about 1860. Michael Igo, a miner, had with a partner bought a lot on Mill Street in 1847 and built a house. There is no evidence to connect Thomas and Michael with the other Igos.[2]

Martin Duffy and John Igo remained in the area until they died. Duffy and his family resided in Crow Hollow until 1868, when they moved back to St. Clair. He was, in the words of his biographer,

> . . . a substantial citizen and was held in high esteem by all who knew him. He took an active and praiseworthy interest in all matters pertaining to the public welfare, was especially interested in educational matters, served as school director of East Norwe-

gian township for several years, and was also a school director and tax collector in St. Clair borough.[3]

He continued to work as a laborer in the mines and was finally killed by a fall of coal in Johns' Eagle Colliery in 1876 at the age of sixty-eight.[4] Of John Igo's fate we are less well informed. Starting out as a laborer, by 1860 he was a contract miner. In 1870, at the age of fifty-seven, he was still working in the mines, now as a laborer again.[5] His name does not appear in the 1880 census.

A similar pattern of extended-family migration and settlement appears in the records of other ethnic groups. Family biographies similar to the Irish cases can be assembled for the Welsh, the Germans, and the English. We may begin with Thomas Phillips, an "enterprising, money-making Welshman" who emigrated to the United States sometime before 1864. He may have been the same Thomas Phillips who lived in St. Clair in 1862, worked in a mine at Wadesville a mile away, and wrote an informative letter back home that has fortunately been reprinted in a collection of Welsh immigrant letters.[6] In any case, one Thomas Phillips acquired an interest in a colliery at Summit Hill, in Carbon County, and became superintendent there. In 1864 he "succeeded to" a general store at Hyde Park, near Scranton, and appointed as manager a man named John Williams. By 1876 Phillips was worth about $100,000. In that year, back at St. Clair, he came to the rescue of a "relative" named Daniel Williams, whose general store had failed. Phillips bought the stock at the sheriff's sale and transferred it to Christopher, Daniel's son, aged about twenty-three, who had been a clerk in his father's store. The credit-rating agency that reported on the transaction declared that the new business of Christopher Williams "will be safe with endorsement of Thomas Phillips."[7] Daniel Williams, his wife, and children (eventually, at least nine of them) had been living in St. Clair since 1860 at the latest, when the census listed him as a merchant. He had been born in Wales and emigrated to the United States about 1842. Evidently, a Phillips had married a Williams and the connection was traced through a woman.[8]

For a German case, we may take the Frantz connection; but this is in fact the only clear case in the 1850 records of a German extended family emigrating to America and settling together in St. Clair. About 1845 (to judge from the ages of children born in Pennsylvania) a man named Adam Frantz, fifty-nine, and his wife, Catherine, also fifty-nine, emigrated from Prussia along with four sons, Adam (thirty-five), Jacob (twenty-six), Valentine (twenty-five), and Christian (twenty-four). They jointly purchased a lot and built houses. By 1850 all the sons were married and had children, owned their own houses, and were occupied as miners. Jacob was elected to the borough council in 1850. The elder Adam and Catherine died between 1860 and 1870, aged seventy-four or greater. By 1870 two of the sons, Adam and Valentine, had also died; both widows lived separately in houses owned by themselves, Adam's relict, Mary, being supported by her three unmarried sons, laborers in the mines, and Valentine's Magdelena taking in boarders. Jacob and Christian continued to prosper. Jacob now was a miner who owned his own house in Johns' Patch at the north end of town, where he and his wife lived with two miner sons and an Irish girl employed as a domestic servant. Christian was the most prosperous of all, being the owner and operator of a small colliery west of town near Wadesville valued at $15,000. In 1874 a Jacob Frantz (perhaps the older Jacob, perhaps his son, perhaps one of his two nephews) had his thigh broken and his body crushed by a fall of coal in Johns' Eagle Colliery. By 1880 all the brothers were gone and only one of old Adam's children, Jacob, and his wife and one son remained in St. Clair, together with one of the younger Jacobs and his family. Old Jacob, now sixty-one, was still working as a coal miner.[9]

Our last example is a complex cross-ethnic extended family involving English, Scots, Irish, and Welsh over at least three generations. The presence of the Tempest-Stephenson connection in St. Clair first becomes visible in the 1850 census, which lists a Joseph Tempest, miner, age thirty-eight, from England, as head of a household including his wife, Catherine, from Scotland, also thirty-eight, their five boys, all born in England except the last (aged one year), plus a twelve-year-old girl with a German name who was probably a servant, and a boarder, a miner from England. By 1860, after siring a daughter, Joseph had died and the widow Tempest was keeping a boardinghouse for coal miners which she owned in the south end of town. Her oldest son, Thomas, had gone off to Australia about 1859 and married an Irish woman named Bridget Mack. The rest of Mrs. Tempest's children, with the exception of the eldest, were living with her, the two older boys mining coal. She employed a Welsh servant girl; and about 1861 a second son, Joseph, married a Welsh girl. By 1866 or '67 Thomas had returned with his Irish wife and four children and in 1868 joined John Siney and twelve other miners, of varied ethnic backgrounds, to found the Workingmen's Benevolent Association.[10] In 1870 the family was considerably dispersed. The widow Catherine, now fifty-nine, had gone to live with an English coal miner, a forty-nine-year-old widower named William Stephenson who occupied a house across the street from her boardinghouse, along with his handicapped son, John, a mine laborer; Catherine's own daughter, Hannah, sixteen and now a schoolteacher; and a fifty-nine-year-old woman from Scotland named Elizabeth Phillips. Catherine's son James had married William Stephenson's daughter Maria, and it is tempting to speculate that the Scottish washerwoman was also a relative of hers or Stephenson's.

During the '70's the Tempest brothers all had their own households. Four of the brothers were miners and one was the town constable. In October of 1870 Joseph was badly burned in gas explosions in the Wadesville Shaft.[11] And in 1874 James was recommended to the Pinkerton detective in St. Clair (assigned to watch the miners' union for signs of terrorist activity) as a suitable "butty" when the spy began looking for work. The spy started to work as a laborer for James in the Wadesville Shaft, but was soon thrown out of work by James' going on a spree. They started again a week later, but James was injured by a fall of coal and the job lapsed again. The spy was finally put out of his job by James on account of James' "going to work with his brother." "Work is scarce now owing to partial suspension of the P. and R. mines," reported the spy.[12] The reader will note that loyalty to kin took priority over loyalty to an unrelated partner even though the partner was a member of the same union.

By 1880 all the Tempests had left St. Clair except the aging widow Catherine, who by now had married William Stephenson, and James' daughter Isabella, age nine, who lived with her grandmother and grandfather. William Stephenson, now fifty-nine, was still mining coal. The rest of the Tempests had moved to Shenandoah, a larger mining town about eight miles to the north. By then one of the brothers, Martin, the constable, and one of the wives, James' Maria, had died, and James had married his widowed sister-in-law Matilda and he and his son lived with her and her children. Brothers Thomas, Joseph, and Andrew had large families of seven or eight children. All four brothers were still coal miners and all the boys over ten years of age worked as slate pickers, mule drivers, or laborers.[13] One of these slate pickers, nine-year-old Henry ("Harry"), became a famous stage minstrel and an informant to folklorist George Korson.[14]

OTHER BENEVOLENT ASSOCIATIONS: ODD FELLOWS, SONS OF TEMPERANCE, AND MASONS

Fraternal organizations supplemented the extended family as a source of aid to the individual household. These "secret" societies flourished in nineteenth-century America; with their exotic dress, degrees of status, and arcane rituals of initiation, they provided ordinary men (women were regularly excluded from all but auxiliaries) with an identity as a member of a great, hierarchical, international organization devoted to noble, if somewhat vague, moral principles such as brotherhood, loyalty, and charity. Most of the larger societies paraded in their livery on the Fourth of July and at other occasions of patriotic ceremony; the Odd Fellows of St. Clair, for instance, marched in white gloves and dark suits. Many sponsored subsidiary organizations devoted to causes, such as temperance, that were believed to lead to community improvement, and all provided aid to members and their relicts in distress.

In St. Clair the first lodge to be organized, and the only one in town in 1850, was Mineral Lodge No. 285 of the Independent Order of Odd Fellows. Of the ten original members, two were illiterate miners from England and Wales, two were Pennsylvania-born blacksmiths, one was a prosperous carpenter, and one a clerk. The second-ranking officer of the lodge, Jacob Metz, the carpenter, was also the first president of the town council. Another member, John Seitzinger, a blacksmith by trade, was also a justice of the peace. Both Metz and Seitzinger belonged to large, local extended families. Clearly, it was a lodge for prosperous, respectable workingmen, for family men, for men who aspired to community betterment.[1]

The Independent Order of Odd Fellows has been referred to as "the poor man's Masonry," and indeed it would seem to have been patterned after the older secret society. Odd Fellowship was first organized in England in the eighteenth century and was brought to the United States in 1817 by a member of a Manchester lodge that had split from the parent organization in protest against the excessive "conviviality" of its meetings. The order flourished in America under the leadership of the English emigrant and by the time he died (in 1861) numbered more than 200,000 members in the United States. Like the Freemasons, the Odd Fellows had their secret passwords, grips and signs, and rituals of initiation. The initiate, after admission by ballot, was blindfolded and placed in chains while the members marched around the room; after his blindfold was removed, he was required to look at a human skeleton, illuminated by torchlight, and to meditate upon death. New members could rise to three higher degrees within the lodge, known as Friendship, Love, and Truth.[2]

The *Miners' Journal* saluted the Odd Fellows of Pennsylvania in a small article in October 1850, praising the society for its charitable works, which were "much greater than people imagine." During the year, the 404 lodges counted 38,193 members and accumulated aggregate dues of

$206,268. The principal benevolent activity of the order was to provide financial assistance to its members (aid had been extended to 5,748 "Brothers" to the amount of over $75,000). Smaller amounts were paid to cover the funeral expenses of deceased Brothers (of the 350 members who had died, 308 were buried at the society's expense); widowed families received subventions, and some orphans were educated.[3] And the society also expended funds for the burial of non-members. This particular aspect of the society's commitment to community improvement was expressed in St. Clair in 1865, when the society bought four acres of land and established a public cemetery on the hill at the southwest end of town.[4]

The second secret fraternal order in St. Clair was the Mount Horeb Division of the Sons of Temperance. (Mount Horeb was the mountain of God in the desert of Sinai where Moses received the ten commandments.) The parent organization was founded in 1842 by men and women dedicated to reforming drunkards and dissuading the public from the use of alcohol. The Sons of Temperance too had their own secret rituals, but were not as formal as most other fraternal organizations. In 1851, however, a group split off from the Sons of Temperance, calling itself the Good Templars. Like the Odd Fellows, the Good Templars recognized three degrees—in their case, Heart, Charity, and Royal Virtue—and incorporated religious prayers and songs into their ritual.[5]

The Order of Free and Accepted Masons was the third fraternal organization to establish a lodge in St. Clair. Anthracite Lodge No. 285 was founded in April 1854. Its charter members and first officers were for the most part members of the town's elite: colliery owner William Milnes, who in 1853 had bought Hickory Slope from John Pinkerton; Charles Lawton, building contractor, sawmill owner, and chief burgess; Theodore Thorne, a prosperous plasterer and landowner from New Jersey; George Stahl, a German-born carpenter; John Geiger, operator of a sawmill (probably Milnes' or Lawton's); Jonathan Johnson, owner of the hotel where the better class of boarders lived; and William Littlehales, an English-born colliery superintendent. Milnes was the Worshipful Master and during official sessions of the lodge wore the emblem of the square, symbolizing morality; Charles Lawton, Senior Warden, wore the level, symbolizing the equality of all Freemasons; and Theodore Thorne, the Junior Warden, wore the plumb, signifying righteousness.[6]

European Freemasonry tended to be atheistic, anti-clerical, conspiratorial, and revolutionary, and it was this reputation that led to the persecution of American Masonic lodges during the evangelical revival of the 1830's, when in fact some lodges admitted free-thinkers. By the 1850's, however, American Freemasonry had managed to combine its arcane symbols and rituals with a conservative social stance. Masons had to believe in God, an afterlife, and the Bible; they had to be male; they had to be free, white, and twenty-one. In addition to the already mentioned "jewels" worn by the officers, in the local lodges a number of other ritual objects were displayed, most representing a tool of the mason's craft, each symbolizing moral and spiritual principles. The three "great lights" were the Bible, signifying faith, truth, and hope; the Square, representing morality; and the Compass, standing for spirituality. The hooded initiate could not see the jewels; his temporary blindness was a lesson to the candidate that the senses cannot lead man to spiritual enlightenment and that worldly passions must be curbed. The altar was decorated with three "lesser lights," representations of the sun, the moon, and the Worshipful Master. The altar, a symbol of sacrifice, was supposed to express the Mason's surrender of self-interest (and candidates were not supposed to be motivated to join by hopes of pecuniary or social advantages to be obtained from membership). Over the altar was a canopy of clouds, through which an opening in a ladder reached to a starry firmament. This symbolized the wish of the Mason to reach heaven by ascending the ladder of degrees of perfection. Other symbols of the craft had analogous ritual uses and meanings. The white lambskin apron, which was worn at official functions and in which members were buried, bespoke purity and honor. The rope tied around the disrobed initiate's neck as he took the Masonic oath of the Entering Apprentice degree represented submission and fidelity to the order. (It was this secret oath, and the threat of terrible mutilations to follow if the member revealed Masonic secrets, that led many laymen to suspect the order and in Catholic eyes justified the Church for prohibiting membership. The Presbyterians, the Lutherans, and some other Protestant denominations also opposed Freemasonry.) The hood reminded the candidate of his former state of benighted ignorance before receiving the "light." The all-seeing eye (similar to the figure on the Great Seal of the United States) showed the Grand Architect's omniscience and his constant oversight of man's works. The acacia represented eternal life.

The Masons, perhaps more than the other orders, were a conspicuous public presence in any town that supported a Blue Lodge. At public holidays, whenever there was a procession—on the Fourth of July and New Year's Day, at the least—the marching units of the Masons joined with other orders, and with fire companies, the militia, and the brass bands. They strutted up and down the streets of the little towns, dressed in bright reds and yellows, greens and blues and purples, bearing the symbols of their order, and carrying large banners showing scenes symbolic of civic virtue and progress. In later years, Masons strove to erect a Masonic hall in every community, where, in addition to sessions of the order itself, all sorts of public meetings could be held, but in these early days in Pottsville and St. Clair they and other benevolent associations had to rent quarters in hotels, bank buildings, or the town hall.[7]

The benevolent activities of the Masonic order were not channeled as precisely as were the Odd Fellows' charities. The Masons took care of their own indigent, sick, aged, and dead too, but they also made *ad hoc* contributions to a variety of worthy causes. The founding members were men who could be expected to exert their energies toward the public good. We have noted who were the founders of the St. Clair Lodge; in the county seat, Pulaski Lodge No. 216, chartered in 1831, as one of the county histories put it, "included in its membership many of the best men in Pottsville." Captain Thomas J. Baird, Carey's brother-in-law and coal-lands agent, was one of the first members; other community leaders may be mentioned too—Andrew White, pioneer colliery operator; Judge Strange N. Palmer; the Rev. Daniel Washburn, rector of Trinity Episcopal Church; William Kendrick, colliery operator; Henry Russell, land agent for Carey, and so on. Chapters of the Scottish Rite enrolled, among others, William Milnes, Jr., son of the founder of the St. Clair Blue Lodge. The Odd Fellows of the region, not to be too brightly outshone by the Masons, over the years strove to improve their social standing. In commendation of Pottsville's Odd Fellows Lodge (instituted in 1829 and no doubt the lodge to which St. Clair's Odd Fellows repaired before founding their own in 1847) one of the county historians wrote in the 1880's: "From a membership composed mostly of miners at its inception, there are but three living members at present (1881) who are known to have followed that occupation."[8]

The lodges evidently functioned overtly as a kind of middle-class siphon-and-sprinkler system, absorbing dues and ceremonial charges from their members and disbursing them as benefits to their less fortunate members and as investments in improvement projects on behalf of the community as a whole. It cannot be doubted that the lodges also provided the opportunity, and the moral incentive, for an informal "old boy" network within the respectable Protestant community. This network acted as a kind of credit reference bureau for its members, as a clearinghouse for news of economic dangers and of opportunities for investment; membership, and especially membership in the advanced degrees of Masonry, was a testimonial to good character, as important as or more important than affiliation with a religious congregation.

But the obvious practical benefits of membership in this limited social-security system for artisans and businessmen do not entirely account for its form. In doctrine, symbolism, and ritual, the secret fraternal organizations, like the college fraternities growing up in America at the same time, evoked archetypal images. The rituals of initiation and of promotion to advanced degrees were rites of passage in a secret, hierarchical organization, a vast family, a network of adoptive kin into whose embrace the initiate was born during the dark night of initiation. It is difficult to estimate the proportion of the workingmen of St. Clair who in the 1850's belonged to one or another; to judge from the published accounts, it might be no more than 20 percent. Of the remainder, some could in principle expect to join, if they felt the need. But there were some who could never join, who were prohibited from joining by their Church, and most of these were the Irish, who needed help more than anyone else.

TABERNACLES AND TAVERNS

Mine workers had the reputation of being a hard-drinking lot, prone to boisterous singing and drunken brawling in the local saloons on Saturday night. Peter Lesley, the pious geologist, was distressed by the low morality, and particularly the fondness for alcohol, of the miners whom he first encountered in 1839 on his excursions into the mines near Pottsville.[1] But Eli Bowen of Mount Carbon, in his *Pictorial Sketch-Book of Pennsylvania* (published in 1852), made no mention of drunkenness as a problem in the section on the "Moral Condition of Miners" and claimed that Pennsylvania miners were morally superior to miners of any other country:

> They have abundance to eat, good clothes to wear, and *money in their pockets*. A more generous-hearted people, more devoted to their friends, and faithful to their domestic attachments, does not live.[2]

But Bowen was something of a chauvinistic booster of American industry and this rhetoric was prefatory to a condemnation of the English system of forcing women and girls to work half naked in the mines, debased in values, vulgar and obscene in language. The truth of the matter is that there were both drinkers and non-drinkers in St. Clair; the former patronized the hotels and saloons and bought beer and liquor to consume at home; and the latter went to the more severe Protestant chapels and the meetings of the Sons of Temperance and prayed for the salvation of their brethren.

Perhaps the most intensely devout among the church people were the

Welsh—one might even say that they were devotedly contentious, for they were schismatic among themselves as well as apt to fall into angry disputes with "the Papists" over baptism (adult baptism by immersion vs. infant baptism by partial immersion). The first churches in St. Clair were built by Welsh miners: the Welsh Congregationalist in 1840 at the south end of town; the Welsh Calvinist at the north end in 1846; and the Welsh Baptist about 1847, a remodeled carpenter shop, replaced by a proper church building in the middle of town in 1853. To judge from the size of the congregations indicated in the local histories, they were prosperous churches and must have embraced most if not all of the Welsh-born population. Sermons were delivered and hymns were sung in Welsh; as late as the 1880's, both English and Welsh were used in the Sunday School.[3]

After the raising of the Welsh churches, the other denominations quickly followed. The usual order of events was for a congregation to organize under the patronage of a Pottsville church and to hold its meetings in private houses or schools until it had sufficient members to pay for the purchase of a lot and the construction of a place of worship. The Primitive Methodist church was built in 1847; the Methodist Episcopal in 1849; St. Bonifacius Roman Catholic (for Germans) in 1852; and St. Mary's Roman Catholic (for Irish) in 1864.

The Primitive Methodists had the distinction of being, in America, not only a working-class church but the coal miners' special denomination.[4] Primitive Methodism had begun in England in the early years of the nineteenth century as a movement to bring back open-air preaching—what in America was called the camp meeting—to increasingly respectable pew-renting Methodist congregations. The established Methodists, convinced that more souls were conceived than saved at camp meetings, expelled the Primitive Methodists. Under the leadership of Hugh Bourne, and influenced by the field preaching of the American evangelist Lorenzo Dow, the Primitive Methodists flourished among the spiritually neglected working people of the Midlands, drawing them away from their traditional "paganistic" parish wakes, where all sorts of orgiastic excesses were alleged to occur. The first wave of English miners to emigrate to America included a number of Primitive Methodists and by 1829 the English Conference had resolved to "colonize" America. Missionaries, male and female, were sent over and a congregation was organized in St. Clair as early as 1831; it met in the old schoolhouse on Cemetery Hill, west of town. In 1845 and 1846, Hugh Bourne himself toured the American circuit and for a short time served as the designated minister to the congregation at St. Clair. St. Clair continued to hold one of the larger Primitive Methodist congregations and in 1850 took its turn as the site for the denomination's annual conference. These conferences, to which elected delegates were sent by the local congregations, assigned ministers to the various churches on a rotating basis, so that no one remained long in one place. The conference also approved the book of discipline, which, among other things, prescribed the minister's duties and daily schedule: seven hours sleep per night, six hours study per day, and eleven hours preaching, family visiting (twenty visits per week the maximum), and performing other pastoral duties, with meals squeezed in as opportunity arose. The minister's salary was on the order of a mine laborer's wage: unmarried male preachers got $100 per year, unmarried females $60, and married males $260 per year plus a $26 annual allowance for each child under fourteen. The affairs of the local congregation were managed by a board of trustees. The St. Clair board in 1852, for instance, appointed two men as a committee of ushers to maintain good order during services, "to keep the doors, and take up the cent collection, and keep out the dogs and babies, or keep them quiet."[5] The local congregation also disciplined its members; in St. Clair in 1847 a certain sister was sentenced to "remain silent three months longer."[6] Ministers could and did intervene and adjudicate domestic disputes—for instance, persuading a nagging wife, who demanded that her temperate husband bring her a ration of beer each day from the grog shop, to join the ranks of the teetotalers.

Leadership among the Primitive Methodists did not usually come from the community's economic elite, but sometimes it did, as in the case of the Donaldsons at Tamaqua. Here the town's leading colliery operator was a Primitive Methodist; he provided land for the church and gave it his support until he was killed in a gas explosion in 1859. By and large, however, the ministers themselves were usually not formally educated in college or seminary; they were generally poor, plain-spoken, and zealous. In St. Clair a leading layman was William Yeo, an English miner who had come over during the 1840's, and who helped finance the purchase of the land for the 1847 church by buying half the lot from the church for $100, with the stipulation that if he sold it for more than that amount, the balance would go to the church. The Carey group helped by selling the land at a reduced price. Yeo was also one of the ushers assigned to keep out babies and dogs and later served as a trustee. In the 1870's, when a new church was built (the foundation of the old one had been damaged by a mine cave-in), the Masons helped financially and the cornerstone was laid with Masonic ceremonies.

The religious style of Primitive Methodism was enthusiastic. Members of the congregation might spontaneously clap hands and ejaculate hallelujahs during the sermon. Conversions of the tempestuous sort were actively sought at periodic revivals where both male and female, black and white evangelists preached hellfire and redemption. The differences with established Methodism were not doctrinal. As the Reverend Dr. John H. Acornley, erstwhile minister at St. Clair, put it in his history of Primitive Methodism in America:

> The mission of Primitive Methodism is to all classes, but especially to the poor. Wherever life is thickest, wherever poverty is greatest, wherever sorrow is commonest, wherever crime is blackest, there she ought to be, telling of Jesus and His love . . .
>
> The grand old doctrines proclaimed with such earnestness and power by the fathers, she still continues to preach, and she is never willing to tone down one atom of the truth.[7]

It was a church that conceived itself to be Methodist as John Wesley had intended it to be, essentially a church for workingmen and -women, egalitarian, inspired by song and spiritual drama. And, as in England, these characteristics would contribute to the milieu in which radical unionism began to develop in the later 1860's.[8]

The next congregation to form was the more conservative branch of Methodism: the Methodist Episcopal Church in 1848. Like the Primitive Methodists, the Episcopal Methodists were mostly English, but their principal sponsor was the Johns family, proprietors of the Eagle Colliery, who were among the first members and who were Welsh. The Sunday School was also organized by Thomas Johns. Besides the Johns, other early members included two carpenters, a clerk, a well-to-do merchant, two prosperous widows, two miners, and one Irish laborer—a "middle-class" congregation in St. Clair terms.[9]

The last of the denominations to establish themselves in St. Clair in the 1850's were all high churches. St. Bonifacius Roman Catholic Church was built in 1852 and dedicated in 1853 by Bishop Neuman. Its parish included not merely St. Clair borough but also neighboring New Castle, Norwegian, and East Norwegian townships, and it was intended specifically to provide for the religious needs of the many Catholic immigrants from the southern German states. The pastor spoke German and Latin but only broken English, if any English at all (to judge from his efforts to render English place names in Germanic syllables: e.g., "Wehtsvil" for Wadesville and "Kroholla" for Crow Hollow). Some Irish nevertheless attended mass, presented infants for baptism, and claimed other ritual services at St. Bonifacius. In 1853, St. John's Reformed Church was organized to serve the needs of Protestant German immigrants and Pennsylvania German Lutherans in the area. As in the case of St. Bonifacius, the first pastor was German-born and German was, and remained for many years, the language in which services were conducted and records kept. It was a small congregation, numbering only fifty-five members in 1858, and grew slowly.[10] The last of the churches built in the 1850's was the Episcopalian Church of the Holy Apostles. The vestry was organized in 1848, largely in response to the efforts of Joseph Lawton, and Lawton also served as superintendent of the Sunday School. In addition to the Lawtons, the family of Joseph Foster, a landowning miner from England, and Richard Coryell, M.D. (who would later marry a daughter of one of the Johns brothers), were among the first Episcopal families.[11]

But what of the Irish Catholics in St. Clair? Their religious needs were, in the 1850's and early '60's, somewhat neglected by the diocese. Although they formed the largest number of Catholics in the parish of St. Bonifacius, about 3,000 souls—far more numerous than the Germans—they were left without an English-speaking church with an Irish pastor for more than a decade, until St. Mary's Roman Catholic Church was built for them in 1864. In the meantime, they were expected to make use of St. Patrick's in Pottsville. This church had been established as early as 1828 and a cathedral had been completed in 1838. The pastors were Irish (Fitzpatrick, McCarty, Maginnis, Walsh . . .) and the congregation largely composed of the Irish miners and their families in Pottsville and the surrounding district. The few German Catholics in the area at that time were attended by a missionary from Reading, who held services for them in St. Patrick's, but, the arrangement proving to be unsatisfactory, a separate church for the Germans in Pottsville was established in 1840.[12] Although the Irish of St. Clair were welcome at St. Patrick's, it must have been inconvenient to trudge two or three miles over dirt roads, in all kinds of weather, to get to a church with an Irish priest. A few families made do with the German pastor in St. Clair, calling on him for the administration of the necessary sacraments at birth, marriage, and death, but most did not. Many Irish families, one suspects, existed in a kind of religious limbo until 1864, considering themselves to be Catholic, and availing themselves of the indispensable sacraments at times of life crisis, but identifying themselves with no congregation and falling outside the pale of parish financial support. The separation of the Irish from the German congregation of St. Bonifacius did not end with death: Irish and German bodies were buried in separate parts of the graveyard, separated by a low stone wall.

But the Irish—or at least Irish men—could avail themselves of another, strangely parallel set of institutions that catered to the spiritual and social needs of the community: the taverns and other drinking places. It is perhaps not a coincidence that the terms "tabernacle" and "tavern" have the same Latin root. But probably to most of the residents of St. Clair, to speak of the House of God as comparable to the Den of Iniquity, to place the Lord and Lucifer in the same category, would have seemed blasphemous. And yet the very zeal with which temperance men and women attacked these resorts of Satan suggests that the tavern was viewed as an institution of great power, a dangerous competitor. For both tavern and tabernacle were places where men raised their voices in song; both administered the same beverage as sacrament.

Early in the town's history, it was realized by virtually everyone that liquor was a dangerous article in the collieries, where a drunken man's accident might bring death and destruction to all. At the Pine Forest Colliery and the Mill Creek Colliery, a couple of miles south of St. Clair, in 1851, Snyder and Milnes prohibited liquor and Parvin did the same at his slope shortly thereafter. The *Miners' Journal* was delighted:

> No liquor is allowed to be used on the premises. It is stipulated with every man who engages at these collieries, that he must remain sober or lose his situation. The consequence is a different state of affairs exists here from that about those collieries where the use of liquor is unrestricted. The workmen attend punctually to their business, they do more labor, save their pay and render their families comfortable and happy, by judiciously expending it for their benefit, instead of squandering it foolishly in dissipation. Their houses are neat and clean—their furniture though scanty, nevertheless in good order, and everybody exhibits the wonderful difference between the condition of collieries where rum is and where it is not.

Where rum "is," the *Miners' Journal* observed, there are "scenes of riot and disorder—quarreling, and sometimes blood-shed."[13] And soon the use or sale of liquor around a colliery was universally grounds for dismissal.

The six taverns of St. Clair in 1850 had much in common. All were substantial establishments, the ground level containing, in addition to a bar and tables for drinkers, a dining room and (usually) meeting rooms, some of them large enough to be called "hall"; upstairs there were bedrooms for visitors and permanent residents. They were, in fact, hotels, and provided a multitude of functions, only one of which was the serving of alcoholic beverages. Another feature shared by the taverns was location in relation to the churches. All of the taverns were located west of First Street (down which coursed Mill Creek); all of the churches stood east of First Street, which thus served as a kind of spiritual meridian. Not surprisingly, the new school (built in 1847) stood on the east side, and so did the Johns and Lawton mansions. Curiously enough, all of the hotel buildings have survived; this cannot be said for all of the churches, the school, or the Lawton mansion.

The oldest tavern was the Cross Keys, which went back to 1829, when the work crews building the tunnel for the Danville and Pottsville Railway required temporary quarters. A two-story, mansard-roofed structure at the corner of Third and Hancock, then the main road through the town, it was occupied by the proprietor, Daniel Frack, and his wife and three children, all five Pennsylvania-born. Four other people lived there: a sixteen-year-old girl, who probably worked as a domestic servant; a male laborer, who probably was a paying guest; a young man of twenty-four, a painter, and his nine-month-old daughter, no doubt also paying guests. (Who was nursing the baby is not clear.) Daniel Frack moved on a few years later to found Frackville, another coal town, north of the mountains about five miles away.

Five other hotels were built in the years when St. Clair was being developed by the Carey interests, between 1843 and 1850. They were all on the new, wide main street, Second Street, and three stood in the north end of town where the stores and artisans' shops clustered. In 1850, in the north end, the landlords were Jonathan Johnson, Mark Shirk, and John Betz. Johnson's hotel was occupied by New Jersey–born Johnson and his Pennsylvania-born family plus five male boarders, one of them the town's leading physician, Richard Coryell. Johnson's place was a brick, two-story, mansard-roofed corner building. Two blocks to the south on Second, facing each other on opposite corners of Carroll, stood the hotels maintained by John Betz and Mark Shirk, who, like Frack and Johnson, lived with their families on the premises. Shirk's hotel had the distinction of being the first voting place in St. Clair. Shirk had seven guests, and Betz four. Betz and his wife were German-born and so were all of their guests except a two-year-old child living there with her father, who, like the other residents, was a miner. Shirk and his family were Pennsylvanians.

At the south end of town there would soon be two more hotels. The one at Second and Patterson had just been built and had no guests when the census enumerator arrived; its proprietor was an Englishman, James

Wood, who occupied the building with his wife, two sons (both miners), and four daughters. He had lived in this country for about eight years. And, finally, just beyond the south borough line on the road to Mill Creek and Port Carbon would be built, within a couple of years, the establishment of twenty-nine-year-old, Irish-born Martin Dormer and thirty-three-year-old, Irish-born Thomas Canfield. The Dormer-Canfield place was a large brick building, located in virtually perpetual shade on the downhill corner of the intersection, and included a "saloon" in addition to the usual attached hotel, and a brewery; on the hillside across the street, Dormer later laid out Dormer's Park, a grove where groups could rent space for picnics, concerts, dances, and other entertainments. Dormer's hotel would later become notorious in St. Clair as a reputed hangout of the Molly Maguires, who allegedly met there on their travels between Port Carbon and Shenandoah. Martin Dormer's older brother Patrick, who operated a hotel in Pottsville in the 1870's (soon moving back to St. Clair to manage the hotel there), would figure prominently in the testimony of the Pinkerton detective James McParlan at the trials of the accused Mollies. The Dormer brothers in the 1850's were young pillars of the community—members of the St. Bonifacius congregation and public servants, Martin serving for a time as the postmaster of St. Clair, and Patrick as county commissioner.[14]

Indeed, if we look over the "taverns" and "hotels" of St. Clair in 1850, we do not find them to be rip-roaring saloons. Rather, they appear to have been more on the order of boardinghouses where a respectable resident family cared for permanent guests, mostly temporarily unattached males and females or widowers with children. In two instances (Johnson and Shirk) the male residents were all professional persons, merchants, or tradesmen; Daniel Frack's male boarders were a painter and a laborer. In the case of the German-born proprietor, the guests were German-born miners. But the Dormer-Canfield place was another story. At the beginning Dormer owned and operated the brewery and Canfield the hotel and saloon. Canfield, however, was by trade a canal boatman, often absent from home, and during his absences his wife, Catherine, managed the saloon and hotel. Their tavern did not conform to the pattern of the quiet, respectable inn. Being just outside the borough line, it was safe from the local magistrate's jurisdiction, but not from the county's, and in 1856 Catherine Canfield was prosecuted by the district attorney and convicted of keeping a "disorderly house."[15] The boardinghouse hotels remained in St. Clair as places of respectable residence and refreshment. But saloons gradually became more common. By 1876 there would be twenty-one drinking places self-styled as "saloons" in the town directory, in addition to thirteen "hotels." The population had merely doubled since 1850, but the number of liquor-dispensing establishments had increased five times.

But the Canfield conviction reminds us that there was still a third kind of drinking place: the so-called "disorderly house." The "disorderly house" was invariably kept by a woman (although the property owner might be her husband) and at late hours provided "nice young men" with drinks and the social services of a small bevy of female boarders. "Disorderly house" was in fact the legal euphemism for brothel. In 1851 there were two establishments in St. Clair that came to the attention of the county court of quarter sessions. Charles Lawton, chief burgess, made the complaints. The first case was brought against Mary Sitler.

> Witness testified to the "general character of the house" and some "swore positively" that they heard dancing and fiddling tunes, at all hours of the night, that at these times they saw the girls fighting, pulling hair, and drinking spirits, and some of the nice young men stated that they remained there courting the ladies until the small hours of the morning.

The evidence, although sufficient to convict Mrs. Sitler of keeping a "tippling house" (an offense not mentioned in the indictment), was not conclusive on the "disorderly house" charge and she was acquitted by the jury. The judge warned her to expect a different verdict the next time. Not so fortunate was Jenkin Edwards. Edwards suffered from a "personal infirmity" (whose nature was not specified in the newspaper account) that made him an object of sympathy to the jury. "Poor Jenkin," averred the *Miners' Journal,* "is but a cypher in his own house, consequently many honest persons wished the wife was only placed in his position." The evidence in this case was stronger and "poor Jenkin" pleaded guilty, was assessed a minimal fine of $5, and, in want of the money, and his wife failing to assist him, was hustled off to jail. And at the same session Mrs. Elizabeth Parry of Pottsville was also convicted of keeping "a disorderly and tippling house" and fined $50. "She boarded several ladies who gave Social Cotillion Parties, which adjourned at three or four o'clock, a.m., and sometimes at day break."[16]

A PLACE OF SONG

St. Clair had no opera house (although there was one in Pottsville), but its residents made it a place of song nevertheless. English miners had their own traditional genre, the "collier's rant," which was quickly taken up by immigrant miners of all descriptions and became known as the "the miner's ballad." The devout Protestants sang hymns. The Primitive Methodists in particular brought from English fields and chapels the practice of loud singing of newly composed hymns set to popular tunes.[1] The Welsh had their own high tradition of bardic composition and minstrelsy and they applied these skills not only to the local *eisteddfod* or music fair, where prizes were awarded the most skilled musicians and composers, but also to hymn singing in their own churches. The Germans gathered in St. Bonifacius to hear music played on an organ made (after his arrival in 1855) by St. Clair's own resident organ builder, Maurus Oestreich; a chorus of parishioners no doubt sang Gregorian chants from the loft that looked down over the pews stretching from wall to wall between the stained-glass windows. The Odd Fellows had their own special odes and hymns in honor of their departed dead and in celebration of their values ("Truth," "Faith," "Wisdom"), which they sang in their own hall and on public occasions. The schoolchildren sang their school lessons and even the stage driver set off in the morning bellowing his own chanty.[2]

But much of the music was neither private nor sacred. Of special importance were the parades that formed part of the celebration of each event in the annual calendar of public ceremonies. Some parades were performed by special groups, such as the benevolent associations and the militia, for the entertainment and edification of the local community, on dates of special importance to the group itself (such as the anniversary of the death in 1861 of Thomas Wildey, founder of the American Odd Fellows). But there were also the celebrations of the community in general, such as New Year's and (later on) the Fourth of July, and on these days the marching units of the various orders joined with local brass bands playing marches and rousing popular tunes. They paraded through St. Clair, Port Carbon, Wadesville, Mount Laffee, and all the other little towns and patches, and wound up marching down Centre Street in Pottsville amid cheering crowds of onlookers lining the streets. On these occasions the uniformed, or at least regalia-wearing, marching units of various St. Clair organizations—the local militia company, known as the Wetherill Rifles, the Odd Fellows, the Masons, the Sons of Temperance, the German and Hibernian benevolent societies, and eventually the volunteer fire companies—would merge with their peers in the general procession, each, however, preserving its own identity in the line of march. Thus, for example, in Pottsville on the Fourth of July in 1855, the order of parade numbered thirty-three units, civil and military, and included no less than five brass bands.[3]

It is not the blizzard of sound created by brass bands, psalm singers, and chanting schoolchildren that has attracted the special interest of observers, however, but rather the songs and ballads of the miners, sung in the mines, in barrooms and saloons, on the steps of the general store, and on the green in remote patches, by mining men and their women and children. These ballads are now best known through the works of George Korson, a Pottsville newspaper reporter who in the 1920's recorded, preserved, and published in a series of books and phonograph records a collection of dozens of the genre. Two of the principal "minstrels of the mine patch" whose compositions were published in Korson's books came from the St. Clair area: William Keating from Oak Hill near Mount Laffee, in whose mines men from St. Clair worked, and Harry Tempest, who spent his early boyhood in St. Clair before moving to Shenandoah. Their songs and ballads were dedicated to bar owners and their working-class patrons, and they celebrated the amoral realities of the miner's life, funny or tragic. The boyish-looking William Keating sang songs that evoked tears and laughter because, in a mood mellowed by beer and whiskey, they recalled familiar scenes, personalities, and events. Social criticism was muted; the theme was the silliness of risk, the randomness of tragedy, the irrelevance of disaster to the miner's love of home and family. Growing out of Keating's experiences as a mule driver at Wadesville, his ballad "The Driver Boys of Wadesville Shaft" is typical of the genre. As published by Korson, there are innumerable stanzas detailing the pranks and exploits of a group of madcap mule drivers (some of them undoubtedly boys from St. Clair, half a mile away); only a small selection can be presented here:

> The driver boys and the stable boss,
> From my song should learn a lesson,
> And now I'll begin with the bottom men,
> For some of them needs a dressin'.
> There's easy-going, fat Jack Betzs.
> Jack jokes and loafs all day,
> While old "Dutch" Hen is humpty-backed
> Pushin' cars from the cage away. . . .
> "The breaker is waiting'; this won't pay,
> Move those empties," Betzs will shout.
> Then Dutch Hen will say in his dutchified way,
> "Be der Lawd Kyist der twack is blocked out!"[4]

It is worth noting that Keating repeatedly draws attention to the economic and human cost of inefficiency. Henry Flynn, the mule driver; Willie Brennan and Bossy Donnaghan, the stable boys; Matt Reddington and Dutch Hen, the boys who push cars on and off the elevator—are all described as contributing to the colliery's failure to make money. Flynn is lazy; Brennan and Donnaghan are afraid of the mules; Matt Reddington drops a coupling on Dutch Hen's foot.

As early as the 1870's, miners' ballads became popular in music halls in the larger cities. Some of the most successful songs were written for the stage, including "Down in a Coal Mine," probably the most widely known of all the ballads, and well liked in the anthracite region despite its literary origin; even the ladies sang "Down in a Coal Mine" as they promenaded on St. Clair's Second Street of an evening. It begins as follows:

I am a jovial collier lad,
and blithe as blithe can be,
For let the times be good or bad
they're all the same to me:
'Tis little of the world I know
and care less for its ways,
For where the dog star never glows,
I wear away my days.

(Chorus)

Down in a coal mine, underneath the ground,
Where a gleam of sunshine never can be found;
Digging dusky diamonds all the season round,
Down in a coal mine, underneath the ground.[5]

And in the 1890's Harry Tempest from St. Clair sang "White Slave of the Mine" in Daniel L. Hart's play *Underground*. Dan Hart was mayor of Wilkes-Barre and Sam Boyd, composer of the song, was a Wilkes-Barre newspaperman.

I'm a little collier lad,
Hardworking all the day,
From early morn til late at night
No time have I to play.
Down in the bowels of the earth
Where no bright sun rays shine,

You'll find me busy at my work,
A white slave of the mine.[6]

As the anthracite ballads circulated in the mass media, a selection for pathos seems to have occurred as the nation became increasingly aware of the need for industrial reform. But pathos in the mass media was complemented by the ribaldry of some of the songs sung in the saloons. Only bowdlerized and truncated fragments remain; of these, the best known are the few lines printed by Korson:

My sweetheart's the mule in the mines,
I drive her without reins or lines,
On the bumper I sit,
I chew and I spit,
All over my sweetheart's behind.[7]

THE OLD COUNTRY IN THE NEW WORLD

Most of St. Clair's residents in 1850 and for many years thereafter were either born in Europe or, if born in the United States, brought up by foreign-born parents. Those immigrant families brought with them important parts of the ways of life in their lands of origin. Consequently, St. Clair in the early days was a patchwork of ethnic groups stitched together by the common culture of the coal region that all immigrant groups shared.

This common culture included a virtually universal technology and material culture. Central to the economy was a modified form of the standard British coal-mining technology, knowledge of which was brought over by experienced English, Welsh, and Scottish miners, supplemented by imported English manuals on such subjects as pumps, ventilation, plans of working, methods of sinking, etc.

Members of all ethnic groups soon learned the map of the regional organization: that is, the physical layout of canals, roads, and railroads that joined the mines, the mine patches, the mining towns, the regional centers, and the county seat, and the corresponding economic and political network that managed the whole system and connected it with markets and competing coal regions and centers of money and political power, in Philadelphia and New York, in Mauch Chunk and Wilkes-Barre, and in Harrisburg and Washington. They all traveled the same roads, rode the same trains, and, once naturalized (and sometimes when not), voted in the same elections. They all knew the social roles and ranks of miners, laborers, engineers, lawyers, mine operators, coal agents, landowners, and railroad and canal officials. They all recognized that there were great inequalities of wealth and power, and, being European in origin, undoubtedly saw a clear-cut class structure. But undoubtedly they also believed that some working people, or their children, would climb the ladder of success.

All ethnic groups, as we observed earlier, shared fundamentally the same kinship system in ideology and in practice. This made possible a small but significant number of inter-ethnic marriages, at least thirteen in St. Clair by 1850, that take on an added importance when one recognizes that any such marriage made possible a widely ramifying network of economic alliances between members of two ethnic communities. The most common of these inter-ethnic unions involved an English-and-Welsh couple: in six instances a Welsh husband and an English wife, in two the reverse. There were two Irish cases: a Welsh man and an Irish woman, and an Irish man and an English woman.[1]

For practical purposes, the English language was also a part of the shared culture. Many Welsh and German families continued to speak in their native tongue at home and among fellow ethnics in the street, there were Welsh and German newspapers in Pottsville, and church services were for years conducted in Welsh and German; nevertheless, the language of the schools, of government, and of business was English. A minimal facility in English—however modified by Old Country dialect, in the case of Irish brogue, or by marginal fluency, in the case of the newly arrived Germans—was necessary for getting along. Some immigrants, like Maurus Oestreich, the organ builder, insisted on the use of English by all the family even at home.[2]

The religious differences were, so far as one can tell, more conspicuous than important to working people, certainly less threatening to them than to the more evangelistic middle-class businessmen. Welsh Baptists might deeply deplore the failure of the Catholics to practice adult baptism by total immersion; the Protestants generally suspected the Papacy of dark plots against religious freedom. But, in a practical sort of way, the congregations of the different denominations got along well. There were no riots; no churches were set afire; all the pastors agreed on the importance of temperance, even though some were teetotalers and some were not. And good people were recognized, whatever their faith: when Maurus Oestreich's Catholic wife died, one of the Protestant ministers praised her from the pulpit as a "good woman," a gesture gratefully remembered by her descendants. One suspects that a general ethic of ethnic tolerance was promulgated in the community as a necessary condition of getting along.

Such an attitude of good-natured tolerance of alien ways certainly was applied to some of the more superficial differences between those of different national origin. Games and entertainment are an example. Footraces and boxing matches were a universal pastime, and whole mines emptied out when Buffalo Bill's Wild West Show came to Pottsville. Beginning in 1858, cricket teams were organized in the various towns and competed in the summer on a regular schedule. St. Clair had its cricket club, along with Pottsville, Port Carbon, Schuylkill Haven, Wadesville, Tamaqua, and other places as well. Some of these cricket clubs tended to be middle class in membership and included some of the best-known names in the participating communities: Colonel John Macomb Wetherill; Harry, the son of George W. Snyder; James Bannan; Charles Lawton; Henry Pleasants, the mining engineer; Carey's agent, Henry Russell; two sons of E. W. McGinness, Daniel and Theodore (who made an 800-foot hit, the longest ever recorded in Pottsville!). Pottsville teams even traveled to Philadelphia to meet the players of the renowned Germantown Cricket Club. The popularity of the game was not confined to lawyers, financiers, and mine operators, however; working people also played and teams were organized by fire companies, machine-shop employees, and miners. Baseball was introduced after the Civil War, however, and in the 1880's the interest in cricket began to wither away.[3]

English and Irish workers also introduced one of the Old Country blood sports, cockfighting. A cockfight was reported in St. Clair as late as 1874, with an audience of miners, and gamecocks were bred especially for the pit.[4] But betting on cockfights was hardly a respectable middle-class recreation in nineteenth-century St. Clair and, in fact, the Pinkerton reports and testimony are the only evidence of its existence there. The Irish union leader John Siney, when met at a cockfight, felt it necessary to explain that he did not keep birds himself and was merely a spectator.[5] Such a form of amusement would not have appealed to many religious workingmen either, who, like the German Maurus Oestreich, preferred to engage in family singing and to take the children to the circus when it came to town.

Food preferences also gave occasion for amused and critical commentary. One mildly annoyed Welshman complained about an Irish neighbor's love for potatoes in a letter to a newspaper back home:

> I know a man from near Merthur who is laboring for an Irishman in these works and, from his appearance, I suspect that he did nothing but plant and pull up potatoes before coming to this country. This old sinner lives near where I stay and he thinks so

much of the potatoes that one gets no peace from him even on the Lord's Day and he is continually busy with his hoe and his rake.[6]

The Irish in turn patronizingly referred to the Welsh as "soup drinkers" and no doubt some commented disparagingly on the English taste for mutton.

Cultural differences such as these could be expected gradually to fade as neighbor ladies borrowed recipes and miners and laborers watched each other's games, joined in each other's songs, and in the spring watched each other march on their national saint's days, the Welsh in honor of St. David and the Irish of St. Patrick. But there was a domain of cultural difference among the four national groups that would prove to be significant later on, and would, indeed, contribute to the Molly Maguire confrontations between Irish and Welsh street gangs and between all of these and English, Welsh, and German mine managers, local police, and the military. And these troubles, in turn, made it easier in the 1870's for the Reading Company to purchase 80 percent of the Schuylkill coal lands and to suppress, temporarily, the miners' union. These crucial cultural differences had to do with traditional conceptions of legitimate authority and of acceptable subordination, and of citizens' privileges and responsibilities, that the several ethnic groups brought with them to the United States from their European communities of origin.

The German immigrants came mostly from the principalities in the southern and eastern parts of the country—Bavaria, Alsace, Rheinbayern, Hesse, Saxony. Germans were mostly town dwellers, even the peasant farmers, accustomed to life in ancient villages and small cities, often walled, that went back to medieval and even Roman times. It is difficult to generalize about Germany prior to the unification under Bismarck, for the country was divided not only politically among its principalities, but also regionally in religion and language; as the anthropologist Robert Lowie has put it, the old Germany suffered from an unrestrained parochialism of the sort "that recognizes no kinship or solidarity beyond the range of the village church bell." Nonetheless, within the walls, the social structure was extremely tight. Minute distinctions of rank governed social relations, even in the smaller towns, where a vestigial guild system still controlled craft specialization and ranked artisans as apprentices, journeymen, and masters, and where farm workers were separated into hierarchical categories, with the rich landowning farmer at the top, descending through successive levels of hired help to the illegitimate swillery maid and cow girl at the bottom. A myriad of regulations by church fathers, town councils, and princely courts governed daily life and movement, and courts and lawyers adjudicated numerous petty disputes. Conscription into the army was a common fate of the young men.[7]

Broadly speaking, then, St. Clair's German immigrants of the 1840's and '50's came from the least-industrialized, predominantly Catholic part of the country. They were used to life in small towns rather than on remote country farms; and they were accustomed, if not to working the land, to getting a living as artisans and shopkeepers. In addition to the extended family, strong loyalty was focused on the village itself. And, most important for their mode of adaptation in America, they were accustomed to submit, albeit with grumbling, to the network of governmental bodies that regulated the town's affairs. They were pre-industrial peasants and artisans, but they were accustomed to civic and economic discipline.

When Germans came to the St. Clair area, they tended to seek out, or re-create, life situations for themselves that initially perpetuated this European past. Thus the Germans living in the St. Clair area squeezed into the town. Including both the borough and the patches in New Castle and East Norwegian townships, there were fifty-seven German households, and forty-nine of these resided in the town; the eight others were all located in Crow Hollow, the nearest of the patches to St. Clair. Furthermore, the Germans in 1850 were far more likely to be tradesmen than the Irish: of ninety-one employed adult German immigrant males, fifteen (or 16 percent) were artisans and shopkeepers. Among the 362 Irish workers, only fourteen (or 4 percent) practiced a trade.[8]

Something of the burgher quality of the ideal German lifestyle in St. Clair is revealed in the family history of the Oestreichs. A family of cabinetmakers and organ builders, the Oestreichs had lived for generations in the small town of Oberbimbach, near Fulda, in Hesse. Maurus, the progenitor of the St. Clair Oestreichs, emigrated from Germany in 1855 as a youth of nineteen in order to avoid conscription. Other members of his family also came to the United States in the following decade, but none of them settled in St. Clair. Maurus established himself as a carpenter, married Katherine Anschutz, a German girl from Crow Hollow, and proceeded to raise a family and to prosper. He built the organ for St. Bonifacius and other Catholic churches in Pottsville and the surrounding towns, and he built and repaired church furniture, such as altars and crucifixes. But he made his fortune by turning his skills in carpentry to use as a contractor for the construction of coal breakers. He believed firmly in the importance of conforming to the requirements of life in a new country, and to that end, after St. Mary's was built, he encouraged some of the family to switch to the Irish parish. At least one of his boys married an Irish girl. When the Civil War came, he volunteered and fought through to the end; after the war he became a leader in the veterans' organization (the Grand Army of the Republic) and gave speeches on Memorial Day. A strong believer in education (he is said to have briefly attended a university in Germany), he sent his son to the University of Pennsylvania, where he earned his M.D.

While her husband was pursuing his successful career, his wife was busy with domestic matters. In addition to bearing and raising ten children, Katherine kept the house on North Second Street in a typically German style. The family lived mostly in the kitchen and dining room on the first floor, with open curtains and flowers on the windowsill facing the sidewalk, beside the bicycle shop and hardware store at the front (where Mrs. Oestreich sold ice cream). The "parlor" above was reserved for Sundays; on all other days its door was closed and the shades were drawn. A prudent woman, when her daughters' dresses were worn out, she ripped the seams, turned them inside out, and resewed them on the reverse side. And she required her sons, once a week, to scrub down by hand the brick paving in the back yard and alley in order to remove the "slippery greenness." But Mrs. Oestreich (the "good woman" of the pastor's encomium) also had a professional career of her own as a midwife and curer; on Sundays her husband drove her around the town and out to the mine patches, visiting the sick and bringing them food delicacies and herbal concoctions.[9]

Maurus Oestreich, and other Germans like him, had come from an essentially pre-industrial burgher society whose social ambience emphasized rank and duty and strong local loyalty. These values made entry into the formal economic and political order of the new country relatively easy. The transition from pre-industrial tradesman, building organs and altars, to industrial contractor raising up coal breakers was accomplished with little difficulty in Oestreich's case; and these same values no doubt made it possible for German mine workers to graduate in a short time from underground jobs to surface trades. The closest the Oestreichs' children came to participation in the ranks of industrial labor was working as breaker boys in their youth. They hated it; the acid water on the coal, they complained, made their hands red and sore.

But for two of the other ethnic groups—the English and the Welsh—the transition from the pre-industrial to the industrial world had already been accomplished. The vast majority of these British immigrants came from the mining districts of South Wales and the north of England—Lancashire, Yorkshire, and Durham—where the Industrial Revolution had proceeded farther than anywhere else in the world. The English in particular, as their forest fuels became scarce, had been engaged in the intensive mining of coal since the sixteenth century. By the eighteenth century, English coal miners had developed a specialized subculture of their own, often compared for its uniqueness to the customary lifestyle of English sailors. The typical English miners lived a somewhat isolated existence in mining villages that huddled about the pits (the prototype of the American mine "patch"). In the eighteenth century, before the great expansion in the market for coal and the consequent increase in the size and impersonality of colliery operations, the relations between masters (many of them lords of the realm) and pitmen were ordered by traditional rules determining wage rates, the right of the miner to a minimum income averaging fourteen or fifteen shillings a week through the year whether "the works went on or not," work hours, house rents, free coal, fines for sending up dirty coal, and so forth; magistrates enforced these traditional understandings. The village and its colliery constituted a social and economic unit comparable to a plantation. Among the workers, there existed a clear hierarchy, with the miners who worked at the face of the coal, the "hewers," at the top, and the "putters," the inexperienced men and boys and girls and women who pushed the trams loaded with the corves (baskets) of coal along the rails, at the bottom. Young recruits to the mine were subjected to initiation rites that were apt to involve decorating the genitals with grease and coal dust, symbolizing subordinate rank in the colliery's pecking order. Adult male miners were sometimes able to earn more than mere subsistence wages, and spent some of it, of course, on drinking, gambling, and attendance at the bloodier spectator sports such as bull-baiting and cockfights.[10] But there were other traditional modes of displaying one's success. One was the purchase of large and expensive carved mahogany furniture—bedsteads, chests of drawers, and chairs—that graced the clean, bare interiors of humble miners' dwellings. And another mode of conspicuous consumption was the wearing by pitmen, on holidays or on visits to the larger towns like Newcastle, of a gaudy livery characteristic of the mining district where the pitman was employed. The prosperous miner in the Newcastle area, for instance, affected a flowery display (an irony perhaps reflected, in the St. Clair area, in the names given to veins and localities, like "the Flowery Field" and "the Primrose Vein"). An early nineteenth-century observer, John Holland, recorded the dress the pitmen on holiday in Newcastle-upon-Tyne "formerly" wore:

> Their holiday waistcoats, called by them *Posey Jackets,* were frequently of very curious patterns, displaying flowers of various dyes: Their stockings mostly of blue, purple, pink, or mixed col-

ors. A great part of them used to have their hair very long, which on work-days was either tied in a queue, or rolled up in curls; but when drest in their best attire, it was commonly spread over their shoulders. Some of them wore two or three narrow ribbands round their hats, placed at equal distances, in which it was customary with them to insert one or more bunches of primroses or other flowers.[11]

In Staffordshire, on the other hand, it was shiny buttons rather than flowers:

Their working dress consists of trowsers and tunic of flannel; but their holiday clothes are generally of velveteen, rather profusely decorated with shining metal buttons: like their Newcastle brethren, they pique themselves on their garters, which are of worsted, very gay in colour, and so tied on that a great part as if by accident, appears, below the knee.[12]

And there were other features noted by Holland that express a well-established miners' culture in England: a custom of substituting opprobrious nicknames for legal names, not only in address but in reference; and the prevalence of miners' drinking songs and ballads—the "colliers rant"—very similar to the ones recorded by Korson.

But the semifeudal paternalistic relations between masters and workers was breaking down as English coal mines became deeper, bigger, and more dangerous. Before 1840 the typical British colliery employed fewer than fifty men, and even in the north, in Durham and Northumberland, the best-developed coal region in the kingdom, there were only twenty pits that employed more than 200. But in twenty years 200 men became an average figure. The deeper the colliery, the more extensive were the workings and the more difficult the problems of drainage and ventilation. The variations in the market cycle alternately depressed and raised wages as production slowed down and speeded up. To protect their interests, and to stabilize relations in the old mode, miners began to petition and even to strike, but strikes were met with violence and the importation of strikebreakers, often from distant parts such as Ireland, Scotland, or Wales. Unions were still treated by the courts as illegal combinations, but the masters encouraged their employees to organize benefit societies that insured miners against loss of wages as a result of accident and paid burial expenses. And, of course, the Primitive Methodists were encouraging miners to see themselves less as feudal retainers of the mine owner and more as God-fearing, respectable, and educated (or at least educable) citizens.[13]

Thus it was from a context of economic change that English miners were coming to the United States in the 1830's and '40's. They were men (and women) used to industrial discipline: early rising, specialization of labor, strict measurement of output, access to "privileges" (such as housing and fuel) conditional upon continued employment, a measure of collective responsibility in event of illness or injury, and some experience with union organization and class-conscious political activity. They accepted the presence of hierarchy in the organization of work as well as of society. But they resented the disorganizing effect of periodic layoffs and reductions of wages that, the masters now said, were necessitated by market conditions. Asked how he compared America with England, an English miner writing in the 1840's from somewhere "near Pottsville" said:

> With respect to that, I must say I would rather have this country by far than England, upon the whole, for several reasons, first, I would rather have the work, second, because provisions are cheaper. Third, because wages are always likely to be better than in England. Fourth, because we are always peaceable at our work compared with England. The times have been very hard, it is true, since I came, and during the winter there has been no money; but we had plenty to eat; and now, I trust we shall have cash winter and summer. . . . Dear friend, I am and ever shall feel grateful to you for the kind offer in your letter to get me back if this country did not suit me. But I am satisfied that the country is better for working men in general than England; the water is better than I have ever tasted about Staly Bridge; and I am lead to think it is better than any I ever tasted in England if possible. The land is one hundred dollars an acre, uncultivated, all about the coal region; I do not know what it is fit to cultivate. I have cultivated twenty-roods; and I can have hundred if I like, so long as I stop here, all for nothing. I pay half a dollar a week for the house.

There was a strike going on as he wrote, but still he was cheerful. "There is a better chance to get through a turn out here than in England, because the people are not so much afraid of their masters as they are in England." The strike was aimed not at resolving grievances about working conditions or work discipline, but at getting better wages from the mine operators. The English miner accepted the new industrial system, but in the United States he demanded more money for his work.[14]

The Welsh also came from an industrial region, albeit one more recently brought into the orbit of coal and iron. Most of Wales is a hilly country, not unlike the Appalachian highlands of Pennsylvania, and, before ironmasters and colliers began to exploit its mineral resources, rather a poor land. South Wales, particularly Pembrokeshire, had some anthracite, buried in deeply folded seams as in Pennsylvania, but until its use in smelting iron was discovered, the hard coals were neglected in favor of the rich bituminous beds to the north and east that supplied coke to great ironworks and steam coal to railways and steamships. In the 1840's and '50's the valley of Aberdare was growing rapidly as a colliery center, and a number of the Welsh residents of St. Clair and its neighborhood emigrated from there and from nearby Merthyr Tydfil. A few, including the Johns family, came from the anthracite district in Pembrokeshire. Clearly, St. Clair's Welsh population, and that of the surrounding districts, emigrated from the coal country of South Wales; most if not all of the men were experienced miners or practiced trades necessary to the operation of collieries and ironworks. They might not have had the depth of involvement in the culture of mining that the English immigrants had, but they were just as well trained in modern methods of mining. And they had the reputation for being "decidedly religiously inclined."

The main motive for emigration for the Welsh miners, as it was, presumably, for the English, was to escape from a situation of economic instability in the new, impersonal, market-dominated coal economy. Despite the constant long-term increase in the demand for coal, the seasonal and cyclical ups and downs of the market meant periods of unemployment or reduced wages in a land with a minimally developed system of social service. For some, it appeared that even unemployment in America was better than regular employment in Wales:

> . . . there are dozens if not hundreds who have not had a day's work in five or six months. As this country is better than Britain, generally, they have plenty of food and their board is furnished with delicacies which are not even seen on a workingman's table in Wales even when they are working regularly.

In Aberdare there was an emigration company that gathered up the hopeful emigrants and shipped them off "almost for nothing." One miner described the way the system worked:

> Another word about the plan adopted by some of the companies in the county mentioned for bringing emigrants here from Britain

and other places and leading them here to confusion. I knew before I left Aberdare, that N. M. Jones, Cymro Gwylit, had been raised to be an agent in some emigration society and that he is transporting men to the western world almost for nothing. Once I called at his office at Cross Inn, Trecynon—God save us all!—it was full of men who had come from every part of the valley, some to ask when they would start and others to get their name on the list and my instructions were to find what his conditions were. As near as I can remember, the chief agent in Britain at Liverpool received passage certificates from the company and passed them onto the various agents up and down the country. Names were taken together with the number in the family, for example, a husband, wife and two children, money was handed over to bind the agreement and all they had to do was to keep themselves in Liverpool until the emigration company took them to their destination. A house and everything would be waiting for them. After they reached the other side, they would work a year for the company, which deducted a quarter of their earnings every month until all the passage money was paid.

He went on to complain that in some cases the emigration companies brought Welsh miners over as strikebreakers "at the expense of the master."[15]

The Welsh thus were emigrating, like the English, in the hope of finding in America not freedom from industrial discipline, but stability of employment and better wages. They were already beginning to rely upon the strike as a device for persuading "the master" and to recognize the value of solidarity, of union organization, in confrontations with capital. Some Welsh even considered that the "unwavering loyalty of the Welsh in time of strike" was a part of the national heritage and spoke proudly of "the unbending determination of the old nation in such struggles."[16]

In contrast to all the rest, the Irish of St. Clair came for the most part from a land neither industrial nor urban. They were born not in the factory districts of Ulster nor in Dublin nor in the coastal towns of the south, but in the countrysides of Galway, Cork, Sligo, Cavan, and other agricultural counties.[17] Except for the region around Belfast, Ireland was still a preindustrial country most of whose population lived on small farms scattered among the fields, some owned by the farmer himself and some rented from absentee landlords (usually English). The Irish emigrated not because they expected to find another, slightly better Ireland in the New World, but because they were being forced away. Some were being evicted by land-lords who planned to enclose their estates and turn the land to pasturage for beef cattle, expecting a better profit from the sale of meat than from the collection of rents from cottagers. And some were being evicted for non-payment of rent, or were being forced to sell their holdings because the potato blight was ruining one of the country's staple crops. The estates of the Crown were shipping many off to America free of charge, whole vil-lages at a time; others scraped together, or borrowed, passage money suf-ficient to escape the enclosures, the workhouse, and the famine. Many went to England, where some stayed while others moved on, to America, Australia, or other countries; many came to America directly.

The typical Irish countryman did not identify with the state, which was an English governmental apparatus that worked largely in the interest of English, or Anglicized Irish, landlords. Nor did he identify with the town, which was apt to be an old English garrison site with a veneer of English and Irish shopkeepers. Policemen and courts were instruments of oppression. Without access to any modern industry at all, he had no ex-perience whatever in the work discipline of collieries and mills, where overseers and managers exercised an authoritarian prerogative to hire and fire, to lower wages arbitrarily, to set rigid hours of work, to dock piecework wages for poor quality, and to chastise workers verbally for violations of rules governing drinking, smoking, and the observance of safety proce-dures. He had no experience with craft unions and benefit clubs, so fa-miliar to the English, Welsh, and Germans. More exclusively than the others, the Irish countryman organized his work, his financial obligations, and his social relationships around a network of cooperative extended families, and to these he turned when he was in trouble. Cooperation meant, in "Hibernia," that related households exchanged labor during the mowing, the "boys" from one farm working for their uncles and cousins on another. And this friendly cooperation was repeated at weddings and wakes, when relatives got together, all contributing food and services to their uncles and aunts and cousins and in-laws according to traditional rules of exchange. Reciprocity was required and relatives who failed to live up to their traditional obligations were apt to be reminded by force—perhaps a beating by irate in-laws resentful of a man's neglect of their sister, or bullets fired through the window of a cottage whose aged childless owner had failed to devise it to the proper nephews. Even the few Irish shop-keepers in town were caught up in the web of kinship, dependent upon country cousins for their trade, obligated to entertain them on their visits to town and to hire young rural kinsmen when assistants were needed.[18]

Thus, in contrast to the other ethnic groups, with their allegiance to town and colliery and their reliance on union and club, the Irish were "clannish." Their wakes and weddings were family, not community, events; to kinsmen they turned in case of accident, or illness, or financial need; and injuries to a kinsman were a matter for kinsmen to avenge. Thus, in the winter of 1851, when an Irishman about fifty years of age—"an old man"—was killed by a train near Coal Castle north of St. Clair, his Irish relatives became so threatening that the engineer was warned not to take his engine into the town. No matter that the man had allegedly been drunk and had fallen off the cowcatcher on which he was hitching a ride. As the *Miners' Journal* reported:

> The deceased was extensively related, and had many friends about Coal Castle. They were greatly incensed by the accident, the more so because the same engine had run over and cut off a man's arm. . . .[19]

This was all very well for those Irish who did have kinfolk living nearby. But for the growing number of young, unmarried Irish males without parents or brothers and sisters or cousins, it was a lonely, strange, and threatening new world.

Yet, with these differences in political custom and industrial experience, there seems to have been a general sense among working people that ethnic boundaries were of minor importance in the face of chronic disaster. The common danger alienated the workers and their families from the landowners and the operators, but it promoted solidarity within each class. In the next two chapters we shall see how the two classes went about creating a new cognitive world in response to the problems of mining anthracite.

IV

ILLUSIONS OF THE COAL TRADE

The first response of the industrialists to bad news about the coal trade was denial that the fault was theirs. Pessimistic reports by geologists about the places where landowners and operators had sunk their mines were passed off as mere theories concocted by mischievous college professors who had failed to consult experienced miners. Market prices that fell below the cost of production were blamed on tariff policy or transportation rates rather than on high production costs. Among the St. Clair developers, Enoch McGinness and Henry Carey were selected as heroes of the coal trade not primarily because they were daring industrial developers but because they created comforting illusions. McGinness touted a geological theory that contradicted certain findings of the state geologist and put forward in their stead a doctrine that inspired a generation of colliery operators to sink deep shafts in the wrong places. And Carey assured the coal trade that the low profit margin and high failure rate of Schuylkill County collieries was the result not of excessively high production costs, but of outrageously low tariff barriers against British iron. These two illusions were jointly responsible for the persistence of the operators in trying to extract coal from formations that were too deep, too steeply pitched, too gassy, and too extensively faulted to permit safe and economical operation.

HENRY CAREY AND PROTECTIONISM

Although Henry Carey did not begin to entertain pro-tariff views until 1842, he may well have been introduced to the pro-tariff doctrine, and to the idea of investing in the coal trade, some years earlier by a German refugee, Friedrich List, an associate of his father's. List was already famous in Europe—perhaps notorious would be a better word—for his radical economic views. In lectures and books he had preached the unification

184

of the German states by means of a program of internal improvements, particularly roads, canals, and (eventually) railroads, and of legal reform, including the elimination of internal customs duties and the protection of nascent German industries by high tariffs. He accompanied General Lafayette on his triumphal tour of the United States in 1825, thereby gaining the acquaintance of the political and economic elite of the country. Settling in Pennsylvania, he quickly became a close friend of Stephen Girard (and may even have advised Girard to make his purchase of coal lands in 1830). And, most particularly relevant to the history of St. Clair, his advocacy of the protective tariff for developing nations brought him, in 1826, to the attention of the Pennsylvania Society for the Encouragement of Manufactures and Mechanic Arts, a pro-tariff political-action committee headed by C. Jared Ingersoll and Matthew Carey. The society employed List to write a series of pro-tariff pamphlets. These quickly caught the attention of American statesmen; List became an adviser to Henry Clay. Matthew Carey's son Henry must have known List and read his works and it is perhaps not an accident that Henry Carey virtually duplicated List's career, entering the coal trade shortly after List and developing a school of economic nationalism that applied List's theories to American conditions.[1]

List had another, more particular contribution to make to the development of the coal trade, however. He was one of the pioneers of railroad construction in the anthracite district and an early investor in coal lands in the Pottsville Basin. In 1828, List was a resident of Reading, a community of German-speaking craftsmen south of the Blue Mountain, where he edited a German-language newspaper. List had studied some geology during his early years in Germany. In company with Isaac Hiester, a local physician with a medical degree from the University of Pennsylvania, he explored the region around Tamaqua, some miles east of Pottsville. Recognizing that the outcrops signified more extensive veins under the surface, they purchased a large tract of coal lands, and then proceeded to secure an amended canal charter that permitted the construction of a railroad to connect Tamaqua with Port Clinton on the Schuylkill Canal, twenty-two and a half miles away. Hiester served as president and List as vice-president of the new company, the Little Schuylkill Navigation, Railroad, and Coal Company, and both served on the board of managers. They secured the services of one of the leading civil engineers of the day, Moncure Robinson, to survey the route and superintend construction. The line was opened officially at a grand celebration at Port Clinton in November 1831; but by that time List was on his way to Europe as U.S. Consul at Leipzig. His mission there was to open the European market for American anthracite.[2]

Carey's interest in tariff protection may have been awakened by List in the late 1820's, but he retained the public image of a free-trader for another fifteen years. In 1835, as his acquisition of coal lands began, he declared with Benthamite optimism (and a side glance at Adam Smith's preoccupation with mere wealth) that "the great object of political economy, and its chief claim to attention, is *the promotion of the happiness of nations.*"[3] Most of his book *Essay on the Rate of Wages* was devoted to proving that the free American economy was the most favorable in the world for the workingman as well as the capitalist.

> Secure in person and property, comparatively free from taxation, unrestrained in action, comparatively so in all matters of trade, and very industrious, the people of this country, applying their labour in the way which they think will produce the largest reward, find their capital rapidly augment; the consequence of which is, that mines are opened in all directions, new lands are brought into cultivation, railroads and canals are constructed and machinery is applied in every way to increase the produce of labour. Capital flows from all quarters to this country, where it can be best paid for, and, increasing the demand for labour, finds employment not only for the vast natural increase of population, but for great numbers who are led to seek there an improvement of their condition. The fund out of which the labourer is paid is larger, and his wages are consequently greater, than in any other country.[4]

By Carey's criteria, America was the happiest of nations. After 1842, however, he poured forth an unceasing stream of pro-tariff books, pamphlets, letters to newspapers, and personal correspondence with influential public figures, and in the famous "Carey Vespers" promoted his views in person. Carey's conversion to the protectionist doctrine—popular among textile manufacturers long before it was applied to the interests of the coal trade— would seem to have been prompted by two events. First, by 1842 it had become apparent that the Carey group's investment in the coal tracts about Pottsville were not going to be profitable and that the mines at St. Clair would have to be developed instead of those at Guinea Hill and Westwood. And, second, the successful use in Pennsylvania after 1839 of the hot-blast process for smelting iron with anthracite suddenly made the idea of a protective tariff irresistibly appealing. Coal men did not seriously fear that England would flood the market with British coal. But if British iron could be made more expensive, the market for Pennsylvania iron smelted with anthracite would undoubtedly expand, permitting both higher prices and increased production. And a protective tariff of some importance was in fact instituted in 1842.

Representative of Carey's arguments are his essays on *Coal, Its Producers and Consumers.* They were written in 1854 (the last signed in Pottsville on September 29, 1854) and published under the pseudonym "An Owner of Coal Mines." In that year, anthracite prices (i.e., the price paid by the dealer to the colliery operator) had risen to their highest point in a decade in New York ($6 per ton for white-ash and $5.75 for red-ash from Carey's mines at St. Clair). There was public complaint about these high prices and Congress was being petitioned to remit the current 30 percent *ad valorem* tariff on imported coal. The imported coal was bituminous, not anthracite, and the total import for 1852 and 1853 was only 414,523 tons, while the total quantity of domestic anthracite shipped to market was 10,098,000 tons—twenty-four times as much. At the present time, Carey concluded, a duty of $3 per ton on pig and $6 per ton on bar iron would be more helpful to the coal trade than $50 per ton on imported coal. Carey then went on to review the experience of earlier years, when opposition to the tariff on coal and iron had conspired with periodic economic crises to embarrass the coal trade. The years from 1837 through 1842 had been ruinous; then the market rose, only to collapse again in 1848 through 1851, as a result of a decline in the iron trade. The market thus went up and down; yet Carey's statistics showed that anthracite production steadily increased, year after year, from about 1,000,000 tons in 1841 to over 5,000,000 in 1853. And why did not coal production vary with the rise and fall of the economy? Because, Carey explained (no doubt on the basis of his own business experience), the colliery operator had to plan two or three years in advance:

> Until recently, it has generally, as we are informed, been calculated that coal might begin to be sent to market in about a year from the time the spade had been first put into the ground. With the gradual development of the trade, however, more extensive and expensive works are found to be requisite, and it is precisely as capital has thus been applied to the business, that the commodity has been cheaply furnished. Many of the works recently established have cost, as we are informed, from $50,000 to $100,000, while one that is as yet but very partially in operation [i.e., the St. Clair Shaft], we are assured, already cost much more than the latter sum. To expend so large an amount of money on a spot upon which but few can work, requires, of course, much time. . . .

The result was successive waves of ruin. Thus, for instance, the landowners, mine operators, and canal and railroad companies that had invested some $60,000,000 in the coal trade in the 1830's were in 1841 almost universally ruined by "British free trade." Anthracite sold for less than it cost to produce:

> The actual cost of a ton of coal, however, at that time, paying any reasonable wages to the people engaged in mining it, and any fair compensation for the labor of transportation, could not have been less than three dollars, or nearly the price at which it sold, leaving nothing for the owner of the land, nothing for the wear and tear of machinery, nothing for the use of railroads and canals, and nothing for the commission merchants.

Carey went on to paint an apocalyptic landscape of the coal regions in the 1840's:

> ... the whole of the great coal region was one vast scene of desolation. Mines everywhere abandoned, and machinery everywhere going to ruin. Houses were tenantless. Rails were being worn out, and roads were becoming impassable for want of means to repair them. Canal boats were being used up, and none were being built. . . . It was, however, as is always the case with the periods of British free trade, a time of harvest for the middle men dealers in coal. They could do a large business on a small capital, and the coal operators were so distressed that they were willing to accept money on any terms.

Indeed, Carey's theme was a paean of praise for those engaged in the coal trade and a jeremiad against all those—free-traders, coal dealers, New York newspapers, "penny-a-liner" journalists, unthinking domestic consumers of coal—who were responsible for the unsteadiness of the market. *"It is a steady and growing market that we need, and not increase of price."* In his characteristically paranoid style, he accused the public of a kind of conspiracy against "our trade which is at once the most important and most difficult of all you know."

> All the profits that ever have been realized in the coal region have been put back again. Were you here I could show you that scarcely any one has ever carried anything away with him. Landowners

expend their rents, and operators their profits, when they have any, in preparations for further improvements, and so it is with canal and railroad stockholders; and were a proper estimate now made of the labor and capital that have been applied to the improvement of the land, it would amount to a hundred millions of dollars, *or more than would pay for all the shipping employed in the foreign trade*. Nevertheless, this great trade is treated as if we were a set of paupers soliciting contributions from the people whom it has enriched, while it has beggared nearly all the people who have contributed the labor and capital by which it has been built up.

And he concluded, "The more good we do, . . . the more enemies we make."[5]

Carey's arguments, hardly different in style from editorial polemics in the *Miners' Journal,* gained added credibility with concerned readers because Carey placed them in the context of a larger philosophical system. Carey saw himself as America's premier political economist, in the tradition of Adam Smith; Malthus and Ricardo were his competitors; he did not hesitate to "swear like a bargeman" when opposing opinions were cited from the works of John Stuart Mill and Herbert Spencer. He regarded his views as products of "social science." Carey took seriously the idea that if it is to be called a science, the study of society must be based on the assumption that social life is governed by the same laws as those revealed by the natural sciences. But this was a vacuous proposition and Carey advanced nothing more in the way of example than metaphorical language, suggesting analogies between planetary motion and human migration, or gravitation and the tendency of human beings to associate. He paid little attention to scientific method beyond recommending the more extensive use of statistics in social science; but he did pioneer in the use of such statistics and in systematic comparisons of national economies. Carey considered himself, and some of his followers considered him, to be an intellectual giant, and he believed that his great discovery—that the laws of society are identical with the laws of physics and chemistry—put him in the company of Galileo, Harvey, and Newton.

If we strip away the pseudoscientific scaffolding of Carey's thought, however, we find an interesting set of ideas. Carey believed that it was in the nature of man to "associate," and that from "association" come all the good things, all the utilities, that man desires. Association was not very clearly defined, but in most contexts it seems to have implied an economic exchange between diverse partners, each bearing a different service, commodity, or idea. Maximum division of labor entailed maximum exchange capability and maximum productivity. As population increased too, the possibilities of association and therefore of productivity increased (thus denying the dismal predictions of Ricardo and Malthus). Capital and labor would prosper together rather than compete for ever diminishing resources. Government, like foreign trade, should be small and unobtrusive, leaving people free to form spontaneous associations. Furthermore, the productivity of the soil (and of mineral deposits, including coal) increased rather than decreased over time because, he argued, only the inferior soils and surface deposits could be cultivated in the early years of a society; reaching the rich, forested soils (and deep measures of coal and metal) required the higher technology that only advanced societies could provide. Carey declared this principle to be the "great fundamental truth" of social science.[6]

Carey applied this conception to his own investment policy (or perhaps it was the other way around). St. Clair had been settled before the bottom lands along Mill Creek because hillsides covered with scrub were always easier to develop than heavily timbered lowlands. Recalling his first visit to St. Clair, he described it as being, in 1835, an economic frontier:

> If, passing northward from the Schuylkill River, we trace its little tributary, Mill Creek, to its source, we see miles of fine meadowland, still covered with the original timber, with but here and there a patch of cleared land: while on the hillsides may be seen occasional little farms, the houses on which bear every mark of considerable age. Arriving at the little town of St. Clair, . . . the site of which three years since was covered with timber growing on land fitted to make the finest meadows, but much of it then a mere marsh, we see, far up the hill, the residence of the first owner of this large body of fertile land, and may judge for ourselves the original character of the soil selected for cultivation from the small pines and hemlocks on that immediately adjacent; and yet the style of the house proves him to have been of the better class of the settlers of half a century past, when population was thin, and good land abundant, but wealth scarce.[7]

In Carey's eye, wilderness would inevitably give way to cultivation and industrial development. In the first volume of his *Principles of Political Economy* (published in 1837) he described the future of St. Clair, and of the rest of the world, as a vista of unlimited splendor. Not for him the dismal economic doctrines of Ricardo and Malthus, who foresaw an endless tragedy for the bulk of mankind as population increased and wages fell to starvation levels in a cruel play of checks and balances. For Carey, the past fifty years of mankind's experience, coinciding with what would soon be called the "Industrial Revolution," had shown that investment of capital in new machinery could produce unlimited wealth for the worker as well as the capitalist.

> We now possess no means of measuring the extent of the powers of the earth. It produces now vastly more than it did half a century since, and the close of the present century will see it rendered greatly more productive than at present. When we cast our eyes over the surface of the globe, and see how large is the portion that is yet *totally unoccupied*—how large a portion of that which appears to be occupied is really so, only to the extent that its powers can be reached with the worst machinery, and that the chief part of those powers is, as yet, unappropriated, . . .—that twice, or thrice, ten, or twenty, or fifty times the population could be supported, even with our present agricultural knowledge, on land that is now partially cultivated—and that there is a great extension of production as science is brought to the aid of the agriculturalist, we cannot hesitate to admit that the productive power of land exists in *measureless quantity.*[8]

And this principle of unlimited production applied to coal mining as well as to agriculture, as British experience showed:

> If the owner of a coal mine . . . follow the example of the farmer, in investing a portion of the produce in the continuation of his shaft, he finds new seams of coal, and a continued increase in the ability to yield rent, as has been the case with the coal mines of England. The shafts are constantly being sunk deeper, accompanied by constantly increasing value in the land, which is vastly greater now, when they are obliged to go to the depth of 100 or 150 fathoms, than they were half a century since, when such expenditure was unnecessary. . . . The lower strata of coal are in the situation of the dormant powers of land subjected to cultivation. When coal mines are worked with indifferent machinery, capable of extracting the coal from only a moderate depth, the land is soon worked out, and abandoned. Increased capital en-

ables the miner to descend double the distance, and the value is now greater than at first. A further application of capital enables him to descend successively 300, 500, 600, 1000, or 1500 feet, and with every successive application the property acquires a higher value, notwithstanding the quantity of coal that has been taken out.[9]

In the natural course of events, the optimum development of the power of association would occur in relatively small regions. Nowhere was Carey very precise about the size of these regions, and it is evidently an enveloping concept; the community may be as small as a township, as large as a state, or even include the whole nation. But the essence of the idea is that there should be a community with a rich, diversified economy, such that industry and agriculture may exchange products in an internal trade. One of Carey's letters on the subject of the protective tariff, published in the *Miners' Journal,* described the concept of the communal association as it normally existed in America:

> All our institutions find their foundation in local development, tending to the creation of thriving towns and villages in the neighborhood of our vast deposits of lead, copper, zinc, and iron— there making a market for the products of agriculture, and giving occasion to the improvement of our great water powers, to be used in the conversion of [cotton] and wool into cloth, and wood, coal, and ore into knives and axes, steam engines and railroad cars.[10]

Carey lived from 1833 to 1855 in the small town of Burlington, New Jersey, across the Delaware River from Philadelphia, but his image of "local development" was based on the New England village and on the image of the English mining town enshrined in Baird's dream of Westwood. Surrounded by farms, each village had its own shoemaker, blacksmith, mason, and other artisans, its own savings bank where artisans and farmers accumulated their money in order to open shops, to buy land, or even to set up a cotton mill with the help of small investors—"shoemakers, seamstresses, farmers, lawyers, widows, and orphans." As one of his more perceptive biographers has characterized Carey's view:

> In the perfect community every townsman would own his house and lot, with perfect security of person and property, and there

would prevail an intense civic pride in good management. Local demands for labor would offer inducements to youth. Timber would be cleared, fertile acres farmed, manure applied to poorer lands, swamps drained to make meadows; dairy products would be increased for consumption in nearby towns; sawmills would attract sawyers to consume food raised on the farms, while blacksmiths, tailors, hatters, printers and other craftsmen would further diversify the economic life. Intensive agriculture, including mechanized farming methods, would result in the division of farms into smaller but more efficient units; railroads [in part locally owned] would be feeder lines to bring in iron and coal, and thus create more capital.[11]

And indeed St. Clair grew in much the way Carey described the Yankee village, except that coal took the place of farming in the town's economy.

St. Clair in 1873

193

This small-town imagery was akin to the utopian socialist imagery that inspired the followers of Robert Owen at New Harmony and of Fourier at Brook Farm (and Carey may have been influenced, as Horace Greeley was, by the Fourierist "Associationists"). But, unlike the socialists, Carey blandly assumed that there was a natural harmony of interests between agriculture and industry and between capital and labor which only artificial interventions could disrupt. Carey did not believe that unemployment was a serious problem; he called it "labor competition" and considered it to be a temporary difficulty that would be removed by the natural growth of the economy. His system required competition between capitalists; it required it between workers as well. Only monopoly was wrong. Labor unions, and strikes over wages and hours, he deplored as interruptions of the growth of business, but limited-liability corporations were expressions of the principle of association. Public poor relief, and private charity as well, he opposed sternly (although he was supportive of miners' safety legislation) as interference with the natural self-healing principle of association. He objected to the abolition of slavery by legislation, on the ground that the growth of the economy, by making slaves more valuable and thus more expensive to maintain, would eventually make them more costly than free labor, and at that time the peculiar institution would come to a natural end. And he was a consistent opponent of excise and income taxes; the less government, the better. Government should confine its intervention in the lives of the citizenry to the preservation of life and property from crime, to the maintenance of adequate armed forces, and—of supreme importance— to the collection of duties upon foreign imports.

Carey deplored some of the social evils that afflicted urban America— pauperism, prostitution, crime, gambling (including financial speculation), poor housing and sanitation—but he did not attribute them to class exploitation. There was one single cause for any disparity between ideal and real: the British system of free trade. He believed that it was British policy to reduce the rest of the world to colonial or neo-colonial status by a system of "free trade" that kept the underdeveloped countries selling Britain their raw materials—agricultural and mineral products—and buying back British manufactured goods. In order to destroy any nascent industry, the British would sell at low prices or even at a loss. The result was the inhibition of the free working of the principle of association, the abortion of the division of labor, and the stifling of economic growth. Utopia could only be realized, and preserved, by setting up a tariff wall around America that protected the natural process of local development. International trade in general, and even internal trade requiring costly transport, was to be avoided; transportation was a "tax" on commerce. After 1840 most of Carey's writing and conversation was devoted to this one topic: with the concentration of a monomaniac, he attributed every ill to Britain and free trade, and promised every benefit from the protective tariff.

Carey regarded Great Britain as the great international oppressor. As an Irish nationalist, son of a refugee from English-occupied Ireland, he opposed not only the British in Ireland but also British worldwide neo-colonialism. The doctrine of free trade, developed by the classical econo-mists of England, he considered to be a specious rationalization of British economic domination of the world economy and a false justification for the pauperization of labor. With the images of British women and girls labor-ing half naked in coal mines and British children chained to cotton-spinning machinery in Manchester ever present—the American press never ceased to point out the negative face of the Industrial Revolution in England—Carey argued that only the protective tariff could save American labor from such degradation and poverty. The tariff would keep out cheap goods produced by underpaid Europeans and permit—nay, force—the American capitalist to pay higher, and ever rising, rates of wages. "The object of protection," he said, "is to produce dear labour." But with American labor adequately paid, and constantly employed, by prosperous capitalists, the American workingman could not only feed, house, and clothe himself and his family properly, but could also cultivate his mind and sensibilities. The individual worker would be a sturdy individualist, selling his labor by free contract, needing no public charity nor union nor protective legislation to support his interest.

Carey's narrow preoccupation with the protectionist issue in most of his writing meant that, despite the titles of his supposedly general works, *Principles of Social Science* (1858–1859) and *The Unity of Law* (1872), he had little impact on academic social science and the social-science move-ment. The social-science movement was essentially an effort to apply sci-entific method to social reform, focusing on the conventionally recognized social problems of the day: crime, prostitution, illiteracy, intemperance, and disease. The American Social Science Association was founded in 1865 and spawned a number of still-existing professional associations—the American Economic Association, the American Political Science As-sociation, the American Sociological Association, and the American Acad-emy of Political and Social Science. Carey never published in the *Journal of Social Science*, the original association's organ, and never participated as more than an "honorary member." His chief impact on academia probably was achieved through the agency of Joseph Wharton, another Philadelphia coal-and-iron millionaire, who, when he founded the Wharton School, dictated that the principle of protectionism be communicated to its students. The Wharton School in its early years was indeed unique among business schools in teaching not only economics but also sociology and political science. But Carey's work had little to do with the development of modern academic social science. His views were rarely mentioned, and then not with favor, by the leaders of American sociology in the latter part of the nineteenth century. And pioneering sociological studies of the anthracite region by Peter Roberts, a Yale graduate student from Scranton, whose dissertation was supervised by William Graham Sumner, took a view wholly different from Carey's old "harmony of interests." Roberts was an avowed apologist for capitalism, a lapsed utopian socialist converted to the view that "self-preservation is the first law of nature." Sumner was a staunch free-trader and the prototypical Darwinist, and his student Roberts in *The Anthracite Industry* (1901) and *Anthracite Communities* (1904) depicted a coal district red in tooth and claw, with degenerate Irishmen and ignorant Slavs struggling for survival against each other and the common foe, the coal corporations. Sumner in his introduction to the first work even described the region's family life, schools, and churches as "strange or hostile to our civilization."[12] Roberts was writing, of course, about a later generation than Carey's, a generation that by the time of his second book had seen the great strike in 1902 and had come to realize that there were serious social conflicts in the coal fields whose perpetuation boded ill for American industry. Carey's general optimism and his readiness to offer tariff protection as the sovereign remedy for all social ills could have no place in the social Darwinist tradition.

But if he was ignored by social scientists, Carey was a charismatic leader to businessmen and their political representatives. The protectionist doctrine was irresistibly attractive to the rulers of the coal-and-iron trade. It absolved the employer of blame for low wages, dangerous working conditions, and intermittent unemployment; it declared that the employer was forced against his will to skimp and cut corners because the tariff was too low and in consequence foreign competition depressed the market. And, of course, a languishing iron industry was a threat to the national defense. But, on the other hand, the coal operators and ironmasters were doing something about the problem by signing petitions and supporting the campaign of right-thinking political representatives. Carey's personal reputation was enormous and he became the central figure of the "Pennsylvania School" of political economy. He was quoted and paraphrased at length in the pages of the *Miners' Journal* and in Daddow and Bannan's *Coal, Iron, and Oil* (1866). Horace Greeley, editor of the *New York Tribune,* and E. Peshine Smith, an attorney who became adviser to William H. Seward, were devoted followers, and in 1853 Smith even published a college text-book propounding Carey's views. Carey's friend Stephen Colwell, a Pennsylvania ironmaster and evangelical Presbyterian layman, published influential protectionist tracts along lines similar to Carey's. David Ames Wells, a writer of popular manuals on the sciences aimed at the "working classes," repeated Carey's views on protectionism in an American edition of Charles Knight's *Knowledge Is Power* (1857).[13]

Carey was also able to promulgate his views to distinguished guests at the famous "Carey Vespers," the most notable salon in America. Among the local men of affairs who were regulars at the vespers were Condy Raguet, free-trader and former United States minister to Brazil; Henry Vethake, professor of moral philosophy and political economy at the University of Pennsylvania; Judge William D. Kelly ("Pig Iron Kelly"), staunch advocate of protectionism in Congress; Joseph Wharton, and other prominent editors and political economists of Philadelphia. Well-known politicians like Ulysses S. Grant, James G. Blaine, and General Robert Patterson sat at the round table when they were in town, and visiting literary folk, including Charles Dickens and Ralph Waldo Emerson, made it a point to visit with Carey when they passed through Philadelphia. A contemporary description of the vespers at Carey's brick row house on Walnut Street gives something of the flavor of these occasions:

> Mr. Carey had so many books that he turned his front and back parlors (the drawing and dining rooms) into a library. The entire place was filled with literature and works of art. In the back parlor stood two white marble statues: the one of Truth, the other of Silence. In the centre of the room was the famous Round Table. Every Sunday at two o'clock three bottles of exquisite hock wines were deposited at the feet of these statues: a Marcobrunner and bronze Johannisberger at the feet of Truth, a Dom Deehanay at the feet of Silence . . . his guests were due at three o'clock and were always remarkably prompt. So soon as two or three guests arrived Mr. Carey and his company took their seats at the Round Table. Before each person stood a red Hungarian glass. The first bottle, the Marcobrunner, was then opened and passed around, when the conversation began. At the end of about an hour the second bottle, the Johannisberger, was opened and passed around. At the end of another hour, the third bottle, the Auglese, was

opened and passed around. When the bottle was exhausted, the company usually broke up.[14]

But perhaps Carey's most loyal and enduring convert was his own nephew Henry Carey Baird, son of Eliza Baird of Pottsville. In the fall of 1857, young Baird, then thirty-two, read his uncle's article on "Money" in *Hunt's Magazine* and, interested, went on to read his uncle's books. Baird experienced a sudden change in world view; he was so excited he was almost sleepless at night. He now realized that the laws of human behavior were "as fixed and immutable as the laws which govern the movement of the planets" and man, if he acted in accordance, would be released from his chains and "perfect harmony will exist in all the movements of mankind." He thought *The Harmony of Interests* (1852), with its emphasis on Carey's theory of "association" as the basis of economic behavior, the most important book of the century. "I have been convinced of the truth of this theory," he confessed, "by an irresistible storm which I never before experienced, and which cannot be adequately described."[15]

So charismatic a figure as Carey could not be kept from participating in the active political arena. Although Carey did not enjoy speaking in public and consistently refused to run for public office, he was considered for a time as a possible Vice-Presidential candidate and was touted by his friends as a potential Secretary of the Treasury. He corresponded, both privately and in public letters, with many of the most influential state and federal legislators and executives. A particularly close associate was Senator Simon Cameron, erstwhile ironmaster, a former Know Nothing anti-Catholic, the political boss of the Pennsylvania Republican Party, and, as Senator, a loyal advocate of protectionism in the halls of Congress. Carey did not personally like Cameron, called him a "shirt of Nessus" (unbearably painful), and he would later write to President Lincoln, urging him not to appoint Cameron as Secretary of War because Cameron was so dishonest.[16] But Carey was not one to avoid mixing business with politics and in 1858 he brought Cameron in as a partner in the acquisition, for the sum of $72,300, of the lands of the North American Coal Company. It is not clear how much, if anything, Senator Cameron put up. Another partner in this venture was the aristocratic leader of Schuylkill County Democrats, Pottsville attorney Francis W. Hughes. Hughes had read law with George W. Farquhar, amassed a fortune from legal practice and the coal trade, and had served in the state senate and as Secretary of the Commonwealth. A third partner was Carey's neighbor, friend, and political confidant William D. Lewis, an old Whig businessman who had served as

Collector of Customs of the Port of Philadelphia and at twenty-two had served as Henry Clay's private secretary during the negotiations to end the War of 1812. Carey's associate in the St. Clair Tract, Abraham Hart, was the fourth partner. Cameron and Hughes, the active politicians, were not named as "Trustees" in the published report of the reorganized company and seem to have functioned as silent partners. This acquisition gave Carey, as chairman of the trustees, and Hart as treasurer, administrative control of the North American and thus of virtually all the coal land between St. Clair, Pottsville, and Port Carbon, a total of about 2,000 acres of coal reserves, placing Carey and his partners for a time among the largest owners in the region.[17]

Simon Cameron as a politician, of course, had friends in Pottsville. He knew Benjamin Haywood well, did favors for him in Washington, and persuaded him to construct an ironworks in Dauphin County, Cameron's home ground. He himself, in fact, had been a partner in an ironworks in Luzerne County a few years before. In June 1858, Cameron and the president of the Reading Railroad escorted a distinguished diplomatic party including the French Ambassador and Lord Napier, Minister Plenipotentiary from Great Britain, on a tour by special train of the Pottsville industrial district. In addition to a walk through Haywood's Palo Alto Rolling Mill, "the entire party visited several collieries at St. Clair, and inspected them."[18] Cameron had been returned to the Senate in 1856 as a Republican and he was an ardent opponent of the weak tariff of 1857, which reduced duties 20 percent. His argument was calculated to secure him the support not only of the men of capital, particularly in the iron-and-coal trade, but also of the laboring men whom they employed. Cameron urged the workers to vote the pro-tariff Republican ticket because it was in their own and the country's interest. Despite Carey's professed loathing, Cameron frequently stopped in for a glass of wine and a political chat with Carey when he was in Philadelphia, for Cameron's views on the tariff and its blessing for the working class were in perfect accord with Carey's own. Together they talked endlessly in the smoke-filled rooms, persuading their colleagues that the Republican Party platform must include a strong-tariff plank.

It is easier to recognize Carey's contribution to an evolving American political ideology that considered the protective tariff, low taxes, and free labor to be the keys to economic paradise, than to measure the impact of his ideas on the town he founded, St. Clair. His values were not unique, and other, less articulate town fathers set up similar communities. Nevertheless, Carey clearly obeyed his own principles. In the real-estate development program he initiated after 1842, when he was converted to protectionism, he deliberately encouraged the purchase of town lots (surface rights only) by a diversity of interests: miners and mine operators, of course, but also an ironmaster, engineers, hotel keepers, tradesmen of all kinds, different churches and schools and fraternal orders, and a variety of immigrant ethnic groups with somewhat different traditional skills. He nurtured a variety of new mining technologies; and, as McGinness said to him, he liked to "go deep." St. Clair from the first was a prime example of the application of Carey's principle of association, an organization of diversity, a rich if somewhat disorderly network of economic and social exchange in a small region. In this it was far different, and far more fit to survive, than the dreary mine patches around it, patches consisting of identical, cheaply built, rental houses along muddy, unpaved streets strung out along a railroad under the shadow of the breaker. Only miners and laborers and a few churches and stores located themselves in the patches; and when the colliery closed down, the patch was abandoned, the houses rotted away, and in a few years the patch itself passed into oblivion. St. Clair, by contrast, would in time survive the closing of its mines.

St. Clair, however, was no utopia, and its fate was determined in part by forces that had no place in Carey's model world. Carey correctly perceived the growing conflict between the underdeveloped countries (such as the United States, Ireland, India, and Turkey) and the imperialistic industrial state (Great Britain); but his picture of the better life behind tariff walls was an eighteenth-century landscape, with shepherds and farmers on one side, and mechanics and miners on the other, and a small town with church steeples in the background. He did not in his writings come to grips with the realities of class conflict; he did not perceive the advance of a proletariat, an army of laborers without trade skills or property, alongside his farmers and mechanics; he did not allow for the possibility of permanent unemployment; he did not recognize the growth of monopoly, even though he finally sold all his property at St. Clair to the avowedly monopolistic Philadelphia and Reading Coal and Iron Company. An awareness of these things would come to younger men.

GEOLOGICAL FACT AND COAL-TRADE FANTASIES

When the Carey group arrived, the anthracite fields of Pennsylvania had already become an object of intense interest to some of the most competent scientists and engineers of the new republic. The elder Benjamin Silliman, influential editor of the *American Journal of Science and Arts,* made a personal horseback survey of the mines in the Wyoming Valley and about Mauch Chunk in 1830.[1] Within a few years, eminent men, or men destined to become eminent, from two main fields of knowledge—geology and chemistry—began to devote their time to the better understanding of coal and its uses. In contrast to the situation in another developing industry, cotton manufacturing, now becoming important in the northeastern states, the exploitation of coal from the first required an intensive input of scientific and technical skill. When Carey entered the field, therefore, he was well aware that a major research-and-development effort was under way.

Scientific interest in the newly popular American coals began in the 1820's with physical and chemical analyses and the comparison of coals from different districts. The results were regularly published in the standard scientific journals of the day. Benjamin Silliman compared the coals of Rhode Island, the Lehigh River valley, and the Schuylkill district early in the 1830's; Henry Darwin Rogers and Alexander Dallas Bache analyzed the ash of the hard coal from Tamaqua and compared it with a bituminous specimen from the western part of the state in a paper published in 1834.[2] Geological interest developed soon after and the Geological Society of Pennsylvania, newly formed in 1832, repeatedly petitioned the legislature to authorize a complete geological survey of the commonwealth. Virginia and New Jersey had already commenced such surveys and in 1836 Pennsylvania followed their example. Such an expenditure of funds fitted the established policy of state financing of public works like canals, turnpikes, and harbors, which stimulated the extension of private enterprise into hitherto unexploited regions and pulled together the state's regions into an effective economic network. Even capitalist Henry Carey—like his father, Matthew, a vociferous propagandist for canals—approved of public works. So the bill, passed in March 1836, authorized a five-year survey to be conducted by a state geologist, geological assistants, and chemists. The state geologist, appointed in 1836 and continuing to act as director of the survey until the final report was eventually printed in 1858, was Henry Darwin Rogers.

The choice was superb. At twenty-seven, Rogers was professor of mineralogy and geology at the University of Pennsylvania and director of the Geological Survey of New Jersey, which had begun in 1835 and would be completed in 1838. His elder brother William was director of the Geological Survey of Virginia. The two men collaborated closely in the field, in the development of theory, and in publication. Two other brothers, Robert and James, were noted chemists and authors of an early chemistry textbook; Robert would become the Pennsylvania survey's chief chemist. And Henry's entry into geology actually came *via* chemistry. Trained in that field by his father, a physician who had fled Ireland, as did Henry Carey's father, after the abortive rebellion of 1798, he had begun his career as a professor of chemistry, including two years at Dickinson College at Carlisle, Pennsylvania, near Harrisburg. Henry was an admirer of utopian socialist Robert Owen, and, finding little sympathy for this point of view at Dickinson, he resigned and in 1832 went to England with Robert Owen's son, Robert Dale Owen. Young Owen, a geologist, took him to meetings of the Royal Geological Society of London, where he met Lyell and other leading scientists. He converted to geology as a profession, joined the Geological Society, and on his return to the United States in 1833 began giving lectures on geology at the Franklin Institute, and soon after at the University of Pennsylvania.[3]

Rogers recruited a remarkable corps of field and laboratory assistants during the first six years (1836–1842) of fieldwork, and an equally distinguished group assembled to complete the survey in a second round of four seasons (1851–1854). Of the twenty-three men who served with Rogers as technical or scientific staff in the ten summer "campaigns," eleven were later to become members of the American Philosophical Society (to which Henry Carey and his brother-in-law and business partner Isaac Lea already belonged); they and others went on to enjoy long and influential careers on the faculties of American colleges and universities and in the national scientific societies, including the American Geological Society, the American Association for the Advancement of Science, and the National Academy of Sciences; and three of them were to become important contributors to the development of the anthracite and iron industries. Seldom has a state been served by such an outstanding scientific cadre.

Because the existing quarries, tunnels, and drifts into its coal formations provided the geologists with unexcelled opportunities to observe the successive strata of rock and coal, much of the survey was conducted in the southern anthracite region. This meant that each summer a little band of enthusiastic young men armed with picks, notebooks, and knapsacks swarmed into the mines, recording data for the two Professors Rogers to analyze and interpret. They lived much of the time in rented rooms at the Mount Carbon House in Pottsville, dispersing by day to their sites of observation and reassembling at night to talk excitedly into the small hours about geology, chemistry, and paleontology. Of particular importance were the valley of Mill Creek and its surrounding hills, on account of the multitude of openings all the way from Broad Mountain down to the Schuylkill at Port Carbon, and Mill Creek Valley eventually became one of the three principal geological sections published in the final report. Peter Lesley and Peter Sheafer were mainly responsible for the fieldwork and drawings of this part of the survey.

Peter Lesley was a tireless letter writer and his communications to father, stepmother, grandmother, sister, brother, and aunts reveal much about the little community of surveyors. They were young gentlemen, well brought up in middle-class homes, liberally educated and well read, some of them—like Lesley—religiously inclined, and all passionately devoted to the advancement of science. They were also apt to be extremely patronizing in their attitude toward the towns and townspeople, miners and mine operators, among whom they did their work. Twenty-year-old Peter Lesley's letter to his sister from Pottsville in April 1839 expresses some of the tension felt by the young man, bred to think about the finer things, now confronted by life in what his wife, a few years later, would call "a dirty little coal hole":[4]

This morning, Henderson and I, tired of moping, tried the second time to visit the Delaware mines [just a few hundred yards west of St. Clair]. They are about three miles from here; so on the way thither (and we didn't go "a la locomotive") there was so much to be seen,—(for you must remember, H. is a natural philosopher, tho' by no means a pretty one, I means his face, for his thoughts and mind are beauty itself) so many toads' spawn to magnify, and newts' backs to examine, and wonder at their golden specks, and spiders "walking the water, like things of life"; so many flowers to cull, and birds to listen to, that I forgot I was a dirty geologist about to seek the lower regions, Ulysses-like, in some one of the muddy Averni, of this Carbonic and almost Sardonic region, in my enthusiasm after Daphnes and water bugs. . . . You can scarcely imagine how beauty and deformity, art and nature, sweetness and filth, sterility and mud, are strangely mixed in this singular place.[5]

Lesley was upset by the low moral standards of the coal miners and by their habitual drinking of hard liquor; and he told amusing anecdotes about the ignorance and peculiar ideas of the common folk. "Did I ever tell you that Rogers had a letter sent by a man to him as State Genealogist? That was rather better than the bill I got from a blacksmith for mending my wagon, and made out to the debit of the Theological Survey of Pa."[6] But his Christian compassion also led him to favor measures to improve the physical and moral condition of the working class. He wrote favorably, for instance, of Carlyle's essay on Chartism, which he approved, finding the conclusion that Chartism was inevitable as a "stepping-stone to rights . . . correct and interesting to us who think of nations as composed of the lower as well as the upper and middle classes of society."[7]

The first products of the survey were a series of six annual reports, ending with an 1842 report outlining future work needed to complete the survey. But the legislature declined to appropriate the necessary funds, and the project was abandoned until 1850, when Peter Sheafer, by then politically well connected and a prominent mining engineer and geological consultant, was able to persuade the legislature to provide funds for four more seasons of fieldwork, during which he and Peter Lesley concentrated their attention on the anthracite districts. The final report was published in 1858, largely as a result of the uncompensated exertions of Rogers himself, who supervised the writing, drafting, and eventual printing (in Scotland) of the two ponderous volumes.[8]

The First Geological Survey of Pennsylvania was something of a landmark in the history of geology, for it produced a new theory of the structure and formation of mountain chains, based on the direct evidence of stratigraphy as it was revealed in the mines and mountain passes of the Appalachians, of which the parallel ridges that contained the anthracite region formed the northeastern terminus. This theory was first expounded in 1842 in a famous address by the two Rogers brothers together before the Association of American Geologists and Naturalists, remembered by one who was present as "the most lucid and elegant effort of oral statement to which I ever listend."[9] This address, and its publication next year, made the two brothers world famous. Lyell, who had toured the anthracite fields with Henry Rogers from Pottsville through Tamaqua to Mauch Chunk the year before, was present at the meeting, was deeply impressed, and asked the brothers to send a summary of their paper to the Manchester meeting of the British Association for the Advancement of Science, where it was read and discussed by the leading British geologists.[10]

The Rogers theory of mountain formation explained a phenomenon prominent in the Appalachian chain that was not adequately accounted for by the then prevailing paradigm. The traditional view was that mountains were created either by horizontal contraction of the earth's crust during cooling, or by direct vertical uplift, the force in the latter case deriving from the pressure of molten rock and hot gases driving into lines of weakness in the crust. But these models did not account for the prevalence of "overthrust faulting" in the Appalachians, particularly in their southernmost ridges. Instead of the strata of these mountains and valleys showing, in cross-section, a regular pattern of symmetrical undulations, the sides sloping alternately southeast and northwest, the northwest slopes were thrust toward the vertical and often beyond so as to underlie the southeast (the "rule of the steep north dip"); thus in some localities all the strata sloped southeastward. The Rogers brothers argued that neither horizontal contraction nor vertical uplift could account for this condition. Instead, they postulated the existence of both a vertical force and undirectional lateral force, provided by slow, wavelike billows in the subterranean ocean of semifluid magma, that produced great fractures in the crust and, like breakers on a beach, thrust the long crustal blocks nearest the point of propagation against those behind them, tilting the latter toward the vertical or even folding them back so that all the strata lay in parallel. These principles were soon demonstrated on other mountain chains. Henry Rogers visited Europe again in 1848 and showed that the structure of the Alps, whose strata, like the Appalachians, also leaned to the north, could best be explained by wavelike deformations of the crust moving from south to north.[11] The Rogers Appalachian model quickly became the accepted paradigm. Henry Rogers' biographer, J. W. Gregory, a distinguished geologist, wrote in 1916 that it was the "foundation of the present theory of mountain formation."[12] And it was not really superseded until the advent of the theory of continental drift, or plate tectonics, in the 1960's.[13]

The Rogers brothers' surveys in Virginia and Pennsylvania also revealed the existence of a vast, continuous coal field, of which again the anthracite region was only the northeastern corner, that extended roughly 700 miles from north to south, and hundreds of miles from east to west. The structure and extent of this great coal field were not described at length until the 1858 report appeared, but some initial descriptions of parts of the Pennsylvania field were presented in the annual reports, and particularly the annual report for 1838, which devoted ten pages to "the Anthracite Coal Measures." Rogers here made an effort to show how the Appalachian overthrust structure affected the anthracite district, and especially the Pottsville Basin, which, being at the southeastern edge of the mountain chain, and nearest the point of origin of the magma waves, was most dramatically affected. When the mountains were formed, the southernmost coal measures, of course, experienced the most severe overthrust pressures (which were also responsible for hardening the coal) and in addition suffered a general downward thrust as both the north- and south-dipping blocks of conglomerate piled up on top of the coal measures of the Pottsville Basin, leaving them "buried, in a more or less crushed condition," several thousand feet below. Eons of erosion followed, wearing down the hills and eventually allowing the veins to crop out on the surface. Thus the geological cross-sections from Broad Mountain south across the five miles of the Pottsville Basin to Sharp Mountain—as is clearly demonstrated by the Mill Creek, Silver Creek, and Tamaqua sections eventually published in 1858, 1866, and 1895—showed a multitude of easily accessible outcrops, currently being exploited by superficial quarries and tunnels, overlying a complex system of vertical and nearly vertical veins, all gradually sinking deeper and deeper toward the south. At the north, on the flanks of Broad Mountain just above St. Clair, the forty-foot-thick Mammoth Vein cropped out on the surface; to the south, on the flanks of Sharp Mountain, where Pottsville stood, only the thinner veins appeared, greatly crushed and faulted, and the deepest undulation of the Mammoth Vein lay thousands of feet below.

To Rogers, this condition boded ill for the further successful development of the coal measures of the Pottsville Basin. Because of depth, the best veins of the basin were accessible only at the northern rim; the extensive outcrops at Sharp Mountain gave access only to inferior coal. He stated his opinion in the 1838 annual report:

I would wish distinctly to make known my belief, that, throughout this tract of the coal region [i.e., the Pottsville Basin], the causes, alluded to above, must render the business of mining these nearly vertical and overtilted seams, precarious in a high degree. My own conviction is, that those peculiarities in the structure of the Sharp Mountain, constitute, from their frequency, a general rule, having perhaps, a few rare exceptions, which will hardly, I conceive, unless indeed, they are distinctly known to be exceptions, justify the expense of mining the coal, in case it must be done by tunneling. . . . Thus, in the vicinity of Pottsville, the intelligent colliers have long been aware of the relative unproductiveness of the north dipping portions of the strata, though from not recognizing the cause, the fact has not been admitted as a general rule, to the extent which it deserves, and injudicious enterprises are, therefore, often undertaken in total disregard of it.[14]

The financial implications of this warning were extremely serious. Further capital development of the coal measures between Sharp Mountain and the foothills of Broad Mountain, into which millions of dollars had just been poured, the state geologist now suggested, might be too risky for prudent businessmen to undertake, except at the outcrops along Mine Hill, three miles north of Pottsville. Rogers' language, to be sure, was cautious, allowing for some success by "intelligent colliers" and, apropos the seams in Sharp Mountain, conceding "it would not necessarily follow, that some portions of them might not well repay the cost of mining." But the general picture was negative: "as a general rule" the coal in Sharp Mountain was worthless; and north of the mountain a crustal block fifty miles long and five miles wide had experienced an "enormous downthrow," leaving the coal measures of the Pottsville Basin "in a more or less crushed condition," with much of the coal damaged and the veins extensively pinched and faulted.

The 1838 publication was intended for a wide audience; like other state reports, it was issued in both an English and a German edition. And no one who read it could doubt the gravity of its message of warning. Those who had already invested tens or even hundreds of thousands of dollars in coal lands would, if the coal in their tracts proved to be inaccessible, see their property revert in value to a few dollars an acre, and could expect their royalties to shrink to nothing. Mine operators and miners would drift away to better but more distant districts; the price of coal in Philadelphia would rise, thus reducing the demand; the Reading Railroad and the Schuylkill Navigation Company might go bankrupt, and the streets of Pottsville, that new Athens in the wilderness, would be reclaimed by the forest.

Relations between Rogers' bright, flippant young geologists and the local coal-trade gentry became a little more distant. But probably the principal retaliation against the geologists took place in Harrisburg in the roominghouses of the legislators and on the floors of the Senate and House. Rogers' qualifications as a scientist were impugned and he was called a charlatan by one senator who voted against a bill to fund further work by the survey:

> Mr. Speaker, I shall vote against this appropriation on the ground of its unfairness to other sciences of like nature with this geology. The bill, sir, makes no provision for phrenology, physiognomy, animal magnetism, and the highly important science of water-smelling; it is partial, and I will vote against it.[15]

The survey was abruptly terminated by the withholding of funds in 1842, after six years of work, although the original program had called for ten years. Peter Lesley attributed this to the ignorance of the "practical" miners; to him, it had been a case of casting pearls before swine:

The mines of the State were (with some most honorable exceptions) bossed by the commonest miners from foreign and quite
different geological regions, who had suddenly exchanged the
character and position of hewers of coal and pumpers of water at
home, for the character and position of mining engineers in
America . . . they were as unwilling to accept as they were unable
to acquire a correct knowledge of our geology, so different from
their own, and hated professional geologists because these had
never lived in childhood, pick in hand, underground,—because
they taught new things hard to comprehend,—and because they
denied the propriety of mining the coal of Schuylkill County on
the plan of the collieries of South Wales, or of employing the
ancient methods of the Cornish tinworks to the brown hematite
banks of the Lebanon Valley. The jealousy of professional and
"theoretical" interference with traditional and "practical" usages
. . . was in 1842 in all its vigor; and was shared by the landed
proprietors, the directors of the companies and the general superintendents of collieries and mines. A wave of suspicion and
dislike, pushed before it by the First Geological Survey through
its whole progress, brought it at last to a dead stop.[16]

Rogers' first draft of a final report was delivered to the office of the secretary of the commonwealth for publication in 1847, but no funds were
appropriated and the new round of fieldwork in 1851–1854 required extensive revisions. Funds paid to a private publisher in 1855 were embez-
zled. The legislature finally agreed to grant Rogers $16,000 and the
copyright if he would agree to publish the work himself and provide the
state with 1,000 copies within three years. This he accomplished, at considerable personal expense and trouble. Finding no Pennsylvania press
capable of executing the fine copper-plate engravings and color lithographs
required for the maps, he carried the whole manuscript to Scotland for
publication. And there he remained, for powerful British friends had him
appointed Regius Professor of Natural History at the University of Glasgow.

Meanwhile, the warning contained in the 1838 report was being quietly ignored. The *Miners' Journal* took no notice of it. The reason was an
understandable reluctance by large landowners, particularly Carey, Lea,
and Hart, the Wetherills, and the Delaware and North American Coal
companies, who owned most of the coal land in the center of the Pottsville
Basin between Sharp Mountain and Mine Hill, to abandon their investment. They had, perhaps, purchased some of the most difficult and dan-

gerous coal measures in the world; but courage, technological ingenuity, and the further investment of capital would, they hoped, triumph in the end. And, anyway, perhaps Rogers was mistaken. Revisionists were at work, minimizing the seriousness of the warning.

The principal theoretician to oppose Rogers was Enoch McGinness. For years before the successful sinking of the St. Clair Shaft, he and a number of other operators had claimed that the great white-ash veins, and particularly the Mammoth Vein that outcropped at Mine Hill, underlay the whole district between Broad and Sharp mountains. This view did not contradict the Rogers brothers, who went further and argued that the same veins of coal formed the several strata of the entire anthracite and bituminous coal fields of the eastern United States. But John Beadle, who had opened the Gate Vein at Pottsville (the same vein on which Carey's York Farm and Guinea Hill slopes had been sunk), argued that the Mammoth Vein undulated, along the several anticlinal axes discernible on the surface, *at readily accessible depths,* between Sharp Mountain and Mine Hill. And it was this theory that inspired Alfred Lawton and Enoch McGinness to sink their test pits in the late '40's and early '50's. Peter Sheafer, the geology consultant to the North American Coal Company, also sank a test pit, but he recognized the validity of Rogers' pronouncements concerning lands south of the Mammoth outcrop at St. Clair. He could hardly do otherwise, having done much of the fieldwork himself. And he advised the company that "some portions" of the anthracite region were "in such a disturbed condition . . . as to be rendered unreliable, thus greatly qualifying the common opinion of general profusion and inexhaustibility."[17] But he believed that at the northern rim of the Pottsville Basin the Mammoth Vein could be reached at a "reasonable working depth." McGinness, however, believed that he would reach a basin on the Mammoth, not just a shelf on the edge of an abyss, when he was sinking slope and shaft in 1853. Thus when the shaft met Mammoth coal on a southward pitch of only 12°, it appeared to McGinness and others that he had barely missed the horizontal bed at the center of the syncline by a few dozen yards; and he was prepared to drive the neighboring slope itself on down "to Bottom of Basin."[18] Four days after Carey's mining engineer, John Maddison, visited the property in December 1853, the *Miners' Journal* exultantly reported:

> The coal was reached in this shaft at the depth of 450 feet, where the veins lie nearly flat, having but little dip. The coal is very pure and hard. The shaft is located near the middle of the Carey prop-

erty, and opens an immense field of coal in every direction, which will require ages to exhaust.[19]

As McGinness' literary mouthpiece, Eli Bowen, and other admirers expressed it a year later, McGinness and others believed that the Mammoth and other white-ash coal veins that outcropped on the foothills of Broad Mountain

> could be reached at a depth not too great for practical and economical working . . . throughout the entire Basin.
>   . . . the great White-ash Coal Measures, instead of being reachable only at the Northern rim of our Coal Basin, as formerly supposed, are so at all desirable points throughout its entire area. . . .[20]

And so were dismissed the "old theories and prejudices" of Rogers and his group. A few years later Bowen even published a fanciful geological cross-section of the Pottsville Basin demonstrating that at its deepest point, under the center of the town of Pottsville, the Mammoth Vein bottomed out at 900 feet from grass, well within "workable reach," Rogers, Sheafer, and the First Geological Survey to the contrary notwithstanding.[21]

But Rogers was not mistaken. And Rogers was not wrong about another matter: the origin of coal. Here too his views were disputed, this time on religious grounds, and it is not unlikely that the perception of Rogers as an atheistic utopian socialist who blasphemously denied the biblical account of creation contributed to the continuing rejection of his opinion on the economic value of the coal in the Pottsville Basin. In *The Geology of Pennsylvania* (1858) Rogers reviewed the evidence in a short section on the "Origins of the Coal Strata."[22] As a few others had suggested before him, Rogers concluded from the chemistry of coal, from the character of the fossil plant remains in the coal and in the intervening strata, and from the nature of the clays and slates, that coal must have been formed from peat bogs in the Carboniferous period. Each vein of coal represented a peat bog, largely composed of the remains of ancient tree-like club mosses, that had been submerged by a sinking of the land relative to the ocean and then covered by a deposit of silt. Eventually compressed by the weight of overlying strata, and heated by the hot, molten matter below the crust, the layers were transformed into soft coal and slate. The transformation into hard anthracite and the tilting and breaking of the strata were the result of the later movements of the crust described in his theory of mountain building. This "peat-bog theory" is essentially the same as that maintained by today's geologists, with the modification that the temperature (about 300° Fahrenheit) necessary to drive out almost all volatile matter and thereby produce anthracite can readily be accounted for without catastrophic events. It can be reached simply by placing soft coal at a sufficient depth. The crustal temperature increases at a rate of 1° Fahrenheit every fifty feet, so that at a depth of three miles (approximately the original thickness of the Appalachian coal field) temperatures on the order of 300° Fahrenheit can be expected.

Rogers' naturalistic approach was offensive to the pious Eli Bowen, Schuylkill County's self-styled resident "Professor of Geology." In a popular book published in 1865 under the title *Coal and Coal Oil; or, The Geology of the Earth, Being a Popular Description of Minerals and Mineral Combustibles,* Bowen attempted to reconcile Biblical creationism with the extended time span shown by geological science. He suggested that the six days of Genesis were actually six geological epochs and thus dispensed with "simultaneous creation," allowing for successive creations, each particular to its own epoch. This formula preserved the idea of progressive change while it cast aside the concept of evolution. Rogers' geological survey he attacked as "perhaps the most stupendous scientific trash ever collected together" and he belittled Isaac Lea's discovery of "dinosaur footprints" in strata bearing ripple marks, saying that if Lea had ever fished in the Schuylkill Navigation Company's dam at Tumbling Run, he would have found annelid worms capable of making those marks, and that Bowen himself had found the "marine sauropus" responsible for the footprint.[23]

Bowen presented his own theory of the origin of coal in a series of books and pamphlets beginning with *Physical History of the Creation of the Earth and its Inhabitants; or, a Vindication of the Cosmogony of the Bible from the Assaults of Modern Science* in 1861. But probably the work best known in Schuylkill County was his *Coal and the Coal Trade,* published in Pottsville in 1862 by Benjamin Bannan and dedicated to George de B. Keim instead of, he observed, "Major Wetherill," who was away at the wars but who would otherwise, Bowen averred, have laid aside his sword and enjoyed an old-fashioned after-dinner argument with him upon the merits of "the different geological hypotheses herein disclosed." Bowen denied the peat-bog theory and instead proposed that coal was formed from the tars and resins secreted by fermenting vegetation on the floors of the Carboniferous forest in the third "Day" of Creation. This liquid, tarry matter was carried away by streams and rivers and deposited as a "thick viscid agglomeration" at the bottom of vast lakes and bays. Eventually this layer

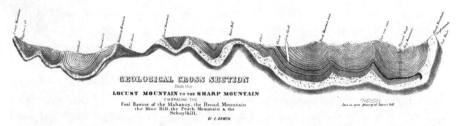

Bowen/McGinness conception of the geology of the Pottsville Basin, 1862

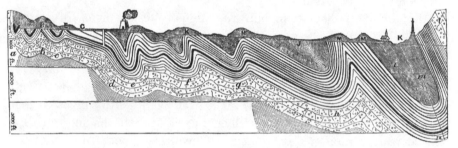

Daddow's conception of the geology of the Pottsville Basin, 1866

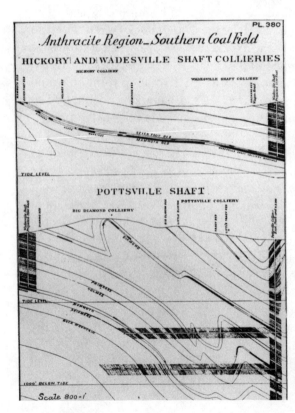

Geological illusions: The Bowen/ McGinness theoretical cross-section shows the Mammoth Vein bottoming out under the town of Pottsville at about 900 feet. The actual measured depth at the Pottsville or Twin Shafts Colliery, just south of St. Clair, was about 1700 feet, and under Pottsville itself, two miles farther south, several thousand feet. Note the fault in Mammoth Vein at intersection with lower tunnel.

Geology of the Pottsville Basin as revealed in the Second Geological Survey of 1895 of tar would be covered by silts and sediments, and then another run-off of tar would cover the lake bottom again. The transformation into coal was achieved not, as Professor Rogers suggested, by driving off inflammable gases by heat, "but by the transformation of the gases into new compounds, and into a denser body," under the pressures associated with the building of the Appalachian Mountains.[24]

Samuel Daddow, St. Clair's resident poet and mining engineer, carried Bowen's thesis forward in a chapter of his and Bannan's handbook of mining, *Coal, Iron, and Oil,* published in Pottsville by Bannan in 1866. Daddow conceived of a shallow sea literally covered from shore to shore with an incredibly fast-growing layer of *Sigillaria* leaves, similar to lily pads, nourished by vines rooted in the ocean floor. So rapidly did this vegetation proliferate that, in contrast to Rogers and Lyell, who thought in terms of millennia, Daddow conceived of a coal bed three feet thick as requiring, "instead of 1,000 years," not even as many months—"perhaps not as many weeks." He estimated thus that the thirty-foot-thick Mammoth Vein was formed in 180 years![25] The actual conversion of the vegetable mass to coal happened underwater. The seepage upward, from the hot underlying rock that formed the inner crust of the earth, of petroleum and natural gas brought these materials into contact with the gases and tars being expelled from the mass of vegetation at the bottom of the shallow sea. The product of this mixture, by means of as-yet-unknown chemical processes, was coal. Anthracite, Daddow argued, was chemically differentiated from bituminous coal while still in a liquid state. He concluded with a backhanded compliment to Rogers:

> We might extend this chapter to an indefinite length in explanation of those great chemical processes of Nature, and in giving many other theories of our coal formations; but, while aiming to be practical, we are in danger of giving more speculation and theory than fact.
>
> In justice, however, to Prof. H. D. Rogers, whose eminent position and laborious researches among our coal-fields entitle his opinions to respect and regard, we give his theory of their formations, which will be found in the Appendix. It covers the ground of the terrestrial vegetation, peat-bog, and drift theories, or combines them all.[26]

But "for want of space" Rogers' theory had to be omitted from the appendix. Instead, we find as the closing words of the book a direct attack against the new, atheistical science of geology:

THE VOLCANIC THEORY herein advanced will give a new and, we hope, a correct starting point to the science of geology. We have always thought the main theories of the science to have been conceived in error by modern sophists and infidels, who invented them as arguments against the truth of revelation and the Bible. Even those who have battled manfully and successfully for the truth seem to have accepted the theories framed by its adversaries, and sought no other guide to the NATURAL PROCESS of Creation. We cannot resist quoting the words of an old and celebrated Cornish miner, whose implicit faith in the truth of revelation made him its staunch defender and a powerful opponent to its revilers. We do not endorse all his sentiments, nor embrace his sweeping denunciations of geology and geologists; but we do think, as he did, that the science was not only conceived in falsehood, but against the truth, by the enemies of religion, and that it has been developed under all the difficulties of the original error. The science itself we consider the grandest study open to the human mind, and its great masters, who have elucidated so many wonderful truths from its dark arcana, are entitled to our highest respect and admiration. Nevertheless, our voice is given against the errors of infidelity, whether adopted by geologists or the teachers of men; for we believe that the WORKS OF CREATION will agree with the WORD OF GOD.

"Permit us to inquire what benefit mining has received from all the writings, lectures, societies, premiums, researches, and labors of our large body of theoretical geologists? If I am wrong, please to set me right; but, I declare, I know not a single instance where any good has emanated from their exertions, to the value of a swabbing-stick! All the progress made in the discovery and working of mines has been without their help. . . .

"I shall be borne out in stating my firm conviction that no skeptic ever made a good geologist; and, whatever those men may think of themselves who dare to write in contradiction to the Word which the Creator has graciously condescended to bestow on his creatures, they are no better than practical atheists in the judgement of all men 'who believe and know the truth,' and their writings are calculated to inflict a serious injury on society and sap the foundations of Christian faith."[27]

The response of professional geologists to this sort of rhetoric, and to

Daddow's geological theories, was expressed by Lesley in his *Historical Sketch of Geological Explorations in Pennsylvania and Other States:*

> . . . all that is valuable in Daddow's Book on Coal was taken from Rogers' Report of 1858, with the addition of chapters filled with geological nonsense, against the influence of which upon their minds students and miners should be warned. The author is now dead; therefore, severer criticism is improper. But a needful lesson is taught by the fact that, had the report of the First Survey been published in a cheap and handy form and become thus universally distributed and discussed, it would never have been supplanted, in its role as a textbook of geological knowledge for the citizens of Pennsylvania, by a mischievous travesty, disgraceful to the author and the age.[28]

Thus the warning was rejected and the recognition that the stony truths of geology were as immutable as the iron laws of economics was delayed until a generation later, when a countryside littered with abandoned mines gave testimony that Rogers had been right all along.

THE MIND OF ENOCH MCGINNESS[1]

In addition to his views on geology, Enoch McGinness has left us a copious record of his thoughts about the coal trade, of his calculations of risk and of anticipated profit, of his feelings toward his companions and rivals in the business, even of some of his social values. McGinness' letters to Henry Carey, about 250 of them from 1852 to 1862, have been preserved, and they afford an opportunity to observe McGinness as he made some of his business decisions. The letters, of course, have to be understood in their context. McGinness was always trying to persuade Carey to continue his support of old ventures and was frequently urging him to invest in new ones, and so things are missing from the letters that would not serve this purpose, such as bad news (like another gas explosion). Just how typical McGinness was of the whole class of colliery operators in Schuylkill County it is difficult to say. But, for the town of St. Clair, representativeness is beside the point, because for a couple of decades McGinness himself, his creations the St. Clair Shaft and Slope, and his ideas about the value of vertical-shaft mines and the geology of the Pottsville Basin were dominant factors in the lives of its citizens. So knowledge of how Enoch McGinness made decisions in situations that involved the risk of catastrophe, decisions that in some cases resulted in catastrophe, is essential in understanding the fate of one town and its environs.

The images of himself that McGinness presented to Carey in these letters were often contained in contrasts between himself and his rivals for Carey's favor. These rivals usually were persons whose opinions and business policies differed from McGinness'. He had a particular aversion to Kirk and Baum, who had abandoned the St. Clair Shaft and Slope Colliery, leaving it idle and full of water, while blaming McGinness for having botched it up in the beginning. Carey, stuck with a ruined colliery, lost rents, and a lawsuit, was trying to rent the colliery in 1861, but its bad reputation was making it difficult to find a tenant. When Carey, frustrated, accused McGinness of having "crippled" the colliery, McGinness defended himself with spirit. The fault lay with Kirk and Baum. In conversation with F. W. Hughes (now a partner with Carey in ownership of "N.A.," the reorganized North American Coal Company), the failings of Kirk and Baum—stupidity and obstinacy—were amusingly sketched.

> I asked him what he thought was the reason they did not do more business. His reply was the place was too big for their *Brains*. I told him that might be a part of the difficulty but it was not the leading one. But the greatest trouble was that K. was very nearly related to his (*Hughes*) wife, and the rest of the Sillymans, and he partook largely of dispositions that most of them was troubled with. *Stubbornness*—and B. was very much of the same sort and both K. & B. thought they were always right, and frequently suffered in consequence, and were the means of making other suffer with them. Hughes admitted there was a great deal of truth in my opinion of them as he knew they were both very selfwilled and that K. particularly would sacrifice nearly everything for an idea. Which will not do for the coal business just now.[2]

In another letter he charged that Kirk's wife's relative William Silliman was the real manager of the colliery, and said, "K. is stubborn B. is pompous." And at the end of the year, he reassured Carey again:

> Banish all your fears. St. Clair is all right yet, or will be very soon. I was turned out of it by croakers when I was shipping 100 cars a day—because Russel said I slept too long in the morning, and I was therefore good for nothing but the place first rate. But now

with tennants who might as well be asleep all the time R. no doubt has come to the conclusion the fault is in the colliery and not in K & B because their eyes are open, but is very evident they neither see nor think correctly. And therefore for your interest I advise you to have it controlled by someone who can think as well as get up in the morning.[3]

The real point of distinction, however, was the issue of loyalty: Kirk and Baum eventually deserted the colliery when it was in trouble, in marked contrast to McGinness, who (as he reminded Carey time and again) was ever the faithful retainer.

Loyalty, as McGinness presented it, was not just fidelity to contract. It was personal, part of the patron-client relationship between himself and Carey, in which McGinness the client was constantly begging his stern and critical patron not to treat him so harshly and also was repeatedly pleading with Carey to back him financially in some new venture. After the North American Coal Company canceled his lease of the Diamond Colliery in September 1861 and McGinness protested, Carey wrote McGinness a sharp note charging him with trying to "*drag* money" out of him. Turned out after having, in his view, built a new colliery for the owners at his own expense, McGinness replied with an almost tearful plea for understanding:

> I . . . am doing my very best. . . . You know very well there is nothing in my power I would not do for you or Mr. Hart, but impossibilities I cannot do. You write that you are very much bothered. This I know, and felt at the same time I am more troubled than any one else. And am very sensitive when you *scold* and can scarcely live. If it were in my power I would pay every debt the N.A. [North American] owes, for I know there is not a better investment in the *country* . . . and I am as near killed as I can be to live.[4]

This somewhat masochistic tone occurs in other letters, including an unhappy confession a few months later that he dreads even to open a Carey letter for fear it will contain "a chapter of faults," and the renewed plea, "Don't whip the horse that does his best for you."[5]

Loyalty also included, for McGinness, a kind of regional patriotism. As we have seen, in his geological theories McGinness was an outstanding exemplar of the local booster spirit. He loudly defended "good Schuylkill men" and deprecated those who belittled the Schuylkill coal trade, under-

estimated the value of the coal remaining in the Pottsville Basin, or criticized the St. Clair Shaft. They were "croakers." In the early 1860's, when
he was employed as collection agent for Carey's North American Coal
Company and he and his son Dan were attempting to operate collieries on
the company's estate, he was especially bothered by such fair-weather
friends as Francis W. Hughes and Burd Patterson. Hughes, one of the
owners, was saying that the Pottsville district, in the center of which lay
the North American Coal Company's tracts, was ruined, and he was reported to be seeking to sell his interest.[6] And Burd Patterson was spreading
word that the coal trade south of Broad Mountain was all washed up, and
that "there is only one man this side of the mountain who is making any
money in coal"—William H. Johns.[7] And McGinness hated "shavers" (e.g.,
bankers who discounted his notes), who typically had "a very small soul"
and placed no value on McGinness' capacity to develop mines; they would
prevent the development of the North American if they were in charge of
its finances.

The moral quality that good Schuylkill men possessed, and which was
denied to croakers and shavers, was "grit."[8] Grit was the willingness to
take risks in the advancement of a great cause like the development of the
North American Coal Company's coal lands. The moral importance of courage for the industrial community was explicitly recognized by McGinness.
Just after he lost his lease on one colliery, but was about to open a new one,
he set forth his code of values. He had come to the conclusion that

> *daring men* after all are the men who make things move. It is not
> the men who are mere money getters that are the most useful to
> the community at large . . . in these times when every other in-
> terest is suffering so severely we must not expect too much from
> coal. *But like the Silver Mines of Mexico, Coal mines are still
> valuable* in this Basin though the countries may be in a state of
> *Anarky.*[9]

The most successful of the "mere money getters," of course, was Johns.
Johns could not "be accused of having an over amount of *brains*," but still
he had been "fortunate" and therefore was commonly considered "wise
above many others who have more real business ability than a dozen such
men."[10] In contrast to some like Kirk and Baum, Johns sold his coal for
whatever he could get for it in the market. Kirk, who in some ways had grit
("stubbornness" was McGinness' word for it in Kirk's case), fixed a price,
and if the market fell below it, he simply piled his coal on the ground. "He

would sooner lose than sell below his price." But wily Johns "does not do this." McGinness explained:

> Milnes frequently states his prices to Johns and they verbally agree to sell at the prices named but if Johns does not get orders enough at the prices, he arranges the price so that it will bring the orders, which sometimes makes Milnes very cross, but that does not stop Johns from shipping coal—at prices that he seems content with.[11]

The coldly rational capitalist was not McGinness' model for emulation. As he repeatedly explained to Carey, he was not in the coal trade simply for money. He was also moved by the ambition to be of use to the community in this "age of utility"—to leave each project, whether richer or poorer, with the satisfaction of having proved he was right and of having made a preparation for the success of others. Thus, after he and Dan lost the Wallace and Rothermel Colliery after driving through a fault at their own expense, he wrote Carey a rationalization of his decision that mingled pride in being technically correct with pride in serving the interest of the owners:

> Such a party as K & B would have abandoned the C & C [i.e., the Wallace and Rothermel colliery on the Carey and Chamberlain Tract] in the worst kind of a fault and with the coal market in a terrible condition had they have happened to have been operating instead of myself. And let the owners lose the money invested there. And all the knowing ones would have said it was right in them as there was no coal there. And no one could expect it so deep down as some yet say. But I was *fool* hardy enough to go on until I ruined myself and just as I got where the investment could be saved to the owners I must leave with very little thanks from some of them. But I have the satisfaction of having proved I was right, poor pay as this may be it is some consolation for the place now is in infinitely better coal than when I was obliged to leave it three months ago—Eshelman did not put the coal there but is taking it out. And it will continue to be taken out by him or someone else until it pays the owners all I ever told them it would. I did not put the fault there but I drove through it *for the very purpose* of trying to prevent the loss of money put in by the owners.[12]

In his next project, the shaft on the Primrose, similar motives applied in advance:

> All I have shall be staked on the Primrose, in N.A. *for I know it is* where I am looking for it and I am determined to show it to the unbelievers as well as the faithful and *true*.[13]

This was to be "the great project of my life" that would finally make him *"one of the coal operators* of this region." It would seem that McGinness kept in mind from the very beginning of an enterprise the future reward of esteem from "the faithful and true" for his technical knowledge, his loyalty, and his grit. The prospect of such ego enhancement may even have been enough to get him started on risky projects. He was living the myth of the industrialist-as-hero.

What made projects risky in McGinness' eyes was lack of capital. From the beginning of the St. Clair Shaft venture in 1852, when he had only $4.50 to his name, to the Primrose Shaft, the last great project before his death in 1867, McGinness was always short of capital. This he viewed as a normal enough condition; as he pointed out to Carey, "the two men here [William H. Johns and William Kear] who have been most successful in mining coal, had no capital to start with."[14] There were three ways to secure capital: by taking on monied partners, carefully chosen for compatibility; by borrowing cash from patrons, friends, and banks; and by contracting to pay for machinery and buildings only after some delay. The need for ready cash was pressing in the period of several months between breaking ground and opening the first breast, for the contract miners hired to sink the shaft or slope, dig the sump, and drive the attendant gangways, headings, and airways had to be paid regularly or they would quit. Some suppliers—perhaps of props, perhaps of machinery, or track, or wire rope— might require cash on delivery. Short-term notes had to be paid on time or his credit would decline. And while the coal dug out of a slope was in principle salable, it was small in quantity and difficult to market until the breaker was complete and the railroad company extended its spur to the chutes. The projected date when the breasts had been opened and good coal was being shipped out at the rate of, say, 1,000 tons a week was also the projected date when notes fell due and contractors had to be paid. If anything stalled the project and coal was not being shipped in sufficient quantity to satisfy creditors by this deadline, then a second and potentially chronic stage of financial crisis began. Miners were not paid on time, dunning creditors were put off with promises, the landowner was persuaded to accept a delay in the quarterly rent payment, new loans were arranged to get the cash to pay off old notes. Eventually, if sufficient coal was not sold, the landowner would cancel the lease for non-payment of rent and the other creditors would force the hard-pressed operator to sell his machinery, supplies, and improvements.

Under these circumstances, financial worries could be preoccupying and could cloud the judgment. This McGinness understood well enough when he saw it in others. After the explosion and fire in Parvin's Slope in November 1859, he explained that the problem was the haste with which Parvin, or one of Parvin's bosses, was trying to get at new coal. The slope was being sunk down to a new lift and the air hole, which ran parallel to the slope, was being extended. But when the slope neared its new level, work on extending the air hole ceased and instead a loading platform and sump were dug and a "trial gangway" was driven to prove the coal. This left the air hole incomplete. McGinness talked darkly of "bad management" and explained to Carey:

> This whole difficulty was caused by the oversight or more properly by the carelessness of not having the air hole put through, so that there would have been a circulation of air, instead of which no fresh air could get to the bottom of the workings, because there was no connection between the slope and airway within fifteen yards of the bottom, which should have been done before or while the sump was being made.[15]

But when McGinness was asked for advice on how to manage Parvin's Slope, he was just as daring as Parvin. Just before the explosion, he advised Carey, concerning Parvin's Slope, to "stop leaving half the coal in for Pillars for air and keeping up water which is one of Mr. Russell's humbugs."[16] And two months after the explosion, and against the opinion of George K. Smith, the engineer, he was himself driving a trial gangway east in Parvin's Slope, with Carey's permission, because "I know it is the cheapest way of ascertaining whether there is any good coal near."[17] Parvin's need to open the new lift cheaply and quickly, of course, was determined by his financial difficulties.

Just as McGinness' letters frequently contained sad complaints about owing money and being short of cash, so also many displayed cheerful calculations of profits soon to be realized. These calculations vastly overestimated any likely rate of return. Thus, for instance, in June 1855—a couple of weeks before a gas explosion in the St. Clair Shaft set in train a series of embarrassments that culminated in October in his loss of the colliery—McGinness wrote a characteristic letter to his patron that is worth quoting in full for its mixture of bad news and sunny optimism:

Pottsville June 2, 1855

Henry C. Carey Esqr.

Dear Sir

I received yours this morning and will endeavour to answer it to the best of my ability. In the first place I am very sorry that I am detaining you from your trip across the water and but for the unforseen accident of cutting the spring in the slope none of the charges could have been laid to me. And since the unfortunate occurrence I am very sure I have done all I could to remedy the evil as soon as possible. I have put in 360 feet of new pump and broke the main shaft of the engines. And in twenty hours had it pumping again. And have put a new shaft in the other engine and it will be ready to hoist on Monday so that I will have one engine to pump and one to wind with so there need be no delay on account of water. And as regards loosing the lease all I have to say is that I shall do my best to keep it if I fail to do so and any one else has a better right to it or is more deserving of it let them have it and I will get rid of a vast deal of trouble. I have fought it for four years and have now got it in shape to produce about 12000 tons per month. So if I don't make anything out of it somebody else will. And I am very much mistaken in the owners of St. Clair if I am not allowed to make a very handsome fortune out of it, the shaft done 300 Reading cars this week which is about 1400 tons and will increase. The slope has done as much and no doubt can do it again. And as there is plenty of ground open in the slope there will be no necessity for driving any more gangway this summer and therefore the coal should be produced cheaply and no doubt can so that the two places should make five or six thousand dollars a month clear. And that would very soon put me out of debt, but until the last month the shaft has never paid expenses but now it is beginning to pay, and will pay fast if the slope had gone on the last month all would have been right now. And that is now ready to work again it will soon come out right. I would be very glad to pay Mr. Harts Mortgage notes off as they mature but really I am not able to do it now but hope to do so soon.

And as to Holmes place that will all be right. I have put between 2500 & 3000 dollars in money lumber & machinery and will have it all ready by the time red ash coal is wanted at paying prices. Holmes gets nervous and uneasy and goes off before he is ready. I took some money out a week ago today to pay his men but he did not come to me to get it and as I was engaged with the broken shaft I had no time to go after him and on Monday morning he told he [*sic*] had stopped his inside men and would give me until 4 o'clock on Tuesday to pay his men. Now the truth is his men ought to have been stopped a month sooner and not been put in again until the outside work was ready. And now it will all come right if the slope starts right again and I have no doubt it will. I think you can go to Europe without any misgivings.

Yours truly

E. N. McGinness[18]

Particular attention should be paid to his quantitative estimates of profit. He was predicting that very soon the shaft and slope together would be producing 12,000 tons per month and that this amount of coal would yield him a profit of $5,000 to $6,000 a month "clear" (i.e., presumably above the cost of production, transportation, royalties, and commissions). With this level of income he would easily be able to pay his debts. But the reader may note that he was calculating on a profit of 42 to 50 cents per ton even though contemporary authorities agreed that the profit rate of a successful mine was 10 to 12 cents per ton. The reader may also note the preoccupation with finances, the emphasis on "cheap" methods of production, the allusion to "fighting it" (i.e., the mine), and the expression of satisfaction at having won the battle even if someone else made the money.

How McGinness' values and circumstances combined to produce one disastrous explosion in a mine may be seen in the letters that describe the course of events at the Diamond Slope on the North American Coal Company's estate between December 1859, when his men began to dig, and May 1861, when he lost the lease.

In the fall of 1858, McGinness was hired by Carey and the trustees of the North American Coal Company to serve as their agent to collect rents and to supervise the work done by the several operators of mines on the North American Coal Company's lands and on Carey's several other tracts (the St. Clair Tract, the "80 Acres" adjoining St. Clair, and the Carey and Chamberlain Tract on Mill Creek). The contract was for two years and provided for an annual salary of $2,500. Also McGinness in the fall of 1859 was instructed by the North American Coal Company to sink a slope on the Diamond Vein in the Mill Creek Tract, east of the creek, and was instructed by Carey to clean up and reopen the old Wallace and Rothermel Slope on the Lewis Vein, in Carey and Chamberlain's tract, which had been burned out, flooded, and abandoned five years before. It was in his capacity as Carey's agent that McGinness investigated the cause of Parvin's gas explosion and blamed it on Parvin's failure to complete the last fifteen yards of the air hole before starting a trial gangway.

The financial arrangements for opening the collieries on the Lewis and the Diamond veins were simple. The cost of opening both collieries was borne by the owners, who advanced some of the money in cash (borrowed from a Pottsville bank), authorized McGinness to write notes drawn on Carey, Hart, and others, permitted him to spend as needed the rents he collected from other collieries on lands held by the Carey interests, and allowed him to use the proceeds of any coal he was able to sell. Accounts were examined periodically, but he could spend money at his own discretion, relying on his own judgment of what to spend it on and when. The amounts were significant. By March 1860, for instance, he had spent well over $13,500 on the Lewis. He himself received no remuneration (other than his salary as agent) while the collieries were being opened, but would receive a one-eighth share of the royalty revenue after the colliery was leased to a tenant operator.

Toward the end of November 1859, with Parvin starting to get water out of his burned-out mine, and McGinness near completing the drainage of the burned-out Wallace and Rothermel, McGinness started to sink the slope on the Diamond. In January he assured Carey that he was proceeding "as fast as possible."[19] By early April, he told Carey, things were going well. The workmen digging the slope were sending up eighteen railroad cars of good coal per week, the rails in the slope were being laid, and the hoisting engine was nearly ready. By the beginning of May they were down 150 yards and expected to bottom out in seventy-five more.

But rumors of trouble with the new slope were reaching Carey; McGinness had to refute the lie that the Diamond Vein had no good coal. True, the vein was too thick at the start (thirteen to fourteen feet), which made it difficult to timber, and slate and stone were mixed in with the coal; and then it narrowed to four feet "or less."[20] To be sure, it was not really *good* coal, but there was a lot of it. . . . And it turned out that the vein bottomed out at 275 feet instead of 225 as predicted, so that there were more delays. On July 2 he reassured Carey again: "I don't think there is anything about the Diamond that should alarm you. I now have the gangway started east and west and have no doubt it will be in good coal soon."[21]

What McGinness had not so far revealed to Carey was that he had failed even to begin to sink an air hole and had instead contracted with John Holmes to drive the gangway east in a search for "good coal." He had over the course of seven months thus created precisely the same situation that he had identified as the source of Parvin's explosion. Holmes' men worked slowly, no doubt hampered by lack of air. The inevitable explosion occurred about two a.m. on the 18th of July. Because of the hour, no one was injured, but the roof was blown off the engine house, much of the slope timbering was knocked down, and debris littered the mine. McGinness' first apologetic letter to Carey ("I am sorry to inform you that we had an explosion of firedamp last night . . .") minimized the loss—"it may take a week to repair the damage."[22] And his next disclaimed any responsibility: "I am very sorry we had the accident but it was one of the unaccountable things, to happen when there was no work opened."[23] But after more careful examination—not completed until the 26th—the magnitude of the disaster was revealed. "It will require some time and $1000 to clear the slope . . . and at the same time I will have the air hole driven, which will cost about $400." And he added, "for which there is no money . . . it may be possible it can be done from rents, tho' of this I am not certain."[24] It did not help that another Mill Creek operator who should have been paying rents had run into "a little fault." Carey and Hart were eventually forced to pay for the repairs. On the 3rd of September, McGinness reported:

> at the Diamond we are driving out the airhole by contract $450. When that is done the gangway must be driven further . . . the explosion has driven the work back very much but it is now cleared up, as you and Mr. Hart directed but how am I to pay on the 10th $900—I don't exactly see, it must be done somehow.[25]

But trouble continued to dog the project. There was too much water flooding the mine for the pumps, which probably had been damaged in the explosion, to get rid of, and this interfered with driving up the air hole. A new pump didn't arrive until January. Six months after the explosion, the air hole was finally completed and work in the gangways could start again. But now there was no money to pay Holmes or his men, so in April 1861 Holmes' miners turned out. At this point McGinness threw up his hands and walked away, telling them not to bother coming back. A new operator now took over the colliery. . . .

McGinness' letters both before the explosion and after reveal a great deal about his state of mind and, read in conjunction with other information about his career, make it possible to understand why he failed to drive an air hole. Lack of adequate funding at the start was not the reason: the air hole would cost no more than $450, a small fraction of the $20,000 he already had in cash and credit. What was at stake for McGinness was the company's satisfaction with his performance and confidence in his geological theories. And in practice this meant pleasing his patron, "Mr. Carey," whose disapproval, as we have observed, McGinness already feared with almost phobic intensity. Pleasing Carey meant, first of all, proving that the North American Tract contained good, easily accessible coal, proving it quickly, and proving it cheaply, within the budget. Thus at the very beginning he assured Carey that he was sinking the slope "as fast as possible" and that his policy was "to find out as cheaply as possible where the good coal is." As the slope progressed, it became apparent that he was not in "good coal" (McGinness chose not to call it a "fault"), but he promised that good coal would be found when they reached the bottom of the Diamond syncline, either in the Diamond or in the adjacent Orchard Vein, easily accessible by a tunnel.

McGinness *could* have had the air hole driven in sections of fifty yards or so as the slope descended, by cutting headings off from the slope and then working them up; or he could have refrained from driving a trial gangway until the air hole had been driven up after the slope reached bottom. But he was in a hurry. By spring, not yet having found good coal, he was husbanding funds in order to drive trial gangways as soon as bottom was reached. And funds were in fact low when he started Holmes' crew off in their ill-fated search for good coal. To be sure, he knew that failure to put in the air hole before driving a gangway was "careless" and "bad management," as he had called it in Parvin's case a few months earlier. But McGinness regarded the risk of a gas explosion as less serious *to him* than the risk of losing Carey's confidence by asking him for money to drive up an incomplete air hole while still in bad coal.

McGinness could in fact have raised the money for the air hole by using his wife's testimonial silver service and his own gold watch as collateral on a loan, as he did for another purpose later. But he had another concern by that spring: his sons. He had just fixed up Theodore as a coal merchant in New York; and he was committed to helping Dan, who in May had taken the operating lease on the old Wallace and Rothermel, to make a success as a coal operator. Thus money McGinness might have spent driving up the air hole he used to help his son. A former clerk with no personal experience in colliery management, Dan was almost immediately in trouble. The mine began to produce coal in May, but the airways proved to be too small to ventilate the workings adequately, and from the middle of June to the middle of July the mining of coal had to be stopped while a counter-gangway was driven to supply air. This emergency cost Dan $1,200. All then went well for six weeks, but everything stopped again when the gangway came to a dead fault. Again at great expense, Dan spent three months from September through November driving through solid rock to find the vein. During that time he had no income, could not pay his men their back pay or his rent to the North American Coal Company, and had to mortgage the colliery to his father for $1,500 to get cash to pay the special crew driving the gangway. His father put in $400 more in cash and he borrowed from Carey or one of Carey's associates another $500. The whole episode left Dan $3,000 in debt. Then the railroad refused to assign cars because he owned money for tolls, and the chutes filled up, preventing the miners from sending up more coal. After the matter of tolls was arranged, the colliery operated for two weeks, but in mid-January the breaker broke down, stopping all shipments for weeks. In April the air failed again and Dan was able to do nothing but drive up another air hole "day and night" for two weeks. In June things slowed down once more because one of the mules was injured. Then the hoisting cable broke and Dan had no money to buy wire rope. To take care of this, father Enoch finally put up his wife's testimonial silver service as collateral on a $500 loan. By September, Dan owed $8,000 in back rents, plus thousands more in miscellaneous debts and back pay to his men; he was selling coal at less than it cost him to produce it, just to keep cash flowing, because it cost him $400 per month to stand idle. In September the owners of the tract decided that he was not a good investment, had the work stopped by court order, and reassigned the lease to the mine operator to whom Dan owed $3,000 for driving through the fault. Dan and his father were suddenly out of business, in debt, and broke, after having—at least in their own opinion—finally gotten the old colliery in working condition again. The critical blow to Dan's venture was the fault. Until he could get through the fault, he was not able to mine coal and his breaker stood useless. Dan's father argued that driving through the fault had saved the owners $20,000 and he tried to persuade Carey and his associates to reimburse him and his son for their expenses. But they refused. It was not fair, said McGinness. "As the owners are all *rich* I don't think it right that Dan should be ruined for their benefit."[26] As for himself, he reported to Carey that he was ruined. "$4 50/100 is all I have left tonight."[27]

But, strangely enough, $4.50 was exactly what he allegedly had left when he started the St. Clair Shaft! And he was already engaged in sinking another shaft (at Carey's expense once more) on the Primrose, to prove to all the "croakers" like Russell and Patterson, and all his fortunate but stupid rivals like Johns, Milnes, and Kirk and Baum, working the Mammoth outcrop to the north, that there *was* good coal on the North American below. Patterson might say that everything south of Broad Mountain was in fault. But all that Schuylkill County really needed was a few "daring men. . . ."[28]

CELEBRATING THE INDUSTRIALIST AS HERO[1]

The moment is not long past when a new genre of heroes was created in the Western world to fit the demands of an industrial society. The hundred years between 1750 and 1850, in England and America, saw the elevation of the industrialist, and his allies in political and commercial life, to a status rivaling the traditional military heroes of the past. For an expression of the eighteenth-century pre-industrial position, we can do no better than turn to Adam Smith, who in 1759 published his *Theory of Moral Sentiments,* a work well received by his contemporaries and destined to pass through many editions. Smith argued that people are motivated in significant part by a desire to secure the esteem of their fellows by means of virtuous conduct; he was stating an early version of the "exchange theory" of twentieth-century sociologists. But as exemplars of heroic virtue Smith mentioned only great military leaders, of both ancient and modern times, and the Duke of Marlborough received his highest accolade on account of his unparalleled "coolness and self-command" and his lack of "excessive self-estimation and presumption." (Modesty was a necessary accompaniment of heroism, in Smith's view.) Smith's choice of Marlborough is an interesting one, for Marlborough's reputation was at that time under a cloud on account of alleged irregularities in his political and financial affairs. But Smith focused *only* on his military conduct, evidently regarding political and economic behavior as irrelevant to virtue. The relative moral unimportance of economic behavior—after all, it was merely the expression of man's innate "propensity to truck, barter, and exchange one thing for another"—is noteworthy. The welfare of the community, in economic matters, was owing not to the daring of heroic investors (he regarded investment in mining ventures as merely foolish speculation) but to the "invisible hand" of economic law that guided individual actions toward the common good. Similarly, he showed relatively little interest in the progress of mechanical invention, discussing it under the rubric of the "Division of Labor," and concentrating attention mostly on the contributions of workmen who wanted to lighten their task. A critical improvement in the steam engine (the automatic steam-valve control) was ascribed to an unnamed boy who wanted "to divert himself with his playfellows" instead of attending to his task of opening and shutting the valve by hand. Newcomen, Smeaton, and Watt—steam-engine inventors and heroes of a later day—were not mentioned by their eighteenth-century contemporary. But, as others have remarked, Smith was not fully aware that an Industrial Revolution was occurring all around him, despite his recognition of economic progress.[2]

The eighteenth-century pre-industrial position may be summarized as follows. Enlightened Europeans accorded the status of hero to men—occasionally to women too—who, at great risk to their own lives, property, or reputation, undertook a course of action that was intended to preserve, or enhance, the welfare of the community, and particularly the nation as a whole. Victory was not necessary; heavy casualties among both followers and enemies were allowable; courage, perseverance, and good intentions were enough. For the most part, these conditions could be satisfied only by service in war and in the exploration of new lands. Ancient and legendary heroes possessed these attributes and newly created heroes—such as Admiral Nelson and General Washington and Christopher Columbus—did too. Merchants, industrialists, statesmen, and philosophers might be lauded as great men, but they were not heroes.

But seventy-five years later, Englishmen (and Americans and Frenchmen) were acutely aware of an Industrial Revolution all about them, and the cult of the economic, non-military hero was in full swing. The leading English exponent of the cult was Samuel Smiles, a physician with experience as a railroad official, who wrote his popular lives of the engineers to celebrate a new kind of hero. Smiles viewed the engineer as the man who, by developing new sources of energy, by inventing new machines, by opening new lands to cultivation, and by devising new means of transportation, opened up benighted regions to the light of modern civilization and brought order and health to ignorant, lawless, hungry, and diseased millions. Such benefactors of mankind were a special breed, emerging from the ranks of the rural working class, largely self-taught, and nobly courageous. The first exemplar of this type to receive Smiles' treatment, in 1857, was George Stephenson, the coal miner, mining engineer, inventor of a successful miner's safety lamp, and developer of one of the first successful steam locomotives. Smiles' rhetoric in describing Stephenson's trial of his lamp, as he advanced into a gassy mine with his lighted lamp in hand, defines the character of the industrial hero in vivid terms and explicitly compares him to the military hero:

Stephenson, advancing alone, with his yet untried lamp, in the depths of those underground workings, calmly venturing his life in the determination to discover a mode by which the lives of many might be saved, and death disarmed in these fatal caverns, presented an example of intrepid nerve and manly courage more noble than that which, in the excitement of battle and the collective impetuosity of a charge, carries a man up to the cannon's mouth.[3]

Smiles' book was published in an American edition in the same year. He went on to write competent and readable biographies of other engineers, and he also wrote books on the improvement of character with titles like *Self Help, Duty,* and *Thrift.* His emphasis throughout was on the goal of development—the development of wild, uncultivated, uncivilized lands, and the correlative development of men of character. He articulated a mystique of industrial progress, seeing it as the means by which poverty, ignorance, violence, and vice could be eradicated, and prosperity, education, cooperation, and virtue take their place. His heroes, largely drawn from poor rural circumstances, developed their own characters and achieved wealth; and with dauntless courage and indomitable perseverance they worked to make a good life possible for others. Smiles saw the process of economic development as a complex unfolding that required the services not only of inventors but also of engineers and investors, not only of mechanicians but also of scientists. It was no mere Horatio Alger or Tom Swift the Boy Inventor kind of fable that he was creating, but a valid myth for the times that celebrated the heroic virtues appropriate to the goal of industrialization. As confidence in industrial society itself has declined, of course, so has Smiles' standing as a literary figure; but that is another story.

George Stephenson as hero was introduced to the educational system of Schuylkill County most emphatically on the occasion of the thirteenth annual meeting of the Schuylkill County Teachers' Institute in December 1875. The sessions were held in Pottsville and attended by the teachers and principals of all the public schools in the county (including St. Clair). During these institutes the schools were closed for the week so that the teachers could receive special training in the theory and method of education. After the day's work of discussing the philosophy and mechanics of education, there were evening entertainments. Traditionally, the second evening was devoted to a lecture about a famous man—a military hero or literary lion, generally; the previous year the subject had been Sherman's

March to the Sea. But on this occasion the speaker, a Mr. William Parsons of Dublin—a popular figure on the Lyceum circuit—chose to substitute for the announced subject, dramatist Richard Sheridan, his own personal friend, the "brave hero of the mine," George Stephenson. Most of the hour and a half was devoted to Stephenson's later exploits, but the introduction told the story of how Stephenson as "a little boy" risked his life to save miners in a burning pit. In a final fit of eloquence, the speaker attributed America's entire prosperity, her freedom, her glowing future as the finest achievement of the human race, to George Stephenson and his locomotive.[4]

Sentiments of admiration for the heroes of industrial progress were expressed, albeit somewhat ambivalently, by St. Clair's resident poet, Samuel H. Daddow, in an early volume of verse. Daddow's father was an immigrant Cornish miner who had for a time operated a small colliery near Mount Laffee, and young Samuel worked in his youth as a laborer and miner at Oak Hill, nearby. But Daddow managed to hire on as a clerk in the company store, where he was able to find time and privacy to continue a program of self-education that led him to a job as reporter for the *Miners' Journal*. He was the principal author of what was for a time the major American treatise on coal-mining methods (*Coal, Iron, and Oil,* published by Bannan in 1866) and went on to become a highly paid mining engineer and the co-inventor and manufacturer of a squib (a type of fuse) used by miners all over the world. As he prospered, he moved to St. Clair and with his family occupied one of the best houses in town, on South Second Street; he was a leader in the Methodist Episcopal Church and taught Sunday School. Daddow was a high achiever of humble origins, motivated to succeed in the middle-class world.[5]

In 1853, under the pseudonym "Alpha Lyra" (an alternative name for Vega the Harp, near the North Star, one of the brightest constellations in the heavens), Daddow offered to the Pottsville public a book of verse entitled *Trevaro and Other Occasional Poems*.[6] He prefaced it with a diffident introduction, apologizing for his lack of a "classic education" and of "cosmopolite and refined manners," the consequences of a "a toiling life," and denying that he was a "mute inglorious Milton," though yet daring to claim a "strong mind." His "greatest ambition" was to be "an acknowledged Poet." "Most of the poems in this collection," he wrote, "were either written for amusement, or the gratification of some of my own intimate acquaintances, at the end of toiling days by the light of the solitary lamp; after the performance of arduous duties, in a continued business, in the rough realities of which exist but little of Poetry, and less of leisure." And who were Daddow's "intimate acquaintances"? We can know some of them from the dedications of the poems. In addition to parents, uncles and aunts, and a number of young ladies to whom at one time or another he had been sentimentally attached, he dedicated several pieces to influential older men. Among these were two Pottsville ministers; one was a St. Clair schoolteacher; two were principal colliery owners at St. Clair (Thomas Johns and William Milnes), and two more were well-known mine operators elsewhere in Schuylkill County (John C. White in the Swatara Valley to the west and David P. Brown, Daddow's

Samuel Harris Daddow (1827–1875)

former employer in the Mount Laffee area). He also honored two fellow workmen of St. Clair—a miner and a shoemaker. And in broadcast fashion he dedicated his elegy on Henry Clay to "the gentlemen of Pottsville" who originated the project to erect the monumental statue of Clay on a hillside overlooking the town.

A number of Daddow's poetic effusions were tributes to the charms (and charmers) of Mount Laffee, the little mine patch where he grew up and first worked in the mines. The most extensive is a piece entitled "Old Mount Laffee, or the Home of Our Childhood," dedicated to "Mary." He introduced the verses by describing "old Mount Laffee" as "a now nearly deserted village . . . which was once partially destroyed by fire," and he noted that the name was lately applied to a new hamlet half a mile away, "as notorious for its rudeness and strife as the former was for its picturesque beauty, rural sports, and charming quietness."

> Old Mount Laffee! sacred spot!
> Lovely still though lonely;
> Ruined is thy garden plot,
> Nature's garden only:
> Where the thistle lifts his head,
> Bloomed a bed of roses;
> Where their trailing beauty spread,
> The violet reposes.

Daddow's nostalgia for his childhood's Eden had its obverse in a moral condemnation of social conditions in the coal region, intimated in the introduction, and made explicit in his concluding description of an unfinished play, *Old Galagher the Coal Operator, or the Miners of Mt. Luffco.* The play, announced Daddow, would exemplify "a Miners" life in its reality and show the effects of intemperance, immorality, and oppression; it had for its motto, "A bad master makes a bad steward and *vice versa.*"

Daddow's moralistic patriotism could not let him see miners except as exemplars of some civic vice or virtue. When he came to write his "miner's songs," dedicated to colliery operators, he switched from the view of miners as intemperate, immoral victims of oppressive mine owners to miners as heroic contributors to the success of the American economy and national defense. One is enough to quote here:

> We dig by day and we dig by night,
> For the Iron ore and the Anthracite—
> For the ore so gray, and the coal so bright;
> Sing ho, for the ore and the Anthracite!
>
> The Sailor's life has its round of charms,
> The storm and chase with their wild alarms;
> And he sings as the boatswain pipes to arms,
> "Ho! ho! for the sea with its mystic charms."
>
> The soldier fights for a scanty hire,
> Yet pants for the strife and the battle's fire;
> As he to the rampart's heights aspires,
> Sing—"ho! for the strife and battle's fire."
>
> The Farmer treads o'er his furrowed land,
> And scatters seed with his careful hand,
> And sings as he twists his shining bands,
> "Ho! ho! for hearty harvest hands."
>
> The Miner pants for no gory goal;
> In vain to him may the battle roll;
> Yet his manly heart and his fearless soul
> Sing—"ho! success to the gleaming coal."
>
> We dig by day, and we dig by night
> For the Iron ore and the Anthracite—

> For the ore so gray, and the coal so bright;
> Sing ho! for the ore and the Anthracite.[8]

But, despite its artificialities, the book expresses a real tension between the gains and losses of industrialization. There is a genuine sense of confrontation—"Good in Evil, Evil in Good," to use the title of one of the poems—that finds perhaps its clearest expression in two pieces, one entitled "The Apotheosis of Knowledge" and the other, "The Aspen or Tremble Tree."

"The Apotheosis of Knowledge" is written around the aphorism "Knowledge is power." Drawing inspiration from a Baconian kind of expectation of technological progress resulting from the accumulation of knowledge, he recites the accomplishments of the past, and intimates the triumphs of the future, including the airplane:

> She shall yet usurp the eagle's pinion,
> And men shall drink 'neath Pennsylvania's
> mountains
> And ere they thirst again, Sierra's golden fountains.

The similes are generally violent: knowledge is successively depicted as whirlwind, storm at sea, urban conflagration, prairie fire, ship of war; knowledge "will subject all Nature to our use and pleasure." But he suddenly concludes this somewhat bombastic tribute to "the superiority of mental over physical strength" by citing as the ultimate gift "the knowledge of the truth in God and in his holy word."

But Daddow was also aware of the cost of progress, not only in the coal region but more generally. One of his favorite spots, treasured in "the casket of our mind," was saluted in "The Aspen or Tremble Tree." This aspen stood near "a crystalline well by the mine" where he and Jenny once played, near their home in Mount Laffee, in their happy childhood; but now (in 1853) "modern improvements have destroyed the tryst, and husband the silver laugh of the purling streamlet." The poem is a lament over the destruction of nature by knowledge:

> The Aspen is gone—it will tremble no more!
> The hand of Progression has rooted it up! . . .
> For the barrel-staved well's with dark coal covered o'er,
> And the stream is as slow and as sluggish as sin.
> Yet often we think of the place and the time,

When the waters replied to the winds in the tree,
    When the chirruping wren had just finished his rhyme,
    And still was the hum of the honey-cloyed bee.[7]

It is tempting to interpret the imagery chosen by the devoutly Christian Daddow as symbolic of the Garden of Eden and of man and woman driven out after eating the fruit of the tree of the knowledge of good and evil. But we may suspect that, perhaps not in full awareness, Daddow was entertaining a somewhat more Manichaean conception of the modern industrial world; he accepted the inevitability of human suffering as the result of progress.

Daddow articulated some of these implications in a later work, a short story published in *Lippincott's Magazine* in 1870. "Noncarra's Bad Luck" is a tale about a Cornish tin miner and his two sons, who are working a claim 2,000 feet deep in the earth, below the coastal town of St. Agnes (where Daddow was born).[8] Daddow sets up the plot as a competition to find the optimal solution to a decision problem in a situation involving risk and uncertainty. Events are set in motion by the sudden and unexpected discovery, by Uncle Nicky Noncarra and his two sons, of "a magnificent lode of tin," just two weeks before the end of their three-months' contract period. During this contract period, because the company did not expect unlucky Uncle Nicky to find much tin, he was entitled to a high percentage of the value of what he did find. The three men differ in their response, and Daddow goes to great pains to attribute these to differences in character. Uncle Nicky is a small, wiry man of sixty who has mined tin with minimal success since he was ten years old. "Fifty years he had spent like a mole, digging blindly in the earth." His oldest son, Black Joe, dark and hairy and strong as a bull, has a vicious temper and is not very bright. The youngest son, Salathe—obviously the author's ideal self—is "his mother's son—fair and noble in appearance." "Around his forehead clustered curls of rich brown hair, and a short beard concealed his face just enough to give it a manly appearance . . . quick intelligence beamed from his eyes. . . ." This androgynous paragon had (again like the author) educated himself while his illiterate father and brother were carousing and attending cockfights.

But now Salathe is ready to challenge his father and his brother. When the old man and his elder son propose spending the last two weeks of the quarter working like large, industrious moles to get out as much of the "great blocks of almost pure tin" as possible before they lose the gallery to others in the bidding, Salathe angrily denounces the plan. Why should they not get all the silver? He proposes a different strategy: to cover over the rich lode, continue the appearance of unrewarding toil, and maintain their poor repute as unlucky miners until the contract period is over. Then they will contract for the same high percentage as before, and will have three months instead of two weeks to mine their ore. After arguing down his father and his dull brother (who becomes ever after Salathe's "slave"), Salathe's strategy is adopted. There are risks in it, of course: someone may discover the concealed lode by accident during the viewing and bid for the contract; the company may reduce the rate; they may wear themselves out working twenty-four hours a day in two shifts for three months; the other miners may be jealous. But at last the new contract is theirs, they reveal their good luck, the other miners applaud the fact that at last one of their number has triumphed over "jealous capital," and when the company tries to reduce the rate, all the miners threaten to strike. Three months later they retire with "a fortune such as had seldom fallen to the lot of a common miner, and which a lifetime of hard work and close economy could not secure to men in his condition of life." The old man, exhausted, remains feeble, and Black Joe becomes an alcoholic, but they buy little farms and live out their lives "in quiet frugal comfort." Their children go back to the tin mines. Salathe, however, who has drunk only pure water during the ordeal, becomes rich and famous:

> His career was onward and upward. His actions were honorable and his purposes noble. After a long and useful life, well spent in serving God and loving his fellow man, he closed his eventful days peacefully and calmly, full of faith in the life to come.

There are two points to be made about this little piece of spiritual autobiography. One is that after becoming a successful businessman Daddow still clung to his "evil in good, good in evil" philosophy, calmly accepting the inevitability of poverty for most miners, and seeing wrong neither in a successful turn of sharp practice (if not of fraud) nor in the human cost of success. Noncarra's little parable is ostensibly about Cornish miners, but it would seem to apply equally well to Pennsylvania colliery operators (the situation of miners, even contract miners, was never such that a fortune could be made). And what it says, in effect, is that most coal operators are doomed to fail as a result of two factors working in combination: sinking their mines in poor veins and fearing to take business risks. Only good luck can provide a potentially profitable location; only the daring and ruthless entrepreneur can turn that potentiality into a fortune.

But the ambience of respect for the economic hero was communicated not only in classrooms, books, and popular journals. There was a world of more public symbols, displayed in ceremonies, entertainments, and statuary, in which we can see deliberate efforts being made to articulate a merging of the images of military and economic patriotism.

One of the settings in which the coal trade celebrated its heroes was the testimonial dinner; and no better examples are provided than the dinners in honor of Enoch McGinness and Henry Carey.

After the St. Clair Shaft had begun to send its first carloads of coal to market, a testimonial dinner was held in Enoch McGinness' honor, on October 13, 1854, at the Mount Carbon Hotel in Pottsville. After the dinner a "Tea-Service of Silver, of the most costly and magnificent design," was presented to him by the district's Congressman, F. W. Hughes, on behalf of the gentlemen of the coal trade. Then Hughes went on to state the reason for the occasion. It was intended, he said,

> as a memorial of their appreciation of the energy and intelligence that, surmounting all obstacles, whether of prejudice or theory, have demonstrated the accessibility for practical working, of the great White-Ash Coal Measures throughout the entire [Pottsville] Basin. . . . You have vanquished difficulties, and have demonstrated the inexhaustibility of this Coal Basin as a resource for Anthracite Coal, and have shown the vast and munificent provisions of Providence for a supply of fuel for all the purposes of the thronging myriads that in future generations will inhabit this continent. This is your work, sir; this your proud monument— more lasting than brass—enough for the just ambition of any one.[9]

Hughes went on to emphasize the vast importance of McGinness' accomplishment in proving that the great white-ash veins, "instead of being reachable only at the Northern rim of our Coal Basin, as formerly supposed, are so at all desirable points throughout its entire area." He exulted that every acre of land "could be made to yield a product from sixty to one hundred thousand tons of Coal!" And he sketched out a utopian view of "that vast industrial population" that in centuries to come would throng the mountains of Schuylkill County and would transmit the impact of Schuylkill coal "throughout the world."[10]

McGinness responded with becoming modesty, thanking his friends for standing by him "through good and through evil," admitting to his own financial interest in the enterprise, and assuring his listeners (and creditors) that he expected to send to market 1,000 tons of coal per day from the St. Clair Shaft. He then handed over the tea service to Mrs. McGinness and sat down.

Now came the toasts from the company of coal men, which included virtually every important figure connected with the trade. McGinness' patrons, Abraham Hart and Henry Carey, praised his energy, skill, and industry; and Carey took occasion to observe that McGinness had been "laughed at as a visionary" just as he, Carey, and Burd Patterson had been nearly twenty years before, when they proposed to sink the first slope. Carey warmed to his identification with McGinness as a prophet without honor and, in words reminiscent of Matthew Boulton in the previous century ("We sell what the world wants—power"), declared his own apotheosis of *cheap* power:

> We, Mr. Chairman, supply cheap fuel to the housekeeper; we supply power to the shipowner and the manufacturer; and it is to our cheap power that the Nation is indebted for its ocean steamers and its factories. Yet, on every occasion, we are treated as enemies rather than as *friends!*[11]

The toasts, long, well prepared, and undoubtedly written for publication, went on for hours, always celebrating the courage of the many men—not McGinness alone—who had battled to build the coal trade. But again and again McGinness was saluted for his "Sagacity, Energy, Perseverance." He was hailed by the agent of the Wetherill group, John Macomb Wetherill, as "the Columbus of Schuylkill County" for having proven a geological theory (previously derided by Wetherill) as important, perhaps, as the rotundity of the earth, and for having brought to successful completion "undoubtedly, the greatest work of mining in the United States." Throughout the proceedings, the theme was the courage and perseverance of the pioneers of the coal trade in "the rescue of their country from the dominion of the beasts of the forest, to place it under the rules of enlightened life." The celebration did not end until after midnight. The proceedings were published by Bannan as a book within the year, with editorial comments by the popular writer Ele (Eli) Bowen, under the title *The McGinness Theory of the Schuylkill Coal Formation.*

In 1859 it was Henry Carey himself who was treated to a public testimonial dinner. Although Carey was known to insiders as one of the founders of the coal trade, it was not as an owner of coal mines that he was honored, but as a political economist and particularly as an influential

advocate of the protective tariff. Carey's agonistic rhetoric struck a re-
sounding chord in the hearts of virtually everyone connected with the coal
trade. He blamed the very real hardships of the trade not on the trade itself
but on outsiders, and placed responsibility for solving the trade's problems
on other shoulders. They might not read his other books on political economy and social science, which argued the case for protectionism in somewhat more abstract language; but they knew that Carey was their man in
the high councils of the new Republican Party and a powerful commen-
tator on public affairs. He was one of them, he had served with them in the
ranks, striving to develop his own coal properties. But his special value, his
status as a hero of the coal trade, rested upon the economic doctrines with
which he fought to establish a favorable political and financial climate—
and with which, like Enoch McGinness, he provided a nourishing illusion.

And so, in the spring of 1859, on the eve of a visit to Europe, Carey
was invited on a triumphal tour of the northern coal region. He was wined
and dined and toasted and listened to in a series of coal towns from Mauch
Chunk, Wilkes-Barre, Scranton, and Pittston to the great ironworks at
Danville. The invitation by George W. Scranton, S. T. Scranton, and others
was typical; it saluted him as a scientific genius who had placed the policy
of protection at the heart of the discipline of economics.

> *Dear Sir*—The undersigned, citizens of Luzerne county, have
> watched with pride and interest the preeminent part you have
> taken in defence of the Protective policy. We believe that your
> labors mark an era in the science of political economy. To your
> researches and lucid arguments are we indebted for the explosion
> of the absurdities of Malthus, Say, and Ricardo, in regard to the
> inability of the earth to meet the demands of a growing popula-
> tion. American industry owes you a debt which cannot be repaid,
> and which it will ever be proud to acknowledge. Regarding you as
> one of the foremost champions of the great doctrine of protection,
> which lies at the foundation of our national prosperity, and is
> especially identified with the leading interests of our honored
> Commonwealth, we shall be happy to welcome you in our midst,
> and we, therefore, cordially invite you to name a day when it will
> suit your convenience to pay a visit to this region, prior to your
> departure for a foreign land.[12]

On his return to Philadelphia, the celebration was brought to a climax
in a lavish testimonial dinner party at La Pierre's Restaurant. The names

of his friends who arranged the party included many of the industrial elite of the metropolitan area: Samuel Reeves, iron founder; William Elder, physician, lawyer, and newspaper editor; Steven Colwell, railroadman and economist; Simon Cameron, land speculator and politician; John Price Wetherill, paint manufacturer and owner of coal lands; Joseph Ripka, cotton manufacturer; John and William Sellers, locomotive builders; Abraham Hart and Henry C. Baird, publishers; J. B. Lippincott, publisher; Matthew Baldwin, locomotive builder; Edward Biddle, financier; John Tucker, president of the Reading Railroad; and dozens of others. The hall was spectacularly decorated with symbols of Carey's contributions to science and industry. At one end, emblazoned upon the wall, was the motto "PROTECTION TO AMERICAN LABOR" and at the other the words "HARMONY OF INTERESTS." Pyramids of fresh-cut flowers decorated the table, hung from the chandeliers, and flanked the chair of each of the 150 guests. But the *pièce de résistance* was a display of "ornamental confectionary" in sugar and chocolate, produced in the pastry room of the hotel and placed in front of Carey himself—a candy locomotive drawing a train of candy cars loaded with candy coal and pig iron. The speeches went on for hours and were still going on when the reporter for the *North American and United States Gazette,* which devoted its entire front page to the story, left, exhausted, vowing that "The Carey Dinner . . . will not soon be forgotten by those who participated in it."[13]

To understand fully the meaning and importance of the testimonial dinner parties honoring Enoch McGinness and Henry Carey, we must retreat somewhat in time and survey a wider field. The custom of holding such ceremonial banquets in honor of men of achievement no doubt goes back into antiquity, but for the coal trade these symbolic occasions perhaps began with the completion of the first chartered lateral railroad, the Little Schuylkill Navigation, Railroad, and Coal Company, in 1831. The program of the celebration followed a form that was to become standard: a procession, a dinner, and toasts which took the form of brief eulogistic speeches. The procession was a traversal of the twenty-one-mile route from Port Clinton to Tamaqua by two horse-drawn, flag-bedecked "pleasure cars" occupied by sixty principals and a corps of buglers. On their arrival at Tamaqua, they were greeted by the sight of fifteen cars loaded with coal from the company's mines, over each of which a white flag fluttered. In front of the cars, drawn up in ranks, stood forty or fifty sooty underground miners in their work clothes, "who, with stentorian voices, roared three cheers as the procession came opposite." Leaving the grimy miners behind, the company repaired to Keasby's Hotel, where half were seated to "an excellent dinner" (the lesser members of the party were left unfed until later). After the cloth was removed, the toasts were drunk with "enthusiastic applause." These toasts complimented the men of enterprise who had projected and carried through what was, at the time, the longest railway in America. The principal honors went to Friedrich List and Moncure Robinson, through whose efforts, as we have noted earlier, the line was carried through. The rhetoric would become familiar:

> By their resistless power "the wilderness has been made to smile and the desert to blossom." Before their march the dark and almost impenetrable thickets through which the Tamaqua (Little Schuylkill River) had wound its course for unnumbered years, have disappeared; and the river itself had abandoned its accustomed channel to make room for the construction of a work which will rank high among the public improvements of the country.[14]

And one cannot leave the neighborhood of Little Schuylkill without recalling that the atmosphere of enthusiasm for railroads as the glory of the age did not leave the area soon. Almost fifteen years later, the Reading Railroad built a large engine house at Schuylkill Haven, just upriver from Port Clinton. It was in the form of a rotunda, 126 feet in diameter and 80 feet high, crowned by a cupola whose roof stood 117 feet above the ground, with a spire rising to an undetermined height above that. The building, resplendent with pilasters and Grecian consoles and Venetian latticed windows, was alleged to be the fourth-largest rotunda in the world, smaller only than the Pantheon at Rome, Santa Maria del Fiore at Florence, and St. Peter's, again at Rome. Thus did the coal trade strive to emulate the great human achievements of classical antiquity.[15]

The genre of ceremonial dinners for the heroes of the coal trade reached full bloom at the completion of the Philadelphia and Reading Railroad Company's line to Pottsville in the winter of 1842. Some of the most prominent citizens of Pottsville, including such Carey associates as the Potts brothers, the Bannan cousins, Andrew Russell, Charles Lawton, and Francis B. Nichols, invited the directors and officers of the Reading to a "Public Dinner and Ball" on Tuesday evening, January 11, 1842. In return, the railroad invited 1,000 persons from Schuylkill County to ride the company's train to Philadelphia on Monday, the day before, and return in time for the celebration in Pottsville.

It was to be an arduous experience for the hardy souls who embarked in the cars at eight o'clock in the morning. After a thirteen-gun salute at dawn, the forty-three open cars, painted a bright yellow, were entered by three companies of militia, four bands, and 1,200 citizens. Snow had fallen during the night, so a special locomotive preceded the train to clear the tracks; and a second train of fifty-two cars loaded with coal from Carey's York Farm Colliery, operated by Potts and Bannan, followed behind. After numerous stops, at which artillery salutes were fired and thirty more cars, loaded with celebrants and militia companies, were added, the train finally crawled into the Broad Street depot in Philadelphia at seven at night. The travelers now formed into a procession that marched on foot the ten blocks to the Stock Exchange, bearing banners with the following inscriptions:

> The opening of the Philadelphia, Reading and Pottsvile [*sic*] Railroad.

> The Philadelphia and Pottsville Railroad Company can never be *in* fault—so long as they have the rich deposits of the Schuylkill Coal Region to draw upon.

> We penetrate the Mountains to bring out treasures to add to your comfort and prosperity—On which [banner] was the Miners' Coat of Arms, the Pick and Shovel.

At the Exchange, most of the multitude dispersed to the warmth of hotels, boardinghouses, and the lodgings of friends, but a small party of about 100 remained for a banquet at the Washington House.

Next day the train returned after dark to Pottsville, late again, and minus a company of militia and two bands that had missed the train. There the dinner and ball went off with spectacular success. The ball excited particular comment for the brilliance of the lighting, the elegance of the decorations, and the delightfulness of "the congregated beauty of the Coal Regions."

But the spirit of the occasion was most eloquently expressed by the toastmaster, Pottsville attorney George W. Farquhar, an expert on the economics of iron and coal, whose address, opening the session of toasts in honor of the Reading Company's achievement, stated the theme of the industrialist-as-hero in emphatically utilitarian terms. His words, which echo Jeremy Bentham's advice to Wellington to be not only the "hero of war" but also the "hero of peace," are worth quoting:

> We live, Mr. Chairman, in an age of utility, and men and measures are estimated by the benefit or injury they cause. This is the result of an increased degree of intelligence, for just in proportion as we become enlightened, do we reverence the real benefactors, and condemn the malefactors of society. The vulgar glory of con-

querors has had its day, and the better informed mind turns with
disgust from fields of carnage. The benevolent spirit of the age
will tolerate no longer that war should be waged for mere ambition or glory. Its humanity revolts at suffering needlessly inflicted.
At no period, have the arts of peace been throughout the world so
highly cultivated and appreciated. A general improvement in science, and the comforts of social life is the consequence. The true
philosopher, the philanthropist will still glow at the recollection of
victories won in the great cause of human rights, but he has no
sympathy for mere conquerors; no homage for genius, perverted
to enslave or destroy. He envies neither Genghis Khan his pyramids of skulls, or Napoleon his Russian Campaign. He may ad-
mire the powers of a Machiavelli, or a Metternich, but he will
regret that unlike Sully or our own Franklin, their abilities were
not directed to benefit their species. Living, then, at a period
when men and things are estimated by the usual and benevolent
purposes they subserve; let us try by that test, to what extent our
guests are entitled to the grateful consideration of our country.
Let us see whether their railroad has added to the value of the
State, or the social happiness and comforts of its citizens.[16]

The most conspicuous symbol of the economic hero in Schuylkill
County was the Henry Clay monument in Pottsville. The monument was,
and is, a colossal iron statue of the American statesman, set upon a cast-
iron column, that stands sixty-six feet in total height from the base to the
top of the head, and twice that above the main street of the town. It is
visible from the north for miles, and dominates the town below it even
today, dwarfing public buildings and churches. Henry Clay was a hero to
the industrialists of the coal regions for one reason: his steady advocacy, in
the face of southern opposition, of the protective tariff that supposedly
nourished the rapidly growing Pennsylvania iron industry and thus the
coal industry that supplied it with fuel. Just as in cotton-manufacturing
towns there were mills named after him, so in the anthracite district there
was a town named for his estate, Ashland, and a mine named for the man
himself. When Clay died in 1852, John Bannan, a leader in Pottsville's
civic and educational affairs, and Samuel Silliman, landowner and mine
operator of St. Clair, proposed erecting a monument in his memory. The
construction, raising, and dedication were arranged by a variety of committees in which the men in the coal trade were prominent, including a
number from or associated with St. Clair—John Macomb Wetherill, Andrew
Russell, Dr. Coryell, Adam Kline, Jonathan Johnson, William Milnes, and

F. W. Hughes. Invitations to participate were distributed nationally. The completed monument was dedicated on the Fourth of July 1855. The grand procession was composed of thirty-three units, starting with six military units (including the Scott Rifles from St. Clair), extending through a long list of bands, occupational categories, and benevolent associations, and ending with "citizens mounted." It was a drunken and joyous celebration of the union of military and economic patriotism. And the resemblance of the monument to Nelson's Column in Trafalgar Square is unmistakable.[17]

The "great thoughts" expressed by the orator of the occasion concerned what might be called a second American Revolution. The first, launched in 1776, delivered the country from *political* subordination to Britain. The second, begun in 1812, freed the United States from *economic* subordination (or what might today be called a neo-colonial dependency). In that process Henry Clay is depicted as playing a dual role: as the patriotic Congressman who urged the nation to enter the War of 1812; and as the architect of the so-called American System that combined self-sufficiency in agriculture with independence in manufacturing, particularly by means of the protective tariffs of 1824 and later.[18]

The poet of St. Clair, Samuel Daddow, expressed the view in somewhat terse verse:

> With Henry Clay
> Has passed away
> Kentucky's mighty one—
> The Ashland sage
> Star of his age—
> Columbia's darling son.

Daddow's book of poems, published two years before the Clay statue was erected, shows the statue in its frontispiece.[19]

Promotional literature extolling the contributions to national greatness made by men of industry was common not only in the coal regions. On a national scale, it was voiced perhaps most effectively by J. Leander Bishop in his classic *History of American Manufactures* (published in Philadelphia in 1864). He took it as his goal to rescue from oblivion the "true history" of the men whose industrial innovations and enterprises built up "the fair fabric of our national civilization." He sought to give not merely an account of their material contributions, but also an appreciation of their lives:

The Henry Clay Monument

... what were their everyday pursuits, how they lived and supported their families, and shaped the character and directed the channels of American labor, as well as to know their lineage and connections, for whom they voted, and how they fought. Unfortunately, history has been too little cognizant of anything but the public acts or words of the world's benefactors; while often the more instructive examples of their struggles and triumphs, the heroism of their daily life, is consigned to a narrower influence.[20]

Most of the earlier celebrations of economic man explicitly contrasted the military hero of the past and the peaceful hero of the present day. The modern hero's contribution to society was not conquest but prosperity; as George Farquhar put it, "we live in an age of utility," and today's benefactor was a proper Benthamite who added to the sum of man's well-being. As Carey expressed it, the proper object of economic endeavor was to increase not the wealth but the happiness of nations, and he deplored the British tendency to elevate to glory military heroes rather than heroes of peaceful statesmanship. But, as the decades passed, the distinction began to blur and the image of the military leader and the entrepreneur began to merge. More and more commonly, at least in the coal regions, the industrialist was also a military man or at least a conspicuous contributor to the military strength of the nation. Coal became a patriotic fuel.

Perhaps the first intimation of this union of Mars and anthracite was contained in Nicholas Biddle's toast, at the Pioneer Furnace celebration in 1840, to Old Pennsylvania, which had "plenty of Coal to warm her friends" and "plenty of Iron to cool her enemies." The theme was, in a sense, the resolution of the plot of Wetherill's comedy, *Mars in Mahantango,* which concludes with the militia commander marrying the daughter of the colliery operator. The union of economic and military virtue became public and explicit in the ceremonial dedication of the Henry Clay monument, for Clay presented a Janus-like image, old War Hawk of 1812 behind, great statesman and proponent of the American System—including the protective tariff—to the fore.

But these rhetorical flourishes were converted into serious social policy by the militarization of the coal fields that accompanied the Civil War. During the tense winter days preceding the first summer of the War between the States, the conjunction of Mars and anthracite stood forth conspicuously. There was an "Inauguration of an American Flag" upon the steps of the county courthouse in Pottsville on February 22, 1861 (Washington's birthday), and a procession followed by speeches. The procession was as usual led by military units, now including the "Wetherill Rifles of St. Clair" and the "Marion Rifles of Port Carbon," led by Captain Allison (the engineer whose daughters taught school in St. Clair). John Bannan, of course, was the organizer; he was now a colonel himself. The speech, supporting the Union, was richly embroidered with allusions to "a noble history" and to "the illustrious deeds" of the hearers' ancestors.[21] During the war, men prominently associated with the coal trade served along with others, many of them as high-ranking officers, and they tended to retain their titles after the war. Secretary of War Cameron, Colonel Wetherill, and General Pleasants were well known as operators and landowners, and there were a number of others in the region. Furthermore, after 1866 all, or at least most, local superintendents held commissions from the state in the Coal and Iron Police and commanded their own companies' forces. Thus captains of industry were apt to be captains at arms as well.

The implications of this shift of the industrialist's image from the non-military toward the military are important. If it was not just a change in the public image *of* the industrialist but also a change in self-image *by* the industrialist as well, from the operators of 1845 to those of 1875, then calls for a tighter industrial discipline were really appeals to a military morality. The scenario unfolds like one of Wetherill's plays. The operators are captains of industry leading an army of workers into battle with nature in order to extract black gold from the depths. Both officers and men naturally take risks, the one class financial, the other physical (although a few operators and numbers of superintendents and bosses were in fact killed and injured in mine accidents). But there are casualties in all wars; the army's task is to press on, to dig out the dusky diamonds as fast as possible. Any holding back, or refusal to obey orders, is tantamount to mutiny, to be put down if necessary by force. The commander does what he can to feed, clothe, and house his men decently. But safety is not the aim of war, and, anyway, good soldiers somehow manage to survive; it is the unskilled, inattentive, careless raw recruits who die. And, naturally, no soldier sues his commanding officer for ordering him into a battle in which he is wounded. Eventually the campaign ends, the exhausted colliery closes down, the commander gets his gold and is awarded his hero medal, and the old soldier, his wounds healed, retires contentedly to his cottage in the beautiful green hills of Schuylkill County.

The prospect of being publicly honored for helping to develop an industry that was essential to the prosperity of the county, to the economy of the state, and to the defense of the nation, no doubt added to the pleasure of making money and diminished the pain of losing it. The industrialist-as-hero theme was a system of non-financial rewards that helped the coal trade recruit and retain its investors, colliery operators, and political friends. But there was another function that played a more equivocal role in the economy of the coal trade. The literary plaudits and the dinners and the statues celebrated not any and all brave heroes of the mine. It celebrated precisely those who not only exemplified the heroic virtues of the new age but also promulgated two of its most necessary illusions: that the geology of the Pottsville Basin was favorable to underground coal mining; and that the protective tariff would relieve the trade's financial problems. A third illusion—that careless miners, rather than negligent operators, were responsible for mine accidents—was promulgated by other means.

Illustrations, from early photographs, published in 1885 in the Annual Report of the Inspector of Coal Mines, *showing miners, laborers, and breaker boys at work in the Kohinoor Colliery near Shenandoah*

V

THE POLITICS OF SAFETY

Henry Carey and Enoch McGinness, and men like them, did not include the human casualties of colliery accidents in their optimistic calculations of profit and the happiness of nations. Privately they were able to recognize the role of poor colliery design and maintenance in creating the conditions for financially unfortunate events such as fires and explosions. In the public arena, however—for instance, in the pages of the *Miners' Journal*—the blame for colliery damage, as well as death and injury was regularly placed on the shoulders of "the careless miner." Not until a county-wide miners' union was formed in the late 1860's, able to lobby effectively in Harrisburg, was safety legislation passed by the Pennsylvania legislature.

DEATH AND DISABLEMENT IN THE MINES

During the years before 1869, when official casualty statistics were first published, the general public as well as the mining population were well aware that coal mining was a dangerous occupation. The *Miners' Journal* regularly published accounts of mining accidents. It is difficult to estimate how many casualties went unreported in the *Journal*, but if we compare newspaper reports with the official list of casualties published annually by the state after 1868 as part of the *Report of the Inspectors of Coal Mines*, we can calculate a rough figure. In 1869, for the period of nine months from April through December, the *Miners' Journal* reported 16 deaths in Schuylkill County mines; the report of the mine inspectors for the same months of 1869 listed 56 fatalities. The *Journal* reported few non-fatal injuries; the state report listed 91. Clearly the *Journal*'s fractional, selective reporting minimized public awareness of the degree of risk involved in coal mining. But the *Journal* did list 4 fatalities that were missing from the official tally, so the actual total was at least 60. If the *Journal* had listed 56 fatalities, and found the same proportion of deaths unreported by the state, then there would actually be 14 deaths not reported by the mine inspectors, making an estimated total of 70 fatalities. This suggests that the official casualty figures for 1869 underestimated the number of fatalities by approximately one quarter and very probably underestimated the non-fatal injuries by an even larger factor. The definition of a reportable injury was vague at best, but perusal of the casualty lists reveals that only serious injuries—severe burns, amputations, major fractures—were reported. Some miners listed as "burned by fire-damp explosion" were later to be found at work; on the other hand, a mere broken arm did not necessarily constitute a reportable accident. And some "injured" miners undoubtedly died later of their injuries; but these delayed fatalities were not reported at all in 1869. If delayed fatalities were added to the list, the underestimate would exceed 25 percent.

The official statistics for the complete year of 1870 revealed the fact—shocking to chauvinistic Americans—that casualties in the four southern counties of the anthracite district of Pennsylvania were much more frequent, per ton of coal mined, than in Great Britain: one death per 49,174 tons versus one per 103,000 tons. The mine inspectors' report listed 129 killed in accidents and 298 injured, and the published tonnage casualty rates were calculated on that basis; but the deaths recorded by the inspector actually numbered 157 because the 129 did not include 28 injured persons who were noted in the "injured" list as having "died subsequently of the results of injuries." Furthermore, the *Miners' Journal* reported 17 deaths in 1870; of these, 2 were not included in the government report. If we apply an undercount ratio of 2/17 to the official list of 129 immediate fatalities, we must add another 15, bringing the total of deaths to an estimated 172, higher by about one third than the number used to calculate the official tonnage-per-fatality ratio. Applying the same factor (1.33) to injuries, these rise to 396. Recalculated, the American rate climbs to one death per 36,875 tons mined and sets the American fatality rate at three times the British figure.

But these are averages for the four counties of Schuylkill, Northumberland, Columbia, and Dauphin. If we look at Schuylkill County alone where most of the deep mines were located and most of the coal was mined, the rates are much worse. The inspector's report for 1870 lists 112 killed and 252 injured in Schuylkill. If we apply the same corrective factor (1.33) in Schuylkill alone as we did to the figures for the whole southern field, they rise to 149 killed and 335 injured. In Schuylkill County as a whole, with 3,938,429 tons of coal mined, the tonnage-per-fatality ratio is only 26,432. Within Schuylkill County, the corrected fatality figure for the Pottsville district (within which fell St. Clair) is 62; coal production was 2,072,845 tons; the tonnage-per-fatality ratio was thus 33,433. Comparing this with the British average of one fatality to every 103,000 tons mined, we find that in the Pottsville district a miner was about three times as likely to be killed as his British counterpart, and those in other parts of Schuylkill about four.

The casualty probabilities (based on corrected figures) are also impressive. Estimating the total colliery labor force in the southern field at 30,000 (the mine inspectors' report figure), we find that the probability of a colliery employee being killed in one year (1870 data) was .0058, or about half of one percent, and of being seriously injured .013 or about one percent. In Schuylkill County, with 21,000 employees and a higher rate of casualties, the rates were .0071 and .0161, approaching 1% and 2% respectively. But most of these deaths and injuries—at least 137 out of the 157 deaths officially reported and described in the mine inspectors' report—happened underground. Inasmuch as the underground work force was routinely estimated as one half the total for the colliery, we have a situation where about 90 percent of the casualties are occurring among 50 percent of the men.

Whether one uses the casualty figures published in the mine inspector's annual reports, or attempts to correct them to a "truer" (and inevitably higher) number, one finds that in 1869 and 1870 the order of magnitude is about the same. But the casualty record seems to have improved in the Pottsville district through the 1870's and 1880's. Unmodified figures from the annual report for 1880 list only 15 fatalities in the Pottsville district and a total tonnage of 1,882,796 tons, yielding a tonnage-per-fatality ratio of 125,519. In 1890, for the Pottsville district, there were 17 fatalities listed and 2,579,160 tons reported, yielding a tonnage per fatality ratio of 151,715. Perhaps in later years better medical facilities and more scrupulous attention to safety eventually had a beneficial effect.

The foregoing figures are regional averages; the experience of particular mines might be higher or lower. Looking at the four major collieries in operation in the St. Clair area in 1870—Pine Forest, Eagle, St. Clair Shaft, and Wadesville Shaft—we find a total of 7 deaths and 28 injuries officially reported. With an inside work force of approximately 568, the *uncorrected* casualty rate for deaths and injuries combined was 6.1 percent. Most of these casualties, however, were concentrated in two collieries, the St. Clair Shaft with 3 deaths and 11 injuries, and the Wadesville Shaft, with 2 deaths and 12 injuries. The death rate for the 126 inside workers at the St. Clair Shaft for this year was 3/126 or 2.4 percent and the injury rate

11/126 or 8.7 percent; the total casualty rate for inside employees was 11.1 percent. For the Wadesville Shaft, with 205 inside workers, the rates were 2/205 or 1.0 percent for fatalities and 12/205 or 5.9 percent for injuries; the rate for total casualties was 6.8 percent. These casualty rates, furthermore, are based on uncorrected figures; if they were increased by one quarter—the approximate correction factor used before—the rates would go up correspondingly, with the St. Clair Shaft combined rate rising to 14 percent.

The year 1870 was a bad one for the St. Clair and Wadesville shafts and good for the Eagle, which had no deaths and no injuries reported, and the Pine Forest, with no deaths and only three injuries. But the Eagle and the Pine Forest over the years also had a substantial, if variable, rate of deaths and injuries. In the fifteen years from 1870 through 1884, the Eagle had a total of 11 reported deaths and 23 injuries, or 2.3 casualties per year; with an inside force of about 132 men, this yields an average combined rate, based on uncorrected figures, of 1.7 percent. With corrected figures, the rate would rise to 2.3 percent. For the Pine Forest, uncorrected figures yield a combined rate over this period of 5.1 percent and a corrected rate of 6.8 percent. Comparable figures cannot be calculated over this same period for the Wadesville and St. Clair shafts because the St. Clair Shaft was abandoned in 1874 and the Wadesville Shaft was out of production much of the time from 1871 through 1876 as a result of a series of explosions, underground fires, and floods. During the last eight years, however, from 1876 to 1884, the Wadesville Shaft was in production again, and its combined rates were 4.5 percent uncorrected and 6.0 percent corrected.

It must be remembered that these casualty figures are based on experience *after* the passage of the 1869 Mine Safety Act and the imposition of some reform. But what were the numbers like in the two decades preceding? The anecdotal accounts in the *Miners' Journal* do reveal that death and injury were common, but the accidents reported there are only an unknown fraction of the total. Fortunately, we do have a quantitative estimate, however, by a correspondent in the *Miners' Journal* in 1858, who wrote from Tamaqua in support of a Miners Hospital and Relief Association:

> Taking for a basis the number of accidents that occur in this region in the course of a year at 2140 which is a low estimate, one-third of that number may be so maimed as to be totally unfit for their usual occupation, 721 men, many of them with families without the means of support. You may calculate also out of the

above number of accidents, one-third result in death, which will leave nearly 700 widows and 1400 orphans annually, without provision or support.[1]

The Tamaqua correspondent estimated the number of workers at 12,000, a reasonable figure. But the casualty rates revealed in these figures are very much higher than those issued in the mine inspectors' reports for 1869 and later: in each year, 6 percent of the "persons employed either in mining, preparing, or conveying" coal (not just underground workers) were killed, 12 percent either killed or crippled for life, and 18 percent either killed, crippled, or seriously injured with the prospect of sooner or later returning to work. According to this estimate, a colliery employee had a less than even chance of surviving for twelve years; he could expect to be killed or crippled for life in six. And these estimates included surface workers as well as miners; the corrected rates for underground miners, laborers, mule drivers, and door boys would presumably be much higher, on the order of 10 percent killed per year, and proportionate rates for the other categories. Applying these rates to St. Clair, with approximately 600 colliery workers in 1850, one would expect 108 accidents in the five or six collieries in and around the town, with about 36 fatalities.

Rates such as these are on the order of military losses in combat, and the comparison was remarked on at the time. In addition to rhetorical flourishes by such versifiers as Daddow, who extolled miners in naval and military metaphor, and the anonymous composers of popular ballads like "The Miner's Doom," practical miners expressed the same opinion. Thus John Maguire of Crow Hollow commented in his reminiscences of mining in the 1850's, '60's, and '70's:

> Considering the numerous accidents in mining and the dangers involved, and comparing the risks of a miner with those of a soldier, Mr. Maguire used to assert that a miner is a soldier every day he works, while the man in the army is only taking risks when he goes to the front, which is only occasionally. Looking back over a long period of mining, the dangers he recalled having passed through were very, very many, and he realized that the miner may expect, in the natural course of events, to ultimately meet his death in the performance of his duties.[2]

And Jack Johnson, a miner from Luzerne, said much the same thing in "The Miner's Life" in 1884:

You can talk about the railroads,
the danger they go through
Warriors and sailor boys,
I know it's very true.
They have good air to work in,
for the roof they have the sky:
There's no one braves the danger
like the poor miner boy.
They have bad air to work in,
shattered pillars and bad top,
They don't know the moment
when a fall on them might drop,
A little lamp to show them light—
that is their brightest hope,
See the danger they go through
coming up a shaft or slope.
When a miner is at work
in a gangway or a breast,
His mind is never easy
if he sits down to rest,
For fear some careless comrade
the gas he might ignite
And cause a great explosion,
and then you would see a sight.
There are other dangers
poor miners often dread:
Water in abandoned slopes,
perhaps not far ahead.
There are instances where they struck it
they hadn't time to fly,
Brought death and destruction
to the poor miner boy.
Way down in the coal mines,
in the bowels of the earth below,
Where the sun it never shines
or gently wind does blow;
If you went there it would make you stare
and fill your heart with dread,
To see the dangers they go through
to earn their daily bread.[3]

And even the ever popular show tune "Down in a Coal Mine" repeated the ominous refrain of peril:

> How little do the great ones care,
> who sit at home secure,
> What hidden dangers colliers dare,
> what hardships they endure;
> The very fires their mansions boast,
> to cheer themselves and wives,
> Mayhap were kindled at the cost
> of jovial colliers' lives.[4]

Let us examine the *Miners' Journal* reports of accidents for St. Clair miners in 1861, a year in which Schuylkill's coal production fell below 2,800,000 tons for the first time since 1853. With production languishing as a result of the onset of war, one might expect a low level of casualties. Actually, the *Miners' Journal* reported 7 deaths and 16 major injuries. Four of the deaths and 13 of the injuries were the result of firedamp explosions; the other 3 deaths were caused by the breaking of chains while men were being hoisted up the shaft. All were accidents underground.

If we assume that the *Miners' Journal* failed to report the same proportion of deaths in 1861 as in 1869, then the number 7 should be increased by a factor of 70/16, yielding a corrected figure of 31 fatalities. Assuming an inside work force in 1861 in the same proportion to production figures as in 1870, or 398 men, the fatality rate in the four major St. Clair mines must have been approximately 7.8 percent. But this general estimate does not adequately indicate the situation. The majority of the deaths and injuries occurred in the traditionally dangerous mines: Kirk and Baum's St. Clair Shaft and Slope and the Milnes' Hickory Slope. At these mines the casualty rates, using uncorrected figures (4 deaths and 14 injuries) and allowing one-quarter of the underground workers to Kirk and Baum and one quarter to Milnes, are 2 percent killed, 7 percent injured, and 9 percent combined; using corrected figures, the rates soar to 9 percent killed, 32 percent injured, 41 percent combined!

Such numbers stretch the imagination. Perhaps the correction of 70/16 needed to bring the *Miners' Journal* tally, on a county-wide basis, into agreement with the official figures for 1869 and 1870 is too high for communities close to Pottsville. Perhaps the editors had more nearly complete reports from St. Clair than from, let us say, Ashland or Shenandoah. But evidently the dangerous mines at St. Clair, even when they were closed most of the year, could still produce a fatality rate somewhere between 2 and 9 percent and a combined casualty rate between 9 and 41 percent for underground workers. Figures such as these lend plausibility to the Tamaqua correspondent's 1858 estimate of 6 percent fatalities, 12 percent injuries, and 18 percent combined casualties.

Also suggesting that these high figures are not unreasonable are the mortality rates for the general population of the county. In 1853, in the county medical society's annual report in the state society's *Transactions*, it was stated that the county's crude death rate, despite the healthiness of the population as a whole, was 1.44 percent. This figure was above the state average, in the rapporteur's opinion, but it would have been much lower, he claimed, "if we deduct the large number of deaths which occur from accidents."[5]

Another source of casualties to the mining population was, of course, the industrial disease "miner's asthma." Local physicians recognized a variety of lung disorders that they believed were caused, or aggravated, by the breathing of coal dust, stone dust, powder smoke, and methane and carbon-monoxide gas. As early as 1856, in the annual report of the county medical society, the growing incidence of miner's asthma was recognized as a major public-health problem:

> . . . you find but few miners at all advanced in life, who are not laboring under some disease of the chest, but more particularly asthma. . . . [6]

Dr. Carpenter, the Pottsville physician, writing in 1869, argued that the chronic inhalation of firedamp and choke-damp (carbon dioxide) produced a characteristic neurological syndrome including dyspepsia, tremors, vertigo, and palpitation "entirely independent of organic disease." Carpenter was not in a position to consider the possibility that what he observed was a psychosomatic response to prolonged anxiety comparable to what would later come to be called, among troops in battle, "combat fatigue." But he too was most concerned about miner's asthma and its debilitating and often fatal course:

> A peculiar asthmatic character of cough is generally noticed; emphysema is detected on physical exploration, and the sputa are black, often streaked with blood. Miner's asthma is chronic bronchitis, with thickening of the air passages, emphysema and ner-

vous distress in breathing. These chronic troubles may last a lifetime, without being rapidly fatal, or necessarily so. But acute pneumonia supervenes in many cases on some exposure and is very apt to prove fatal. If not, a chronic softening of the lungs may occur, in other words, phthisis, which is a frequent disease among these men, and generally an incurable one.[7]

The coal editor of the *Miners' Journal*, in an article on "The Hygiene of Coal Mines" (published in a textbook on public health in 1879), put the problem in more dramatic language:

> . . . the deeper the workings penetrate the less water is found and the drier and more dusty the coal becomes. Any one who has seen a load of coal shot from a cart, or has watched the thick clouds of dust which sometimes envelop the huge coalbreakers of the Anthracite region so completely as almost to hide them from sight, can form an idea of the injurious effect upon the health of constant working in such an atmosphere. . . . Ventilation mitigates this evil, but does not obviate it. . . . Every fresh stroke of the pick or the hammer, every shovelful of coal moved, every fall of a dislodged mass, causes a fresh cloud of dust, until the ventilating current would need to flow with a force little short of a hurricane to keep the miner's lungs supplied with unvitiated air.

And he quoted an Ohio mine inspector, Andrew Roy, on the short expectancy of life in a dusty mine:

> . . . After six years' labor in a badly ventilated mine—that is, a mine where a man with a good constitution may from habit be able to work every day for several years—the lungs begin to change to a bluish color. After twelve years they are densely black, not a vestige of natural color remaining, and are little better than carbon itself. The miner dies at thirty-five years, of coal miner's consumption.[8]

Statistical information, however, is not available on the prevalence of "miner's consumption" in this period.

The social implications of casualty rates of the order of magnitude indicated above, and of a probably high rate of death and disability from lung diseases, are considerable. Death or serious injury to the married

257

miner left a wife and children with an immediate problem of finding means of subsistence in a community that did not provide relief from public funds except in the poorhouse. Most of the miners were married and had children—in 1870, for instance, 72 of the 112 men reported killed in the county had wives, and their deaths left 72 widows and 252 children. These relicts coped in various ways: some were helped, temporarily, by one or another benevolent association; some widows took in boarders or opened little candy stores or drinking places; some certainly remarried; some moved in with other households of an extended family, or sent children to live with such relatives. But one must suspect that casualties were outrunning the ability of the extended-family system and the benevolent associations to provide relief for the disabled, widowed, and orphaned.

BUSINESS FAILURES

The failure rate among colliery operators was extraordinarily high. The principal economic historian of the Schuylkill coal trade, Clifton K. Yearley, found, in a sample of over 300 Schuylkill County collieries in the period 1820 to 1875, that 95 percent failed within five years; the median life expectancy of a colliery business was less than one year.[1] The demise of a colliery did not mean that the works closed forever, of course, only that a given operator went out of business, losing his lease and either selling his surface real estate and equipment or seeing it sold for him at a sheriff's auction. The pages of the *Miners' Journal* bulged with advertisements of collieries for sale by the sheriff. As Franklin B. Gowen, the president of the Reading Railroad and of its subsidiary Coal and Iron Company, and himself a former colliery operator at Mount Laffee who failed when his mine caught fire, remarked in 1875: "Three men retired from the business of coal mining with money . . . one of those died in an insane asylum and another had softening of the brain."[2] It is difficult to avoid the conclusion that most operators lost money over the years and eventually failed, and that the operators as a class were providing their consumers with coal at a price below what it cost them and their creditors to mine, prepare, transport, and sell to the consumer.

Part of the problem was the low margin of profit on a ton of coal. There were occasional good years, but by and large the net profit per ton during a year in which coal was mined without interruption was on the order of 10 to 12 cents. Eckley B. Coxe of Hazleton testified at length concerning costs and profits during a U.S. Senate hearing in 1888. Coxe was a large operator with a million dollars invested in nine collieries; he was also a well-educated, scientifically trained man, the recipient of an M.A. degree from a German school of mine engineering, and the translator of a standard German engineering textbook (Julius Weisbach's *Manual of the Mechanics of Engineering, with an Introduction to the Calculus*).[3] Coxe testified:

> I suppose there is in this country no man who has given more attention to the details of cost of mining anthracite coal than I. It has been the study of my life. I am naturally a mathematician. If I had not been forced into coal mining by my surroundings I would have been a professor of mathematics. The coal we have mined in the last two years, without allowing any interest on our capital, anything for depreciation (and you gentlemen will agree with me that a coal mine does not grow better from constant working) has cost within twelve cents of what we got for it. That is, the difference between what the coal cost and what we sold it for was almost twelve cents. Now, although it is impossible to tell exactly every cost that should enter into the cost of coal, as near as I can make it out it was about twelve cents a ton margin on the coal that we had made during last two years. It requires an enormous amount of capital, which should bear interest, to get out the coal and keep up all the departments. We have made no charge for interest on the plant and no charge for depreciation of the plant. In other words, gentlemen, if we had had the money that we have put in the mining invested in a mortgage at five percent, and had we done nothing, we would have been better off in the last two years.[4]

Coxe's figures might perhaps be questioned on grounds of special pleading: he was explaining, during a strike, why the colliery operators could not afford to pay the workers the wages they demanded. But other sources support Coxe's estimate. Peter W. Sheafer in 1864, in a brochure advertising the profitability of the Hickory Colliery, assured prospective investors that the mine normally earned a profit of 10 cents per ton.[5] The mine inspector in his annual report for 1871 estimated that the average cost of mining, preparing, shipping, and paying royalty on a ton of coal delivered to Port Carbon was $2.68, not counting "loss of animals, breakage in machinery and incidental expenses." The base price of coal at Port Carbon in that year was $2.75. He concluded that "unless a colliery is exceedingly favorably circumstanced, it is impossible to make our deep mines pay."[6] Benjamin Bannan in 1869 declared that during the past forty years, coal operators had lost money in twenty years; in 1862 only six colliers remained solvent.[7] And a recent economic historian essentially supports Yearley, Coxe, Sheafer, and the mine inspector. Using data from other coal companies, he found that in the decade prior to the 1888 strike, profits per ton for companies operating without major interruptions ranged from 10 to 25 cents per ton. The latter figure, on coal sold at the breaker at $1.60 per ton, was provided by a firm reputed to be the most profitable in the anthracite region.[8]

The low profit margin made the colliery vulnerable to anything that interrupted the shipment of coal. By careful management, the operator could make 10 or 12 cents per ton on his coal; if he shipped 100,000 tons in a year, his maximum capacity, he would make $10,000. But down time at the average colliery amounted to three months out of the year. And if by some mischance he was closed down for six months and only shipped 50,000 tons, he did not make $5,000 but considerably less, because he still, according to Enoch McGinness, had to spend about $400 per month just to "stand."[9] (Other estimates of the cost of an idle colliery were higher: in 1871 William Kendrick, then operating the St. Clair Shaft, declared it cost him $150 per day.)[10] Even when producing no coal at all, the pumps had to be kept working night and day to prevent the mine from filling up with water; coal had to be mined or purchased to fuel the steam engine; the breaker and other surface structures had to be guarded by a night watchman; the horses and mules had to be stabled, fed, and cared for by at least one stable boy; minimum royalties had to be paid and creditors somehow satisfied. The frequency of interruptions resulting from "accidental" causes and from strikes was very high: as Eckley B. Coxe put it, "There is no business on the face of the earth subject to as many casualties."[11]

Thus the operator had actually two problems: first, the day-to-day problem of efficient business administration during regular operation, of managing as well as he could to sell his coal at a profit in the face of the vagaries of the market, ups and downs in rail and canal tolls, and all the difficulties of labor relations; and, second, the safety problem of preventing the unanticipated "casualties" that would stop his mine and precipitate him into failure even if he had been doing well hitherto. Unfortunately, the two problems were interdependent: maximum profit could only be achieved by spending no more than the minimum on casualty prevention; maximum safety could only be secured by accepting less than maximum profit.

With few exceptions (of which the Johns family and their Eagle

Colliery were one) the operators chose to solve the dilemma by minimizing expenditures on safety. The result of this policy of putting aside the best in safety practice for the sake of lowering operating costs was so high a frequency of physical disasters and of bitter labor confrontations that eventually the commonwealth of Pennsylvania and the federal government intervened.

INSURANCE

Although the insurance industry might in theory have helped both miners and colliery owners, in fact it gave little or no help to the workers and was of limited use to the landowners and colliery operators.

Miners were regarded as poor risks for life insurance. Dr. Carpenter, after fifteen years' experience with miners' accidents and diseases, considered that miners' life expectancy was short, few surviving beyond age fifty-five. He urged those of his colleagues who, like himself, were called upon by insurance companies to give advice on applications for life insurance, to provide "just views of the risks run in mining occupations here." Mining was more dangerous than railroading, and he concluded:

> On a full review of the whole subject, I could not conscientiously advise any life insurance company to do business among miners, except on short periods of risk, and at large increase of percentage.[1]

Life insurance was available, on the other hand, to mine operators (for instance, Enoch McGinness' life was insured for $10,000), mine owners, and other folks in less dangerous occupations.

The purveyors of insurance to the coal trade made available, in addition to life, disability, and household policies, four major types of industrial coverage: for the operator, transport, fire, and employer's liability, and for the landowner, insurance against loss of royalties.

The *Miners' Journal* regularly carried advertisements by insurance agents. The issue of July 21, 1860, for instance, contained a notice by Clementina Smith's brother Horace, acting as agent for the Liverpool and London Fire and Life Insurance Company and other Philadelphia-based companies. It was addressed particularly to "Coal Operators," who "would find it advantageous to insure their colliery structures in reliable Companies." Names cited as "references" (presumably satisfied customers) included John Tucker, president of the Philadelphia and Reading Railroad and of the Mill Creek and Mine Hill branch; operators John R. White and George W. Snyder; state representative James H. Campbell; and Judge R. M. Palmer. Similar notices were published by the Anthracite Insurance Company, which included on its board of directors such well-known figures in the coal trade as D. Luther, Lewis Audenried, and J. E. Baum (at the moment struggling with the operation of the St. Clair Shaft), and the Franklin Fire Insurance Company, which in 1864 had Isaac Lea on its board.

We can obtain some idea of the way in which risk in the coal trade was conceived by professional insurers, such as these, by looking at sample policies and contemporary reviews of the state of the art in the insurance business. First, let us examine a royalty-insurance policy taken out by Henry Carey and his partners in March 1859.[2] The policy, issued by the People's Fire Insurance Company of New York, insured the Carey group for one year "against loss or damage by fire to the amount of Four Thousand Dollars in their Rents" expected from the St. Clair Shaft Colliery. Similar policies were issued to Carey by The New York Fire and Marine and the Manhattan insurance companies. The premium in each case was $100, calculated at a rate of 2.5 percent of the amount insured. The structures covered were all above ground, specifically "Breakers, Engine and Hoisting Apparatus," whose destruction by fire would prevent the working of the mine and the shipping of coal and would result in a "total loss of the rents" normally to be expected. The conditions attached to the policy further explained the parties' understanding. During any period of down time greater than twenty days, caused by a breaker fire, the companies agreed to pay the insured at the rate of $18,000 per year until the sum of $12,000 was paid out; thus in effect the Carey group was insured against any loss of royalties for eight months, long enough for the breaker to be rebuilt by the operator. The length of time—i.e., the repair or rebuilding time—for which the companies were liable had to be estimated within ten days of loss and agreed to by all parties or submitted to binding arbitration. If the works were suspended for other reasons (e.g., a strike or a mine fire), the company would cancel the policy and refund the premium for the unexpired term.

Operators also were able to purchase fire insurance on breakers, at least from the 1850's on, usually for amounts equal to half the cost of construction. When the breaker at Johns' Eagle Colliery was burned in 1878, for instance, allegedly by the hand of an arsonist, the *Miners' Journal* reported that it had been insured for half its value. But the underground workings of a colliery, constantly changing and expanding, and always subject to rot, corrosion, and destruction from crushes and explosions, were inherently uninsurable. By 1881, experience would seem to have made breakers appear a little more risky, for in that year a guide published by the Continental Insurance Company, after warning agents against "Coal Mine Property" in general—"Decline as a rule"—suggested a rate of 3.5 percent for coal breakers.[3]

But these premium rates were in actuality extraordinarily low. Carey's 1859 rate of 2.5 percent was comparable to the rates in the 1840's and '50's on cotton factories (the Columbia Insurance Company, specializing in textiles, headed by C. N. Buck, charged 2 percent) and wooden barns (also 2 percent).[4] And the Continental's 3.5 percent rate on breakers in 1876 (written in a book published in 1881) appears to be downright cheap, compared to rates quoted by insurance expert J. A. Fowler, who put cotton and woolen mills at 4 percent and planing mills at 8 percent.[5] When we review the actual experience with breaker fires in Schuylkill County, and in the neighborhood of St. Clair in particular, we find that the St. Clair Shaft breaker burned down twice in its twenty-year history, the Eagle breaker burned at least twice in about twenty-eight years, Repplier's breaker at the Mammoth Colliery burned at least once, and there may have been breaker fires at Pine Forest, the St. Clair Slope, and the Hickory not recorded in my notes. The newspapers reported a breaker destroyed by fire every few weeks among the approximately 200 breakers in the county. The true rate, at a modest estimate, must have been nearer 5 percent than 3.5 percent. Such a figure is suggested by the comments of F. C. Moore, author of the 1881 manual mentioned above, in his subsequent work, *Fire Insurance and How to Build*. In a chapter on how to evaluate manufacturing structures presenting "special hazards," his comments on coal breakers and other coal-mine property (such as engine houses, workshops, and miners' dwellings) were negative: "The company will want full advice before issuing policy. . . . Have not been profitable as a class. . . . The class of help employed usually involves a serious moral hazard."[6]

The actual probability of loss by fire, as it was estimated by underwriters, was, of course, not the same as the rate used in calculating the premium; supposedly it was lower, but in actuality it could be higher. Insurance authorities regarded the problem of relating risk to premium as a muddle. The revered Horace Binney, in his address in 1852 at the observance of the centennial of the Philadelphia Contributionship for the Insurance of Houses from Loss by Fire (founded by Benjamin Franklin in

1752 and managed by Binney for the past thirty-nine years), complained bitterly about the casual fashion in which premium rates were set. He was reflecting on the state of the art in the fire-insurance business and was eager to introduce the best statistical methods then available, those that had been applied to vital statistics to produce the mortality table. Rate setting for fire insurance at present, he said, was done in a hit-or-miss way, each company setting its own rates on the basis of its own experiences:

> The present method seems to be that of trying a set of rates for a certain term of time, and if they result in loss to the parties insuring, to raise them. . . . [7]

What Binney wanted to see was a truly scientific approach: systematic collection of data on fires and buildings, on a national scale, by an independent body, continuously into the future, enabling underwriters to know the "true" probability of loss for the various classes of risk over a long enough period to permit the business to become profitable.

City, state, and national boards of underwriters did eventually, toward the end of the 1860's, begin to perform at least some of these research functions, and toward the end of the century developed increasingly detailed schedules for classifying structures according to the presence of risk features, each of which contributed a certain amount to the rate. But twenty-some years after Binney's address, rate setting for fire insurance was still a muddle. J. A. Fowler, the authority on the history of insurance in Philadelphia, in 1876 published a little pamphlet on the fire-insurance premium. Standard practice, he said, was to calculate the expenses of management at 30 percent of the premium; in other words, to load the "fire cost" about 43 percent. The "fire cost" in turn theoretically included both the anticipated cost of paying off claims and the company's profit. But in fact, Fowler claimed, the fire cost provided no profit at all:

> Normally . . . the profits which a company actually makes on its rates is solely the interest earned on the premium fund; and however different single years and exceptional cases may look from this, in the end it comes to about this, and to about this in successful companies.[8]

Thus, in Fowler's opinion, the actual probability of loss was 70 percent of the premium rate as conventionally set. The point of Fowler's pamphlet was that the fire-cost/office-cost ratio should be variable, depending on the risk, rather than uniform. But we need not concern ourselves further with his proposals for reform; it is his premise that is important to this discussion—the assumption that 70 percent of the rate was fire cost (i.e., fire probability as estimated by the underwriter).

Applying this figure to the rate quoted in 1859 for the St. Clair Shaft, we are led to the conclusion that the underwriters for three fire-insurance companies were insuring the breaker, only four years after it had burned down, and six years before it burned down again, on the assumption that a breaker fire had an annual likelihood of occurrence of 1.75 percent. Certainly a breaker built on top of a shaft with a furnace at the bottom must have been considered more hazardous than a breaker that served a slope and was connected with the entry only by an inclined plane; so the generality of breakers would in 1859 have been individually rated no higher, and possibly lower, than the St. Clair Shaft. Yet the rate seems extraordinarily low. Part of the problem in setting realistic rates was perhaps the recency of the invention. Breakers had been commonly used only since 1844, when Battin's first breaker was built, and thus the maximum time span for collecting statistical data on breaker fires was only fifteen years. But the Philadelphia Board of Fire Underwriters was not organized until 1852, in response to Binney's address in that year; before that time, companies could only consult their own claim experience, and in all likelihood no one collected records on fires in uninsured breakers. Without a history, breakers were simply lumped in with the other classes of less incendiary commercial and manufacturing structures. In effect, companies were insuring a new technology without any statistical basis for setting rates and initially were setting the rates too low.

Presumably, most of the companies were able to absorb the losses until such time as the experience of the insurance industry indicated that rates on well-built, well-managed breakers had to be increased and high risks declined altogether. But the low initial rates may have had the secondary effect of assuring colliery operators, mine owners, and others in the coal trade that the risks of loss were lower than in fact they would prove to be.

THE "CARELESS MINER" AND THE EROSION OF EMPLOYER'S LIABILITY

After an accident or disaster, the general reaction of landowners, operators, and their representatives in the legal, real-estate, and journalistic professions was to place the blame on the carelessness of miners. At St. Clair, comments by such people after firedamp explosions invariably blamed the careless miner. Thus, after the first explosion at the McGinness Shaft on June 11, 1855, which burned five men (one of them was not expected to live), agent Andrew Russell advised Carey, "no injury done the works—air good in the mines it was the result of carelessness." Echoing Russell, the *Miners' Journal* attributed the blast to "sheer carelessness."[1] Four months later, three miners were killed in the same shaft and two others severely burned. The *Miners' Journal* explained carefully that it was the miners' fault, not only in this, but in "all the recent explosions":

> It appears that the mining boss had examined one of the breasts and informed the miner, who was engaged in working it, of the fact [the presence of gas], cautioning him at the same time, not to go into it.—But disregarding the warning, the most reckless and unpardonable carelessness, he ascended the breast with a naked lamp flaming on his cap and *unlit Safety Lamp in his hand*.
>
> It is singular that all the recent explosions should be so clearly traced to carelessness on the part of the miner. But we know them—even the best miners to be reckless and fearless, and we are only surprised that explosions, still more terrible in nature, do not often occur.[2]

In 1859 another explosion in a breast in the shaft burned three men and two boys, "some of them severely," and as usual "the incautious exposure of a naked lamp by a miner" was given as the cause by the *Journal*.[3] No mention was made of the fact that if the ventilation system had been adequate, an explosive mixture of firedamp and air would not have formed.

The testimony of St. Clair miners who rose to positions of managerial responsibility, as boss miners or superintendents, is particularly interesting because it shows a *sang-froid* which in itself might be deemed careless, coupled with the routine criticism of the careless miner. Edward Herbert of St. Clair, for instance, was an English miner who came over in his thirties about 1859. By 1870 he was married, a father, and a "boss miner"; by 1877 he was the "superintendent" of one or another of the St. Clair mines, including the Wadesville Shaft. In the mid-1870's, Mr. Herbert was interviewed by H. C. Sheafer, the coal editor of the *Miners' Journal*, who was preparing his article on "The Hygiene of Coal Mines." The interview was quoted in detail:

> Mr. Herbert was asked if he had ever been "blown up" by a fire-damp explosion. He replied: "Oh yes, a few times, but I never was hurt much"; and then gave the following as his experience

with mine explosions; "I have occasionally gone into fire-damp (carburetted hydrogen) so pure that it could not explode except at the edges, where it mixed with the air. I never went far, and I never stayed long, and I always shut my eyes and held my breath until I came out again—just went in a little way to get my tools, or something like that. When I happen to be in an explosion, my practice is to shut my eyes, hold my breath, and try to get as near the floor of the mine as possible. Men are often so scared when they see the fire flash, that they open their mouths and holler; then they in

John Maguire (1845–1912)

hale the flame, and that kills them; it burns their lungs and they never get over it. . . . Another queer thing about an explosion of gas is, that just where you would expect it to have the most effect it has none at all. I have known men to be driving gangway, for instance, and get so far beyond the air-current that fire-damp would gather in the 'face.' . . . By and by some careless fellow would fire the gas, and men fifty or sixty feet back along the gangway would be burned to death, while those close to the face would not be hurt."[4]

John Maguire, the inside boss at the Pine Forest Colliery, had a career not unlike that of Herbert, beginning as an underground miner and going on to positions of responsibility in union work, as a state mine inspector, in colliery administration, and ultimately as a division superintendent for the Philadelphia and Reading Coal and Iron Company. Maguire's father was made superintendent at the Pine Forest Shaft about 1867 by George Snyder; this was the first time an Irishman had been appointed to the position of mine boss in that area, and the action may have contributed to the friendly relations of labor and management that seem to have prevailed at the colliery. Maguire's "Reminiscences . . . after Fifty Years of Mining," collected and published by another erstwhile miner, Joseph Patterson, display a curious mixture of attitudes. As an administrator he was extremely conscious of risk and very exacting in his safety measures. He recited with relish how a little boy tending a pair of ventilation doors in a certain mine physically blocked the passage of the state mine inspector at one door until the other had been closed after a trip of cars went through. He was following the rule that the two doors were never to be open simultaneously. The inspector was well pleased and told the superintendent, "You have got a splendid boy tending those doors out there." Maguire's editorial remark about the incident, in the last paragraph of his memoir, was solidly in favor of stricter compliance with regulations:

This is a sample of the discipline sought to be attained in a well regulated mine, where the thoughtless or negligent act of one may disastrously affect the safety of all.

But these responsible sentiments of the aged Maguire do not represent Maguire's attitudes in his twenties, when he was assistant boss under his father at the Pine Forest Shaft. He describes himself carelessly igniting a pocket of gas with a naked light in the upper part of a breast. Fortunately, the pocket was pure gas; it burned only around its edges, and eventually smothered itself, while Maguire stared, fascinated, at the "cloud of rolling flame, which looked as terrible as the reputed flames of Hades." But the most revealing anecdote is his account of how he cleared some workings of water and gas. As a result of heavy rain and snow melt in the spring of 1870, the abandoned "old works" in the upper levels above the Seven-Foot and Mammoth gangways had filled with water, blocking the upcast airway to the fan, and, to make matters worse, a crush in the Mammoth gangway stopped ventilation in the east gangway too. As the mine inspector put it, "the air could not be measured for want of motion, and, in fact, there was no regular ventilation." The gangways and breasts filled up with firedamp and "the situation of the miners was a critical one." The inspector left orders that only safety lamps could be used. In an effort to clear the mine, it was decided to drill bore holes from the Seven-Foot Vein up into the abandoned higher workings to drain the water down into the Seven-Foot, whence it could be removed by the pumps. As inside boss, John Maguire led a team of men in heroic forays into the half-drowned, gas-filled mine. But did he follow the safety rules? Not at all: he took with him on one occasion a surface fireman, untrained in underground work, who abandoned him at the critical moment and ran away to the surface; he used naked lights until he reached what in his judgment was the danger zone (his judgment proved to be correct); and, against his father's direct orders, he fired a shot to open a bore hole because he thought (again, as it turned out, correctly) that the gas had cleared. Maguire was taking chances with his own and others' lives in the interest of saving the mine and of proving his manhood. And in fact some miners called him on it. When he was firing the forbidden shot, it happened that the miners' union was on strike; the strike committee had permitted a team of men to drive the bore hole, for the sake of future jobs, but had set a condition that the team quit as soon as the hole was large enough "for a man to go through." Young Maguire, "anxious to be the first to get into the old gangway," did not wait to let the team enlarge the bore hole and dress the sides, but wriggled himself through, with difficulty, covered with mud and water. When he got back down, he ordered the men to enlarge it, but they refused, saying that they had been directed by the union to work only until they had made a hole large enough for a man to go through. "You call yourself a man, and you have gone through. Our work is done. We dare do no more." And they left the hole incomplete. Young Maguire's father was very angry because his son's feat of derring-do had resulted in the bore hole being left unfinished.[5]

The first mine inspector, the Englishman John Eltringham, another former miner and lately a colliery operator at Ashland, commented on the carelessness of many miners in the presence of firedamp:

> It is the perilous business of the miners, very frequently, to work in this element, knowing well the dreadful element that surrounds him at his work, and his feeble capacity to cope with it in its inflammable form, beside the danger he has to encounter after an explosion, in the form of choke-damp; that his life depends as much on his fellow-workman's carefulness as on his own; and yet, to see with what degree of carelessness he hurriedly enters the district where death hangs on the smallest spark, and goes about his business as if no such danger ever existed, and often contrary to positive instructions and regulations; thus endangering his very life for the sake of earning a subsistence to maintain his family.[6]

It is obvious, however, with respect to firedamp explosions, that the "careless miner" with his naked light could not ignite the gas if the ventilation system, for which the operator was responsible, had done its job. Of course, there were careless miners and careful miners guilty of moments of carelessness, who entered old workings against the rules in order to urinate or defecate, or who climbed up into gassy breasts against the fire boss' orders, or who failed to use safety lamps when they were told to do so because they could work faster with naked lights. But in every explosion there was the contributing factor of an inadequate ventilation system for which the operator, the superintendent, the engineer, and the inside boss were responsible, and which the individual miner could control only to the most limited degree. Thus for the operators and their associates routinely to blame the miners alone for explosions which could have been prevented by better ventilation was obviously a self-serving position. By placing the responsibility for prevention on the miners' shoulders, and demanding of them the moral qualities of prudence and foresight, the operator community avoided the "extra" expense of the extensive "dead work" involved in extending gangways and headings, installing large fans, and enlarging air holes.

There was, however, another reason for blaming the "careless miner." In English common law, for centuries, masters had been held liable for injuries suffered by their servants if the accident had been the result of the employer's negligence; but negligence by the servant that caused or contributed to the accident was an allowable defense by an employer. This legal principle worked well enough before the Industrial Revolution. Apart from some ship's masters, few private middle-class employers had a large number of servants; the gentry kept some domestics and farm workers, master tradesmen had several apprentices and journeymen, merchants and professional men a few clerks; and the relationship between master and servant was apt to be close and supervision constant. But with industrialization came organizations that counted hundreds and even thousands of employees, with several tiers of managerial hierarchy between the employer and the employee, whether in textile factory, railroad, ironworks, or colliery. Under these new circumstances, English and American courts acted to protect the rising class of industrial entrepreneurs—so necessary to the economic growth of nations—from personal-injury suits following industrial accidents. In 1836 in England, and in 1842 in Massachusetts, the "fellow servant" rule was articulated in precedent-setting court decisions. This rule asserted that an injured employee could not hold his employer responsible if the accident was caused by the action, or inaction, of a fellow employee. The reasoning behind this decision invoked a third principle of employer innocence: assumption of risk. According to this rule, the employee—conceived as a person who was free to leave his master's employment if he considered working conditions unsafe—by continuing to work with negligent fellow servants was assuming the risk on his own responsibility. Soon this rule would be extended to include risks imposed by an employer who did *not* provide a reasonably safe work place.

The consideration that the employee was in fact constrained, by a fear of losing his income, from either refusing to work in hazardous circumstances or from resigning his job, was not admitted as relevant.[7]

The ready acceptance by the courts in mid-nineteenth-century England and America of the three "wicked sisters"—contributory negligence, the fellow-servant rule, and assumption of risk—virtually nullified the effectiveness of the employer's-liability principle. Although the principle remained, the employer—or his insurance company—was able, in an overwhelming majority of cases—on the order of 90 percent—to evade the payment of claims. And when claims were settled, after long months of court delays or haggling with an insurance company, the payments were minuscule in comparison with the enormity of the injuries.[8] The shift in responsibility from the employer to the victim himself, his family, and ultimately to state-mandated workmen's-compensation programs, is an evolutionary change comparable in significance to the change worked by the Elizabethan Poor Laws, which removed the burden of charity from the householder and made the indigent the responsibility of the parish.[9] And just as the moral and emotional concomitants of the Poor Laws were important, so, we shall argue, were the moral and emotional effects of the abrogation of employer's liability.

One consequence of the narrowing scope of employer's liability was the effort by some insurance companies to introduce disability insurance. Policies were issued directly to employees, insuring them against expense and loss of wages resulting from accidental injury. One company, advertising in the *Miners' Journal*, gave a list of claims settled in Schuylkill County:

> *Robert C. Hill & Co.*, General Agents New York Accidental Insurance Co., have paid weekly compensations for disability as follows: James D. Crawford, Wilksbarre, thrown from carriage dislocating right shoulder, paid six weeks compensation, $300; cost Crawford $2.50. Robert Humphrey, Supt. St. Nicholas, sprained in lifting Gangway timbers, paid 6½ weeks compensation $162.50; cost Humphrey $30. James Stewart, Supt. Coal Breaker, Locust Gap, pistol-shot through right hand, paid 2 weeks compensation, $25. Lucian H. Miller, carpenter, Cressona, foot injured getting off an Engine, paid $5 compensation.[10]

These policy holders would seem, in at least two of the four cases, to have been relatively prosperous, as supervisors at collieries. Whether many ordinary miners and laborers could afford such insurance, however, would seem to be doubtful, and disability policies were not regularly advertised.

A more serious effect was to render ambiguous what was meant by an employer's obligation to exercise reasonable care to provide his servants with a safe work place. What is reasonable care and how safe is safe? And, at a colliery, is a contract miner a servant? In effect, the colliery operators acted as if they had done their duty as soon as they had opened the mine and erected the breaker in whatever fashion they pleased. The 1869 and 1870 mine safety laws, which we shall consider in detail later, can be seen as efforts to define more precisely what constituted a reasonably safe work place; collieries failing to meet these standards were *ipso facto* liable for accidents resulting from inadequate ventilation, improper design, and other violations. The injured and the survivors of the dead could and did still bring suit as individual claimants. But now the state had entered into the situation as a third party, with power to inspect, advise, fine, and close down non-compliant collieries.

Although state intervention was really another step toward relieving the operator and the miner alike of the burden of adversary proceedings, it was, as we shall see, resisted bitterly at the time. No state had enacted mine safety legislation before Pennsylvania, and the federal government had entered into the regulation of private industry, in the interest of public safety, only twice. The federal actions had been the passage by Congress of laws in 1838 and 1852 regulating the construction, maintenance, and operation of steamboat engines. These engines, often worked at extreme pressures by captains racing their ships on inland waters, exploded frequently with terrible consequences. Between 1816 and 1848, no less than 2,563 persons were killed in the United States in steamboat explosions, most of them passengers.[11] But these laws were intended primarily to protect an "innocent" general public, many of them women and children. Federal safety legislation for coal mines was not passed until the act of 1952, which dealt only with factors conducive to major disasters. In 1969 a comprehensive coal-mine safety law superseded the 1952 act, providing for standard regulations, inspections, and sanctions on all aspects of mining. And, of course, in 1970 the even more comprehensive Occupational Safety and Health Act was passed, finally bringing into reality the national code for all industries that Eckley B. Coxe had called for a century earlier.[12] In the meantime, in the decade 1910–1920, most of the states—including Pennsylvania—had passed workmen's-compensation laws, which provided the worker with no-fault insurance for industrial accidents.[13] In effect, after about 130 years of debate, the old common-law principle of an employer's personal liability has been largely replaced by federal safety regulation and no-fault workmen's-compensation insurance.

In the period of the 1840's through the 1880's, however, the colliery operator and his colleagues in the coal trade were, we suggest, still experiencing a moral dilemma over safety and employer's liability as acute as the anxiety of the Elizabethan householder who turned a beggar woman away from the door because the parish was now responsible for her keep and then worried lest she cast the evil eye on his cattle and kin. And the operators' response to this dilemma was one factor that distorted their perception of the values associated with expenditures for ventilation and other "safety" features at the mines.

The process of self-mystification was straightforward. Self-interest prompted the operators to minimize the traditional responsibility of the master for the safety of his servants, and the legally acceptable way of doing this was to blame most accidents on the carelessness of the servants themselves. Such a divestiture of responsibility had the additional function of contributing to the illusion that the problems of the coal trade were not the fault of operators or landowners. As a mechanism of defense against the resulting guilt over abandoning traditional loyalties, the careless servants were eventually perceived as hostile, alien, destructive agents of a vast international conspiracy known as the Molly Maguires. Such a myth-constructing process had happened before in American history, in the rise of anti-Masonry at just the time that urban master craftsmen were cutting the ties of paternalistic responsibility that bound them to their journeymen and apprentices and were substituting for the traditional familistic industrial morality the "free" labor contract and the factory. In response to the resulting dilemma of conscience, Paul Johnson has suggested, the masters—and to some extent the workers—turned to evangelistic religion, which in its emphasis on an individual religious experience of salvation, man to God, one on one, both legitimated the idea of the free labor contract and allowed the industrialist to turn over his workers to the care of a benevolent deity.[14] The wave of middle-class fear of an international Masonic conspiracy, allegedly deriving from the deistical, anti-clerical theories of the enlightenment and fomented by anti-British French and Irish radicals, thus can be looked upon as the paranoid residue of the evangelical awakening of the 1820's and 1830's.[15] Many of the operator class were old enough to have experienced the second Great Awakening and the anti-Masonic furor; virtually all were churchgoing Christians, many of them temperance men, a few pulpit-pounding evangelists themselves. Many, of course, were members of Masonic lodges, now that Freemasonry and Odd Fellowship were respectable again. But very few were Catholic, even fewer Irish Catholic. For the Irish Catholics had—for the men of the coal trade—taken the place of Freemasonry as the evil empire of the 1860's and 1870's.

The paranoid scapegoating process at a time of social change, when people are experiencing a sense of compulsion to live up to old moral obligations even while they are ignoring them in day-to-day behavior, is a common human event. It accompanies many social movements and is apt to flare up when law and order lapse (as they did at Salem in Massachusetts during the interregnum of 1684–1692). But what is interesting in this case is its association with the industrialization of the United States, first, in connection with replacement of domestic and shopkeeper industry by the factory system, and, second, in consequence of an aborting of the principle of employer's liability. One wonders whether comparable flurries of scapegoating have accompanied other aspects of the Industrial Revolution, not only in the United States but around the world, as entrepreneurs have felt themselves compelled to abandon one or another traditional obligation in order to minimize costs.[16]

In the case of the coal trade, however, there was a curious twist. Most operators seem to have become prisoners of their own mythology. By classifying ventilation, prop work, detached breakers, second exit shafts, and the miners' hospital as humanitarian but costly "safety" measures, the operator placed them mentally in an account separate from the books he kept for necessary business expenses incurred in the sinking of the mine and the day-to-day operation of the colliery. To introduce "safety" measures into his business accounts would not only have increased costs but would have been an admission of previously unsafe conditions and thus of liability. Thus even one spontaneous lapse in the direction of improving the safety of the colliery could serve as a precedent in a court case or as an example cited by a witness before a legislative committee. And, of course, it could also arouse a sense of guilt. Hence were derived from multiple compulsions the implacable resistance of the operators against "safety" measures and the incredibly callous (to an outside observer) response to injury and suffering. The operators and their allies acted as if making the slightest move toward improving the safety of the collieries and helping the sick and injured would ruin them.

This attitude, however, itself virtually guaranteed ruin. For the same accident that killed and maimed a few workers usually damaged the colliery also. We have already seen how, after most major accidents, an escalating series of financial embarrassments resulting from lost sales, increased labor costs, and the expenses of repair eventually resulted in the business failure of the operator. Thus "safety" expenditures were actually indispensable business expenditures too. But, protected from worry about liability by the myth of the careless miner, the typical operator sought to get by with minimal protection from disaster.

THE RISE OF THE MINERS' UNION

The apparent indifference of the operators and the courts to safety issues evoked from the miners, in addition to turnouts and demands for higher wages for work in hazardous mines, a political response. Unable to control individually, by their own effort, the safety of the work place, and faced with a refusal to accept responsibility for safety on the part of the colliery operators, the miners of St. Clair at first, and of other coal towns later, began to call for legislative action to regulate the industry. This response of labor to perilous working conditions was far more realistic than the response of capital to the risk of disaster-caused failure. Capital constructed a delusional ideology; the underground miner applied economic and political pressure to the operators in the interest of safety.

St. Clair has a special place in the history of the American labor movement because of the formation in 1868 of the Workingmen's Benevolent Association of St. Clair, or "WBA" as it was familiarly called. The WBA and its various successors in the anthracite fields were important not so much for priority as for success. Many more-or-less short-lived unions had been formed from the 1840's on, both in the anthracite district and in the soft-coal fields to the west, and some—especially during the Civil War—had by means of strikes been temporarily successful in maintaining or raising wages. Miners' unions were organized by industry rather than by craft, bringing together both skilled and unskilled workers of all kinds, not just the skilled practitioners of a single trade, such as carpenters, masons, and machinists. Perhaps because it had ideological links with the older, and sometimes more radical, trade unions like the International Molders' Union in the United States, and with the Chartist and cooperative movements in Great Britain, the WBA during its brief heyday from 1868 to 1875 was able to unite a wide front of anthracite-colliery workers under a banner calling for social change. Mobilized by the inspired leadership of John Siney, the WBA members were able to work effectively for changes in the way an entire industry operated, successfully lobbying for safety legislation and hospital facilities, and establishing a system of collective bargaining in the coal fields over such issues as the sliding scale of wages, arbitration procedures, and the settlement of grievances. Although Siney wanted to carry the union farther into national labor organizations and third-party politics than his fellow unionists in Schuylkill wanted to go, and although the union did not survive the Long Strike in 1875 (of which more later), the WBA proved that a union of colliery workers, organized on an industry-wide basis, could not merely strike effectively on wage issues but could influence the social policy of a commonwealth. It was an inspiring legacy.

In the early years, it is not possible to distinguish purely economic from safety motives in workers' demands for higher wages, for one tactic for coping with a dangerous mine was to turnout, or institute a slowdown, until the operator paid miners extra wages to enter his mine. Two of Enoch McGinness' experiences will serve as examples. After the explosion and fire in the St. Clair Shaft in June 1855, McGinness had trouble with the men working in the shaft, and this trouble contributed to his failure four months later. In August he wrote to Carey:

> Yesterday forenoon a Miner had his leg broken in the Shaft and all the rest came out at noon and consequently we lost the day or most of it and I think without any good reason for it. The Shaft has not done as well since the explosion as it ought to have done but that is one of the things I could not avoid. . . .[1]

Again in 1861, while he was opening the slope on the Diamond Vein south of St. Clair without an air hole, the mine blew up. In consequence, he had to pay higher wages than before. A year later the mine still was not turning a profit, but he had hopes (vain ones, as it turned out) of making it pay:

> by gradually working labour down we shall be able to make it pay for getting and the rent upon it. . . . We now have a very careful inside Boss and therefore have avoided explosions of firedamp and have had [no] men injured in the least so far this summer and we do not have to pay higher wages on that account as some do and as we formerly had to do.[2]

Clearly, a demand for a higher rate of pay was not uncommonly prompted by the miners' perception of dangerous conditions in the work place, particularly the threat of firedamp explosions resulting from inadequate ventilation.

As we have seen, however, neither the threat of disaster nor the cost of higher wages was sufficient to motivate most operators to do what had to be done to correct ventilation and other safety problems. The realization that uniform safety rules and provision for inspection were necessary on an

Unidentified St. Clair miners

industry-wide basis first surfaced at St. Clair in 1858, when at a public meeting a resolution was passed recommending an annual state labor convention that would formulate "legal and just rules and regulations" to be enforced at all Pennsylvania collieries.[3] Sentiment was widespread in favor of such "regulations," and a flood of petitions sought to persuade legislators in Harrisburg that safety legislation was needed. And so in the spring of 1866 not one but two bills were presented to the House of Representatives, respectively entitled "An Act for the protection of miners and laborers in Schuylkill County" (No. 855) and "An Act for the better protection of life from the results of mining in Schuylkill County" (No. 1327). Both bills were amended to bring Luzerne County under the provisions of the law and both were passed by the House and sent on to the Senate for concurrence. No. 1327 died in the Committee on Judiciary and No. 855 was rejected by voice vote on the floor of the Senate.

The contents of the two bills were different. No. 1327 was intended to protect both workers and the general public from falling into open shafts, slopes, air holes, or test pits "of greater inclination than fifteen degrees." The mine operator was required to erect a substantial picket fence six feet or more in height around any pit, and in the case of abandoned workings, the landowner had a similar obligation. Delinquent parties were to be prosecuted by the district attorney, and township supervisors had the right to post guards at the owners' expense. No. 855 would have required the governor to appoint two inspectors of mines for Schuylkill County (and presumably two more for Luzerne, although the printed bill only mentioned Schuylkill). They were to be "practical miners of good repute and large experience in mining operations in Schuylkill County." Each mine in the county was to be visited by an inspector and his assistants, "giving precedence to those reputed to be most dangerous," who would examine the condition of its entry, gangways, breasts, drainage, and ventilation. Certificates specifically enumerating safe and unsafe parts of the workings were to be issued. Particular attention was to be paid to the ventilation: "in all cases where foul air is designated they [the operator] shall forbid all admission to said locality by inexperienced workmen on the objection of any miner working therein and that part of said mine shall not be further worked . . . only to remedy the danger until on subsequent inspection it shall be certified safe." The miners could take the initiative in enforcing safety, for the law provided that if any three or more miners made a written complaint to the inspector, he was to make a special visit, as a result of which he could stop work in the dangerous area until the condition was corrected. If an inspector was negligent and as a result a worker or workers died, a bond of $500 posted by the inspector was to be forfeited and given to the families of the victims. Even heavier penalties could be levied upon the operator if he neglected or refused to have a reported hazard "speedily removed." If a miner were killed or even materially injured as a result of the operator's negligence, the operator could be fined $500 and held liable for damages in addition—the money, if necessary, to be collected by the court by lien on his property, and the whole paid to "any miner laborer or driver working in said mines." Furthermore, in regard to areas certified as hazardous, it was made unlawful "by threat of discharge or otherwise to force any employee into such dangerous locality against his own judgement or personal risk under a penalty of one hundred dollars."[4]

Objection by operators and their senatorial supporters no doubt prompted the negative vote on the bill, which not only promised to add substantially and immediately to the cost of mining, but also gave the miners a powerful voice in the day-to-day operation of the mines. Furthermore, by stating emphatically that the miner had a right to a safe work place, it made the operators responsible for the health and welfare of their employees.

The issue of where the responsibility for the safety of miners should be placed lay behind another legislative controversy, the struggle to establish a miners' hospital. The high casualty rates and the prevalence of "miner's asthma" suggested to many persons acquainted with the region that a special medical facility, supported by levies upon operators or by the state, should be constructed to help sick or injured miners, who rarely had the funds to pay for more than emergency medical care.

As early as 1842, the *Miners' Journal* was publicly calling for the erection of "an establishment for the benefit of superannuated miners and others injured in the work." Benjamin Bannan editorialized:

> it is not uncommon to see men carried along our streets some-times dead, and frequently horribly mangled in consequence of accidents in the mines. And we have many worthy industrious men in this district so crippled and maimed as to unfit them for labor entirely.

The *Journal* noted that one family of operators, the Youngs, had recently left a legacy for the founding of a miners' asylum or hospital, but that it was insufficient for the purpose. So the *Journal* proposed that the canal and railroad charge an additional one cent per ton on all coal carried, the collection being set aside for the support of the proposed institution.[5] This idea was agitated for several years, but the boards of directors of the transportation companies did not act, "although everyone seemed to favor the plan." In 1845 and 1846 the *Journal* brought the matter to its pages again, with no result.[6] Early in the 1850's, the transportation companies were asked to subscribe to a miners'-hospital fund, but most if not all of them (specifically including the Mill Creek and Mine Hill Railroad) declined.

After a lapse of several years, the *Miners' Journal* in 1858 again pointed to the need for a miners' hospital comparable in size, specialties, and quality to the Pennsylvania Hospital in Philadelphia:

> We want an Institution into which the wounded miner will be placed, and receive the treatments his state demands, not as at present be confined to a badly ventilated room in his cabin, and run the risk of medical treatment or not, as the case may be. The large percentage of mortality among the mining population, may be traced to the want here of an Institution where all the conven-iences for an operation and for correct treatment, are at hand, and where the practitioner can treat his case with a chance of suc-cess.[7]

In response, the anonymous correspondent in Tamaqua whose casualty statistics we cited in an earlier section offered a proposal for a combined "Miners Hospital and Relief Association." The hospital would be financed, as the *Journal* had long proposed, by a penny-a-ton surcharge on coal, collected by the transportation companies, and a penny-a-ton deduction from rents collected by landowners. A system of outdoor relief for crippled miners and railroad and canal men, and for widows and children, would be financed by a contribution of 15 cents per month from all workers who wished to join the association, plus voluntary subscriptions from coal dealers, landowners, and others interested in the trade. This proposal too failed to receive an enthusiastic official response.[8]

At last, in 1870, under pressure from the WBA, the Pennsylvania legislature considered an act authorizing the construction of a Hospital and Asylum of Schuylkill County. The board of managers was to include three members from Pottsville and one from each of the twelve major coal towns, including St. Clair. And it was to be financed by a one-cent-per-ton surcharge on transportation tolls and a one-cent-per-ton surcharge on the dealer's price to the consumer (thus exempting the landowner). When the tax fund amounted to $500,000, tax collection would cease. Part of the fund would pay for buying the ground, erecting the buildings, and furnishing them, and the remainder would serve as a permanent endowment to provide operating expenses.[9] But the legislature did not approve. A similar act was proposed by former Wadesville miner and Labor Reform Party representative John Morgan in 1874. The act was finally passed in 1879 and the hospital was at last built in 1882 near Ashland—forty years after Benjamin Bannan made the idea a public issue in the pages of his newspaper. And even this final success was allegedly the result of a political deal. The political triumvirate ruling the Republican organization in the commonwealth—Senator Cameron, his son Donald, and Matthew Quay—were interested in the passage of a bill of their own. One of Schuylkill County's representatives was in a position to determine its fate, and the price he demanded for cooperation was Republican support of the hospital bill. The Camerons at last delivered.[10]

Despite its reluctance to provide direct relief for miners by safety and hospital legislation, the commonwealth did find a way to provide some indirect relief. In 1859 there was enacted into law an act extending to miners in Schuylkill County (not other mining counties) the principles of the more general "mechanics' lien law" passed in Pennsylvania in 1849. This act provided that in the event of the sale, transfer, or insolvency of any colliery, colliery employees' back wages up to $100 had first claim on the proceeds of the estate. One of the speakers for the bill, a representative from Schuylkill, spoke poignantly about how the never ending succession of business failures affected the poor miner:

> Although many millions of dollars have been and continue invested, as capital in railroads, canals, collieries and improvements of every description necessary to its vast coal productions, there are very few coal operators who have ever been able to retire upon a competency. On the contrary, the large lists of sheriffs' sales, continually recurring, show how unfortunate the majority who engage in mining are. And when failures take place, as they so frequently do, the liabilities are often very large, and the losses fall with great and peculiar severity upon the miners and laborers. These men pursue their dangerous avocation in the darkness of the mines, and shut out, as they are, for a great portion of their lives from the light of day and the intercourse with their fellow men, they have no opportunity to learn anything of the financial condition or pecuniary difficulties of their employers. When the sheriff levies upon and sells a colliery under an execution, it falls with crushing force upon the poor operatives, uninformed and unprepared as they are. When their wages are swept away from them by a landlord's warrant or the execution of a watchful and diligent creditor, their families and themselves suffer actual want.[11]

Inasmuch as many of these bankruptcies and sheriff's sales were precipitated by disaster in the mine, the payment of back wages was a necessity for injured miners in need of medical care and for widows left to support children.

But even this concession did not come easily. It was the result of a massive defection in 1858 of miners in Schuylkill County from their traditional party of choice, "the Democracy," in favor of the new Republican Party, which was also the party of most of the mine operators. The bill had the public support of such major leaders among the operators as Brown, Heckscher, Borda, and St. Clair's own George Snyder. The Republicans, campaigning in Schuylkill County under the banner of "The People's Party," had staged large rallies in the coal towns around Pottsville just before the October elections. A "People's Meeting" in St. Clair was held at Wood's hotel on Saturday, September 18, and the speakers were local leaders, among them the district's Congressman, J. H. Campbell, and two former colliery operators, Benjamin Haywood and C. L. Pinkerton. Haywood delivered a "telling speech" in favor of "Protection to Home

Industry," which was the only true path to prosperity, and which could be secured only by putting out of office those "enemies of free labor," the Democratic Party. Pinkerton, however, came directly to the point of the miners' lien act, reading aloud:

> . . . the pledges given by the candidates for the Legislature, to use their influence for the passage of an act to secure priority of claim to miners and laborers. . . . [12]

To judge from the names of the twenty-four officers elected by the meeting, the People's Party in St. Clair was mainly English, Welsh, and German; the Irish remained for the most part supporters of "the Democracy." But in 1858 enough former Democrats voted for the Republican and People's Party candidates, not only in Schuylkill but across the county and the state, to enable the Republicans to take control of the state legislature and to put through the miners' lien act.[13]

Another reason for the political restlessness of the colliery workers was the growing polarization of capital and labor over the issue of collective action. The businessmen associated with the coal trade had as early as 1832 organized themselves into a Coal Mining Association of Schuylkill County, whose board of trade was a committee that issued annual reports (printed, of course, by Benjamin Bannan) on improvements, prices, tonnages, and financial conditions affecting the anthracite community. The officers of the association were the people whom one might expect, many of them the Careys' and the Wetherills' associates: Thomas Baird, Burd Patterson, Francis B. Nichols, Andrew Russell, George H. Potts, Charles Lawton, John Pinkerton, and Benjamin Bannan, among others. The constitution, bylaws, and rules of order, printed by Bannan in 1855, provided that any coal operator in the county shipping at least 1,000 tons per annum might become a member. Dues were set at a rate of 50 cents per 1,000 tons shipped. In a curious marriage of the operators and shippers, the board of trade, elected by the operators, was to consist of one or more representatives of each of the eleven branch railroads. And this board of trade was empowered to use the monies of the association "in such manner as may appear to them most conducive to the interests and objects of the Association." These monies were not very considerable, for if member operators shipped as much as a million tons in a year and paid dues at 50 cents per thousand, the association's income would be no more than $500, from which the secretary of the board of trade received a salary of $200, plus 5 percent of the dues collected. But the association provided both a public digest of economic and technological information and a private forum for the discussion of political isssues relevant to the interests of the members.

The board of trade could also mobilize the operators to take concerted action when the members were threatened by impending restrictive legislation, by toll increases on the canal or the Reading Railroad, or increasingly, by strikes and the organization of miners' unions.[14]

Brief local turnouts by miners had, as we have seen, been a common response to accidents and disasters and to wage disputes ever since the beginning of the coal trade in Schuylkill County. But the first regional strike occurred in 1849, when the "Bates Union" was formed under the leadership of John Bates of St. Clair. The organizing of this union was prompted by the example of the Coal Mining Association. As a striking English miner put it in a letter to a friend:

> The masters formed a Union last summer, something like a Secret Order, and that was the cause of the strike. So we followed their footsteps, and we shall form a society called the "Association of the Miners and Labourers of Schuylkill County."

When the coal merchants in Philadelphia and New York refused to pay the price on coal demanded by the operators' association, "all the coal masters . . . turned out . . . and would not let their coal go down to the city." The dispute lasted six weeks and ended when the operators got the price they wanted. Then the miners took their turn. "As soon as they were agreed, we stood out, and we have got all we asked," including payment in cash at those collieries accustomed to paying their men in scrip redeemable at the company store. Plans for the union went enthusiastically ahead, with a formal constitution and bylaws and a dues schedule.[15]

Now the union's strategy became political. Operating on the theory that over-production was indeed the root of the problem, as the operators themselves had argued, the Bates Union resolved on a symbolic turnout. On the Fourth of July, a union parade marched from St. Clair through Pottsville to the picnic grounds at Deer Park, south of the town. Gathering adherents as the crowd proceeded, the number of marchers eventually reached 4,000 to 5,000. At the union meeting, presided over by Bates, a number of resolutions were passed, including a call for a brief three-day suspension. The rationale for this quasi-strike is worth quoting because it echoes so clearly the line taken by Henry Carey on "the harmony of interests":

> Resolved: That we believe our interests and the interests of our employers are so connected and identified that it would be impossible to separate them—both require adequate protection, and

must languish without it, and the absence of such general legislative protection from our government make it more necessary for
us to devise means to protect ourselves.

Resolved: That all work is suspended till Monday, the 9th day
of July, believing such a suspension is required for our own good,
for the good of our employers, and for the interests of the coal
region.[16]

But the union disintegrated during the following year. Bates, the
leader, who received a salary of $12 a week and the use of a horse and
buggy, became the target of resentment by mine workers whose earnings
fell below that level of relative affluence. He was accused of collusion with
the operators and of conspiring with politicians for a political career of
his own (as, indeed, a conscientious Chartist might be inclined to do).
Disillusioned by the rejection of his leadership, in 1850 Bates left
the region, followed by charges that he had run away with the union
treasury.[17]

The next eight years were not prosperous ones for the coal trade,
despite ever increasing demands for coal. By 1858, wages had fallen again,
the company stores had been brought back, and organized labor protests
were heard once more. In May, production at the Ashland collieries was
cut back sharply, and in response Ashland's miners not only struck for
higher wages, but marched "through the country, coercing men who are
satisfied with their situations, to stop work."[18] This militant response was
not displayed at first by the miners of St. Clair, who, according to the
Miners' Journal, advised the Ashland strikers to "make a Demonstration at
the ballot-box next fall for a Protective Tariff and against Democratic
wages. . . ." This "advice" was tendered at the public meeting noted earlier. The Ashland miners endorsed the St. Clair miners' proposal for labor
conventions, but also urged that the current strike be extended to a "general strike by all persons employed in and about the Anthracite Collieries
of Pennsylvania." The Ashland miners, perhaps again in deference to the
St. Clair miners' more moderate position, resolved that during the strike

we keep within the bounds of the fair laws of our country,—not to
get drunk, bellow, make threats, give insults, stop those who wish
to work from doing so, annoy persons, or other things unlawful or
imposing, so that our employers, or any evil-disposed persons may
not find any blame in any of our actions during our "strike" for
our rights.[19]

But placards bearing the figures of pistol and coffin posted at blackleg collieries, warning the workers to turn out or be killed, gave the strike an ominous tone; and the strike collapsed in May at St. Clair and in June at Ashland after leaders were arrested.[20]

The denouement at St. Clair came on May 21 and 22. The strikers marched about with drums beating and flags waving on the 21st and by afternoon had managed to shut down all the St. Clair collieries. But on the evening of that day William Milnes, operator at the Hickory Slope, called upon the county sheriff to disperse the demonstrators gathered on Parvin's Hill, overlooking Hickory and the St. Clair Shaft. The sheriff turned to the military "to assist him in maintaining order and making arrests." An entire regiment of militia was mobilized, consisting of four companies (one of cavalry, one of artillery, and two of infantry, including St. Clair's), and marched from Pottsville to St. Clair. There the sheriff's proclamation was read to the demonstrators and five men were arrested on the charge of riot. Actually, they had succeeded in stopping a colliery at Mount Laffee by "stoning the men from the breaker" and had returned to St. Clair and in succession stopped Milnes' Hickory, Johns' Eagle, and finally Snyder's Pine Forest (although here they met with some considerable objection from the workers). The St. Clair Slope and Shaft were already shut down from mechanical problems. Four of the arrested were convicted; one was sentenced to pay court costs, and three to pay costs and serve sixty days in prison.[21]

This memorable military expedition proved to be a political bonanza for the Republicans. The *Miners' Journal* was able to ridicule the county Democratic establishment as being responsible for "The Great Battle of St. Clair" and published a long spoof, profusely illustrated, that made fun of the overreaction by the sheriff and the militia. Supposedly written by a correspondent of the London *Times* just returned from the Crimea to report on "stirring events, as they transpire in the Western World," the piece was published under the heading "War Correspondence."[22] Benjamin Bannan, the *Miners' Journal*, and the county People's Party were able to present themselves as the true friends of the miners by opposing the use of militia to suppress a peaceful demonstration. The image of public sympathy for the strikers was, indeed, so persuasive that when John Maguire, who was present on Parvin's Hill as a lad of thirteen, recalled the event fifty years later, he "supposed" that the men arrested "were given a hearing and set free."[23]

A few weeks later, after the furor had died down, the *Miners' Journal* editorialized on the subject of turnouts. Bannan was astute enough to

realize that the threat to capital lay not in strikes for higher wages at
Ashland and St. Clair, but in the Chartist principles advocated by "Mister
Price," editor of the Minersville *Workingman's Advocate*. Bannan spoke
out against the company-store order system, but he criticized turnouts as
mere folly, doomed to fail. He advised labor to negotiate politely with management. As soon as the market for coal improved, the operators would be
glad to raise wages:

> . . . there must be reason and moderation on both sides. We are
> aware that there are cases of oppression and injustice to workmen
> on the part of employers, and where such exist, the workmen
> should appoint a committee to wait upon their employers, and
> insist firmly but courteously, upon redress of their grievances. We
> are confident that all grievances will be sooner redressed, and an
> advance of wages if possible, be accorded with more alacrity, if
> such a course be adopted.

Bannan's vitriol was spent mostly on the "the Minersville clown" who
claimed to represent "the working classes" in his partisan newspaper. It
was the publication of an organ of class consciousness, and the proposals
therein contained for regional labor organization with political power, that
Bannan really opposed:

> Any paper arrogating to itself the organization of an industrial
> class, is narrow in its views, hostile in its tone, and a mischief
> maker between men who should labor in harmony. . . . Every word
> spoken or published tending to alienate employee and employer,
> is like casting a firebrand among inflammable material. Desola-
> tion and ruin follow.

Bannan, on the other hand, and by implication the People's Party, believed
in cooperation between employers and employees not only in the present
trying times, when both classes must suffer and make concessions, but in
better times as well, when both should prosper together.[24]

The Republicans were, in fact, again making a determined and temporarily successful effort to win over the miners of Schuylkill County.
Locally, the party was known as the "the People's Party" until 1860, when
for the first time it used the term "Republican" in the campaign to elect
Abraham Lincoln. Although the Republicans were to enjoy a century of
domination of the governmental apparatus in Harrisburg, their victory in

Schuylkill County was short-lived, with the combined Irish and Pennsylvania German vote returning the county to Democratic hands again in 1862. The temporary Republican ascendancy in Schuylkill was probably the result of traditionally Democratic voters' disillusionment with the party's weak position on the protective tariff in the years following the panic of 1857. The People's Party platform as expounded by Bannan's *Miners' Journal* had five planks: a strong protective tariff (publicly symbolized by the Henry Clay statue towering over Pottsville); non-extension of slavery; internal improvements at the expense of the federal government (the state had just sold its public canal system to the railroads); restriction of Irish Catholicism's influence in politics (by stricter enforcement of election and naturalization laws); and prohibition of whiskey.[25]

What was the effect of all this Republican newspaper rhetoric, all the drums and flag waving, the bands and marches and mass meetings, in the town of St. Clair? St. Clair was particularly vulnerable to Republican appeals, it would seem. It was the wealthiest of the county's townships and boroughs, as measured by per-capita value of real estate, and although it also ranked number two in percentage of foreign-born, more than half of these foreign-born, as we have seen, were English, Welsh, or German rather than Irish Catholic. The People's Party vote in the local elections in 1856 was 50 percent; by 1858 it had moved up to 59 percent; in 1860, swayed by Lincoln's popularity, it had risen to 67 percent. But with the war, and the unpopular draft (and with Bannan serving as county draft commissioner), the Republican vote in St. Clair in 1861 fell to 46 percent; similar drops were registered in townships and boroughs across the county. The simplest explanation for the roughly equal popularity of the Democrats and Republicans with St. Clair voters is that the town's voting population contained a smaller proportion of Irish Catholics than did other, more Democratic, towns.[26]

During the war, there were some strikes in Cass County, whose mining population was predominantly Irish, and one of them—in 1862—was put down by a battalion of regular infantry.[27] (But the strikers got their wage demands anyway.) After the war ended in 1865, the demand for coal slackened sharply and the operators cut back production and reduced wages. In Schuylkill County the operators proposed to reduce the wages of miners by 35 percent and of laborers by 25 percent. A Welsh miner wrote back to a hometown newspaper, "It is believed that the idea is to destroy the workmen's union and thè workmen know this and are determined to stand up for it. As far as I can see the motto on both sides is, 'A pull, a strong pull, and a pull all together.' "[28] But apparently this pre-WBA union, about which little is known, was not prepared for "a pull all together" and the Schuylkill miners, their resources already depleted by unemployment, accepted the wage cuts without calling a general strike.

The first enduring and effective miners' union in Schuylkill County was organized in St. Clair in 1868 in the wake of a brief strike in January and February of that year at the Eagle Colliery.[29] The board of trade had selected the Eagle, now under the direction of young George W. Johns, to initiate what it hoped would be a general reduction of wages. Johns announced that wages would be reduced by 10 percent beginning January 1, 1868. The men turned out and after six weeks Johns capitulated. The men returned to work at the old wages. During this strike at the Eagle, a miner named John Siney became prominent as an eloquent exhorter and ingenious organizer. When some of the men began to drift back to work after a few days, Siney rented Walker's Hall and had all the men assemble there all day every day "in convention." This roll-call effectively deterred potential blacklegs. Siney also organized a grand "subscription ball," the proceeds of which went for the relief of the strikers' families. The whole successful exercise, conducted so peacefully and with so firm a spirit of solidarity, encouraged the participants to form a more enduring organization. They petitioned the county court for a charter for a labor union similar to the English unions with which Siney and others were familiar; but the petition was rejected on the grounds that it violated state law. On the advice of Lin Bartholomew, an influential Pottsville lawyer and Republican politician (during the war he served as private secretary to Simon Cameron when Cameron was Secretary of War, and in 1868 he was elected to the state House of Representatives), a revised petition was submitted in April for a benevolent association, comparable in its stated objectives to others like the Odd Fellows and the Masons. It was being formed, the petition said, "in order that the stranger may find the kind attention and fostering care of a brother when he needed assistance, and be encouraged in resolutions of morality and sobriety at all times."[30] On these grounds, the new union, named the Workingmen's Benevolent Association of St. Clair, could collect dues for a fund that would pay sickness and death benefits and provide poor relief to members (who might, of course, otherwise have been reduced to poverty during a long strike). The charter was granted by the court in June 1868. This organization was the nucleus of the first county-wide miners' union.

The seventeen charter members of the WBA were all foreign-born. The president, elected after Siney withdrew his name, was Ralph Platt, an older English miner from Rochdale, near Manchester, where he had worked as a weaver and had organized a co-op; he was also a teetotaler. Thomas Pilling, a fellow Lancastrian with whom Siney had boarded when he first arrived in St. Clair, was treasurer. The Pilling family lived in one of the patches, either Ravensdale or Crow Hollow, just outside the borough limits. In 1868, Thomas Pilling was fifty-two years old and had lived in the St. Clair area for twenty years or so. The secretary was Levi Orme, age twenty-seven; John Orme, age fifty-eight, another member, was Levi's father. They were a classic example of the respectable mining family. The Ormes had arrived in St. Clair from Wigan, Lancashire, about 1854 and it was Levi who had invited Siney, whom he presumably had known in Wigan, to come to St. Clair. John Orme and his sons were prominent in the town. The father, a miner, owned a substantial house assessed (in 1870) at $650, and four of his sons—Seth, twenty-three, Pilot, twenty-one, Esau, eighteen, and Washington, thirteen—lived at home; Levi and Peter lived separately with their wives. They were a religious, law-and-order, patriotic family. The father named his sons for Biblical figures, except for the last, who received the name of America's most revered leader. The eldest son, Seth, lost his leg in a mine accident in 1862 at the age of fifteen, and then learned the trade of shoemaker; he eventually opened a shoe store, which was not notably prosperous (he received a dubious credit reference in 1876 because of his alleged "irregular habits").[31] He married in 1872, was a member of the Episcopal congregation, served as postmaster for a time, and was active in two lodges, the Knights of Pythias and the Improved Order of Red Men, in which he served as the Keeper of the Wampum for the Schuylkill Tribe. Pilot Orme, a mine laborer in 1870, was active in the affairs of the Primitive Methodist church, becoming in 1881 the superintendent of the Sunday School. Esau, a mule driver in 1870, was killed by a fall of coal in the Hickory Slope three years later. Washington in 1870 was a mine laborer and in December of that year was crushed and run over by a train of wagons in the St. Clair Shaft; his subsequent fate is not recorded. Peter apparently was not living in St. Clair when the census was taken in 1870, but he had moved back with his family by 1880 and was employed as a coal miner. Of Levi's career, in addition to his later travels with Siney on union business, we know little beyond the fact that he volunteered and was wounded during the Civil War, was married twice, and in 1868 ran unsuccessfully for sheriff of Schuylkill County.[32] It may be noted that of the father and six sons, at least two were severely injured in the mines and one killed.

Thomas Tempest, another of the charter members, was one of the Tempest extended family described in the third chapter. There were five

Tempest brothers in their twenties and thirties living in St. Clair in 1870, all English-born: Martin, a constable, and four miners, Andrew, James, Joseph, and Thomas. Of these, Thomas was the most widely experienced, having lived with his Irish wife in Australia mining gold for several years, and he was wont to lecture his fellow unionists learnedly on mathematics, basing his conclusions upon and drawing illustrations from "what he had learned while working in the gold mines in far away Australia." In the early 1870's, all the Tempests picked up and moved to Shenandoah. The known Tempest casualties in the mines are comparable to those of the Orme family. Of the five brothers, three were seriously injured. Thomas, a very big, strong man who could cut and load fifteen tons of coal in a day without a laborer's help, was overcome by gas and nearly killed in the Kehley Run mine fire in 1880. Joseph was seriously burned in a gas explosion in the Wadesville Shaft, along with five other men, in 1879. James was seriously injured by a fall of coal in the Wadesville Shaft in 1874 and "had a very narrow escape from death" (this accident was, incidentally, not included in the *Annual Report* of the mine inspector). And Martin died, of causes not known to the writer, before the move to Shenandoah. And of the five brothers' sons, two had been killed and two injured in colliery accidents around Shenandoah by 1885.

Other English miners among the charter members included Adam Omerd, Robert Wilde, John Gittins, William Howarth, John Cowan, and Daniel Hughes, all of them except Howarth (twenty-four) in their forties or late thirties, all married, and all with children except Omerd. Omerd, whose wife kept a beer shop, was the most prosperous of the lot, owning real estate valued at $4,000 and personal property worth $3,500. His wife was listed as owning $2,600 in real estate. Cowan's wife also kept a beer shop. Robert Wilde's wife kept a candy store and he too owned his own house. All of the men were literate but Wilde—and John Siney.

Thus eleven of the original sixteen were English, all married men, most of them middle-aged, all but one literate, and some were among the town's more prosperous citizens. Solomon Reese, age thirty-five, from South Wales, was also married, a father, and literate. Of the three Irish-born members, all in their thirties, two (Robert Bowers and Siney) had lived in England before coming to America, and two (Bowers and Timothy Crowley) were married and had children; only Siney was unmarried and illiterate. Of William Scholes we have no record.

But it is about Siney that we know most. He was born in Ireland, son of a tenant farmer who was evicted by an English landlord during the famine year of 1837. The family moved to England and settled at Wigan, an industrial suburb of Manchester, where John at the age of seven was put to work in a cotton mill. At sixteen, after refusing to accept a wage cut, he was apprenticed to a brickmaker, and in his twenties he went to work as a full-fledged journeyman in the brickyards around Wigan. Here he helped to organize the local brickmakers' union and was elected president year after year for seven years. Then, in 1862, his wife died, leaving a two-year-old child, and a year later the loss of cotton shipments from the American South cast a pall over business activity generally in the area. So in 1863 Siney emigrated to America to join old Lancashire associates at St. Clair and try out his luck for the first time in the coal fields. By 1868 Siney was ready to organize the miners on the basis of a matured theory of labor relations, which he was able to apply soon to the events that transpired during a county-wide strike over the eight-hour issue.

A law had been enacted in 1867, to take effect July 1, 1868, making eight hours a legal day's work. Most operators opposed the legislation and insisted that wages be reduced in proportion to time. Early in July the mines at Ashland and in the Mahanoy Valley turned out, demanding the eight-hour day with no corresponding decrease in wages—in effect, a 20 percent increase. Strikers marched from colliery to colliery, and within two weeks the county's mines were all shut down. Henry Russell wrote Carey on the 9th of July that not only the collieries but the ironworks were being struck:

> The eight-hour "raiders" are now going through the region, stopping business of all kinds. All the St. Clair mines were stopped yesterday. Lanigan has rec'd notice to blow out his furnace in 60 hours. The "raiders" are the scum of the "Molly Maguires." A riot is feared.[33]

By the end of the month, machine shops at Ashland were closed down and the "raiders" were advancing on the mines around Scranton and Pittston. Rumors of actual violence, apparently untrue, were published in Philadelphia papers, but the *Miners' Journal* denied the charges.

Once again, some of the most influential political theorists among the workers were to be found in St. Clair. On the 15th of July a committee of "many workmen" from St. Clair (no doubt the officers of the newly formed WBA) addressed a letter to the *Journal*, deploring the misrepresentations of the strikers' actions and setting forth their own position. It articulated clearly a theory of class relations that seemed on the surface similar to

Carey's views on the harmony of interests but also contained a firm commitment to collective action by labor:

> The strike is now general, and is likely to continue until an im-
> provement in prices will warrant concession to the demands of
> the men. For it is certain that only an advance of prices will
> warrant a reduction in the hours of labor and an increase of the
> wages of the miners. . . .
>
> The true interest of capital and labor is to harmonize as much
> as possible. It is true that capital and labor are mutually depend-
> ent, but in antagonism, not governed by prudence and reason,
> capital can take care of itself better than labor. We have always
> advocated and still advocate the most liberal wages, and so should
> every business man, for when labor is well remunerated, general
> trade is most prosperous. We sincerely hope that the present
> deadlock will speedily pass away with brighter prospects for both
> employer and employee. In the meantime the surest way for
> working men to secure adequate wages for their labor, and to
> control their hours of work, is to petition Congress for the imme-
> diate adoption of the protective policy. Without it business must
> languish and working men must suffer. It is an unchangeable
> law of political economy that unless the domestic industry of a
> country be adequately protected, the demand for labor must de-
> crease and wages reach starvation point.[34]

The strike was settled in August on terms of compromise: the miners
agreed to a return to the old ten-hour day (the law provided for such
contractual arrangements) and the operators agreed to a 10 percent advance in wages. This was not the result that the local organization in St.
Clair had favored, however; to the members, the eight-hour issue was the
important point, and for it they were willing to accept a wage reduction. In
their view, the strike had failed to achieve its object because of a lack of
organization. The "raider" tactic of men armed with clubs marching from
colliery to colliery created an image of turbulence, struck fear into the
hearts of potential sympathizers, and stiffened the backs of the board of
trade. The lack of a general union was responsible for the fact that most of
the miners of the northern district did not join the strike. There was no one
voice to speak and negotiate for all. There was no central treasury to collect
dues and to maintain a fund to provide relief to the strikers and their
families.[35]

At the end of the strike, the temporary president of the St. Clair WBA moved away to Hazleton and Siney was elected in his place. It was a casual sort of election. On a Saturday night in mid-August, John Maguire, then assisting his father as inside boss at the Pine Forest, William Pilling, Siney, and others were standing on the post-office corner chatting, and Pilling told Siney he had been thinking of nominating him for president of the union. Siney demurred, but Pilling insisted he was the right man. So Siney was elected the next Monday.[36]

Siney moved fast to enlarge the organization. He was already well known to strikers across the county from having served as chairman of the July strike convention at Mahanoy City and as one of a delegation from that meeting to visit Luzerne to try to persuade the northern miners to join the strike. The mission failed (the Luzerne miners remembered that the Schuylkill miners had refused to join them in 1865) and Siney learned that regional jealousy was more important than ethnic antagonism in inhibiting collective action. But Siney proceeded to call a county-wide convention of delegates from all the mining towns to organize a county union. It met in St. Clair in the first week of September and succeeded in establishing a Workingmen's Benevolent Association of Schuylkill County comprising twenty-two districts, from St. Clair (number one) to Tower City (number twenty-two). The executive board of the union was composed of a delegate from each of the districts; and the new board elected Siney chairman of the board at a very substantial salary, $1,500 per year. Liberated from the need to earn his daily bread in the mines, Siney was able now to visit the mining districts of the county with his aide, Levi Orme, to converse on the subject of the coal trade with men of all classes, from laborers to colliery owners, and to think.[37]

THE FIRST MINE SAFETY LAW

The first item on Siney's agenda in the winter of 1868 was a mine safety law. After traveling about the county with Levi Orme visiting the miners at one colliery after another, collecting signatures to a petition that grew to be fifteen feet long, Siney and his committee took the petition and a draft of a safety act to the state legislature in Harrisburg. In January, Senator William Randall, Democrat from Schuylkill, presented the petition from the county's miners to the Senate, but action was taken first by the House, where the county's representatives, including Philip Breen, a storekeeper from St. Clair, deluged the legislators with petition after petition from

Schuylkill and Luzerne. Early in March 1869, the House passed "An act for the better regulation of mines, and for the protection of the lives of miners in the county of Schuylkill" and sent it over to the Senate.[1] It was in the Senate debate on the bill on March 31 that the politics of the situation boiled to the surface. Noting that the House bill applied only to the county of Schuylkill, George B. Coleman, the senator from Lebanon County, proposed an amendment to strike the word "Schuylkill" and insert "State of Pennsylvania," making the act apply generally to all anthracite mines and all bituminous mines as well. Coleman was one of the most distinguished members of the Senate, a Republican, part owner of the famous Cornwall iron mine and of various blast furnaces, foundries, and steel mills. Coleman was also known for his strong religious convictions and for his humanitarian activities; during the Civil War he had served on the Sanitary Commission and in 1869 was a member of the State Board of Charities. But the senator from Luzerne, Samuel G. Turner, a Democrat and a coal dealer, rose to claim a point of privilege: he said he had not read the bill, had never seen a petition in its favor, and his constituents had not had an opportunity to consider the matter, and therefore the provisions of the bill should not be "forced upon" his county. After Turner's invocation of the privilege to consult with his constituents, a number of other senators, including Senator Randall from Schuylkill, backed away, admitting that although in principle the bill should be general, it was "rough treatment" to force it upon an unwilling county. Schuylkill County, with its older, deeper, more dangerous mines, needed protection more than Luzerne. Thus reassured, the senator from Luzerne went on to make statements that must have been somewhat difficult for his listeners to believe:

> I am pretty familiar with the mining operations in Luzerne County, and I can now remember but one instance where firedamp explosions resulted in injury to miners in that county . . . the time is approaching when it [this bill] may be needed for Luzerne County. . . . I feel as much disposed to aid in protecting and preserving the lives of miners as any man. I know of one small district in Schuylkill County where there has been an explosion of firedamp, resulting in the loss of seventy lives.

The senator can hardly have been unaware that in 1860 an explosion in the Eagle Shaft at Pittston had killed five men and that in 1866 alone there had been at least two firedamp explosions in Luzerne, killing three and injuring nine. Nor could it have been easy to accept his claim that he had never read the bill. But one senator could not easily call another a liar to his face. Coleman, however, was quick to point out the paradox in Turner's position:

> Here is that Senator, representing one of the largest mining re-
> gions of the State, who has never read the bill. He also says there
> are no explosions of firedamp in that county. This bill does not
> refer only to that, but also to lowering and elevating the miners,
> to riding on the cages, &c. My object in this thing was that it
> should go before the committee, where we could prepare a gen-
> eral bill. I do not therefore see the point of the Senator's objection
> after he has told us he has never read the bill and does not know
> what is in it.[2]

But Senator Turner's objections to the amendment to make the bill apply generally across the state were persuasive. As the senator said, "important interests" were involved. When it came to a vote, both Coleman and Turner demanded a roll-call. The amendment was rejected, fourteen to twelve, with Senator Randall joining Turner among the "Nays."[3] With the Luzerne County issue out of the way, the Senate now proceeded to pass a bill applying only to Schuylkill County, the House concurred, and Governor Geary signed it into law on April 12, 1869.

The 1869 safety law, modeled generally after English mining law, did three things: it specified certain minimal safety standards for the ventilation, hoisting, and steam-engine systems; it placed responsibility for safety on the shoulders of the landowner, operator, and management, and classified failure to comply with the safety regulations of the act as a misdemeanor, punishable by fine and imprisonment; and it created the office of inspector of mines, who had the duty to inspect all collieries, to give orders where necessary to bring them into compliance, to record and investigate all accidents, and to write an annual report to the governor. Some of the specifications were a little vague. Each colliery had to provide "an adequate amount of ventilation and of circulation of pure air to dilute and render harmless all noxious gases therein." But some provisions were more exact, such as the requirement that furnaces

> shall be so erected as to prevent ignition of the coal in the mines;
> the fire of the same shall be fed with fresh air, and the vitiated air
> of the mine shall not be allowed to come into contact with the
> furnaces [sic], but shall be made to pass into the upcast air course,
> at a point far enough above the fire to insure against the ignition
> of the firedamp which said return air current may contain. . . .

And others would seem to have described and given the force of law to conventional best practice, such as self-closing doors, bottom-to-surface signaling, adequate upcast airways, annual boiler inspections, underground maps, and flanges on hoisting drums. But some desiderata, such as dual outlets and non-combustible furnace flues, were not even mentioned.

It was probably in regard to the social organization of the colliery that the act was most innovative. It made the colliery at once a safer and a more disciplined place. The miner suffered a significant loss of control over his work place; and the supervisory employees were no longer free to make certain decisions, for the mine inspector could order things done and could shut down the mine if they were not. The inside boss not only was authorized, but was required, to keep the miner out of "his" breast if, in the boss' judgment, it contained unsafe quantities of gas. The colliery had to provide, maintain, and control the use of the safety lamps; no longer was the safety lamp's use at the discretion of the miner. If a miner rode on a cage, wagon, or car loaded with coal, he was guilty of a misdemeanor and subject to a $50 fine. If the mining boss failed to perform his duties (for instance, by permitting the men to ride on the cars), he too was guilty of a misdemeanor and subject to the same $50 fine. Thus the status of the contract miner changed; he was now less an independent "company," a subcontractor who hired his own help to do a job without supervision, and more an employee subject to colliery rules and to orders from the inside boss. And the status of bosses changed too, from easy-going senior partners of the contract miners to foremen in coal factories. From now on, the contract miner was increasingly extruded from the class of independent artisans and reduced to the level of operative in a mill that produced coal. Furthermore, no longer could the coal operators of Schuylkill County fully exculpate themselves for gas explosions by blaming them all on the careless miner. Now the operator was—in theory, at least—guilty of a misdemeanor if an inadequate ventilation system permitted methane gas to accumulate sufficiently for a careless miner to set off the explosion. But, paradoxically, this meant also that the operator demanded greater discipline in his work force, thereby further increasing the social distance between the two classes.[4]

THE AVONDALE DISASTER

It was only a few months after the passage of the Schuylkill County safety law that a disaster occurred that forced the legislature to pass even stricter legislation.[1] It happened at the Steuben Shaft at Avondale, near Plymouth

Workers and superintendent at the Eagle Colliery

in Luzerne County, where the safety law did not apply, thanks to Senator Turner's exertions on behalf of the operators. The mine was a new one, constructed in 1868 by the multi-colliery Nanticoke Coal Company, a subsidiary of the Delaware, Lackawanna and Western Railroad, which was owned by the Scranton interests and was one of the three large coal, iron, and rail corporations operating in the northern field.[2] During the summer of 1869, for three and a half months, the colliery employees were out on strike, but they returned on Friday, September 3, and worked the mine that day and Saturday. On Monday morning, the colliery started up again as usual and the underground work force, numbering 108 men (including the inside boss), began sending up coal from the bottom of the shaft some 300 feet below. About nine o'clock the engineer who ran the steam engine that raised and lowered the cage went up to the head house at the top of the breaker, directly over the shaft, to oil the pulleys on which ran the wire rope. The head house was so full of smoke and heat that the engineer could not enter. He reported this to the superintendent, who made light of the problem, saying that the fireman below was starting up the ventilation furnace with wood. But within minutes flames were shooting into the head house, then into the engine house (driving out the engineer), and soon the entire wooden breaker was enveloped in flames; the men and boys inside had to jump, some from considerable heights. Within about half an hour, the shaft was choked to a depth of about forty feet with burning timbers, burning coal, and twisted metal.

The colliery was not well prepared to cope with disaster. It had no fire

Removing bodies after the Avondale Colliery disaster

department of its own; the only water thrown on the fire in its early stage, before the general conflagration, was a bucketful from the blacksmith shop, and that exploded into steam in the super-heated shaft. After the breaker and engine house had collapsed, fire companies with steam fire engines began to arrive from Plymouth, Kingston, Wilkes-Barre, and even Scranton, and these put out the remaining surface fires. Thousands of people—relatives of the victims, would-be rescuers, and mere spectators—crowded around the ruins, making the work of the fire departments difficult. By 7:15 p.m.—ten hours after the fire started—the debris clogging the shaft had been removed and two miners descended in a bucket to the bottom. They were followed by two more Welsh miners, who, after sending a message up for tools, were asphyxiated. This new tragedy ended rescue efforts for the evening. It appeared that there was small likelihood that the entombed 108 were still alive, unless they had been able to barricade themselves behind air-tight doors in a remote part of the mine.

Early next morning, two separate rescue programs were under way: one, to continue to send men down the shaft to explore the mine as much as the ventilation would allow; the other, to drive a tunnel through solid rock from a neighboring mine into the back parts of the Steuben, where it was hoped the men had taken refuge. A great deal of equipment had by now been assembled—steam engines, air pumps, and lengths of chain and hose—and all the miners from miles around had quit work and assembled in mining clothes, ready to form rescue parties. A rescue team of fifty men was organized; the area around the shaft was roped off and guarded by police; and by eleven o'clock a steam fan was forcing fresh air into the mine through a canvas duct. Now the rescue team began to enter the mine, in small groups of two or three men, each able to work in the poisonous air for only a few minutes.

What they found below was shocking. The furnace, which had probably started the fire in the wooden shaft, was still burning; and not only was it aflame, but its coal heap nearby was also burning furiously, fed by the fresh air now coming into the mine, and was sending its gases backward through the return airways into the breasts and gangways. A fire hose was set so as to play upon the furnace, but this procedure produced such noxious gases that all the rescue party had to be removed until the fire was out and the smoke cleared. Conditions did not permit further exploration of the mine until three o'clock in the morning of the 8th— nearly two days after the original accident. On the 8th and the 9th, the 110 bodies were brought out. A few bore the marks of fire and blast, but most had been asphyxiated or killed by smoke inhalation as they sat behind their useless barricades, waiting for rescue.

The Avondale disaster was the greatest coal-mining catastrophe to happen in America up to that time and it became front-page news all over the United States and Europe. National magazines—e.g., *Harper's Weekly* and *Frank Leslie's Illustrated Newspaper*—ran articles with sketches, drawn on the spot, of dead bodies and tangled debris. Thousands of persons thronged to the site to help, to pray, to assist in the work of relief committees that sought to aid the widows and orphans. Ballads were composed to lament the tragedy and at least one was still remembered when George Korson collected his folksongs in the 1930's.[3] Among those who traveled to Avondale while the bodies were being brought from the mine was, of course, John Siney, who made a speech to a crowd of miners that profoundly impressed young Terence V. Powderly from Wilkes-Barre. Among other things, Siney said:

> Men, if you must die with your boots on, die for your families, your homes, your country, but do not longer consent to die like rats in a trap for those who take no more interest in you than in the pick you dig with. Let me ask if the men who own this mine would as unhesitatingly go down in it to win bread as the poor

Street scene in Avondale after the colliery disaster

fellows whose lives were snuffed out beneath where we stand and who shall hence forth live with us only as a memory. If they did, would they not provide more than one avenue of escape. Aye men, they surely would and what they would do for themselves they must be compelled by law to do for their workmen.[4]

You can do nothing to win these dead back to life, but you can help me to win fair treatment and justice for living men who risk life and health in their daily toil.[5]

Seeing Siney standing with his back to a rock on that hillside over Avondale, his hands extended to the crowd, was the electric experience that, like young Baird's reading of Henry Carey, determined Powderly's future as a leader of the Knights of Labor.

When I listened to John Siney, I could see Christ in his face and hear a new Sermon on the Mount. I there resolved to do my part humble though it might be, to improve the condition of those who worked for a living.[6]

The investigation of the tragedy by a coroner's jury was clouded by intimations and charges, circulated in the public press, that Irish arsonists had set fire to the shaft from the mouth of a tunnel that opened into the upcast about forty feet below the breaker. After throwing kerosene onto the wooden brattices and setting them on fire, they allegedly had escaped through the tunnel before any alarm was given. But this theory was disputed by a mine operator whose colliery was adjacent to the disaster. Somewhat patronizingly, he discounted stories of bad blood between Irish and Welsh miners at Avondale:

> There may have been some little clannish feeling, and some harsh words may have passed before the occurrence of this disaster, but they were only words without any meaning. Irishmen are a warm-hearted set and impulsive, and often at times may say things they do not mean. Their tongues especially, when they have been imbibing a little stimulants, say much more than their hands dare do. I have known the men at this mine for many years; they are not bad men, and would not do such an act. The shaft took fire from the furnace, and no other way.[7]

These ethnic accusations, as well as the story that the fire was started by the stable man accidentally setting fire to a bale of hay with his lantern while he was descending into the mine, were set aside by the jury. The verdict was that the fire originated from the furnace, from which burning debris entered the air shaft and set fire to the brattices at the bottom.[8]

No one will ever know for certain how the fire began, but the furnace theory would appear to be in keeping with the evidence. The inside foreman had been heard to express his fears of the strong draft carrying burning brands into the wooden flue, even though the furnace was set about seventy-five feet away from the bottom of the shaft. The practice of relighting the furnace with wood every Monday morning was regarded as inherently dangerous, at least by some experts, because it built up highly inflammable soot in the flue. The fireman was a man new to the job, hired since the strike and inexperienced. People who inspected the mine after the disaster were highly critical of the placing of a furnace in an airway propped and bratticed with dry wood.

There is, however, a problem with the theory that the fire started when the furnace was being primed with wood: the discrepancy between the hour when the furnace was actually lit, about 6:30 a.m., and the time when the fire broke out in the breaker, about 8:45 a.m. Also the outside foreman testified at the inquest that the updraft was weak that morning. There is also the problem of accounting for the deaths of at least three men from what may have been blast injuries rather than asphyxiation or smoke inhalation (bleeding from the mouth in the case of two stable boys, contusions and lacerations of the face in a miner found alone in a gangway). Apparently the flue was not provided with a dumb drift (required by the 1869 law in Schuylkill but not in Luzerne). Perhaps the fire began with a gas explosion that originated in the furnace as gas-laden return air passed over the flames, killed those nearby, scattered hot coals into the nearby coal heap, igniting it and sending a billow of flame up the shaft, setting fire to its wooden, soot-laden walls.

But, as virtually everyone conceded, investigating the exact cause of the fire was not the main issue. The main issue was the fact that the mine safety law of 1869 did not require a second outlet. Even if the law had applied to Luzerne, the 110 dead men would still be dead because the 1869 law did not require a second shaft or tunnel. The importance of having a dual outlet—standard British practice for years—became the focus of attention. The outside foreman testified at the inquest that the inside foreman, who lost his life, had told him as work started that day, just two hours before the fire, that

> he intended to drive a tunnel so as to make a second entrance to the mine, and to take men in and out that way; it would have been nearly done then but for the suspension. . . .[9]

And the neighboring operator, who served as special correspondent for the *Philadelphia Press*, publicly promised to make a second entrance at his own mine as quickly as possible and demanded a law requiring a double outlet "to protect those engaged underground from being imprisoned without a possibility of escape. . . . If we give the men an inlet, we must give them a safe outlet." He even urged a march on Harrisburg:

> If all those engaged in mining coal could have seen and gone through what I went through last week they would make up their minds that they could do no greater service to their fellow workers (the miners) than to go to our legislative halls and get enacted such laws as would remedy this evil.[10]

THE MINE SAFETY LAW OF 1870

The embers of Avondale had barely cooled before Democrats and Republicans were exchanging accusations of callousness, if not criminal responsibility, for the great calamity. The Republican *Pittsburgh Gazette* suggested that the miners of Luzerne might well be tempted to take revenge upon the Democrats in the legislature, regarding "their lost comrades as murdered men"—murdered, in effect, by Senator Turner and those of his Democratic colleagues who had voted against extending the 1869 safety law to Luzerne. The Democratic *Harrisburg Morning Patriot* replied heatedly that the bill had been introduced by Democrats from Schuylkill, and it contrasted Republican Governor Geary's "obtrusive electioneering visit to the mourners at Avondale" with his silence on the subject of mine safety in his annual recommendations to the legislature. The *Patriot* accused the Republican-dominated legislature of the last decade of

> legislating too much in the interest of the capitalists and coal mine operators who paid handsomely for votes to give a moment's thought to the humble and begrimed toilers beneath the earth.

It alluded to the "criminal indifference" of the "owners of mining shares." And it demanded a new safety law to cover all anthracite-mine workers.[1]

In addition to demands in the public press for "legislative safeguards in coal mining," and no doubt personal communications to that effect as well, a miners' committee returned to Harrisburg to lobby for additional legislation. The committee consisted of John Siney, Thomas Williams, an English miner from Luzerne who served as secretary of the general council of the WBA, and Henry J. Walls, the successor to recently deceased William H. Sylvis as head of the International Molders' Union. Siney had known Sylvis briefly, and Walls had appointed Siney to a committee that advocated the government takeover of the mines, thereby giving him national prominence. According to Andrew Roy, an early historian of the miners' union movement, the miners' committee came to Harrisburg "with a bill providing for the proper security of the health and safety of miners, which was promptly enacted into law."[2] Actually, however, the matter was not so simply arranged.

On the 5th of January 1870, Governor Geary presented, as one of his legislative recommendations to the legislature, a request for the enactment of a general, stringently enforced law requiring the best possible ventilation system and other safety provisions. Senator Turner, fighting for his political life, took the lead in responding to this challenge. He first moved successfully to have the Senate establish a Committee on Mines and Mining, separate from Manufacturing, with which it had hitherto been classed. Then, as chairman of the new committee, Turner began to prepare a safety

bill that would bear his name. He let it be known that he had communicated with authorities in Europe and from them had secured copies of "all
the existing laws" bearing on coal-mine safety. He was invited to a "con-
sultation" by the four great coal corporations of the middle and northern
fields, and he met (in Harrisburg) with Siney's committee, now without
Walls but enlarged to include other union representatives from Luzerne,
Columbia, and Northumberland counties. The *Philadelphia Press*, reporting on these developments, let Turner appear as the political hero of the
hour, "the prime mover" in the effort to achieve mine safety. A cloak was
drawn over the fact that he was the same Senator Turner who had opposed
extending the 1869 law to his own county; indeed, the *Press* implied that
he had attempted to help the miners in 1869. And in total contradiction of
his stand the year before, it depicted him as motivated by compassion at
the sight of suffering around him:

> The rapid and profitable increase of coal mining has begotten a
> recklessness, which has resulted in disasters such as those at the
> Avondale and Stockton mines, and has produced such narrow
> escapes as those at the Jersey and Nottingham mines. All of these
> occurrences, except the Stockton disaster, occurred in Senator
> Turner's native village. It is but natural, therefore, that he should
> seek to provide against this class of accidents.[3]

The Mines and Mining Committee struggled to harmonize the differences
it found between the demands of the union and the protests of the operators "so as to save the companies from heavy expense and to preserve the
lives of the miners." The bill was passed unanimously by the Senate on the
17th of February, by the House on the 3rd of March, and signed into law
the same day by Governor Geary.[4]

The new law was essentially an expansion of the 1869 law, setting out
more specifically the lists of required and prohibited acts.[5] But it did differ
in three important points. It prohibited boys under the age of twelve from
working in the mines. It specifically required that every existing mine,
and, of course, all mines sunk in the future, have available to the miners
"at least two shafts, or slopes, or outlets" at least 150 feet apart. And in
furnace-ventilated mines, the breaker and engine house could not be built
over the furnace shaft. In existing mines with only one outlet, work on a
second outlet was to start immediately after the passage of the act, and
continue with three shifts working twenty-four hours a day until completion. After four months, mines still not in compliance were to be shut down

until the second outlet was completed (in Turner's original draft, the time limit was July 1, 1871).[6] Certain senators—not Turner or Randall, or at least not publicly—tried, in April, to circumvent this last strong enforcement section by proposing an amendment to a supplement to the act, rescinding the four-month limitation and requiring instead only that the operator show "reasonable diligence" in the prosecution of the work. The amendment passed the Senate (against Turner's and Randall's votes), but failed in the House. It was a party vote in the Senate, all the Democrats but Turner and Randall voting for the amendment and two thirds of the Republicans voting against it.[7]

THE EFFECTIVENESS OF THE MINE SAFETY LAWS

One immediate consequence of the circumstances surrounding the passage of the mine safety laws of 1869 and 1870 was that Samuel G. Turner, Democrat, did not return to his seat in the Pennsylvania Senate when his three-year term ended in 1871. In general, the Republicans would appear to have improved their image as friends of the workingman, by showing themselves capable of balancing their support for industry and commerce with fairness to labor in matters of safety in the work place. In the aftermath of Avondale, Governor Geary was re-elected in the fall of 1869, and although Schuylkill County as a whole went for his opponent, all three wards in St. Clair favored Geary, the combined vote being 534 for Geary and only 268 for Asa Packer, the great coal operator and ironmaster of the Lehigh Valley.

The technical effectiveness of the act of 1869 was probably slight. The man appointed to the post of mining inspector of Schuylkill County was John Eltringham, the superintendent of the famous Pioneer Colliery at Ashland. The qualifications would almost seem to have been drawn with him in mind, for the act specified that the inspector must have been "intimately connected" with anthracite mining in Pennsylvania for ten years and "have had experience in the working and ventilation of coal mines where firedamp is evolved." In his published report on his own colliery, Eltringham declared:

I have managed these mines these last ten years, and am certain the explosive element here is as active and in as large a body according to the extent of the openings as in any English mines I am acquainted with. . . .[1]

305

Eltringham's published report of his activities during the last nine months of 1869 revealed that he visited many (141 in all—about three fourths) of the collieries in the county, and in most of them made a thorough inspection. In many places, he gave instruction for "reforms" in the ventilation system, particularly requiring that doorways and brattices be made more nearly air-tight, enlarging airways, requiring the use of Davy lamps, and recommending the use of mechanical fans, to which he was partial, having had great success with a Beadle fan at the Pioneer.

Eltringham affected a man-to-man style. Joseph Patterson, a miner who wrote his memoirs in later years, remembered him vividly in that first year:

> He was from very near my home in the old country, and on his first tour of inspection I gazed on him with a great deal of interest and curiosity. I had seen mine inspectors before, but they were awful beings, far removed from ordinary mortals, for they represented the British Government, appointed by Her Royal Majesty, and she was something to be spoken of only with bated breath. Surely this jovial, commonplace man, who spoke familiarly to everybody about the colliery, did not know his business. Why he had no dignity of office at all. How could he expect that people would mind him when he told them what to do and what not to do? My previous inspectors had been clothed, not in purple, but in official blue flannels, while the ordinary miner wore but white. This man wore any old thing, and you could not distinguish him by his dress from the common miner or laborer.[2]

But he did genuinely solicit cooperation from miners as well as operators, and at each colliery took with him a practical miner appointed by the union, who accompanied him on his tour "and afterwards kept track of the things that were to be done toward improving matters." Patterson noted a certain tendency in Eltringham to measure everything by his own convenience, however.

> Airways and traveling ways were then, because they were paid for exclusively by the yard, driven very small. Mr. Eltringham was a very rotund personage, about as broad as he was long. It took quite a good sized opening to let him through. And, of course, when he had difficulty in squeezing through a passageway, he instinctively emphasized his orders to the mine superintendent to make those airways larger.[3]

Eltringham was the first mining inspector in the United States and, as Patterson observed, he had no American precedents to follow and was free to make up his own rules and standards for the industry (for the law itself was indefinite). One crucial standard was the amount of fresh air that had to be introduced, and stale air that had to be exhausted, from a mine. Here Eltringham set a standard that must be regarded as both grossly inadequate and obviously self-serving. The Pioneer Colliery—his own colliery— was ventilated by an underground, steam-powered Beadle fan that exhausted foul air from the upcast at a rate of 18,137 cubic feet per minute (and evidently sucked a lesser amount of fresh air into the downcast). Eltringham in his report declared that "the speed of the air current in this mine is the standard fixed for the county." That this amount of air was insufficient for the Pioneer workings is proved by Eltringham's own report, which reveals that "the average percent of gas in the mine was 25 percent of the volume" (measured at the upcast). Indeed, Eltringham was almost boastful about the gassiness of his mine and the virtue of the Beadle fan, claiming:

> Owing to the large amount of explosive gas evolved in this mine, every known method for ventilation was attempted but nothing satisfactory resulted from these experiments until the Beadle steam fan was resorted to . . . [now] the mines can be worked with little or no fear, under the regulations I had adopted.[4]

The "safeness" of the Pioneer mine may actually have been a paradoxical consequence of the total inadequacy of the ventilation. Keeping in mind that methane mixed with air becomes explosive at 5 percent concentration, and ceases to be explosive at 13 percent, it would appear that there was so much gas in Mr. Eltringham's mine that in much of the workings it simply could not explode—it was too rich a mixture.

Published results of the application of Eltringham's standard to the mines about St. Clair are available only for the St. Clair Shaft and the Wadesville Shaft. At the St. Clair Shaft, he found the concentration of gas to be 12 percent and the ventilation "3/4 times slow" (which means that air movement in the upcast was only 13,603 cubic feet per minute).[5] At the Wadesville Shaft, the gas percentage was also 12 percent and the ventilation was described as "4½ times slow," which means that only 4,030 cubic feet per minute were being moved through the upcast.[6] Furthermore, all of the gas in the upcast was added to the air stream after the fresh air entered the downcast, so the amount of fresh air actually introduced must be reckoned as less than the outcast by exactly the gas percentage.

Thus the Pioneer's fresh-air intake was 13,603 cubic feet, the Wadesville Shaft's only 3,546 cubic feet. Eltringham was concerned about gas in both St. Clair mines and issued detailed instructions for the care and use of Davy lamps, the location of fans, and the enlarging of airways, but his reports on the St. Clair mines were in general favorable, and he noted that the operators were very cooperative. At the St. Clair Shaft, "all . . . instructions are promised to be faithfully respected. . . . Every precaution to secure the safety of the miners is attended to."[7] At Wadesville, "Every reform proposed for the better ventilation and protection of the lives of miners is taking place as rapid as possible."[8] At the Pine Forest, in the new shaft mine, "The gas is not as yet in too large a body to create any serious fears."[9] And at the Eagle, which he praised for its sound management, "there is but little gases evolved."[10] Eltringham could be severe, as at the vast Heckscherville Deep Slope, with ten miles of gangways and 900 breasts, where the air was "9½ times slow," the ventilation "poor," and there had been a recent fatal gas explosion, and at the Beechwood at Mount Laffee (air 7½ times slow, gas 20 percent), where eight men were burned in an explosion in the fall, despite regulations prohibiting the use of naked lights.[11] Thus it would appear from Eltringham's report that his own Pioneer Colliery, with its 18,137-cubic-feet-per-minute ventilation, was moving more air than most.

But the problem revealed in Eltringham's report is the gross inadequacy of the ventilation standard he was applying to the county. It was well known to mining engineers and to persons acquainted with British mining practice that for mines the size of the Pioneer, the St. Clair Shaft, the Wadesville Shaft, the Pine Forest, and the Eagle, the fresh-air intake should be on the order of 100,000 to 200,000 cubic feet per minute, seven to fifteen times Eltringham's standard. Eltringham, by picking his own colliery's ventilation rate as the standard for the county, exempted his own colliery from the need to spend time and money on a larger fan, although its inadequacy was plainly shown by the ominous figure "25 percent gas." We shall not speculate here on Eltringham's motives, but he can hardly have been unaware of British best practice and he was probably familiar with Daddow and Bannan's *Coal, Iron, and Oil*, published three years earlier, which asserted that "a deep mine" required about 100,000 cubic feet per minute of fresh air, and which cited three British mines that used air at rates of 104,000, 166,000, and 176,000 cubic feet per minute respectively.[12] In H. M. Chance's work on *Mining Methods and Appliances*, published in 1883, it was observed that "the amount of air circulated is rarely less than four or five times the amount specified in the act," and in the Wilkes-Barre district, from 200,000 to 250,000 cubic feet per minute of fresh air was not uncommon in the "most fiery" collieries.[13] Twentieth-century minimum standards specify on the order of 200 cubic feet per minute per man in "gaseous" mines, which for the Pioneer Colliery, with about 275 men and boys underground, would mean a 55,000-cubic-feet-per-minute flow.[14]

Eltringham was still mine inspector when the safety act of 1870 went into effect. His 18,137-cubic-feet-per-minute standard was revised and refined for the new law, which required "not less than . . . thirty-three hundred feet per minute, for every fifty men at work in such a mine, and as much more as circumstances may require. . . ." For a mine with 275 men and boys underground, the law required 18,150 cubic feet per minute, nearly the same figure as Eltringham's standard, and less in places with a smaller work force. The new law thus in effect permitted the same inadequate ventilation systems that had passed inspection in 1869 and had been common practice for a generation in Pennsylvania. To be sure, "circumstances" might "require" more air, but in whose judgment? In Eltringham's judgment (and, after he reduced his inspection district to Ashland, in the judgment of the legion of his successors).

In March 1870, Eltringham was publicly accused by the executive board of the WBA of failing to enforce the law. Presumably, Siney and other members were acting on the basis of complaints made through union channels. The board charged that Eltringham did not close down collieries with inadequate ventilation or crumbling pillars. In a defensive reply in the *Miners' Journal*, Eltringham admitted that he permitted collieries to operate "whilst the ventilation of the colliery was in progress" and that he did so out of compassion for the poor miners "who could not afford to lay idle." He charged, in his turn, that during the recent strike the union would not permit work to continue on "air courses, safety roads, and other improvements." He went on to explain that he always invited the miners to complain if the operator and his superintendent and bosses were not following his instructions. He stated explicitly that new inlets were to be no less than thirty-six square feet in area, and outlets the same, and that the movement of air should be no less than "20,000 to 18,000 cubic feet per minute in mines where the pressure of gases amounting to 16 or 20 percent existed." As usual, he claimed that the "prevailing evil" was "careless, hasty, and incompetent persons," and he complained that Siney, with whom he had "frequently exchanged views relating to miners' interests, etc.," had failed to keep him informed of problems as he had promised to do.[15] Presumably, Eltringham's policy of "compromise" and of refusing to close dangerous mines when "with care the mine could be worked" continued.

There does not seem to have been negative comment in the press about the inadequacy of the ventilation standard set in 1869 and 1870; at least, the *Miners' Journal* was silent on the subject. And after Avondale the prohibition in the 1870 law of one-entry mines and of furnace ventilation where the breaker and engine house were built over the shaft may have seemed to answer the most essential ventilation-and-safety issues. But the 1870 law was severely criticized in other respects.

One of the first critiques was a highly publicized paper on "Mining Legislation" read by Eckley B. Coxe at the general meeting of the American Social Science Association in Philadelphia in October 1870. Speaking with the combined authority of the scientist and the practical business-man, Coxe minced no words. In the excitement caused by the Avondale disaster, he claimed, "the State legislature passed, in haste and without proper study of the question, an act, which is both defective and incom-plete." (He made no mention of the 1869 law.) After reviewing the hun-dreds of years of European mining legislation and praising the European corps of well-trained, uniformed inspectors, he pointed out that even in European coal mines terrible accidents occurred in which hundreds of lives were lost. He then analyzed accidents under three categories: those resulting from the "ignorance or carelessness" of those in charge; those caused by the "ignorance or carelessness" of the miners; and those which neither managers nor workers could have foreseen and prevented. With regard to the responsibility of operators, in addition to providing adequate ventilation, he mentioned the need to protect the miner while he was traveling to and from his work place in the mine. But he was eloquent on the subject of the careless miner:

> But there is another class of accidents, which occur even when all
> reasonable precautions have been taken. They are those occa-
> sioned by the thoughtlessness, imprudence, and foolhardiness of
> the workmen. Some men, when accustomed to climb ladders, do
> it almost mechanically, and are very apt to have their thoughts
> elsewhere when moving in dangerous places, and, while in a sort
> of brown study, will step off ladders or platforms and be dashed to
> pieces. Others again are so anxious to show how much stronger,
> braver, or more active they are than their fellows, that they will
> constantly put themselves in unnecessary peril by climbing where
> they ought not to. There is also a class of workmen who are
> naturally careless, and who will always be leaning over the side of
> the cage, putting their heads or arms out, etc., forgetting that
> they may at any moment be killed or maimed by a projecting rock

or timber. Accidents of this kind cannot be prevented by legislation; it is only by raising the standard of education among the miners, by instructing the boys, and by providing schools for master miners, that their number can be diminished.

In particular, he blamed casualties from falls of rock or coal on miners' carelessness and impatience with setting props and firing excessively large powder charges. And he claimed that in Pennsylvania coal mines, lung diseases were less a risk than in European metal mines, because "the miner works always in very pure air"!

All this led Coxe to argue that the 1870 law was a bad law and should be replaced by new legislation, state and federal, that applied to all industries and not just mining alone. Furthermore, the safety law should be satisfactory to operators as well as workmen. "It is important to the whole country," he averred, "that the mines be required to make no useless expenditures, as this will cause an increase in the cost of production. . . ." Mining inspectors should be graduates of schools of mining legislation, obtain the post by competitive examination, and be subject to an appeals board which could overrule the inspector and even "suspend some of the provisions of the act" if necessary. But his most emphatic demand was for tighter discipline in the mines:

> It is of the very greatest importance that the men should be obliged by law to obey the orders given them in regard to mining, timbering, use of lamp, etc., by those placed over them. No law and no care of the inspectors will be of much avail if the men are at liberty to disobey the instructions given them in regard to their work, the use of their lamp, or the precautions to be taken to avoid accidents. In all the mining codes of Europe there is a provision compelling the directors of mines to adopt rules for the management of the works, and these, when approved of by the inspector, become part of the mining law, and everyone is obliged to obey them. Unfortunately, there is no such clause in the law lately adopted in Pennsylvania.[16]

The *Miners' Journal* reprinted Coxe's paper within three months after it was delivered. The *Journal*'s editors too were unhappy with the 1870 law. They had, in fact, published a draft of the act in January 1870 that provided a generous sixteen months, instead of the original four, for compliance.[17] In February, again before passage, they deplored the excessive emphasis on ventilation and argued (correctly) that falls of coal, not gas explosions, caused most of the casualties in the mines.[18] Through 1871 and 1872 (years of considerable tension between the WBA and the operators) they pointed to the recklessness of miners as the root cause of accidents and to the consequent need for discipline.[19] After the calamitous gas explosion at Pittston in 1871 that killed seventeen men, the paper blamed Thomas M. Williams, the union official and sidekick of John Siney, now mining inspector for Luzerne, for lax administration of the law in order to give miners work after a long strike.[20] Again, in October 1872, the paper called for strict control of the miners and for better inspectors. Thus it was with some satisfaction that in August 1873 the *Journal* reported that a number of miners were arrested at the Hickory Colliery for a violation of the mining law—riding on a cage more than ten men at a time.[21] And again in September the *Journal* urged that the setting of prop timber be taken out of the hands of the reckless, hasty miners, who skimped on "dead work," and be made the responsibility of special crews.

This renewal of the claim that it was the careless miner rather than the careless operator who was responsible for mine accidents had no immediate effect on legislation. In the next ten years, supplements to the act simply tightened its requirements for adequate inspection and compliance. But the kind of criticism of the 1870 act launched by Coxe and the *Miners' Journal* probably helped to obscure that law's fundamental deficiency: its specification of 3,300 cubic feet per minute of fresh air for every fifty miners as the basic standard of ventilation. This standard permitted mines to operate legally with explosive mixtures of methane and air in their return airways and thus ensured the fires and explosions that in the 1870's closed down for long periods the St. Clair Shaft, the Pine Forest Shaft, the Hickory Slope, and the Wadesville Shaft, and would lead eventually to an abandonment of the town by many miners looking for work. The wonder is not that so many fires and explosions took place, but rather that the underground workers were so extremely careful that firedamp fatalities did not occur every day. There were some moments of recklessness, and some reckless men, to be sure, but they must have been very few for work to proceed at all, for as long as it did, in the fiery mines of St. Clair.

The other aspect of the public criticism of the 1870 law that echoes a wider theme is the demand for stricter discipline in the mines. There was a rising tide of feeling in the coal region, at least among the "respectable" elements of society, that not only were miners reckless, they were also lawless. The outer towns and patches, especially where Irish Catholic colliery workers were the predominant part of the population, were perceived as sinks of iniquity, as dangerous Hibernian enclaves of rum, Romanism, and rebellion, as arenas for innumerable crimes of violence. Thus calls for stricter colliery discipline were part of a more general demand for an effective sovereignty, a super-ordinate authority capable of bringing law and order to the coal regions of Schuylkill County. Once again, the problem was defined, by the operators and their social allies, as one of worker rather than operator irresponsibility. So from the politics of safety let us move to the politics of violence.

VI

JUSTICE AND VIOLENCE

In the mid-1850's, the *Miners' Journal* had a regular correspondent in St. Clair, a young schoolteacher with the *nom de plume* "Kate." A native of the town, Kate wrote sentimentally of its bustling success, its "grand and awful" scenes of disaster, especially the burning of the breaker at the St. Clair Shaft, its Sunday Schools and temperance societies, and its efforts at civic improvement, such as the planting of trees along the sidewalks and the passage of an ordinance against goats running free. But in 1856 Kate announced her engagement to be married and her plans to live in the South. Part of her reason for "running off so suddenly," she wrote, was a feeling of unease about the town. "St. Clair, though still flourishing and gay, does not seem to me now what it once did." A Christian temperance woman, Kate blamed the social deterioration of the town on drink; but the condition that she found intolerable was public rowdiness:

> I want the streets made passable before I return to St. Clair, and I want the police to keep the *rowdies* off the corners. It would not be amiss, indeed, to keep them quiet too, but I should be satisfied if these nuisances were abated and seven-eighths of the taverns closed up, or even if someone would keep a "black list" of those who lead the rising generation to ruin, through "groggeries" and "gambling dens."[1]

Seventeen years later, another of the *Journal*'s St. Clair correspondents was making essentially the same complaint:

> St. Clair is cursed with a gang of young roughs who go by the name of the "chain gang." They make a practice of insulting and assaulting people.[2]

314

The police did their best, arresting flagrant offenders and hauling them before the magistrate, who levied fines and made them sign peace bonds. But the ever present disorder in the streets, compounded by the occasional rape, drunken murder, arson, mugging, break-in, and highway robbery, maintained a high level of public concern with violence. As in other coal towns, the good people of St. Clair carried arms as well as the ruffians. One Welsh miner put it succinctly in a letter home in 1865: "Revolvers are ready weapons here with the ordinary people."[3] John Siney was reported in the press to have lost two revolvers when his house burned down. The eminently respectable Maurus Oestreich, organ builder, contractor, and devout Catholic, regularly walked with a sword cane and, on occasion, a revolver. On the road from Pottsville to St. Clair one night, he came upon a group of men loitering about a fire with a large dog. Not waiting to be attacked, Oestreich shot the dog, warned the men to stay away, and marched by with his gun drawn.[4]

In this kind of impromptu street violence, St. Clair and other coal towns were probably not different from other industrial neighborhoods of the period. It is impossible to gain adequate statistical information on crime in communities like St. Clair, but St. Clair was probably a basically orderly, if somewhat noisy, place with a very small police force and a large number of well-armed citizens, some of them drunk. But a type of crime was occurring there, and in other towns in the region, that would in coming years stimulate intense fear, prompt the formation of vigilante committees, and lead finally to the spectacular "Molly Maguire" trials. This crime was the exacting of retributive justice by outraged Irish communities—sometimes homicide, sometimes a beating, sometimes arson. In later years, this kind of crime would be connected with a semi-mythical Hibernian organization called the Molly Maguires. But at the beginning, before fantasies of a secret terrorist organization became rampant, Irish "outrages" were just *ad hoc* conspiracies to even the score.

Let us examine the case of a retributive-justice murder committed in 1846, allegedly by an Irish miner who worked at Lawton's colliery in St. Clair.

THE MURDER OF JOHN REESE

John Reese, a Welshman living in Delaware Mines—the mostly Irish mine patch strung out along the tracks of the Mount Carbon and East Norwegian Railroad, just over the ridge from St. Clair—shot and killed an Irish

neighbor, one Thomas Collahan, in 1846. He was arrested (actually res-
cued from a threatening mob of Irishmen), held in prison for several
months, tried, and acquitted early in December on the ground that he had
acted in self-defense. During his stay in prison, he suffered a broken arm
and some sort of mental collapse (his wife later said he was "out of his
mind"). During the trial and her husband's subsequent incarceration for a
couple of weeks in a "madhouse," his wife stayed in Pottsville, but she
made arrangements to take a house in St. Clair afterward for herself and
the children. After Reese was released from the hospital, he was to go to
stay with his sister Mary in Roaring Creek, a mine patch in Columbia
County. But Reese first wanted to visit for a night with his brother, who
lived in Wadesville. So one morning right after Christmas—it was the 30th
of December—at his insistence the family walked straight up the tracks
toward Wadesville, through their old neighborhood in Scalpington and
Delaware Mines, where Collahan had been killed. It was a slow-moving
group: the injured John Reese with one arm in a sling and an umbrella in
his other hand, his wife, Ann, his sister, Mary Humphreys, and his sickly
daughter, Mary Ann, gingerly picking their way along the ties. They stopped
to shake hands and chat politely at several houses in Delaware Mines. The
last house was old Mrs. Brennan's. Mrs. Brennan came out, inquired about
their health, chattered about the children, and asked John Reese, who did
not look at all well, if it was really he. When John Reese acknowledged that
it was indeed he, she nodded to a man silently standing nearby, leaning on
the handle of a miner's pick, looking down at the ground. Under his cap,
this man's face was white, "whiter than snow"; Mary Humphreys thought
"he looked like a man that had no blood in his body." Mrs. Reese and the
other women recognized the man as Martin Shay, a bachelor who lived
with his aunt and uncle a few doors from the Reeses in the patch just
below; he had once been in their house to buy a glass of porter. Then the
Reese party started up the railroad tracks again.

A short distance along the tracks, Martin Shay came running up,
brushed past the women, and caught up with Reese. He swung the pick,
catching Reese on the side of the head with the iron, ran on up the track,
and disappeared over the hill. Reese fell down the railroad embankment
into frozen Norwegian Creek, where he lay helpless and unconscious;
Reese's sister held his head off the ice on her lap, and cried "Murder" and
"Help" to the Irish men and women who stared at the scene, some of them
standing in a crowd with clubs in their hands, just watching, others star-
ing out of doors and windows. But no one would aid them, not even people
Mrs. Reese called by name. Mrs. Brennan's son turned away, laughing; a
woman clapped her hands and said "good for him"; a squad of Irish mili-

tiamen whooped and hollered and laughed. The women thought they were all to be killed. Meanwhile, the daughter had run off toward Wadesville to get help, but before this help arrived a black man driving a string of empty coal cars came by and he helped to put Reese in one of the cars. Then a rescue party arrived from Wadesville. They took him to his brother's house, where he died about three in the morning. That night Mrs. Reese told the police that the man who killed her husband was Martin Shay, and a reward was offered for his apprehension.

Although the death of "the Welshman" did not provoke much concern in the Irish community, the authorities were very much disturbed by this revenge slaying because it was seen as a direct refusal by some Irish to accept the legitimacy of the county's system of justice. The *Miners' Journal* expressed alarm:

> Seldom have we been called upon to record an instance of more daring and cold blooded murder than the above. The circumstances under which the deed was perpetrated, in open day light—in view of several dwellings—in the midst of the deceased's family—without provocation or quarrel, all tend to stamp it as one of those diabolical acts which overwhelm the mind by the magnitude of its atrocity. It is but a short time since this unfortunate man, acquitted by an impartial jury on the ground that he acted in self defense, returned to the home of his family with health and reason shattered. He is now dead, we fear the victim of a deadly and implacable revenge.
>
> In view of all the facts our authorities ought to offer a large reward for the apprehension of the murderer, and to spare no exertions to procure his speedy arrest. While such miscreants are at large there is no security for person or property.[1]

Shay was arrested three days after the crime, on Saturday, the 2nd of January 1847, as he came out of Alfred Lawton's drift after work. He worked in breast number twenty-five as laborer for his uncle (and landlord), James Brennan of Scalpington. John Moore, the inside boss, and constable Joseph Geisse took him into St. Clair to Frack's Tavern in his work clothes, and there Mrs. Reese identified him as the man who killed her husband. Shay was allowed to dress, and was then taken to a hearing before Squire Reed, a magistrate in Pottsville, where Mrs. Reese changed her mind and said she wasn't sure the murderer was Shay. Later, during the trial, she declared that she had changed her testimony only because she feared for her life on account of threats from people in St. Clair and in the crowd, and persuasions by an Irish constable, who kept by her side, saying, "Don't swear this young man's life away." But eventually her recollection became firm again and Shay was indicted for murder and bound over for trial.

The trial was held in June 1847. The three Reese women—Mrs. Reese, Reese's daughter, and his sister—positively identified Martin Shay as the man they saw kill John Reese. A good deal of suggestion was insinuated into the record, during the examination of these witnesses and of others from the Delaware Mines–East Mines–Scalpington area, about threats against Reese's life and about Irish hostility toward English and Welsh generally. All this collateral testimony made it appear that Shay was merely the executioner in a conspiracy to take Reese's life. The commonwealth's attorneys, a redoubtable trio that included F. W. Hughes, John Bannan, and James Campbell, made discrepancies in the witnesses' identification— uncertainty about the color of his pantaloons, his cap, his vest, his shirt— appear minor. And they proved, from the testimony of a defense witness, the surveyor Samuel Lewis, who had made a map of the roads between Pottsville and St. Clair, that Shay could have climbed up the thirty-seven-foot air hole and left the mine unnoticed, changed his clothes, committed the murder around four o'clock, and returned to leave the mine with his uncle at six. It was only seven-eighths of a mile from the air hole at Lawton's mine, through which Shay allegedly left and returned, to the upper end of Delaware Mines where Reese was killed.

The team of defense attorneys was headed by an able and respected lawyer, E. O. Parry, who customarily served the elite; Henry C. Carey was one of his regular clients. But the defense brought to the stand a parade of witnesses who laid the rebuttal testimony on so thick that in the end the jury could not believe any of it. Several men from Lawton's mine, including the English inside boss, John Moore of St. Clair, swore that they had seen Shay at work in breast number twenty-five that day at or about the hour when Reese was killed. Shay's uncle, James Brennan, claimed that Shay was there in the breast with him all day except for a few minutes when he went to borrow a prop at the next breast; but the Welsh miner who had been working that breast confessed under cross-examination that he remembered no such incident. Both Shay's uncle and his aunt also vouched for his character, a bit left-handedly, perhaps. Shay had come from Ireland to live with them in August 1845, and after half a day's work in the mines he was taken ill, lay sick in bed for six weeks, and was unable to work or even walk for five months; part of the time he went about on all fours. Brennan thought Martin Shay was too meek and mild a person to commit murder: "I never knew him to quarrel, or to get drunk, or to give insolence to any person." A neighbor said Shay never went out much among men, but played with boys of thirteen of fourteen and "he couldn't kill a chicken." Furthermore, Shay had no reason to kill Reese. He was not related to Collahan (at least, not so far as anyone knew), and the Welsh Reese and the Irish Brennan households were on good next-door-neighborly terms; in fact, until the murder, "I never saw any disunion between the Welsh and Irish." The Brennans got their water from a spring on Reese's property and the Brennans invited the Reeses to a christening. Although he could not attend because his wife was away, John Reese even cooked the goose for the christening feast "because we had not the means of cooking it at our house."

Then five women—Shay's aunt, the Mrs. Brennan who identified Reese for the assassin, a couple of neighbors, and a lady who sold beer in Pottsville—provided other suspects. The four residents of the mine-patch community all said that a mysterious dark-haired stranger named Cummings, presumably a relative of Collahan, had been seen lurking suspiciously about both before and after Reese's death. He looked, they all agreed, remarkably like Martin Shay. Mrs. Harris of Pottsville recalled that another man had declared to her that if Reese was acquitted "he would be killed anyhow . . . any man that kills another ought to be killed." She suspected him of the murder of Reese. And she said his name was James Cummings and that he worked at the Delaware Mines. Mrs. Brennan, on the other hand, said that the man she saw was named Devine but that he was related to a Mrs. Cummings whose maiden name was Collahan. Martin Devine worked at St. Clair and he too looked like Martin Shay. Her son Michael Brennan then testified that it was Martin Devine who was loitering near the house just before the murder, leaning on a pick. But the cross-examination had to be interrupted because of Michael's "sickness produced by intoxication," and both he and his mother were committed to jail on the charge of being accessories to the murder of John Reese. The next day Michael admitted that he had been told during the trial "that I must say these things or Shay would be hung." The commonwealth now brought in new witnesses, including Martin Devine's alleged employer, who testified that no man of that name or description lived in the neighborhood or worked at the Delaware Mines. And they recalled the Welsh miner, who had previously failed to support Shay's alibi, and who now remembered hearing James Brennan say, as they left at the end of the day, that Martin Shay, who was not among them, "went out between 2 and 3 o'clock."

During the summation for the prosecution by John Bannan, Shay became unwell and had to be removed from the courtroom twice. In the end, after three and a half hours, the jury, composed of two Englishmen and ten Germans, found Shay guilty of murder in the first degree. After an appeal for a new trial was turned down, the judge sentenced him to be hanged.[2]

The case of John Reese is significant because it exhibits a procedure for exacting retributive justice by an Irish community in the face of what it regarded as a hostile constabulary and a biased judge and jury. The course of events is not difficult to reconstruct. A Welshman killed an Irishman and got off scot-free after claiming self-defense. The Irish community might have been satisfied by his broken arm, his madness, and his plan for separation from his wife and voluntary exile to another county, where he would live with his sister and brother-in-law. But, in defiance of threats against his life if he stayed, he chose to walk through the very mine patch in which the killing had occurred and in which the victim's friends and relatives lived. An assassin, already appointed, was notified and, disguised in borrowed clothes and with his face whitened to make him more difficult to recognize, met Reese at the prearranged spot, where Mrs. Brennan positively identified him. The man killed his victim and then ran off, unpursued. When Reese's womenfolk proposed to identify the killer, they were threatened. Alibis were secured from the accused man's Irish co-workers and even an English boss. Community witnesses, neighbors of both Reese and Shay, gave Shay a good character and described the Reeses as friends and neighbors of the Brennans, with whom Shay lived. And, finally, several community witnesses described not one but two mysterious strangers—relatives of the widow of the man shot by Reese, or of Collahan himself—who either threatened Reese or were actually identified as the murderers.

Nearly thirty years later, in the same court in Pottsville, men were tried for crimes of revenge allegedly committed with the same rationale and a similar *modus operandi*. But in 1876 these crimes would be attributed to a criminal organization known as the Molly Maguires. And eventually this folk-justice tradition was caught up in the political struggle between the miners' union and the Philadelphia and Reading Coal and Iron Company and its president, former district attorney Franklin B. Gowen.

THE *MINERS' JOURNAL* AND THE
ANTI-IRISH-CATHOLIC MOVEMENT

Conspiracies to exact retributive justice on those who outraged the Irish community, like the vendetta that went awry in the case of John Reese and

Martin Shay, were not common events. The kinds of crime that filled the columns of the county newspapers were of a different sort: highway robberies and domestic break-ins by gangs of "Schuylkill Rangers"; assaults by groups of offended Irishmen on non-Irish patrons and proprietors of inhospitable public houses; and the usual parade of domestic shootings, stabbings, and beatings. (The Schuylkill Rangers were not a single organized band; the term was applied to a class of armed robberies, with accompanying non-fatal assault, by gangs of up to ten men.) Although a general lawlessness of the Irish was implied in the testimony at the Shay trial, there was no particular editorial comment on the matter at the time.

But early in the 1850's Benjamin Bannan began to articulate in the pages of his *Miners' Journal* a political theory that cast the Catholic Irish in the role of conspirators against the common weal. First of all, the Catholics, he believed, voted in a block for candidates of the Democratic Party, thus defeating Bannan's Whigs. Most of these Catholic votes were Irish, and many of them were fraudulent, being cast by men who were not citizens or were otherwise unqualified. And behind the local Catholics loomed the Pope and Rome, ever scheming to destroy Protestantism and, in particular, to hand the British Isles back to the Celts and the Inquisition. Bannan was an ardent Welsh Presbyterian. He charged that "the controlling power of the Catholic Church" opposed the protective tariff; he complained that Catholics showed disrespect for the Sabbath; and, of course, he roundly condemned Catholic efforts to take public funds to support parochial schools. A passionate temperance man, he accused the Irish Catholics of being the principal patrons of the county's 636 taverns (one for every nine voters) and blamed Irish intemperance for the alleged fact that most of the county's paupers and convicted felons were Irish Catholics. He sought, indeed, to drive all Catholics out of the Whig Party. He was, in effect, co-opting for Whiggish use the anti-Catholic, anti-Democrat sentiment concurrently being exploited by the Know-Nothings, who in Pennsylvania formed the short-lived (1854–1857) Keystone American Party. Along with other anti-Democrats in Schuylkill, Bannan in 1856 supported the anti-Catholic, anti-Democrat, pro-Republican People's Party and later, as the anti-Catholic issue declined in saliency in comparison with anti-slavery feeling, joined the Republican Party itself.[1]

The term "Molly Maguires," which was later to become the rubric for an alleged Irish terrorist organization, seems to have been given local currency in Schuylkill by Bannan in 1857.[2] After frauds were discovered in Philadelphia's 1856 presidential election, a number of Irish Catholic inspectors were indicted. Bannan charged that a secret Irish Catholic organization controlled the Democratic Party:

The Miners' Journal *Building, ca. 1863, with the Henry Clay Monument in the background*

Every one of these inspectors were Irishmen, belonging no doubt to the order of "Molly Maguires," a secret Roman Catholic association which the Democracy is using for political purposes. The Philadelphia *Transcript* says this Association commenced in Boston and now extends all over the country, controlling all the nominations of the Democratic Party in our cities and in some parts of the country. . . .

So powerful and notorious has this Association become, that no less than two Catholic Priests in Philadelphia have called attention to it.

The honest thinking citizens of all parties ought to unite in putting down such a "secret association" as this. . . .[3]

The term "Molly Maguire" seems to have come into use in the rural south of Ireland during the early famine years and was taken up by, and applied to, groups of peasants who retaliated against landlords, agents, magistrates, bailiffs, process servers, constables, and even the military—all either Englishmen or Irish collaborators—who had been guilty of injustices to poor Irish peasants and their families. (In Wales, such resistance groups were called "Rebecca.") In Ireland in the 1840's, the term "Molly Maguire" was used specifically to denote bands of young men dressed in women's clothing, with faces blackened by burnt cork or otherwise disguised, who beat or killed gamekeepers, servers of eviction notices, cottage-wrecking crews, and other agents of the establishment. Whether there was a secret society by the name of Molly Maguire or whether it was merely the term applied to the culturally sanctioned way of exacting retributive justice, whose mere regularity suggested to some the likely existence of a parent organization, is not clear. But what is clear is that in the 1830's and 1840's local branches of a totally separate, large, international organization were being established in America. This society, named the Ancient Order of Hibernians, was a benevolent association reserved for Irish Catholics, who were excluded from the Masons and Odd Fellows and other fraternal societies of English and Protestant origin. Like the others, the Ancient Order of Hibernians had its secrets: initiation rites, handshakes, passwords, and toasts. And, also like the others, because it required members to take secret oaths, the AOH was technically proscribed by the Catholic Church.[4]

The organization to which Bannan was referring in 1857 by the label "Molly Maguire" was probably the Ancient Order of Hibernians, to which many Irish Democratic politicians in America undoubtedly did belong. But by using the name given to Irish night raiders, fighting their guerrilla war against the British, for a perfectly ordinary fraternal organization, Bannan was managing to lump together all Irish Catholic lay leaders into some sort of secret conspiracy that was violent and terroristic and also at the same time, in its penetration of the Democratic Party, insidious and corrupting of the political system. Increasingly, for Bannan, the enemy became the local Irish, less and less international Popery and Romanism. He paid no heed to the Catholicism of most recent German immigrants. Bannan's conspiratorial image of 1857 was eventually to blossom forth in the 1870's in the Pinkerton Detective Agency investigations, and subsequent trials, of the Molly Maguires.

As another part of the image of the Irish Catholic, Bannan's paper constantly presented, as news, amusing or lurid anecdotes of Irish behavior. Funny stories were run on the back page, with Irish men and women expressing some antic notion or other in stereotyped brogue. There were, to be sure, jokes at the expense of other ethnicities. But on the inner pages, reserved for local news, Irish crime was featured. Thus, in 1851, Bannan reported a "regular old-fashioned Irish fight" at the Seven Stars tavern, when twenty drunken Irishmen attacked "persons of the house."[5] On the night after the Fourth of July 1850, "a party of Irishmen" stoned a small group of respectable citizens at Mount Carbon and were dispersed only by a volley of pistol fire.[6] Again at Mount Carbon, the following year, the Whig governor of Pennsylvania, escorted by a number of deputies including Edward Carey, George Repplier, Jeremiah Boone, Charles Willson Peale, and three gentlemen from St. Clair, was physically attacked. Bannan blamed "locofoco" Democrats (who in his system of thought must have been Irish).[7] Week after week, year after year, the *Miners' Journal* painted for its middle-class, Whiggish readership a picture of the Irish as an incompetent and criminal underclass. Although in the decade and a half that followed the trial of Martin Shay there were no similar examples of retributive justice going to the extreme of premeditated murder, the image of Molly Maguire lingered on in Bannan's thunderous prose. No doubt it had little direct effect in the mining towns and patches, where poor men and women of differing ethnicities had to get along together as individuals, but it was laying the basis for an explosion of antagonisms in the future.

That future came with the Civil War.

THE MILITARIZATION OF THE COAL FIELDS

The perception by the operators that they were faced with a dangerous element that threatened the stability of the industry led to their first calling upon the military in the year 1858 at "The Great Battle of St. Clair," which was described in the last chapter. The coming of the Civil War rendered such scenes more common and more serious as Unionist, abolitionist, radical Republicans charged compromising Democrats, particularly the Irish miners, with being disloyal "copperheads." Many foreign-born, non-naturalized miners, on their part—and no doubt many new citizens as well—saw no reason to leave their families to fight and die in another country's civil war.

In the early months of the war, when it was believed that the industrial North would quickly overwhelm the agricultural South, the ranks of the northern army were filled by voluntary enlistment. The procedure during the Three Months' Campaign in 1861 was simple. An aspiring officer, with or without prior military experience, issued a public call in newspapers and posted handbills for men to enlist under him as captain of a company. Thus, for instance, fifty-two-year-old Pottsville attorney and speculator in coal lands Charlemagne Tower advertised for a company and succeeded in actually recruiting two. He led his men into battle once and then resigned, leaving his lieutenant, Henry Pleasants, a Pottsville mining engineer, to take over the company. Other familiar names from the class of operators and professional men who led men into battle during the three-month campaign include Colonel John Macomb Wetherill, Major Edward Carey Baird, and Surgeon Major John T. Carpenter, the Smith family's friend in Pottsville, who later became prominent as an organizer of army hospitals.[1]

Wetherill had been elected to his militia colonelcy in 1851, commanding Scott's St. Clair Infantry, and now he moved on to higher echelons, leaving the Wetherill Rifles of St. Clair to the command of Captain Edward Frane. These early volunteer units received mostly men with English, Welsh, and German names, but some Irish were enlisted. An examination of the seventy-five-man Wetherill Rifles company roster reveals about half a dozen Irish-sounding names (Dormer, Donovan, McHugh, McLafferty, O'Neill, McGowen), but none of them can be identified from census schedules as residents of St. Clair. A second St. Clair company, the Lafayette Rifles, also includes several Irish names (Brennan, Dougherty, Kelly, Dolan). Citizens of St. Clair also contributed money to support the families of volunteers. The list was headed by William H. Johns, the most generous donor at $250, and he was followed by virtually all the colliery operators, hotel keepers, tradesmen, and professional men: engineer John Holmes, $50; Drs. Coryell and Andrew Carr, $25 and $5 respectively; coal operator George S. Repplier, $25; baker Jacob Gwinner $50; storekeeper Charles Lawton, $10. The town's contribution added up to $1,767, about 7 percent of the entire county's collection.[2]

The units recruited for the Three Months' Campaign were incorporated into the regular army later in 1861. It was the 48th Pennsylvania Regiment that took Henry Pleasants, now Lieutenant Colonel, and Enoch McGinness' son Daniel, adjutant. And another name, soon to assume extreme prominence in the county's affairs, was that of George Washington Gowen, colonel of the 48th Regiment, who was killed in 1865 near Appomattox seven days before the surrender. Afterward his name was given to the Pottsville post of the Grand Army of the Republic. He was the younger brother of attorney Franklin Benjamin Gowen, soon to be district attorney and then president of the Philadelphia and Reading Railroad.[3]

The issue of Irish copperhead sympathies came to a head in 1862 after a conscription act was passed. Benjamin Bannan was appointed draft commissioner for Schuylkill County, responsible for compiling a census of men of draft age and for verifying claims to exemption. In 1863, Charlemagne Tower, Pottsville lawyer and part owner of millions of dollars' worth of coal lands, was appointed military provost marshal, with the rank of captain, to enforce compliance within the county. And Franklin B. Gowen was elected district attorney. Clearly, the leaders of law enforcement and guardians of the Union cause in Schuylkill County were men closely identified with the coal trade and intimately connected with the military themselves, for Bannan was the father-in-law of Henry Pleasants, Gowen was the brother of Pleasants' commanding officer, and Tower himself had formerly been Pleasants' commander. The 48th Regiment had, as it were, a rear guard in the coal regions. But trouble carrying out the provisions of the 1862 conscription act began almost immediately in Schuylkill (as it did across the country). Although Bannan was able to compile a household census, from which conscripts were selected, one of the trains carrying drafted men to the induction center at Harrisburg was blocked by rioters at Tremont. The Irish in Cass Township refused to be conscripted at all. Excitement ran so high that all the collieries in Schuylkill and Luzerne were stopped by turnouts. Bannan sent word to Governor Curtin, who telegraphed Secretary of War Stanton to the effect that a conspiratorial "league" of 5,000 men had formed that must be put down before it spread. Bannan believed that disloyal Democrats were secretly urging men not to fight in "an abolition war" and were spreading inflammatory rumors that the northern "capitalists" were planning to use freed slaves as scabs in northern industries to replace men striking for higher wages.[4] Eventually Lincoln promised veteran troops if necessary, but suggested that he would be satisfied to see the law "appear to have been executed." Understanding the suggestion at once, Bannan proceeded to have affidavits of enlistment forged to show that the Cass Township quota had already been filled by volunteers. As Alexander McClure, then state draft commissioner, observed in his memoirs many years later, "it was an imperious necessity to avoid a conflict between the Molly Maguires and the troops."[5] But for the Irish it was a victory for the little man, who had nothing to gain from the war while the "glory and the plunder" went to the capitalists "for whose interests they are flinging away their lives."[6]

Next year, in July 1863, a national conscription act was passed. Resistance was immediate. In New York City, hundreds were killed by troops in bloody battles with slum rioters. In Schuylkill, the commander of the local regulars (two companies of the "Invalid Corps" of wounded soldiers assigned to home-guard duty) reported to Washington that the miners of Cass Township had organized an anti-draft army of 2,000 to 3,000 men, commanded and drilled by discharged veterans, and possessed not only of small arms but some pieces of artillery. They had threatened, it was said, "to burn down the houses and coal breakers owned by Republicans" and had served "cautionary notices" on prominent citizens including Benjamin Bannan. The army sent additional troops and, under cover of military force, conscription was effected by late August. By then hatred was intense on both sides. The military feared that if the troops were withdrawn, Pottsville would be "laid in ashes and a thousand barbarities committed."[7] But the immediate target of the draft resisters' revenge seems to have been the colliery operators and mine superintendents who cooperated with draft officials and the military occupation, particularly those operators who supplied the authorities with colliery pay lists, from which the names of eligible draftees could be selected. The first to suffer death from this cause of retributive justice was an operator named George K. Smith of Audenried in Carbon County, who was shot in the head in the presence of his family. This was the same George K. Smith who had worked for Henry Carey as consulting engineer at the St. Clair Shaft a couple of years before. Several suspects were arrested, but were set free by an angry mob.[8]

St. Clair men in the Union service, as volunteers or conscripts, were numerous, especially in the 48th Regiment, whose ten companies were all made up of Schuylkill County men, and in Company A and Company F of the 80th Regiment, in which re-enlistments from the Wetherill Rifles and the Lafayette Rifles of St. Clair were placed. Irish names were particularly common in the 48th Regiment. The 48th saw some of the heaviest fighting of the war, including Second Bull Run, Antietam, Fredericksburg, the Wilderness campaign, and the siege of Petersburg, where the miners under Lieutenant Colonel Pleasants' command tunneled under the Confed-

erate fort and exploded the famous—or infamous—"Petersburg Mine."
Colonel Gowen was killed in the disastrous charge through the crater.
Company H, for instance, where Lieutenant Edward C. Baird and Ser-
geant Daniel McGinness served, lost thirty-six men killed during the four
years of war, about 13 percent of the men who ever served in the company,
or about 3 percent per year. Wounded and missing, of course, were larger
in number. All in all, service in the 48th during the Civil War would seem
to have been almost as dangerous as working in the mines back home.[9]
From St. Clair, with a total population of 4,475 in 1860, at least 182 men
served. Of the twenty-five who fought with the 48th, seven lost their lives:
four were killed in battle or died of wounds suffered in battle, two died of
disease, and one was a suicide. Other units suffered fewer casualties, but
it is probably a reasonable estimate that 10 percent of those who went away
to war from St. Clair died of wounds or disease, and that another 20
percent were wounded.[10]

Nothing in rosters of Schuylkill County companies suggests that Irish
miners did in fact fail to bear their full share of the burden of service and
casualties. Irish names appear in profusion, along with English, German,
and Welsh. But after the war the bitterness of some Irish conscripts and
their families toward the mine operators and other middle-class officialdom,
and the latter's fear of a secret army of disaffected Irishmen, festered on,
building toward its grim denouement. Attacks on mine superintendents
became more common, and two of them, both occurring in 1867, involved
persons with a close connection to St. Clair. The first incident, in February, involved J. C. Northall, then the engineer in charge of the sinking of
the Wadesville Shaft, now almost complete. (Northall would later that year
become superintendent of the Hickory Slope and then the St. Clair Shaft
and Slope.) Northall and his family lived in Tamaqua, where on the night
of February 11 his house was attacked by a drunken Irish mine worker,
John Donahue, employed by Northall, and a small group of Donahue's
friends. Northall was not at home at the time, but the house was occupied
by his wife and two small children, their servant girl, and one William
Cole, his wife, and their two children. About 11 p.m., Donahue and some
friends banged on the door of the house, waking up the families. Donahue
wanted money from Northall to go to a funeral at New Philadelphia, a
decrepit mining town several miles away. Donahue went to the back door,
where Cole met him. They exchanged words through the door and then
Cole set the dog on Donahue. Donahue fell to the ground, pulled free, and
ran off, but half an hour later, back he came with his friends. First Donahue
tried to break in the back door. Terrified, the ladies hid in a closet with

their children while Cole and the servant girl rushed to the windows. Cole fired his revolver and yelled, "Help! Murder!" while the assailants fired pistols into the house. A crowd began to assemble, so Cole and the girl, thinking it was safe, opened the front door to go out. They were met with gunfire, one shot passing through the girl's dress. Donahue rushed at Cole with a sword; Cole warned him off with a revolver; Donahue then threatened the crowd with a sword, threatening to "cut their bloody heads off." A volley of shots was fired from the crowd, now swollen to twenty or twenty-five men, and Donahue fell, mortally wounded.

One man was tried for the killing: Thomas Border, who lived close by. The jury—which included St. Clair hotel keeper Amzi Brown—acquitted Border after a strong defense marshaled by former district attorney and Democratic leader F. B. Gowen and by Republican leader Lin Bartholomew. The *Miners' Journal* editorialized somewhat smugly:

> The verdict of the jury in this case has met with general approval, for it is the belief of all the respectable people in this community that Thomas Border and in fact all the men who came to the assistance of Mrs. Northall, Mr. Cole, Miss Higham and the children, when the cries "Help, Murder" rang out upon the midnight air, did simply their duty. If a desperado lost his life in his attempt to commit murder at Northall's house, he met a merited fate.[11]

But not all outrages ended so satisfactorily. Immediately preceding the account of the Northall trial, in the same issue of the *Journal*, was an account of the murder of William Littlehales, Jr. In this case, no suspect was ever brought to trial, although the county commissioners offered a $5,000 reward; the case would come to be regarded as another in the long list of unsolved "Molly Maguire" killings. Littlehales was a son of the English-born William Littlehales of Pottsville, who for many years, with his son, had operated small collieries in and about St. Clair. In 1865 the younger Littlehales had become superintendent of the Glen Carbon Coal Company, in Cass Township, and had moved his family there in the winter of that year. He was in the habit of paying the men monthly in cash, and at first carried the payroll, about $3,000, up from the bank in Pottsville in a sulky; but in view of the mounting number of highway robberies, he had by March of 1867 begun to carry it by rail "in the cars." On Friday, March 15—the day before payday—he made the mistake of driving into Pottsville in the sulky, as he had previously been used to do the day before payday, to transact some personal business. He left town by sulky early that afternoon, telling friends that he would be back next day in the cars to pick up the payroll. But he never reached home. About half a mile from his residence, on a secluded section of the road, he was waylaid, shot, and killed. After death his eyes were blown out, perhaps by thieves angered at not finding the payroll. The body was discovered, but not recognized at first, by a physician who was riding up to the Littlehales' residence to attend the man's son, whose leg had been amputated just below the knee two weeks before, in consequence of being run over by railroad cars. The *Miners' Journal* painted the pathetic scene at the home: the hysterical widow on one bed, the corpse of her husband on a second, and the mutilated body of her son on the third.[12]

Such inflammatory acts as these brought public concern, at least among Bannan's respectable readers, to a boil. In 1866 the legislature had passed an act establishing a special police force in the coal regions, wearing badges stamped with the words "Coal and Iron Police," and recruited, paid, and controlled by colliery owners and ironmasters. The Coal and Iron Police were primarily intended to protect property, however.[13] In 1867 the legislature was petitioned for further action to reduce "the terrible prevalence of crime in Schuylkill County." The *Journal* published an itemized list of fifty murders committed from 1863 through March 1867 (three of them, all Irish killed by Irish, in St. Clair). Several of these deaths were women murdered by their husbands, including one from St. Clair; some died "by cause unknown"; and of the victims with Irish names, most were killed by men with Irish names as well. The editor included John Donahue's death as one of the fifty "murders." Few were "Molly Maguire" outrages, but these were highlighted in the list and attributed to "the incarnate fiends who rule the County."[14] In effect, all killings were associated by proximity in time to the Molly Maguire stereotype. In response to the hue and cry, and in the face of threats to establish vigilante committees (even the *Journal* favored these), the state legislature passed an act to set up a special 100-man police force and a new court district with its own jury panel to suppress violent crime in Schuylkill and three adjacent counties.[15] Thereafter, for about five years, violence was said to have diminished remarkably, but whether it was the result of an increasingly muscular justice system, or of the presence of the Workingmen's Benevolent Association, with its ability to negotiate grievances, would be difficult to say.

Clearly, the decade between the "Great Battle of St. Clair" in 1858 and the passage of the Court, Police, and Jury Act in 1867 saw a marked deterioration in the image that Schuylkill County's elite had of the moral status of its working population. By 1867 the military had been called in at least twice to put down organized resistance to the draft, an organized Republican political campaign had been launched and maintained against the alleged alliance between the Democratic Party and the Irish Catholics, and a secret order of Hibernian terrorists named the Molly Maguires had been identified in the public mind with attacks by Irish miners upon English and Welsh mine bosses and superintendents. The latter image was peculiarly ominous. As the *Journal* put it:

> Unless this terrible state of affairs is checked, but few men will feel that they dare accept situations at collieries, while capital and population are driven from the county.[16]

THE PINKERTON SPY IN ST. CLAIR

For the most part, the WBA enjoyed respectful press coverage in Schuylkill County, even during strikes and tense negotiations. Both political parties courted the labor vote, although the Democrats appealed especially to Irish Catholic miners and Pennsylvania German farmers, and the Republicans to Protestant workers of English and Welsh descent. The union was widely seen as a responsible organization that had united workers of different faiths and national origins, had substituted grievance committees for retributive justice, had restrained wildcat strikes, and had disciplined its members to refrain from acts of violence during the strikes that the union did call. Even during the tense days in 1876, when the Molly Maguires were on trial, counsel for both sides agreed on one thing: that the union had been a force for good and had not used the Mollies as its enforcers. For the defense in the Thomas case, Republican Martin L'Velle claimed, somewhat extravagantly, that the "honest body of men called the union" had ended capital crime between 1868 and 1873:

> Immediately prior to 1873, while the Miners' and Laborers' Union was in the heyday of its prosperity in this county—I say the union, and God bless it for the good work it did in this community—there was not a transgression or serious crime of any character in our county for years. . . .

And even prosecuting attorney George Kaercher vehemently agreed, saying that the two societies—the Molly Maguires and the labor union—"are not to be mentioned in the same breath," and that after the dissolution of the union in 1875, the Mollies were left "unchecked, uncontrolled, and unwatched." And he too praised the working people who had made up the union. "There does not exist today upon the face of the earth a more honest, a more intelligent, and more law-abiding population than the working men of Schuylkill County."[1] One of the accused Mollies, who testified in his own defense, explained how the union worked to resolve grievances and abort revenge:

> A: Johnny Boyle, who came from the west in the spring, went to work in Loss Creek, but I believe the boss didn't want him there and they sacked him, and they wanted me and another man to go and shoot him, and two men from Philip Nash.
>
> Q: Do you mean two men from your own division [of the Molly Maguires]?
>
> A: Yes, sir.
>
> Q: And two men from Philip Nash's division?
>
> A: Yes, sir.
>
> Q: To go and shoot the boss?
>
> A: Yes, sir; and I told them I would not. I told them that the man never done anything to me, and that I didn't want to hurt him, and that Johnny Boyle could get work somewhere else; that if anything was wrong with Johnny Boyle I would let the Union reinstate him back; the Union was in force then.[2]

Even special counsel for the prosecution Franklin B. Gowen, formerly district attorney in Pottsville and now none other than president of the Philadelphia and Reading Railroad, who had earlier made an earnest effort to smear the union with the Molly Maguire label, made no such explicit charge in 1876.

But Gowen's earlier effort to incriminate the union must be examined. In March 1871, in the course of a Pennsylvania Senate investigation into the right of the Reading Railroad to double its rates on coal, Gowen defended the action from the charge that it threatened the public interest by explaining that the decision had in fact been taken with the welfare of the commonwealth in mind. It was necessary, he said, "to rescue a great industry, the largest in Pennsylvania, namely, the coal mining interest, from the control of an association that had almost destroyed it . . ."— namely, the Workingmen's Benevolent Association. The railroad, by raising its rates, had merely prevented the operators from giving in to the wage scale demanded by the union. And Gowen went on to intimate that the WBA was one with the Molly Maguires:

There never, since the middle ages, existed a tyranny like this on the face of God's earth. There has never been, in the most despotic government in the world, such a tyranny, before which the poor laboring man has to crouch like a whipped spaniel before the lash, and dare not say that his soul is his own. Can it be for a moment supposed that we, in whose hands are millions of dollars, invested by women and children, who depend for bread upon it, shall stand idly by without making some little effort to save it? Such a thing has never been heard of before under Heaven. I do not charge this Workingmen's Benevolent Association with it, but I say there is an association which votes in secret, at night, that men's lives shall be taken, and that they shall be shot before their wives, murdered in cold blood, for daring to work against the order. At Trevorton, six or eight weeks ago, a man, working outside of this organization and against their order, who was sitting quietly beside a sick neighbor, was shot and killed by a bullet through the window of the house. Last week there was an attempt to kill a man working outside of this organization, by igniting a keg of powder under his house, and he was then shot. *I do not blame this association*, but I blame another association for doing it; and it happens that the only men who are shot are the men who dare to disobey the mandates of the Workingmen's Benevolent Association. Is this to last forever? Can there be no redress? Can it be that in the Commonwealth of Pennsylvania, which has this great body of coal, this great industry, which has supported the Commonwealth of Pennsylvania, which has paid its taxes, is to be singled out and made subservient entirely to the dictates of the workingmen? It is, then, gentlemen, good-bye to the credit of Pennsylvania, good-bye to the coal mining and manufacturing industries. Let every man give it up and go home and be a poor man. . . .[3]

Three days later, Bannan made the accusation explicit in an editorial. Criticizing another newspaper's editor, Bannan said:

He says that the Molly Maguires do not belong to the W.B.A. This is not true; they all belong, because they could not get any work whatever if they did not. There are but two classes in this Region—members of the W.B.A., or what they term blacklegs. The correspondent says: "the 'Buckshots' and 'Molly Maguires' are the self-constituted detectives and judges for the Workingmen's

Benevolent Association, although not members of the order." This is true, so far as the acts of these persons are concerned, and it is also this class that the quiet and orderly men dread so much, and always obey when ordered to stop work; but when the writer says that they are not members of the organization, he states what is absolutely false. They are the Danites of the leaders, and whenever the *Monitor*, the organ of the leaders denounce any person, the Danites are ready to execute the order.[4]

Gowen's concern about the Molly Maguires, as well as the union, was not merely that of a railroad president whose trains carried coal. It was not public knowledge, but since 1868 he had been buying up coal lands in Schuylkill County with his own money and with funds supplied by other investors. The plan was to create a corporate subsidiary to the railroad, a coal-and-iron company, which would take over these purchases and make others on its own. No sooner was the Senate investigation over than the state legislature passed a bill incorporating the Laurel Run Improvement Company and authorizing it to operate collieries and ironworks (which the parent railroad-company charter excluded). The Philadelphia and Reading Coal and Iron Company, as the new corporation quickly was renamed, by the end of 1871 owned over 100 square miles of coal land and by 1875 over 150, amounting to about 80 percent of the coal lands in Schuylkill County, and nearly a third of the entire anthracite field. The stakes in the Reading plan—of which we shall say more in the next chapter—were very high, and Gowen was no doubt genuinely fearful of interference from obstinate unions and unsettled social conditions.

Gowen's preoccupation with the idea of a tyrannical union in league with a vast terrorist organization prompted him in 1873 to hire the Pinkerton Detective Agency to investigate the connection. This agency, headed by Allan Pinkerton, undertook commissions from insurance companies, banks, railroads, and other business concerns that needed anything from detective work to the protection of a private army. Already famous nationally for its battles with western outlaws, especially the Jesse James gang, the agency simply hired new secret agents or armed guards as new contracts were made. The Philadelphia office handled the contract with the Reading Railroad, and assigned a number of men to the Molly Maguire case. Detective James McParlan and some other agents concentrated their attention on the Irish districts north and west of St. Clair. But one agent, P. M. Cumming, was sent to St. Clair to infiltrate the headquarters of the Workingmen's Benevolent Association and reveal its hidden ties with the

Molly Maguires.[5] To be sure, Siney had at the 1871 hearing—where he was interrogated by the irrepressible Gowen himself—denied any involvement of the union with Molly Maguirism. The union had no secret signs or passwords; but, of course, he could not guarantee that no union member was a member of any secret society. And his answers were lame when he tried to distinguish between union discipline, sanctions against blacklegs, and Molly Maguire outrages.[6] Thus Cumming should have been able—in Gowen's and Pinkerton's view—to produce evidence linking Siney and the union with the great Irish criminal conspiracy.

But Cumming failed to find any substantiation whatever and he was never put on the stand during the trials. The summaries of his reports to Gowen, prepared by Benjamin Franklin, the chief of the Pinkerton agency in Philadelphia, have survived, however, and provide intimate vignettes of working-class life in St. Clair in the 1870's. Allan Pinkerton wrote to Gowen at the end of March 1874, introducing an operative from Illinois who was now assigned to "special duty in regard to ascertaining the workings of the Workingmen's associations in the coal Region." Mr. Cumming had been, although "a Scotchman," a member of the Dublin police force and, since coming into Pinkerton employ, had already spied on the Miners' National Association and secured a membership card from it. Cumming left the Pinkerton office in Chicago and went to Cleveland, where he conferred with John James, the secretary of the Miners' National Association, but missed Siney, the new president. James gave him some information about the association, including a claim that it was honest, and let him look at the membership roster. Cumming noted that the roster included information on any member's criminal record and his movements through the states of Pennsylvania, Ohio, Indiana, Illinois, and Missouri, and thus the member (and any unsuspected Molly) could be "traced up very easily." James advised Cumming to look for work in Schuylkill County, where, despite the generally bad business conditions, the mines were still open because "the miners had settled with the operators and had never known what the panic was." On the 26th of February, after brief stops at Pittsburgh and Philadelphia, Cumming reached St. Clair "with instructions to hunt for work and get into the Miners National Union." He was to remain in St. Clair for a year.

Cumming's first order of business was to meet "Mr. Sina." He waited for two days, even turning down a job opportunity at the new Twin Shaft, in order to obtain Siney's "advice regarding obtaining some work." Finally, as Cumming's rapporteur put it, "The operative succeeded in finding Mr. Sina—at a cock fight in St. Clair." Siney explained, a bit defensively perhaps, that "he did not take any active hand in cockfighting—although he liked to see a good fight." After the contest Cumming followed Siney to his boardinghouse, where he formally presented his credentials, and Siney promised to speak to his old boss in Johns' mines—"not so dangerous as the others"—which were not going to start up, however, until the middle of March. Siney indulged in a little boasting about his success and seemed especially pleased that he had forced certain Catholic priests to retract public statements accusing the union of being "a secret and oath-bound organization"—in other words, of being Molly Maguires.

> He represented that the Schuylkill County [union] is now the best in the United States—that they had now fought successfully the larger operators in the County—viz: Mr. Gowen and others—and so long as he was connected with the miners he would continue fighting on every issue. That the Catholic clergy had denounced the conclave [National Association] from the altar as a secret and oath bound organization. That he had to tackle the Divines in question and had got them to retract their words from the pulpit.[7]

Siney left a few days later on his duties as president of the National Association, and was to be met with in St. Clair only occasionally after that. But Cumming met Mr. Johns, who predicted that there would be no difficulty in finding work in the spring. And Cumming found other informants to explain to him the sliding scale and the basis and the current status of union-operator relations. His own landlord, Peter Hall, explained the local situation with regard to the Molly Maguires, saying that the Mollies were numerous around St. Clair but were "kept down" by another secret society known as "the Chain Gang."[8] The Chain Gang was a loose association of experienced Irish miners from County Kilkenny (where lay the only coal mines in Ireland), together with a few Welshmen, that clashed with the Mollies in a number of towns in the coal region. Hall, one of the rare Catholic Republicans, had other interesting things to say about the Mollies—that there were some Englishmen among them, that they "belonged to no church, although very bitter against non-Catholics," and that for Cumming, a total stranger, to go "farther up the mountain," where the Mollies ruled, "would be almost certain death."

Peter Hall's boardinghouse, located on Third Street between Carroll and Lawton, virtually in the shadow of the breaker at the St. Clair Shaft, was an excellent vantage point for a Pinkerton operative. Hall was an Irish-born miner in his mid-forties who had migrated to St. Clair in about 1852 after a brief stay in Scotland. He had prospered and owned a large house valued at $2,500. He and his wife, Bridget, and their six children took care of the house and (in 1870) five boarders, all Irishmen, all miners and mine laborers. As a miner, Hall was undoubtedly a member of the union, which he explained and praised to Cumming.[9]

When Siney returned from a visit to Ohio a few days later, Cumming sought him out. In addition to union business, Molly Maguire came up again, in connection with a murder recently committed in St. Clair. Thomas Russell, a mine laborer and secretary of the local union chapter, had, a few days before, killed his stepfather, teamster Martin Nash, who had been "chief among the M.M.'s." Nash, who was nearly sixty, was living with Russell's mother and thirty-eight-year-old Russell in a house in "the patch"; all of the family were Irish. Nash had complained to the magistrate a few days before that he had been beaten and threatened with death by Russell. The reasons for the son's hatred of his stepfather were obscure and the method of execution peculiar: Russell had apparently hanged him in the stable.[10] At the funeral a large number of Molly Maguires were in attendance and the people at Hall's were frightened. "Everybody speaks in whispers about the murder for fear of being overheard." Later Cumming learned from Mrs. Hall, who heard it from Nash's sister Bridget, that the reason Nash was murdered was that he had resigned from the Molly Maguires. During an illness he had sought absolution from the priest and had been refused until he renounced his membership in the "M.M.'s" (no doubt the Ancient Order of Hibernians). He accordingly left the order and "from that time until his death he had no peace" with Russell.

Cumming lost interest in the Nash murder after Russell was jailed and a new union secretary was appointed; Russell last appeared in Cumming's reports as having a brother named William "who keeps a house of ill-fame in Philadelphia." And no further mention was made of the Molly Maguires except for a brief note in November 1874 about a gunfight in Mahanoy City between the Molly Maguires and the Sheet Iron Gang. His informant, William Nash of Lanagan's Patch (possibly Martin Nash's son William), said that after George Major was shot, the priest offered to raise a vigilante committee of 200 men to "put the M.M.'s down." But the operative's reports on the "Miners Secret Organizations" did not in fact report any connection between the Ancient Order of Hibernians or the Molly Maguires and the union. Cumming did not even provide the names of the nine members of the AOH in St. Clair in 1874:

Casey, John
Dormer, Pat—Saloon keeper
Flannery, Pat

Heenan, James
Mill, Frank
O' Neil, Frank—Secretary
O'Regan, Jack [presumably John Reagan, bodymaster]
Roach, Pat
Ward, Martin—Treasurer

These names were probably supplied by the Pinkerton agent in Shenandoah, James McParlan, who did join the AOH, and whose reports and testimony incriminated several men on the St. Clair list, and others in the neighborhood.[11]

What Cumming *was* able to do was to keep the Pinkerton agency and Gowen informed of the state of disorganization in the union in advance of the Long Strike in 1875. These reports of union weakness may have encouraged the Reading forces to persist in their effort to break the union. Cumming was also interested in union violence. Although he saw no violent acts committed, he reported a good deal of violent rhetoric, much of it consisting of threats by Siney against strikebreakers. Siney was very much concerned about the importation of "Italian Cutthroats" to break a miners' strike in western Pennsylvania, and his language was sprinkled with words like "fight," "war," "outrage," "revenge," and "death." He was also greatly incensed at disloyalty within the ranks of labor. When he learned of an assault upon a strikebreaker by some union men at Johnstown, Siney said (according to Cumming):

> the only fault he found with it was that they did not kill him "and every bugger that would blackleg." That it was not only the blackleg they would kill, but that they would shoot Morrel [the mine operator] as sure as he was a living man. Siney said this with great determination and looked the operator square in the eye as much as to say that he would approve of the deed if committed.[12]

And on a later occasion he denounced spies and double agents within the National Association, saying that the officers (he himself was the president) were not asleep and would "hunt these men to death."[13]

None of these reports of union plans and rhetoric contributed much to the Molly Maguire dossier, and in February Cumming was withdrawn to the Philadelphia office. His failure was, according to Allan Pinkerton, the result of an excessive fondness for beer. To replace him Gowen now sent a former newspaper reporter named H. B. Hanmore, who was not a Pinkerton detective and who submitted his reports and bills directly to Gowen.[14] With two other Pinkerton operatives having infiltrated the union at St. Nicholas and Shamokin, reports on union affairs kept coming in to the Reading headquarters in Philadelphia. But, evidently briefed by Gowen, Hanmore kept his eyes open for the Molly Maguire connection.

Hanmore's chief assignment was to track down the incendiaries who fired the breaker at the East Shaft, just west of St. Clair, on the night of February 15, 1875. Posing as a newsman (and in fact he actually had dispatches published in the *Philadelphia Times*), Hanmore checked in with General Henry Pleasants (promoted after the war by President Grant in recognition of his bravery at Petersburg), made friends with John Welsh, Siney's successor, and hired as an assistant and guide a young man, Thomas Joyce, who lived with relatives in a shanty "under the shadow" of the East Shaft. At first Joyce led Hanmore to believe that the arson was the work of the Molly Maguire organization, and introduced him to alleged members of the dread order "without informing them that I knew of their identity." For a time Hanmore believed from "hints" that Joyce was on such good terms with the Mollies that "he can if he will reach the East Shaft incendiaries." But the Molly Maguire connection faded away after Joyce discovered a new lead. Hanmore finally told Gowen that he was satisfied that the fire "was not the result of any regular 'Mollie Maguire' system but was started by these drunken fellows on the spur of the moment to 'get square' with the Company on General Principles."

"These drunken fellows" were a party of seven or eight unemployed Irishmen who had been drinking at the house of a Mrs. Weaklin near the Twin Shafts the night of the fire. According to Joyce, rumor had it that these men had been refused jobs at the colliery and, all drunk, had left the house just before the fire; but it was necessary to find hard evidence. Joyce's method was to charm the information out of Mrs. Weaklin and her daughter. Hanmore reported to Gowen:

> Young Joyce is on the road to that discovery:—he is making love
> to Mrs. Weaklin's daughter with all the intensity of a Leander.
> The young lady (!) remarked "it was strange it was not found out
> who set the shaft fire." The old lady (Mrs. W.) said it was a
> "strange proceeding, entirely." I think we are on the scent.[15]

But the young men moved away to a reservoir construction project near Harrisburg before they could be arrested, and by the end of the month

Joyce's researches had proved that these men were not the guilty parties anyway, because they had remained in the house until after the fire. But now Joyce reported a new clue. Writing directly to Gowen, he revealed that there were "Men from St. Clair" drinking on the hill overlooking the shafts on that fateful night who probably set the fire to get revenge after being turned down for a series of jobs. He knew the name of one and if only Mr. Gowen would send a check for some money, he could get the men drunk enough to confess. . . .

Actually, Joyce had made the same proposal to Hanmore with respect to the first group of suspects. Joyce, in fact, was doing very well. On the strength of his promise as a detective, General Pleasants had got him a job at the Twin Shafts. And there was the prospect of the $10,000 reward. Gowen, realizing that he was probably being swindled, discontinued the correspondence and turned his attention to sterner stuff.

"MCKENNA" PENETRATES THE ANCIENT
ORDER OF HIBERNIANS

The Ulster-born Irish detective who three years later was to become the commonwealth's star witness in the Molly Maguire cases—and a star in the Pinkerton organization too—arrived in Pottsville in December 1873. His name was James McParlan (although sometimes he called himself James McFarlan, and in Schuylkill he was known as James McKenna) and his mission was to infiltrate the Ancient Order of Hibernians. He had already done some research for Pinkerton on Irish secret societies and had submitted an essay on the Molly Maguires, tracing them back to the famine, and even further, to the days of the Ribbonmen and the rebellion of 1798. He concluded in advance (and incorrectly) that the supposed benevolent association was merely a new name for the same old terrorist organization.[1]

McParlan established himself in Pottsville and then began a series of one-week trips to various places in the region where he might be able to pass himself off as a murderer and forger and a former member of the AOH seeking to join a local branch. His first visit was to St. Clair, where he stayed at Taggart's hotel in the north end of town.[2] Hearing rumors that Patrick Dormer was a "Sleeper" (i.e., a Molly and a member of the AOH), he promptly repaired to Dormer's saloon just over the borough line and proceeded to charm his way into the gigantic saloon keeper's confidence. Speaking and singing in a broad Irish brogue, McParlan lurched around

340

the saloon, dancing a jig, downing whiskey, singing a Donegal ballad celebrating the killing of land agent Bell by Pat Dolan's Mollies, playing cards, fistfighting with a man he caught cheating at cards, telling stories, passing what he alleged to be counterfeit money, and dropping hints of past affiliations with the AOH. He played the wild Irish lad so convincingly that Dormer was won over and, a month later, introduced him to "Muff" Lawler, the "bodymaster"—the chief officer—of the AOH branch in Shenandoah. Lawler kept a tavern, ran an employment agency for miners, and raised his own breed of gamecocks (known as "muffs"). Lawler sponsored McParlan for membership in

James McParlan (a.k.a. James McKenna), the Pinkerton spy

the AOH and the detective was duly initiated into the Shenandoah lodge.[3]

McParlan now discovered that the Shenandoah lodge, and several others—Girardville, Mahanoy City, Mount Laffee, St. Clair, and Tamaqua, in particular—had been virtually taken over by ruffians. Many of the respectable Irish members had dropped out in compliance with stern public warnings from the Church dating back at least to a pastoral letter from the Bishop of Philadelphia in 1864 condemning the AOH as a secret society and threatening with excommunication any Catholic who remained a member. As a result, there remained only a few hundred—between 300 and 600—members in the county in 1874. This presented the organization with a serious financial problem. The dues and assessments normally required for operating expenses (hiring a hall, paying delegates' expenses to regional meetings, and the like) and for its charitable activities were shrinking at the very moment when the criminal members sought to use the organization not only as a cover for conspiracies to murder but also as a source of getaway money and legal defense funds for the assassins. It is quite possible that St. Clair teamster Martin Nash was killed, after resigning from the organization, in public retaliation for his withholding of future financial support. Traditional local leaders of the AOH, like John Kehoe, the Democratic politician of Girardville, Pat Dormer, the publican of St.

Clair, and Muff Lawler, the hiring contractor of Shenandoah, no doubt wanted to be on good terms with everyone, and Dormer and Lawler were even said to have managed to join the Odd Fellows. So some of the older leaders stayed, hoping that the criminal element would somehow clear out and that the Church would relent and take the society into its good graces.

The members of the AOH were by no means all miners. In St. Clair, of eleven known members—the nine men on McParlan's list plus Nash and Russell—at least three were not miners (Pat Dormer, saloon keeper; Frank O'Neil, secretary and later acting bodymaster, shoemaker; and Martin Nash, teamster). Martin Ward, the treasurer, was a respectable contract miner who owned his own home, was not mentioned in any of the trial testimony or detectives' reports, and was still living in St. Clair in 1880. Only four of the members of the St. Clair AOH were implicated in the crimes of the Molly Maguires: miner Thomas Russell, James Heenan, Frank O'Neil, and Jack O'Regan, a laborer. Pat Dormer enters the story of the Mollies only as a colorful character in Allan Pinkerton's account of McParlan's introduction to the coal regions. Concerning John Casey, Patrick Flannery, Frank Mill, and Patrick Roach, no information is to be had from either the census records or the accounts of the crimes of the Molly Maguires.[4]

Between the time of his initiation into the AOH in April 1874 and his flight, in fear of his life, in March 1876, McParlan was able to overhear and take part in the planning of several murders and murder attempts, and to participate in the discussions of rewards and escape procedures afterward. He was able to build up an intimate account of the Molly Maguire organization and of the rationale and procedures for obtaining retributive justice. In regard to procedure, a member with a grievance presented his case to his local bodymaster; the bodymaster arranged the appropriate retaliation. The administrative structure of the AOH, with its provision for a senior officer (the "bodymaster"), a secretary, and a treasurer in each lodge, and its hierarchy of county, state, and national delegates, gave to an amorphous collection of Irish street-gang members numbering perhaps 150 men and boys a semblance of discipline. But only a semblance: treasurers were absconding with funds, secretaries took no minutes, deputized assassins refused their assignments, and drunken Mollies fought with each other, and with the fellow-Irish Chain Gang, as enthusiastically as they beat up the Modocs, a rival Welsh gang. In spirit, however, the pattern of violence perpetrated by the AOH-affiliated Mollies was no different from the violence meted out by anonymous Irish assassins a generation earlier in the name of retributive justice.

McParlan was the only Pinkerton detective to testify at the Molly trials; it is his exploits that have become legend, the stuff of lurid popular narratives from Allan Pinkerton's own semi-fictional *The Molly Maguires and the Detectives* (1877) to Sir Arthur Conan Doyle's Sherlock Holmes mystery *The Valley of Fear* and the modern movie *The Molly Maguires.* But while McParlan was conducting his lonely investigations with a view to arrests and trials of individuals, a larger number of Pinkerton agents, together with the Coal and Iron Police, were preparing to meet force with force, not only as vigilantes terrorizing Mollies, but as a private army mobilizing against anticipated labor violence. Militia were called out to guard the collieries at Shenandoah and Hazleton during the Long Strike, and both vigilantes and private police acted in the fall of 1875, when, after the failure of the Long Strike in June and the collapse of the union, union discipline was no longer available to handle labor grievances and to suppress attacks on company property and managerial personnel. As we have seen, spying on the union was extensive. In addition to Cumming at St. Clair and Hanmore in Pottsville, Pinkerton agent William McCowan joined the union at Shamokin, and "W.R.H." at Frackville; and Robert J. Linden, an assistant superintendent in the agency, took up his post in Ashland in May 1875, where he was to watch for threatened union violence and coordinate the work of the Pinkerton men with the Coal and Iron Police, in which he obtained a commission as captain. Unknown to General Pleasants, Linden's commanding officer in the police, Linden also had charge of a secret fifteen-man commando force within the police ranks, half of them Pinkerton men.

The threat of labor violence was real enough. The WBA had two enemies, the blackleg and the colliery operator, and while its senior officers publicly disavowed acts of violence, there was a great deal of private talk and some action. Threats against Gowen's life became commonplace and there were occasional acts of vandalism, breaker fires, car derailments, and the like, most of them reliably attributed not to the Molly Maguires or to WBA officers but to impatient union members. There were warnings of general carnage to come if any efforts were made by the railroad to import large numbers of strikebreakers. And no doubt a few blacklegs did get beaten for working in spite of the union. But the impressive fact is that the detectives to a man, including McParlan, despite their suspicion of a link between Molly Maguire terrorism and union objectives, failed to report any evidence of violence ordered by union officers. It would seem that the union was generally effective in restraining its members from violent acts that would give them a bad press and harden the determination of their opponents.

But immediately after the end of the Long Strike in June 1875,

McParlan began to report murders planned and executed by the Molly faction within the AOH. By the end of the summer, six murders of Welshmen and Germans had been carried out with the connivance of the organization, and McParlan had been unable to prevent them. Allan Pinkerton, still furious at his inability to capture Jesse James and his gang in Missouri, and smarting from the bad publicity his agency received after Pinkerton agents bungled an attempt to assassinate the James brothers (a bomb hurled into their mother's house blew apart their eight-year-old brother and tore an arm off the mother's body, but did not touch Frank and Jesse, who were not even there), determined to use terror tactics to stop the wave of violence. Reflecting on the earlier success of Pinkerton guns against the Reno gang in Indiana, he proposed a commando strike against the Mollies. The Reno gang, captured by the Pinkertons, had been hanged by a mob of vigilantes. Fearing that jury trials would result in acquittals of the Mollies, he advised his general superintendent in Philadelphia:

> The only way then to pursue that I can see is, treat them in the same manner as the Reno's were treated in Seymour, Indiana. After they were done away with, the people improved wonderfully and now Seymour is quite a town. Let Linden get up a vigilance committee. It will not do to get many men, but let him get those who are prepared to take fearful revenge on the M.M.'s. I think it would open the eyes of all the people and then the M.M.'s would meet with their just deserts. It is awful to see men doomed to death, it is horrible. Now there is but one thing to be done, and that is, get up an organization if possible, and when ready for action pounce upon the M.M.'s when they meet and are in full blast, take the fearful responsibility and disperse.
>
> This is the best advice I can give you. I would not keep this letter in Philadelphia, but if you want to preserve it, send it over to New York. Place all confidence in Mr. Linden, he is a good man, and he understands what to do.
>
> If you think it advisable, bring the matter before Mr. Gowen, but none other than him.
>
> In case of failure, bail may be required. Mr. Gowen will be able to furnish it by his understanding it.[5]

This extraordinary document was perhaps the charter for the notorious "massacre at Wiggan's Patch" in December 1875. In one half of a large duplex at the patch, near Shenandoah, lived an Irish extended family, the

O'Donnells and the McAllisters. The head of the household was the widow O'Donnell; her two unmarried sons, James ("Friday") and Charles, also lived there, and her daughter Ellen, with her husband, Charles McAllister, and her baby, and Charles' look-alike brother James. There were also three unrelated male boarders. James McAllister and the two O'Donnell boys had been identified by McParlan as the murderers of Thomas Sanger, a mine boss, and William Uren, a miner, at Raven Run earlier in the year; and Charles McAllister was known to be the assailant of a seriously wounded man who recovered. Another O'Donnell girl, not present, was wife to John Kehoe, the "county delegate" of the AOH and the leading figure among the Schuylkill Mollies. At three in the morning of December 10, a band of masked men brandishing pistols burst into the house, searching for the McAllister and O'Donnell brothers. In the melee of breaking into sleeping rooms, Ellen McAllister was shot and killed. James O'Donnell was wounded but escaped and James McAllister escaped; both remained fugitives. Charles McAllister fled temporarily into the house next door, but returned to his wife and child.

No one was ever convicted of the killing. John Kehoe charged that a vigilante group from Mahanoy City was responsible, and Mrs. O'Donnell identified a respected butcher as one of the gang. (And vigilante groups were operating in other places; even in St. Clair, armed civilians patrolled the streets and stopped people on suspicion.) But charges were dropped. Some suggested that Kehoe himself was behind the attack because he was disturbed by Charles O'Donnell's mental trouble after the Sanger-Uren killing. Others believed there was a feud between the Wiggan's Patch gang and a gang at Gilberton and that the killing was in revenge for the beating of a Gilberton man by O'Donnell's crowd. But James McParlan, at least initially, seems to have believed that it was the work of Linden's special force, for he offered his resignation the same day as the murder. He was particularly upset by the killing of Mrs. McAllister:

> Now I wake up this morning to find that I am the murderer of Mrs. McAllister. What had a women to do in this case. Did the Sleepers in their time shoot down women. If I was not here the vigilant committee would not know who was guilty.[6]

He gloomily looked forward to "burning and murdering all over . . . and I am sure the Sleepers will not spare the women so long as the vigilants has shown the example."[7]

But the expected bloodbath never took place; McParlan's resignation was not accepted; and next year the trials of the Mollies identified by McParlan began. And the vigilante committee that attacked Mrs. O'Donnell's house at Wiggan's Patch, whether local civilians or Linden's strike force, kept their counsel.

THE GOMER JAMES CASE

In September 1875, after an epidemic of murders and attempted murders, McParlan advised his Philadelphia contact, Benjamin Franklin—and Franklin sent the advice on to Gowen—that the carnage was the result of the failure of the miners' union, which had collapsed, its funds exhausted, after the Long Strike in the winter and spring of 1874–1875. The circumstances will be discussed in more detail in the next chapter; here we are concerned with the effect of the union's demise on the level of violence in the mining districts.

During the heyday of the WBA, "each man got his turn," irrespective of ethnicity. But now, as the collieries reopened with no union to take up grievances, the Irish were having "rough times." McParlan reported that the Irish were being discharged or assigned to work breasts in places "where they can make nothing." And he declared flatly, "there was very little killing adoing while the Union stood, but now it is quite the reverse."

In the two months from July 5 to September 2, there were six Molly Maguire murders. None would seem to have been part of any coordinated terrorist plan, although five of the victims held positions of authority and none was Irish. Benjamin Yost, a Tamaqua policeman, was shot in revenge for a beating suffered at his hands by the AOH bodymaster in Tamaqua. Thomas Gwyther, justice of the peace at Girardville, was shot while trying to arrest an alleged Molly after a barroom brawl in Girardville. Gomer James of Shenandoah, an unemployed miner and former constable, was shot in revenge for his alleged killing of a Molly two years before. Thomas Sanger, the Raven Run mine superintendent, was shot for reasons not at all clear (McParlan had failed to learn of the plot beforehand). William Uren, a miner boarding with Sanger, was not an intended target and was shot merely because he was walking to work with Sanger. And John P. Jones, mine superintendent of Lansford, in Carbon County, was killed in revenge for blacklisting a Molly miner.

The Gomer James case, which involved a probable former resident of St. Clair as victim and the St. Clair and Mount Laffee AOH bodymasters as accomplices of the fugitive killer, fairly represents the motives of the Molly

Maguire murders: the demand for retributive justice in an atmosphere of ethnic discrimination by the authorities and bitter resentment by those who felt that they had been systematically denied their rights. And the *modus operandi* was still, even with the AOH administrative apparatus now available, reminiscent of the murder of John Reese by Martin Shay thirty years before.

In 1860 a Peter James and his wife, Sarah, were living in St. Clair with their seven children, ranging in age from one to seventeen. The eldest son, "Goma," was thirteen. Peter James was a miner and he, his wife, and the eldest two children had been born in Wales, the rest, including Gomer, in Pennsylvania. Their neighbors were mostly Irish.[1] But by 1870 the James family had moved away, and the next time we hear of a Gomer James is in 1873 when, now a "young man" of twenty-six (exactly the age to be expected of the St. Clair "Goma") and a miner, he allegedly shot and killed an Irishman, Edward Cosgrove.[2]

The circumstances were sadly typical for a mining town where many men carried handguns, got into drunken fights in bars, and then carried the fights into the streets. Gomer James was a small man, with light hair, dark eyes, and a slight mustache, who had a reputation in some quarters for quarrelsomeness and for making threats with a revolver. For a time he was a policeman. The year before, he had been nearly killed by a man who fired at him at such close range as to burn his face with powder. On the evening of August 11, Gomer James was drinking porter in company with a German policeman at a saloon near the center of Shenandoah. He left about 11:30 and walked up the street to the house of Benjamin Yost, where he sat on the porch with Yost and two other men, talking about "business." In about a quarter of an hour, their attention was drawn to three men scuffling on Main Street, who turned out to be Edward Cosgrove, Thomas James, and Tom Jones. Tom Jones broke away and ran down Center Street, pursued by the other two, who caught up with him, knocked him down, and began kicking him in the face and head and "yelling like Indians." Meanwhile Gomer James, recognizing that it was a friend who was in trouble, started off to help. Jones was unconscious by the time James reached him and the two attackers were running up Center toward Main. James drew his revolver and fired two shots at the retreating Cosgrove and Thomas James and then ran after them. At the corner of Center and Main, he stopped and allegedly fired a third shot. In any case, a ball hit Cosgrove about the ear; he fell and was dead in a few minutes. Finally the constable who had been drinking with Gomer James emerged from the saloon and fired two more shots at some unidentified figures retreating down Center toward the Lehigh Valley Railroad depot. This constable may have imbibed more than the bottle and a half of porter he admitted to; he spoke little English and may not have understood what was happening; he did not see the original scuffle; he apparently thought the first two shots had been fired by Cosgrove or by one of the unidentified pair that he fired at.

Gomer James was arrested next morning and, after a local coroner's jury declared that Cosgrove died "from a pistol wound received at the hands of Gomer James," he was taken to Pottsville. At a hearing before Squire Reed, five witnesses from Shenandoah testified, and their testimony was summarized in the *Miners' Journal*.[3] There was no question that James fired the first two shots; whether he fired the third, and fatal, shot remained unclear. No one other than Thomas James admitted seeing him fire a third shot; one witness said that the third shot came from somewhere down Main Street, on the other side of Cosgrove; and the German-speaking constable said he saw someone else fire the shot. Nevertheless Squire Reed deemed the evidence strong enough to hold James for trial on a charge of murder. Next week Lin Bartholomew, James' chosen attorney, asked the squire to admit him to bail, arguing that the evidence showed that his client had not fired the fatal shot, and anyway, if he had, he was acting in the course of making a citizen's arrest and should be charged with no more than involuntary manslaughter. The district attorney opposed the motion, declaring flatly that James killed Cosgrove and that the motive was revenge against the men who had beaten his friend into unconsciousness. The court next day denied bail.[4]

The editorial sympathies of the *Miners' Journal* were now manifestly on James' side. After early assertions that James was a ruffian, the paper began to describe him as an innocent man and repeated the popular opinion that the fatal bullet must have come from the gun of Constable Schrader, who admitted firing two shots (that no one else heard). And the *Journal* even suggested, four days after the killing, that the Mollies were after James, raising money for special counsel to help the prosecution. "It looks as if the hounds were on James' track." Edward Cosgrove, it implied, was no great loss to the community, being "a bad man and a rampant Molly Maguire" who, because of his membership in the "infamous clan," had been excommunicated by the Catholic Church and (so the *Journal* was told) even denied the last rites.[5]

But James' case did not come up for trial during the fall session of the county's Criminal Court. Instead, on the 15th of March, seven months later, the case was heard by a special session of the Court of Oyer and Terminer. This was a questionable jurisdiction, because, according to law, this court could sit only during the first week of June, and F. W. Hughes, now associated with Bartholomew for the defense, pointed the error out to the court. The judge overruled him. Presumably the court assignment, and Hughes' complaint, were legal stratagems to provide a basis for appeal in case of conviction. But the jury did not convict. Convinced by testimony that "proved that James could not have fired the fatal shot," the jury returned a verdict of acquittal, and James walked out "a free man."[6]

But not entirely free. Cosgrove's relatives now applied to the Shenandoah bodymaster, Muff Lawler, for retributive justice: the "execution" of Gomer James. The lodge met, decided to kill James, and appointed Cosgrove's cousin and another man to carry out the sentence. But Cosgrove's cousin backed out, and when the victim's own relative refused to take the responsibility, the other man declined too. Lawler did not bestir himself to get the job done and appeared to the more militant members to show something of a lack of sympathy with their wishes. As a result, he was expelled from the AOH and a few weeks later severely beaten. The new bodymaster, Frank McAndrew, did not pursue the matter either, however, and James remained in Shenandoah. Not until May of the next year, during the absence of McAndrew, who had gone temporarily to the northern district to look for work, was the plot revived. The detective McParlan, appointed acting bodymaster, was approached by two Mollies who demanded that James be executed. McParlan felt that he had to agree. After two attempts to kill James had failed, James left the county for a couple of months. But in August he was back at work as a carpenter in Shenandoah. And on August 14, while serving beer at a fire-company picnic, James was shot at point-blank range by one of the Shenandoah lodge's more effective hitmen, Thomas Hurley, a Shenandoah miner. While James lay dying, Hurley walked away in the crowd, which included by his own admission at least ten people who knew him, among them his own mother.[7]

Hurley now demanded reward money "to enable him to flee the region." The matter was discussed at a county convention of bodymasters at Tamaqua on August 25, and it was at this meeting that certain citizens of St. Clair and Mount Laffee were implicated as accessories to murder. Actually, St. Clair men had been involved in the prior plot, for James Heenan, one of the St. Clair company of militia, had offered to lend his uniform to an assassin so that he could "get a chance at James without being suspected." The offer was declined.[8] The Tamaqua convention, after some delay—a competing claimant insisted *he* had shot James—decided to give Hurley his money. Present at these deliberations were Frank O'Neil, the acting bodymaster at St. Clair, and Jeremiah Kane of Mount Laffee.

Hurley now took flight and was not found again until he was arrested in Colorado; he was reported to have committed suicide while there.[9]

McParlan's reports implicated a number of people, including himself, in the plot to kill Gomer James and in the decision to reward Hurley afterward. Although the fugitive Hurley could not be tried, it was never-theless possible to prosecute his associates as accessories after the fact. On the 6th of May 1876, six men, including Frank O'Neil of St. Clair, were charged with having assembled at Tamaqua on August 25, 1875, to reward Thomas Hurley for the murder.[10] The trial began on the 16th of August 1876 and continued for a week. The defense employed the usual tactic of claiming that someone else, not Hurley, had shot James, but when one of the defendants was brought to the stand as a defense witness, he con-fessed under cross-examination. It took the jury only a quarter of an hour to find all the defendants guilty.[11]

The hand of the law rested lightly on the Mollies of St. Clair. O'Neil was out of jail within two years and by 1880 he had followed John Reagan into exile.[12]

THE GREAT SHOWCASE TRIAL

During each of the dozen or so trials of individual defendants on charges of murder, some information was developed about the way in which the Molly Maguires had been operating within the Ancient Order of Hiberni-ans, particularly after John Kehoe became the county delegate. The pros-ecution wanted to convict not just some individual ruffians who had committed capital crimes, but the AOH itself. The ultimate aim of Gowen and his legal colleagues was to destroy what they regarded as a secret, revolutionary, terrorist organization. So a showcase trial was arranged.[1] John Kehoe was withheld from the docket in other cases, where he might have been charged as a co-conspirator, in order to be the principal defend-ant—as the AOH's principal officer in the county—in a trial artfully con-trived to give the best chance of conviction. The crime chosen was not murder but conspiracy and attempted murder, felonies that did not entail the death penalty and so were more likely to draw a guilty verdict from jurors possibly reluctant to condemn a man to be hanged. If the evidence in such a case were to consist largely of proof of membership in and attendance at meetings of a murderous secret order, and a guilty verdict were returned, it would be tantamount to a conviction not only of the individual defendants but of the order itself.

The matter at issue was the attempted murder of a Welshman, William M. "Bully Bill" Thomas. The defendants were John Kehoe, Schuylkill county delegate of the AOH and bodymaster at Girardville; Christopher Donnelly, county treasurer; Michael O'Brien, bodymaster at Tuscarora; James Roarity, bodymaster at Coaldale; Dennis Canning, Northumberland County delegate and bodymaster at Locust Gap; Frank McHugh, secretary at Mahanoy City; and four members from Shenandoah, John Gibbons, John Morris, Thomas Hurley, and Michael Doyle. (The latter two were fugitives from the law and were tried *in absentia*.) Notably absent from the list was Frank McAndrew, the Shenandoah bodymaster who had participated in making the final arrangements to kill Bully Bill, but who later saved McParlan's life as the detective was ending his stay in Shenandoah and was preparing to testify. He seems to have been rewarded by a tacit agreement not to prosecute. Despite his apparent complicity in other conspiracies as well, McAndrew was never tried. The lawyers for the prosecution were an imposing team: the district attorney, George E. Kaercher; the president of the Philadelphia and Reading Railroad, Franklin B. Gowen; former Democratic state senator and state attorney general, the eminent attorney Francis W. Hughes; and the son of George W. Farquhar, Guy E. Farquhar. The defense attorneys were also distinguished, although perhaps not as prominent: former Judge of the Court of Quarter Sessions James Ryon, unsuccessful Republican senatorial candidate Martin M. L'Velle, and S. A. Garrett. And among the jurors (mostly men with German names) were two from St. Clair: Welsh-born John J. Thomas, a fifty-five-year-old coal miner, widower, and relatively prosperous property owner; and William Wilcox, an English coal miner, aged fifty-six, also a property owner, with a wife self-employed as a dressmaker. Judge Walker presided.

The basic facts in the case were these. In Mahanoy City on the night of October 31, 1874, a fire in the center of town had brought out both fire companies, one manned by Welsh and German "Modocs" and the other by Irish Molly Maguires. As usual, after the fire was put out, the two companies fought each other in the street. In attempting to quell the melee, the chief burgess, Welshman George Major, fired his pistol and killed a dog. Someone then shot Major, and Major, before he fell, got off two more shots of his own, one of them allegedly lodging in the skull of a young Irishman, Daniel Dougherty. Major died after naming Dougherty as his assailant, and Dougherty was promptly arrested. Dougherty was examined by several doctors, including Pottsville's John Carpenter at the behest of the *Miners' Journal*. Carpenter declared that Dougherty was only shamming, but the bullet was finally removed from his skull during the trial and displayed to the jury. There was so great a hue and cry against Dougherty that his trial was moved to Lebanon, south of the mountains, and there a jury acquitted him after the defense proved that the bullet from his head had not been fired from Major's gun and produced the usual parade of witnesses who swore that another man, John McCann (now said to be in Ireland), had fired the fatal shot. And, in fact, McParlan later declared on the witness stand in another case that Dougherty was innocent and McCann the murderer.

But, precisely as in the John Reese and Gomer James cases, the relatives and friends of the murdered man were not persuaded of the innocence of the accused; this time, however, it was an Irishman acquitted and Welshmen avengers. The kinsmen of the dead Major, William and Jesse Major, and a Welsh tough—"Bully Bill" Thomas—were reported to be on Dougherty's trail and in May of 1875, according to Dougherty, made an attempt on his life, some of the bullets even passing through his clothes. Accounts of the attack deeply disturbed John Kehoe, who felt that they represented the concerted action of a Welsh secret order, the Modocs, and he talked wildly of sending a company of armed Mollies into the streets of Mahanoy City to shoot it out with them. But on more mature reflection Kehoe decided to call a county meeting of bodymasters on June 1 in Mahanoy City to hear Dougherty's complaint, "try" the Majors and Bully Bill, and plan their demise.

In preparation for this convention, Kehoe on the 30th of May 1875 met at his house in Girardville with McParlan and John Reagan of St. Clair. Reagan had gotten a ride up with Dr. Andrew Carr of St. Clair, who had been summoned to care for Kehoe's wife and child, just born with a harelip. (Carr, at the moment in the throes of swearing off alcohol, declined a drink and instead offered the company cigars.) He no doubt was unaware that Thomas Hurley, the killer of Gomer James, was planning to go down to St. Clair and either kill or badly wound him because Carr had sued Tom Hurley's father to recover a debt. Reagan's contribution to the discussion was the nomination of "a good man" from St. Clair for "a job of that kind" to shoot Bully Bill and the Majors. Two days later, on June 1, Kehoe convened the bodymasters in Mahanoy City (including, once again, Reagan of St. Clair). Dougherty's grievance was heard there and it was agreed that his pursuers had to be killed in order to save his life. McParlan (now acting bodymaster at Shenandoah) and two other bodymasters were appointed a committee to recruit a team to kill Thomas, and two young men volunteered to kill Jesse and William Major. But the committee spent nearly a month in organizing the team of assassins, part of the delay being

the result of McParlan's strenuous efforts to avoid being forced to participate in the shooting. Eventually, on June 28, 1875, the attack on Bully Bill
took place at the stable where he worked. Four men approached the door-
way and pumped perhaps a dozen bullets wildly at the Welshman, first
shooting him in the chest from a few feet away and then at point-blank
range after he jumped at them. Two horses were killed and Bully Bill fell
under one of them, shot once in the chest (the bullet glanced off a rib),
once in the fingers (he grabbed the gun), and twice in the neck. He
survived.

William M. Thomas was tough (he was a professional pugilist), but he
was not a good citizen. Since returning from the Civil War, he had repeatedly been in trouble with the law. The people of St. Clair knew him as one
of a gang of pig thieves; he escaped from the arresting officer and ran away
to Ohio for about a year to escape prosecution. In Mahanoy City he was
arrested on a charge of robbery. A month or so after the unsuccessful
attempt on his life, he and an Irishman got into a gunfight in the main
street in Mahanoy City. Thomas was shot in the cheek and a bystander, a
German miner waiting for his wife, was killed. Thomas was tried and
acquitted of that crime (no doubt giving the Mollies another reason to kill
him) and it was during his time in court and jail that he recognized two of
his assailants in the earlier attack.

On the basis of Thomas's complaint and McParlan's reports about the
conspiracy, the persons accused of planning and attempting the murder of
Bully Bill were picked up in May and tried in the showcase trial at Pottsville
in August 1876. Although the facts of the conspiracy were brought out in
the testimony, and clearly called for a guilty verdict, the prosecution's
questioning was deliberately designed to elicit additional descriptive information about the history and organization of the Ancient Order of Hibernians. Its constitution and bylaws were introduced in evidence; its method
of planning crimes was explored in detail. By the time the defense was able
to call in its character witnesses, the cross-examining prosecution attorneys had cast the order in so evil a light that public knowledge of a man's
membership in the AOH amounted to a bad reputation. The defense charge
that McParlan was in fact the real criminal who had instigated and planned
all the murders and assaults, and thus entrapped innocent men, seemed a
trivial issue when everyone knew that the real defendant in this trial was
the AOH itself.

Thus the examination of witnesses and exhibits was only scaffolding
for the main structure of argument: the passionate denunciation of the
AOH by one of the best courtroom orators of the day, Franklin B. Gowen.

In grand rhetorical style, Gowen laid out the history of the order, describing how it began in agrarian resistance to British colonial rule but moved on to become an international terrorist organization:

> . . . it has been reserved for you to be singled out to try not merely the question of the guilt of particular persons, but the far more transcendent issue of the guilt of the society itself which is now on trial for its life. The lives of these men who sit around this table are not in jeopardy, because the punishment of the offence with which they are charged, so far as the individual actors are concerned, is simply the punishment of imprisonment at hard labor. Therefore, you try no men for their lives, but upon your verdict rests the question, which is of far more importance to the people of this county, and the people of this State, whether this society shall not be adjudged to an instantaneous and ignominious death.

As it functioned in Schuylkill County, he said, the society practiced what would later be referred to as organized crime:

> The purpose was to make the business of mining coal in this county a terror and a fear; to secure for the leading men in this society profitable positions, and the control of large operations at every colliery. The purpose was to levy blackmail upon every man engaged in industrial pursuits in this county, so that the owners, under the terror which this organization had acquired, would gladly purchase peace and immunity, by having one or two, or more of these men in prominent positions in every colliery, and employ as many of their confederates, members of this organization, as possible, to protect their property from the villainy of their own Order.

But what might it not have soon become? Gowen painted an apocalyptic scene:

> Every man of character and reputation and integrity would have been driven into other regions, and this great theatre of industry, this boundless deposit of mineral wealth with which God has blessed the region in which you live, would have been, for aught I can see, transformed into a desert. With these conspirators in the possession of everything that was of value, they would have

354

driven out all honest industry, shooting down, either in the darkness of the night or in the broad daylight, as they became bolder, any man who dared to oppose the dictates of their decrees. Can you doubt this? Can you believe, if a state of society such as has been shown to you here, upon this witness stand, had continued for one or two years longer, that this county would not have been the pesthouse and the lazarhouse of the United States, controlled and ruled by a class of men to whom human life was no more sacred than the life of the worm they trod beneath their heel? What would have been your condition, and that of all of us, but for the check which has been received from the officers of the law who have been engaged in the punishment and detection of crime? This county would have been a refuge for every outlaw in the United States, and in the world. It would have been an Alsatia in which every man who committed crime was safe, the moment he crossed its boundaries. This organization now numbering in this county five or six hundred, would have swelled its numbers to tens and twenties of thousands; and would have become so strong that it would have openly defied the law, and then only after open defiance of the law, its extermination would have been assured.

He declared that for unprincipled ferocity the Ancient Order of Hibernians had no parallel in human history:

Was there ever such an organization heard of? Search the pages of history and go back over the records of the world, and I will venture to say you will never find in any society, claiming to be civilized, such an adjudication to death, and by instruments of vengeance as ghastly and as horrible, as this society wielded for the murder of their fellow men.

And he could descend from these heights of windy rhetoric to the green meadows of his fellow Irish countrymen, pointing out that he shared with "those of the land from which my father came" a fondness for verse, and commiserating with the mother and father of one of the defendants, young Frank McHugh:

We have called here from among the prisoners, right out of their midst, the youngest member, young Frank McHugh, whose father and mother I knew well from eighteen to twenty years ago up to the time I left this county, as decent, respectable, worthy, honest people, who I am sure left undone nothing to bring their children up in the fear of God, and to make them honest and respectable members of society. There is no more glaring and terrible commentary upon this society, and its effects upon the people of this county, than is here offered in this case of young Frank McHugh. A young fellow only twenty years of age, having an education rather better than the most persons in his sphere of life are able to receive from their parents, was drawn into this organization, and you may readily believe that when he joined it, as a young man only seventeen or eighteen years of age, he did not believe he was joining a criminal organization. I do not believe that young men, sons of honest parents, whose fathers and mothers are known to be good people, become criminals of their own will. It is from keeping bad company, from associating with men such as those who compose this association of Molly Maguires that they are led into crime. There can be no doubt that this young man, when he joined the society, believed he was simply joining an Irish Catholic beneficial association, yet bad company ruined him.

He went on at great length about the future sufferings of the wives and mothers of the defendants. He called Frank McAndrew (who was not a defendant but was a member of the society) the "one good man" who saved McParlan's life and urged the district attorney to grant him "immunity from punishment" in future cases. He accused the pro-union "labor reformers"—a short-lived political party—of being Molly Maguires. And he wound up explicitly charging Kehoe, Roarity, and others of the defendants with being "murderers." At that, the counsel for the defense moved that the judge declare a mistrial, but the judge overruled the motion.[2]

Kaercher, the district attorney, was less fulsome in his rhetoric but more hyperbolic. He urged the jury:

You have in your keeping the peace of one of the greatest counties in the Commonwealth. This case involves the life or the destruction of one of the greatest criminal organizations of which any mention can be found, and I will say to you now, that before I conclude the remarks which I shall make in this case, I shall show to you from the testimony, that never since the world began has there existed a more villainous society or more horrible organization than the one the leaders of which we have brought for trial.

He asserted that the Mahanoy City convention on June 1, 1875, "will stand as a picture of murder which has never been surpassed since time began." And he summarized his analysis of the Ancient Order of Hibernians with the most extreme comparison of all:

> It was a horrid and murderous fiend, which strode through our streets, and through our towns, and left its victims scattered along the highways. It was Apollyon himself.[3]

There was little that defense counsels Ryon and L'Velle could do in their summations against this blast of oratory. They did their best to defend the AOH as being basically a benevolent, charitable organization no different from the Masons or the Odd Fellows. They praised the Irish people and lauded the now defunct Workingmen's Benevolent Association as a powerful influence for law and order in its day. They compared the public excitement to the anti-Masonic hysteria of the 1830's and they tried to discredit McParlan, questioning his truthfulness and charging him with being responsible for all the crimes that followed the end of the Long Strike in 1875, crimes committed so that he could solve them and gain a name as a detective. But to no avail. The jury voted to convict, after deliberating for twenty minutes, "with a recommendation for mercy in the case of Frank McHugh."[4]

The proceedings of the showcase trial were promptly printed, including verbatim transcripts of the testimony, in a 262-page book by the "Miners Journal Book and Job Rooms." It appeared about midway in the series of trials that ran from January 1876 to November 1877. In all, twenty men were hanged, starting with ten in one day on June 21, 1877, and ending with John Kehoe, who was convicted of murder in another case, and who died on December 18, 1878, after failing in a lengthy series of appeals.

Although Gowen, Pinkerton, the Catholic hierarchy, and the middle-class establishment generally regarded the trials and the twenty executions as a triumph of law and order, there were many in whose mouths a bitter taste remained. Maurus Oestreich, the St. Clair carpenter and breaker contractor, passed down the view in his family that "many are of the opinion that justice was not completely served at the end of the Pottsville trial, and that certain mine officials and financiers should have taken their place before the bar of justice and stood trial in their turn."[5] The members of the Ancient Order of Hibernians in other parts of the country were outraged and defended the organization zealously. Many if not most Irish people saw the trials as just another example of religious and ethnic bigotry. Organized labor denounced Gowen and the Reading company's repeated insinuation that Molly Maguire violence was union violence. (Pinkerton agents also spied on the Knights of Labor as soon as it began to organize mining locals and they spread the rumor that it was both Molly Maguire revived and also a part of the international communist conspiracy.) Plainly, the spectacular trials, Gowen's histrionics, and the mass executions suggested to some that the Mollies, however guilty some or all of them may have been individually, were being used as scapegoats, sacrificed in the name of law and order when it was actually the prosecutor who had fomented the social disorder for which the Mollies were blamed.

WHO WERE THE MOLLY MAGUIRES?

A fair assessment of the Molly Maguires as revealed in detectives' notes and trial testimony is difficult even today. As Harold Aurand and William Gudelunas have pointed out, the image now has acquired a "mythical quality" from the diversity of political positions that the Molly Maguire episode has been used to support.[1] But one feature of the Molly Maguire organization still shines clearly through the smoke of ideological battle: it was regarded by even its most violent members as a mechanism for Irish Catholics to achieve retributive justice in a hostile world. The reports and testimony of McParlan do not reveal a gang of professional criminals planning bank and train robberies, extorting protection money from collieries, smuggling liquor, or kidnapping for ransom. There were no rapes or beatings of women. Members showed some participation in the political process as Democrats, much of it quite irregular, with the aim of advancing the local interests of the Irish. There was apparently no AOH involvement in union activity at all. Mostly the notes and testimony show a preoccupation with issues of justice and injustice. Tom Hurley, who killed Gomer James, opposed killing a mine boss when bodymaster McAndrew wanted him dead for firing an Irishman. The boss, said Hurley, was justified in discharging the man because he had in fact been insolent.[2] The precipitating reason for assigning a team to kill the Majors and Bully Bill was that, when one of the Majors shot at Dougherty on a Mahanoy City street, the policemen who witnessed the event from a spot only a few yards away made no attempt to arrest the would-be assassin.[3] The conclusion was simple: Dougherty, who had just been acquitted of a charge of murder (a murder of which he was in fact innocent), could expect no help from the police. As Kehoe put it:

> ... these Modocs done just as they pleased, and it did not seem as if an Irishman could get any law in Mahanoy City; that he would have to take the thing in hand and clear them out.[4]

Another Molly refused to kill a mine boss for firing an Irishman because the union could get him his job back.[5] And the punishment was generally meted out in proportion to the injury. Thus a mine boss at Wadesville merely threatened that he would not give work, when the mines opened, to any man who went to Mahanoy City on St. Patrick's Day to parade with the Ancient Order of Hibernians. A committee visited the boss and gave him "a very good licking."[6] In Shenandoah the Mollies were even credited with settling civil disputes (at some cost in misappropriated school funds).[7] There is not enough evidence to delineate in detail the scale of offenses for which various degrees of violent retaliation were appropriate, but it would appear that killing an Irishman and being acquitted by the court, trying to kill an Irishman and not being arrested by the police, and taking away a man's living were capital offenses, whereas mere verbal threats justified no more than a severe beating. Women and children were never attacked even when they were witnesses. And the victims were always selected because, allegedly, they had personally given an injury to a specific individual; they were not attacked as random targets merely because they were members of a class or ethnic group. Nothing suggests that the attacks on mine bosses and the notorious "coffin notices" were part of a terrorist plot to take over the coal trade. There was, however, some intrusion of private greed into the practice of posting, or mailing, death threats. Thus, for instance, Reagan, bodymaster at St. Clair, had the Shenandoah bodymaster post a threatening notice in front of the long chute at Turkey Run Colliery:

> To the Union men now in the Union. I would have you take your tools out of this place. This is my first notice but if I have to come back again it will be a difficult requisition.

The purpose of this warning was to open up jobs for Reagan and his brother by driving out "Cornishmen."[8]

Another major function of the organization was to help members get out of trouble with the law. The county convention could levy contributions on the various divisions to hire lawyers to defend Mollies on trial or to provide "reward" money to help an assassin escape. Balls were organized by Frank O'Neil in St. Clair, for instance, to raise money for the legal defense of Mollies on trial.[9] Although such activities were roundly condemned by the *Miners' Journal* and prosecuting attorneys, they hardly seem to be illegal or even remarkable. Somewhat less acceptable was the practice of rounding up defense witnesses, often women, to provide false alibis. Gowen complained bitterly about this habit, which had made his career as district attorney so difficult in the early 1860's. Alibis were not offered, however, during the Molly trials in 1876 and 1877, perhaps because of pre-trial threats to punish perjured witnesses. Allegedly, legal defense funds and false alibis were automatically provided for any Molly accused of anything, irrespective of guilt; but, on the other hand, AOH members could be, and some were, expelled upon conviction of major crimes. Whether a serious effort was made to ascertain guilt or innocence before extending aid, the records do not reveal. Lack of respect for the judicial process was no doubt intensified by what seems to have been the general practice of excluding persons of Irish descent from juries, at least in cases involving Irish defendants.

Irishmen believed, with some justification, that they were discriminated against in the labor market by some mine officials, and that Irish people in general could not expect justice from police and the courts. It is not surprising that some of the more militant chose to use the organizational structure of the AOH as a means of more efficiently exacting retributive justice against those who had injured them and their friends. The conceptions of justice, and of how to obtain it, were no doubt imported from Ireland and reflected Irish experience with English administration; what the county organization of local AOH officials made possible was more rapid communication and the trading of "jobs" to provide unrecognizable assailants. The drunken brawling and random firing of weapons that McParlan's accounts feature so prominently obscure the sober purpose of the Molly Maguire faction within the AOH: to make sure that those who hurt innocent Irishmen did not go unpunished and to protect Irish defendants from prejudiced judges and juries.

Whence came the delusions of Gowen and his legal colleagues, who saw the AOH as a satanic cult bent on destroying Christian civilization? In part the delusion rose out of a Protestant cultural tradition. Their words echoed the charges against the Masonic order a generation before, and more generally appealed to the images of the Catholic Inquisition and of the Beast in Rome that had become nearly universal bugaboos in Protestant households since the Reformation. But the myth of the Molly Maguires had other, more venal functions for Gowen, Bannan, and their allies. It tended to discredit an already broken union, by innuendo if not by open accusation. And in perhaps the most dangerous obscuration of all, it continued the tradition of placing the blame for the problems of the coal trade on forces outside the trade itself. Like British free-traders, Irish Mollies—being Democrats, free-traders too—were charged with bringing death and destruction to an American industry from an evil Old World.

JUSTICE DENIED

If the courts of Schuylkill County in 1876 showed their readiness to bring accused Irish murderers to trial and execution, in 1877 they revealed a marked unreadiness to prosecute and convict colliery officials for negligence directly responsible for fatal accidents.

On May 9, 1877, a major explosion of firedamp in a section of the Wadesville Shaft killed six men and injured six others. A considerable amount of information about the circumstances of this accident has been preserved because the proceedings of the coroner's inquest were published as well as the mine inspector's report. The event led to an indictment for manslaughter of the chief mining engineer of the Philadelphia and Reading Coal and Iron Company, General Pleasants, and the superintendent of the colliery, Edward Herbert of St. Clair.[1]

The Wadesville Shaft had been designed by that highly respected geologist, Peter W. Sheafer, and had been sunk under the direction of a reputable engineer, J. C. Northall. It was touted as the greatest colliery in the world. But, as we have seen, it was troubled by ventilation problems and gas explosions from the day it opened in 1868. Its gangways connected with the old, abandoned gangways of the Hickory Slope, which generated large quantities of firedamp and which had been left with crippled ventilation by the Milnes. In 1871 and again in 1872 it was closed down for extended periods because of underground fires that had to be extinguished by turning off the pumps and letting the mine fill with water, and three more fire and flood disasters in 1878, 1881, and 1882 led to the closing of the mine in 1886. The year 1877, the year of the explosion that is the subject of this section, was the Wadesville Shaft's best year, with 150,261 tons shipped to market. The accident evidently happened at a time when the superintendent was pressing for higher production.

The explosion took place in the Mammoth Vein in a section of the mine called Lundy's gangway. Lundy's gangway was the westernmost sector, a mile on the surface from the downcast and the upcast air shafts, and considerably more than a mile by the tortuous windings of the air through at least two levels. It had been opened only recently, but after the breasts had been driven up a short distance, the miners encountered a fault that made completion of the breasts impossible. A further awkwardness was the poor condition of the top slate, which collapsed here and there, allowing pockets of methane to collect in the roof, thus requiring the construction of "slant batteries" to direct air into these pockets. Even more ominous was the fact that the slate separating the Mammoth from the overlying Seven-Foot Vein was thinner than usual, and on occasion sections of the Seven-Foot coal, as well as the top slate, crashed down into Lundy's gangway. So the decision had been made to rob the pillars and abandon the sector. Work crews had been engaged in this process for several months when the accident occurred.

One of the factors that made robbing the pillars a delicate process was the constant alteration of the airways. As weakened pillars collapsed in crushes, existing doors and batteries were removed or destroyed and new routes had to be created to ensure a continuous flow of fresh air throughout the sector. Even under the best of circumstances, robbing pillars was a tricky business. But in Lundy's gangway this normally tricky business was becoming critical because of an interacting series of management errors, mechanical failures, and geological accidents that interfered with the air. To begin with, the fan in the upcast, which normally drew air through this part of the mine at 40,000 cubic feet per minute, had broken down and the mine was dependent on "natural ventilation." Natural ventilation worked well enough in a small mine in the winter, when the air inside was most of the time warmer than outside and therefore naturally formed an ascending column in the upcast. But now the season was changing; and in May the outside temperature was apt to be higher than inside, in effect forming an inversion layer over the mine. To make matters worse, the colliery's stock of brattice boards and brattice cloth had run out and the new supplies ordered from the Coal and Iron Company's central depot had not yet come in. These supplies were needed in order to repair breaches in the door-and-brattice system of the intake airway. No one knew just how much gas there was in Lundy's gangway because Superintendent Herbert had not measured it as state regulations required; and, in fact, he had never measured it because the colliery did not possess the necessary instruments. The fire boss made his daily visit to that part of the mine sometime after ten o'clock. Unwarned of the presence of gas, and with only general instructions to use their safety lamps "on cloudy days, when the barometer was likely to be falling," or when they heard rockfalls, the miners were working with naked lights.[2]

About ten o'clock in the morning of May 9, according to survivors, a fall of rock was heard; it was a large piece of Seven-Foot coal that suddenly blocked the return air course just as it left Lundy's gangway. At that moment the victims were at their jobs, robbing pillars and repairing airways, at the several positions indicated on the map on page 365. A few seconds after the fall of coal, an explosion occurred somewhere between points 1 and 2, presumably set off by a miner's lamp. The blast and fireball were violent enough to kill men hundreds of feet down the gangway, at point 6′, and to injure others even farther away. The doors and brattices were, of course, destroyed and after-damp (carbon monoxide) and firedamp made it impossible to live in the workings until days later, after an air course was re-established and a temporary fan rigged up.

A coroner's inquest opened next day. It met for three days in Walker's Hall in St. Clair, and the jury, composed of men from the vicinity, included John Siney. The first witnesses were Edward Herbert, the acting superintendent (apparently his tenure in the job was in question), and Sampson Parton, state mine inspector. Herbert candidly revealed that the fan had broken down, that brattice boards and canvas to repair the airways were lacking, and that he had never measured the methane concentration by instrument. Herbert, a middle-aged family man with a son in college, superintendent of the Episcopal Sunday School, and a leading Mason in the town, could hardly lie before his neighbors about facts that were common knowledge to the miners. We have already met him as an expert on the subject of gas explosions. Parton, however, was a defensive and uncooperative witness who refused to answer inconvenient questions, and he and Siney exchanged sharp words. Parton, who had not visited Wadesville for six months, did not want to admit that there were any unsafe conditions in the mine, no doubt because the existence of such conditions would reflect on his competence in his job. After some sparring about assuring miners that if they testified they would not be fired, a parade of miner witnesses did appear and revealed the lax administration of the colliery. The coroner's jury released its written report a week after the accident. The report was severely critical of the colliery's slipshod management and of the mine inspector's negligence in not enforcing the law.

From the evidence produced we are satisfied that the part of the mine where the explosion took place was considered very dangerous by both bosses and men, and that it shows great neglect on the part of the bosses in not ordering the men to work with safety lamps exclusively—believing, as we do, that had the men been so working the accident would not have occurred—the evidence showing that the men invariably obeyed when ordered by the bosses to work with safety lamps. We are also satisfied that the requirements of the ventilation law were not complied with, and the owners of the colliery are censurable for not complying with the same. We are of the opinion that had there been extra doors as the law requires, there is a possibility, at least, that the lives of two of the men might have been saved. The mine inspector, Sampson Parton, who is a sworn officer of the law, and clothed with the highest authority—whose commands according to the law should be imperative, and whose orders no one is supposed to disobey, has been grossly neglectful of his duties in not visiting this colliery oftener and compelling the owners to comply with the law.

Parton's rejoinder, published along with the coroner's jury's report, charged that Siney had directed a biased investigation:

The entire investigation was conducted by a man known to be an agitator in our midst; prejudiced alike against myself and the Philadelphia and Reading Coal and Iron Company, the owners of the mines.

He exculpated the superintendent entirely and explained the rareness of his own visits on the ground that he had sixty-six collieries under his charge.[3]

There were two consequences of the coroner's report. The first was that General Pleasants, Superintendent Herbert, and several subordinate bosses at the Wadesville Shaft were indicted by the coroner a few months later on manslaughter charges. When in January 1878 the district attorney attempted to bring the case to trial, however, he found that the former witnesses in the case now refused to testify. The *Philadelphia Press*, although unfriendly to the charges brought by "John Siney, the Labor agitator," and fearful that if the verdict was adverse to the company it would "beget many more of the same kind," did suggest that perhaps the reluctant witnesses would not speak against the company "through fear of losing their situations." General Pleasants was reported to treat the matter

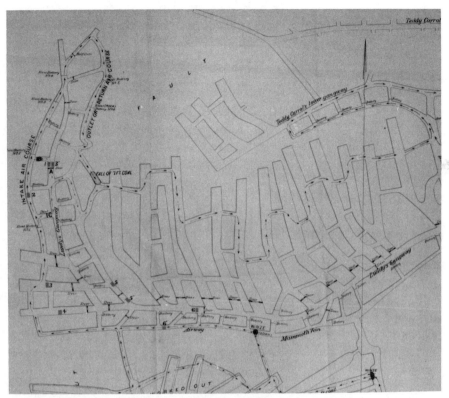

Survey of a part of the Wadesville Shaft Colliery, showing the mine workings and ventilation of the locality where the explosion of fire damp occurred on May 9th, 1877. Arrows indicate direction of air currents before and after the fall of coal. Nos 1 through 6 indicate where the bodies of miners were found. Nos. 3', 5', and 6' indicate where men were working if their bodies were found elsewhere. The distance from No. 1 to No. 6 along Lundy's gangway is approximately 450 feet.

with "indifference and contempt."[4] Gowen arrived in Pottsville to defend his company on the trial date, and legal maneuvers led to a postponement.[5] Although the case never did go to trial, it may have been the first time that high company officials were charged before a Pennsylvania court with responsibility for a mining accident.

But the second consequence was that nothing at all further happened. Pleasants, Herbert, and Parton remained in the same employment as before. In 1880, Herbert was still a mine superintendent, Sunday School superintendent, and Worshipful Master of Anthracite Lodge No. 285. And

Parton wrote an account of the accident, in the 1877 mine inspector's report, that completely eliminated any reference to problems in the ventilation of the colliery, or failure of the fire bosses to measure the gas and to require safety lamps in Lundy's gangway, and instead blamed it all on the miners who were killed. Parton theorized that the afternoon before the fall of Seven-Foot coal, miners robbing pillars had opened the doors at A and B, thus depriving the upper part of the workings of ventilation, and on the morning of the accident had left open another door at C, permitting gas to descend the airway to point 2, where a naked lamp exploded it. He concluded with a pontifical statement that completely exonerated the colliery (and himself) by blaming the victims for contributory negligence.

It is difficult to avoid the conclusion that in this case, accidental death and injury were a form of violence perpetrated on miners by an inept and careless organization, and that justice was arbitrarily denied. A district attorney was prepared to go to trial on a manslaughter charge; but the case was dropped. And the state mine inspector in his annual report suppressed the facts about the colliery's failure to maintain the ventilation and blamed the disaster—predictably—on the careless miner once again.

Equal justice was a commodity in short supply, and violence in ample, in Schuylkill County in the 1870's.

VII

A STATE CALLED ANTHRACITE

Out of the struggles between capital and labor, between landowners and colliery operators, between the Catholic Irish and the Protestant British, there was emerging in the anthracite region a social order new to America. Based on a perception by both unionists and capitalists that a higher level of sovereignty, social control, and industrial discipline was required for mutual survival, this new order began to emerge in the 1870's. Among the most articulate of its architects were two men of Irish background, the union leader from St. Clair, John Siney, and the railroad president, late of Mount Laffee and Pottsville, Franklin B. Gowen. Although they did not live to see the structure completed, by the beginning of the new century a politically astute observer could write of the whole anthracite region:

> A community of interests and the ties of labor unions have so bound the counties together that they constitute a sort of separate and distinct state, called by its inhabitants "Anthracite."[1]

A big union and a cartel of coal, iron, and railroad corporations banded the diversities of religion, national origin, and social class together into a state within a state. But even this social juggernaut was unable to transcend the difficulties of geology and technology that brought ruin, first, to the industries of the Pottsville Basin and, ultimately, to the whole anthracite trade.

ST. CLAIR IN 1870: DEMOGRAPHY AND CULTURE

St. Clair, as it entered the new era, looked very much as it had twenty years before. In 1870, as in 1850, the horizon was dominated by coal breakers and culm banks. The town itself had roughly doubled in size, the new blocks of houses extending southward along the banks of Mill Creek; expansion in any other direction was blocked by the presence of collieries and steep hillsides. It was still a noisy, sooty, dusty coal town; but it provided its residents with some amenities—fresh running water from Mine Hill piped into the houses, a system of fireplugs and two volunteer fire companies to use the water from them, a borough cemetery, street lamps, and an indulgent borough council that used the balance in the town treasury to forgive taxes on poor and ailing citizens.[1] And it was a town that knew itself now as a center of attention, famous for the mining establishments that attracted distinguished visitors from the whole world. Thus in June 1867 four members of the Japanese trade commission then visiting the country, in pursuance of the recently signed commercial treaty, made a trip to St. Clair at the suggestion of the Secretary of State "for the purpose of inspecting the Coal mines of this County." Escorted by John Northall from Wadesville, James Lanigan, the owner of the furnace in St. Clair, and other local worthies, the Japanese, with their interpreter, inspected the workings at the Hickory Slope and the Pine Forest collieries. The *Miners' Journal* paid the usual compliment:

> The Japanese are very ingenious, and readily adopt foreign inventions. They have recently constructed a steamboat, engine and all. On the completion of the Pacific Railroad we have no doubt that the commercial relations between this country and Japan will become important and valuable.

The visitors, dressed in formal Japanese style, created quite a sensation at the Hickory as they stood watching the coal cars coming up out of the slope, and were soon surrounded by a crowd of young slate pickers, who characterized them as "rum-uns." At the Pine Forest, the first commissioner was taken down to examine the gangways and observe the process of mining in the breasts and the use of the lamps, and he even "mined a piece of coal" himself. Then, with soiled hands and sooty clothing, but still enthusiastic for more knowledge, the commissioner toured the breaker, observing the breaking, screening, and picking processes and the way the coal was dumped from chutes into cars.[2]

Probably no later visitors compared with the Japanese in exotic charm, but the St. Clair collieries were, year after year, inspected by public figures and important groups. In 1872, Horace Greeley, the prominent New York editor and aspiring politician, came to Schuylkill County. He spent some time in the Pioneer Iron Works in Pottsville and then was shown the "great works" at the Wadesville Shaft, in which he professed to be "deeply interested" despite the fact that they were in one of their periodic shutdowns. He also visited the Pine Forest Shaft and inspected the breaker. But the *Journal* felt compelled to warn its readers that, despite his admiration for the "black diamonds" of Schuylkill County, Greeley was showing signs of indecision about the protective tariff.[3]

Next year a group of officers of the Philadelphia branch of the Catholic Benevolent Union—all Irish—held their meeting in Pottsville and during their stay took the tour of the mines about St. Clair, visiting the Wadesville Shaft (again not in operation) and the Eagle drift and slope. At the bottom of the slope, they wanted to sing "Down in a Coal Mine" (first performed and published the year before), but no one knew the words, so one of the party sang the *"Marseillaise"* instead. Finally a miner was found who knew both the words and the tune and he was prevailed upon to perform. After this underground *musicale*, the party was hoisted up, clutching lumps of souvenir coal they had "mined" themselves, and went on to enjoy a banquet at a tavern nearby. These Catholic dignitaries were, in contrast to some other observers, more interested in the social than in the economic or technical aspects of mining, and professed to be "vastly astonished at the realities of a coal mine." They "vowed that hereafter they would never grumble at the high prices of coal."[4]

It would be interesting to know what some of these visitors thought of the little town, but no accounts by travelers seem to have survived. The *Miners' Journal,* however, from time to time published thumbnail sketches of various coal towns, including St. Clair, and one from the late '60's is at hand. Like an earlier account, it took a moralistic view, praising and blaming with enthusiasm. The piece testifies to the continuing tension between tavern and tabernacle:

> This borough is . . . well laid out, the streets intersecting at right angles. The buildings are mostly frame, a large number having been erected during the past season, and others were remodeled; but in architectural beauty the place is far behind Pottsville. There is a population of about 7,000, of various nations and tongues, such as American, German, English, Irish and Welsh, the foreign element greatly prevailing. This is the mining district, and here Coal is King. Collieries are all around us. . . . Great heaps of coal dirt close by the town, attract the eye. In brisk times immense quantities of coal are sent to market from this neighborhood. . . .

The road passes through here to Palo Alto where the long trains are formed. There is one blast furnace here, and the recent discoveries of iron ore in the neighborhood, give promise of iron works before long.

We have churches enough in the place, if they were only more efficient. Satan and his cause seems to be on the ascendant: few towns perhaps are more cursed with intemperance; drinking houses of all kinds abounding, and when all other kinds of business is dull, the rum traffic flourishes. Oh! it is fearful to think how many husbands and fathers, sons and brothers, frequent these dringing [sic] hells, spend time, money, brains and conscience, pawn soul and body to the devil. We have several temperance organizations that are doing something to mitigate the evils of this monster vice. Recently a lodge of Good Templars has been opened, which bids fair to be very useful.[5]

The impression given by these sketches, and by the occasional notes of fires, crimes, and public events, is that St. Clair in 1870 was simply a bigger version of the St. Clair of 1850. But an examination of the census schedules for 1870 suggests that some important changes were under way.[6] The population of the borough was now recorded as 5,711, of whom 2,925 were males and 2,786 females. This was considerably less than the 7,000 that the correspondent claimed in 1867, and one is reminded of the complaints made earlier about the 1860 census, which gave the town only 4,900 as opposed to the estimate of 5,500 by "good judges." At that time, the St. Clair correspondent accused the enumerator of sloppy work:

> Numerous families were not visited at all, the censusman having taken the very uncertain method of collecting at one house, the statistics for a number of others. It is thought that a true census will show a difference of several hundred.[7]

Such observations as these imply a 20 percent undercount. As before, there was an excess of males (139), mostly concentrated in the age groups of working miners, but the excess in 1870 is little greater than it was in 1850 (115), despite the two-and-a-half-times increase in total population. This would suggest that in 1870 a smaller proportion of the town's male population was living as unattached bachelors in hotels and rooming-houses. There was also a difference in the proportion of foreign-born. In 1850, 1,235 persons or 56 percent of the population were foreign-born; in

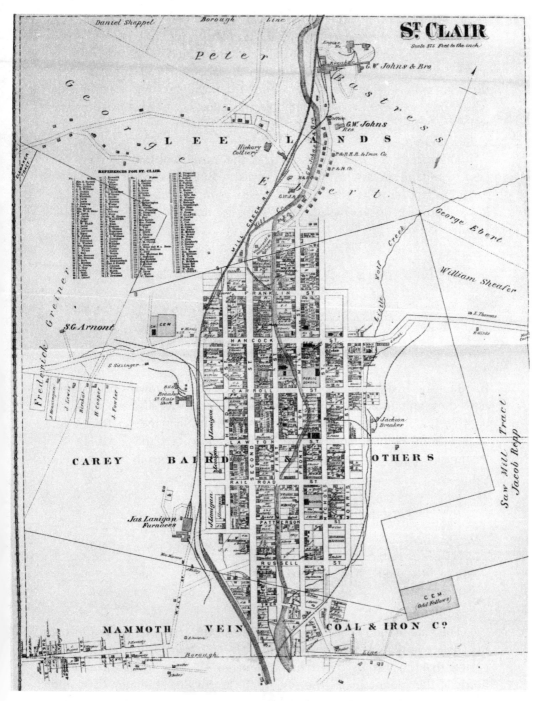

Property map of St. Clair, 1875

1870, only 2,288 or 40 percent were foreign-born. Very few 1850 residents (including both native and foreign-born) can be identified in the 1870 census, 328 in all (15 percent of the 1850 population). But, interestingly enough, the Irish-born made up the largest proportion of these survivors of the 1850 cohort (30 percent). As before, the town was almost exclusively white; only one black extended family was counted, headed by the same individual recorded in 1850, and now including married children and some grandchildren.

The principal countries of origin of the immigrant families were the same: England, Ireland, Wales, and Germany. But there had been a change in the proportions. In 1850 the Irish had been the most numerous, followed by the English, Welsh, and Germans; now the English-born outnumbered the Irish.

TABLE 7: *Ethnicity of Foreign-born, 1870*

	Irish	English	Welsh	German
1850	493	272	227	227
1870	685	691	538	338

In 1850, the Irish-born amounted to 22 percent of the town's population; now they amounted to only 12 percent. There was also a sprinkling of other nations of origin: 20 persons came from Scotland; 11 from Canada; 3 from France; and 2 from British Guiana. Of the 3,421 U. S.-born residents of St. Clair in 1870, the fathers were born in the following countries:

TABLE 8: *Birthplace of Fathers of U.S.-born, 1870*

	U.S.	England	Ireland	Wales	Germany	Other
NO. OF CHILDREN	818	380	761	259	444	759
PERCENTAGE	24	11	22	8	13	22

The explanation of the relative decline of the Irish component in the St. Clair population may be what the *Miners' Journal* repeatedly suggested, that the post-1850 Irish had "colonized" the new towns and patches north of the mountain, in the region of Girardville, Mahanoy City, and Shenandoah, where they were able to control local Democratic politics, including school boards, and obtain more favorable jobs. The decline of the Irish in St. Clair no doubt was partly responsible for the borough's swing in the Republican direction at election time.

The 1870 census recorded the occupations of most of the town's 2,786 females. In addition to 876 infants and females "at home and unemployed," there were 555 females attending school and 1,355 employed. Most of these, 1,044, were "keeping house," but 311 were gainfully employed. Nearly half of these, 147 in all, were domestic servants or housekeepers. The next most popular employment was in the textile trades; 73 women were listed as seamstress, dressmaker, milliner, or "tailoress." There were 18 washerwomen. No less than 26 women were storekeepers (especially candy stores) and 2 were store clerks. But an even more common profession was keeping a beer shop; 31 women kept beer shops, saloons, or hotels. There were 12 female schoolteachers and 1 nurse; and 1 girl worked as a slate picker.

For the 2,925 males, in addition to the 691 unemployed (including both infants and adults), the 1 listed as "retired," the 1 as "keeping house," and the 452 attending school, there were 1,780 gainfully employed. The largest number of jobs, of course, was in the colliery occupations, which accounted for 1375 men. There were 474 "miners," 195 "laborers at Mines," 389 "laborers" (presumably most but not exclusively underground miners' laborers), 162 slate pickers, 71 driver boys, and 45 engineers. There were 19 bosses and superintendents and 5 colliery operators. The remaining 15 were a miscellany of colliery clerks, watchmen, carpenters, firemen, and "working at coal mines." But in contrast to 1850, when colliery jobs outnumbered those in other trades by a ratio of five or six to one, in 1870 the ratio of colliery to non-colliery jobs was about three to one, with 405 men working outside the collieries. Most of these were in the standard trades: teamster (35), blacksmith (31), carpenter (50), shoemaker (24), butcher (9), cabinetmaker (13), plasterer (10), and smaller numbers of such craftsmen as carpet weaver, saddler, druggist, house painter, tinsmith, stonemason, wheelwright, barber, baker, molder, sawyer, tailor, watchmaker. There were 40 merchants of various kinds—groceries, dry goods, boots and shoes, clothing, tobacco, tinware, lumber, flour and feed; and there were 20 clerks in stores. Twenty-six men kept saloons and hotels. Six men worked at the iron furnace. There were 24 railroad workers. Among the ranks of professional and semi-professional men, there were 3 physicians, 9 schoolteachers, 12 hotel keepers, 6 clergymen, 2 justices of the peace, 1 photographer, 1 surveyor, 3 telegraph operators, 1 life-insurance agent, and 1 agent for the water company.

Clearly, St. Clair had now an even more diversified economy than in 1850, providing a wide range of goods and services for its own resident mining population and for the population of the nearby patches, including Crow Hollow, Ravensdale, Mill Creek, and Wadesville. The number of establishments furnishing alcoholic refreshment—beer shops, saloons, and hotels—kept by men and women was, as the town's critics charged, extremely high, no less than forty-five, but they no doubt catered to a large number of out-of-towners as well as the residents.

Another change in the character of the town was a shift in the relation between ethnicity and occupation. One of the striking features of the social structure revealed in the 1850 census was the segregation of the Irish colliery workers into the lower-status jobs. Of the 191 Irishmen then in the mines, 167 were laborers and only 24 contract miners; the English and Welsh, by contrast, had most of the better jobs, the ratios being seventy-three to ten and seventy-three to six respectively. By 1870, although they were still at a disadvantage, the situation of the Irish had somewhat improved. Counting only foreign-born in the census schedule categories "coal miners" and "laborers at Mines," we find that many more Irish were now contract miners; in fact, a majority of the Irish workers in these two categories were now full-fledged "miners."

TABLE 9: *Miner/Laborer Status and Ethnicity, 1870*

	Irish	Welsh	English	German
MINER	78	134	180	40
LABORER	58	20	22	17

TABLE 10: *Property Ownership and Ethnicity, 1850 and 1870*

	Irish		Welsh		English		German	
	1850	1870	1850	1870	1850	1870	1850	1870
NUMBER OF FOREIGN-BORN MEN AND WOMEN	493	685	227	538	272	691	227	338
NUMBER OF OWNERS OF REAL ESTATE	9	131	20	97	27	107	16	107
PERCENT OWNING REAL ESTATE	2%	19%	9%	18%	10%	15%	7%	32%

Another noteworthy change is the declining number of German-born miners, 45 in 1850 and only 40 in 1870. (Compare Table 3, page 134, with Table 9 above.) This change occurred despite an increase in the number of German-born residents from 227 in 1850 to 338 in 1870. The Germans were, evidently, moving out of mining into other occupations and the Irish were in effect taking their place.

The improvement in the social circumstances of the St. Clair Irish is reflected also in the statistics for education and property ownership.[8] In 1850, of 338 Irish children under the age of sixteen (including both Irish-born and born in the United States with Irish-born father), 65 or 19 percent were listed as having attended school in the past year. The figures for English, German, and Welsh, by contrast, ranged from 30 to 40 percent. In 1870, of 772 Irish children, 312 or 40 percent were in school, and the English, German, and Welsh percentages were still in the 30 percent range. The Irish improvement, however, had been achieved by Irish girls, of whom 48 percent were in school, while only 19 percent (the same percentage as in 1850) of the boys attended school, still far below the figures for boys of the other groups. A similar pattern of improvement appears in regard to ownership of real property.

These impressions can be amplified by data from the county tax assessments for these years.[9] Using ownership of more than one lot and/or house as an index of sufficient affluence to invest in income-producing property, we find that multiple ownership among the foreign-born is distributed as follows in 1851 and 1870:

TABLE 11: *Multiple Property Ownership and Ethnicity, 1851 and 1870*

	Irish		Welsh		English		German	
	1851	1870	1851	1870	1851	1870	1851	1870
NUMBER OF MULTIPLE PROPERTY OWNERS	16	76	19	62	27	76	22	69
PERCENT OF MULTIPLE PROPERTY OWNERS	19%	27%	23%	22%	32%	27%	26%	24%

From all these figures, one must conclude that not only did the Irish presence in the town decline in relative numbers between 1850 and 1870, but that the Irish who remained were, on the average, better educated and more prosperous. But significant disadvantages remained.

MIDDLE-CLASS CONTROL OF TOWN AFFAIRS

From the relative reduction of the Irish presence in the town, the flourishing of crafts, and commerce in other things than coal, we can perhaps
infer that St. Clair was becoming more and more a middle-class market
town, a central place with its own small hinterland of mine patches. Earlier, there had been a tiny elite—primarily the Johns and Lawton families—and a large population of poor immigrant miners, with relatively little
in between in the way of tradesmen, merchants, and professional men.
Now only George W. Johns and his extended family were left of the original elite; the mining population had perhaps doubled, mostly from England and Wales; but the major change was the growth of a middle class
of tradesmen, merchants, professionals, and colliery superintendents, who
now dominated the local government and the social and cultural life of the
town. The merchants, tradespeople, and professionals depended largely on
the mining families for their income, of course; but the miners depended
upon the willingness of the middle class to extend credit during hard
times. The relationship was an essential one and it was clearly recognized
by both classes. Indeed, one of the functions, if not an original intent, of
the Workingmen's Benevolent Association of St. Clair was to regularize the
relationship between the middle class and the miner. During the spring
strike in 1871, at a union meeting in St. Clair, a series of resolutions was
unanimously adopted, including two that testify both to the awareness of
a kind of class distinction between miners and merchants, and to their
mutual dependence:

> Resolved . . . That we tender sincere thanks to our friends, the
> merchants, for their assistance, pecuniary and otherwise, and we
> shall request them to furnish at their convenience, after resump-
> tion, a list of delinquent customers belonging to the WBA; and

> Resolved . . . that no member of the WBA of this district shall be
> entitled to a traveling card or certificate of membership who will
> not fully and satisfactorily compensate the merchants who have
> furnished him with provisions during this and former struggles of
> our association.[1]

The middle class of St. Clair was dominant in the popularly elected
borough council in the late 1860's and 1870's. After passing only a few
ordinances in the first sixteen years of the borough's existence, the council

East side of St. Clair, looking north to Mine Hill

in 1867 was spurred to pass a small blizzard of twenty-one ordinances aimed at cleaning up the town and making it more respectable. Among other things, the firing of guns of any kind was prohibited; carrion, offal, garbage, trash, and stove ashes were henceforth not to be thrown into streams, gutters, streets, or alleys; dirty or smelly food was not to be sold; vandalism of street lamps and fire hydrants was enjoined; minors were not allowed to "have communication" with any hose company; "all dogs and bitches running at large" had to be muzzled; snow had to be cleared from sidewalks; and the owners of the tract on which stood the St. Clair Shaft and Slope (i.e., Henry Carey and Eliza Baird) were required "to clean and keep in good order the water course and drain through which the water is discharged from their collieries." Infractions of these rules were punished by small fines of $2 to $25. The same council established and published for the first time a set of "Rules of Order" for business meetings of the council. After this revolutionary effort to bring the borough within the pale of middle-class respectability, new ordinances were passed with fair regularity, regulating the same kinds of things as before: the size and depth of graves; the conduct of markets; the paving of sidewalks and the setting of curbstones; the imprisonment of vagrants.

The president of the council in 1867 during the passage of the ordinances to render St. Clair respectable was one H. B. Sessinger, superintendent of the St. Clair Shaft and Slope collieries. Information is also available about a number of council presidents both before and after Sessinger's incumbency. In the following list, we note only name, date of service, occupation, and value of real estate owned (as given by the census):

Jacob Metz (1850)	carpenter	$4,000 in 1850
Charles Lawton (1850)	contractor	not known
Amzi Brown (1857–1858)	hotel keeper	$2,650 in 1860
H. B. Sessinger (1867)	superintendent of St. Clair Shaft and Slope collieries	not known
Charles R. Johnson (1869)	hotel keeper	$4,500 in 1870
Paul Atwood (1869)	teamster	$3,000 in 1870
Clay Evans (1873–1874)	storekeeper	not known
William Prosser (1875)	shoemaker	$1,200 in 1870
Rees Davis (1877)	blacksmith	$3,000 in 1870
Michael Hillan (1879)	liquor merchant	not known
Seth Orme (1879)	boot and shoe dealer	not known

One might perhaps have expected that council presidents would be property owners and successful tradesmen or merchants, but what about other members of the council? Let us take the five members of the council in 1870:

Joseph Atkinson	huckster	$4,000
Paul Atwood	teamster	$3,000
Thomas Lewis	mine boss	$1,500
David Morgan	shoemaker	$800
Thomas Williams	coal miner	$1,500

378

Again we find property owners, a majority of tradesmen and merchants, and an absence of Irish names. Sampling council membership in other years of the 1870's, one finds English, Welsh, and German names, but very few Irish—Michael Hillan, a tavern keeper in John's Patch and Siney's friend, was apparently the sole Irishman on the council during the decade.[2]

Some of the council presidents and members had extensive influence in the town in other ways. Thomas Lewis, the mine boss, for instance, served on the council for eight years but for at least ten years was town supervisor. Seth Orme, whom we have noticed earlier as an inveterate joiner of fraternal societies, was for a time the postmaster. Charles Johnson's hotel was one of the principal establishments in town. But perhaps the best example of a rising middle-class booster of civic improvement was Clay Evans, council president in 1873–1874, and council member in other years as well. Born in Pottsville in 1844, he served as a private in the 48th Regiment in 1864, and by the end of the war had risen to the rank of captain; after the war he remained an officer in the national guard. In 1867 he married Emily Allison of St. Clair, the sister of Robert Allison. After a short spell clerking in Boone's store, in 1872 he opened his own grocery and dry-goods store. He was a charter member of the Grand Army of the Republic post in St. Clair. He served on the school board and was elected to the state legislature for the 1879–1880 term.[3] And he, together with his friend Richard Brown (superintendent of St. Clair Schools and a temperance advocate), in 1870 helped found the St. Clair Scientific and Literary Association, which initially met weekly in the Creek School House to debate such questions as "Should the United States seek to increase its territory?" Other founding members included twenty-one-year-old Daniel Lewis, newly launched as proprietor of a general store, Daniel Crawshaw, an engineer, and W. T. Richards, a store manager. The editor of the *Miners' Journal* was so moved by this evidence of the spirit of improvement that he saluted the new society as likely to be equal even to the Pottsville association:

> Let all enter into it with a will, and it will be a success. Let the old, let the young join, let all who favor the onward march of the times, contribute in establishing and successfully maintaining an institution, having in view an object worthy so much attention and consideration. We may congratulate St. Clair. . . .[4]

The founding of the Scientific and Literary Association was one expression of a theme to which most middle-class St. Claireans subscribed:

that to participate in the onward march of the times required knowledge. Like the citizens of hundreds of other little American towns, the men and women of St. Clair were insatiable consumers of information. The town supported a bookstore, kept by that ubiquitous civic benefactor, John Holmes, and his brother.[5] Prominent lecturers included St. Clair and other mining towns of Schuylkill in their circuit, including the Irish nationalist Charles Stewart Parnell and one Father Burke, whose lecture on "Light and Shade of Irish Character" gave "inexpressible pleasure" to his "warm-hearted countrymen."[6] Traveling theatrical companies visited the town.[7] The formal musical arts were cultivated with what seems to have been nearly universal participation, at least by the more refined element. Every church had its organ and its choir; formal concerts were held in St. Clair Hall with imported singers and musicians; there were at least two home-town glee clubs and a cornet band, and there were formal balls at Walker's Hall where "all the beauty and fashion of St. Clair" attended in their "extremely elegant" toilets. And the town's poet, Samuel H. Daddow, in his verse celebrated the progress of the age and announced that knowledge is power.[8]

THE RITUALS OF CIVIC SOLIDARITY

But these were middle-class ways of self-improvement and recreation, inaccessible to the poorer colliery workers, who, even if they had the inclination, had neither time, energy, nor money—let alone the self-assurance—to participate. Public social intercourse between the classes was, however, promoted on certain ritual occasions. There seems to have been a tradition, active at least in the 1850's, of ceremonial exchanges of food and gifts between colliery workers and the colliery superintendent. Thus in 1866 the employees of the St. Clair Shaft and Slope gave H. B. Sessinger, the resident superintendent, a rosewood box of Swiss drawing instruments, made of silver and costing $135. In return, the employees were "generously entertained" at the company office.[1] And on New Year's Eve in 1867 John C. Northall, superintendent of the Hickory Colliery, gave a supper to the miners employed by the company.[2] But the most important of the rituals of civic solidarity were three: parades, and particularly the Fourth of July parade; church attendance, especially on the high holidays; and turning out into the streets at times of disaster. On these occasions, men, women, and children of all social stations and ethnicities met and mingled, affirming their common identity as Americans, as Christians, and as neighbors.

Waiting for the Fourth of July parade

Parades with marches in regalia had for years been held on national saints' days by ethnic fraternal organizations. In St. Clair, however, the Fourth of July up to 1867 had been a rather lackluster holiday, celebrated by picnics held separately by the Sunday Schools of the half-dozen or so churches. (In the county seats of Orwigsburg and Pottsville, by contrast, elaborate parades by militia as well as Sunday School classes had been popular since the 1840's at least.) In 1867, however, the patriotic order of Junior Sons of America paraded for the first time, and the following year GAR Post 47 proposed a general parade by all the town's societies. A joint committee of all the groups decided favorably and appointed Adjutant N. M. McIlwain of Post 47 as marshal and Lieutenant Clay W. Evans as assistant marshal. The parade was scheduled to start at seven a.m., while the air was still cool, at Holmes Hall in the south part of town. At daybreak, in order to wake everybody up, cannon were fired at various points in the hills surrounding the borough, church bells rang loudly, and the steam whistles at the various collieries shrieked unceasingly. Sleepy people stumbled out of their houses, some in fright, expecting to discover a conflagration. With everyone now out in the streets, anxiously waiting for the grand display, the parade formed and proceeded up Front Street. The order

381

of march included eight contingents: the St. Clair Union Brass Band; Mineral Lodge No. 285, Independent Order of Odd Fellows; Post 47, Grand Army of the Republic; Camp 75, Patriotic Order of Junior Sons of America; Perseverance Section, No. 16, Cadets of Temperance; Eagle Temple of Honor, No. 47; Hope Hose Company; and Columbia Hose Company. The brass band, dressed in new uniforms, played stirring tunes that, in the opinion of the *Miners' Journal* correspondent, created "an inspiration of patriotic fervor" and caused "the love of American Government and her glorious institutions to burn more brightly within the breasts of true and loyal subjects." Mineral Lodge 285 and Post 47 were attired in "citizens dress" but wore white gloves; Perseverance Section and Eagle Temple, however, wore full regalia. The fire companies, which had been organized only the year before, paraded in uniform, Hope Company in red shirts and Columbia in blue, all wearing dark pants, belt, and white gloves, and drawing their carriages. People cheered, flags waved, and banners fluttered above the street. After the procession returned to Holmes Hall, the chaplain called for three cheers for the "union as it is," colliery supervisor H. B. Sessinger read the Declaration of Independence, and the marshal promised an even greater demonstration next year. It all proved that "St. Clair can get up a jubilee" that compared favorably with that of any other town in Schuylkill.[3]

The churches, of course, were supposed in Christian doctrine to be places where all social classes mingled in common devotion, but they were also bastions of ethnicity. There were, however, two occasions when some blending of congregations occurred. The most regular of these was at Christmastime, when all St. Clair was invited on Christmas evening to attend the annual concert organized by the Sunday School at the Methodist Episcopal church.

> The M.E. Sunday School of St. Clair claim Christmas evening as peculiarly theirs from a long annual observance, and the public seems to enjoy their entertainments as much as the school, judging from the patronage extended to them.[4]

Attending services at another denomination's place of worship was a common Christmas practice in some other parts of Pennsylvania as well, permitting even Catholics and Protestants some admission of their mutual Christianity.

The other religious occasion for the celebration of community solidarity, mingling Catholic and Protestant, Irish, Welsh, English and German, and all of the social classes, was the revival. Revivals attracted thousands to campsites around Pottsville; special trains were provided by the Reading. Revivals were not intended to recruit for any particular denomination, but to persuade lukewarm and lapsed Christians and, indeed, atheists of the peril of their souls, to invite rebirth, and to encourage renewal of fellowship in some congregation. Revivals were so clearly a testament to the idea of a community of Christians that even racial and gender barriers came down. An extraordinary example of this ecumenical spirit was the camp meeting held at Cressona, just south of Pottsville, in the summer of 1874, where the "colored lady evangelist" Mrs. Harriet A. Baker preached to an audience (presumably assembled by rail from far and wide) that swelled to 16,000 blacks and whites together and saved souls of both races. Her message so impressed the pastor of the Primitive Methodist church at St. Clair, J. H. Acornley, that he and the pastors of the Primitive Methodist churches in Pottsville and Mahanoy City invited her to stay and do the Lord's work in Schuylkill County for a while. She remained in the county for two months, "preaching the Gospel of Christ and lecturing on the story of her life," and then went on to do evangelical labor in black and white churches in several northeastern states, sponsored by a number of denominations, including Primitive Methodist, Methodist Episcopal, Baptist, United Brethren, and African Methodist. Eventually she retired from the field to take charge of St. Paul's African Methodist Episcopal Church in the Pennsylvania German industrial town of Lebanon, just a few miles south of the coal region.

The Reverend Mr. Acornley was so impressed by Harriet Baker that some years later he wrote and published a biography of her, revealing her romantic genealogy and the visions that propelled her into the ministry, showing the evangelical milieu to which St. Clair was exposed and to which it responded positively.[5] Her great-grandmother on the maternal side was an "Indian squaw" married to an Englishman; her grandmother, a slave, killed her master and mistress with an ax after they had whipped her, while she was pregnant, so severely that her "entrails protruded." Harriet and her husband escaped from slavery to Columbia, Pennsylvania, about 1848; her husband, captured after the passage of the fugitive-slave law, was bought free for $750. After her children died in 1872, when she was about forty-two years old, she went on the road as an evangelist, as she had longed to do ever since the age of twelve, when she had a conversion experience. On her mission, she was guided and inspired by a vision of personal salvation, which served as a kind of charter for her efforts to save others:

On the occasion she dreamed she was in the middle of a great sea, out of sight of land, standing on a platform, with nothing to be seen but the blue sky above and the deep waters beneath, the sea gently swelled until the platform upon which she stood floated away to a place just large enough to rest her two feet upon. . . . She was left alone looking up to the heavens for help, and as she looked, she saw a small cord coming down out of the clouds, and swinging lower and lower until it got within her reach; she imagined she heard a voice say "lay hold," but she was afraid, and hesitated. As she hesitated the cord swung to the south, and as it passed her, she thought she heard the voice say again, "lay hold" and then it continued to swing from north to south. She cried mightily for help, and again she heard the voice say "lay hold," her fears vanished in a moment, and as the cord passed her again, with a mighty effort she sprung and laid hold with both her hands. Consciousness left her, and she was carried away to the north, and when she came to herself, found that she had been set down in a strange land, among strange people, and she imagined she heard the same voice command her to tell the multitude of her wonderful deliverance and with a heart overflowing with gratitude and joy, she recounted in the hearing of the people . . . how . . . she had been so graciously delivered from the sea.[6]

More visions came about the time of her daughters' deaths, when she was wrestling with the urge to leave her family for the mission field, and she experienced the classic vision of the god on the mountain. In church one evening she was carried away in spirit to Mount Calvary, where she saw the Redeemer, the thieves, and the Roman cavalry. Then the vision shifted and she saw rise before her an exceedingly high mountain.

Behind this mountain was a great reflection which lit up both the heavens and the earth. And as she stood gazing in astonishment at the marvelous light, she imagined she saw the Lord Jesus standing on the top of the mountain clothed in bright raiment, with a glorious crown upon his head, streams of light flowing therefrom in dazzling rays. . . . The Savior looked upon her with a smile she will never forget, and spoke to her in a voice mellowed with sweetness. He reminded her of how He had delivered Joshua, and assured her He was the Captain of the host which had come to deliver her. She realized that He was the same God today, was

384

filled with Divine glory, and springing to her feet she gave full expression to the joy of her soul. She praised God who had revealed such wonderful things to her, and shouted glory! glory! glory![7]

According to Acornley, her sister and husband and others in the town who had abused her for wanting to be an evangelist saw lightning flash through the church and the shock of thunder. And so the people decided to "loose the woman and let her go."

Her actual sermons, separated from the autobiographical accounts of visions and miracles, were pretty much standard fare, recounting the life of Jesus and singing the praises of the Lord, aimed at individual salvation rather than world regeneration. How many she saved in St. Clair is not known. But her mere presence perhaps was a reminder to all professed Christians in the town that all are equal in the eye of the Lord.

A more somber occasion that brought the classes and ethnicities together was the spectacle of mass mortality. A passionate act of assembly in the streets took place whenever disaster in the mines took many lives at once. Such a scene happened in May 1877 when the explosion in the Wadesville Shaft (described in the last chapter) killed six men and seriously injured six others, most of them residents of St. Clair. The newspaper accounts described the typical event following a mine disaster:

> The news of the explosion spread like wildfire and as all the people living in the vicinity of the shaft have relations working there, they immediately rushed pell mell to the mouth of the shaft.[8]

But the major assembly took place at the time of the first funerals, on May 11, when three men were buried. "Business was generally suspended and everybody turned out to do honor to the dead." The first to be buried was John Durkin, a Civil War veteran. The cortege formed at his brother-in-law's house on Second Street in St. Clair and proceeded to St. Mary's Catholic Church, marching slowly, the band with muffled drums playing a dead march, the militia carrying reversed arms. At the church, the cortege was met by a delegation from two militia companies of Pottsville along with a drum corps. Speaking over the coffin in the church, Father McEnroe "preached a short discourse on the life of the deceased and sketched his gallant military career." Then the coffin was placed again in the hearse and the procession moved up the hill to the Irish Catholic cemetery. After the coffin was placed in the ground, the militia companies fired a salute over the grave. Next, Herbert Moore was carried to his final resting place in the Odd Fellows Cemetery, accompanied by a similar procession, headed by the Primitive Methodist minister in a buggy before the hearse, and escorted by a cortege consisting of Lincoln Lodge No. 92, Knights of Pythias, and Mineral Lodge No. 285, Independent Order of Odd Fellows, and friends and relatives in carriages and on foot. The last to be buried was William Kirk, of Third Street, whose remains were accompanied to the Catholic church and then to the cemetery by the same procession that had escorted Durkin.[9]

But the most impressive of the communal rituals in honor of the dead was the raising of the Soldiers' Monument. After the Civil War, some of the St. Clair veterans set up Post Number 47 of the Grand Army of the Republic, named for John Ennis, Second Lieutenant, of the Lafayette Rifles of St. Clair, and the post quickly undertook to raise a monument to honor the men and boys of St. Clair who served, and in some cases gave their blood, in the Union army and navy.[10] The initial method of raising money was to present dramatic performances. In the fall of 1870, the play *Pride* was enacted by members of the post, with great success, and the money from the sale of tickets was spent purchasing an initial block of burial lots, surrounded by an iron fence, in the newly created Odd Fellows Cemetery at the south end of town. Next year, the post presented a week's run of another play, a "popular military drama," *Winchester, the Spy of Shenandoah*, the cast again being drawn from the ample supply of "talent and ability" said to be available in St. Clair. The scenery was painted by Charles Rohrbach, the town's sign painter, formerly of the Wetherill Rifles. The funds collected were placed in the post's Monument Fund.[11] But more in the way of general community participation was needed, and so a St. Clair Monument Association was organized. At its second meeting, in Holmes Hall, with Dr. Coryell in the chair, a plan was proposed for soliciting private contributions and for holding a town fair at which the churches and fraternal orders would sell food and sundries, the proceeds to go to the Monument Fund. The fair was held in due course during the week before Christmas in 1872, and raised enough money to pay the $2,600 price to Seasholtz and Shenton, sculptors of Pottstown, for the monument and engraving.

The monument was dedicated on Thanksgiving Day 1874. It was a white marble shaft, about twenty-five feet high, surmounted by a statue six feet six inches tall of a soldier at parade rest, and it stood on the cemetery hillside, looking down over the town. The base was inscribed with the names of soldiers from St. Clair who served in the War of the Rebellion. The symbolism of unity was explicit: on each corner near the base of the shaft was displayed, in bas-relief, "a bundle of reeds . . . bound together, indicative of the Union and its strength." The parade that proceeded through "an immense concourse of people" to the dedication ceremony at the foot of the monument was no doubt the longest ever to wind its way through St. Clair streets, composed of about thirty bands, not only from St. Clair but the rest of Schuylkill County as well. At the dedication, Dr. Coryell introduced Governor Hartranft, who made a few remarks about the bravery of the men of Schuylkill. The Honorable Lin Bartholomew then eulogized the dead, observed that the monument represented "the principle of patriotism without which there is nothing noble on earth," and uttered a prayer for peace and the end of hatred. Waxing more and more eloquent, he assured the crowd that the men being honored today had saved "the cause of civil and religious liberty on the face of the globe. Their failure meant the banishment of liberty forever." He urged that the sons of these fathers emulate their glorious deeds. Then there was band music, and finally a speech by the ever available orator Benjamin Haywood, who was "greeted with cheers." Haywood supervised the unveiling of the statue, spoke of "the wives and children waiting for the return from the war of him who never, never came again," and appealed for contributions to defray the expenses still remaining despite energetic collections by the ladies of St. Clair. After the choir sang "Rest, Soldier, Rest," the immense crowd slowly separated.[12]

The projectors and committeemen who carried this project through represented a fair slice of the town's occupational classes, from Dr. Coryell, the wealthy physician and heir of William H. Johns, to two (possibly three) coal miners who served on the original GAR committee. One of these men, William Davis, a Welshman, had lost a leg in an accident in the St. Clair Shaft in 1869; another, John Taylor, was perhaps the same man as the miner of that name who would be severely injured by a premature blast of powder at Beechwood Colliery in 1878.[13] There were two John S. Thomases listed in St. Clair in the 1870 census, one a Welsh watchmaker, the other an English miner. The miner would be injured at Beechwood in 1878, his hands severely burned in a gas explosion.[14] One other committeeman, English-born Seth Orme, had earlier been a miner but had lost a leg in a mine accident in 1862.[15] The other members of the GAR committee and the Monument Association Fair committee included Richard Brown, the one-armed high-school teacher and school superintendent, two store clerks, a merchant tailor, a state policeman, and a flour-and-feed dealer. No Irish names appeared; they were all English, Welsh, or German.

But, whatever may be inferred from the absence of Irish from the planning group, it was certainly not the intention of the GAR or the Monument Association to ignore the sacrifices made by Irish soldiers in the war. Irish, English, Welsh and German names were listed without distinction on the monument itself. And the rhetoric surrounding the appeals for financial support invoked the concept of a St. Clair united in patriotic opposition to the "late Rebellion," freely offering life and treasure for the government's use in the defense of "our flag and honor, free institutions, free press," mothers and daughters too working with "zeal and patriotic fervor" equaled only by the women of the Revolution.[16] The monument became a symbol of monolithic solidarity: the present was united with the past, the living with the dead, and class and ethnic divisions were no more. No doubt it was expressive of a yearning for an organization of the extreme diversity of cultures and classes and individual economic interests in the town, a call for unity in the face of all the disputes over safety and union building and ethnic prejudice, a cry for order to quell the violence in the night streets. But the monument represented a sentimental resolution of conflict; it did not address the hard mechanics of creating new institutions. And, like the Clay statue, the Soldiers' Monument was a partisan symbol, for there were many who had opposed the war. It would require more than symbols of unity to resolve the social conflicts that afflicted the coal region.

JOHN SINEY AND LARGE-SCALE LABOR ORGANIZATION

John Siney believed that workingmen, long exploited and degraded by capitalists, were now becoming aware of their situations and of the means for improving it. "Our eyes are being opened," he wrote. Social justice could be established not by random violence, but by large, well-disciplined organizations, including cooperative stores, mills, and mines, a national industrial union, and a national political party devoted to the cause of the workingman.[1]

For Siney, the workingman was the miner, the foundry worker, the shipyard worker—in general, the employee of the wealthy capitalist or the corporation. What defined the class was not manual labor but wage labor. Wage laborers were dependent on one employer who monopolized their services; self-employed mechanics or artisans provided goods or services to many customers. Self-employed craftsmen such as carpenters, machin-

ists, and stonemasons, like butchers
and bakers and candlestick makers,
belonged to an old system of industry and now, in places like St. Clair,
constituted a middle class between
the miners at the bottom and the
mine operators and landowners on
top. The striking colliery worker had
little in common with a prosperous
carpenter like Maurus Oestreich,
who built coal breakers, patronized
the Catholic church, and served as a
member of the borough council.
Siney was a child of the Industrial
Revolution and, along with the English socialists, recognized that the
essential tension was between the
capitalists and the employees who in
brigades of hundreds manned the

John Siney (1831—1880)

capitalists' mills and mines and lived in their company towns. He did not use
the word "proletariat," but it was the proletarian worker, not the self-
employed master carpenter, machinist, stonemason, watchmaker, or other
traditional tradesmen, whom he wished to mobilize in a movement for industrial justice.

Siney's language in his public statements invoking the idea of social
justice was strong, even violent. He repeatedly cast up to the readers of his
newspaper the contrast between the warm, cozy homes of the capitalists
who profited from the miners' work, and the dark, dangerous, underground
working places of the miners, who dug coal for a pittance, barely enough to
feed wives and children. Throughout his career, his public utterances were
garnished with bitter denunciations of the rich for their indifference to the
sufferings of the poor workingman and his family. The new union miner,
aware of his rights and of his power, "will suffer no longer to be driven to his
work like a sheep to the slaughter." A new world was dawning:

> Let us show to the world that the miner is not such a degraded
> animal as is generally supposed—lives in the mountains to ac-
> commodate city folk and to enrich large corporations, at the risk
> of health and life, in dismal coal pits for whatever paltry pittance
> they see fit to give us.[2]

He depicted the nature of labor's position in frustrating labor negotiations with stubborn mine operators as a defense of manhood against an enemy bent on castration. For instance, in a "review of the situation" at the start of a strike against the Philadelphia and Reading Coal and Iron Company, he declared that to avert a strike he had done everything "in keeping with our honor and our manhood." He charged that "nothing but a total surrender of manhood and independence will satisfy the wishes of the President [Gowen] of this mammoth corporation." He accused the coal-trade cartel of planning "the subjugation of the people" and of having annihilated "every spark of manhood" in the miners of the northern field and of "depressing and degrading" the men of Schuylkill. The companies, he said, were planning to "annihilate" the union in order to "make the people *lick* the dirt from *their feet*." He appealed to the "impartial public" to decide between "a defenseless people and this all powerful corporation." And he repeatedly used military metaphors to describe labor conflict (although he and the union prohibited actual violence), talking about "war," a tactical "retreat," the need to store up "ammunition."[3]

A somewhat more systematic exposition of what seems to have been Siney's position was set forth in the first annual report, for 1872–1873, of the Bureau of Statistics of Labor, a new Pennsylvania state agency. Siney had hoped to be appointed commissioner at a $4,000 annual salary, but the post went to Republican politician T. J. Bigham. The report, largely devoted to anthracite mining, contained a sympathetic history of the WBA, details of the miners' standard of living (mostly data on wages and housing), some abstracts of questionnaires returned by both miners and operatives, and several statements by experts on "the labor question." It was in general strongly biased in favor of labor in "the great struggle in which labor is engaged." Siney may have been consulted in the writing of the report, but the most eloquent indictment of the present industrial system was provided by an anonymous "ship joiner," a "journeyman mechanic," who probably was Siney's friend Richard Trevellick, a former shipyard carpenter. In a ten-page essay, the literary mechanic carefully explained that labor was forced to work excessive hours and did not receive a fair share of the profits of enterprise, and that working people were beginning to realize that their "supposed equality" was chimerical and their education a deliberate fraud. The behavior of the prosperous in forcing wages down "would disgrace the lower animals in a struggle for a bone." Injustice, in fact, was universal and inevitable in the competitive industrial system.

The effect of long hours and low wages upon the working-class community was the anonymous workman's final subject. Exhausted and often sick or injured, workingmen were prone to "drunkenness, dissipation, and idleness," and their wives and daughters were forced into prostitution and misery. Demoralized and alienated workers were difficult to organize into effective unions, and, in fact, in the anonymous workman's experience, the demand for higher wages generally came first from those who attended religious services because of the necessity churchgoers were under "of keeping a Sabbath suit of clothing for themselves and their children and meeting church expenses." He went on to ask why the workers could not meet their own and the middle classes' expectations of piety, respectability, and education. The answer was that all the things that respectable people did in their spare time—such as going to church, attending lectures, reading books and newspapers, taking excursions—*required* spare time (and spare money):

> How can a laboring community, which does not finish its evening meal until half past seven or eight, be expected to comply, in their exhausted condition, with the social decencies, a change of dress, etc., necessary to attend the prayer meeting or any evening gathering of the various organizations which bring the different classes of society together? The very thought is repulsive to all except to the most determined minds.
>
> These workmen who are able by evening liberation from labor to form a connection with our churches, masonic and reformatory organizations, make acquaintance with those who are above them in their style of living. They incidentally visit them at their homes, and, seeing articles of use, ornament and luxury, intelligent interest and strong desires are excited. Short hour days thus raise wages by powerfully tending to create a class who, by improved minds and hopes, will earn more as a body . . . pressed [on] by the most powerful stimulus, the desire for social elevation. . . .[4]

The testimony of the anonymous workman shows the other side of the coin that Siney was looking at when he talked of the degraded and brutalized condition of labor. The goal of these early labor reformers was not to preserve a traditional, segregated, patriarchal tradesman's culture, but to raise the status of the man who already worked for wages. As his biographer put it in one of a series of "American Labor Portraits" published in 1873 in the *Workingman's Advocate*, Siney was one of the "progressive school" who "sympathizes with all movements which work to the moral or social elevation of the workingman."[5]

To a workingman who had grown up in the cotton mills and brick-yards of Lancashire, the tools needed to bring about that elevation were already familiar. Some were a century or more old in practice, traditional modes, along with church membership, of bringing improved security and solidarity to the working-class community; some were relatively new out-growths of the social conflicts attending upon industrialization. The friendly society (or, in America, the benevolent association) was a well-established method of providing aid to the unemployed, the sick, and the widowed. Trade unions—as opposed to ad hoc, temporary strike organizations—with permanent officers, grievance committees, dues, membership cards, and constitutions and bylaws—had been part of the British labor world for a century or more (and the Combination Acts that prohibited them from 1799 to 1825 merely forced the unionists to combine secretly).[6] More recent was the entry of labor directly into the political process during the years of the Chartist movement, which, among other things, supported demands for universal manhood suffrage and election reform (the ballot box being the key to political power and labor legislation). And still more recent was the rise of utopian socialism, particularly of the Owenite per-suasion, with its successful dissemination of the idea of cooperative stores and cooperative mines and mills. All these British ideas for organizing and elevating the laboring class, along with the similarly intended evangelistic programs of the Primitive Methodist and Baptist churches, were alive in St. Clair when Siney arrived in 1863. And all of them seem to have been particularly salient in the years from 1868 to 1870 (just after the borough council had undertaken its own campaign to clean up and quiet down the town).

Perhaps the first idea to materialize in institutional form was the co-operative. In January 1867 the Union Cooperative Association of St. Clair was formally organized, with Edward Herbert (ten years later to be the superintendent of the Wadesville Shaft) as president and W. T. Richards (three years later a co-founder of the Scientific and Literary Association) as treasurer and store manager. The general store proved to be a great suc-cess. It started out with a capital of $4,400 from the sale of stock; at the end of the first year the capital from stock subscriptions had increased to over $11,000. Sales for the year were over $69,000 and there was a net profit of over $2,800, which was used to pay a 7 percent dividend on stock, 9 percent rebate on purchases by stockholders, and 4.5 percent on pur-chases by non-members.[7]

By the spring of 1870, Siney himself was caught up in a plan to start a cooperative mine. The proposal was originally made to Siney by members of the molders' union, which had set up cooperative foundries in Pennsylvania and New York, as a means of circumventing exploitive coal merchants. Siney pointed out the advantages of a producers' cooperative, which did away with middlemen, at a WBA convention in Mahanoy City, and the delegates voted to start such a colliery. Siney negotiated with the operator of two collieries on the Girard Estate, near Ashland, but the parties could not agree on the royalty terms, and the plan fell through. Again in 1875, Siney proposed a cooperative mine, this time to the third annual convention of the Miners' National Association in Cleveland, of which he was then president. The Miners' National Association was a country-wide federation of local unions, formed in 1873, which, its leaders hoped, would formulate the policies of labor, coordinate strike actions, and provide financial support to striking locals. Siney spoke in messianic terms of the great experiment of the cooperative movement, comparing it in importance to the invention of the printing press, the steam engine, and the telegraph.

> In cooperation I see the revolution of the entire social fabric in the generation to come . . . cooperation is a great democrat. . . . The wages system keeps us slaves, and to perpetuate it with our remedies, which only touch effects, is to make our children heirs to an inheritance men should be ashamed of. It is a blot on our age—the fact that we keep running in the same old ruts as did our forefathers. I claim we have wrongs we can right. I claim we have a higher end in life than simply to live and enjoy the fruit of others toil. I claim there are thousands in our ranks who are ripe to adopt the scheme of the cooperative movement and look to this body to make the start.[8]

At the instruction of the convention, a committee on cooperation appointed Siney and Andrew Roy, an eminent mining engineer from Scotland, to make an adventurous month-long journey to Tennessee to inspect cheap coal lands. Roy, a self-educated miner, had emulated Siney in Ohio, preparing the first mine-safety bill for that state, and accepting appointment as the first mining inspector. After interviewing colliery operators, visiting with the governor, and personally examining possible sites for the venture, Siney and Roy prepared a report for the committee. It was an elaborate proposal for a cooperative settlement on a site with timber and agricultural land to supplement income from coal in slack times. Again he was somewhat grandiose in his plans, proposing to raise $5 apiece from each of the 4,000 members of the Miners' National Association—enough to purchase 50,000 acres, start the settlement, and attract additional capital for an enterprise nearly as large as that of the Philadelphia and Reading Coal and Iron Company in Schuylkill. He spoke of "the advantage of owning in our own right a portion of God's footstool" and touted the plan as the way out of labor's "present troubles." He pointed out that there would be no manager like Gowen with a $30,000 salary nor officers "accustomed to the driving of fast horses and faster women." To Siney, the plan was a moral and ritual duty:

> Should we let this opportunity pass we ought to cease finding fault with men who do not pay us that which we think we are entitled to receive for labor we perform.[9]

But the appeal was futile. While Siney was soliciting subscriptions, the Miners' National Association was crumbling, its treasury empty and its members out of work. And so the plan for the cooperative mining colony in Tennessee had to be abandoned. Later, in 1876, Siney fielded another cooperative scheme, this one to raise goats—1,000 goats to each member, to be cared for by imported Mexican goatherds—in the hills of western Texas. But this venture too came to naught.

Although his dreams of leading a cooperative revolution never came to anything, Siney was signally successful, at least for a time, in organizing miners' unions, and his work served as an inspiration and a guide for other unions that followed. From the very beginning Siney believed in large labor unions. In language reminiscent of the *Communist Manifesto,* he asserted, in a letter to the *Miners' Journal* in December 1868, "The object of the Workingmen's Benevolent Association is to unite in one band of brotherhood all who earn their bread by hard toil—more especially the miners and laborers of Pennsylvania."

Siney had little sympathy for the helter-skelter methods used in many of the labor actions in the coal fields, where the absence of an overall organization meant either that the workers in each colliery or district went out on their own, or that the strike spread like a wave, being pushed along by bands of armed men threatening to burn and maim and kill their fellow workers if they did not turn out. Siney believed in large, centralized, well-disciplined unions that could set policy for an entire industry, call a strike in advance to take effect simultaneously throughout the industry, and engage in collective bargaining with the representatives of capital. Thus he sought to organize, and served as presiding officer of, successively larger unions: the Workingmen's Benevolent Association of St. Clair; the Workingmen's Benevolent Association of Schuylkill County; the Miners' and Laborers' Benevolent Association (for the entire anthracite region); and the Miners' National Association. Such unions would transcend local and some ethnic jealousies (Siney himself opposed admission of blacks into the national union) and would stand firm against attempts by the capitalists to split the ranks of labor. Siney also believed that in order to obtain general public support, the union movement must divest itself of the image presented by the "eight-hour raiders." Some in Schuylkill from the first called the members of the WBA "Molly Maguires" and "Buckshots." But Siney, even in his first letter to the *Miners' Journal* in December 1868, had been emphatic in his denunciation of labor violence:

> By the rules of the association all acts of violence are strictly forbidden, and any member found guilty of such will not only be expelled from the association, but from the county also, and we hope soon to say, from the six anthracite counties, for where our laws go they will carry with them strict adherence to social law and order.[10]

Instead of setting fire to the breaker, or beating up the superintendent, miners who felt they had been treated unfairly were urged to tell their stories to the colliery's grievance committee. This position not only encouraged the churchgoing, law-abiding miner to join the WBA without fear of connecting himself to a gang of arsonists and assassins, but also reassured operators and property owners that their investments were safe with the union itself policing the land. Some months later, the *Miners' Journal,* which had all along encouraged Siney by printing his letters, editorially came out in favor of his union, despite its success in forcing up wages. "We urge," it said, "all the working men to join the Workingmen's Benevolent Association throughout the region."[11]

Siney was, however, very cautious about the strike as a method for bringing capital to terms. The WBA struck successfully several times in its early years over wages, hours, and working conditions. But strikes, if prolonged, could be ruinous and frightening experiences for the miners and their families, and Siney opposed striking except as a last resort. He preferred negotiation, collective bargaining, between committees representing the union and the operators, leading to signed, industry-wide agreements. And if negotiations proved to be fruitless, he believed that binding arbitration by an impartial third party, acceptable to both sides, was a better solution than the strike, even if it meant an unpalatable compromise. Arbitration, indeed, was a "cardinal principle" with Siney. And even if neither negotiation nor arbitration could resolve the confrontation, a strike still should not be called unless market conditions were favorable and the union strike fund was adequate to support the miners during a long suspension. A failed strike was more damaging than accepting "unacceptable" terms because it threatened the union itself. Siney's public letters commonly contained exhortations to "keep our columns unbroken," to retreat if necessary and store up "ammunition" for the next engagement, to maintain a "solid phalanx," to "save the organization" even if to do so caused Siney "to be branded with infamy."[12]

These views on union strategy made Siney, despite his passionate speeches, more a negotiator and an administrator than a demagogue. With a $1,500 union income, well dressed, sporting a goatee, he sat in meeting after meeting with the great and near-great of Pennsylvania's industrial and political world, and tried earnestly to understand the financial problems and political schemes of his union's capitalist oppressors. But much of his effort had to be expended in transforming an unruly mob of miners into an organization with an effective central administration. Siney and his lieutenants patiently visited towns and patches all over the county, explaining and persuading suspicious miners to his point of view. Joseph Patterson, who first met Siney on such a mission, described how the union educated its members:

> Its officers and lecturers went about the region discussing the past and present conditions and the future prospects of the anthracite coal trade, and the causes affecting it. They lectured on the past and present condition of labor in Europe and in the United States, contrasting the two, and endeavoring to account for the difference. They discussed legislation affecting labor interests, not only as regards the miners, but other callings as well. They were usually men of more than ordinary intelligence, and while self-educated mostly, they were men of wide observation, reading and experience. Quite a number of them, although denounced at one time as ignorant demagogues, rose later on to positions of great responsibility, which positions are the usual and ordinary objects of the ambitions of mining men, and held such positions successfully for several decades.[13]

A second organizational problem was discipline. An effective union could not put up with impromptu strikes and violence; not only did they give the miners a bad press, they made collective bargaining impossible.

Operators would not make an agreement with a union that could not guarantee compliance by the men. Miners guilty of violent acts were officially expelled from the union, and probably the instigators of unauthorized strikes were dropped as well. According to Patterson, new miners were told that they "had to join the Union." But the principal disciplinary problem was the control of "blacklegs"—strikebreakers—who might be either newly imported hands or, in the more difficult cases, union members desperate to make money to feed their families. The official position of the union was that no force could be used against them. Joseph Patterson described the moral pressure that was employed in its stead:

> How did we treat blacklegs? Well, during a long stoppage perhaps one percent of the men would break away from their fellows. Of course, we had feeling against them. We had absolutely no love for them. They were ostracised. We would not talk to them socially. If we met in a tavern we would not drink with them. When the strike was over we refused to go to work until they were discharged. Then they had to come and make their peace with the Union, and the Union fined them heavily. Their life for a considerable time thereafter was certainly not a happy one. They were a despised lot, and deservedly so from the stand point of the stalwart miner. Those whose interests their defection served did not admire them.[14]

No doubt there were occasions when blacklegs were beaten, their houses fired on, and death threats issued. But the union's legal position in the matter of punishing blacklegs was awkward. Unions had been legalized in Pennsylvania by the Act of May 8th, 1869, and three years later a second act provided that a union-led strike was not considered a criminal conspiracy, provided, however, that union members did not "hinder persons who desire to work for their employers from doing so, or other persons from being employed as laborers."[15] This law prohibited the union from disciplining its own members for strikebreaking, let alone outsiders, and the problem was made worse by the ambiguity of the term "hinder." Siney himself was later prosecuted under the act.

Siney was realistic about power and politics, however, and realized that the size of an organization in itself helped to protect it from the application of unjust laws. His little Workingmen's Benevolent Association of St. Clair, first chartered in 1868, had within a couple of years grown into the Miners' and Laborers' Benevolent Association of Schuylkill County, with 20,000 members registered in twenty-two districts, administered by a twenty-two-member executive board with Siney as president. But Siney wanted more. He was, in the opinion of the anonymous author of his 1873 "Labor Portrait," "one of the few men who believe in general organization." He was "always impressed with the necessity of national organization" and he never lost an opportunity to "agitate the question" of a national union of miners.[16] At the meeting of the National Labor Congress in Cleveland, Ohio, in 1873, he argued the case so effectively that when in October 1873 the Miners' National Association was organized, Siney was elected president. Six months later, he resigned the presidency of the M&LBA of Schuylkill County and moved to his new offices in Cleveland.

The MNA was a true industrial union, organizing all colliery workers above and below ground, and also all workers in gold, silver, lead, copper, and other mines—"all men who are employed in and around the mines of the United States." It would not compete with other unions, such as the M&LBA, but would rather serve as a protective umbrella over them, using the dues it assessed from the local members as a national strike fund. But to do this effectively, Siney realized, required planning. The MNA had to have the right to approve or prohibit local strikes and to stagger their schedule so as not to exhaust the fund in one catastrophic general miners' strike. Siney never really had an opportunity to develop his theories on the national industrial union, however, because the MNA collapsed, its treasury depleted, in 1876.

Siney's third strategy for securing social justice to the workingman was political action. As we have seen, the miners' lobby in Harrisburg was effective to some degree in persuading the legislature to pass mine safety legislation in 1869 and 1870 and probably helped to pass other laws favorable to labor, including the act legitimizing unions in 1869 and the Miners' Hospital bill later in the '70's. But the miners' lobby would obviously be more effective if the workers could elect their own senators and representatives to the legislature in state capitals and in Washington, rather than depend on the good will of two political parties already beholden to large corporations and wealthy capitalists. To bring about such a revolutionary change in the composition of legislative bodies required the formation of a new political party for workingmen.

Siney may not have known that this gambit had been tried at least once before in America, in the 1830's, when the Workingman's Party, inspired by the rhetoric of Thomas Paine, Fanny Wright, Robert Owen, and other utopian anti-clericals and socialists, fielded candidates in Philadelphia and New York. But this party had withered in the wake of the financial panic of 1837. Now a number of reform parties were springing up, most of them inspired less by the utopian socialist tradition than by the success of practical unions in raising the political consciousness of working people, not only in industry but also (by the Grange) in agriculture.

Siney's first venture in politics occurred in 1870, when he attended the fifth annual meeting of the late William H. Sylvis' National Labor Union as a delegate from Pennsylvania. Originally a free-trade Democrat and friend of Democratic Senator Decatur Nice, Siney was apparently converted to a more radical political stance at this convention.[17] He supported the new president, Richard Trevellick, in his call to the convention to take up Sylvis' program for direct political action by labor and became a member of a committee that formulated the principles of a new political party, the Labor Reform Party. Although internal squabbles were destroying the National Labor Union, the new party took root in various localities, including Schuylkill County. There in 1871 Siney and C. Ben Johnson, the radical new editor of the M&LBA's official organ, the *Anthracite Monitor,* organized the Schuylkill branch of the Labor Reform Party, with Siney as president. The party fielded candidates for the state legislature in the fall election, and, although none of them won, the election returns were encouraging. In 1872, the Labor Reformers chose to nominate Republican candidates. Next year, they nominated their own slate at a local convention that included four delegates from St. Clair: German-born John Weber, a schoolteacher who had been endorsed for election to a local office by the *Miners' Journal* the year before; William J. McCarthy, an Irish hotel keeper; Thomas Behan, an Irish miner, M&LBA member, and Siney's father-in-law; and Thomas Russell, secretary of the M&LBA local, and the notorious member of the Ancient Order of Hibernians who was to murder his stepfather, Martin Nash, the following year.[18] In 1872, Siney presided over the National Labor Reform convention that nominated candidates for President and Vice-President. The platform adopted by the convention included assurances that "productive capital" and labor could easily become friends if they united against the common enemy, usury, and a strong endorsement of the protective tariff, which endeared Labor Reformers to Republicans and the *Miners' Journal*. There was the usual plea to liberate the laboring masses from the chains of slavery to the monopoly of wealth by such measures as the issuance of a national "greenback" paper currency, restrictions on the importation of "cheap Chinese labor," cessation of the harsh federal policy toward the South, a one-term Presidency, breaking up monopolies, enforcing laws requiring stricter accountability by public officials, and increased government regulation of railroads. They testified to their solidarity with the farmers' Granges and, in a curious recognition of the class difference between "laborers" and "mechanics or artisans," declared that the Labor Reform principles should be attractive to them too: "our cause . . . is their cause."[19]

Siney spent most of his time in 1874 and 1875 away from St. Clair, attending to the affairs of the MNA, but on his return to Schuylkill in 1876 after the collapse of both the WBA and the MNA, he became involved in the affairs of a successor to the Labor Reform Party, the Independent Party, also known as the Greenback Labor Party. Siney was elected as the first chairman of the local party, which was dominated by old Labor Reformers. In Schuylkill, Greenback Labor clubs were formed in all the towns, including St. Clair, and the party gained a powerful spokesman when former Democrat Francis W. Hughes joined along with his nephew Francis P. Dewees. From 1876 to 1878, when he fell ill, Siney devoted much of his time to speechmaking and committee work for the Greenback Labor Party.

The third-party movement in its various transformations, with its demands for an inflationist paper currency, anti-monopoly legislation, and recognition of the rights of labor, gave Siney some strange bedfellows. Not only was he personally associated with Hughes; Henry Carey and Henry Carey Baird also joined in the creation of the Independent Party that followed the disintegration of the Labor Reform organization, and Carey's ally in Congress, protectionist William D. "Pig Iron" Kelly, became an outspoken supporter. Even Simon Cameron betrayed a sympathy for Greenbacks. And from the other side of the political fence, Siney was no doubt influenced by many of the prominent labor leaders whom he met, including William Sylvis, the left-wing leader of the Iron Molders' International Union, who had formed a local at Tamaqua in 1864 and had made many visits to Pottsville, and Terence Powderly, the benevolent head of the Knights of Labor, who favored worker cooperative ownership of mines and mills. Back in Schuylkill County, one of his "most confidential friends," according to Siney's biography in the *United Mine Workers Journal*, was fellow Irishman John Holmes, the St. Clair engineer and sometime coal operator. Another adviser, whom Siney supported against bitter criticism from more conservative laboring men, was Ben Johnson, editor of the *Anthracite Monitor*. Johnson was apparently something of a communist and allegedly used the pages of his paper to advocate the principles of the First International. To judge from his joining in a committee report advocating the nationalization of the coal trade, Siney must be considered as more than a simple populist. But his consistent advocacy of law and order and of conventional politics as the medium for change would separate him from the more militant advocates of class warfare, and from 1871 on, the *Anthracite Monitor* virtually ignored Siney. But in this era, political positions on the issue of communism had not hardened anyway. Writing in the *Irish World,* Henry Carey's literary heir, his nephew Henry Carey Baird, wrote somewhat sympathetically about the left in a little article published in 1878. A dedicated worker in the Greenback movement himself, he, like the industrial worker and the communist, feared finance capitalism: "the great possessor of money has become the real autocrat, the potent tyrant of our age."[20]

Some years later, a novel was published, loosely based on the life of John Siney, entitled *The White Slaves of Monopolies; or, John Fitzpatrick, the Miner, Soldier and Workingman's Friend.* No author's name is to be found on the title page, but the familiarity of the writer with the details of the coal trade suggests a Schuylkill County authorship. The political stance of the work—anti-monopoly, anti-corruption, anti-immigration—accords well with the view of Francis P. Dewees, and Dewees was already something of a popular writer, having published his sensational *The Molly Maguires* in 1877, right after the trials in which his uncle served as a prosecuting attorney. Perhaps Dewees was the author of *Fitzpatrick.* In any case, the work provides thinly fictionalized accounts of what the writer saw as the plots of Gowen ("Col. Thomas") and the Reading ("the Excelsior Railroad Company") to monopolize the Schuylkill coal trade; of the crooked politicians ("Hon. Obeisant Crafty") who did Thomas's bidding in Harrisburg; and of the brave union organizer and anti-monopolist John Fitzpatrick. The account of Fitzpatrick (i.e., Siney) lobbying for the first ventilation act in 1869 reveals how an observer outside the union saw Siney's character and policy:

> John was deputed on a mission from colliery to colliery, circulating petitions to the legislature setting forth the dangerous manner in which the coal operators conducted their mines. He again traversed the anthracite region, gaining signatures and preparing the way for a general organization of the miners and laborers into a Benevolent Union; one that would make their power felt throughout that region; a union that would discipline the miners and laborers, suppress the tendency to lawlessness, divest its members of National prejudices, and assimilate under an intelligent and well-managed organization the whole working force of not only the coal regions of Pennsylvania, but the wage workers connected with the mining of coal in the United States. This was no easy task, but all the energy and talent he possessed were

thrown into the work. Funds were raised, and a regular bureau of correspondence was carried on with laboring men and miners and wage workers in all sections of the State. Judicial officers, prominent lawyers, and politicians were written to, and nothing left undone which the limited funds at their command could suggest to bring the subject of the health and safety of the miners before the Legislature. . . .

He could not be well excelled as an organizer—methodical, systematic, intelligent, conservative, persuasive, and logical in his speeches; honest and upright in his deportment. While he was hated by the companies, he commanded their respect. He was not only opposed by the operators or companies, but some of the men thought he did not advocate sufficient force, but relied too much upon law and order.[21]

The sketch goes on to the Avondale disaster, Fitzpatrick's speech, and the passage of the second mine safety law.

What is particularly interesting in the *Fitzpatrick* novel is the attention paid to the success of the hero—a partial success, to be sure—in introducing union discipline to unruly miners. The same point was made by both defense and prosecution counsel during the Molly trials; and it was expressed very forcibly in 1873 in the first publication of the Bureau of Statistics of Labor. In his history and evaluation of the WBA, Commissioner Bigham quoted a letter from a miner responding to a questionnaire issued by the bureau. The writer of the letter was a highly literate miner living in a four-room company shack, with no garden or outhouse, on the land of the Philadelphia and Reading Coal and Iron Company. He advocated shorter working hours because they promoted health, moral as well as physical, and gave "time and courage to seek mental culture, and thus elevate the man." And his evaluation of Siney's union suggests that, however successful the union might be in achieving economic and political goals, it had already introduced a new dimension to working-class culture in the coal regions:

I have have [*sic*] had four years' experience with "trade unions," as a member of the Miners' Union of Schuylkill County. I regard it as an excellent institution. Its effect has been to create harmony and unity among the workmen. Their frequent meetings, debates, and regular order of business, develops rapidly the reasoning powers of the order and intelligent regard for their own and the rights of others. Its beneficial features secure its membership against want when in misfortune, and imbue them with a hopefulness that only the sense of mutual helpfulness can give. . . . The vices of the old system with us, that may be said to have been almost entirely eradicated by the union, may be summed up thus:

1st. A lack of sympathy with each other, that often led to ruinious competitions, one man underbidding the other for his work, leading to passionate rivalries and bitter revenges. These would extend from individuals to classes of nationalities, one class always arrayed against another and, through their mutual jealousies going into conflicts and strikes without just cause, making demands not found in reason, and producing an idle and demoralized condition among workmen.

2nd. Strikes during the years preceding our organization were often without sufficient cause, always demoralizing, and seldom of advantage to either employer or employed. Often trivial grievances on the one side and the other would result in strikes, differences that but for the bad blood existing, should and might have been settled by calm and friendly discussion between the parties. Except in few instances, the strikes that have occurred since our organization have not been so much for advanced wages as for the defense of some principle of the Union, involving in the issue its right to exist at all. The strike is held to be now the remedy to be used only as a last resort.

Without citing statistics, the commissioner went on to say that "the general expression" of all the returns on this subject was "substantially" the same.[22]

As we shall see, the union founded by Siney did not survive beyond 1875, when it was broken in the Long Strike. But Siney's most important legacy was not the particular accomplishments of the WBA and the M&LBA but the idea of the large industrial union and the development of a higher consciousness of class, of pan-ethnic solidarity, and of norms of union discipline that served as the basis for more enduring organizations, culminating in the United Mine Workers, in subsequent decades. The State called Anthracite required Siney's kind of union organization.

FRANKLIN B. GOWEN AND THE NEW INDUSTRIAL ORDER

Siney's counterpart on the side of capital was Franklin Benjamin Gowen, former district attorney, attorney for the railroad, and, finally, president of the Philadelphia and Reading Railroad and policy maker for its subsidiary, the Philadelphia and Reading Coal and Iron Company. Gowen was initially important because the Reading, with its control not only of the main trunk railroad from Port Carbon to Philadelphia but also of the parallel canal of the Schuylkill Navigation and of the feeder rail line that ran through St. Clair, completely monopolized access to market of all St. Clair coal. But after 1871 and 1872, when his coal-and-iron company bought up the mineral rights to all the land in and around the borough (and most of the rest of Schuylkill County as well), he appeared to many to be, as a later president of the Reading Company put it, "pretty much of a dictator."[1] He was able to open or close the St. Clair collieries, to raise or lower transportation charges, and (in company-operated mines) to determine the rates that the men were paid. How Gowen exercised this power over St. Clair and other coal towns in Schuylkill was determined by a social philosophy that some called ruthless and others realistic.

Gowen was very much a product of Schuylkill County, where he had experienced—perhaps "endured" would be a better word—the ups and downs of the coal trade in his early twenties. His father, a successful Philadelphia merchant prominent in Democratic politics, had apprenticed him, after an excellent education at a fine boys' academy in Lititz, to a Lancaster coal dealer. When Gowen was only nineteen, his employer sent him up the Susquehanna to Shamokin to manage an iron furnace. After several years at the Shamokin furnace, Gowen married and, with his savings, entered into a partnership with a coal operator in Pottsville. They leased the East and West Mount Laffee collieries on January 1, 1858, and Gowen's younger brother George (later the Colonel Gowen killed in the Civil War) came up from Lititz to keep the company books. The Gowens lived on fashionable Mahantango Street and young Frank became one of the organizers of the Pottsville Literary Society, reciting Poe's "Raven" at the first meeting and at the second lecturing on "The Triumphs of Genius." In 1859 he was elected president.

But this happy time ended suddenly with an explosion and fire at the East Mount Laffee Colliery. The colliery had to be flooded, then pumped out, and by the spring of 1859 the partners were running out of cash. In September another gas explosion, which set fire to a keg of powder, killed four men and burned three more.[2] Gowen advertised for new partners, but no one wanted to invest money in the venture and in October the sheriff sold the colliery to D. P. Brown to satisfy the creditors who had brought $20,000 in judgments against Gowen in county court. Nothing daunted, he read law for a year, was admitted to the bar in 1860, and immediately entered the lists as a Democratic campaign speechmaker and Fourth of July orator. In 1862 he was elected district attorney, but his private law practice was coming along so successfully that he resigned in 1864 after a singularly inactive term of office during which, among other things, the unsolved murder occurred for which he would help to prosecute John Kehoe fourteen years later. He was by this time earning about $8,000 per year, the second-highest-paid lawyer in the county, and was well able to pay for a substitute to avoid the draft. In 1865 he was retained by the Philadelphia and Reading Railroad as its counsel in

Franklin Benjamin Gowen (1836–1889)

Pottsville, his income jumped above $13,000, and the following year it reached $18,000. In 1867 he was invited to head the Reading Company's legal department and the family moved to Philadelphia. In 1869 he replaced the ailing president, Charles E. Smith, as acting president, and in January 1870, at the age of thirty-three, Franklin B. Gowen was elected president in his own right of the Philadelphia and Reading Railroad.[3]

Gowen became associated with the Reading Company at precisely the time when across the anthracite region there moved a wave of sentiment in favor of increased social orderliness with rules enforced by a central authority. It is necessary to know something about this moral context in order to understand Gowen's administrative philosophy.

In St. Clair, we may recall the spate of clean-up and tighten-up ordinances passed by the middle-class borough council in 1867, when H. B. Sessinger, the superintendent of the St. Clair Shaft and Slope collieries, was council president. About the same time, the town's GAR post, under the leadership of schoolteacher Clay Evans, was promoting patriotic observances, like the expanded Fourth of July parade and the Soldiers' Monument. The state legislature authorized the Coal and Iron Police and special courts for Schuylkill County. John Siney was impressing on WBA members the imperative need for discipline, self-restraint, and non-violent tactics in prolonged labor disputes. And soon the greatest law-and-order drama of them all, the investigation, trial, and hanging of the Molly Maguires, would culminate a decade of intense public concern with the need for unity and discipline.

And the coal trade itself needed unity and discipline. Observers had as early as 1858 been urging that the chaotic conditions brought about by the pattern of under-capitalized small operators be replaced by planned regional development under the control of large corporations. In an address to the Pottsville Scientific Association on June 19, 1858 (printed in the *Miners' Journal* a couple of weeks later), P. W. Sheafer pointed out that future mining in the Pottsville Basin would have to employ the deep-shaft method exemplified by the Carey shaft at St. Clair. In Schuylkill the cost of sinking a 600-foot shaft, at a rate of $75 per linear foot, was $45,000; and he pointed out that in Great Britain the successful deep-shaft mines required a starting capital of up to half a million dollars. Few small operators could raise this kind of money. Therefore he suggested for Schuylkill a policy of confederation to raise capital for the larger, well-equipped, efficient deep-shaft mines needed to exploit the deeply buried white-ash coals once the easily reached superficial beds were exhausted:

> It is doubtless unfavorable to the profitable working of our coal beds that there is frequently both a want of capital and of the proper concentration of that which exists. Certainly no method of mining coal can be less economical than to fit out a number of separate operations upon comparatively small estates, with all the necessary engines and other improvements, instead of selecting a suitable point from which the coal of several adjacent tracts could be worked by one large operative, equipped in the best manner. This policy can only be carried out effectually by the *union of the proprietors of adjacent tracts*. Indeed, the pursuit of the coal below the water level, requiring increased capital, has already tended to the concentration of the business of mining in fewer hands, and as the necessity of shafting to the lower coals becomes more apparent, the discussion, among those interested, of an enlightened system of harmonious action is more and more frequent.[4]

And again in a pamphlet on the *Geology of Schuylkill County*, published about 1869, he suggested that in order to stop the wastage of approximately two-thirds of the coal in the ground, the first measure should be to consolidate land ownership and colliery operation and end the "butty" system:

First.—The owning of the land by the operators would make them careful to mine all the coals. As tenants for a limited term of years, their object is merely to take out that coal, and in such a manner as will cost them little, and bring them much.

Another measure to ensure that high degree of interest and discipline needed to "mine all the coals," even in leased collieries, should be a revised type of lease that gave the *owner* supervision of "the methods of mining, ventilation and drainage," the length of breasts, and other technical details. Other suggestions called for "larger collieries, and fewer of them, with perfected machinery," and, finally, "more capital," which would make it possible

> to open the mines for extensive and exhaustive working, by driving the gangways to the extreme ends of the territory, and then mining towards the outlet, so as to obviate the necessity of retracing our steps and robbing the pillars.[5]

Sheafer later became the manager of all the mines of the Philadelphia and Reading Coal and Iron Company and of those on the Girard Estate.

The value of stricter social control was also celebrated by an old Pottsville operator, Charles Miesse, in his semi-autobiographical book, *Points on Coal and the Coal Business* (1877). Reflecting on coal towns he had known, he took a position in favor of extreme social control:

> Sometimes the government of the mining village partakes of the monarchial system or that of the republican. Where it is entirely governed by the owners, the former is the case; and when it is a free village left to drift into a borough government by council, the latter is the form. There is always more order and quiet, social, and moral interest about it, when controlled by the owner or manager; and more of the abandonment to freedom, and riot, or go-as-you-please about it, when left to govern itself. This fact is indeed suggestive; it brings down to a small scale that which one would suppose ought to follow from the systems in the government of nations. Much as we love our country, even to shed our own life's blood for its maintenance against the monarchial system, we are forced to admit that a mining village governed by an absolute one-man power partakes of more genuine law and order than that governed by the free system.

And he later stated succinctly:

> The government of a mining village, in the hands of one-man
> power, displays a beautiful example of a controlled, and well gov-
> erned people. Drunkenness and disorder are scarcely known. Pi-
> ety and morality, the rule of life, are adopted, and obeyed with
> cheerfulness.[6]

In a nation that had just suffered a prolonged and cruel war, preceded
by long and acrimonious disputes over such issues as states' rights, nul-
lification, and the powers of the federal government, a pervasive dread of
disorder and a striving for centralization and social control might not be
unexpected. But, while such sentiments may have contributed to the
movement, the roots of the ethos of social control emerge from deeper
ground—from a sense that the continued progress of the Industrial Revolution, the advance of science, the constant raising of the standard of
living, required more discipline than had been needed in the pre-industrial
age. Such a view was certainly being communicated to the public-school
students of St. Clair. Long before the war, the coal districts of Schuylkill
County (in contrast to farming areas) were enthusiastic supporters of educational institutions, public and private, and eagerly adopted the public-
school system provided by the state laws of 1836 and 1854. What was
communicated, in the way of values, in these schools? Although Ruth
Elson in her survey of the moral content of nineteenth-century schoolbooks notes the almost universal presence of national military and political
heroes, headed by George Washington, she emphasizes the distinction
between the hero and the great man (Washington was a hero because he
was brave and the father of his country; Franklin was only a great man
because he was merely wise and successful).[7] But the presentation of the
hero as an object of emulation was restrained in the primers for pre-
pubertal readers; the moral message conveyed in the primers emphasized,
above all, obedience.

Bannan's New Columbian Primer, published in the 1830's in Pottsville
and in Philadelphia by Lippincott, drenched the young reader in praises of
docility. The first part of the book consisted of alphabetical lessons: a page
with a letter, a syllable beginning with the letter, a picture of an animal or
person designated by a word beginning with that letter, and then a moral
lesson. Thus, Lion: "The lion is the noblest of all beasts, and can be tamed
like a cat or dog." Horse: "The horse is a useful animal, and on account of
his docility is loved and petted by his master." Naughty Boy: "James was
a naughty boy, and, like all disobedient children, was punished for break-

ing the looking glass with his ball." "William and Lucy were good children, and their mamma praised them for their industry. Lucy would sit and sew, while William watered the flowers." Following the alphabetical section came pages of moral aphorisms, aimed perhaps at more advanced readers, stating one after the other such principles as "true merit is always modest," "virtue is its own reward," "honesty is the best policy," "good and bad habits formed in youth commonly go with us through life. . . ."

Little Harry's Indestructible Reading Book, printed in Philadelphia on indestructible linen cloth in 1857, was a little bit more literate, but conveyed the same moral lesson. A star figure was Harry himself. Blind Harry, struck by lightning at sea, is "patient and does not complain, but gives thanks to his Father in Heaven for his many blessings. . . . We should learn of him to be patient, and to submit to the will of God in all things. This is true wisdom." The picture caption notes ambiguously: "Poor Blind Harry is all alone."[8]

Blind obedience as a martial virtue was even celebrated in an address on "Culture of the Moral and Intellectual Faculties of Man" on the occasion of the opening of the Arcadian Institute at Orwigsburg in 1854 (published by Bannan). The keynote speaker said, among other things, that the value of history was to enable us to see ourselves as

> . . . soldiers in the ranks, to whom our great Captain has not revealed the plan of battle . . . as the vast army, enveloped in mystery, moves forward, each soldier knows that he is only to *obey* orders, while the design, yea even the *success*, of the battle is concealed from his knowledge.[9]

It would seem, then, that training in heroism was deferred until the secondary grades, perhaps at puberty, by which time the young reader had already been well instructed in the necessity of discipline and obedience to the will of those in legitimate authority. (This separation must, in effect, have left the working-class children with training in docility but not in heroism, if most working-class children left school after the primary grades.) But speakers at the annual teachers' institutes clearly affirmed the importance of inculcating aspirations for giving not merely faithful but distinguished service to the community, in the advanced grades. Thus Miss Sanford on the purpose of teaching history: "Another object in teaching history is to inspire a love for a noble life." And later, again on the goals of teaching: to inculcate "Love of Success. By this we are led to contend for glory."[10]

In the spring of 1858, on the occasion of the public examination of the pupils of the No. 1 school in St. Clair, under the care of Theodore R. Johnson, in Reading, Writing, Arithmetic, Orthography, Grammar, Composition, Geography, and Natural Philosophy, Mr. Johnson delivered a commencement address later published by the *Miners' Journal*. In it he drew his pupils' attention to the inspiring image of the young scientist studying alone in his quiet room, soon to discover "a long-hidden mystery of nature," the revelation of which would be "productive of much benefit." What factors would operate to prevent the pupils of St. Clair from achieving similar fame and glory as benefactors of mankind? Sickness, yes— parental indifference, yes—but the main obstacle was "obstinacy and disobedience." Mr. Johnson went on to condemn disobedience in the most general terms as the "MONSTER" that not only hurt the cause of education but was the cause of "strife and contention" in families, and, indeed, was in general "the bane of society." He complained of the rowdies on the corner, and pitied the criminal in his cell, and sorrowed over the "repentant daughters of vice," all poisoned by the venom of disobedience. Indeed, disobedience was a threat to the country itself, for "a more terrible and dangerous foe to the great cause of *liberty* could not exist." And he went on to compare the laws of man to the laws of nature:

> *Be obedient*. One of the first laws of God is obedience. The planets and all the heavenly bodies obey the laws which regulate them in their motions around their respective centres. The fruit trees and all vegetables, *obey* the voice of nature, and put forth their leaves and blossom at her bidding, and yield their abundance to man. . . .
>
> In fact look around, above, or beneath you; or even wherever you may direct your thoughts, and you will find that all things are governed by laws which they must obey. Then, children, why should you not obey the laws of your parents and teachers; you who were created in the image of God, and have the power to discriminate between right and wrong? *Why,* I ask again, should you be allowed to run lawlessly and without restraint, setting at defiance all rules or laws that should regulate your conduct, brewing discord and strife wherever you are, and destroying the harmony and goodwill, which should exist in your presence? No reason can be assigned. If your parents, your teachers, your friends, and everything around you, obey laws, and those same laws secure to you all the blessings that you enjoy then your good sense ought to teach you to obey; if not, you ought to be taught to obey; and if you will not learn, then you *must feel the penalty of disobedience, and be forced to obey*.[11]

This impassioned rhetoric conveys more than mere authoritarianism in a zealous, evangelical Christian teacher. There is a sense of unease about the state of society. The issue is not the salvation of the disobedient child's soul from everlasting hellfire and damnation; it is rather that a higher level of civic discipline is needed, on the street, in the school, in the home, and in the work place. As Carey said, the social system has its own inherent laws, as natural as those of physics and chemistry, and obedience to them is necessary to make the system work.

Thus it was in a coal trade complaining about the chaos of small collieries, and in a coal region where many people sensed a need for greater social control by central authority, that Franklin B. Gowen developed his ideas about how to save the anthracite industry. In no one document are these thoughts written down; they must be inferred from practical business decisions, persuasive speeches, and observations recorded by friends and enemies.

So let us consider the viewpoint of one of the great architects of industrial capitalism in nineteenth-century America. Gowen presided, for about fifteen years, over what was at the time one of the largest concentrations of men and machinery in the country, and he was guided in his operation of that enterprise, the conglomerate of corporations and allied businesses that clustered about the Reading Railroad, by two cardinal principles. One of these was faith in technological progress; the other, a belief in size. The former, no doubt growing out of his early experience in operating an ironworks and a colliery, led him to insist on technological experiment and improvement on the railroad and in the mine. He was an early member of the American Institute of Mining Engineers. In his obituary, his fellow engineer and colliery operator Eckley B. Coxe praised his employment of scientists and engineers, who developed, among other things, a device for reducing anthracite waste by burning coal dust. Gowen had it installed in the road's locomotives. Coxe paid particular tribute to the importance Gowen placed on research and development:

> Mr. Gowen was thoroughly convinced of the value of scientific training, and in hearty sympathy with every endeavor to elevate the professional standard of engineers. This was the secret of his interest in the Institute, which he held to be an effective agency in that direction. As an employer of engineers, he selected men worthy of confidence, and then trusted and supported them loyally. The testimony of all who ever served under him, will be found unanimous in this respect, and, on the other hand, the record made by the scientific employees of the Reading Coal and

Iron Company, proves that the confidence of its head was not misplaced or abused.[12]

But the most spectacular of Gowen's adventures in technological development was the gigantic mine that he sank near St. Clair in the 1870's. The twin shafts of this colliery—to be described in more detail later in this chapter—were proclaimed in his annual report of 1874 to the stockholders of the Philadelphia and Reading Railroad to be the entrance to untold wealth. He explained its significance in almost utopian language:

> The extent of territory tributary to these shafts is so great that there can be but little doubt that at least one hundred millions of tons in the several veins already opened can be worked through them, and that for almost an indefinite period the proposed colliery will become one of the most productive known. When it is considered that the deposits of coal thus opened and proved extend throughout the entire length of the southern coal-field principally underlying lands bought at exceedingly low prices, and heretofore considered by many as comparatively valueless, and which are within one hundred miles of tidewater at Philadelphia, the importance of the developments made by the shafts cannot be over-estimated.[13]

But most of Gowen's thinking was directed to the problems of law and order, of social justice, of state and national policy created by the new world of large, competitive transportation and energy corporations in which the Reading was playing an important role. Gowen was not, personally, a wealthy tycoon, and when he retired in 1886 he had amassed only a modest fortune of half a million dollars, far less than many of his contemporaries. As he confided to Francis Dewees of Pottsville, "I never was very fond of money," and there is no reason to doubt his word, when one considers the fortunes being amassed by the Morgans, the Vanderbilts, and the Rockefellers of his day.[14] To the contrary, he seems to have been a man satisfied to live on a salary and maintain a not-at-all spectacular way of life with his family in the quiet residential neighborhood of Mount Airy. His hobbies were not gambling or race horses, but reading, attending the theater, translating German poetry, and composing limericks. He was a Democrat in politics and a close friend of the Democratic politicians of Schuylkill County, including Lin Bartholomew and Francis W. Hughes. As a Democratic delegate to the state constitutional convention in 1873, he was conventionally conservative, opposing the prohibition of alcohol, female suffrage, and the secret ballot.

But on the subject of the size and power, the rights and duties, and the internal management of large corporations, he was a very thoughtful man. Gowen consistently tried to find a formula that would permit desirable corporate extension without sacrificing personal freedom and civic virtue. Such a quest had both a personal and a theoretical interest, in an age when small businessmen could charge that public statements by corporate officers were merely

> . . . the sullen murmurings of a powerful corporation, whose inspirations and aspirations are thought to be somewhat monarchical; who, through the aid and instrumentality of venal Legislatures and mercenary Executives, are insidiously, in conjunction with kindred corporations, sapping the very vitals of the nation, crushing individual enterprise, laboring to [render] representative government a scorn and byword.[15]

And Gowen was free in admitting his own discomfort in this climate of opinion:

> I have been subjected for some years to the humiliation of occupying a position in which I am forced to infer that almost every man who comes to see me supposes I am a monster and an oppressor. I endeavor to control my temper as well as I can; and whenever I can find somebody to take my place I shall be happy to go back to practicing law, and to get into some decent business again. Whenever a corporation makes a proposition to any set of men, they invariably suppose you are going to cheat them, and there is something terrible back of it.[16]

Judged by his own actions, Gowen believed that corporations not only had a right to, but should, grow to some optimal size—a size, that is, at least sufficient to ensure a regional monopoly of its service to the public. This meant a plant valued at tens of millions of dollars; to establish such a plant it was not merely legitimate, but desirable, to borrow heavily. Large size was necessary because it entailed both increased productivity and efficiency and possessed the advantage of economies of scale; and all this in turn led to reducing prices and increasing consumption. To reduce wasteful competition among regional monopolies, he proposed "combinations"—essentially cartels—that fixed prices and allocated shares of the market, thereby preserving the local monopolies. It was a vista of a continuously expanding economy able to support a continuously expanding debt by ever increasing productivity.

But, Gowen recognized, the public was not entirely wrong in its fear of corporations. Three evils were common in the corporate management of his day: dishonest acquisition of wealth by corporate executives; unjust discrimination against competitors or clients by raising prices or refusing services; and corruption of legislatures and public officials by bribes, threats, and other forms of illegal influence. Gowen himself, at least in his early years as president of the Reading, had used the threat of selective toll increases to force uncooperative coal operators to accept his labor policies. But as his career continued, he saw this discrimination technique—employed extensively by his rivals, the Pennsylvania Railroad and Standard Oil—as a social evil, and in his last years he spent much time as an attorney trying to persuade legislatures to outlaw it. Railroads and pipelines, he argued, were common carriers, and combinations of national monopolies in restraint of trade were "criminal conspiracies" that must be broken up. Thus he favored a strong Interstate Commerce Commission to regulate corporations when they exceeded their appropriate bounds of economic sovereignty.[17]

Gowen seems to have tried to govern the Reading according to these principles. He banned the issuance of free railroad passes—a common form of influence peddling—to any but employees of the line. He claimed—contrary to popular suspicion—that, unlike the Pennsylvania, the Reading influenced the legislature by persuasion rather than by bribes. (But he was not above setting Pinkerton men on the trail of the state senators who were investigating the company. Their reports were as intimate as McParlan's on the Molly Maguires, detailing the legislators' eating and drinking habits as well as their opinions and prejudices about the Reading, and even following them into the brothels of Atlantic City.[18]) He did not deny the use of his railroad to operators who were in open competition with the Philadelphia and Reading Coal and Iron Company and, except during the labor dispute, did not "discriminate" by selectively raising their tolls; at least on paper, competitors were charged the same tolls as the PRCI. He opposed using the power of the cartel to force prices of anthracite up to extortionate levels. He asserted that neither he nor any other official of the company was getting unduly rich, at least as might be evidenced by conspicuous consumption such as being "loaded with diamonds, driving fast horses, indulging in dissipation, or making an ostentatious display of wealth."[19]

It would be possible to argue, indeed, that Gowen thought of the

Reading Railroad and its auxiliary PRCI as a kind of public utility, authorized to maintain a monopoly within its own domain, but subject to constraints imposed by the public interest. Although the bureaucratically managed Reading system became a byword for red tape, Gowen strove for efficiency. When he set up the railroad's own vast coal wharves at Port Richmond, thereby cutting out the unproductive and relatively inefficient middlemen, the coal merchants, he lowered the price of his coal by one dollar, on the theory that lower prices meant larger sales; and when the competing operators complained of unfair competition, he offered to sell their coal too at the same price plus a nominal charge of 10 cents per ton, provided they picked and washed their coal to Reading standards. Standards for coal preparation in PRCI collieries were raised and Schuylkill anthracite, hitherto suffering from a reputation for dirt, soon became more attractive to buyers. On one occasion, he compared the Reading with the cooperatives organized by New York dairy farmers, in that both were distributing direct to consumers by eliminating the middleman. And during the floor debates at the Pennsylvania constitutional convention in 1873, he even suggested that not only was some government regulation of the railroads needed, but that the best system would be for the government to own and operate the railroads—when and if government became as efficient and honest as business.[20]

But while Gowen insisted that big corporations had a responsibility to the public and needed government regulation to make sure they lived up to that responsibility, he was fiercely opposed to interference from other corporations or militant labor unions. Particularly with respect to labor was Gowen painfully ambivalent. On the one hand, he seems to have insisted on certain standards of fair treatment for employees of both the railroad and the coal-and-iron company. He refused to maintain company stores and the workers were paid in cash, a policy formed years before when he was a colliery operator at Mount Laffee. A company system of workmen's compensation was established that did not require workers' contributions. No company blacklist was maintained and even opponents like Siney could obtain work at PRCI collieries. When individual miners complained to Gowen about unfair or incompetent bosses, the matter was routinely referred to General Pleasants for investigation, with the reminder that "no injustice is permitted to be done by any one of our Superintendents." No garnisheeing of miners' wages was allowed on behalf of local doctors or businessmen. And he instituted strict rules against ethnic discrimination:

> If, however, there is any authenticated case of the discharge of a
> man because he was an Irishman, or because he was a Catholic,

or because he belonged to the Catholic Workingman's Society, we would instantly dismiss the Superintendent who had made the discharge; and if there are any just grounds even of suspicion that there is any movement among our Superintendents to discriminate in any manner against Irishmen or against Catholics, we will see that the proper steps are taken to prevent it. I have already issued an order upon this subject which I thought would do some good. . . .[21]

And non-militant labor organization was not only not proscribed, it was even welcomed because it permitted rational negotiation of wage rates and grievances and, when agreement failed, it provided the discipline necessary for labor to abide by decisions made by an arbitrator.

But Gowen had an extreme fear of labor organizations that used violence to enforce strike discipline and drive away strikebreakers. The image of the Workingmen's Benevolent Association as a militant labor union merged, as we have seen, with the vision of the Ancient Order of Hibernians as a satanic conspiracy bent on violating all law and decency and reducing the Reading Railroad and the PRCI to the status of helpless vassals. Gowen's concept of the dread Molly Maguire organization may, indeed, have been the product of his own ambivalence about the corporation itself, thrown like a shadow over the entire territory of the Reading organization. And, once articulated, it became part of the regional mythology, attributing to the hapless Mollies just those qualities of rapacity and stealth which the critics of monopoly had been charging to the Reading itself.

But, whatever were the psychological processes involved, Gowen became the deadly foe of the Workingmen's Benevolent Association and then the Knights of Labor. After the demise of the WBA, he invoked a more modern image of international conspiracy, that of "communism," charging that the labor agitators of 1875 had been followers of Engels and Marx:

I believe ninety-five out of every one hundred of the men employed about the mines in the coal region are decent, orderly, law-abiding, respectable men; but there is among them a class of agitators—a few men trained in the school of the Manchester cotton spinner—men brought here for no other purpose than to create confusion, to undermine confidence, and to stir up dissension between the employer and the employed. . . . I stand here to arrange before you a class of two or three men out of every one hundred who, by their machinations and by their agitation, have held in absolute idleness and starvation thousands and thousands of men for months.[22]

And later Gowen had Pinkerton men infiltrate the Knights of Labor, who, Pinkerton and Gowen believed, were also communist-inspired, part of another international conspiracy. His conversion to this view came during the five-year struggle among the WBA, the operators, and the Reading, that resulted in the emergence of a company state.

THE RISE OF THE COMPANY STATE

The story of the Reading takeover has been so well and repeatedly told that there is no need to do more here than recite the major events in the context of St. Clair's own experience.[1] The Reading's goal, well defined even before Gowen's presidency, was to achieve, first, a monopoly of transportation between the southern anthracite district and Philadelphia, and, second, such control of coal production as would ensure regular profits to the railroad. It was Gowen's realization that coal production could not be made dependable as long as the region remained a crazy quilt of small landowners and small operators that prompted the Reading to become the sole landowner and the principal operator. All this fitted Gowen's general philosophy of a regional monopoly, rather like a public utility, efficiently managed in the interest of both the stockholders and the general public. But the ruthlessness with which he crushed opposition from unsympathetic landowners, operators, and labor unions made him appear more like a not-too-benevolent dictator than an honest, public-spirited corporate executive.

The Reading's monopoly of transportation to Philadelphia was achieved in 1870, when the Reading leased the Schuylkill Navigation Company's canal for 999 years. But the coal lands upon which the Reading depended for its traffic down to Philadelphia were vulnerable to penetration by the Lehigh Valley Railroad from the east, and the Pennsylvania Railroad from the west, and when these lines began to lay track, and even to buy up coal lands, in the southern field, and when the operators (including Enoch McGinness) began to organize a People's Railroad to carry Schuylkill coals to the lucrative New York market, the Reading felt that it had to act in self-defense by buying up the lands itself.

It had long been rumored that Reading stockholders were interested in coal lands. As early as 1861, Enoch McGinness was expressing fears that the landowners' neglect of their properties in the south part of

Schuylkill County would force the Reading and the Lehigh railroads to take the district over, use it up, and then abandon it for the Mahanoy field.[2] It was reported that the Reading had an interest in the old Delaware and North American coal companies.[3] But the Reading, in contrast to the Lehigh, the Lackawanna, and other railroads in the eastern part of the state, was prohibited by law from owning or developing coal lands. As late as 1869, Gowen had been publicly opposed to the Reading adventuring in coal, and urged that an act authorizing railroads to enter the coal business should be amended to exclude Schuylkill County from its provisions. But two years later, in 1871, after frustrating dialogues with uncooperative coal operators who unnecessarily, in Gowen's view, prolonged strikes and cost the railroad money, Gowen changed his mind and lobbied through the Pennsylvania legislature an act to incorporate the Laurel Run Improvement Company. This company was, in vague language, authorized to mine coal and iron, and, most importantly, its stock could be purchased by any railroad, including the Reading. The Reading promptly purchased all of the Laurel Run stock, issued an initial $25,000,000 in bonds for the purchase of coal lands, and changed the new company's name to the Philadelphia and Reading Coal and Iron Company.[4]

With P. W. Sheafer as adviser, the company's agents now set out in great haste to buy coal land. By the end of the year 1871, the PRCI had acquired 70,000 acres; by 1874, another 40,000 had been added; by 1880, the total amounted to 160,566 acres, or 251 square miles. In this pandemonium of buying, good coal land was bought up with bad, and some 69,417 acres were eventually reported as "probably containing no workable coal." In some places, both surface and underlying mineral rights were acquired; in others, only the residual mineral rights. Most of the land lay north of Broad Mountain, from the Mahanoy-and-Shenandoah area west to the Susquehanna about Shamokin, but 18,269 acres lay south of the mountain, from Tamaqua west to the Lykens Valley. St. Clair, of course, lay in this region, and there the company bought up all of the Carey group's land in the St. Clair Tract, most of it being merely mineral rights under the borough; all of the Seitzinger and Wetherill tracts; and all of the land of the Mammoth Vein Coal Company.[5] Thus, from 1872 on, all of the collieries in which the miners of St. Clair were employed were operated by lessees of the PRCI or by the company itself, including the Pine Forest, Eagle, Hickory Slope, St. Clair Shaft and Slope, Wadesville Shaft, and the small workings on the old North American, Delaware, and other tracts to the south and west of the town. The cost of this acquisition of coal lands and mineral rights, at an average price of about $300 an acre, amounted to something on the order of $45,000,000, provided mostly by the railroad, which went into debt for this amount (and more for improvements and operating costs).

A large part of the Reading's reason for going into the production end of the coal trade, in addition to land ownership, was the series of strikes that, as we have seen, escalated in mutual animosity until the Reading and its subsidiary had bought the land, displaced many of the old operators, and crushed the union. When the union broke up in 1875 and the Mollies were convicted in 1876, the company state in Schuylkill reached its maturity. Let us review the process.[6]

There were strikes in Schuylkill in 1869, 1870, and 1871; then a period of uneasy peace in 1872, 1873, and most of 1874; and, finally, a combination lockout and strike—the catastrophic Long Strike—that lasted from late November 1874 to June 1875. The first strike, in May and June 1869, was almost utopian in its intentions. Siney and the WBA argued that over-production was the source of the industry's financial problems and that therefore the only way to secure better prices for the operators and higher wages for the workers was for labor and capital to form a partnership to control production. The strike would deplete the market, and when the price of coal had climbed to $3 per ton, the miners would go back to work at higher wages. For the first time, a sliding scale of wages was proposed, with the wages of labor rising for every increment in the price of coal above a "basis" of $3. The union proposed to hold the price up by a voluntary slowdown after the end of the strike. And they demanded a closed shop and management recognition of local grievance committees. The strike was general throughout the coal regions. When the price of coal did in fact rise in Schuylkill and Lehigh, the two sides agreed on the $3 basis and the sliding scale, compromised on the closed shop, ignored the grievance-committee issue, with the operators agreeing not to fire union leaders and the union agreeing not to insist on the firing of blacklegs. But the major operators in the northern region refused to accept the basis and the sliding scale. As the strike continued, with rumors of Chinese strike-breakers and evictions of strike leaders from company houses, the strikers became more militant and the companies hired hundreds of special police to protect property and blacklegs. By the end of August the miners were returning to work with no basis but a higher wage.

The Schuylkill operators, dismayed by the union's success, quickly reorganized the Anthracite Board of Trade and opened negotiations for an 1870 contract that accepted the $3 basis, but provided for a reduction of wages if coal prices fell *below* the basis as well as a raise if they went above. The union rejected the proposal and called a strike in January 1870. This strike dragged on until the end of July, with the increasingly embittered parties unable to agree on any compromise. When the authority of the board of trade over the member operators seemed in danger of diminishing, the Reading Railroad disciplined backsliding operators who dared to return to work on the union's terms by raising their freight tolls 20 percent. Eventually, after repeated consultations between Gowen—whose railroad was suffering financially from the strike—and representatives of the board of trade and the WBA, including both William Kendrick (operator of the St. Clair Shaft), and Siney, a compromise was reached. Known as "Gowen's Compromise," it provided for the $3 basis, with an 8.25 percent rise in wages for each 25-cent rise in the price of coal, and an 8.25 percent drop in wages for each 25-cent fall in the price of coal, down to a floor of $2 per ton. This sliding scale and other provisions were spelled out in a written labor contract, the first to be signed in the industry.

But the strike of 1870 weakened the WBA. Its northern members in the Wyoming district had failed to join the suspension; and the president of the Reading Railroad had successfully intervened. And Gowen's definition of the industry's problem was very different from Siney's and the operators'. Whereas both Siney and some of the operators believed that the solution was to raise prices by restricting production, Gowen thought that reducing production costs and selling (and shipping) more coal was the way to prosperity. And Gowen had a stranglehold on the industry by his power to raise freight rates at will. This he demonstrated during another long strike, from January to May 1871. By this time, convinced of the need to take control of the industry, Gowen was quietly buying up coal lands and not so quietly stiffening the backs of the operators by raising freight rates to prohibitive levels whenever the board of trade began to waver in its opposition to the union. To the north, where the strike began, violent attacks on strikebreakers resulted in the dispatching of militia companies, who eventually were ordered to fire on a mob of strikers. The northern union split along ethnic lines when the collieries in the northern region fired all their Welsh miners in a temporarily successful effort to divide and conquer. Gowen, as we saw earlier, turned the legislative investigation of the freight-rate issue into a theater in which to accuse the WBA of using the Molly Maguires to let loose a reign of terror on the coal regions. Finally, following the suggestion of Gowen and Eckley B. Coxe, and with the concurrence of Siney, binding arbitration was agreed to by the WBA and the board of trade. Judge Elwell of Columbia County was the arbitrator, and his eventual decision was a compromise not unlike Gowen's the year before. He set the basis at $2.75, with wage rates at basis somewhat lower than in 1869, and with a sliding scale that permitted wages to go up or down by 33 percent. But this agreement was sabotaged by a series of wildcat strikes that resulted in the abandonment of the sliding scale for the balance of the year.

The Reading and the other railroads were by now committed to taking control of the coal trade by establishing an industrial hegemony over the entire anthracite region. In 1872 the major carriers—most of whom were by now coal producers too—formed the first of the anthracite "combinations."[7] The cartel allocated to each of its members a share of the total market and specified the number of tons it was authorized to ship. Still shuddering from the strains of the 1871 walkout, the union accepted the operators' terms in 1872 and 1873, but in January 1874, in the midst of the depression, there were month-long strikes in Schuylkill and Wyoming over wage reductions. The PRCI continued to operate its collieries despite the deteriorating economic conditions, honoring an agreement to give the miners ten months' work a year. But both sides were gearing for battle— a battle, Siney knew, the Workingmen's Benevolent Association could never win. His letter, written as president of the Miners' National Association, warning local unions that the MNA could not encourage strikes at this time, alienated his old comrades in Schuylkill and called down upon him the obloquy that made his last year so painful:

> To sum all up in a word, we say suffer every indignity that can be heaped upon you, sign every kind of paper the bosses present you, and do not think to combat them now. Organize secretly if you are not permitted to do so publicly, but do organize. The bosses do not fight you openly; they cannot blame you if you adopt their tactics. Those who have accomplished great good had to bear great opposition. Remember those of old who, struggling for freedom, had to move cautiously and judiciously; do ye also the same. We advise you thus, for to strike now is, as it were, fighting the wind. Reserve your prowess and your power until the opportune time, and then let us burst the bands assunder. For the present let there be no strikes.[8]

The Long Strike of 1875 that ended in the demise of the union actually began with a suspension of the PRCI collieries called by Gowen in November 1874 because the Reading wharves were overflowing with coal. The railroad combination also advised operators who insisted on remaining open that the carriers would accept no coal after December 1, 1874. The operators' association offered a new contract that reduced wages by 10 percent to 20 percent and removed the floor below which wages could not fall. But, despite Siney's warning, the WBA decided to call a strike. This was precisely what the Reading and the other great corporations wanted. Ignoring all counter-offers, they employed more and more Pinkerton detectives, hired more and more Coal and Iron Police, and, when frustrated strikers attacked trains and breakers, brought in the militia, who patrolled the streets, railroads, and collieries at trouble spots like Shenandoah and Hazleton. And while all this was going on, spies like McParlan in Shenandoah and Cumming in St. Clair were collecting information about the union and the Mollies, in the vain hope of finding them to be two sides of the same coin. The operators, backed by Gowen, never gave way and never met with union representatives, and, finally, toward the end of June 1875, the workers began drifting back to work on the operators' conditions. The WBA, its treasury empty and its policy discredited, was dead.

The experience of the miners of St. Clair during the strike years from 1869 to 1875 was one of gradually diminishing solidarity. In the spring of 1870, a Welsh miner in St. Clair, David L. Griffiths, wrote back to Wales about his disillusionment with the men of Luzerne, who had not joined the strike called by the WBA.

> We had a correct picture of the strike in Pottsville, Pennsylvania, by the editor of the *Miners' Journal,* that is a picture of a cow on paper, the masters holding its horns and pulling forward and the miners holding its tail and pulling with all their might and the men of Luzerne quietly milking it as busy as bees. Everyone admits that in union there is strength and one would think that after getting thirty thousand together there was strength enough but our strength was defeated and will be defeated because it is the masters who have the money and it is but folly to think of beating them. We do not know how it will turn out but I can say that the workmen are sorry that they did not accept the offer of the masters; but now it is too late. We have always seen plenty of repentance after strikes; undoubtedly the effects will be felt next winter by some families if it is a hard winter.[9]

Next year another Welshman, Benjamin James, wrote from St. Clair in February describing real suffering:

> Many of the works have been idle since before Christmas and with little hope of them restarting. Many of the works have not been open for more than four months in the past year and, when

working, the miners have not earned wages corresponding to the high prices of everything in this country. Hundreds of families are as poor here as ever they were in the Old Country. . . .

. . . I have been here two years and traveled as much as those who have been here twelve because I have been out of work so often, as the workmen are either on strike or on suspension nearly all the time. . . . The truth is that there is too much coal going to the market to meet the demand. As a result the price of coal falls until the coal operator is unable to pay the basis of the regular wages for the miners. So he prefers to stop working rather than pay money out of his pocket, and on the other side, the miner prefers to be idle in the house rather than working underground in the gas, sulphur, and coal dust for next to nothing. So it develops into a general suspension on both sides. Before a family can pay off the debts from the previous strike there is a suspension again.[10]

By the time Pinkerton agents reached St. Clair in February 1874, the union was in disarray. At the beginning Charles Rohrbach (the painter who made the scenery for the plays put on by the Monument Fund) told agent Cumming that the union had improved the "character" of the miners. As he reported it,

since the commencement of the Union they had minded very much previous to that they were a very tough class. That every other day there would be a meeting of the men and an advance asked by them—whether entitled to it or not, but that now they trust all their business to their committee men and seem to settle down to it. That what they now earn they seem to take care of and that the Union was beneficial to both miners and operators.[11]

But now Siney was resigning to take up his duties as president of the Miners' National Association; he visited St. Clair on and off, but was not playing a major part in the affairs of Schuylkill County any longer, and by the end of the year he was almost universally hated for his advice not to strike and his refusal to spend national-union funds if the M&LBA started an unauthorized suspension. A union meeting called by Siney to discuss affiliation with the national union ended in a "continuous wrangle."[12] Still trying to enforce the closed shop, the local branch threatened to strike at the Wadesville Shaft unless the company fired some men who would not join the union. But by April 1874 the treasuries of the locals were nearly empty, miners were so hungry for work that even those few still working in the St. Clair Shaft, with four feet of gas in the breasts, were reluctant to complain to the mine inspector for fear he would close down the mine, and the men were cursing and swearing about paying their union dues. In November, as rumors spread that the operators intended to reduce the basis to $2, there was further discussion in the union over whether it was wise to strike. It was "the general opinion at St. Clair" that if there was a strike, it could not last longer than one month because some of the miners no longer cared about the union anyway and those who did could not afford the financial hardship any longer than a month. The anti-strike faction believed that if the strike lasted three months or longer, "it will break up the union."

The strike proper began in January 1875, some weeks after most of the collieries had shut down. By February 7, when Cumming's reports ceased, the union's solidarity with the storekeepers—so lavishly praised by Siney in better years—had broken down. Cumming reported on that date "that a great many of the Miners are getting to be pretty hard up for money, and that the storekeepers are refusing to credit them. . . ." Needless to say, ballads emerged about this time touting union strength, like "The Long Strike," collected from a miner who took part:

> In eighteen hundred and seventy-five, our masters did conspire
> To keep men, women, and children without food or fire.
> They tho't to starve us to submit with hunger and with cold,
> But the miners did not fear them, but stood out brave and bold.
>
> Now two long months are nearly o'er—that no one can deny,
> And for to stand another month we are willing for to try,
> Our wages shall not be reduced, tho' poverty do reign,
> We'll have seventy-four basis, boys, before we'll work again.[13]

In later years, Joseph Patterson, the secretary of the M&LBA during the Long Strike, recalled the agony of defeat. In going back to work in June, the miners accepted a wage schedule 26.5 percent below the 1869 arrangement, and in subsequent years the average wage declined further, until in 1877 it was 54 percent below the 1869 basis. Patterson's recollection of the time was painful:

> How bitter, how very bitter and humiliating was the defeat sustained by the miners in 1875 is hard to impress upon those who did not experience it. . . . The pain of having to yield was only

exceeded by the hunger and suffering produced by a struggle of six months, during which time nothing was earned to provide bread for the miners' families. Famine drove the men into submission. It was a terrible thing to submit to a twenty percent reduction on contract work. Evil days had come. We went to work; but with iron in our souls.[14]

And the anonymous balladeer who published some verses under the title "After the Long Strike" in a Pottsville paper in 1878 looked forward to a continuous decline in the miner's standard of living under the rule of the Reading:

> Well, we've been beaten, beaten all to smash,
> and now, sir, we've begun to feel the lash,
> as wielded by a gigantic corporation,
> which runs the commonwealth and ruins the nation.[15]

By 1876, after the breaking of the union and the conviction of the Mollies, the Reading system, including the railroad and the coal-and-iron company, held an unchallenged, near-perfect monopoly of the Schuylkill coal trade. It produced most of the coal in its own collieries, carried all of it on its own railroads or its own canal, delivered it at Port Richmond to its own wharves, ships, and dealers. Its prices were maintained by the successive "combinations" that guaranteed it the largest share of the trade of any member corporation, from 20 to 25 percent; at its zenith in 1893, in fact, after (temporarily) acquiring control of other railroads, the Reading owned or controlled 70 percent of the anthracite shipments in the state. Whether achieved by honest lobbying or other means, its influence in the legislature and the governor's office was formidable.

Within the coal fields of Schuylkill County and parts of adjacent counties, the PRCI was a strict administrator. At the company's collieries, "rules and regulations for the government of the workmen" were "conspicuously posted . . . warning their employees of the duty required of them to observe and obey." Compliance was "strictly" enforced. The eight rules were a mixture of wise administrative orders to ensure compliance with the ventilation laws (IV, V, and VII), a public effort to protect employees from unjust dismissal by ethnically or personally prejudiced supervisors (VIII), and regimentation of the employees' time (I, II, III, and VI).

> I. At any time between the hours of six and seven o'clock in
> the morning empty wagons will be furnished for the purpose of

letting to the bottom of all shafts and slopes the persons employed in them.

II. No empty wagons will be furnished either for the purpose of hoisting or letting down men between the hours of 7 a.m. and 12 p.m., and between the hours of 1 and 5:30 p.m., unless by special instructions of the inside foreman. The engineers and top and bottom men will be held responsible for the carrying out this rule.

III. All persons employed by the day, either inside or outside, are expected to work ten hours for a day's pay, or fifty-eight hours per week for a week's pay. Any persons working less than this will receive wages proportionate for the time worked. The same rule to apply in all cases where overtime is worked, unless by special agreement with the mining superintendent.

IV. In all workings where there is firedamp evolved, and naked lights used, no person or persons other than the inside foreman and fire boss must pass the first check door without the consent of the fire boss. Where nothing but locked safety lamps are used no persons other than the inside foreman or fire boss will enter any of the workings until permitted to do so by the fire boss.

V. All safety lamps must be handed into the lamp house each evening for inspection and repairs. Persons using safety lamps will be charged with the cost of repairing when ordinary care has not been exercised in their protection.

VI. Persons not employed at the colliery are positively forbidden from speaking to, or in any way interfering with, the employees during working hours.

VII. All the rules and regulations of the ventilation laws to be fully enforced by the bosses and workmen.

VIII. No workman is to be discharged except for incompetency, bad workmanship, misconduct, drunkenness, or other good cause given by him. By order of the superintendent of the company's coal mines and collieries.[16]

The company's control of the mine towns and patches was less visible but no less extensive. Apart from being the economic mainstay of the entire region by virtue of direct employment and the purchase of local goods and services, the company wielded an enormous power comparable only to a state's right of eminent domain. The company could, after giving due notice and fair compensation, remove surface structures, including houses, roads, bridges—in principle, even entire communities—if it was necessary to do so in order to mine the coal to which it had acquired mineral rights. It had not been necessary for the company to buy the surface of its domain; it could, in effect, expropriate the surface at will. Social control, in addition to being implicit in the "law and order" guaranteed by the state (which included the use of the militia as a last resort), was also enforced by uniformed, armed Coal and Iron Police paid by the company but appointed as peace officers by the state, and, less overtly, by a secret police force, the Pinkerton Detective Agency, which specialized in quelling labor disturbances, and whose operatives in any locality could be quickly mobilized and augmented to any number desired.

Vested with a right akin to eminent domain over 250 square miles, endowed with police powers, possessed of a monopoly of a sector of the coal trade similar to that of a public utility, and assured of ready access to the state's legislative and administrative bodies, the Reading system was almost a state within a state. But nonetheless it was bleeding to death from the same lesion that had ended the careers of so many other coal operators, large and small: the impossibility, with the technology then available, of mining coal at a profit in the steeply pitching veins of Schuylkill County at any but a few special locations.

A COMMON RUIN

By 1872 the private landowners in the St. Clair area had been bought out, including the Carey and Wetherill groups and the Mammoth Vein Consolidated Coal Company, successor to Carey's interests in the old North American tracts. The PRCI's initial policy in administering these lands and the rest of its holdings in Schuylkill and the adjacent counties seems to have been a relatively conservative one: to continue to lease the colliery rights to individual operators at prevailing royalties (on the average about 30 cents per ton), thus ensuring the income not only from freight tolls but also from rentals. On paper, in advance, this no doubt appeared to be a very advantageous arrangement. In 1872, in the Pottsville district alone, the PRCI owned the mineral rights under some fifty-eight collieries that produced something over 1,051,000 tons of coal. Rents should have earned the company about $300,000. But these collieries were not really very efficient. The average output was only about 18,000 tons for the year and nineteen of the fifty-eight produced less than 1,000 tons. The PRCI's competitor, the Lehigh Coal and Navigation Company, owned only four collieries in the Pottsville district, all in the neighborhood of Tamaqua or farther east, but they produced over 240,000 tons, for an average 1871 output of about 60,000 tons per colliery. The reason for the sharp discrepancy was, of course, that these Reading holdings were in the Pottsville Basin. The only collieries in the entire basin producing better than 60,000 tons in 1872 were those at or near the line of the Mammoth outcrop in the neighborhood of St. Clair: Wadesville Shaft, Eagle, Pine Forest, Beechwood, and St. Clair Shaft. At all of these except the Eagle, where the Johns remained, the PRCI had installed William Kendrick as operator, no doubt buying out Snyder and the other operators on Kendrick's behalf; and Kendrick was the operator at no less than eleven others.[1]

Between St. Clair and the outskirts of Port Carbon and Pottsville, down Mill and Norwegian creeks, lay the lands once owned and mined by the Delaware Coal Company and the North American Coal Company, now all gobbled up by the PRCI with (or perhaps without) the advice of its able geologist, Peter W. Sheafer. It was here, on the Delaware Tract, that anthracite had first been commercially mined; and it was here, on the North American, that Carey and Patterson sank the first slope and McGinness tried and failed in his patron's effort to renew mining at Mill Creek. But the region had for a decade been a wasteland of ruined patches, tumbledown breakers, eroding culm banks, and abandoned holes. As early as 1862, Eli Bowen wrote, in the dedication of his pamphlet *Coal and the Coal Trade:*

> It can afford you no satisfaction to look upon the grand old mountains and picturesque gorges and valleys that surround you, for they are strewn with the fragments and ruins of a great trade . . . gloom, and dreary aspect of decay and ruin . . . everywhere meets the eye and saddens the heart.[2]

The reader will recall Burd Patterson's remark, so much resented by McGinness, that mining south of Broad Mountain was defunct. And by 1870 the mine inspector, John Eltringham, could reflect on the abandonment of Repplier's colliery at New Castle in terms reminiscent of "The Deserted Village":

> The abandonment of these mines threw several hundred persons out of employment, who until then found their chief support by labor at the colliery. Many such melancholy examples are to be met with all along the valley of the Schuylkill, from Tamaqua to

Tremont . . . this large district is at present, comparatively, in a state of being nearly abandoned.[3]

And in 1871 the mine inspectors' annual report called for a "new order of things" in the Schuylkill coal trade:

The enormous expenditures incurred in developing our deep mines, in former years, have driven our large coal companies out of the business, and left the lands waste, the mines idle, and the buildings to rot. Very many melancholy evidences can be met with in the Schuylkill valley today. The petty little land-sale drifts, suffered to be worked on their surfaces, have consumed all the young and old timber, which, had it been properly protected for the last twenty-five years, would now be of intrinsic value to new developments.

A new order of things must take place for the redemption of our mining interests, which will be sufficiently powerful to grapple with this monster, and create a new form of things that will redeem the region and make it prosperous and interesting. There is not an equal amount of territory in the State or nation, which affords greater facilities and advantages to the investment of capital in any and all of the different branches of business, such as furnaces, rolling mills, nail mills, cotton mills, potteries, machine shops, agricultural manufactories, boot and shoe manufactories, and any other business that requires water or steam power for its purpose. Its coal, water and railway facilities cannot be excelled elsewhere. There need be no doubt but that hands, for any or all of these enterprises, can be obtained, if only capitalists will open to us a business for our surplus population, which would then become self-sustaining, which is not the case at present in many localities.[4]

The PRCI, however, did not plan to abandon mining in the Pottsville Basin and turn to manufacturing; it planned, instead, to rehabilitate the coal trade there, partly by encouraging small collieries doing a few hundred tons a year, partly by taking over operation of the larger collieries itself, partly by closing down expensive failures. By 1876 the company directly operated twenty-two collieries in the Pottsville district and leased fifty-five more, many of them very small. In 1873 the St. Clair Shaft was acquired by the company and almost immediately closed down, presumably because its technical problems made safe and profitable operation impossible. About 250 employees, most if not all of them residents of St. Clair, were thrown out of work. By 1875 the company was operating Pine Forest, the Wadesville Shaft, and the huge Beechwood Colliery at Mount Laffee. Johns continued at the Eagle with a work force reduced from about 200 to 165.[5] The company collieries were administered by William Kendrick as overall business manager and General Pleasants as system superintendent and mining engineer. The individual collieries' day-to-day business was directed as before by resident superintendents. The consolidation of a large number of collieries under one central bureaucratic administration presumably made possible certain economies of scale in the purchase of supplies and the keeping of books; it also invited the inevitable problems of organizational failure, such as breakdowns in the ordering and delivery of supplies and failures to repair machinery.

But the company's main plan for revitalizing the Pottsville district did not rest upon the continued operation of the same old collieries. According to his friend Eckley B. Coxe, Franklin B. Gowen early in 1869, shortly after he was elected president of the Philadelphia and Reading Railroad Company, determined to build a giant colliery to exploit the deep veins of coal under the lands of the former Delaware Coal Company and the North American Coal Company—i.e., in those very tracts between St. Clair and Pottsville that were now, "to a certain extent, abandoned." A very large, very deep shaft would penetrate to the Mammoth Vein and gangways would be run off east and west to exploit the Mammoth and other overlying veins throughout the several square miles of the two tracts and even into adjoining tracts, thus opening up virtually all the coal in the district between St. Clair on the north and Pottsville and Port Carbon to the south. All this was allegedly projected before the Coal and Iron Company received its charter from the legislature and thus before the company had purchased any of the mineral rights in question.[6]

This grandiose scheme was not, however, original with Gowen. It had been publicly proposed by Eli Bowen in his 1862 book as the cure for the economic desolation of the region of Pottsville. The work was dedicated to Pottsville's George de B. Keim, a close friend of Gowen since 1858, his aide after Gowen assumed the presidency of the Reading, and himself the first president of the PRCI and for a time president of the Reading itself. After explaining that the ruin of the coal trade was the result of the reliance upon slopes, he proposed a "plain and simple" remedy:

We must organize companies with large capital, to sink enormously deep and permanent shafts—shafts that will cut through not *one* vein merely, but a dozen veins or more, before a single pound of coal is allowed to be sent to market.

Let us suppose such a company to be organized. It will be located at Pottsville, with a stock capital of $500,000, one half of which should be paid up in cash. It should have a run of lease from Westwood to Port Carbon, a distance of four miles. The shaft at Pottsville should go down to the bottom of the basin, say two thousand feet in depth, more or less. As the shaft goes on down, gangways should be run at each end of the ground. At a depth of two thousand feet probably not less than fifteen veins of coal will have been cut through, *with right and left breasts up to the surface,* or, in other words, with the shaft in the angle of the V, there would be coal on both sides of the gangway, instead of one side, as in the case of slopes, so that each vein would really be *doubled,* and therefore equal to *two slopes* at the same depth.[7]

This plan was in fact the one selected by Keim and Gowen, when the PRCI came into being, for the rebuilding of the coal trade in Pottsville district.

Gowen was resolved not to make mistakes of the kind McGinness had made, by sinking a shaft in haste, with inadequate capital and superficial study. He was prepared to make "a great outlay of money" and knew that it would take "a long time" to open the mine, but he believed that the result would be a colliery that would produce daily "a very large amount of coal for a long series of years." General Pleasants was put in charge of the initial geological survey and technical planning. At first Pleasants proposed a single-shaft colliery on the McGinness plan, but the Avondale disaster and the mine law of 1870 forced him to provide instead for two shafts. The location chosen was just outside St. Clair, about 200 yards west of the borough's southwest corner, in the area of the old East Mines and Scalpington, but the colliery was usually referred to as the Pottsville Twin Shafts or the Pottsville Colliery. The two shafts, timber-lined below the brick-and-masonry top forty feet, about 700 feet apart, were located along the strike of the basin. The East Shaft, intended solely for raising coal, served as the downcast; it was the smaller of the two, approximately sixteen feet by fourteen feet. The West Shaft was larger, about twenty-six feet by fourteen feet, and was divided into three compartments, two for hoisting and one for the upcast airway. An eighteen-foot Guibal-type suction fan provided ventilation. The plan was to intercept the Mammoth Vein at an estimated depth of 1,500 feet, just above the synclinal axis so as to provide space in the coal for sumps.

The most "interesting and novel" part of the plan for sinking the twin

Head frame of the East Shaft at the Pottsville Twin Shafts Colliery

shafts was the simultaneous use of several diamond drills for making the holes for blasting. The holes were drilled 300 feet deep in the solid rock and were then filled with sand; the sand was later removed section by section to provide for the insertion of explosive. Each drill hole was about one and one half inches in diameter; the East Shaft contained twenty-five of them, the West Shaft thirty-five. Near the surface, the drills were driven by steam, but at the lower depths compressed air was substituted in the interest of comfort and safety. The average rate of drilling was (theoretically) thirty to forty feet per day, working twenty-four hours a day. Local firms built the machinery: Snyder's Iron Works the larger engines, Allison's machine shop the compact rotary engines that drove the drills, and the Pennsylvania Diamond Drill Company of Pottsville the drills themselves. By April 1873, after a year of work, the East Shaft had reached a depth of 530 feet and the West Shaft 400.[8]

The Reading's great project proceeded in a glare of initially favorable publicity. In addition to journalistic acclaim, professional opinion was extremely favorable. Mine inspector John Eltringham in 1870 learned of the company's plans to save the Pottsville district and greeted with unbounded enthusiasm General Pleasants' experimental use of the diamond drill to prove the accessibility of the Mammoth. Once again, Rogers and other un-American geological theorists were put in their place, and hope for the future of the Pottsville Basin was renewed:

> Though this large district is at present, comparatively, in a state of being nearly abandoned—to the stranger it would appear so— yet by recent and successful developments at Phoenix Park, in boring, by the Pennsylvania Diamond Drill Company, under the direction and counsel of General Henry Pleasants, C. and M. Eng. of the company, has accomplished the undertaking and has established the certainty of the underlying seams of the basin by boring 750 10/12 feet to the D or Skidmore vein. The correctness of General Pleasants' conclusions has demonstrated the much desired results and sets aside all mongrel theories, cherished by skeptics, of the great depth of these veins. General Pleasants has won for himself an enviable reputation in the history of the rebellion, in mining under and blowing up the forts at Petersburg, Va. He has likewise set aside the arguments so often advanced by these would-be-miners, by his late developments at Phoenix Park. Schuylkill County fostered many boastful characters, who stultified themselves on their conceited pretentions to a superior knowledge of mining and scouted the claims of an American to the art. Their own lack of any business capacity, proved by their futile endeavors to accomplish anything, except the ruin of their employers, is manifest in their career through the coal region. So far for an American.[9]

Eckley B. Coxe, in an address to the American Institute of Mining Engineers in May 1872, hailed the Twin Shafts project because of the careful study and preparation by General Pleasants:

> This undertaking differs in this respect from most of the mining enterprises that have been started in the United States. We generally begin operations without fully understanding all that is to be done, and then solve as best we can any problems that may present themselves during the progress of the work. The latter mode of proceeding involves, of course, very often, much useless expenditure, and sometimes ends in failure. I think therefore, that this enterprise is worthy of notice as an example of the way in which such mining operations should be undertaken.[10]

And the reports of the mine inspectors annually contained a notice of progress. The report for 1873 included a section that showed the East Shaft down to 704 feet and the West at 542 by the end of the year. The 1874 report lauded the project for having proved the existence of the largest anthracite deposit in the world, four miles wide and twenty-five miles long, "in the vicinage north of the noble little city of Pottsville." By the fall of 1874, the East Shaft had reached a depth of 1,127 feet and the West 930. And at last, in December 1874, a bore hole from the East Shaft reached the Mammoth at a depth of 1,980 feet. The mine inspector saluted the accomplishment:

> The improvements and machinery used will far exceed anything of the kind ever erected in this county before. The shafts are a success in their style and finish, and the community take a great pride and interest in this great undertaking.[11]

And the *Miners' Journal* exulted:

> The importance to Pottsville of the success of this great and plucky undertaking by the Reading Company cannot be overestimated. It makes Pottsville the great mining city of the future. For years and years to come, hundreds of men will be at work here, taking the black diamonds from this inexhaustible supply. It takes no great stretch of the imagination to see in operation here the largest and finest colliery in the world.[12]

But soon there was a measure of caution in the praise being dutifully doled out. The 1875 mine inspectors' report also noted that the West Shaft—the shaft for hoisting men, mules, and supplies, and intended for the upcast—had only reached the Primrose at 1,600 feet. Separated from the Mammoth Vein by hundreds of feet of rock and coal, the ventilation incomplete, the project was stalled after four years of enormous labor and expense. And there the West Shaft stayed, sunk down to the Primrose, with a useless 410-foot bore hole, containing broken and jammed bits, descending to the Mammoth below the loading platform. The colliery once hailed as the salvation of the Pottsville district was proving to be a catastrophe.

Efforts were made to work the coal at the 1,600-foot depth. A gangway on the Primrose was completed, connecting the East and West shafts and establishing ventilation and coal-hoisting capability. Then gangways were opened east and west on the Primrose, about 1,000 yards each way, until they were stopped by faults. A tunnel was also driven north in the expectation of meeting the Mammoth on its south dip in about 500 feet, but because of an unexpected syncline, the tunnel passed over the Mammoth and Seven-Foot veins without cutting them. Continuing on a quarter of a mile to the north, the tunnel finally intercepted the Mammoth and other veins, but the coal was in such a crushed condition that it was useless. By 1881, when the annual report published an extended article on the "Pottsville Colliery," it was necessary to admit that "some mistakes have been made" and that "the quantity of coal in this piece of territory is much less than the projectors anticipated finding." Amid reports circulating both in this country and abroad "that the capital invested is lost, and that the colliery is an entire failure," the mine inspector stoutly asserted that the colliery would be a productive one "for many years to come."[13]

The statistics of coal production published in the annual reports tell the story of the Twin Shafts colliery's lack of success. The years 1872, 1873, and 1874 were occupied with sinking the shafts and building the surface buildings, so no coal was mined until 1875. In the first ten years of production, from 1875 through 1884 (when the Reading suffered its second bankruptcy, after the first in 1880), the tonnages were:

1875	1,810	1880	39,062
1876	25,020	1881	16,478
1877	48,501	1882	42,625
1878	2,574	1883	59,562
1879	27,781	1884	12,458

The colliery was "suspended" in 1885. During its short ten-year life as a working colliery, the Twin Shafts, which had been expected to produce 750,000 tons a year indefinitely, shipped a total of only 275,871 tons. Even the St. Clair Shaft had done better. What had been vaunted as the greatest colliery in the world, as the salvation of the Pottsville district, had at last proved the wisdom of Henry Darwin Rogers' warning issued nearly fifty years before.

The Twin Shafts fiasco was not the only drain upon the PRCI's finances. We have already (in Chapter II) seen the difficulties encountered at Wadesville, Pine Forest, and the St. Clair Shaft and Slope. Similar problems plagued the PRCI's enterprises, as operator or landowner, in other areas. The PRCI's books have not been available to scholars recently, but they and the Reading's papers were studied by Gowen's biographer, and he has left a very clear picture of the company's losses.[14] From 1871 to 1874, Gowen borrowed about $48,000,000 to purchase coal lands and "develop" them, which presumably includes the outlays at the Twin Shafts, improvements at such sites as Wadesville and other company-operated mines, and loans to lessees to bring their collieries up to the company's high standards. Although the Reading system's efficient management and wage reductions allegedly reduced production costs at company collieries from $2.51 per ton in 1873 to $1.35 per ton in 1876, the company constantly lost money on its operations (to say nothing of the $3,000,000 paid out annually on its indebtedness). In the five years from 1875 through 1879 the PRCI lost money at a rate of $600,000 to $750,000 per year. Although the railroad continued to make a profit, it could not sustain the crushing burden of debt and operating losses suffered by its wholly owned subsidiary, and took refuge in bankruptcy and receivership in 1880 and 1884. Gowen weathered the first storm, but lost his position as president in the second. And even after the company was reorganized, the PRCI continued to lose money. In the opinion of Gowen's biographer, the first year that it showed a profit was during the First World War.

St. Clair did not fare very well under the regime of the PRCI. The shutting down of the St. Clair Shaft and the abandonment of Lanigan's Furnace in 1873 put about 300 men and boys out of work, and efficiency measures at the Eagle and Pine Forest by 1877 had reduced their complements by about thirty and twenty respectively. A few of these men were doubtless hired on during the sinking of the Twin Shafts, and a few more between 1876 and 1884. But the Twin Shafts never, even in its best years, hired more than 315 hands, and most of the time less than 200. The Hickory Slope was abandoned in 1874. The Wadesville Shaft, when it was working, employed as many as 570 men, but it was suspended on account of mine fires and flooding much of the time, being closed down during most of 1871 and all of 1874 and 1875; in the latter two years, it was not recorded as producing any coal at all. Thus, in the years leading up to and including 1875, the Wadesville Shaft must have added to St. Clair's burden of unemployment by as many as 300 to 500 jobs. The Long Strike in the first six months of 1875 idled those who still had jobs at the Eagle and Pine Forest.

The cumulative impact on St. Clair was disastrous. By 1875, something on the order of 500 of St. Clair's 984 colliery workers were, seemingly, permanently unemployed. With half of the colliery workers out on strike, and the other half with no jobs to go to after the strike ended, the town's merchants and artisans were also facing ruin. The result was an exodus as miners, merchants, and artisans emigrated, many of them—like the Tempest family, whom we noticed earlier—seeking their fortunes in Shenandoah and Mahanoy City. Precisely how many moved away it is impossible to say, but the 1880 census reveals a substantial loss in population as compared to 1870. The total population enumerated in 1870 was 5,711; in 1880 it had fallen to 4,149, a difference of 1,562 souls. Better than 25 percent of St. Clair's population had left the town. In 1870 there were 474 men listed as "coal miners"; in 1880 there were only 320, a difference of 154.[15]

Furthermore, the decline in the fortunes of the coal trade affected the ethnic groups in different ways. In 1880 the census revealed that for the first time there were more Irish-born contract miners than either English or Welsh, and the Germans had virtually withdrawn from mining:

TABLE 12: *Miner/Laborer Status and Ethnicity, 1880*

	Irish	Welsh	English	German	1880
MINER	78	73	72	18	Foreign-born
MINE LABORER	32	20	24	5	
MINER	35	9	12	13	Pa.-born, fa.
MINE LABORER	96	26	25	28	foreign born
MINER	1	0	1	0	Other U.S.-born,
MINE LABORER	2	1	0	1	fa. foreign born

Also there were more U.S.-born contract miners with Irish-born fathers than all other first-generation miners combined (35 to 34). Clearly the Germans and the British were moving out of mining into service occupations, such as the various skilled trades and shop-keeping. Counting both place of birth and place of father's birth as indicators of ethnicity, we see the figures for artisans and merchants.

TABLE 13: *Artisan/Merchant Status and Ethnicity, 1880*

	English	Welsh	German	Irish
ARTISANS	15	7	28	9
MERCHANTS	19	10	6	4

Thus the Irish-born and their U.S.-born children, who made up 27% of the town's population in 1880, held only 11% of the artisans' and merchants' jobs, while the Germans, who constituted 14% of the population, held 35% of these jobs. Evidently the Irish, who in the previous generation had been relegated to laborer's status in the St. Clair mines, now were inheriting the better mining jobs, while the other ethnic groups were abandoning mining for careers as artisans and shop keepers.

No doubt there was a revival of hope in 1876, when the Twin Shafts Colliery began to produce some coal, but the demise of that establishment in 1884 and the closing (for fifteen years) of the Wadesville Shaft in 1885 left the town from 1885 on with only two collieries operating—the Eagle and the Pine Forest. Together they could employ no more than 400 men and boys.

Thus, for all practical purposes, ended mining on the lands south of the Mammoth outcrop at St. Clair. The southern part of the Pottsville Basin, below St. Clair, whence the first anthracite was shipped to market little more than half a century before, had been ravaged by eager colliery operators, all seeking wealth, and all failing. The miners' union had been broken and the PRCI had gone into bankruptcy. Ignoring the warnings of scientists, disregarding the principles of best practice, deluded by a mythology they and their friends had created, the operators had ruined themselves and decimated the communities around them.

EPILOGUE

THE SURVIVAL OF ST. CLAIR

The principal figures in our history, whose lives most importantly affected the town of St. Clair, did not long survive the town's crisis in the 1870's. Enoch McGinness, in fact, did not even live to see the abandonment of his pioneering mine, the St. Clair Shaft; he died in 1867 while engaged in sinking a shaft into the vein of black band ore at the south edge of St. Clair.[1] Samuel H. Daddow retired from management of the Erie Railroad's coal estate in 1874 and died in St. Clair in March 1875 after a brief illness.[2] In 1879, at the age of forty-eight, John Siney died in poverty at his house in Crow Hollow of miner's consumption—black-lung disease, in all likelihood—complicated, we may suspect, by disappointment at the rejection he suffered at the hands of former union comrades.[3] Henry Carey passed away peacefully, also in 1879, working on articles and personal correspondence almost to the last minute. As his memorialist described it, it was the ideal departure of a gentleman scholar:

> Only five days before his death, Dr. S. Austin Allibone received from him an article on the use of the word *fortnight* and its synonyms in several languages and varied uses, which was marked by clearness, pertinency, and niceness of verbal distinctions worthy of the divertisements of leisure in his best days; and, with his habitual observance of the amenities of social life, he continued to visit and receive his friends to within two weeks of his departure. His death was not premature, nor was it surprising either to himself or to those nearest to him; but at the last it was, in some sense, sudden. He was spared the helplessness of protracted illness. Gently, tranquilly, he passed into his last sleep.[4]

John Kehoe was hanged a week before Christmas in 1878 for a murder allegedly committed sixteen years before[5]—and he was pardoned posthu-

439

GENERAL VIEW of WADESVILLE COLLIERY - YEAR 1930

Wadesville Colliery in 1930, a few years before its final shutdown. Only the pumping station at extreme left remained in 1986.

mously by the governor of Pennsylvania nearly 100 years later. Gowen's life ended, as one might have expected, even more spectacularly: he shot himself in the head in a Washington hotel room in 1888. He left no note, and his reasons for suicide are a matter of speculation; some suspected revenge by Mollies who escaped the hangman's rope, but there was no evidence of foul play.[6]

St. Clair itself, however, did survive the loss of half its coal mines and the emigration of a quarter of its population. Although mining virtually ceased south of the town, it continued along the outcrop of the Mammoth Vein and in the shafts just to the south, where the Mammoth could be reached at a reasonable depth. The Pine Forest was worked by the PRCI until it was suspended in 1899. The Wadesville Shaft, which had been kept on stand-by status for fifteen years after it was suspended in 1885, producing only enough coal to keep the pumps working, and employing about fifty men, was reopened in 1900 and continued to operate until sometime in the 1930's. The Eagle Colliery was the most enduring of them all. Perched on its own basin of the Mammoth, north of the outcrop, it was operated by the Johns brothers under the Wetherill lease until 1872, when the mineral rights were taken over by the PRCI; the PRCI renewed the lease and the Eagle was operated by the Johns family until 1889.[7] After a brief interval, the colliery was then leased by the St. Clair Coal Company. The local superintendent, William T. Smyth, expanded the operation eastward toward Silver Creek, and he and his descendants continued to mine coal from deep shafts and slopes until 1957, when the final owner, H. Gordon Smyth, closed the mine down. The St. Clair Coal Company's mine was undoubtedly one of the last major underground mining operations in the anthracite region, for by that date much of the northern field had been flooded when the Susquehanna River broke through the roof into gangways incautiously driven under the riverbed, and the southern and middle fields were turning mostly to strip mining. Strip mining began as early as the 1890's in some parts of the southern field, but it depended for widespread use on the development of large, self-propelled steam shovels and draglines. Superintendent Smyth was deploying steam shovels in stripping operations at St. Clair by 1900.[8]

But St. Clair's survival as a relatively prosperous community depended on more than the continued operation of a couple of collieries. It was a nice example of Carey's principle of a diversified regional economy. St. Clair had a number of new enterprises that took up some of the slack left by the closing of the mines.[9] Samuel H. Daddow was the founder of at least three manufacturing establishments. The Miners' Supply Company, started about 1870 to manufacture the safety squibs invented and later patented by him and Jesse Beadle, was by 1880 selling its products all over the country and had grown large enough to employ thirty-one persons in addition to the owner, widow Esther Daddow, almost all of them girls under twenty (there was a male superintendent, Esther's brother, and two male clerks). Daddow also manufactured Lattimer's patented miner's caps in another little factory; it is said to have at one time made 90 percent of the miner's caps used in the United States. And he established a little shop to make the boxes for shipping squibs and caps. All in all, the Daddow enterprises must have employed on the order of fifty people. The other new employer of some consequence was the Reading railroad, which by 1880 had established, in addition to the depot, a repair shop, office, and yards for rolling stock and had hired at least forty-four people, mostly brakemen, repairmen, and laborers, along with a few superintendents, clerks, and watchmen. In 1875 a German master mechanic, Peter Quirin, established a brass foundry and machine shop that took care of repairs for the machinery of the various collieries about the town; it is still in business today.

Bird's-eye view of St. Clair, from a postcard circa 1890

But the greatest boost to St. Clair's economy came in 1913, when the Reading expanded its repair shops and marshaling yards at St. Clair into "the largest classified coal yards of the world." The St. Clair Coal Yards had sixty-three tracks, a capacity for 2,010 cars, and an engine house large enough to contain fifty-two locomotives. It employed over 1,000 men when working at full capacity. It was here that all the trains of empty cars were made up for dispatching to the collieries north of Broad Mountain, and all the loaded trains were assembled from the lateral branches serving the collieries. Actually, the suggestion that the flat and swampy land at the south end of St. Clair would be a fine site for a railroad distribution center for the Mahanoy and Broad Mountain coal trade had been made as long ago as 1862. But McGinness, ever jealous of the northern field, deprecated the idea in a letter to Carey, saying that there wasn't space enough for the yards.[10]

Important social and technological changes occurred in St. Clair, as elsewhere in the region. In the 1880's the immigration of Slavic-speaking eastern Europeans began and continued into the first part of the twentieth century. New labor organizations, first the Knights of Labor in the later '70's and '80's, and finally in the 1890's the more militant United Mine Workers led by the legendary John Mitchell, replaced the defunct Workingmen's Benevolent Association of St. Clair. The larger operators improved the technology of mining where they could, replacing the old oil

Second Street, St. Clair, looking north

and carbide lamps with electric cap lights energized by battery packs carried on the hip, and electric power was run into the mines to permit permanent lighting fixtures and to replace the mules with electric locomotives. Conveyor belts aided in the labor of loading cars. But steeply sloping seams still made the use of mechanical coal cutters and the longwall method impossible. And then, between the two world wars, the deep mining industry gradually died, crushed by competition from oil and natural gas, and only strip mining remained. But strip mining requires no miners, just a few dynamiters, dragline operators, and truck drivers. And so, even though the hills have been stripped down to the Mammoth on all sides of St. Clair, St. Clair is no longer a mining town in the way that it was when Enoch McGinness prowled the hills and Siney harangued his men at Walker's Hall more than 100 years ago.

Today there is no longer a Mill Creek and Mine Hill Railroad to take the traveler to St. Clair; there is, indeed, no longer a Reading passenger train to take him to Pottsville. From Reading, one must drive a car or ride a bus north on Route 61 alongside the abandoned canal, through Pottsville, and over the old iron bridge into the center of St. Clair. Still farther north, Route 61 will take you to Frackville and on to the outskirts of Centralia, where the fire burns beneath the streets in a long-abandoned mine and the road is closed to traffic. Or from Frackville one might wish to visit Shenandoah, where only recently another mine fire burned so hot that the sidewalks, so they say, would fry an egg and one could see the red glow through cracks in the pavement. The Shenandoah fire was finally checked by stripping out the burning seam; it is said in St. Clair that the Shenandoah fire began more than 100 years ago when Kehley Run Colliery burned underground.

But there are no underground fires at St. Clair; no breakers tower over the town; and most of the culm banks have been torn away. Driving through on Route 61, the casual traveler might not know that this was a mining town at all, except for a sign that identifies the office of the Pine Forest Stripping Company on Second Street, and the coal trucks that roll their way south. It is a pleasant place of about 4,000 people, a suburb of Pottsville, nourishing among the well-kept, white-painted houses a small grove of some seventeen church steeples and domes that are a legacy of the ethnic diversity of the original settlers. But if one stays awhile, one finds more evidence of the past on the side streets. "Johns' Patch" still survives at the north end of the town, in the form of a few remodeled miner's cottages; at the south, Dormer's saloon, now renamed, still invites its clientele of workmen to its long mahogany bar. People still tell tales of the Molly Maguires and how they met at Dormer's, summoned by the unauthorized ringing of the bell of St. Mary's Church, and there planned their evil deeds. The Soldiers' Monument, its inscribed names partly eaten away by acid rain, still towers over the Odd Fellows Cemetery; and the obelisk still stands over Siney's grave in the Irish half of the Catholic cemetery on the other side of the creek. But it is in the hills north and east and west of the town—there is no trace of the once vast railroad yards to the south—that the coal town's past can still be seen. Tramping through the underbrush at the heels of a local guide who knows where the holes are, one can still find remains of Lanigan's Furnace, McGinness' iron mine, and some of the old collieries. The Twin Shafts are covered over with dirt and debris, and timbers and rock tunnels are the only remains of the Eagle, its site now a great hole hundreds of feet deep, stripped down to the rock underlying the Mammoth Vein. But the Pine Forest Shaft is still there, now a pumping station drawing water from the aquifers through which the stripping draglines are descending, and rumor has it that the St. Clair Shaft will be re-opened, to serve as a pumping station too. North of Wadesville, another great hole remains where the gangways of the Wadesville Shaft once ran. All of these strip-mining excavations will be back-filled, leaving grassy valleys where hills once rose. But Wadesville itself, as the headline in the Pottsville *Republican* put it in an article in its May 9, 1986, edition, "awaits destruction . . . as bulldozers advance." Already gone are the Primitive Methodist Church and several houses.

But the sharpest confrontation with the past is to be experienced at the sites of two of the old shafts. Near the top of the hill between St. Clair and Wadesville, a hundred yards or so from the Catholic Cemetery, hidden in underbrush, lie the remains of the Wadesville Shaft. Nothing can be seen above ground but chunks of concrete and steel surrounding the shaft itself. On the day of my visit, the shaft was covered by perforated plates of iron, no doubt old screens from the top of the breaker. My guide dropped a stone through one of the holes; no sound returned. And on the hillside just west of town, at the end of Carroll Street, we found the remains of the St. Clair Shaft. Surrounded by a chain link fence, it is a yawning black hole fifty feet or more across. The sides caved in many years ago; filled with water and blocked by debris, its edge littered with beer cans and broken bottles, McGinness' great creation still stares silently at the sky, like the eye of a sleeping volcano.

APPENDIX

THE DISASTER-PRONE ORGANIZATION

The early decline of the anthracite industry in the Pottsville district was, in this writer's view, not the result of the purely social and economic factors that have been blamed by others who have studied the trade. The panic of 1873 and the subsequent depression did not bear especially heavily on the Pottsville district because the vast Philadelphia and Reading Coal and Iron Company, owned by the Philadelphia and Reading Railroad, chose that time to invest in its development. An official of the national miners' union even declared in 1874 that the miners in Schuylkill "had never known what the panic was."[1] Clifton K. Yearley, in his fine 1961 study *Enterprise and Anthracite: Economics and Democracy in Schuylkill County, 1820–1875,* found the prolonged zealous individualism of the county's entrepreneurs in the face of corporate consolidation among their northern competitors to have been the underlying cause of the decline.[2] And Edward J. Davies' recent (1985) book, *The Anthracite Aristocracy: Leadership and Social Change in the Hard Coal Regions of Northeastern Pennsylvania,* has argued that the trade of the Pottsville district collapsed long before that of the Wilkes-Barre area because the Schuylkill County elite never solidified into a powerful upper class in the same way as did the elite of the northern region, and therefore was unable to maintain control of its local economy.[3] But neither of these studies deals adequately with the roles of rejection of scientific advice, neglect of safety technology, and colliery mismanagement in the approach to disaster.

In this appendix we shall try to develop a cultural and psychological model that will account for the self-defeating behavior of so many landowners and colliery operators who, by their disregard of geologists' warnings and their neglect of well-known contemporary principles of best mining practice, doomed their own mines to disaster and themselves to financial ruin. One is tempted to regard their conduct as irrational; one recalls the lines in the local ballad "The Driver Boys of Wadesville Shaft":

446

In insane asylums madmen rave
But where sensible men go daft,
You'd go nutty too
With that bughouse crew
On the bottom of Wadesville Shaft.[4]

But let us assume that the operators were indeed "sensible men" who made their decisions above ground with the aid of some conventional economic calculus. As we have seen, however, the values assigned to the terms of that calculus were determined not only by such financial and probability figures as were available but also by a variety of private motives and public myths. First we shall consider a present-day psychological model of risk evaluation and decision making which may suggest elements of the calculus. Then we shall try to construct a model not so much of a disaster-prone personality, but rather of a disaster-prone organization in which a culturally acceptable economic calculus, which may be called "optimum scenario thinking," was applied within the constraints of a culturally determined mythology that minimized the awareness of risk and, interacting with the unsteady financial or job-tenure situation of an administrator, dictated the choice of a comparatively unsafe, but comparatively inexpensive, technology.

RISK-SEEKING BEHAVIOR IN DECISION THEORY

The economic literature on rational decision making in a risky world, or, more precisely, on how to allocate scarce resources in order to maximize gains and minimize losses when one knows the risks attending alternative actions, is more normative than descriptive, although there is a growing awareness in the decision-analysis field that more description of real behavior is needed (a point made in the recent report on *Risk and Decision Making* by the National Academy of Sciences).[1] Furthermore, formal decision analysis does not usually take into account the cultural patterns and social conflicts that define what a society conceives as undesirable risk and as the right way to think. There is an anthropological literature on agricultural decision making in peasant societies that carefully distinguishes between normative rationality, as prescribed by economic theory, and the actual mode of thought (sometimes regarded as "irrational" by economists) of peasant farmers.[2] And cross-cultural psychologists have begun to investigate cultural differences in probabilistic thinking. But even such a culturally comparative, descriptive approach as is demonstrated in Mary

447

Douglas' and Aaron Wildavsky's recent essay *Risk and Culture* does not probe very deeply into the mentality of the risk taker; it is more concerned with the social situation and cognitive world of those who engage in public debate than with what goes on in the head of an executive who decides to dump toxic waste in a landfill, or a materials engineer who allows defective pipe to be installed in a nuclear reactor—or a colliery operator who fails to complete the ventilation system in his mine.[3] And, indeed, a good deal of contemporary analysis of "risk management" is written from the point of view of the harassed bureaucrat or corporate executive, for whom public anxiety is seen as the major administrative problem, rather than from the view of the public, for whom bureaucratic and corporate mismanagement, secrecy, and self-serving reassurance are perceived as the source of real threats to public safety.

The literature on coal-mine safety deals more directly with the behavior of miners and managers. A study by the National Academy of Sciences, *Toward Safer Underground Coal Mines*, describes the results of a survey designed to discover factors that differentiated mines with poor and mines with better safety records.[4] Not much progress seems to have been made since the 1870's. Casualty rates for deaths and disabling injuries ("disabling" now, however, includes injuries that would not even be mentioned in Pennsylvania's nineteenth-century mine inspectors' reports) in the 1970's ranged from a low of 8 to a high of 16.7 per 100 men per year; the average was 12. The monograph laid the responsibility on management. Under bad management, workers became "weary and careless." Most of the variation in safety records in the nineteen largest coal companies in the country was attributed to differences in the strength of the commitment to safety by top management, differences in the extent of cooperation between labor and management, and differences in the safety education of miners. There was also a strong positive correlation between mine age and safety (older is safer) and mine size and safety (bigger is safer). But the analysis is so clearly policy-oriented—it strives to answer the question, What can be done to improve safety?—that one wonders whether causal factors in behavioral domains deemed less accessible to management intervention may not have been examined very closely.

The historian William Graebner in *Coal Mining Safety in the Progressive Period* does provide a model of the colliery operators' mode of thought during the years from 1900 to 1920. Although his analysis applies to the bituminous industry, and to a later time than our study, its main point is nevertheless applicable to anthracite. In a thoughtful chapter entitled "The Operator as Victim," he argues that not all safety-neglecting operators can be dismissed as heartless capitalists. Such an explanation of their behavior would be too simple. The bituminous-coal industry really was highly competitive and prices really were low. Thus "industry economics insured that operators would view safety not as efficiency, but as expense to be avoided."[5] Only the largest companies could afford to comply with state safety laws and give support to the new federal Bureau of Mines in its research and standards-setting activities. Graebner's analysis is certainly applicable, as far as it goes, to the nineteenth-century anthracite industry. As we have seen, many operators did skimp on safety measures, in ventilation and timbering particularly, in order to save money. But what skews the analysis, and diverts attention from the other half of the problem, is the general practice of referring to the issue as "safety." Safety—the protection of human life—is indeed the most important issue in the eyes of most observers. But there is a second issue that is, or should be, of major concern to the operators, miners, and general public. And that issue is maintaining the integrity and efficiency of the colliery itself, including the mine, the breaker, the engines, and all the rest. For the gas explosion, flood or fire, roof fall, or broken hoisting cable that killed and maimed the miners also damaged the mine and cost the operator (and often his employees) money. Safety measures protected not only the men but the mine itself and thus the operator's pocketbook. It is easy to understand, by way of a calculus of class conflict, the operator's lack of comradely concern for the miners, but it is not so easy to understand his repeatedly risking the destruction of his own colliery.

It has long been recognized that in making decisions in situations where gain and loss, and the probabilities thereof, can be stated accurately in numbers (as in playing games of chance), people do not always choose the mathematically optimal strategy. They do not always make the decisions that would maximize their chances of success and minimize their chances of failure. When it is possible to obtain a sure but modest gain (as in investing savings), many players have a tendency to neglect somewhat higher-paying but slightly risky alternatives, even though in the long run the alternative will pay more. Conversely, where the possible payoff is very great (as in lotteries), many bettors will regularly invest small amounts even though failure is almost certain. There are systematic cultural differences in response to probability information.[6] Such patterns of risk-aversive and risk-seeking behavior, in situations where the stakes are not matters of life and death, or even of economic survival, have recently been investigated by psychologists Daniel Kahneman and Amos Tversky. Their crucial observation, which is very relevant to the apparent behavior of the coal operators of Schuylkill, is that when their subjects were forced to choose between a sure loss, on the one hand, and, on the other, the substantial probability of a larger loss combined with a small probability of no loss at all, they tended to choose the risky alternative. In the case of the colliery operators, they avoided the sure financial loss attendant upon taking all recommended safety precautions and opted for the more risky, and ultimately more costly, alternative of neglecting safety and gambling that they could "get away with it."

The experiment was described by the investigators as follows:

> To get a sense of risk seeking imagine you are forced to choose between a sure loss of $80 and a risk that involves an 85 percent chance of losing $100 and a 15 percent chance of losing nothing. Faced with this choice a large majority prefer the gamble to the loss. . . . The majority preference is thus an instance of risk seeking.

This example of risk seeking is grounded in a cognitive model, derived from the introspections of psychologists, economists, and mathematicians, that goes back at least to the early eighteenth century and has been employed by economists in the development of utility theory. In the psychology of preferences used in utility theory, the actor (be he consumer, investor, gambler, or colliery operator) is considered to be making a choice of alternative actions based on information concerning the value *to him* of possible, quantitatively measurable gains and losses, and the relative likelihood of these alternative outcomes. The crux of the problem is that the difference in the *value* to the actor of any two outcomes is not a simple arithmetic product of "objective" costs, losses, gains, and probabilities. When the differences in value are functions of differences between losses, the investigators found that in both real and hypothetical situations, involving both money and outcomes other than money, there was a strong tendency for preferences between losses to be risk-seeking. The risk-seeking strategy also prevails over a wide range of magnitudes of loss and of probabilities (with the qualification that the preference may be reversed where the loss under risk seeking would result in a "substantial change in a person's way of life").[7]

The significance of the experimental exercise, however, is not the proposition that most human beings are risk seekers with respect to prospective losses, but that the "true" magnitudes of gain and loss and of probability are so readily malleable into variable values. It may be useful to consider that the actors in the anthracite drama sometimes did acquire information about the "true" magnitudes of possible profits and losses, and of probabilities, associated with various business options. Unfortunately, however, we do not have a clear statement of a complete decision matrix, with continuous probabilities on a scale from zero to one, and magnitudes of gain and loss, from any mine operator confronted with an actual decision. But we have been able to document ways in which operators manipulated such quantities so as to make their choices appear more reasonable to their employers, creditors, and patrons. With respect to gains, they tended to overestimate possible future profits and to overestimate the probability of securing them. On the negative side, they underestimated possible future losses and underestimated the probability of such losses occurring. To the extent that colliery operators did calculate the relative merits of different courses of action, they *may* have acted like Kahneman and Tversky's gamblers, but they may also have been only closet risk seekers, as it were, concealing their risk-seeking behavior from others' eyes, and perhaps their own, by working with false figures that made "truly" bad bets look like safe ones.

But one must keep in mind that these mid-nineteenth-century operators were not administrators trained in a modern business school. They were hampered by the inevitable lack of accumulated records of experience, let alone organized statistical information, in the early years of the industry; their bookkeeping methods were for the most part primitive; and normative decision theory had not been developed by twentieth-century operations research and game theory into a procedure applicable in almost any business. Furthermore, most of the serious decisions a colliery operator had to make were not the neat choices offered to Kahneman and Tversky's subjects, describable in a four-celled matrix of gains and losses partitioned by alternative courses of action. They were rather more like choices in a stochastic network, each choice generating a new array of options and foreclosing other possibilities; they were choices linked end-to-end in a colliery's twenty-year history. The operator thus had to think not just of today's choice but of ultimate outcomes—or at least outcomes a few months in advance, when the seasons changed, rents came due, or the price of coal should rise. One of the deficiences of "rational" decision theory for understanding the problems of system managers lies precisely here. It is not diachronic, as Max Black has pointed out.[8]

If the operator thought of today's decision as determining a whole series of future options, then, one may suspect, he made his choices on the basis of alternative scenarios. We may define "scenario," for our purposes, as a single line of choice through a stochastic matrix, or network of branching possibilities. Such a line of choice is affected by all sorts of personal considerations in addition to the simple calculations of profit, loss, and probability affecting the colliery. The operator, according to this model, might pose to himself this problem: What will the colliery's financial position be six weeks from now on July 1, when the rents come due in the amount of $1,000, if I suspend operations for a week while the fan is being repaired? And what the position if I keep the men at work? The answers cannot really be derived from straightforward numerical calculations of all possible chains of events. The considerations rapidly become so complex, and so many involve time, costs, and probabilities that are impossible to quantify very precisely, that the exercise quickly becomes intuitive. The operator visualizes men working slowly, in bad air, with safety lamps; the natural ventilation grows less and less effective as the summer season advances; if they try to start up the old furnace, it might set off a firedamp explosion, so suppose instead we pipe steam jets into the furnace flue, the way they used to do at the St. Clair Shaft . . . Thus, instead of asking, What is the probability of getting through six weeks without the fan? the question becomes, Can I *imagine* getting through six weeks without the fan? The risk seeker in this model is satisfied with mere possibility; only the unimaginable is impossible. And since he can exercise some control over events (unlike the subjects in Kahneman and Tversky's study), he can act to ensure that the good conditions envisioned in his imaginary possible sequence—a careful fire boss, experienced and responsible workmen, a sober night watchman—are actually present. Or at least he can try to bring about these conditions. He is imagining the optimum scenario.

If decisions were being made by operators on the basis not of formal decision matrices, but of imagined (and therefore possible) scenarios, then the door was open to the consideration of utilities that pertained less to the colliery's books than to the operator's personal interests. The interests most pertinent to the operator's selection of scenario were those that concerned his relationship to people who controlled him financially: landowners, creditors, and employers. These persons set payment and production schedules for the operator and, unfortunately for everyone, the risk of offending them was increased the more time and money the operator spent on such things as ventilation and props. And the displeasure of landowners, creditors, and employers was easily translated into cancellation of lease, foreclosure, and bankruptcy, or (in the case of managers of collieries operated by a large corporation) deprivation of advancement and even termination of employment. The operator thus had, potentially, a powerful motive to skimp on protective expenses that only the most explicit, detailed, and emphatic instruction and supervision by his superiors was likely to overcome.

THE DISASTER-PRONE ORGANIZATION

Any model of the conditions under which industrial disasters occur, whether in nineteenth-century coal mines or twentieth-century nuclear installations, must be based on the assumption that it is not just a person, or a mechanical part, but an organization that fails. Whether the organization be a large, bureaucratically managed corporation like the Philadelphia and Reading Coal and Iron Company, or a loosely administered company like the North American, or a network of colliery workers, operators, landowners, and creditors like McGinness' St. Clair Shaft Colliery, it is always the organization that is responsible for winning or losing. The mentality of people like Enoch McGinness is an essential component of the process, but their fears, aspirations, and calculations are influenced by organizational structure, by the economic situation in which they find themselves, and by the cultural ambience of values and beliefs in which not only they but their organization lives and works.

In the broadest sense, we are looking at an early stage in the Industrial Revolution when human beings on this planet were for the first time burning fossil fuels on a large scale, when iron and steel were for the first time being used in considerable quantities, when steam engines were transforming arts and crafts into high-energy industries and were creating high-speed transportation systems. Large, bureaucratic industrial organizations and complex financial institutions were emerging. But the actual level of risk to life, limb, and property in this new world was not yet clearly realized, if for no other reason than that sufficient experience over time had not yet generated reliable and valid statistical runs. And new and improved methods of reducing risk were just being developed, for the most part in Europe, where the Industrial Revolution began.

In the anthracite-coal trade in America, newly established as an important industry in the 1830's, there were at first three major groups whose interests converged in a way that made application even of European experience with colliery safety and security slow and incomplete. The early investors in coal lands in the 1820's and '30's put their surplus capital into mineral rights as a form of real-estate speculation and then, as the boom subsided, discovered that it was difficult to withdraw without losing money. Compelled to remain, they sought to maximize the return on their investment by maximizing the production from which their rents derived. The colliery operators, not very much interested in the safety of their workers, were not much interested in colliery security either, because security involved "dead work" that cost money and slowed production, and the scenarios they attempted to enact emphasized speed, economy, and large profits. The miners themselves, and particularly the contract miners on piecework, forced, both by economic need and by personal inability to control the ventilation system, to work in unsafe mines, were themselves on occasion careless. Surrounding this arena of financially insecure men, their eyes on production rather than security, was a busy cadre of myth makers attempting to rationalize the process by putting the blame for accidents on careless workers, touting the industry and praising its leaders as heroes, blaming economic problems on British free-traders and Irish terrorists, denying the uncomfortable facts of geology and atmospheric physics. And the regulatory agencies, eventually established to salvage an industry dying by its own hand, tried to aid struggling companies by lax law enforcement.

We have, in the instance of the coal trade in St. Clair and its environs, a case history that I believe represents the forces at work in this period throughout the anthracite region and, in fact, the bituminous coal fields as well. But it is difficult not to find similarities in other industries, the railroads, steamboats, iron, and steel in particular. And I find the anthracite model useful in trying to explain the perennial difficulty of regulating safety and security in present-day industries—nuclear, chemical, transportation, manufacturing, and others—in both capitalist and socialist countries. For these are problems brought on by what is still, by evolutionary standards, an early stage of the Industrial Revolution, before lessons have been learned and the social, psychological, and cultural situation in which the disaster-prone organization is nourished has been fully identified and means devised to correct it when it appears.

Let us now attempt to define the essential characteristics of the disaster-prone organization in terms sufficiently general to include not only the nineteenth-century anthracite industry in the Pottsville Basin, on which the model is based, but other domains of enterprise as well, both private and governmental, capitalist and socialist.

An Organization May Be Said to Be More Prone to Disaster the More Strongly

1) it follows a policy of maximizing productivity while minimizing expenditures for safety (including training as well as plant);
2) it requires bosses and workers (both individually and in teams) to assume responsibility simultaneously for both productivity and safety;

454

3) it encourages these bosses and workers to make safety-relevant decisions without adequate information (and even suppresses negative information) and without formal rules for decision making (thus making "scenario" thinking in situations of risk more likely);

4) it punishes these bosses and workers if production goals are not met, while imposing minimal sanctions if safety is neglected;

5) it endorses a prevailing mythology that praises daring and productive persons more than cautious and protective ones;

6) it endorses a prevailing mythology that blames the industry's problems on conspiratorial outsiders and on disaffected, dishonest, or careless workers.

The first two of these characteristics of the disaster-prone organization were, in fact, clearly recognized early in the British coal industry's history. In an effort to remove the conflict of interest inherent in situations where the same manager is responsible for both production and safety, the duties of the fire boss were separated from the role of the underground mine boss. The fire boss, theoretically, could stop or limit production whenever and wherever he felt that the ventilation was not adequate to eliminate the threat of a firedamp explosion, and his decisions in this matter supposedly could not be revoked by the pit boss. But other aspects of safety—such as props, pillar size and spacing, hoisting equipment—still remained in the hands of men responsible for production. The fire boss' position was continued in America.

We have suggested repeatedly, furthermore, that highly disaster-prone organizations were the norm in Schuylkill County's coal trade, and that mine accidents and disasters not only routinely gave the *coup de grace* to failing collieries but helped to make most collieries unprofitable enterprises. How the coal trade managed to continue for generations while most individual collieries were losing money is an interesting question. Clearly, the anthracite region was producing a commodity of great value to American society; it provided the fuel for initial industrialization. Perhaps the ethos of these disaster-prone organizations in itself spurred them on to produce coal at a loss, rewarding the participants for their useful function not in money but in social approval, and dissuading them from withdrawal from the trade by creating a series of gratifying delusions. America needed the coal and found ways other than financial to motivate its producers.

Thus the function of the industrialist-as-hero theme, of the geological fantasies of Enoch McGinness, and of the delusion that the problems of the coal trade were being caused by aliens, British free-traders, and Irish Molly Maguires, was not only to permit disaster but also to persuade a bankrupt industry and its creditors to continue nevertheless to produce the fuel needed to bring the Industrial Revolution to America.

That may have been all very well in the nineteenth-century coal trade, when the victims of an accident were essentially the miners and their families. The general public in nearby communities was usually not personally threatened by a gas explosion (unless it started a mine fire) or a fall of coal. But in the twentieth-century world, failures to maintain high standards of industrial safety can threaten not only nearby but even distant communities. "Safety" comes to mean public welfare as well as plant security. In this condition, the identification of disaster-prone organizations would seem to be a matter of some importance.

NOTES
BIBLIOGRAPHY
INDEX

ABBREVIATIONS

Libraries and Manuscript Repositories

APS	American Philosophical Society
EMHL	Eleutherian Mills Historical Library (now known as The Hagley Library and Museum)
HSP	Historical Society of Pennsylvania
HSSC	Historical Society of Schuylkill County
LOC	Library of Congress
NA	National Archives
PHMC	Pennsylvania Historical and Museum Commission
SCCH	Schuylkill County Court House
UP	University of Pennsylvania

Persons

HB	Henry Carey Baird
TB	Thomas J. Baird
EC	Edward Carey
HC	Henry C. Carey
EM	Enoch McGinness
AR	Andrew Russell

Biographical Dictionaries

DAB	Dictionary of American Biography
DNB	Dictionary of National Biography
DSB	Dictionary of Scientific Biography
NC	National Cyclopaedia of American Biography

Newspapers

MJ *Miners' Journal* (Pottsville, Pennsylvania)

Government Publications

ARMI Annual Reports of the Inspectors of Coal Mines

Notes

I. MINING ANTHRACITE

1. The physical qualities of coal are reviewed in Rogers, 1858, vol. 2, pp. 970–1000, and Johnson, 1844, pp. 36–181. More modern data are given in Francis, 1961, Krevelen, 1961, and Lowry, 1945, 1963.

THE STRUCTURE AND OPERATION OF AN ANTHRACITE COLLIERY

1. The following general description of mining and coal preparation in nineteenth-century anthracite collieries is based largely on the contemporary treatises of Bowen, 1852; Daddow and Bannan, 1866; Chance, 1883; and Miesse, 1887.
2. The payroll of the Kaska William Colliery (at HSSC), a few miles from St. Clair, from 1851 to 1853 provides detail on job categories and pay scales.
3. Chance, 1883, pp. 357–367.
4. Tolls on the Mill Creek and Mine Hill Railroad may be found in EMHL, Reading Company Papers (Acc. 1520, Box 301). Canal and railroad tolls were regularly published in MJ; see, for example, MJ, 1 March 1851, and Bowen, 1852, p. 229.

SOME PECULIARITIES OF COAL AS A COMMODITY

1. This section was presented as a paper before the Ethnohistory Workshop at the University of Pennsylvania, 29 March 1984.
2. MJ, 24 July 1858.
3. HSP, EM to HC, no date.
4. Yearley, 1961, p. 59.

PROGRESS AND REGRESSION IN COLLIERY TECHNOLOGY 1830–1870

1. In addition to Hedley, 1851, Marlor, 1854, and Moore, 1859, other nineteenth-century British manuals include Holland, 1835, Bagot, 1879, and Atkinson, 1892. One early American publication, Phillips, 1858, purported to explain the "general principles" of British mining practice, but was very vague; nothing of substance on mining methods seems to have been written in America before Daddow and Bannan, 1866, and Daddow was born in Cornwall.
2. Maguire, 1912, p. 310.
3. Hedley, 1851, pp. 20–21.
4. Early cylinder screens are mentioned in Bowen, 1852, p. 190.
5. HSP, Carey Papers, EM to HC, 26 June 1861; Binder, 1974, p. 58.
6. Battin's invention of, and patents for, the coal breaker, and its early diffusion and modification, are given in detail in Pinkowski, 1949. Bowen, 1852, p. 189, pictures an early breaker installed at a drift mine. McGinness' engine is mentioned in MJ, 2 March 1844, and the first installations in MJ, 11 Jan. 1845. See also MJ, 13 and 20 Feb. 1858, for Battin's negotiations with the operators.
7. Daddow and Bannan, 1866, pp. 482–483.
8. Bowen, 1852, p. 190.
9. MJ, 8 Sept. 1855.
10. Bowen, 1857; Daddow and Bannan, 1866, p. 477.
11. ARMI, 1869.
12. See HSP, Carey Papers, EM to HC.
13. Chance, 1883, pp. 359–360.
14. *Ibid.*, pp. 304–305.
15. MJ, 26 Jan. 1861.
16. Allison, 1912; Daddow and Bannan, 1866, p. 789; MJ, 2 Nov. 1867.

17. MJ, 24 April 1858.
18. Agricola, 1950, pp. 200–212.
19. Birch, 1756–57, vol. 1, pp. 133–136.
20. Savery, 1702, pp. 49–50.
21. Information on nineteenth-century British mining practice may be found in Galloway, 1882, and Mining Association of Great Britain, 1957.
22. MJ, 13 Dec. 1856.
23. Galloway, 1882, pp. 228, 245.
24. Standard discussions of ventilation procedures may be found in Daddow and Bannan, 1866, chapters 22 and 23, and in Chance, 1883, chapter 19.
25. See Moore, 1859, pp. 132, 248–250.
26. Daddow and Bannan, 1866, pp. 424–426, 435–436.
27. MJ, 7 Nov. 1868.
28. MJ, 20 Jan. 1870. See also Chance, 1883, p. 125, and ARMI, 1870, p. 187.
29. Chance, 1883, p. 498.
30. *Ibid.*, p. 327.
31. Galloway, 1882, pp. 253–256.
32. NA, Patent Office Records, Patent No. 47694, J. Lowden Beadle, "Importance in Ventilation of Mines," 16 May 1865.
33. Daddow and Bannan, 1866, p. 439.
34. Maguire, 1912, p. 311.
35. See descriptions of some of Beadle's fans in Daddow and Bannan, 1866, advertisement with picture on p. 788, and MJ, 10 June 1865.
36. See ARMI, *passim,* and Chance, 1883, p. 315.
37. MJ, 12 Feb. 1870.
38. Maguire, 1912, pp. 316–317.
39. Some of the Miners' Supply Company records have survived and are located at EMHL, Acc. 500, Box 265. See also the account in MJ, 3 April 1874, and in *Scientific American,* vol. 26 (1872), p. 59.
40. Kline, n.d.
41. Phillips, 1858, p. 36. Spontaneous combustion is now recognized as a continuous danger in coal piles.
42. Chance, 1883, p. 418.

II. THE DEVELOPMENT OF ST. CLAIR

THE OWNER FAMILIES

1. The earliest biographical memoir of Henry Charles Carey (1793–1879) was written by his friend William Elder and published in 1880; it gives the date 1835 for Carey's retirement from the publishing business (see Elder, 1880, p. 32). His nephew Henry Carey Baird in 1885 published a brief memorial in the *American Bookseller* that gives the date as 1836. Later biographers follow Elder (see Green, 1951, Smith, 1951), but Kaplan, 1931, gives the date as 1834.
2. The Carey genealogy is in HSP, Carey Papers, Box 81, F-7.
3. A fifty-page biography of Isaac Lea is included in an exhaustive bibliography of his works by Scudder, 1885. See also the biography of Henry Charles Lea by Bradley, 1931; the obituary in *Science,* vol. 8 (1886), p. 556; and DAB.
4. Lea's early business interests in coal and iron are described in his own introduction to R. C. Taylor, 1855, and in Taylor, 1840.
5. HSP houses the six boxes of the "Military Papers of Thomas J. Baird," and two other boxes of miscellaneous materials, in the Baird Section of the Carey-Gardiner Collection.
6. Hoffman, 1972, pp. 12–14.

7. Information on the various coal-land investments and sales of Carey and his partners are to be found in a variety of sources. Of principal value are the Thomas J. Baird Papers cited above and the box of St. Clair Tract Papers in the Carey Section of the Carey-Gardiner Collection, HSP. Carey's correspondence, also in the Carey-Gardiner Papers, with his agents Enoch McGinness, Andrew Russell, and Henry Russell reveals much about his extensive land holdings, as do several manuscript collections in the HSSC, particularly the Loeser Papers and the colliery folders in the 190.1 series. MJ also contains notes on land holdings *passim*. The figure of $40 per acre for the initial purchases of 1835 is given by the Careys' agent Thomas J. Baird in a letter to Edward L. Carey, 28 April 1838, in HSP, Baird Papers, Box 17, Folder 11.

8. HSP, Carey-Gardiner Collection.

9. See Ellen (Baird) Lawton's correspondence with Henry Carey in HSP, Carey Papers.

10. See Henry Carey Baird's correspondence with Henry Carey in HSP, Carey Papers.

11. See Leslie entries in DAB.

12. HSP, Carey Papers, Box 82, F-6.

13. MJ, obituary of Burd Patterson, 6 April 1867.

14. See Hart biography in DAB.

15. Hussey, 1956, pp. 12–14.

16. These and later details of the Wetherill administration of the coal lands are to be found in the ledgers and correspondence in the Wetherill Collection at UP. A guide to the collection is Hussey, 1942. See also the Wetherill genealogy in Wetherill, 1961.

17. Biographical notices of Charles Mayer Wetherill and John Price Wetherill III may be found in NC.

18. HSP, Carey Papers, St. Clair Tract Papers, royalty agreement between the Wetherills and the Carey group, 24 Dec. 1856.

19. Harris, 1880, pp. 56–58.

20. UP, John Price Wetherill and William Wetherill to George W. Farquhar, 13 Dec. 1837.

21. MJ, 8 Feb. 1851.

22. Biographies are in Munsell, 1881, pp. 306–307, and Wiley and Ruoff, 1893, pp. 458–460.

23. HSP, Carey Papers, Box 82, F-3.

24. Baird's and his family's life in Pottsville, 1817–1842, is described in his letters in HSP, Baird Papers, Box 23.

25. HSP, Carey Papers, AR to HC, 2 Oct. 1855.

26. Carey's early real-estate investments are revealed in the tax assessments for the borough of Pottsville and Norwegian Township, and in property maps. His business correspondence concerning coal, in HSP, Carey Papers, includes long series of letters to and from Enoch McGinness and Andrew Russell and smaller exchanges with dozens of others.

27. The Shickshinny venture is discussed in HSP, Carey Papers, EM to HC, 19 Dec. 1855, 7 May 1856, 23 May 1856, 31 May 1856, and HB to HC, 15 July 1859, 15 Aug. 1859, 19 March 1861.

28. HSP, Carey Papers, HB to HC, 19 Jan. 1862.

29. A copy of Wetherill 1852 is at HSSC.

30. HSP, Carey Papers, AR to HC, 17 Jan. 1859.

THE COLLIERY OPERATORS

1. Yearley, 1961.

2. Hedley, 1851, pp. 20–21.

3. Haywood's biography may be found in Munsell, 1881, pp. 308–309, and Wiley and Ruoff, 1893, pp. 211–213.

4. Snyder's biography is in Wiley and Ruoff, 1893, pp. 457–458. His status as millionaire is recorded in the 1860 U.S. census schedules for Pottsville (NA).

5. HSP, Schuylkill County Pamphlets, #27: Pastoral Report of Daniel Washburn, Rector, for 1855–56.
6. Clementina Smith's visit to Pottsville and Horace's subsequent death are described in a series of letters from 1858 to 1865 at EMHL, W-9, 26146, 26208, 27138, 27181, 27212.
7. U.S. census schedule, 1860, Pottsville, pp. 882–883 (NA).
8. EMHL, W-9, 26208.
9. *Ibid.*
10. EMHL, W-9, 27212.
11. Pennsylvania Senate, 1834, Packer Committee *Report,* p. 73.
12. Milnes' activities at Hickory Slope were monitored by Russell and McGinness and reported regularly to Carey. See HSP, Carey Papers.
13. U.S. census schedules, 1850, Pottsville (NA).
14. See obituary of W. H. Johns in MJ, 19 Aug. 1865. Other data, Munsell, 1881, p. 262. His wife's insanity is mentioned in his will (SCCH), and the household composition in 1850 is to be found in the U.S. census schedule for New Castle Township (St. Clair section) (NA).
15. McGinness' aspersions are in HSP, Carey Papers, EM to HC, 5 Sept. 1861, 23 Jan. 1862, 19 Nov. 1859, and 10 and 12 Dec. 1861.
16. MJ, obituary of Enoch McGinness, 16 Feb. 1867. The McGinness household is described in the U.S. census schedules, 1860, Pottsville; his success as an engine maker is recorded in MJ, 5 Jan. 1850.

EARLY UNDERTAKINGS OF THE CAREY GROUP

1. HSP, Carey Papers, Box 99, St. Clair Tract Papers.
2. HSP, Carey-Gardiner Collection, Baird Section, Box 23, TB to HB, 2 Feb. 1836.
3. SCCH, Pottsville and Norwegian Township Tax Assessments, 1835.
4. HSP, Baird Papers, Box 17, Folder F-11
5. MJ, 10 May and 25 July 1835.
6. MJ, 13 and 27 Feb. 1836
7. MJ, 25 July 1838.
8. The York Farm Colliery is described in detail in MJ, 23 March 1839. Its pre-eminence in size is mentioned in the biography of George H. Potts in Wiley and Ruoff, 1893, pp. 374–376.
9. The Guinea Hill Colliery was described in detail in MJ, 13 April 1839.
10. MJ, 23 March 1839.
11. HSP, Baird Papers, Box 17, TB to EC, 28 April 1838
12. Details of Thomas Baird's administration of the collieries are found throughout his letters to his father, Dr. Henry Baird, from 1836 to 1842 (HSP, Baird Papers).
13. MJ, 27 April 1839.
14. Wiley and Ruoff, 1893, p. 375.
15. Harvey, 1977, p. 56.
16. HSP, Baird Papers, TB to HB, 26 Jan. 1840, 19 Jan. 1841, and 2 July 1841.
17. *American Journal of Science and Arts,* vol. 11 (1841), pp. 370–374.
18. HSP, Baird Papers, TB to HB, 28 April 1838.
19. *Ibid.,* 6 Aug. 1841. See also Carey, 1854, p. 10. Coal prices in 1838 are mentioned in MJ, 30 June 1838, and Binder, 1974, p. 16.
20. MJ, 22 Jan. 1842.
21. *Proceedings of the American Philosophical Society,* vol. 2 (Jan. 1841–June 1843), pp. 229–230.
22. For the sale of the Patterson and Carey interests, see MJ, 26 Feb. 1842, and the Schuylkill County tax records for Norwegian Township and the borough of Pottsville, 1840–1843.

Notes

ANTHRACITE IRON

1. Quoted in Yates, 1974, p. 207.
2. The early attempts to make anthracite iron are described in Yates, 1974, Swank, 1876, and Binder, 1974.
3. MJ, 28 April 1838.
4. HSP, Baird Papers, Box 17, TB to HB, Pottsville, 21 Jan. 1870. Lea's name appears as one of the committee of the board of managers of the Danville and Pottsville Railroad Company that wrote the annual report for 1838 (Philadelphia: Kite, 1839). Thomas Baird mentions him as a co-owner of the Danville Furnace in his letter to Henry Baird, Pottsville, 26 Jan. 1840 (HSP, Baird Papers, Box 23).
5. Swank, 1876, p. 143, and Binder, 1974, pp. 79–80.
6. The story of David Thomas and the Lehigh Crane Iron Company has been best told in Stapleton, 1975. The manuscript business records of the Lehigh Company are located at EMHL.
7. SCCH, tax assessments, 1838–1839.
8. Lehigh Valley Railroad, 1873, pp. 155–156.
9. MJ published bulletins on the construction, failings, and final success of the Pioneer Furnace from the beginning. See issues of 2 May 1838, 27 July 1839, 26 Oct. 1839, 2 Nov. 1839, 14 Dec. 1839, and 15 Feb. 1840. Employment, cost, and production figures were given in the 1840 U.S. Census of Manufactures (NA). The furnace was technically described by Firmstone, 1874. Perry's blowing in on 19 Oct. 1839 was noted in *Hazard's Register,* vol. 1 (1839), p. 27. The source of the ore is noted in Lesley, 1859, pp. 685–686. The success of the pigs at Savery's Foundry is noted in the *Prospectus for the Norwegian Iron Company* (Pottsville: B. Bannan, 1840), copy at HSP.
10. HSP, Baird Papers, Box 23, TB to HB, 26 Jan. 1840.
11. Biddle's toast is recorded in MJ, 1 Feb. 1840; the ceremonies are described in MJ, 25 Jan. 1840.
12. MJ, 26 Oct. 1839.
13. MJ, 18 Jan. 1840.
14. HSP, Baird Papers, Box 23, 6 Aug. 1841.
15. MJ, 11 Jan. and 1 Feb. 1840.
16. See Chandler, 1972. Some aspects of Chandler's thesis are questioned in Winpenny, 1979.

THE ST. CLAIR PROJECT

1. This description of the St. Clair Tract in 1835 has been pieced together from several sources, most notably the *Shenandoah Herald* newspaper articles of Sarah McCool (copy at HSSC) and several early maps: Geddes, 1835; Fisher, 1836; and Samuel Lewis, "Draught of the road between Pottsville and St. Clair . . . June 1847," MS copy at HSSC. Also useful were the St. Clair chapters in Munsell, 1881, and Zerbey, 1934–35. Hare, 1966, contains an account of the construction of the Mill Creek Railroad reprinted from *The Pilot and Philadelphia and Reading Railway Men,* June 1910. Hare's work contains accounts of the various other railroads and canals acquired by the Reading as well as the nineteenth-century history of the Philadelphia and Reading Railroad main line from Philadelphia through Reading and Pottsville to Port Carbon. See also the maps in Geddes, 1835, and Hoffman, 1972, p. 67 (an 1831 "plan and profile" of the Danville and Pottsville Railroad).
2. The sad history of the Danville and Pottsville Railroad Company is given in Hoffman, 1972. See also the company's annual *Report . . . to Stockholders* (Philadelphia: Kite, 1939), copy at EMHL.
3. Pinkerton admitted his own lack of experience in testimony before a Pennsylvania

Senate Committee investigating the coal trade in 1833. See Packer Committee *Report,* Pa. Senate, 1834, pp. 76–77.

4. *Fourteenth Annual Report Made by the Board of Trade to the Coal Mining Association of Schuylkill County* (Pottsville: Bannan, 1846), p. 9. Copy at HSSC.
5. The real-estate development program is revealed in the register of lots sold in St. Clair in HSP, Carey Papers, St. Clair Tract Papers. See also HSSC folder M150.8B, the testimony of Thomas Russell.
6. SCCH, Norwegian Township tax lists.
7. Hare, 1966, reprint of June 1910 issue of *The Pilot.*
8. HSP, Carey Papers, Andrew Russell's "Receipts and Expenditures" from 1841 to 1848; MJ, 23 Oct. 1847.
9. Taylor, 1855, pp. 359–361, gives an account of the early experimental vertical borings.
10. HSP, Carey Papers, EM to HC, 25 May and 9 Dec., 1853.
11. *Ibid.,* 7 Nov. 1861.
12. MJ, 3 and 10 April 1852.
13. HSSC, Report of engineer John Maddison to A. Russell, 27 March 1854.
14. MJ, 31 May 1856.

THE COLLIERIES AT ST. CLAIR

1. HSSC, Maddison Reports, 4 Oct. 1850. Engineer John Maddison's reports to the landowners from 1850 to 1853 describe the progress of work at Johns' Eagle, Parvin's Slope, and the St. Clair Slope and Shaft.
2. ARMI, 1869, pp. 160–161.
3. MJ, 17 April 1858.
4. Beers, 1916, p. 287.
5. HSSC, Maddison Reports, 1 Oct. 1850, 19 June 1851, 9 Nov. 1853.
6. Daddow and Bannan, 1866, p. 768.
7. ARMI, 1869, p. 161.
8. ARMI, 1870, p. 111.
9. HSSC, Maddison's Reports, *passim,* detail the ventilation system.
10. MJ, 1878.
11. MJ, 17 Dec. 1853.
12. MJ, 31 May 1856.
13. Bowen, 1854, pp. 31–32.
14. MJ, 31 May 1856.
15. An underground mine map of the mid-1860's provided detailed information on the history of the mine. See HSP, Carey Papers, St. Clair Tract box.
16. HSSC, Maddison Reports, 23 Nov. 1853, 21 Dec. 1853, 27 March 1853.
17. HSP, Carey Papers, AR to HC, 19 June 1835.
18. MJ, 31 May 1856.
19. HSP, Carey Papers, underground mine map showing crushes in slope.
20. Tonnage figures are derived from several sources: EMHL, Reading Collection, annual reports of Mine Creek and Mine Hill Railroad, 1854 to 1865; HSP, Carey Papers, AR to HC, 1860 to 1863; Daddow and Bannan, 1866, for the years 1864 to 1866; Bannan's *Statistics of the Coal Trade* and Coal Statistical Register for the years 1866 and 1869; and ARMI, 1870 to 1872.
21. HSP, Carey Papers, Box 99, St. Clair Tract Papers, lease HC to EM, 1852.
22. HSP, Carey Papers, AR to HC, 29 Dec. 1860.
23. HSP, Carey Papers, EM to HC, a series of letters from Feb. 1855 to Oct. 1855.
24. HSP, Carey Papers, AR to HC, 8 Aug. 1856.
25. See Carey, 1865, for an account of his troubles with the operators; a technical description of the colliery's condition by mining engineer George K. Smith is appended. HSSC

contains trial testimony by local mechanics, including Robert Allison, about the condition of the colliery during its occupancy by Kirk and Baum, whom Carey sued.

26. Accounts of Pine Forest Colliery are to be found in ARMI, 1870–1885; Munsell, 1881, p. 201; Daddow and Bannan, 1866, p. 766; the 1850 U.S. Census of Manufactures, East Norwegian Township (NA); MJ, 13 Jan. 1855, 16 Aug. 1856, and 9 Jan. 1858. Early tonnages are recorded in the annual reports of the Mill Creek and Mine Hill Railroad (EMHL, Reading Collection). An underground mine map by George Smith is located in HSSC.
27. Maguire, 1912, p. 311.
28. ARMI, 1869, p. 69, and 1870, p. 126.
29. ARMI, 1869–90.
30. Maguire, 1912, p. 314.
31. ARMI, 1869, pp. 69–70, and 1870, p. 126.
32. Packer Report, 1834, p. 77; Munsell, 1881, p. 208; HSSC, Parry Papers, St. Clair folder.
33. See royalty contracts between Milnes and the Carey group in HSP, Carey Papers, St. Clair Tract box.
34. *Scientific American,* vol. 2 (1860), p. 370.
35. HSP, Carey Papers, EM to HC, 22 Aug. 1861 and 23 Jan. 1862.
36. Sheafer, 1864, pp. 13–24; Sheafer, 1867, pp. 393–399; Daddow and Bannan, 1866, p. 765.
37. MJ, 1 June 1867.
38. Sheafer, P. W., and Sheafer, W., 1867.
39. MJ, 2 Nov. 1867.
40. Tonnage figures are given in ARMI for the years noted.
41. The continuing difficulties with ventilation are recorded in ARMI, 1869 to 1885.
42. HSSC, Loeser Papers.
43. Schlegel, 1947, pp. 7–8.
44. Parvin's troubles were analyzed by John Maddison during the early 1850's (HSSC) and recounted in detail by EM in the later 1850's and early '60's (HSP, Carey Papers, EM to HC).

III. A WORKINGMAN'S TOWN

1. The progress of St. Clair as a real-estate development from 1835 to 1854 is recorded in two lists of purchasers and lots sold (one in HSP, Carey Papers, Box 99, "St. Clair Papers," and one at HSSC, "Lots sold by Carey, Hart & Baird in St. Clair"). The lot numbers in these lists are located on two property maps at HSSC, the first made by Peter Simpson in 1850 and the second by Peter W. Sheafer in 1858. Personal information about purchasers comes from U.S. census schedules for St. Clair in 1850 (NA).
2. See HSSC, Parry Papers, A. M. Nichols and John Hughes vs. Kirk and Baum, Dec. 1858, for data on Anna Maria Nichols' suit.

BOOM-TOWN GROWTH FROM 1845 TO 1850

1. MJ, 9 Aug. 1845.
2. *The Act of Incorporation, and Ordinances of the Borough of St. Clair, Schuylkill County, Pa.* (St. Clair: Published by the Council, 1876). Personal information about borough officials is derived from the 1850 census schedules (NA).
3. The Simpson map of 1850 is located at HSSC. Much general information on the businesses, churches, and neighborhoods in early St. Clair may be found in the county histories. The earliest of these histories, *Historical Gleanings of Schuylkill County,* was compiled by Sarah McCool and published serially in the *Shenandoah Herald;* chapters 61–63 concern St. Clair and appeared in 1875. The other major county histories are the anonymously edited Munsell, 1881, and the more recent six-volume *History of Pottsville*

and Schuylkill County, Pennsylvania (Zerbey, 1934–35). Both contain chapters on St. Clair and extensive biographical sections. Biographical encyclopedias of Schuylkill County are Wiley and Ruoff, 1893; Schalck and Henning, 1907, and Beers, 1916.

THE CENSUS OF 1850

1. The schedules of the 1850 U.S. population census of New Castle Township, Schuylkill County, Pennsylvania, contain, in addition to newly formed St. Clair Borough, the town of New Castle and the mine patches in between. The St. Clair portion can be identified by the heading written at the top of the pages by the enumerator. The locations of households can be found in the property-map/sales-list documents mentioned in footnote 1, this chapter, and in other sources, particularly Beers and Cochran, 1875.

ETHNICITY AND OCCUPATION

1. Conway, 1961, p. 185.
2. Aurand, 1980, p. 467.
3. Conway, 1961, p. 194.
4. See Aurand, 1980, for a discussion of the miner/laborer relationship.

THE MINE PATCHES

1. Korson, 1938, pp. 2–3, 13–14.
2. Zerbey, 1934–35, vol. 1, pp. 518–521.
3. The 1850 U.S. population census schedules of East Norwegian Township, Schuylkill County, Pennsylvania, include the separately identified town of Port Carbon and the rural area described here (NA).
4. These patches were enumerated in the section of the 1850 U.S. census schedules of New Castle Township, Schuylkill County, Pennsylvania, that is reserved neither for the town of New Castle nor the borough of St. Clair.

WAGES AND SUBSISTENCE

1. HSSC.
2. 1860 U.S. Census of Manufactures, St. Clair, earnings and production of house carpenters.
3. Personal examination of houses in Johns' Patch, St. Clair.
4. 1850 U.S. Census of Agriculture for East Norwegian Township, Schuylkill County, Pennsylvania.
5. MJ, 27 April 1850.
6. U.S. Census of Manufactures, New Castle Township (1850) and Borough of St. Clair (1860).
7. 1860 U.S. Census of Manufactures, St. Clair (NA).
8. MJ published weekly statistics on the quantity of coal shipped on the Mill Creek and Mine Hill Railroad, and on the other feeder roads, as well as the Schuylkill Canal and the Reading Railroad. Along with this statistical report it provided a brief analysis of the week's news of the coal trade, noting such events as strikes, new legislation, and market fluctuations. The freshet was described in the issue of 7 Sept. 1850.

THE EXTENDED FAMILY

1. Schalck and Henning, 1907, vol. 2, pp. 128–129.
2. In addition to the 1850 census, the Igos appear in the lists of lots purchased in St. Clair (HSP and HSSC).
3. Schalck and Henning, 1907, vol. 2, p. 128.

4. ARMI, 1876, p. 51.
5. 1870 U.S. census schedule, St. Clair (NA).
6. Conway, 1961, pp. 167–170.
7. Middle States Reports, 1876.
8. U.S. census schedules, St. Clair, 1860, 1870, 1880 (NA).
9. In addition to the census records, the Frantz family's career is recorded in ARMI for 1870 and 1874 and in Munsell, 1881, Biographical Appendix, p. 242.
10. Pinkowski, 1963, p. 15.
11. ARMI, 1870, p. 22.
12. HSP, "Molly Maguire Papers," Society Collection. See Cumming's reports of 10 March, 21 March, 1 April, and 14 April 1874.
13. U.S. 1880 census schedules, Borough of Shenandoah, Schuylkill County, Pennsylvania (NA).
14. Korson, 1938, pp. 300–301.

OTHER BENEVOLENT ASSOCIATIONS

1. Munsell, 1881, p. 210.
2. Schmidt, 1980, pp. 243–245; Ross, 1888.
3. MJ, 5 Oct. 1850.
4. Munsell, 1881, p. 210.
5. Schmidt, 1980, pp. 146–148.
6. Munsell, 1881, p. 210.
7. Schmidt, 1980, pp. 119–139.
8. Munsell, 1881, pp. 278–280.

TABERNACLES AND TAVERNS

1. Ames, 1909, vol. 1, p. 28.
2. Bowen, 1852, p. 212.
3. Munsell, 1881, pp. 211–212.
4. Most of the information on the Primitive Methodist Church in America, and in St. Clair, is provided by a onetime minister in St. Clair, the Rev. John H. Acornley (Acornley, 1909). See also the account in Munsell, 1881, p. 211.
5. Acornley, 1909, p. 60.
6. *Ibid.*, p. 51.
7. *Ibid.*, p. 5.
8. *Ibid.*, p. 4.
9. Munsell, 1881, pp. 211–213.
10. *Ibid.*, p. 212. The linguistic limitations of the first pastor are revealed in the parish baptismal record, in which the names and localities of Irish Catholic families are rendered phonetically.
11. Munsell, 1881, p. 212.
12. *Ibid.*, pp. 284–285.
13. MJ, 29 March, 5 July, and 22 Nov. 1851.
14. The foregoing sketch of the respectable taverns and hotels is derived from several sources. Proprietors, names, and locations are given in the county histories by McCool, 1875, Munsell, 1881, and Zerbey, 1934–35; locations are further specified in the 1844–54 lists of lots purchased (HSP and HSSC) and in the property map and directory of St. Clair in Beers and Cochran, 1875; and details of occupancy are to be found in the decennial censuses 1850–80. Dormer's tavern is still a tavern and stories are still told of its service as a Molly Maguire hangout.

15. Columbia University, Butler Library, Charlemagne Tower Collection, Box 24, District Attorney Casebook 1854–57, p. 479.
16. MJ, 15 March 1851.

A PLACE OF SONG

1. See Colls, 1977.
2. Korson, 1938.
3. Elssler, 1910, pp. 409–410.
4. Korson, 1938, pp. 117–122.
5. *Ibid.*, pp. 277–278.
6. *Ibid.*, pp. 114–116.
7. *Ibid.*, p. 65.

THE OLD COUNTRY IN THE NEW WORLD

1. U.S. population census, 1850, Schuylkill County, St. Clair Borough (NA).
2. Oestreich, 1966, p. 63. A copy is held by Robert Scherr of St. Clair.
3. Zerbey, 1934–35, vol. 1, pp. 128–140.
4. HSP, Society Collection, "Molly Maguires," report of agent Cumming, 28 Feb. 1874.
5. Broehl, 1964, p. 163.
6. Conway, 1961, p. 194.
7. See the outlines of German culture in anthropologist Robert H. Lowie's two books, 1945 and 1954.
8. U.S. population census, 1850, Schuylkill County, St. Clair Borough and New Castle and East Norwegian townships (NA).
9. Oestreich, 1966, *passim*.
10. Benson, 1980, p. 217.
11. Holland, 1835, chapter "The Colliers," pp. 286–304.
12. *Ibid.*, pp. 293–296.
13. Benson, 1980, p. 185.
14. In Zerbey, 1934–35, vol. 5, pp. 2078–2079.
15. Conway, 1961, p. 174.
16. *Ibid.*, p. 197.
17. The biographies of St. Clair residents in Munsell, 1881, usually reveal the county of origin for English, Welsh, and Irish immigrants.
18. The foregoing sketch of traditional rural Irish culture and attitudes toward family and authority has been drawn largely from Arensberg, 1968 and from Conrad Arensberg and Solon Kimball, 1940.
19. MJ, 1 Feb. 1851.

IV. ILLUSIONS OF THE COAL TRADE

HENRY CAREY AND PROTECTIONISM

1. List's career in America has been described in Hirst, 1965, and R. W. Brown, 1950.
2. Hare, 1966, reprints of Feb. and March issues of the *Pilot*.
3. Carey, 1970, p. 249.
4. *Ibid.*, p. 180.
5. Carey, 1854.
6. See bibliography for a list of Carey's major works.
7. Carey, 1848, pp. 29–30.
8. Carey, 1837, p. 130.
9. *Ibid.*, pp. 40–41.

469

10. MJ, 11 Feb. 1860.
11. Smith, 1951, p. 20.
12. Roberts, 1901, p. x.
13. See the discussion of Carey's views in Huston, 1983. Carey on "dear labour" is quoted on p. 40. Carey's influence on political and economic thought of the day is dealt with at length by his more recent biographers, Kaplan, 1931, and Green, 1951, and he has been given careful attention in the history of American economic thought by Dorfman, 1946, chapter 29, "The Carey-Colwell School, and by Morrison, 1986."
14. Quoted in Kaplan, 1931, pp. 13–14.
15. HSP, Carey Papers, HB to HC, 2 Nov. 1857.
16. Carey's dislike for Cameron is noted by Green, 1951, p. 170, and Smith, 1951, p. 66.
17. Carey's partnership with Cameron, Hughes, and Lewis is revealed in HSSC, agreement of sale, 25 April 1861; in PHMC, Cameron Papers (microfilm), Report of the Trustees of the North American Coal Company, 20 Dec. 1861; and Smith, 1951, p. 42.
18. MJ, 12 June 1858.

GEOLOGICAL FACT AND COAL-TRADE FANTASIES

1. Fulton, 1947, p. 17. See also Schuman, 1947, pp. 196–197, and Geddes, 1835, p. 17.
2. Rogers and Bache, 1834–37, pp. 158–177.
3. In addition to the brief accounts of his life and career in DAB, DNB, and DSB, Rogers is the subject of a book-length biography: Gregory, 1916.
4. Ames, 1909, vol. 1, p. 254.
5. *Ibid.*, p. 24.
6. *Ibid.*, p. 35.
7. *Ibid.*,
8. Rogers, 1858.
9. J. L. Hayes, New York geologist, quoted in Gregory, 1916, p. 18.
10. For Lyell's visit to the southern coal field see Lyell, 1845, vol. 1, pp. 81–100, and Ames, 1909, vol. 1, p. 36. Lyell's activity in drawing the attention of British geologists to the Rogers brothers' theory of mountain building is noted in Gregory, 1916, pp. 18–19.
11. Gregory, 1916, pp. 16–21.
12. *Ibid.*, p. 16.
13. DSB, "Rogers."
14. Rogers, 1838, pp. 74–77.
15. Gregory, 1916, p. 16.
16. Lesley, 1876, pp. 111–112.
17. North American Coal Company, 1855, p. 26.
18. HSSC, report of engineer John Maddison to A. Russell, 21 Dec. 1853.
19. MJ, 17 Dec. 1853.
20. Bowen, 1855, pp. 3, 5, 8.
21. Bowen, 1862, appendix.
22. Rogers, 1858, vol. 1, pp. 805–808.
23. Bowen, 1865, pp. 54, 246–272.
24. Bowen, 1862, pp. 5–8.
25. Daddow and Bannan, 1866, pp. 68–69.
26. *Ibid.*, p. 81.
27. *Ibid.*, pp. 672–673.
28. Lesley, 1876, p. 156.

THE MIND OF ENOCH MCGINNESS

1. This section was previously published in slightly different form in Wallace, 1985.
2. HSP, Carey Papers, letters of EM to HC, 5 Aug. 1861.

3. *Ibid.,* 5 Dec. 1861.
4. *Ibid.,* 25 Sept. 1861.
5. *Ibid.,* 6 Jan. 1862.
6. *Ibid.,* 8 Nov. 1860.
7. *Ibid.,* 10 Sept. 1861.
8. *Ibid.,* 3 Feb. 1861.
9. *Ibid.,* 29 Aug. 1861.
10. *Ibid.,* 5 Sept. 1861.
11. *Ibid.,* 5 Aug. 1861.
12. *Ibid.,* 5 Dec. 1861.
13. *Ibid.,* 10 Sept. 1861.
14. *Ibid.,* 5 Sept. 1861.
15. *Ibid.,* 30 Nov. 1859.
16. *Ibid.,* 19 Nov. 1859.
17. *Ibid.,* 17 Jan. 1860.
18. *Ibid.,* 2 June 1855.
19. *Ibid.,* 6 Jan. 1860.
20. *Ibid.,* 22 May 1860.
21. *Ibid.,* 2 July 1860.
22. *Ibid.,* 18 July 1860.
23. *Ibid.,* 23 July 1860.
24. *Ibid.,* 27 July 1860.
25. *Ibid.,* 3 Sept. 1860.
26. *Ibid.,* 1 Dec. 1860.
27. *Ibid.,* 10 Sept. 1861.
28. *Ibid.,* 29 Aug. 1861.

CELEBRATING THE INDUSTRIALIST AS HERO

1. Part of this section was previously published; see Wallace, 1981.
2. See Smith, 1976, pp. 13–14, 477, and 1809, p. 343.
3. Smiles, 1868, p. 82. See also Hughes, 1966.
4. Schuylkill County Teachers' Institute, 1876, pp. 18, 21. Copy at HSP.
5. See his biography in Wiley and Ruoff, 1893, pp. 681–683.
6. Daddow, 1853.
7. Daddow, 1853, pp. 108–109, 133–137.
8. Daddow, 1870.
9. Bowen, 1855, pp. 5–6.
10. *Ibid.,* pp. 8–9.
11. *Ibid.,* p. 12.
12. *Philadelphia North American,* 15 April 1859.
13. *Philadelphia North American,* 28 April 1859.
14. Hare, 1966, reprint of the *Pilot* for March 1912.
15. MJ, 5 July 1845.
16. The celebrations in Philadelphia and Pottsville were described in MJ, 15 Jan. 1842. The yellow paint for passenger cars is mentioned in Hare, 1966, p. 52. For Bentham's view on heroes, see Atkinson, 1905, p. 203.
17. Elssler, 1910, pp. 405–417. See also the accounts of the refurbishing of the statue during the summer of 1985 in Ward, 1985.
18. MJ, 7 July 1855.
19. Daddow, 1853, pp. 69–72.
20. Bishop, 1864, vol. 1, p. 9.
21. HSP, Schuylkill County Pamphlets.

Notes

V. THE POLITICS OF SAFETY

DEATH AND DISABLEMENT IN THE MINES

1.   MJ, 18 Dec. 1858.
2.   Maguire, 1912, p. 332.
3.   Korson, 1938, p. 276.
4.   Ibid., p. 278.
5.   Medical Society of Pennsylvania, *Transactions,* 1853, p. 143.
6.   Ibid., 1856, pp. 202–203.
7.   Carpenter, 1868–69, p. 490.
8.   Sheafer, H. C., in Buck, 1879, vol. 2.

BUSINESS FAILURES

1.   Yearley, 1961, p. 59.
2.   Quoted in Yearley, 1961, p. 65.
3.   Coxe, 1870.
4.   Coxe in U.S. Senate, 1889, p. 593.
5.   Sheafer, 1864.
6.   ARMI, 1871, p. 81.
7.   MJ, 18 Sept. 1869.
8.   Campbell, 1978, pp. 107, 124–125.
9.   HSP, Carey Papers, EM to HC, 8 Aug. 1861.
10.   Kendrick in Pennsylvania Senate, 1871, p. 85.
11.   Coxe in U.S. Senate, 1889, p. 623.

INSURANCE

1.   Carpenter, 1868–69, pp. 491–492.
2.   HSP, Carey Papers, Box 99, St. Clair Tract.
3.   Moore, 1881, p. 203.
4.   Fowler, 1888, pp. 362, 397.
5.   Moore, 1881, p. 203; Fowler, 1876, p. 8.
6.   Moore, 1881, pp. 443, 520.
7.   Binney, 1852, p. 53.
8.   Fowler, 1876, p. 5.

THE "CARELESS MINER" AND THE EROSION OF EMPLOYER'S LIABILITY

1.   HSP, Carey Papers, AR to HC, 11 June 1855; MJ, 16 June 1855.
2.   MJ, 6 Oct. 1855.
3.   MJ, 26 Nov. 1859.
4.   Sheafer, H.C., 1879, pp. 237–238.
5.   Maguire, 1912, pp. 318–321, 322–323, 332, 335–336.
6.   ARMI, 1869, p. 13.
7.   See Gersuny, 1981, for a review of the shift in the courts' interpretation of employer's liability. See also Levy, 1957, and Eastman, 1969.
8.   For the coal industry, see Graebner, 1976, p. 148.
9.   Levine, 1973, analyzes the psychological impact of the Elizabethan Poor Laws, using the data given in MacFarlane, 1970, and Thomas, 1971.
10.   MJ, 16 Feb. 1867.
11.   Burke, 1966.

12. National Academy of Sciences, 1982b, pp. 52–58.
13. Graebner, 1976, pp. 149–152; Gersuny, 1981, p. 99.
14. Johnson, 1978.
15. On the middle-class component in the anti-Masonic movement, see Wallace, 1978, and Kutolowski, 1984.
16. See Wallace, 1966, pp. 180–184, and Swanson, 1960, pp. 150–152, for discussion of the relation of witch-fear and lapse of law and order.

THE RISE OF THE MINERS' UNION

1. HSP, Carey Papers, EM to HC, 17 Aug. 1855.
2. HSP, Carey Papers, EM to HC, 8 Aug. 1861.
3. MJ, 29 May 1858.
4. Journals of the Senate and the House of Representatives, Pennsylvania, Acts 855 and 1327; Bills and Resolutions Reported and Printed for the House of Representatives, Act 885 [*sic*] and 1327.
5. MJ, 18 June 1842.
6. MJ, 29 Nov. 1845 and 20 June 1846.
7. MJ, 23 Oct. 1858.
8. MJ, 18 Dec. 1858.
9. MJ, 5 March 1870.
10. Zerbey, 1934–35, vol. 1, pp. 110–116 provides a history of the hospital. See also MJ, 27 March 1874.
11. MJ, 2 April 1859.
12. MJ, 25 Sept. 1858.
13. See Gudelunas and Shade, 1976, p. 73, tables II-J and II-K.
14. EMHL holds the 1855 constitution and bylaws of the Coal Mining Association, and annual reports for 1836 and 1840–1846.
15. Zerbey, 1934–35, vol. 5, pp. 2078–2079.
16. MJ, 7 July 1849.
17. Killeen, 1942, pp. 94–98, contains a general account of the Bates Union.
18. MJ, 22 May 1858.
19. MJ, 29 May 1858.
20. MJ, 26 June 1858.
21. MJ, 29 May and 19 June 1858.
22. MJ, 5 June 1858.
23. Maguire, 1912, p. 333.
24. MJ, 3 July 1858.
25. Gudelunas and Shade, 1976, pp. 63–71.
26. *Ibid.*, pp. 73–85.
27. MJ, 10 May 1862.
28. Conway, 1961, pp. 174–175.
29. Much of the following account of John Siney and the founding of the WBA is based on Killeen, 1942, and on the excellent biography of Siney by Pinkowski, 1963. In addition to consulting primary documentary sources, Pinkowski was able to interview Siney's son and other associates in the St. Clair area.
30. Quoted in Schlegel, 1947, p. 244.
31. Middle States Reports, 1876, p. 1070.
32. Personal information on Siney's associates is drawn largely from Pinkowski and U.S. census schedules for St. Clair, 1850 to 1880, East Norwegian, 1850, and Shenandoah, 1880 (NA). Casualty information is from ARMI.
33. HSP, Carey Papers, Henry Russell to HC, 9 July 1868.
34. MJ, 18 July 1868.

35. *Workingman's Advocate,* 22 Nov. 1873.
36. Maguire, 1912, pp. 322–323.
37. Again, see Pinkowski, 1963.

THE FIRST MINE SAFETY LAW

1. Senate Journal, 1869, p. 745.
2. Legislative Record, 1869, p. 861.
3. Senate Journal, 1869, pp. 848–849.
4. Laws of Pennsylvania, Session of 1869, Act No. 845, pp. 852–856.

THE AVONDALE DISASTER

1. The following description of the Avondale disaster is based largely on the accounts given in the *Philadelphia Press,* 21 and 24 Sept. 1869, *Harper's Weekly,* 25 Sept. 1869, and *Frank Leslie's Illustrated Newspaper,* 25 Sept. 1869. See also Pinkowski, 1963.
2. Accounts of the Delaware, Lackawanna, and Western may be found in Taber, 1980, and Casey and Douglas, 1951.
3. Korson, 1938, pp. 136–139.
4. Pinkowski, 1963, p. 51.
5. Powderly, 1968, p. 24.
6. *Ibid.,* p. 35.
7. *Philadelphia Press,* 21 Sept. 1869.
8. *Harrisburg Morning Patriot,* 13 Sept. 1869.
9. *Ibid.*
10. *Philadelphia Press,* 21 Sept. 1869.

THE MINE SAFETY LAW OF 1870

1. *Harrisburg Morning Patriot,* 18 Sept. 1969.
2. *National Labor Tribune,* 28 April 1888.
3. *Philadelphia Press,* 1 Feb. 1870.
4. Senate Journal, 1870, pp. 389–393; House Journal, 1870, p. 559.
5. Laws of Pennsylvania, 1870, Act. No. 1, pp. 3–12.
6. MJ, 15 Jan. 1870.
7. Senate Journal, 1870, p. 973.

THE EFFECTIVENESS OF THE MINE SAFETY LAWS

1. ARMI, 1869, p. 37.
2. Patterson, 1910, p. 361.
3. *Ibid.,* pp. 361–362.
4. ARMI, 1869, pp. 8–9, 37–38.
5. *Ibid.,* pp. 26–28.
6. *Ibid.,* pp. 28–30.
7. *Ibid.,* p. 27.
8. *Ibid.,* p. 28.
9. *Ibid.,* p. 70.
10. *Ibid.,* p. 160.
11. *Ibid.,* p. 85.
12. Daddow and Bannan, 1866, p. 437.
13. Chance, 1883, pp. 312–313.
14. Beard, 1920, pp. 181–182.
15. MJ, 19 March 1870.

16. Coxe, 1870.
17. MJ, 15 Jan. 1870.
18. MJ, 5 Feb. 1870.
19. MJ, 10 June 1871 and 15 Oct. 1872.
20. MJ, 10 June 1871.
21. MJ, 1 Aug. 1873.

VI. JUSTICE AND VIOLENCE

1. MJ, 3 Jan. 1857.
2. MJ, 5 Dec. 1873.
3. Conway, 1961, p. 176.
4. Oestreich, 1966, p. 86.

THE MURDER OF JOHN REESE

1. MJ, 2 Jan. 1847.
2. The events in the case were described in summaries of courtroom testimony in MJ, 12 June 1847. The sentence is noted in MJ, 26 Sept. 1847.

THE *MINERS' JOURNAL* AND THE ANTI-IRISH-CATHOLIC MOVEMENT

1. Gudelunas and Shade, 1976, pp. 63–69, carefully describe Bannan's ethnic politics.
2. MJ, 10 Oct. 1857.
3. Quoted in Broehl, 1964, p. 86.
4. The best review of the Irish origin of the Molly Maguires is in Broehl, 1964, pp. 1–70.
5. MJ, 11 Jan. 1851.
6. MJ, 5 July 1850.
7. MJ, 27 Sept. 1851.

THE MILITARIZATION OF THE COAL FIELDS

1. See Wallace, 1865, for a review of Schuylkill County "patriotism" in the Civil War. Lists of Schuylkill County servicemen and casualties, regiment by regiment, are to be found in Munsell, 1881.
2. Munsell, 1881, pp. 110–111.
3. Schlegel, 1947, p. 10.
4. MJ, 9 Aug. 1862.
5. McClure, 1905, p. 549.
6. The draft confrontation of 1862 is described in Broehl, 1964, pp. 8–9, and the biographies of Tower (Bridges, 1952) and Pleasants (Pleasants, 1938 and 1961) provide additional information on the personalities involved.
7. The disorders of 1863 and Smith's murder are described in Broehl, 1964, pp. 90–93.
8. Dewees, 1969, p. 49.
9. The record of the 48th Regiment is given in Munsell, 1881, pp. 118–128.
10. The names of St. Clair servicemen who served in the Civil War are inscribed on the Soldiers' Monument in the Odd Fellows' Cemetery. Many names are illegible because of weathering, but fortunately the custodian, Mr. Louis Delker, copied the names down before they disappeared and made the list available to Mr. Scherr and myself. Casualties among these men are noted in Munsell's regimental histories.
11. MJ, 23 March 1867.
12. *Ibid.*
13. Shalloo, 1933, pp. 59–61.
14. MJ, 30 March, 16 April 1867.

15. Broehl, 1964, p. 94.
16. MJ, 16 April 1870.

THE PINKERTON SPY IN ST. CLAIR

1. Commonwealth, 1876, pp. 193, 197, 224.
2. *Ibid.*, p. 256.
3. Pennsylvania Senate, 1871, pp. 19–20.
4. MJ, 11 March 1871.
5. The *précis* of some of Cumming's reports in 1874 and 1875, sent to Gowen by the Pinkerton office in Philadelphia, have been preserved. Half are in HSP, Society Collection, "Molly Maguires," and the rest at EMHL, Reading Company Papers.
6. Pennsylvania Senate, 1871, p. 33.
7. HSP, Society Collection, Molly Maguire Papers, 28 Feb. 1874.
8. *Ibid.*, 6 March 1874.
9. Information on Hall is to be found in the St. Clair census schedules for 1860, 1870, and 1880, and in the property map in Beers and Cochran, 1875 (NA).
10. MJ, 13, March 1874.
11. EMHL, Reading Collection, Molly Maguire Papers, Box 252, printed list of Molly Maguires in Schuylkill County.
12. EMHL, Cumming's Reports, 2 May 1874.
13. *Ibid.*, 11 Nov. 1874.
14. The record of Hanmore's activities consists of eight letters from Hanmore to Gowen, 17 March to 30 April 1875.
15. EMHL, Reading Collection, Molly Maguire Papers, Hanmore to Gowen, 14 April 1875.

"MCKENNA" PENETRATES THE ANCIENT ORDER OF HIBERNIANS

1. The reports and testimony of James McParlan, *alias* James McKenna, have been the principal source of information—and inspiration—to historians of the Molly Maguires and to novelists, particularly Sir Arthur Conan Doyle, whose story *The Valley of Fear* (1915) was based on Allan Pinkerton's mildly fictionalized account, *The Molly Maguires and the Detectives* (1877). Pottsville lawyer James Dewees also published an early account (1877). The literature is extensive; in this treatment, I have largely followed Broehl, who depended on McParlan's reports as summarized for Gowen and located in the Reading Collection at HSP and EMHL, along with those of Cumming, Linden, and others, and on McParlan's testimony (which substantially agrees with the reports) at the various trials.
2. Kehoe case, 1876, p. 14.
3. Pinkerton, 1905, pp. 73–81, tells the tale of McKenna's meeting with Lawler in Dormer's saloon in Pottsville in 1873, but I have been unable to find a Dormer saloon there until years later. Pinkerton's description roughly fits the building in St. Clair, which is still a tavern.
4. Occupations of St. Clair members of the AOH are derived, of course, from census schedules (NA).
5. This remarkable letter was published in Broehl, 1964, pp. 247–248.
6. Quoted in Broehl, 1964, pp. 264–265.
7. Quoted in Broehl, 1964, p. 234.

THE GOMER JAMES CASE

1. U.S. Census, 1860, Borough of St. Clair (NA).
2. MJ, 15 Aug. 1873.

3. *Ibid.*
4. MJ, 22 Aug. 1873.
5. *Ibid.*
6. MJ, 20 March 1874.
7. The plot to kill James, and Hurley's success, were recorded by McParlan; see Broehl, 1964, pp. 175–278, 201–203, 228, 229.
8. EMHL, Reading Collection, Molly Maguire Papers, Memorandum No. 4.
9. Broehl, 1964, pp. 317–318, 358.
10. MJ, Supplement, 12 May 1876.
11. MJ, Supplement, 18 Aug. 1876.
12. MJ, 26 Feb. 1880.

THE GREAT SHOWCASE TRIAL

1. The verbatim testimony, along with attorneys' statements and the judge's instructions at this trial, Commonwealth vs. John Kehoe *et al.*, was printed as a book by Bannan in 1876. See Commonwealth, 1876, *passim.* Except as otherwise noted, the events in the case and in the trial are derived from this work and from Broehl, 1964.
2. Commonwealth, 1876, pp. 176–192.
3. *Ibid.*, pp. 218–231.
4. *Ibid.*, pp. 192–202, 202–218.
5. Oestreich, 1966, p. 85.

WHO WERE THE MOLLY MAGUIRES?

1. Aurand and Gudelunas, 1982.
2. Broehl, 1964, p. 219.
3. Commonwealth, 1876, pp. 174–175.
4. *Ibid.*, p. 30.
5. *Ibid.*, p. 256.
6. *Ibid.*, pp. 30, 130.
7. MJ, 25 Dec. 1874.
8. EMHL, Reading Collection, Molly Maguire Papers, Memorandum No. 1.
9. *Ibid.*, McParlan reports, 14 Oct. 1876.

JUSTICE DENIED

1. The following description of the circumstances at the colliery and the reconstruction of the accident are based on the accounts in MJ, 18 May 1877, *Shenandoah Herald,* 18 May 1877, and ARMI, 1877, pp. 10–14.
2. ARMI, 1877, p. 11.
3. MJ, 18 May 1877.
4. *Philadelphia Press,* 17 Jan. 1878.
5. *Ibid.*, 21 Jan. 1878.

VII. A STATE CALLED ANTHRACITE

1. Quoted in Aurand, 1971, pp. vii–viii.

ST. CLAIR IN 1870: DEMOGRAPHY AND CULTURE

1. St. Clair Borough Council Minutes.
2. MJ, 8, 15 June 1867.

3. MJ, 9, 23 March 1872.
4. MJ, 15 Aug. 1873; data on Hillan are from the 1880 census, the property map in Beers and Cochran, 1875, and Pinkowski, 1963, p. 314.
5. MJ, 12 Jan. 1867.
6. The 1870 St. Clair population statistics are drawn from the U.S. population census, Schuylkill County, Borough of St. Clair, microfilm copy at the Federal Records Center, Philadelphia, Pennsylvania (original at National Archives, Washington, D.C.).
7. MJ, 18 Aug. 1860.
8. In addition to the 1870 census, which records the value of real and personal property, the county tax-assessment books at HSSC also provde information on property ownership. The tax assessments also describe the property (houses, lots or partial lots, animals, vehicles, gold and silver watches).
9. HSSC, tax assessments for 1851 and 1870 (1850 assessments were merged with New Castle Township).

MIDDLE-CLASS CONTROL OF TOWN AFFAIRS

1. *Workingman's Advocate,* 29 April 1871.
2. Data on council membership and presidency are to be found in the published book of ordinances to 1876 (St. Clair Borough, 1878) and in the manuscript of council minutes. Personal data on occupation and ownership of real property come from the appropriate U.S. census schedules (NA) and the biographical dictionaries. See MJ, 3 Sept. 1870, for the list of council members in that year.
3. Evans' biography is to be found in Munsell, 1881, p. R28, and Wiley and Ruoff, 1893, p. 396. See also the 1870 and 1880 census schedules and Middle States Reports, pp. 1068–1069.
4. MJ, 26 Nov. 1870.
5. MJ, 20 Jan. 1872.
6. MJ, 30 Nov. 1872.
7. MJ, 18 Aug. 1860.
8. Daddow, 1853.

THE RITUALS OF CIVIC SOLIDARITY

1. MJ, 3 March 1866.
2. MJ, 4 Jan. 1868.
3. MJ, 11 July 1868; for the earlier years, see MJ, 8 July 1843 and 6 July 1844.
4. MJ, 30 Nov. 1872.
5. Acornley, 1892.
6. *Ibid.,* pp. 35–36.
7. *Ibid.,* pp. 38–40.
8. Pottsville *Evening Chronicle,* 9 May 1877.
9. Pottsville *Evening Chronicle,* 12 May 1877.
10. A general account of Post 47 and the Soldiers' Monument is found in Munsell, 1881, p. 210.
11. MJ, 28 Oct. 1871.
12. Pottsville *Evening Chronicle,* 18, 27, and 28 Nov. 1874; MJ, 28 Oct. 1871.
13. ARMI, 1869, p. 27, and 1878, p. 3.
14. ARMI, 1878, p. 3.
15. Munsell, 1881, pp. 210–211; Pinkowski, 1963, p. 16.
16. MJ, 15 June 1872.

Notes

JOHN SINEY AND LARGE-SCALE LABOR ORGANIZATION

1. Pinkowski, 1963, and Killeen, 1942, *passim,* provide much information on Siney's ideas. The primary sources for Siney's thinking are his letters, published in MJ, *Workingman's Advocate, National Labor Tribune, Philadelphia Press,* and the now unavailable (except for a few issues in the Labor Archives in the Library of the Pennsylvania State University) *Anthracite Monitor,* and in the biographical and obituary notices in the *Workingman's Advocate* for 22 Nov. 1873 and the *United Mine Workers Journal* for 19 Nov. 1900.
2. Pinkowski, 1963, p. 29.
3. *Workingman's Advocate,* 29 April 1871, 24 Jan. 1874.
4. Bureau of Statistics of Labor, First Annual Report, 1872–73, pp. 464–468.
5. *Workingman's Advocate,* 22 Nov. 1873.
6. See Thompson, 1963.
7. MJ, 15 Feb. 1868.
8. Quoted in Pinkowski, 1963, p. 180.
9. Quoted in Pinkowski, 1963, p. 194.
10. Quoted in Pinkowski, 1963, p. 28.
11. Quoted in Pinkowski, 1963, p. 50.
12. *National Labor Tribune,* 25 Jan. 1874.
13. Patterson, 1910, p. 377.
14. *Ibid.*
15. Evans, 1966, p. 240.
16. *Workingman's Advocate,* 22 Nov. 1873.
17. MJ, 7 May 1870.
18. MJ, 31 Aug. 1873.
19. MJ, 12 Sept. 1873. Siney's third-party activities are detailed in Pinkowski, 1963, and the course of the Labor Reform and Greenback movements are described in Evans, 1966, Ch. 9.
20. Baird, 1878.
21. Fitzpatrick, 1884, pp. 259–261.
22. Bureau of Statistics of Labor, First Annual Report, 1872–73, pp. 455–456.

FRANKLIN B. GOWEN AND THE NEW INDUSTRIAL ORDER

1. Schlegel, 1947, foreword by R. W. Brown.
2. MJ, 10 Sept. 1859.
3. Biographical information about Gowen is derived largely from Schlegel, 1947.
4. MJ, 3 July 1858.
5. A copy of Sheafer, n.p., n.d., is located at the Library of the APS. Internal evidence suggests a date circa 1869.
6. Miesse, 1887, pp. 145–146, 155.
7. Elson, 1964.
8. *Bannan's New Columbian Primer* and *Little Harry* are part of the collection of early Pennsylvania schoolbooks at HSP.
9. Thomas Walker's address is also at HSP in the collection of Schuylkill County pamphlets.
10. Schuylkill County Teachers' Institute, Twelfth Annual Session (Pottsville, 1865), copy at HSP in the collection of Schuylkill County pamphlets.
11. MJ, 1 May 1858, p. 4.
12. Coxe, 1889–90, p. 619.
13. Schlegel, 1947, p. 53.

14. *Ibid.*, p. 277.
15. *Ibid.*, pp. 40–41.
16. *Ibid.*, p. 81.
17. *Ibid.*, p. 284.
18. EMHL, Reading Company Papers, Pinkerton reports.
19. Schlegel, 1947, p. 85.
20. *Ibid.*, p. 59.
21. *Ibid.*, p. 176.
22. *Ibid.*, p. 84.

THE RISE OF THE COMPANY STATE

1. See particularly Aurand, 1971, Schlegel, 1947, and Yearley, 1961.
2. HSP, Carey-Gardiner Colliery, Carey Papers, EM to HC, 23 Dec. 1861.
3. Coxe, 1872.
4. Schlegel, 1947, provides detail on Gowen's maneuvers.
5. The coal-land acquisitions of the PRCI are described in detail in Harris, 1880.
6. The events in the series of strikes and negotiations from 1864 to 1875 are narrated in Aurand, 1971, Pinkowski, 1963, Schlegel, 1947, and the Bureau of Statistics of Labor, First Annual Report, 1873.
7. See Jones, 1914, for an account of the anthracite cartel.
8. Pinkowski, 1963, p. 123.
9. Conway, 1961, p. 188.
10. *Ibid.*, p. 189.
11. HSP, Molly Maguire Papers, Cumming's report for 4 March 1874.
12. *Ibid.*, 11 Nov. 1874.
13. Korson, 1938, p. 224.
14. Patterson, 1910, pp. 382–383.
15. Korson, 1938, p. 225.
16. ARMI, 1875, p. 70.

A COMMON RUIN

1. ARMI, 1872, pp. 71–72.
2. Bowen, 1862, dedication.
3. ARMI, 1870, p. 143.
4. ARMI, 1871, p. 81.
5. See ARMI, 1873 to 1876.
6. Coxe, 1873, p. 5.
7. Bowen, 1862, p. 31.
8. Coxe, 1873.
9. ARMI, 1870, p. 143.
10. Coxe, 1872, p. 5.
11. ARMI, 1875, pp. 71–72.
12. MJ, 18 Dec. 1874.
13. ARMI, 1881, p. 22.
14. Schlegel, 1947, pp. 186–197.
15. U.S. population census for 1880, Schuylkill County, Borough of St. Clair (NA).

EPILOGUE: THE SURVIVAL OF ST. CLAIR

1. MJ, 16 Feb. 1867.
2. MJ, 26 March 1875.

3. Pinkowski, 1963, p. 244.
4. Elder, 1880, p. 36.
5. Broehl, 1964, p. 344.
6. Schlegel, 1947, pp. 286–288.
7. Production records in ARMI chronicle the rise and fall of each colliery.
8. The records of the St. Clair Company are located at EMHL. Mr. H. Gordon Smyth, the last operator, kindly lent me the 1900–1902 letter book of William T. Smyth.
9. The account of St. Clair in Zerbey, 1934–35, pp. 648–709, carries the account of the town into the twentieth century.
10. HSP, Carey Papers, EM to HC, 17 March 1862.

APPENDIX: THE DISASTER-PRONE ORGANIZATION

1. HSP, Molly Maguire Papers, Report of P. M. Cumming, St. Clair, 21 Feb. 1874.
2. Yearley, 1961.
3. Davies, 1985.
4. Korson, 1938, p. 122.

RISK-SEEKING BEHAVIOR IN DECISION THEORY

1. National Research Council, 1982a.
2. See, for example, Barlett, 1980, and Wright and Phillips, 1979.
3. Douglas and Wildavsky, 1982.
4. National Research Council, 1982b.
5. Graebner, 1976, p. 154.
6. For reviews of and excerpts from the traditional literature on decision theory, see Page, 1968, and Raiffa, 1968.
7. Kahneman and Tversky, 1982. See also Kahneman and Tversky, 1979.
8. Black, 1984.

BIBLIOGRAPHY

MANUSCRIPTS

American Philosophical Society Library (Philadelphia)
    John Warner Papers
Columbia University, Butler Library (New York, N.Y.)
    Charlemagne Tower Collection
Dauphin County Historical Society (Harrisburg, Pa.)
    Simon Cameron Papers (microfilm supplied by Pennsylvania Historical and Museum
    Commission)
Eleutherian Mills Historical Library (Wilmington, Del.)
    Du Pont Company Papers, Series 1, Part 2-B (Acc. 500), Miners' Supply Company Papers
    (St. Clair)
    Du Pont Company Papers, Series 2, Part 2: St. Clair Mills and St. Clair Powder Works
    Henry Francis du Pont Collection, Winterthur Manuscripts (W-9)
    Lehigh Crane Iron Company Papers (Acc. 1198)
    Reading Collection
        Mill Creek and Mine Hill Railroad Papers
        Molly Maguire Papers
    St. Clair Coal Company Papers
Genealogical Society of Pennsylvania (Philadelphia, Pa.)
    Records of the Holy Apostles Church (Episcopal), St. Clair
Historical Society of Pennsylvania (Philadelphia, Pa.)
    Cadwallader Collection
    Carey-Gardiner Collection
    Society Collection (The "Molly Maguire Papers")
Historical Society of Schuylkill County (Pottsville, Pa.)
    Loeser Papers
    John Maddison Reports
    John Maguire's Notebooks (extracts)
    Parry Papers
    Colliery File
    Kaska William Colliery, Pay Book
    Locality File
    Mammoth Colliery, Pay Book
    Mining Ledgers Collection
Insurance Company of North America Archives (Philadelphia, Pa.)
    Thompson, Derr & Brother Papers

Library of Congress (Washington, D.C.)
    Sanborn Map Collection
National Archives (Washington, D.C.)
    Patent Office Records
    U.S. Decennial Census Schedules, Population and Manufactures
Pennsylvania Historical and Museum Commission (Harrisburg, Pa.)
    Simon Cameron Papers
    Map Collection
    Schuylkill Navigation Company Papers
    WPA Historical Survey, Anthracite Section
Pennsylvania State University
    Labor Archives
Philadelphia City Hall
    Will of Henry C. Carey
Schuylkill County Court House (Pottsville, Pa.)
    Probate Records
    Registry of Wills
    Tax Assessments, St. Clair Borough, 1851–1880
Smithsonian Institution, Museum of American History and Collections
    Extractive Industries Section, Philadelphia and Reading Coal and Iron Company Collection
St. Clair Borough
    Borough Council Records
University of Pennsylvania (Philadelphia, Pa.)
    Henry C. Lea Collection
    Wetherill Papers

NEWSPAPERS

Anthracite Monitor, Tamaqua, Pa. (copies at Labor Archives, Pennsylvania State University)
Evening Chronicle, Pottsville, Pa.
Harrisburg Daily Telegraph
Harrisburg Morning Patriot
Miners' Journal, Pottsville, Pa. (microfilm at Eleutherian Mills Historical Library)
National Labor Tribune
Philadelphia Press
Shenandoah Herald, Shenandoah, Pa.
Splinters, St. Clair, Pa.
United Mine Workers Journal
Workingman's Advocate, Chicago, Ill.

GOVERNMENT PUBLICATIONS

COMMONWEALTH OF PENNSYLVANIA

Annual Reports of the Inspectors of Coal Mines of the Anthracite Regions of Pennsylvania, 1870–1900.
Bureau of Statistics of Labor and Agriculture, First Annual Report, 1872–73. Harrisburg: Singerly, 1874.
Journals of the House of Representatives of Pennsylvania.
Journals of the Senate of Pennsylvania.
Laws and Statutes of the Commonwealth of Pennsylvania.
Legislative Records of the House of Representatives of Pennsylvania.
Legislative Records of the Senate of Pennsylvania.

Bibliography

Report of the Committee of the Senate of Pennsylvania upon the Subject of the Coal Trade, S. J. Packer, Chairman, Harrisburg: Welsh, 1834.

Report of the Committee on the Judiciary, General, of the Senate of Pennsylvania, in the Relation to the Anthracite Coal Difficulties, with the Accompanying Testimony. Harrisburg: Singerly, 1871.

Report of the Inspector of Mines, County of Schuylkill, 1869. Harrisburg: Singerly, 1870.

Report of the Joint Committee of the Legislature . . . to inquire into the affairs of the Philadelphia and Reading Coal and Iron Company and the Philadelphia and Reading Railroad Company. Philadelphia: Helfenstein, Lewis & Greene, 1876.

Rogers, Henry Darwin. *Annual Reports of the State Geologist, 1836–42.* Harrisburg: 1837–42.

Secretary of Internal Affairs, Annual Reports. Part III. Industrial Statistics, 1874–1884. Harrisburg: Hart, 1876–85.

UNITED STATES

Report of the Committee on the Conduct of the War on the Attack on Petersburg, on the 30th day of July, 1864. Washington: U.S. Government Printing Office, 1865.

Report of the Industrial Commission on the Relations and Conditions of Capital and Labor employed in the Mining Industry, Including Testimony, Review of Evidence, and Topical Digest. Washington: U.S. Government Printing Office, 1901.

U.S. *House of Representatives, 50th Congress, 2nd Session, Report No. 4147. Labor Troubles in the Anthracite Regions of Pennsylvania 1887–1888.* Washington: U.S. Government Printing Office, 1889.

COUNTY HISTORIES AND BIOGRAPHICAL DICTIONARIES

[Beers, J. H.] *Schuylkill County Pennsylvania—Genealogy—Family History—Biography.* Chicago: J. H. Beers, 1916.

Boyd, W. Harry. *Boyd's Pottsville Directory . . .* Pottsville: Miller, 1875.

Chambers, George. *Historical Sketch of Pottsville, Schuylkill County, Pa.* Pottsville: Standard Publishing Co., 1876.

Dictionary of American Biography. Allen Johnson and Dumas Malone (eds.). New York: Charles Scribner's Sons, 1928–36. 20 vols.

Dictionary of National Biography. Leslie Stephen and Sidney Lee (eds.) London: Oxford University Press, 1949–50. 21 vols.

[Dives, Pomeroy, and Stewart]. *History of the County of Schuylkill.* Pottsville: Dives, Pomeroy & Stewart [1911].

Gillispie, Charles C. (ed.). *Dictionary of Scientific Biography.* New York: Scribners, 1975.

Munsell, W. W., & Co. *History of Schuylkill County, Pa. with Illustrations and Biographical Sketches of Some of its Prominent Men and Pioneers.* New York: W. W. Munsell & Co., 1881.

National Cyclopedia of American Biography. New York: James T. White Co., 1898–1977. 57 vols. (Vols. 1–49 republished by University Microfilms.)

Robson, Charles. *The Manufactories and Manufacturers of Pennsylvania of the Nineteenth Century.* Philadelphia: Galaxy, 1875.

Schalck, Adolph W., and D. C. Henning (eds.). *History of Schuylkill County, Pennsylvania . . .* [n.p.]: State Historical Association, 1907. 2 vols.

Wetherill, Francis M. *Wetherills' Who's Who.* Philadelphia: privately printed, 1961.

Wiley, Samuel T., and Henry W. Ruoff (eds.). *Biographical and Portrait Cyclopedia of Schuylkill County, Pennsylvania.* Philadelphia: Rush, West and Company, 1893.

Zerbey, Joseph Henry. *History of Pottsville and Schuylkill County, Pennsylvania.* Pottsville: J. H. Zerbey Newspapers, 1934–35. 6 vols.

Bibliography

MAPS

Anonymous. Plan of the St. Clair & Hickory Collieries, c. 1869 (MS in HSP, Carey-Gardiner Collection, Carey Papers, Box 99, "St. Clair Tract").

Beers, F. W., and A. B. Cochran. *County Atlas of Schuylkill, Pennsylvania, from Recent & Actual Surveys and Records.* New York: F. W. Beers, 1875.

Daddow, S. H. Map of the Anthracite Coalfields of Pennsylvania. Pottsville: Bannan, 1866.

Fisher, Samuel B. Map of the First and Second Coal Fields. Philadelphia: Watson's Lith., 1836.

Lesley, J. P., C. A. Ashburner, and F. A. Hill. Geological Map of Schuylkill County. Harrisburg: Second Geological Survey of Pennsylvania, 1891.

Roberts, William F. Map of the Anthracite Regions of Pennsylvania, embracing the first and second and part of the Wyoming coal fields and Montour iron ore range. Hazleton: 1849.

Scott, Walter. Map of Schuylkill County, Pennsylvania [with St. Clair insert]. Philadelphia: James Scott, 1864.

Second Geological Survey of Pennsylvania, Atlas, Part 2, Southern Coal Field Mine Sheets Nos. X and XI. Harrisburg: Meyers, 1889.

Sheafer, P. W. Anthracite Coal Mines in Pennsylvania . . . in 1857 & 1858.

———. A Map of Schuylkill County, Pennsylvania. Philadelphia: Barnes, 1865.

Simpson, Peter. Map of the Borough of St. Clair, 1850. HSSC.

Strauch, G. B., and A. B. Cochran. Map of the First and Second Anthracite Coal Fields. Pottsville: 1871.

PRE-NINETEENTH CENTURY EUROPEAN PUBLICATIONS ON MINING TECHNOLOGY

Agricola, Georgius. *De Re Metallica* [translated and edited by Herbert C. and Lou N. Hoover]. New York: Dover, 1950. Originally published in 1556.

Birch, Thomas. *A History of the Royal Society.* London: Printed for A. Milar, 1756–57.

Savery, Thomas. *The Miner's Friend; or An Engine to Raise Water by Fire.* London: Crouch, 1702.

PUBLISHED WRITINGS BY ST. CLAIREANS AND OTHER NINETEENTH-CENTURY OBSERVERS

Acornley, John H. *Sunshine Among the Mountains: or, The Young Pastor's Wife: Being Memorials of Mrs. Agnes Rebecca Acornley, Wife of Rev. John H. Acornley by Her Husband.* Brooklyn: Howard Daisley, Publisher, 1876.

———. *The Colored Lady Evangelist: Being the Life, Labors, and Experiences of Mrs. Harriet A. Baker.* Brooklyn: 1892.

———. *A History of the Primitive Methodist Church in the United States of America from its Origin and the Landing of the First Missionaries in 1829 to the Present Time.* Fall River, Mass.: B. R. Acornley & Co., Printers, 1909.

Allison, Robert. "Ventilation of Mines—the Steam Jet," *Scientific American,* vol. 2 (1860), p. 370.

———. "Early History of Coal Mining and Mining Machinery in Schuylkill County," *Transactions of the Historical Society of Schuylkill County,* vol. 4 (1912), pp. 134–155.

[American Journal of Science]. "On the gases enclosed in coals," *American Journal of Science and Arts,* vol. 15 n.s. (1825), pp. 472–473.

———. Report of meeting of Association of American Geologists, April 25–30, 1842. *American Journal of Science and Arts,* vol. 43 (1842), p. 184.

Bibliography

Ames, Mary Lesley (ed.). *Life and Letters of Peter and Susan Lesley.* 2 vols., New York: G. P. Putnam's Sons, 1909.

Anonymous. "Cornish Pumping Engine," *American Journal of Engineering and Mining,* vol. 8, 17 Aug. 1869.

——. "Vignettes from the Schuylkill Valley. I," *Lippincott's Magazine,* vol. 13 (1874), pp. 663–678.

Ashburner, Charles A. "New Method of Mapping the Anthracite Coal-fields of Pennsylvania," *Transactions of the American Institute of Mining Engineers,* vol. 9 (1880–81), pp. 506–518.

——. "The Anthracite Coal Beds of Pennsylvania," *Transactions of the American Institute of Mining Engineers,* vol. 11 (1882–83), pp. 136–159.

Atkinson, A. A. *A Key to Mine Ventilation.* Scranton: The Colliery Engineer Co., 1892.

Bagot, Alan. *The Principles and Practice of Colliery Ventilation.* Birmingham: Osborne, 1879.

Baird, Henry Carey. "What Is Communism?" *Irish World,* 1 June 1878.

——. "Biography of Henry C. Carey," *American Bookseller,* February 16, 1885.

——. "The Eight-Hour System," *Journal of Progress,* May 1886.

——. "The Strikes: Their Cost, their Cause, their Cure," *The North American,* May 19, 1886.

[Bannan, B.]. *Bannan's New Columbian Primer, Designed as a Primary Instructor for Families and Schools.* Philadelphia: Lippincott, n.d.

[Bannan, B., ed.] *Statistics of the Coal Trade . . . for 1866.* Pottsville: Miners' Journal Office, 1867.

——. *The Miners' Journal Coal Statistical Register for 1869.* Pottsville: Miners' Journal Office, 1869.

Bannan, Francis B. *Reminiscences of a Long and Happy Life, Fun, Frolic, and Mischief.* Pottsville: 1910.

Bell, I. Lowthian. *Notes of a Visit to Coal- and Iron-Mines and Ironworks in the United States.* Newcastle-on-Tyne: Lambert, 1875.

Binney, Horace. Address [at the] Centennial Meeting of the Philadelphia Contributorship for the Insurance of Houses from Loss by Fire. April 1852. Philadelphia: The Company, 1852.

Bishop, J. Leander. *A History of American Manufactures From 1608 to 1860.* 2 vols. Philadelphia: Young, 1864.

Bowen, Ele [*sic*]. *The Coal Regions of Pennsylvania.* Pottsville, Pa.: E. N. Carvalho & Co., 1848.

——. Eli. *The Pictorial Sketch-Book of Pennsylvania.* Philadelphia: Hazard, 1852.

——. *Off-hand Sketches; a Companion for the Tourist and Traveller over the Pennsylvania, Pottsville and Reading Railroad.* Philadelphia: J. W. Moore, 1854.

——. *The McGinness Theory of the Schuylkill Coal Formation.* Pottsville: Bannan, 1855.

——. "Coal, and the Coal Miners of Pennsylvania," *Harper's New Monthly Magazine,* vol. 15 (1857), pp. 451–469.

——. *Physical History of the Creation of the Earth and its Inhabitants; or, a Vindication of the Cosmogony of the Bible from the Assaults of Modern Science.* Philadelphia: Laird, 1861.

——. *Coal, and the Coal Trade.* Philadelphia: Peterson, and Pottsville: B. Bannan, 1862.

——. *Coal and Coal Oil; or, The Geology of the Earth Being a Popular Description of Minerals and Mineral Combustibles.* Philadelphia: T. B. Peterson, 1865.

Bradsher, Earl L. *Matthew Carey; Editor, Author and Publisher. A Study in American Literary Development.* New York: AMS Press, Inc., 1966.

[Bradstreet, J. M.]. *Bradstreet's Commercial Reports.* New York: J. M. Bradstreet, 1860, 1866, 1870, 1876.

Buck, Albert H. (ed.). *A Treatise on Hygiene and Public Health.* 2 vols. New York: Wood, 1879.

Cameron, Simon. "Protection to American Industry," Speech . . . in the Senate of the United States, March 7, 1870. Washington: Chronicle Print, 1870.

Bibliography

Carey, Henry C. *Principles of Political Economy*. 3 vols., Philadelphia: Carey, Lea & Blanchard, 1837.

——. *The Past, the Present, and the Future*. Philadelphia: Carey and Hart, 1848.

——. *Coal, Its Producers and Consumers*. Pottsville: 1854.

——. *The Harmony of Interests, Agricultural, Manufacturing, and Commercial*. New York: Myron Finch, 1856 (second edition).

——. *Letters to the President, on the Foreign and Domestic Policy of the Union, and Its Effects, as Exhibited in the Condition of the People and the State*. Philadelphia: J. B. Lippincott, 1858.

——. *Letter to the Stockholders of the St. Clair Coal Company*. Philadelphia: 1865.

——. *The Unity of Law, as Exhibited in the Relations of Physical, Social, Mental, and Moral Science*. Philadelphia: H. C. Baird, 1872.

——. *Principles of Social Science*. 3 vols., Philadelphia: J. B. Lippincott, 1888 (first edition, 1858–59).

——. *Essay on the Rate of Wages*. New York: AMS Press, 1970 (original edition, 1835).

Carey, Matthew. *Autobiography*. New York: Eugene L. Schwaab, 1942 (original edition, 1833–34).

Carpenter, John T. *An Essay on the Ectrotic Virtues of Iodine in Varicola*. M.D. thesis, University of Pennsylvania, 1855.

——. "Report of the Medical Society of Schuylkill County for 1856," *Transactions of the Medical Society of the State of Pennsylvania*, n.s., pt. 1, 1857, pp. 176–181.

——. "Report of the Schuylkill County Medical Society, 1869," *Transactions of the Medical Society of the State of Pennsylvania*, 5th Series, vol. III (1868–69), pp. 488–491.

Chance, H. M. "The carbonic acid gas process at the Kehley Run Colliery Fire," *Transactions of the American Institute of Mining Engineers*, vol. 9 (1880–81), pp. 477–479.

——. "An analysis of the casualties in the anthracite coal mines, from 1871 to 1880," *Transactions of the American Institute of Mining Engineers*, vol. 10 (1881–82), pp. 67–77.

——. *Report on the Mining Methods and Appliances Used in the Anthracite Coal Fields*. Harrisburg: Second Geological Survey of Pennsylvania, 1883.

[Colliery Engineer Company]. *The Colliery Engineer Pocket-Book*. Scranton: Colliery Engineer Company, 1891.

[Commonwealth] "The Commonwealth vs. John Kehoe . . . ," Pottsville: *Miners' Journal*, 1876.

Conway, Alan. *The Welsh in America: Letters from Immigrants*. Minneapolis: University of Minnesota, 1961.

Coxe, Eckley B. (translator). *A Manual of the Mechanics of Engineering and of the Construction of Machines, with an Introduction to the Calculus*. By Julius Weisbach, Ph.D. 3 vols. New York: D. Van Nostrand, 1870.

——. "Mining Legislation." A paper read at the general meeting of the American Social Science Association at Philadelphia, October 25, 1870. Philadelphia: Collins, 1870.

——. "Boards of conciliation and arbitration." Read February 16, 1871. *Social Science Association of Philadelphia, Papers of 1871*. Philadelphia: 1871.

——. "A new method of sinking shafts," *Transactions of the American Institute of Mining Engineers*, vol. 1 (1871–73), pp. 261–276. The paper was read in May 1872.

——. "Note upon a peculiar variety of anthracite," *Transactions of the American Institute of Mining Engineers*, vol. 7 (1878–79), p. 213.

——. *Secondary Technical Education: An Address* . . . Philadelphia: Sherman & Company, 1879.

——. *Memorial Address* [for Asa Packer]. Bethlehem, Pa.: Edwin Klose, 1883.

——. "Biographical Notice of Franklin B. Gowen," *Transactions of the American Institute of Mining Engineers*, vol. 18 (1889–90), pp. 618–620.

Daddow, Samuel Harris. *Trevaro and Other Occasional Poems*. Pottsville: J. Robbins, 1853.

——. *Protection vs. Free Trade* . . . Philadelphia: King & Baird, 1855.

——. "Noncarra's bad luck," *Lippincott's Magazine*, vol. 6 (1870), pp. 211–218.

——. "Pillars of coal," *Transactions of the American Institute of Mining Engineers,* vol. 1 (1871–73), pp. 170–182.

——, and Benjamin Bannan. *Coal, Iron, and Oil; or the Practical American Miner.* Philadelphia: J. B. Lippincott, 1866, and Pottsville: Benjamin Bannan, 1866.

Dana, James D. *New Text-Book of Geology Designed for Schools and Academies.* New York: Irison, Blakeman, Taylor & Company, 1877 (first edition, 1863).

Day, Sherman. *Historical Collections of Pennsylvania.* Philadelphia: George W. Gorton, 1843.

Dewees, F. P. *The Molly Maguires: The Origin, Growth, and Character of the Organization.* New York: Burt Franklin, 1969 (reprint of 1877 edition).

Elder, William. *A Memoir of Henry C. Carey.* Philadelphia: H. C. Baird, 1880.

Erickson, Charlotte (ed.). *Invisible Immigrants: The Adaptation of English and Scottish Immigrants in Nineteenth Century America.* Coral Gables, Fla.: University of Miami Press, 1972.

Firmstone, William. "Sketch of early anthracite furnaces," *Transactions of the American Institute of Mining Engineers,* vol. 3 (1874–75), pp. 152–156.

[Fitzpatrick, John]. *The White Slaves of Monopolies; or, John Fitzpatrick, The Miner, Soldier and Workingman's Friend.* Harrisburg: Lane S. Hart, 1884.

Forster, J. M. *Fifth Annual Report of the Insurance Commissioner of the State of Pennsylvania. Part 1. Fire and Marine Insurance.* Harrisburg: Hart, 1878.

Foster, Thomas J. *The Mine Foreman's Pocket Book.* Shenandoah: Mining Herald Company, 1883.

Fowler, John A. *The Fire Insurance Premium.* Philadelphia: Review Publishing Company, 1876.

——. *The Fire Account: Physical, Personal, Moral.* Philadelphia: Review Publishing and Printing Company, 1878.

——. *History of Insurance in Philadelphia for Two Centuries (1683–1882).* Philadelphia: Review Publishing and Printing Company, 1888.

[*Frank Leslie's Popular Monthly*]. "Among the Coal Mines," *Frank Leslie's Popular Monthly,* vol. 3 (1877), pp. 116–126.

Galloway, Robert L. *A History of Coal Mining in Great Britain.* London: Macmillan, 1882.

Geddes, William F. *Comparative Views of the Most Important Anthracite Colliery in Pennsylvania.* William F. Geddes, 1835.

George, Henry. "Labor in Pennsylvania," *North American Review,* vol. 143 (1886), pp. 165–182, 268–277, 360–370; vol. 144 (1877), pp. 86–95.

Gompers, Samuel. *Seventy Years of Life and Labor: An Autobiography.* 2 vols. New York: Dutton, 1925.

Haldeman, H. L. "The first furnace using coal," *Lancaster County Historical Society Papers,* vol. 1 (1896).

Harden, John Henry. Chart showing the production of anthracite coal in the Lehigh, Schuylkill, and Wyoming regions . . . , *Transactions of the American Institute of Mining Engineers,* vol. 5 (1876–77), pp. 504–505.

Harlan, Abram D. *Pennsylvania Constitutional Convention 1872 and 1873.* Philadelphia: Inquirer Book and Job Print, 1873.

Harris, Joseph. *Report upon the coal lands of the Philadelphia and Reading Coal and Iron Company.* Philadelphia: Jackson Brothers, 1880.

Harvey, Katherine A. (ed.). "The Lonaconing Journals: The Founding of a coal and iron community, 1837–1840," *Transactions of the American Philosophical Society,* vol. 67, part 2, 1977.

Hedley, John. *A Practical Treatise on the Working and Ventilation of Coal Mines: with Suggestions for Improvements in Mining.* London: John Weale, 1851.

Heinrich, Oswald J. "The industrial school for mines and mechanics, at Drifton, Luzerne Co., Pa.," *Transactions of the American Institute of Mining Engineers,* vol. 9 (1880–81), pp. 390–395.

Bibliography

Holland, John. *The History and Description of Fossil Fuel, the Colliery, and Coal Trade of Great Britain.* London: Whittaker, 1835.

Hopton, William. *Conversations on Mines, etc. Between a Father and Son . . .* Philadelphia: Lippincott, 1890.

House, Madeline, G. Story, and K. Tillotson (eds.). *The Letters of Charles Dickens,* vol. 3. Oxford: Clarendon Press, 1974.

Hutchinson, E. S. "Notes on coal-dust in colliery explosions," *Transactions of the American Institute of Mining Engineers,* vol. 12 (1884–85), pp. 253–279.

[Iron Masters, Convention of]. *Documents relating to the manufacture of iron in Pennsylvania.* Philadelphia: Convention of Iron Masters, 1850.

Johnson, Walter R. *Report of an Examination of the Mines, Iron Works and Other Property Belonging to the Clearfield Coke and Iron Company . . .* Philadelphia: Lydia R. Bailey, 1839.

——. *Notes on the Use of Anthracite in the Manufacture of Iron.* Boston: Little, Brown, 1841.

——. *A Report to the Navy Department . . . on American Coals Applicable to Steam Navigation, and to Other Purposes.* Washington: Goles and Seatin, 1844.

Lea, Isaac. "On the disturbed condition of the southern coal field," *Proceedings of the American Philosophical Society,* vol. II (1842), pp. 229–230.

[——, LL.D.]. *A Catalogue of the Published Works of Isaac Lea, LL.D. from 1817 to 1876.* Philadelphia: Collins, 1876.

[——, Philip Nicklin, and B. W. Richards]. *Report of the President and Managers of the Danville and Pottsville Railroad Company to the Stockholders, January, 1839.* Philadelphia: Jos. and Wm. Kite, 1839.

Lea, Matthew Carey. "On the first, or southern coal field of Pennsylvania," *American Journal of Science and Arts* (New Haven), vol. XL (1841), pp. 370–374.

[Lea Brothers and Company]. *One Hundred Years of Publishing.* Philadelphia: Lea Brothers and Company, 1885.

[Lehigh Valley Railroad]. *Guide-Book of the Lehigh Valley Railroad.* Philadelphia: Lippincott, 1873.

Lesley, J.P. *Manual of Coal and Its Typography.* Philadelphia: Lippincott, 1856.

——. *The Iron Manufacturers Guide to the Furnaces, Forges and Rolling Mills of the United States, etc.* New York: 1859.

——. *Historical Sketch of Geological Explorations in Pennsylvania and Other States.* Harrisburg: Second Geological Survey of Pennsylvania, 1876.

——. "Memoir of Samuel Stedman Haldeman, 1812–1880," *Biographical Memoirs of the National Academy of Sciences,* vol. 2 (1886), pp. 139–172.

——. *Geological Survey of Pennsylvania.* Harrisburg: 1895.

Leslie, Eliza. *Miss Leslie's Complete Cookery: Directions for Cookery in Its Various Branches.* Philadelphia: Henry Carey Baird, 1856.

[Little Harry]. *Little Harry's Indestructible Reading Book.* Philadelphia: Willis P. Hazard, 1857.

Loiseau, E. F. "The successful manufacture of pressed fuel at Port Richmond, Philadelphia, Pa.," *Transactions of the American Institute of Mining Engineers,* vol. 8 (1879–80), pp. 314–320.

Lyell, Charles. *Travels in North America; with Geological Observations in the United States, Canada, and Nova Scotia.* 2 vols. London: John Murray, 1845.

——. *A Second Visit to the United States of North America.* 2 vols. London: John Murray, 1849.

——. *Life, Letters, and Journals of Sir Charles Lyell, Bart.* London: John Murray, 1881.

McClure, Alexander K. *Old Time Notes of Pennsylvania.* 2 vols. Philadelphia: Winston, 1905.

McCool, Sarah. "Historical Gleanings in Schuylkill County," Chapters LX–LXV, *Shenandoah Herald,* 1875.

McKean, Kate. *Manual of Social Science.* Philadelphia: H. C. Baird, 1866.

Bibliography

Maguire, John. "Reminiscences of John Maguire after fifty years of mining," *Publications of the Historical Society of Schuylkill County*, vol. 4 (1912), pp. 805–834.

Mammoth Vein Consolidated Coal Company. *Reports of the Directors, Trustees, Superintendents, Engineer, etc.*, November 25, 1864. Boston: Wright and Potter, 1864.

———. *Report of Joint Committee and Treasurer's Circular*, April 24, 1866. Boston: Mudge, 1866.

Marlor, Joseph, Sen. *Coal Mining: Investigated in its Principles, and Applied to an Improved System of Working and Ventilating Coal Mines*. London: C. A. Bartlett, 1854.

Middle States Reports for 1876. New York, 1876. Copy at EMHL.

Miesse, Charles. *Points on Coal and the Coal Business*. Myerstown, Pa.: Feese and Uhrich, 1887.

Moore, F. C. *Fires: Their Causes, Prevention and Extinction, Combining also, A Guide to Agents Respecting Insurance Against Loss by Fire*. New York: Continental Insurance Co., 1881.

Moore, Ralph. *The Ventilation of Mines*. Glasgow and London: Hamilton, Adams, 1859.

Morris, Phineas P. "Mining Rights in Pennsylvania. A lecture delivered November 10th, 1860, before the Law Academy of Philadelphia." Philadelphia: Law Academy, 1860.

Munroe, Henry S. "A summer school of practical mining," *Transactions of the American Institute of Mining Engineers*, vol. 9 (1880–81), pp. 664–671.

Neilson, J. B. "On the hot air blast," *Transactions of the Institution of Civil Engineers*, vol. I (1836).

[North American Coal Company]. *Report to the Stockholders of the North American Coal Company*. Philadelphia: John C. Clark, 1848 and 1850.

[———]. *Report of the President and Directors of the North American Coal Company*. Philadelphia: Sickels and Jones, 1855.

Oestreich, Emil. *Maurus Oestreich: A Tribute by His Grandchildren*. Philadelphia: privately printed, 1966.

Patterson, Joseph F. "Old W.B.A. days," *Transactions of the Historical Society of Schuylkill County*, vol. 2 (1910), pp. 355–385.

———. "After the W.B.A.," *Transactions of the Historical Society of Schuylkill County*, vol. 4 (1912), pp. 168–184.

Philadelphia and Reading Railroad Company. *Annual Reports*, 1873–79.

Phillips, G. Jenkin, F.G.S. *System of Mining Coal and Metalliferous Veins Fully Explained; with a Compendium of General Principles on that Science. Productive Consumption and Incidental Statistics on Coal: Together with Geological and Mineralogical Observations*. Illustrated by maps, sections, etc. Philadelphia: The Author (303 Walnut), 1858.

Pinkerton, Allan. *The Molly Maguires and the Dectectives*. New York: Dillingham, 1905. Originally published 1877.

Platt, Franklin. *A Special Report to the Legislature upon the Causes, Kinds and Amount of Waste in Mining Anthracite. With a Chapter on the Methods of Mining by John Price Wetherill*. Harrisburg: The Board of Commissioners of the Second Geological Survey, 1881.

Powderly, Terence V. *The Path I Trod*. New York: AMS Press, 1968 (original edition, 1940, Harry J. Carman, Henry David, and Paul N. Guthrie, Publishers).

Raymond, R. W. "A glossary of mining and metallurgical terms," *Transactions of the American Institute of Mining Engineers*, vol. 9 (1880–81), pp. 99–192.

Riley, Louis A. "Cost and results of geological explorations with the diamond drill in the anthracite regions of Pennsylvania," *Transactions of the American Institute of Mining Engineers*, vol. 5 (1876–77), pp. 303–308.

Roberts, Peter. *The Anthracite Coal Industry*. New York: Macmillan, 1901.

———. *Anthracite Coal Communities: A Study of the Demography, the Social, Educational and Moral Life of the Anthracite Regions*. New York: Macmillan, 1904.

Rogers, Henry D. *An Address on the Recent Progress of Geological Research in the United*

States delivered at the Fifth Annual Meeting of the Association of American Geologists and Naturalists held at Washington City, May 1844. Philadelphia: C. Sherman, 1844.

——. *The Geology of Pennsylvania.* 2 vols. Philadelphia: Lippincott, 1858.

——. "Coal and coal mining," *Harper's New Monthly Magazine*, vol. 29 (1864), pp. 163–168.

—— and H. D. Bache. "Analysis of some of the coal of Pennsylvania," *Journal of the Academy of Natural Science*, vol. VIII (1834).

Rood, Henry. "A Pennsylvania colliery village," *The Century Illustrated Monthly Magazine*, vol. 55 (1897–98), pp. 809–830.

Roy, Andrew. *The Coal Miner.* Cleveland: Robinson, Savage, 1876.

——. *The Practical Miner's Companion.* Columbus: Westbote, 1885.

——. *A History of the Coal Miners of the United States, from the Development of the Mines to the Close of the Anthracite Strike of 1902.* Columbus, Ohio: Trauger Printing Company, 1907.

Ruoff, Henry Woldmar. *Leaders of Men or Types and Principles of Success as Illustrated in the Lives and Careers of Famous Americans of the Present Day.* Springfield, Massachusetts: King-Richardson, 1902.

Saward, Frederick. *The Coal Trade: The Year Book of the Coal and Coke Industry.* New York: Annual publication by author after 1874.

Scudder, Newton Pratt. *The Published Writings of Isaac Lea, LL.D.* Bulletin No. 23 of the United States National Museum. Washington: Government Printing Office, 1885.

Sheafer, H. C. "Hygiene of coal mines," in Albert H. Buck (ed.), *A Treatise on Hygiene and Public Health.* New York: Wood, 1879, vol. 2, pp. 229–250.

Sheafer, P. W. *Geology of Schuylkill County*, n.p., n.d.

——. "Coals and collieries of Schuylkill County, Pa.," *Miners' Journal*, 3 July 1858.

——. *Reports of the Mammoth Vein Consolidated Coal Company.* Boston: Wright and Potter, 1864.

——. "The use of anthracite coal as a fuel," *Journal of the Franklin Institute*, vol. 83 (1867), pp. 314–317.

——. "The anthracite coal fields of Pennsylvania, and their exhaustion." Paper read at the meeting of the American Association for the Advancement of Science, Saratoga, August 1880. Harrisburg: Lane S. Hart, 1881.

——, and William Sheafer. "Colliery shafts," *Journal of the Franklin Institute*, vol. 83 (1867), pp. 393–399.

Simonin, L., and H. W. Bristow. *Mines and Miners; or, Underground Life.* London: Wm. Mackenzie [c. 1868].

Smiles, Samuel. *The Life of George Stephenson and His Son Robert Stephenson.* New York: Harper Brothers, 1868.

Smith, Adam. *An Inquiry into the Nature and Causes of the Wealth of Nations.* Ed. by Edwin Cannon. Chicago: University of Chicago Press, 1976.

——. *The Theory of Moral Sentiments.* Glasgow: Chapman, 1809.

Swank, James. *The American Iron Trade in 1876.* Philadelphia: American Iron and Steel Association, 1876.

Sylvis, James C. *The Life, Speeches, Labor and Essays of William H. Sylvis.* Philadelphia: 1872.

Taylor, George. *Effect of Incorporated Coal Companies upon the Anthracite Coal Trade of Pennsylvania.* Pottsville: Bannan, 1833.

——. *Effect of Incorporated Coal Companies upon the Coal Trade of Pennsylvania in Reply to the Official Statements made to the Legislature of Pennsylvania by the Delaware and North American Coal Companies.* Pottsville: Bannan, 1834.

Taylor, Richard C. *Two Reports: On the Coal Lands, Mines and Improvements of the Dauphin and Susquehanna Coal Company, and on the Geological Examination, Present Conditions and Proposals of the Stony Creek Coal Estate.* Philadelphia: Dorsey, 1840.

——. *Statistics of Coal.* Second edition, revised by S. S. Haldeman. Philadelphia: J. W. Moore, 1855.

Bibliography

Thomas, Samuel. "Reminiscences of the early anthracite-iron industry," *Transactions of the American Institute of Mining Engineers*, vol. 29 (1899), pp. 901–928.

Wallace, Francis B. *Memorial of the Patriotism of Schuylkill County*. Pottsville: Bannan, 1865.

Walton, Thomas H. "Life in coal mines," *Lippincott's Magazine of Literature, Science, and Education*, vol. 3 (1869), pp. 517–521.

Warner, John. "The diamond rock drill," *Journal of the Franklin Institute*, vol. 93 (1872), pp. 314–316.

Wetherill, Charles M. *Report on the Iron and Coal of Pennsylvania*. New York: World's Fair, 1853.

Wetherill, John Price. *Remarks of John P. Wetherill to the Resolution presented by the Memphis Board of Trade, Asking for the Removal of the Duty on Railroad Iron, at a Meeting of the National Board of Trade, held in Richmond, Virginia, December 1, 1869*. Wilmington, Del.: Jenks and Atkinson, 1869.

——. "An outline of anthracite mining in Schuylkill County, Pa.," *Transactions of the American Institute of Mining Engineers*, vol. 5 (1876–77), pp. 402–422.

——. "How anthracite coal is mined," in Franklin Platt (ed.), *Waste in Mining Anthracite*. Harrisburg: Second Geological Survey, 1881.

White, Josiah. *Josiah White's History, Given by Himself*. Philadelphia: Lehigh Coal and Navigation Company, c. 1909.

Wickersham, James P. *Report of the State Superintendent of Public Instruction . . . 1872*. Harrisburg: Department of Public Instruction, 1878.

SCHOLARLY AND TECHNICAL BOOKS AND ARTICLES

Aldrich, Michele. "American state geological surveys, 1820–1845," in Schneer, 1879, pp. 133–144.

Amsden, Jon, and Stephen Brier. "Coal miners on strike: The transformation of strike demands and the formation of the National Union in the U.S. coal industry," *Journal of Interdisciplinary History*, vol. 7 (1976–77), pp. 583–616.

Arensburg, Conrad. *The Irish Countryman*. New York: Natural History Press, 1968 (originally published 1937).

——. and Solon T. Kimball. *Family and Community in Ireland*. Cambridge: Harvard University Press, 1940.

Ashton, Thomas S., and Joseph Sykes. *The Coal Industry of the Eighteenth Century*. Manchester: Manchester University Press, 1929.

Atkinson, Charles M. *Jeremy Bentham: His Life and Work*. London: Methuen, 1905.

Aurand, Harold. "Workingmen's Benevolent Association," *Labor History*, vol. 7 (1966), pp. 19–34.

——. *From the Molly Maguires to the United Mine Workers: The Social Ecology of an Industrial Union, 1869–1897*. Philadelphia: Temple University Press, 1971.

——. "Social motivation of the anthracite mine workers: 1901–1920," *Labor History*, vol. 18 (1977), pp. 360–365.

——. "The anthracite miner: An occupational analysis," *Pennsylvania Magazine of History and Biography*, vol. 104 (1980), pp. 462–473.

——. "Mine safety and social control in the anthracite industry," *Pennsylvania History*, vol. 52 (1985), pp. 227–241.

——, and William Gudelunas. "The mythical qualities of Molly Maguire," *Pennsylvania History*, vol. 49 (1982), pp. 91–105.

Baer, Christopher. "The Miner as Market Victim: 1840–1860," MS, 1979.

——. *Canals and railroads of the mid-Atlantic states, 1800–1860*. Wilmington: Eleutherian Mills–Hagley Foundation, Regional Economic History Research Center, 1981.

Barker, George F. "Biographical memoir of Matthew Carey Lea, 1823–1897," *National Academy of Science, Biographical Memoirs*, vol. 5 (1905), pp. 155–208.

Bibliography

Barlett, Peggy F. (ed.). *Agricultural Decision Making: Anthropological Contributions to Rural Development*. New York: Academic Press, 1980.

Bartholomew, Craig L. "Anthracite Iron," *Proceedings of the Canal History and Technology Symposium*, vol. 3 (1984), pp. 13–53.

Beard, James T. *Mine Gases and Ventilation*. New York: McGraw-Hill, 1920.

Benson, John. *British Coal Miners in the Nineteenth Century: A Social History*. New York: Holmes and Meier Publishers, 1980.

——, and R. G. Neville (eds.). *Studies in the Yorkshire Coal Industry*. Manchester: Manchester University Press, 1976.

Berthoff, Rowland. *British Immigrants in Industrial America 1790–1950*. Cambridge: Harvard University Press, 1953.

——. "The social order of the anthracite region, 1825–1902," *Pennsylvania Magazine of History and Biography*, vol. 89 (1965), pp. 261–291.

Binder, Frederick Moore. *Coal Age Empire: Pennsylvania Coal and Its Utilization to 1860*. Harrisburg: Pennsylvania Historical and Museum Commission, 1974.

Bining, Arthur Cecil. *Pennsylvania Iron Manufacture in the Eighteenth Century*. Harrisburg: 1938.

Binney, Charles C. *The Life of Horace Binney, with Selections from His Letters*. Philadelphia: Lippincott, 1903.

Black, Max. "Making intelligent choices: How useful is decision theory?" *Bulletin of the American Academy of Arts and Sciences*, vol. 38 (1984), pp. 30–49.

Bogen, Jules I. *The Anthracite Railroads: A Study in American Railroad Enterprise*. New York: Ronald Press, 1927.

Boucher, John Newton. *William Kelly: A True Story of the So-Called Bessemer Process*. Greensburg, Pa.: published by the Author, 1924.

Bradley, Edward Scully. *Henry Charles Lea: A Biography*. Philadelphia: University of Pennsylvania Press, 1931.

Bradley, Erwin S. *The Triumph of Militant Republicanism: A Study of Pennsylvania and Presidential Politics 1860–1872*. Philadelphia: University of Pennsylvania Press, 1964.

——. *Simon Cameron: Lincoln's Secretary of War*. Philadelphia: University of Pennsylvania Press, 1966.

Bradsher, Earl L. *Matthew Carey: Editor, Author and Publisher*. New York: AMS Press, 1966 (original edition, 1912).

Bridges, Leonard Hal. *Iron Millionaire: Life of Charlemagne Tower*. Philadelphia: University of Pennsylvania Press, 1952.

Broehl, Wayne G., Jr. *The Molly Maguires*. Cambridge: Harvard University Press, 1964.

Brown, Revelle W. "Friedrich List—The Father of German Railroads—His Residence in Dauphin and Schuylkill Counties, Pennsylvania." Harrisburg: Dauphin County Historical Society, 1950.

Burke, John G. "Bursting Boilers and The Federal Power," *Technology and Culture*, 7 (1966): 1–23.

Campbell, Gilbert Lewis. *Industrial Accidents and Their Compensation*. Boston: Houghton Mifflin, 1911.

Campbell, Stuart William. *Businessmen and Anthracite: Aspects of Change in the Late Nineteenth Century Anthracite Industry*. Ann Arbor, Mich.: University Microfilms, 1978.

Carlson, W. Bernard. "The Pennsylvania Society for the Promotion of Internal Improvements: A Case Study in the Use of Technological Knowledge," MS, 1984.

Casey, Robert J., and W. A. S. Douglas. *The Lackawanna Story: The First Hundred Years of the Delaware, Lackawanna and Western Railroad*. New York: McGraw-Hill, 1951.

Chandler, Alfred, Jr. "Anthracite coal and the beginnings of the 'Industrial Revolution' in the United States," *Business History Review*, vol. 46 (1972), pp. 141–181.

——. *The Visible Hand: The Managerial Revolution in American Business*. Cambridge: Harvard University Press, 1977.

Bibliography

Clothier, I. H. *Letters, 1853–1868, General William Jackson Palmer*. Philadelphia: 1906.

Coleman, James Walter. *The Molly Maguire Riots; Industrial Conflict in the Pennsylvania Coal Region*. New York: Arno, 1969.

Coleman, Terry. *Passage to America: A History of Emigrants from Great Britain and Ireland to America in the Mid-Nineteenth Century*. London: Hutchinson and Company, 1972.

Colls, Robert. *The Collier's Rant*. London: Croom Helm, 1977.

Commons, John R., Jr., U. B. Phillips, E. A. Gilmore, H. L. Sumner, and J. B. Andrews (eds.). *A Documentary History of American Industrial Society*. 10 vols. Cleveland, Ohio: A. H. Clark, 1900–1911.

Couch, Stephen R., and J. Stephen Kroll-Smith. "The chronic technical disaster: Toward a social scientific perspective," *Social Science Quarterly*, vol. 66 (1985), pp. 564–575.

Crippen, Lee F. *Simon Cameron: Ante-Bellum Years*. New York: Da Capo, 1972. Originally published 1942.

Davies, Edward John, II. *The Urbanizing Region: Leadership and Urban Growth in the Anthracite Coal Regions, 1830–1885*. Ph.D. thesis, University of Pittsburgh, 1977.

——. *The Anthracite Aristocracy*. DeKalb, Ill.: Northern Illinois University Press, 1986.

Dorfman, Joseph. *The Economic Mind in American Civilization*, vol. 2. New York: Viking, 1946.

Douglas, Mary, and Aaron Wildavsky. *Risk and Culture*. Berkeley: University of California Press, 1982.

Eastman, Crystal. *Work Accidents and the Law*. New York: Arno Press, 1969. Originally published 1910.

Elson, Ruth Miller. *Guardians of Tradition: American Schoolbooks of the Nineteenth Century*. Lincoln: University of Nebraska Press, 1964.

Elssler, Ermina. "The history of the Henry Clay monument," *Transactions of the Historical Society of Schuylkill County*, vol. 2 (1910), pp. 405–417.

Evans, Chris. *History of the United Mine Workers of America from the Year 1860 to 1890*. 2 vols. Indianapolis: n.d.

Evans, Frank B. *Pennsylvania Politics, 1872–1877: A Study in Political Leadership*. Harrisburg: Pennsylvania Historical and Museum Commission, 1966.

Filbert, J. H. "Joseph F. Patterson," *Transactions of the Historical Society of Schuylkill County*, vol. 5 (1924), pp. 1–10.

Finlay, James Ralph. *The Cost of Mining*. New York: McGraw-Hill, 1910.

Fisher, J. S. *A Builder of the West: The Life of General William Jackson Palmer*. Caldwell, Idaho, 1939.

Folson, Burton W. *Urban Capitalists: Entrepreneurs and City Growth in Pennsylvania's Lackawanna and Lehigh Regions, 1800–1920*. Baltimore: Johns Hopkins Press, 1981.

Foster, Edward Arden. *A History of St. John's United Church of Christ, Saint Clair, Pennsylvania*. St. Clair: mimeograph, 1959.

Francis, Wilfrid. *Coal: Its Formation and Composition* (2nd ed.). London: E. Arnold, 1961.

Fulton, John F. *Benjamin Silliman 1779–1864: Pathfinder in American Science*. New York: Schuman, 1947.

Gerstner, Patsy. "A dynamic theory of mountain building: Henry Darwin Rogers, 1842," *Isis*, 66 (1975), pp. 26–37.

Gersuny, Carol. *Work Hazards and Industrial Conflict*. Hanover, N.H.: University Press of New England, 1981.

Gillespie, Angus. *Folklorist of the Coal Fields: George Korson's Life and Work*. University Park: Pennsylvania State University Press, 1980.

Graebner, William. *Coal Mining Safety in the Progressive Period: The Political Economy of Reform*. Lexington: University of Kentucky, 1976.

Green, Arnold W. *Henry Charles Carey: Nineteenth Century Sociologist*. Philadelphia: University of Pennsylvania Press, 1951.

Green, Victor Robert. *The Attitudes of Slavic Communities to the Unionization of the Anthracite Industry Before 1903.* Ph.D. thesis, University of Pennsylvania, 1963.
——. *The Slavic Community on Strike: Immigrant Labor in Pennsylvania Anthracite.* Notre Dame, Ind.: University of Notre Dame Press, 1968.
Gregory, J. W. *Henry Darwin Rogers.* Glasgow: 1916.
Grob, Gerald. *Workers and Utopia: A Study of Ideological Conflict in the American Labor Movement 1865–1900.* Chicago: Northwestern University Press, 1961.
Grossman, Jonathan. *William Sylvis, Pioneer of American Labor.* New York: Columbia University Press, 1945.
Gudelunas, William. "The rise of the Irish factor in anthracite politics, 1850–1880." Paper read at the 1981 annual meeting of the Pennsylvania Historical Association, West Chester, Pa.
——, and William G. Shade. *Before the Molly Maguires: The Emergence of the Ethno-religious Factor in the Politics of the Lower Anthracite Region, 1844–1872.* New York: Arno, 1976.
Gutman, Herbert G. "The worker's search for power: Labor in the gilded age," in H. Wayne Morgan (ed.), *The Gilded Age: A Reappraisal.* Syracuse: Syracuse University Press, 1963, pp. 38–68.
Hare, Jay V. *History of the Reading.* Philadelphia: Strock, 1966.
Harrison, Royden (ed.). *Independent Collier: The Coal Miner as Archetypal Proletarian Reconsidered.* New York: St. Martin's Press, 1978.
Hartranft, Paul E. *The History of the Public Schools in Schuylkill County.* M.A. thesis, Pennsylvania State University, 1933.
Harvey, Katherine A. *The Best-dressed Miners: Life and Labor in the Maryland Coal Region, 1835–1910.* Ithaca: Cornell University Press, 1969.
Hirsch, Mark G. "Class, ethnicity, and the Irish miners of the lower anthracite region of Pennsylvania, 1850–1880." Paper read at the 1981 annual meeting of the Pennsylvania Historical Association, West Chester, Pa.
Hirst, Margaret E. *Life of Friedrich List.* New York: Kelley, 1965 (originally published 1909).
Hoffman, John N. *Girard Estate Coal Land in Pennsylvania 1801–1884.* Washington: Smithsonian Institution Press, 1972.
[Hudson Coal Company]. *The Story of Anthracite.* New York: Hudson Coal Company, 1932.
Hughes, Thomas P. (ed.). *Selections from Lives of the Engineers . . . by Samuel Smiles.* Cambridge: M.I.T. Press, 1966.
Humphrey, H. B. *Historical Summary of Coal-Mine Explosions in the United States, 1810–1958.* Washington: Bulletin 586, Bureau of Mines, 1960.
Hussey, Miriam. *The Wetherill Papers, 1762–1899.* Philadelphia: Wharton School, 1942.
——. *From Merchants to "Colour Men": Five Generations of Samuel Wetherill's White Lead Business.* Philadelphia: University of Pennsylvania Press, 1956.
Huston, James L. "A political response to industrialism: The Republican embrace of protectionist labor doctrines," *Journal of American History,* vol. 70 (1983), pp. 35–57.
——. "The demise of the Pennsylvania American Party, 1854–1858," *Pennsylvania Magazine of History and Biography,* vol. 109 (1985), pp. 473–497.
Itter, William A. "Early labor troubles in the Schuylkill anthracite district," *Pennsylvania History,* vol. 1 (1934), pp. 28–37.
John, J. J. "The story about one of the first chartered railroads in America," *Transactions of the Historical Society of Schuylkill County,* vol. 1 (1907), pp. 343–411.
Johnson, Paul E. *A Shopkeeper's Millennium.* New York: Hill and Wang, 1978.
Jones, Elliot. *The Anthracite Coal Combination in the United States with Some Account of the Early Development of the Anthracite Industry.* Cambridge: Harvard University Press, 1914.
Jones, Robert. *Analysis of the Strip Mining of Anthracite.* M.B.A. thesis, University of Pennsylvania, 1954.

Bibliography

Jordan, William M. "Geology and the industrial-transportation revolution in early to mid-nineteenth century Pennsylvania," in Schneer, 1979, pp. 91–103.

Kahneman, Daniel, and Amos Tversky. "Prospect theory: An analysis of decision under risk," *Econometrica*, vol. 47 (1979), pp. 263–291.

——. "The psychology of preferences," *Scientific American*, vol. 246 (1982), pp. 160–173.

Kaminsky, John. *Carpatho-Slav Culture and Culture Change in St. Clair, Pennsylvania.* M.A. thesis, Pennsylvania State College, 1951.

Kaplan, A. D. G. *Henry Charles Carey: A Study in American Economic Thought.* Baltimore: Johns Hopkins Press, 1931.

Karaska, Gerald J. *The Pattern of Settlement in the Southern and Middle Anthracite Region in Pennsylvania.* Ph.D. thesis, Pennsylvania State University, 1962.

Killeen, Charles Edward. *John Siney: The Pioneer in American Industrial Unionism and Industrial Government.* Ph.D. thesis, University of Wisconsin, 1942.

Kline, Benjamin F. G., Jr. *Pitch Pine and Prop Timber.* Strasburg, Pa.: privately printed, n.d.

Korson, George G. *Songs and Ballads of the Anthracite Miner: A Seam of Folklore Which Once Ran Through Life in the Hard Coal Fields of Pennsylvania.* New York: Frederick Hitchcock, 1927.

——. *Minstrels of the Mine Patch: Songs and Stories of the Anthracite Industry.* Philadelphia: University of Pennsylvania Press, 1938.

——. *Pennsylvania's Songs and Legends.* Philadelphia: University of Pennsylvania Press, 1949.

——. *Black Rock: Mining Folklore of the Pennsylvania Dutch.* Baltimore: Johns Hopkins Press, 1960.

Krevelen, D. W. van. *Coal: Typology, Chemistry, Physics, and Constitution.* New York: Elsevier Publishing, 1961.

Kutolowski, Kathleen S. "Antimasonry Reexamined: Social Bases of the Grass-Roots Party," *Journal of American History*, 71 (1984), 269–293.

Lauck, W. Jeff. *Combinations in the Coal Industry: Pressure on the Consumer and the Wage Earner of Concentration of Control of Anthracite Reserves, Production, Transportation and Distribution of Anthracite Coal.* Washington: United Mine Workers of America, 1920.

Levine, Robert A. *Culture, Behavior, and Personality.* Chicago: Aldine, 1973.

Levy, Leonard W. *The Law of the Commonwealth and Chief Justice Shaw.* Cambridge: Harvard University Press, 1957.

Lindstrom, Diane. "The industrialization of the East, 1810–1860," *Working Papers from the Regional Economic History Research Center*, vol. 2 (1979), pp. 17–59.

Lowie, Robert H. *The German People: A Social Portrait to 1914.* New York: Farrar & Rinehart, 1945.

——. *Toward Understanding Germany.* Chicago: University of Chicago Press, 1954.

Lowry, Homer Hiram (ed.). *Chemistry of Coal Utilization.* 3 vols. New York: Wiley, 1945 and 1963.

Macomb, Henry Alexander. *The Macomb Family Record.* Camden: Sinnickson, Chew & Sons, 1917.

McCarthy, Charles A. *The Great Molly Maguire Hoax.* Wyoming, Pa.: Cro Woods, 1969.

Metz, Lance E. (ed.). *Anthracite Issue of the Proceedings of the Canal History and Technology Symposium*, vol. 4, 1985.

Michington, W. E. (ed.). *Industrial South Wales, 1750–1914.* London: Cass, 1969.

Miller, Donald L., and Richard E. Sharpless. *The Kingdom of Coal: Work, Enterprise, and Ethnic Communities in the Mine Fields.* Philadelphia: University of Pennsylvania Press, 1985.

Milner, John. *Historical and Archaeological Survey of Frankford Arsenal, Philadelphia, Pennsylvania.* West Chester, Pa.: John Milner Associates, 1979.

[Miners' National Bank]. *Miners' National Bank 1828–1928.* Pottsville, Pa. [1928].

Bibliography

[Mining Association of Great Britain]. *Historical Review of Coal Mining*. London: Fleetway Press, n.d. (20th century, possibly 1920).

Morn, Frank. *The Eye That Never Sleeps: A History of the Pinkerton National Detective Agency*. Bloomington: Indiana University Press, 1982.

Morrison, Rodney J. *Henry C. Carey and American Economic Development*. Transactions of the American Philosophical Society, vol. 76, part 3, 1986.

National Academy of Sciences. *Coal Mining and Ground-Water Resources in the United States*. Washington: National Academy Press, 1981.

——. *Risk and Decision Making: Perspectives and Research*. Washington: National Academy Press, 1982a.

——. *Toward Safer Underground Coal Mines*. Washington: National Academy Press, 1982b.

Nearing, Scott. *Anthracite: An Instance of Natural Resource Monopoly*. Philadelphia: John Winston, 1915.

Nef, John U. *The Rise of the British Coal Industry*. 2 vols. London: Archon Books, 1966 (originally published 1932).

Page, Alfred. *Utility Theory: A Book of Readings*. New York: Wiley, 1968.

Patton, Spiro G. "Railroad versus canal in the southern Schuylkill anthracite coal trade," *Proceedings of the Canal History and Technology Symposium*, vol. 1 (1982), pp. 5–39.

Pinkowski, Edward. "Joseph Battin: Father of the coal breaker," *Pennsylvania Magazine of History and Biography*, vol. 73 (1949), pp. 337–348.

——. *The Lattimer Massacre*. Philadelphia: Sunshine Press, 1950.

——. *John Siney, the Miners' Martyr*. Philadelphia: Sunshine Press, 1963.

Pleasants, Henry, Jr. *The Tragedy of the Crater*. Boston: Christopher, 1938.

——, and George H. Strally. *Inferno at Petersburg*. Philadelphia: Chilton, 1961.

Poliniak, Louis. *When Coal Was King: Mining Pennsylvania's Anthracite*. Lebanon, Pa.: Applied Arts Publishers, 1971.

Powell, H. Benjamin. *Coal, Philadelphia, and the Schuylkill*. Ph.D. thesis, Lehigh University, 1968.

——. "Schuylkill coal trade, 1825–1842," *Historical Review of Berks County*, vol. 39 (1972–73), pp. 14–17, 30–33.

——. *Philadelphia's First Fuel Crisis: Jacob Cist and the Developing Market for Pennsylvania Anthracite*. University Park: Pennsylvania State University Press, 1978.

——. "The Pennsylvania anthracite industry, 1769–1976," *Pennsylvania History*, vol. 47 (1980), pp. 3–27.

Pursell, Carroll W., Jr. *Early Stationary Steam Engines in America: A Study in the Migration of a Technology*. Washington: Smithsonian Institution Press, 1969.

Raglan, Lord. *The Hero*. New York: Vintage, 1956.

Raiffa, Howard. *Decision Analysis*. Reading, Mass.: Addison-Wesley, 1968.

Ross, Dorothy. "Socialism and American liberalism; Academic social thought in the 1880's," *Perspectives in American History*, vol. 11 (1977–78), pp. 7–79.

Ross, Theodore A. *Odd Fellowship: Its History and Manual*. New York: M. W. Hazen, 1888.

Rowan, Richard Wilmer. *The Pinkertons: A Detective Dynasty*. Boston: Little, Brown, 1931.

Sanderlin, Walter S. "The expanding horizons of the Schuylkill Navigation Company, 1815–1870," *Pennsylvania History*, vol. 36 (1969), pp. 174–191.

Schaffer, Jonathan L. "The History of Pennsylvania's Workmen's Compensation: 1900–1916," *Pennsylvania History*, vol. 53 (1986), pp. 26–55.

Schlegel, Marvin W. "The Workingmen's Benevolent Association: First union of anthracite miners," *Pennsylvania History*, vol. 10 (1943), pp. 243–267.

——. *Ruler of the Reading: The Life of Franklin B. Gowen*. Harrisburg: Archives Publishing Company, 1947.

Schmidt, Alvin. *Fraternal Organizations*. Westport, Conn.: Greenwood Press, 1980.

Schneer, Cecil J. (ed.). *Two Hundred Years of Geology in America*. Hanover, N.H.: University Press of New England, 1979.

Bibliography

Schramm, J. R. "Plant colonization studies on black wastes from anthracite mining in Pennsylvania," *Transactions of the American Philosophical Society*, vol. 56 (1966), pp. 1–194.

Schurr, Samuel. *The Mining Industries, 1899–1939*. New York: National Bureau of Economic Research, 1944.

——, and Bruce C. Netschert. *Energy in the American Economy: 1850–1975. An Economic Study of its History and Prospects*. Baltimore: Johns Hopkins Press, 1960.

Scott, Donald M. "The popular lecture and the creation of a public in mid-nineteenth century America," *Journal of American History*, vol. 66 (1980), pp. 791–809.

Seltzer, Robert E. *The History of Education in Schuylkill County, Pennsylvania*. M.A. thesis, Pennsylvania State College, 1931.

Shalloo, J. P. *Private Police*. Philadelphia: American Academy of Political and Social Science, 1933.

Smith, Edwin F. "The Schuylkill Navigation," *Proceedings of the Historical Society of Schuylkill County*, vol. 2 (1910), pp. 475–500.

Smith, George W. *Henry C. Carey and American Sectional Conflict*. Albuquerque: University of New Mexico Press, 1951.

Stapleton, Darwin H. *The Transfer of Technology to the United States in the Nineteenth Century*. Ph.D. thesis, University of Delaware, 1975.

——. "The diffusion of anthracite iron technology: The case of Lancaster County," *Pennsylvania History*, vol. 45 (1978), pp. 147–157.

Stuart, Milton. *Asa Packer 1805–1879: Captain of Industry: Educator: Citizen*. Princeton: Newcomen Society, American Branch, and Princeton University Press, 1938.

Sullivan, William A. *The Industrial Worker in Pennsylvania*. Harrisburg: Pennsylvania Historical and Museum Commission, 1955.

Swank, James M. *Introduction to the History of Iron Making and Coal Mining in Pa.* Philadelphia: the Author, 1878.

Taber, Thomas T., III. *The Delaware, Lackawanna & Western Railroad in the Twentieth Century 1899–1960*, vol. 1. Williamsport: Lycoming Printing Company, 1980.

Taussig, F. W. *The Tariff History of the United States*. New York: Putnam, 1931.

Temin, Peter. *Iron and Steel in Nineteenth Century America*. Cambridge, Mass.: M.I.T. Press, 1963.

Thaler, Richard. "Toward a positive theory of consumer choice," *Journal of Economic Behavior and Organization*, vol. 1 (1980), pp. 39–60.

Thomas, Keith. *Religion and the Decline of Magic*. London: Weidenfeld and Nicolson, 1971.

Thompson, E. P. *The Making of the English Working Class*. New York: Random House, 1963.

Tinkcom, Harry Marlin. *John White Geary: Soldier-Statesman 1819–1873*. Philadelphia: University of Pennsylvania Press, 1940.

Trachtenberg, A. *The History of Legislation for the Protection of Coal Miners in Pennsylvania, 1824–1915*. New York: International Publishers, 1942.

Virtue, G. O. "The anthracite mine laborer," *Department of Labor, Bulletin 13* (1897), pp. 728–774.

Wallace, Anthony F. C. *Religion: An Anthropological View*. New York: Random House, 1966.

——. *Rockdale: An American Village in the Early Industrial Revolution*. New York: Knopf, 1978; Norton, 1980.

——. "The industrialist as hero: An emerging educational theme in nineteeth century America," *Educational Studies*, vol. 12 (1981), pp. 69–83.

——. "Extended family and the role of women in early industrial societies," *Working Papers from the Regional Economic History Research Center*, vol. 5 (1982), pp. 1–12.

——. "The perception of risk in nineteenth century anthracite mining operations," *Proceedings of the American Philosophical Society*, vol. 127 (1983), pp. 99–106.

——. "The Mind of Enoch McGinness," *Pennsylvania Gazette*, 84 (1985), pp. 24–29.

Bibliography

Walter, Joseph. *Hopewell Village: A Social and Economic History of an Iron-Making Community.* Philadelphia: University of Pennsylvania Press, 1966.

Ward, Leo (ed.). *Henry Clay Monument 1852–1985.* Pottsville: Clay Monument Committee, 1985.

Warne, Frank J. *Coal-Mine Workers: A Study in Labor Organization.* New York: Longmans, Green, 1905.

Williamson, Harold F. "Insurance," in Glenn Porter (ed.), *Encyclopedia of American Economic History,* vol. 2. New York: Scribners, 1980, pp. 727–736.

Winpenny, Thomas R. "Hard data on hard coal: Reflections on Chandler's anthracite thesis," *Business History Review,* vol. 53 (1979), pp. 247–258.

Wright, George N., Lawrence Phillips, Peter Whalley, Gerry Choo, Kee-Ong Ng, Irene Tan, Aylene Wisudha, "Cultural differences in probabilistic thinking," *Journal of Cross-cultural Psychology,* vol. 9 (1978), pp. 285–299.

Wright, George N., and L. D. Phillips. "Cross-cultural differences in the assessment and communication of uncertainty," *Current Anthropology,* vol. 20 (1979), pp. 845–846.

Yates, W. Ross. "Discovery of the process for making anthracite iron," *Pennsylvania Magazine of History and Biography,* vol. 98 (1974), pp. 206–223.

Yearley, Clifton K. *Enterprise and Anthracite: Economics and Democracy in Schuylkill County, 1820–1875.* Baltimore: Johns Hopkins Press, 1961.

INDEX

Acornley, John H., 162, 383–5
accidents:
    death and disablement in, 249–58
    miners blamed for, 265–75, 310–12
    see also disasters; explosions; fires
Adams, John Quincy, 67
African Methodist church, 383
"After the Long Strike" (ballad), 425
Agricola, 40, 45
Allibone, S. Austin, 439
Allison, Robert, 37–8, 116–17, 246, 379
Allison Cataract Steam Pump, 38
American Academy of Political and Social
    Science, 195
American Association for the Advance-
    ment of Science, 56, 202
American Economic Association, 195
American Geological Society, 202
American Institute of Mining Engineers,
    411, 433
American Journal of Science and Arts, 84,
    201
American Philosophical Society, 58, 84,
    202
American Political Science Association,
    195
American Social Science Association, 195,
    310
American Sociological Association, 195
American System, 244, 246
Ancient Order of Hibernians, 323, 337–8,
    340–2, 344–7, 349–51, 353–5,
    357–60, 399, 416
anthracite, 7–8
    beds of, 3–6
    as commodity, peculiarities of, 26–30
    and iron, 85–93

mining of, see collieries
    tariff on, 187–8
Anthracite Aristocracy, The: Leadership
    and Social Change in the Hard Coal
    Regions of Northeastern Pennsylvania
    (Davies), 446
Anthracite Board of Trade, 419
Anthracite Communities (Roberts),
    196
Anthracite Industry, The (Roberts),
    196
Anthracite Insurance Company, 262
Anthracite Monitor, 399–401
anticlinal axes, 4, 7, 209
anti-draft riots, 327
Antietam, Battle of, 327
Anzin mines, 45
Appleton (author), 50
arbitration, 395–6
Arcadian Institute, 409
arson, 339
Ashland, 59
    strikes at, 284–6, 291
Association of American Geologists and
    Naturalists, 204
associationists, 194
Atkins, W. W., 73
Atkinson, Joseph, 378
Atwood, Paul, 378
Audenried, Lewis, 262
Aurand, Harold, 358
Avondale disaster, 296–302, 310, 402

Bache, Alexander Dallas, 201
Baird, Edward Carey, 325, 328
Baird, Eliza Carey, 55, 57–8, 64, 65, 72,
    198, 377

Baird, Henry Carey, 58, 60, 66, 68, 240, 401
  and Independent Party, 400
  and protectionism, 198
Baird, Thomas, 55, 57, 64–5, 78–84, 192
  and Coal Mining Association, 282
  and iron smelting, 86, 88–90, 93
  in Masons, 158
Baker, Harriet A., 383–5
Baldwin, Matthew, 240
ballads, 169
  see also specific titles
Bannan, Benjamin, 36, 38, 44, 67, 68, 118, 196, 211, 213, 231, 238, 282, 308, 330, 409
  anti-Irish attitudes of, 321, 323–4
  during Civil War, 326, 327
  and Coal Mining Association, 282
  on iron mining, 93
  link between Molly Maguires and Workingmen's Benevolent Association charged by, 333–4, 361
  on losses by operators, 260
  miners' supply house owned by, 48
  on need for miners' hospital, 279, 280
  and People's Party, 286, 287
  on strikes, 285–6
  as Trinity Church pew holder, 72
  on York Farm expenditures, 82
Bannan, James, 173
Bannan, John, 243, 246, 318, 319
Bannan's New Columbian Primer, 408–9
Baptist church, 383, 392
  Welsh, 160, 172
Bartholomew, Lin, 288, 329, 348, 349, 387, 412
baseball, 173
Bates, John, 283, 284
Bates Union, 283–4
Battin, Joseph, 33–5, 46, 48, 265
Baum, John E., 76, 109, 111, 112, 216–19, 228, 255, 262
Beadle, Esther, 46
Beadle, Jesse, 50, 441
Beadle, J. Louden, 45–6, 48
Beadle, John, 209
Beadle fan, 45–8, 120, 306, 307
Beaver Meadows, 33
Beechwood Colliery, 308, 387, 428, 430
Behan, Thomas, 399
Bell (land agent), 341

benevolent associations, 154–9
  parades of, 168
  see also specific organizations
Bentham, Jeremy, 242
Benthamites, 186, 246
Bessemer process, 59
Betz, John, 165
Biddle, Edward, 240
Biddle, Nicholas, 87, 91, 92, 246
Biddle, Thomas, 91
Bigham, T. J., 390
Binney, Horace, 263–5
Bishop, J. Leander, 244–5
Black, Max, 451
blacklegs, 397
Black Mine Vein, 81, 82, 84
blacks, 372
  at camp meetings, 383
Blaine, James G., 197
Blanchard, William, 64, 65
blasting, 12, 50
Blue Mountain, 3, 4
boilers, 38–9
Boone, Jeremiah, 324
Booth, James C., 57
Borda's colliery, 39
Border, Thomas, 329
boundary system, 44
Bourne, Hugh, 160
Bowen, Eli, 36, 107, 159, 210–13, 238, 428
Bowers, Robert, 290
Boyd, Sam, 170
Boyle, Johnny, 332
Brandywine Manufacturers' Sunday School, 73
brattices, 41–3, 52
breakers, 15–18
  down time of, 28, 29
  at Eagle Colliery, 102
  fires in, 28, 30
  free-market, 27–8
  insurance on, 262–3, 265
  at Pine Forest Colliery, 113
  at St. Clair Slope and Shaft Colliery, 107
  technology of, 33–6
breaker bosses, 23
breasts, 10–12
  firedamp in, 49
  timbering of, 51
  ventilation of, 43
Breen, Philip, 293

Brennan, James, 317–19
Brennan, Michael, 319
Brennan, Mrs., 316, 319
British Guiana, immigrants from, 372
Brook Farm, 194
brothels, 167
Brown, Amzi, 329, 378
Brown, David P., 44, 232, 404
Brown, Richard, 379, 387
Buck, C. N., 263
Buddle, John, 44
Buffalo Bill's Wild West Show, 173
Bull Run, Second Battle of, 327
Bureau of Mines, 449
Burke, Father, 380
business failures, 258–61
    impact on miners of, 280–1

Cadets of Temperance, 382
Calvinist church, Welsh, 129, 160
Cameron, Donald, 280
Cameron, Simon, 198, 199, 240, 246, 280,
    288, 400
Campbell, James H., 262, 281, 318
camp meetings, 383
Canadian immigrants, 372
Canfield, Catherine, 166, 167
Canfield, Thomas, 166
Canning, Dennis, 351
Carey, Edward, 55, 57, 60, 64, 65, 80, 82,
    324
Carey, Elizabeth Sheridan, 58–9
Carey, Henry Charles, 55, 57–60, 64–70,
    85, 116, 158, 173, 318, 327, 377, 401,
    441, 442
    in American Philosophical Society, 202
    death of, 439
    and geological survey, 201, 208
    on happiness, 246
    on harmony of interests, 283
    and Independent Party, 400
    and iron smelting, 88, 89, 92
    and job actions, 276
    McGinness and, 28, 60, 76, 77, 121,
        209, 215–18, 249, 442
    miners blamed for accidents by, 266
    and protectionism, 184–200
    royalty insurance of, 262–3
    St. Clair lots owned by, 124–5, 144
    St. Clair project of, 94, 96–9
    and St. Clair Slope and Shaft Colliery,
        109, 111, 112

Spohn Tract slope sunk by, 80–2,
    428
    and strikes, 291
    testimonial dinner for, 238–40
Carey, Maria, 64, 65
Carey, Matthew, 55, 185, 201
Carey, Patty Leslie, 58
Carey, Susan, 55, 57
Carey-and-Patterson Slope, 80–1
Carey group, 54–60, 64–70, 200, 406,
    418, 427
    churches and, 161
    and Coal Mining Association, 282
    early undertakings of, 78–85
    insurance of, 262
    and iron smelting, 86–93
    sale of St. Clair lots by, 123–5, 128
    St. Clair project of, 93–101, 126,
        165
Carlyle, Thomas, 204
Carpenter, James, 64
Carpenter, John T., 73–4, 256, 261, 325,
    351
Carr, Andrew, 325, 352
cartels, 421
Casey, John, 337
Cass County, strikes in, 287
Catholic Benevolent Union, 369
Catholic church, 172
    and Ancient Order of Hibernians, 341,
        357
    antagonism toward, 321
    German, 160, 162, 175
    membership in Masons prohibited by,
        157, 159
Catholic Workingmen's Society, 416
Centralia mine fire, 443
Centreville Tract, 74
certification of miners, 137
Chain Gang, 342
Chance, H. Martin, 24–5, 44, 52–3,
    308
Chartists, 204, 275, 284, 286, 392
child labor, 147, 148
choke-damp, 256
Christmas services, 382
churches, 159–65
    attendance at, 380, 382–5
    *see also specific churches; denomina-
    tions*
circuses, 173
civic solidarity, 380–8

Civil War, 63, 67, 176, 246, 275, 287, 289, 294, 324–8, 404
  monument to dead of, 386–8, 405
Clanny lamp, 48
Clay, Henry, 185, 199, 232, 243–6, 287
clothing, cost of, 147
Clover, Kitty, 102
Coal, Iron, and Oil (Daddow and Bannan), 44, 46, 196–7, 213, 231, 308
Coal, Its Producers and Consumers (Carey), 187
Coal and Coal Oil; or, The Geology of the Earth (Bowen), 211
Coal and the Coal Trade (Bowen), 211, 428
coal formation, theory of, 210–11
Coal and Iron Police, 247, 330, 343, 405, 422, 427
Coal Mining (Marlor), 31
Coal Mining Association of Schuylkill County, 282–3
Coal Mining Safety in the Progressive Period (Graebner), 448
Coaquenac, 138
cockfighting, 173
Cole, William, 328–9
Coleman, George B., 294, 295
Collahan, Thomas, 316, 319, 320
collective action, 282
collieries:
  and coal as commodity, 27–30
  failures of, 258–61
  mine patches around, 138
  operators of, 70–8
  progress and regression in technology of, 30–53
  at St. Clair, 101–22
  structure and operation of, 8–25
  see also specific collieries
Colliery Iron Works, 72, 73
Columbia Hose Company, 382
Columbia Insurance Company, 263
Columbus, Christopher, 229
Colwell, Stephen, 197, 240
Combination Acts, 392
communism, 400, 401
  Gowen's fear of, 416–17
Conan Doyle, Sir Arthur, 343
Congregationalist church, Welsh, 129, 160
Congress, U.S., 197, 198, 272, 400
Continental Insurance Company, 263

contract miners, 131–2
  ethnicity of, 135–7, 374, 437–8
  wages of, 142–4
contributory negligence, 271
cooperative movement, 392–4
  British, 275
Cornish Bull pumping engine, 18, 37, 39
Cornwall iron mine, 294
Coryell, Richard, 163, 165, 243, 325, 386, 387
Cosgrove, Edward, 347–9
cost accounting, 24
cotton, 26
Court, Police, and Jury Act (1867), 330
Cowan, John, 290
Coxe, Eckley B., 258–60, 272, 310–12, 411–12, 420, 433
craftsmen, 132
  wages of, 141
Crane, George, 86, 88–90
Crawshaw, Daniel, 379
creationism, 211
Cressona camp meeting, 383
cricket clubs, 173
Cross Keys tavern, 165
Crow Hollow, 138
  Germans in, 175
Crowley, Timothy, 290
Crystal Palace Exhibition (New York, 1853), 61
culm banks, 18
  fires in, 52
cultural differences, 171–83
Cumming, P. M., 334–8, 343, 422–4
Cummings, James, 319
Curtin, Governor, 326

Daddow, Esther, 441
Daddow, Samuel H., 18, 36, 44, 118, 196, 253, 308, 380
  and Beadle fan, 46–8
  British authorities cited by, 31
  and Clay monument, 244
  death of, 439
  on Eagle Colliery, 103–4
  geological theories of, 213–15
  on industrial heroes, 231–6
  manufacturing establishments founded by, 441
  squib invented by, 50
Danville, 59
Danville Iron Works, 93

Danville and Pottsville Railroad, 88, 94–6, 165
Dark Water, 138
Dauphin and Susquehanna Coal Company, 56
David, Dennis, 142
Davies, Edward J., 446
Davis, Rees, 378
Davis, William, 387
Davy lamp, 48, 114
death in mines, 249–58
decision theory, risk-seeking behavior in, 447–52
deep-shaft mines, 406
  see also *specific mines*
Delaware Anticlinals, 4
Delaware Coal Company, 5, 98, 208, 319, 418, 428
  mine patches of, 139
Delaware and Hudson Railroad, 27
Delaware, Lackawanna and Western Railroad, 297
Democratic Party, 282, 285
  defection of miners from, 281
  during Civil War, 325, 326
  Gowen and, 404, 405, 412
  Hughes and, 198
  Irish support for, 287, 321, 323–4, 331, 358, 361, 372
  and safety legislation, 293, 294, 302–3, 305
  Siney and, 399
  Wetherill and, 63
De Re Metallica (Agricola), 40, 45
Devine, Martin, 319
Dewees, Francis P., 400, 401, 412
Diamond Colliery, 217, 223–6, 276
Diamond Vein, 4
Dickens, Charles, 197
Dickinson College, 202
disability insurance, 271–2
disablement in mines, 249–58
disaster-prone organization, 453–6
disasters:
  civic solidarity during, 380, 385–6
  frequency of, 30
  see also accidents; explosions; fires
"disorderly houses," 166–7
Dolan, Pat, 341
Donahue, John, 328–30
Donaldson family, 161
Donnelly, Christopher, 351

door boys, 20
  casualties among, 253
  wages of, 143
Dormer, Martin, 166
Dormer, Patrick, 166, 337, 340–2
Doughtery, Daniel, 351–2, 358–9
Douglas, Mary, 447–8
Dow, Lorenzo, 160
"Down in a Coal Mine" (ballad), 170, 255, 369
Doyle, Michael, 351
drainage, 10
drifts, 8–10
  breakers of, 15
  drainage of, 10
  ventilation in, 13, 42
"Driver Boys of Wadesville Shaft, The" (ballad), 169, 446–7
drivers, 19–21
  wages of, 143
Duffy family, 151–2
dumb drifts, 42
Duncan Tract, 66, 80
du Pont, Sophie, 73
Durkin, John, 385

Eagle Colliery, 62, 75, 101–5, 108, 126, 152, 444
  breaker fires at, 263
  deaths and injuries at, 251, 252
  Eltringham's inspection of, 308
  explosions in, 294
  insurance on, 262
  under Philadelphia and Reading Coal and Iron Company, 418, 428, 430, 436, 438, 440–1
  safety practices at, 260–1
  strikes at, 285, 288
  visits by public figures to, 369
Eagle No. 2 Colliery, 76
Eagle Temple of Honor, 382
East Mount Laffee Colliery, 404
education, 408–11
Edwards, Jenkin, 167
eight-hour day, 291, 292
Elder, William, 240
Ellmaker Tract, 62, 118
Elson, Ruth, 408
Eltringham, John, 269, 305–9, 428–9, 432–3
Elwell, Judge, 420
Emerson, Ralph Waldo, 197

employer's liability, 270–5
Encyclopedia of Technology (Appleton), 51
Engels, Friedrich, 416
engine technology, 36–9
English common law, 55, 270
English immigrants, 130, 372
  in benevolent associations, 155
  churches of, 160–1
  in Civil War, 325, 328, 388
  culture of, 171–4, 176–82
  families of, 148, 152–4
  in mine patches, 139–41
  occupations of, 133–5, 137–8, 374, 437
  politics and, 282, 287, 331
  property ownership by, 374, 375
  songs of, 167–8
*Enterprise and Anthracite: Economics and
  Democracy in Schuylkill County*
  (Yearly), 446
Episcopal church, 72–3, 129
Episcopalian Church of the Holy Apostles,
  163
Erie Railroad, 439
Essay on the Rate of Wages (Carey), 186
ethnicity:
  census data on, 130–1, 372
  and cultural differences, 171–83
  and kinship system, 149
  and occupation, 133–8, 374–5, 437–8
  and property ownership, 374, 375
evangelism, 273
Evans, Barton, 123
Evans, Clay W., 378, 379, 381, 405
Evans, Emily Allison, 379
Evans, Evan, 124
Evans, Lott, 128
exhaust fans, 45
explosions, 30, 40, 42
  deaths and injuries in, 255
  in Diamond Slope, 225
  frequency of, 312
  in Gowen's collieries, 404
  and job actions, 276
  miners blamed for, 265–6, 269–70
  in Parvin's slope, 121
  at Pittston, 312
  and safety legislation, 294
  in St. Clair Slope and Shaft, 109, 111,
    112
  in Wadesville Shaft, 120, 361–6, 385–6
extended family, 148–54
Eyre Tract, 65, 80, 85

Farquhar, George W., 63, 198, 242, 246,
  351
Farquhar, Guy E., 351
Farrandsville, 59
  blast furnace at, 88
Federalists, 67
federal safety legislation, 272
fellow-servant rule, 270, 271
fire boss, 21–2
firedamp (methane), 14, 21, 22, 40, 42,
  49, 52
  explosions of, *see* explosions
  lung disorders caused by, 256
  standards for concentrations of, 307–9
  in York Farm Colliery, 83
Fire Insurance and How to Build (Moore),
  263
fires, 52–3
  breaker, 28, 30
  frequency of, 312
  insurance against, 262–5
  at St. Clair Slope and Shaft Colliery,
    111–12
  in Wadesville Shaft, 121
Firmstone, William, 88
First Geological Survey of Pennsylvania,
  84, 204–8, 210, 215
First International, 400
First World War, 436
Fitch, John, 58
Flannery, Pat, 337
floods, 147–8
  in St. Clair Slope and Shaft, 112
Flowery Field Tract, 62, 118, 177
food:
  ethnic preferences, 173–4
  prices of, 146–7
48th Pennsylvania Regiment, 326–8, 379
Foster, Joseph, 163
Four-Foot Vein, 102
Fourier, Charles, 194
Fourth of July parades, 380–2
Fowler, J. A., 263, 264
Frack, Daniel, 165, 166
Frane, Edward, 325
Frank Leslie's Illustrated Newspaper, 299
Franklin, Benjamin, 58, 263, 408
Franklin, Benjamin (Pinkerton agency
  chief), 335, 346
Franklin Institute, 85, 202
Franklin Iron Works, 38
Frantz, Christian, 109, 111, 152–3

Frantz, Jacob, 128, 152–3
Frantz family, 152–3
fraternal organizations, 154–9
  see also specific organizations
Fredericksburg, Battle of, 327
Freemasonry, *see* Masons
free trade, British, 194–5
French immigrants, 372
furnaces, 13–14, 40, 42
fuses, 12, 50

gangways, 10–11
Garrett, S. A., 351
Gate Vein, 81, 93, 209
Geary, Governor, 295, 303–5
Geiger, John, 156
Geisse, Joseph, 317
Geissenheimer, Frederick, 85–6, 88
Geological Society of Pennsylvania, 201
geological surveys, 201–15
Geology of Pennsylvania, The (Rogers),
  210
Geology of Schuylkill County (Sheafer),
  406–7
German immigrants, 130, 372
  benevolent society of, 168
  churches of, 129, 160, 162–3
  in Civil War, 325, 328, 388
  culture of, 172–6, 182
  families of, 148, 152–3
  in mine patches, 139–41
  murders of, 344
  music of, 168
  occupations of, 133–8, 374–5, 437,
    438
  politics and, 282, 287
  property ownership by, 374, 375
Germantown Cricket Club, 173
Gibbons, John, 351
Girard, Stephen, 57, 185
Girard Estate, 88, 149, 393, 407
Girard Tunnel, 95
Girardville, Irish in, 372
Gittins, John, 290
Glasgow, University of, 208
Glen Carbon Coal Company, 329
goaf, 12
gob, 12, 52
Gowen, Franklin B., 326, 329, 367, 401,
  403–17, 435–6
  annual salary of, 394
  death of, 440

and Molly Maguires, 332–6, 338–40,
  343, 344, 346, 350, 351, 353–8, 360,
  361, 405
as Mount Laffee colliery operator, 121,
  258, 404
and rise of company state, 417, 418
during strikes, 420, 421
and twin shafts plan, 430–1
and Wadesville Shaft explosion, 365
Gowen, George Washington, 326, 328, 404
Graebner, William, 448–9
Grand Army of the Republic (GAR), 176,
  326, 379, 381, 382, 386–8, 405
Granges, 399
Grant, Ulysses S., 197, 339
Great Awakening, 273
Greeley, Horace, 194, 197, 368–9
Greenback Party, 400, 401
Gregory, J. W., 205
Griffiths, David L., 422
Gudelunas, William, 358
Guibal fan, 45–8, 431
Guinea Hill Colliery, 82–4, 209
Guinea Hill Tract, 65, 81, 85
  iron ore in, 93
Gumbes, Rebecca, 61
Gwinner, Jacob, 123, 325
Gwyther, Thomas, 346

Halberstadt, Andrew, 64
Hall, Bridget, 337
Hall, Peter, 336–7
Hancock Vein, 93
Hanmore, H. B., 339, 343
hard coal, *see* anthracite
Harmony of Interests, The (Carey),
  198
Harper's Weekly, 36, 299
Harris, Mrs., 319
Harrisburg Morning Patriot, 303
Hart, Abraham, 59, 60, 64, 65, 85, 199,
  208, 217, 222, 225, 238, 240
  and iron smelting, 88
Hart, Daniel L., 170
Hart, El, 112
Hartman Tract, 66
Hartranft, Governor, 387
Hartwell Colliery, 42
Harvard University, 56
Haven, Thomas Albert, 58, 66, 81, 116,
  124
Haven, Virginia Carey, 58

Haywood, Benjamin, 64, 71–2, 75, 81,
    199, 281–2, 387
    and Pine Forest Colliery, 112
Haywood and Snyder, 26, 37, 71, 72, 77
Hazleton, Long Strike in, 343
headings, 43
Heckscherville Deep Slope, 308
Hedley, John, 31, 32
Heenan, James, 338, 342, 349
Herbert, Edward, 226–7, 361, 363–5, 392
Hetherington, Edward, 123–4
Hetherington, Jacob, 124
Hickory Slope, 33, 75, 76, 105, 115–18,
    120, 156, 289, 312, 328, 361
    abandonment of, 436
    breaker fires at, 263
    ceremonial exchanges between miners
        and superintendent of, 380
    deaths and injuries at, 255
    fires and explosions in, 312
    Japanese trade commission at, 368
    profitability of, 259
    strike at, 285
Hiester, Isaac, 185
Hillan, Michael, 378, 379
*Historical Sketch of Geological Explora-
    tions in Pennsylvania and Other
    States* (Lesley), 215
Historical Society of Pennsylvania, 58
History of American Manufactures
    (Bishop), 244–5
Holden, Nancy, 151
Holland, John, 177–8
Holmes, John, 37, 50, 109, 111, 123, 225,
    226, 325, 380, 400
Holmes Vein, 123
Hope Hose Company, 382
Hospital and Asylum of Schuylkill County,
    280
hot-blast smelting technique, 85–6
hotels, 165–6
house rentals, 144
Howarth, William, 290
Hughes, Daniel, 290
Hughes, Francis W., 198, 199, 216, 218,
    237, 244, 318, 349, 351, 400, 412
Humphreys, Mary, 316, 318
Hunt's Magazine, 198
Hurley, Thomas, 349–52, 358

Igo, Patrick, 124, 151
Igo, Thomas, 124, 151

Igo family, 151–2
Improved Order of Red Men, 289
Independent Party, 400
industrialists as heroes, 228–47
Industrial Revolution, 6, 93, 176, 191,
    195, 229, 270, 274, 389, 410, 453,
    454, 456
Ingersoll, J. Jared, 185
inside boss, 21, 22
insurance, 261–5
    and employer's liability, 271–2
International Molders' Union, 275, 303
Irish immigrants, 130, 372
    benevolent society of, 168; *see also*
        Ancient Order of Hibernians
    churches for, 129, 160, 162–3
    in Civil War, 325–8, 388
    as contract miners, 437–8
    culture of, 172–4, 181–3
    discrimination against, 312–13, 320–4,
        346, 347, 360
    families of, 148–54
    in mine patches, 139–41
    occupations of, 133–8, 374–5
    politics and, 282, 287, 331
    property ownership by, 124, 374, 375
    retributive justice among, 315–20; *see
        also* Molly Maguires
    scapegoating of, 273–4
    taverns frequented by, 164
Irish World, 401
iron, 26, 85–93
    and protectionism, 186–7
    on St. Clair Tract, 93–4
Iron Molders' International Union,
    400

Jackson, Andrew, 87
Jackson, Benjamin, 128
James, Benjamin, 422–3
James, Gomer, 346–50, 352, 358
James, Jesse, 334, 344
James, John, 335
James, Peter, 347
James, Sarah, 347
James, Thomas, 347, 348
Japanese trade commission, 368
Jefferson, Thomas, 58
jigs, 17
Johns, George W., 75, 76, 288, 376
Johns, Thomas, 75, 76, 101, 103, 162,
    232

Johns, William H., 28, 71, 75–6, 101, 103, 218–20, 228, 325, 386
Johns Basin, 101, 105
Johns family, 54, 63, 75–6, 144, 336, 378, 428, 430, 441
  mansion of, 165
  and Methodist Episcopal church, 162
  occupations of members of, 132
  and safety practices, 260–1
  see also Eagle Colliery
Johnson, C. Ben, 399, 400
Johnson, Charles R., 378, 379
Johnson, Jack, 253–4
Johnson, Jonathan, 127, 156, 165, 166, 243
Johnson, Paul, 273
Johnson, Theodore R., 410
Johns' Patch, 138, 444
  house rentals in, 144, 145
Johns' Patch Colliery, 153
Jones, Griffith, 37
Jones, John P., 346
Jones, Richard, 89
Jones, Tom, 347
Journal of the Franklin Institute, 31–3, 42, 86, 118
Journal of Social Science, 195
Joyce, Thomas, 339–40
Junior Sons of America, 381, 382

Kaercher, George, 331, 351, 356–7
Kahneman, Daniel, 449, 451, 452
Kane, Jeremiah, 349
Karthaus blast furnace, 88, 89
Kaska William Colliery, 104, 141–4
Kear, William, 220
Keating, William, 169–70
Kehley Run mine fire, 290, 444
Kehoe, John, 341, 345, 350–2, 356, 357, 359, 405
  execution of, 439–40
Keim, George de B., 60, 211, 431, 432
Keim estate, 62
Kelly, William D. ("Pig Iron"), 197, 400
Kendrick, William, 114–15, 158, 260, 420, 428, 430
Keystone American party, 321
Kirk, James S., 76, 109, 111, 112, 216–19, 228, 255
Kline, Adam, 243
Knight, Charles, 197

Knights of Labor, 300, 358, 400, 416, 417, 442
Knights of Pythias, 289, 386
Knowledge is Power (Knight), 197
Know Nothing Party, 198, 321
Korson, George, 138, 154, 169, 171, 178, 299
Krebs, Harry, 128

laborers, 132
  casualties among, 253
  ethnicity of, 133–8, 374
  strikes of, 147
  wages of, 141–4
Labor Reform Party, 280, 399–400
Lafayette, General, 185
Lafayette Rifles, 325, 327
lamps, 14–15
  safety, 48–9
Lanigan, James, 368
Lanigan's Furnace, 436, 444
Lattimer's patented miners' caps, 441
Laurel Run Improvement Company, 334, 418
Lawler, Muff, 341, 342, 349
Lawton, Alfred, 98, 99, 126, 209, 317
Lawton, Charles, 37, 60, 71, 93, 125, 132, 241, 325, 378
  as chief burgess, 128, 167
  and Coal Mining Association, 282
  in cricket club, 173
  in Masons, 156
Lawton, Ellen Baird, 58, 64
Lawton, John, 125
Lawton, Joseph, 58, 64, 66, 121, 125, 128, 163
Lawton family, 54, 376
  mansion of, 165
  occupations of members of, 132
Lawton Vein, 82
Lea, Frances Carey, 55
Lea, Henry Charles, 57
Lea, Isaac, 55–7, 64–6, 84–5, 202, 208, 211
  and Danville and Pottsville Railroad, 95
  and iron smelting, 87–9, 91
Lea, Matthew Carey, 57, 84
Lee lands, 62, 116
Lehigh Coal and Navigation Company, 88–9, 427–8
Lehigh Crane Iron Company, 89, 90
Lehigh Valley Railroad, 417, 418

Lesley, Peter, 159, 203–4, 207–8, 215
Leslie family, 58
Lewis, Daniel, 379
Lewis, Samuel, 318
Lewis, Thomas, 378, 379
Lewis, William D., 198–9
Lewis Vein, 4, 224
Liebig, Justus von, 61
life insurance, 261
Lincoln, Abraham, 198, 286, 287, 326
Linden, Robert J., 343–5
linear processing, 28–30
Lippincott, J. B., 240, 408
Lippincott's Magazine, 234
List, Friedrich, 184–6, 241
Littlehales, William, 156, 329
Littlehales, William Jr., 329–30
Little Harry's Indestructible Reading Book, 409
Little Schuylkill Navigation, Railroad, and Coal Company, 185, 240–1
Liverpool and London Fire and Life Insurance Company, 261
Locustdale Colliery, 46
Lonaconing Furnace, 83
Long Strike (1875), 276, 338, 343, 357, 403, 419, 421, 422, 424–5, 436
"Long Strike, The" (ballad), 424
Lowie, Robert, 174
lumber, 26
lump coal, 16
Lundy's gangway, 362–3, 366
lung disorders, 256–7
Luther, D., 262
Lutheran church, 157, 160, 163
Luzerne lands, 77
L'Velle, Martin M., 331, 351, 357
Lyell, Charles, 85, 202, 204, 213
Lyman, William, 90, 92

Mack, Bridget, 153
Macomb, John 61
Maddison, John, 65, 103, 108–9, 209
Maguire, John, 31, 47, 49, 114–15, 253, 267–9, 285, 293
Maguire, Thomas, 114
Mahanoy City, 59
  Irish in, 372
Major, George, 337, 351–2
Major, Jesse, 352, 358
Major, William, 352, 358
Malthus, Thomas, 189–91

Mammoth Colliery, 39, 66, 121
  breaker fire at, 263
  mine patches near, 139
Mammoth Vein, 4, 101, 112, 113, 115, 117, 118, 268, 440
  accessibility of, 63, 77
  explosion in, 361–2
  McGinness's attempts to mine, 98–100, 107, 108, 209–10
  outcroppings of, 62, 102, 206, 228, 428, 438
  strip mining of, 443, 444
  timbering in, 51
  and Twin Shafts project, 431, 434, 435
Mammoth Vein Coal and Iron Company, 427
Mammoth Vein Consolidated Coal Company, 66, 75, 117, 418
management, wages of, 141
Manhattan Insurance Company, 262
Manual of the Mechanics of Engineering, with an Introduction to the Calculus (Weisbach), 259
Marion Rifles, 246
Marlborough, Duke of, 228
Marlor, Joseph, 31
Mars in Mahantango (Wetherill), 68, 246
Martz, George, 36, 107
Marx, Karl, 416
Masons, 155–9, 161, 168, 288, 323, 357
  movement against, 273
Mays, John, 128
McAllister family, 344
McAndrew, Frank, 349, 351, 356, 358
McCann, John, 352
McCarthy, William J., 399
McClure, Alexander, 327
McCowan, William, 343
McEnroe, Father, 385
McFarlan, James, *see* McParlan, James
McGinness, Daniel, 173, 218, 219, 226–7
  in Civil War, 326, 328
McGinness, Enoch W., 68, 71, 76–7, 113, 173, 200, 239, 260, 417, 428, 431, 443–5, 453, 456
  Carey and, 28, 60, 76, 77, 121, 209, 215–28, 249, 442
  death of, 77–8, 439
  geological theories of, 184, 209–10, 213
  life insurance of, 261
  and Mammoth Vein, 98–100
  Milnes denounced by, 117

slowdowns against, 276
and St. Clair Slope and Shaft Colliery,
75, 93, 105–11
testimonial dinner for, 237–8, 240
McGinness, Theodore, 173, 226
*McGinness Theory of the Schuylkill Coal
Formation, The* (Bowen), 238
McGough, Andrew, 124
McGough, Terence, 124
McHugh, Frank, 351, 355–7
McIlwain, N. M., 381
McKean, Kate, 59
McKenna, James, *see* McParlan, James
McParlan, James, 166, 334, 338, 340–6,
349–53, 356–8, 360, 414, 422
mechanics' lien law, 280
Merrick and Towne, 89
methane, *see* firedamp
Methodist Church, 76
Methodist Episcopal Church, 123, 129,
160, 162, 231, 382, 383
Metz, David, 123
Metz, Jacob, 99, 128, 155, 378
Metz, Joel, 128
middle class, political dominance of,
376–80
Miesse, Charles, 407–8
militia, 168
strike breaking by, 285, 343
Mill, Frank, 338
Mill, John Stuart, 189
Mill Creek, 4, 37, 138, 164
Mill Creek and Mine Hill Railroad, 94,
126, 129, 262, 279, 443
headquarters of, 54
rebuilding of, 97
Milnes, Benjamin, 31, 75, 76, 112,
116–18, 164, 219, 228, 255
Milnes, William, 71, 72, 74–5, 116, 243
Daddow and, 232
in Masons, 156
and strikes, 285
Milnes, William, Jr., 75, 158
mine cars, 10–11
loading of, 13
Mine Hill, 4
mine operators, *see* operators; *specific
names*
mine patches, 138–41
house rentals in, 144–5
Philadelphia and Reading Coal and Iron
Company control of, 426–7

mineral rights, 54, 55
miners, 20, 131
blamed for accidents, 265–75
Daddow's poems about, 233
deaths and injuries of, 249–58
ethnicity of, 133–8, 374–5
as poor insurance risks, 261
songs and ballads of, 169–71
strikes of, *see* strikes
wages of, 141–4
miner's asthma, 256–7, 279
"Miner's Doom, The" (ballad), 253
Miner's Friend, The, 40
miners' helpers, 20
see also laborers
miners' hospital, 279–80
Miners' Hospital Relief Association, 252
Miner's Journal, 27, 31, 32, 34, 38, 39, 42,
44–6, 48, 59, 63, 67, 76, 81, 83, 87–9,
91–3, 102, 106, 109, 118, 125–6, 146,
155, 164, 167, 183, 189, 192, 196,
208–10, 231, 249–50, 255, 257, 258,
261, 262, 266–7, 271, 279, 284, 285,
287, 291, 309–12, 314, 317, 320–4,
329–31, 348, 351, 360, 369–70, 372,
379, 382, 394, 395, 399, 406, 410,
422, 434
Miners' and Laborers' Benevolent Association of Schuylkill County, 395,
397–400, 403, 424
miner's lien act, 280–2
"Miner's Life, The" (ballad), 253–4
Miners' National Association, 335, 336,
338, 393–5, 398, 400, 421, 423
Miner's Supply Company, 50, 441
Mine Safety Acts:
of 1869, 252, 293–6, 302
of 1870, 302–5, 309–12
of 1885, 137
Mining Methods and Appliances (Chance),
24, 44, 52–3, 308
Mitchell, John, 442
Modocs, 342, 351, 352, 359
Molly Maguires, 273, 291, 321, 323–4,
331, 334–61, 414, 416, 440, 456
during Civil War, 327
murders by, 329, 330, 337, 344, 346–50
trial of, 166, 315, 320, 324, 331–2, 343,
346, 350–8, 360, 405–6, 425
Welsh street gangs and, 174
and Workingmen's Benevolent Association, 332–4, 395, 420, 422

Molly Maguires, The (Dewees), 401
Molly Maguires, The (movie), 343
monkey rolls, 17
Moore, F. C., 263
Moore, Herbert, 386
Moore, John, 317, 318
Moore, Ralph, 31
Morgan, David, 378
Morgan, John, 280
Morris, John, 351
Morse, Samuel F. B., 58
mountain formation, theory of, 204–5
Mount Airy College, 59
Mount Carbon and East Norwegian Rail-
    road, 315
Mount Carbon Railroad, 95
Mount Laffee, 26
    Daddow's poems about, 232, 234
    iron ore in, 93
    mine patches in, 139, 140
    parades in, 168
    slope collieries of, 121
mud screen, 17
mules, 20–1
music, 167–71

Nanticoke Coal Company, 297
Napier, Lord, 199
Nash, Martin, 337, 341–2, 399
Nash, Philip, 332
Nash, William, 337
National Academy of Sciences, 202, 447,
    448
National Labor Congress, 398
National Labor Union, 399
Neilson, James, 85, 86
Nelson, Admiral Horatio, 229
Neuman, Bishop, 162
Newcastle, 40, 70, 138, 140
    Germans in, 175
Newcomen, Thomas, 229
Newcomen engine, 37
New Harmony, 194
New Jersey Geological Survey, 201
New York Fire and Marine Insurance
    Company, 262
New York Geological Survey, 56
New York Tribune, 197
Nice, Decatur, 399
Nichols, Francis B., 64, 93, 94, 124, 125,
    241, 282
Nichols, St. Clair, 94

"Noncarra's Bad Luck" (Daddow), 235–6
Northall, John C., 119, 328–9, 361, 368,
    380
North American Coal Company, 66, 77,
    418, 427, 428, 453
    attempt to locate Mammoth Vein by, 98
    Carey acquires lands of, 198–9
    and geological surveys, 208, 209
    McGinness and, 121, 216–18, 223–4,
    226–8
    Milnes and, 75, 116
*North American and United States Ga-
    zette*, 240

Oak Hill Colliery, 75
Oak Hills Tract, 62
O'Brien, Michael, 251
Occupational Safety and Health Act
    (1970), 272
occupations:
    census data on, 131–3, 373
    ethnicity and, 133–8, 374–5, 437–8
Odd Fellows, 123, 155–6, 158, 168, 273,
    288, 323, 357, 382, 386
O'Donnell, Charles, 344
O'Donnell, James, 344
Oestereich, Katherine Anschutz, 175, 176
Oestreich, Maurus, 168, 172, 173, 175–6,
    315, 357–8, 389
*Old Galagher the Coal Operator, or the
    Miners of Mt. Laffee* (Daddow), 233
Omerd, Adam, 290
O'Neill, Frank, 338, 342, 349, 350, 360
open-market relationships, 26
operators, 23
    liability of, 270–5
    see also specific names
Orchard Vein, 226
O'Regan, Jack, 338, 342
Orme, Levi, 289, 293
Orme, Seth, 289, 378, 379, 387
Orme family, 289
Orwigsburg, parades in, 381
outside boss, 23
Owen, Robert, 194, 202, 398
Owen, Robert Dale, 202

Packer, Asa, 305
Packer, S. J., 75
Paine, Thomas, 398
Palmer, R. M., 262
Palmer, Strange N., 158

Palmer, William Jackson, 31, 42
Palo Alto Rolling Mill, 199
panel system, 44
parades, 168, 380–2
Parliament, British, 42
Parnell, Charles Stewart, 380
Parry, E. O., 318
Parry, Elizabeth, 167
Parsons, William, 231
Parton, Sampson, 363–6
Parvin, Francis J., 71, 75, 221, 224–6
Parvin's Slope, 121, 164, 221
Patterson, Burd, 59–60, 72, 80–2, 85, 125,
     428
  and Coal Mining Association, 282
  and iron smelting, 88–90, 93, 126, 129
  and McGinness, 218, 228
  purchase of St. Clair property by, 96
Patterson, Joseph, 267, 306–7, 396, 397,
     424–5
Patterson, General Robert, 197
Peale, Charles Wilson, 61, 324
peat-bog theory of coal formation, 210–11
Pennsylvania, University of, 63, 73, 176,
     185, 197, 201, 202
Pennsylvania Association of Iron Manufac-
     turers, 61
Pennsylvania Bureau of Labor Statistics,
     390
Pennsylvania Diamond Drill Company,
     432, 433
Pennsylvania Railroad, 414, 417
Pennsylvania Society for the Encourage-
     ment of Manufactures and Mechanic
     Arts, 185
People's Fire Insurance Company of New
     York, 262
People's Party, 281–2, 285–7, 321
People's Railroad, 417
Perry, Benjamin, 90
Petersburg, siege of, 327–8, 339
Philadelphia, 4, 54
  cricket club in, 173
  food prices in, 146
  shipping of coal to, 24–5, 28, 84, 143
Philadelphia Board of Fire Underwriters,
     265
Philadelphia Contributionship for the
     Insurance of Houses from Loss by
     Fire, 263
Philadelphia and Reading Coal and Iron
     Company (PRCI), 394, 402, 404,

411–12, 414–17, 427–36, 440–1, 446,
     453
  bankruptcy of, 438
  linear operations of, 30
  Maguire and, 267
  Molly Maguires and, 334
  Pine Forest Colliery sold to, 114
  and rise of company state, 417–22,
     425–7
  St. Clair Tract sold to, 112, 200
  Sheafer and, 407
  strike against, 390
  Twin Shafts project of, 431–6
  and Wadesville Shaft explosion, 361,
     362, 364
  Wetherill estate sold to, 61, 63
Philadelphia and Reading Railroad, 66, 97,
     121, 143, 174, 199, 207, 240, 258,
     262, 283, 326, 401, 404, 405, 411,
     412
  ceremonial dinner for, 241–2
  headquarters of, 54
  and Molly Maguires, 332, 338–9, 351,
     358
  St. Clair Coal Yards of, 442
  Schuylkill Haven engine house of, 241
  tolls per ton of, 24–5, 28
  see also Philadelphia and Reading Coal
     and Iron Company
Philadelphia Times, 339
Phillips, Elizabeth, 154
Phillips, G. Jenkin, 52
Phillips, Thomas, 152
*Physical History of the Creation of the
     Earth and its Inhabitants; or, a
     Vindication of the Cosmogony of the
     Bible from the Assaults of Modern
     Science* (Bowen), 211
Pictorial Sketch-Book of Pennsylvania
     (Bowen), 159
pillars, 12, 50–1
Pilling, Thomas, 289
Pilling, William, 293
Pine Forest Colliery, 47, 49, 62, 72, 75,
     76, 105, 112–15, 117, 119, 267, 268,
     293, 444
  deaths and injuries at, 251, 252
  Eltringham's inspection of, 308
  fires and explosions in, 263, 312
  liquor prohibited at, 164
  mine patches of, 138
  strike at, 285

Pine Forest Colliery (*cont.*)
  visits by public figures to, 368, 369
  under Philadelphia and Reading Coal
    and Iron Company, 418, 428, 430,
    435, 436, 438, 440
Pine Forest Stripping Company, 444
Pinkerton, Allan, 334, 335, 338, 343, 344,
  357
Pinkerton, C. L., 281–2
Pinkerton, John, 96, 115–16, 121, 156,
  282
Pinkerton Detective Agency, 154, 166,
  173, 324, 334–46, 358, 414, 417, 422,
  423, 427
Pioneer Colliery, 305–9
Pioneer Furnace, 26, 59, 73, 89–92, 96,
  246
Pioneer Iron Works, 369
Pittsburgh Gazette, 303
Pittston, explosion at, 312
Platt, Ralph, 288–9
Pleasants, General Henry, 173, 246, 415,
  430
  in Civil War, 325–7
  indictment of, 361, 364, 365
  and Molly Maguires, 339, 340, 343
  and Twin Shafts project, 433
Points on Coal and the Coal Business
  (Miesse), 407
Pomeroy, Benjamin, 90
Pomeroy & Son, 117
pony rolls, 17
Poole, Henry W., 73
Poor Laws, 271
Port Carbon, 24–5, 38, 62
  cricket club of, 173
  parades in, 168
Potts, Charles, 83
Potts, George H., 46, 47, 64, 81, 82, 84,
  85, 282
Potts, John, 89
Potts and Bannan Tract, 66, 93
Pottsville, 54
  churches in, 163
  cricket club of, 173
  food prices in, 146
  Henry Clay monument in, 243–5
  parades in, 168, 381
  Pioneer Furnace at, 59
  revivals around, 383
Pottsville Literary Society, 404
Pottsville Scientific Association, 31, 406

Pottsville Twin Shafts Colliery, 339, 340,
  431–6, 438
Powderly, Terence V., 299, 300, 400
Power, Henry, 40
*Practical Treatise on the Working and
  Ventilation of Coal Mines; with Sug-
  gestions for Improvements in Mining,
  A* (Hedley), 31
precious metal mines, 39–40
Presbyterians, 157
Price (Chartist), 286
Pride (play), 386
Primitive Methodist church, 129, 160–2,
  168, 178, 289, 383, 392, 445
Primrose Vein, 4, 98, 121, 177, 220, 227,
  434–5
Principles of Political Economy (Carey),
  190
Principles of Social Science (Carey), 195
profit margins, 258–60
property ownership, 374, 375
props, 50–2
Prosser, William, 378
protectionism, 184–200, 244
public schools, 408–11
pumping technology, 36–7

quarrying, 8, 39
Quay, Matthew, 280
Quirin, Peter, 441

Raguet, Condy, 197
Randall, William, 293–5, 305
Ravensdale, 138
Reading, 4
Reading Railroad, *see* Philadelphia and
  Reading Railroad
Reagan, John, 338, 350, 352, 359
record-keeping, 23–4
Reed, Squire, 317, 348
Reese, Ann, 316–18
Reese, John, 103, 315–20, 347, 352
Reese, Mary Ann, 316–18
Reese, Solomon, 290
Reese, William, 103
Reeves, Samuel, 240
Reilly, Michael, 128
Reno gang, 344
Report of the Inspectors of Coal Mines,
  249
*Report on the Iron and Coal of Pennsylva-
  nia,* 61

Repp estate, 62
Repplier, George, 66, 71, 121, 263, 324, 325, 428
Republican Party, 198, 199, 239, 280–2, 285–8, 294, 302–3, 305, 321, 325, 331, 372, 399
revivals, 383
Ricardo, David, 99, 189–91
Richards, W. T., 379, 392
Ripka, Joseph, 240
risk, assumption of, 271
Risk and Culture (Douglas and Wildavsky), 448
Risk and Decision Making (National Academy of Sciences), 447
risk-seeking behavior, 447–52
Ritner, Governor, 86
Roach, Pat, 338
Roarity, James, 351, 356
Roberts, Peter, 196
Roberts, Solomon White, 89
Robinson, Moncure, 95, 185, 241
Rogers, Henry Darwin, 72, 84, 201–15, 433
Rogers, James, 201
Rogers, Robert, 201–2
Rogers, William, 201
Rohrbach, Charles, 386, 423
Roy, Andrew, 257, 303, 393
Royal Academy, 58
Royal Geological Society, 202
Royal Society of London for Improving of Natural Knowledge, 40
Russell, Andrew, 65, 70, 72, 76, 121, 241, 243
    and Coal Mining Association, 282
    and McGinness, 216, 221, 228
    miners blamed for accidents by, 266
    and St. Clair Slope and Shaft, 111
Russell, Henry, 158, 173, 291
Russell, Thomas, 337, 342, 399
Ryon, James, 351, 357

safety lamps, 48–9
safety legislation, 272, 277–8
    effectiveness of, 305–13
    see also Mine Safety Acts
St. Anthony's Wilderness, 3
St. Bonifacius Roman Catholic Church, 129, 160, 162–3, 166, 168, 175
St. Clair Coal Company, 112, 441
St. Clair Furnace, 96–7, 125

St. Clair Monument Association, 386–8
St. Clair Scientific and Literary Association, 379, 392
St. Clair Shaft and Slope, 93, 105–12, 119, 124–5, 215, 218, 220, 227, 238, 420, 424, 435, 444, 453
    breaker at, 36, 107
    ceremonial exchanges between workers and superintendent of, 380
    deaths and injuries at, 251–2, 255, 289, 387
    Eltringham's inspection of, 307–8
    fires and explosions in, 111–12, 221–2, 263, 266, 312, 314
    insurance on, 261, 262, 265
    under Kirk and Baum, 76, 216
    Northall as superintendent of, 328
    operating costs of, 260
    under Philadelphia and Reading Coal and Iron Company, 418, 428, 429, 435, 436
    remains of, 445
    Sessinger as superintendent of, 377–8, 405
    sinking of, 75, 77, 99–100, 209
    slowdowns at, 276
    strike at, 285
    ventilation of, 38, 109–10, 452
St. Clair Tract, 60, 64, 65, 77, 78, 126, 199
    beginning of operations on, 96
    collieries of, 101–22
    iron ore on, 93–4
St. Clair Union Brass Band, 382
St. John's Reformed Church, 163
St. Mary's Catholic Church, 129, 160, 163, 175, 385, 444
St. Patrick's Church, 163
St. Paul's African Methodist Episcopal Church, 383
St. Thomas, John, 387
Sanger, Thomas, 345, 346
Savery, P. H., 90, 91
Savery, Thomas, 40
Saw Mill Tract, 62
Scalpington, 4, 139
scapegoating, 273–4
Scharr, John, 128
Scholes, William, 290
schools, 408–11
Schrader, Constable, 348
Schuylkill County Teachers' Institute, 230

Schuylkill Haven:
  cricket club of, 173
  engine house at, 241
Schuylkill Navigation Company, 24, 28,
    54, 59, 207, 211, 404, 417
Schuylkill Rangers, 321
Scientific American, 32, 116
Scottish immigrants, 372
  culture of, 171
  families of, 148, 153–4
  in mine patches, 139, 140
Scott Rifles, 244
Scott's St. Clair Infantry, 325
Scranton, George W., 239
Scranton, S. T., 239
screen bars, 16
Seasholtz and Shenton, 386
Second Geological Survey of Pennsylvania,
    52
Second U.S. Bank, 87
Seitzinger, Jacob W., 60, 61
Seitzinger, John, 99, 155
Seitzinger tract, 418
Sellers, John, 240
Sellers, William, 240
Senate, U.S., 75, 199, 258
Sessinger, H. B., 377, 380, 382, 405
Seven-Foot Vein, 102, 107–8, 112, 117,
    118, 268, 362–3, 366, 435
Seward, William H., 197
shafts, 8–10
  breakers of, 15
  see also specific mines
Shamokin furnace, 404
Sharp Mountain, 4, 56
Shay, Martin, 316–21, 324, 347
Sheafer, H. C., 266
Sheafer, Peter W., 65, 98, 260, 406–7
  and geological survey, 203, 204, 209,
    210
  and Hickory Colliery, 117, 259
  and Philadelphia and Reading Coal and
    Iron Company, 418, 428
  and Wadesville Shaft, 118–19, 361
Sheafer, W. H., 118–19
Sheaffer, Edward, 142
Sheet Iron Gang, 337
Shenandoah:
  fire beneath, 443–4
  Irish in, 372
  Long Strike in, 343
Sheridan, Richard, 231

Shickshinny, 66
Shirk, Mark, 165, 166
Silliman, Benjamin, 200–1
Silliman, Samuel, 70, 243
Silliman, William, 216
Siney, John, 153, 173, 288–91, 293, 312,
    315, 339, 367, 379, 388–403, 415,
    420, 443
  on Avondale disaster, 299–300
  cooperatives advocated by, 392–4
  death of, 439
  in Eagle Colliery strike, 288
  Eltringham denounced by, 309
  grave of, 444
  and Long Strike, 421–4
  and Pinkertons, 335–8
  political action advocated by, 398–401
  safety legislation lobbying by, 303,
    304
  on union discipline, 396–8, 405
  and Wadesville Shaft explosion, 363,
    364
Sitler, Mary, 167
Skidmore Vein, 101, 102, 113
slate pickers, 17, 22, 36
slavery, 194
Slavic immigrants, 442
Slobig, Daniel, 123, 124, 128
slopes, 8–11
  breakers of, 15
  ventilation of, 41, 42, 44–5
  see also specific mines
slowdowns, 276
Smeaton (inventor), 229
Smiles, Samuel, 229–30
Smith, Adam, 186, 189, 228
Smith, Charles E., 405
Smith, Clementina, 73–4, 261
Smith, E. Peshine, 197
Smith, George K., 65, 76, 221, 327
Smith, Horace, 73, 74, 261
Smith family, 325
Smyth, H. Gordon, 441
Smyth, William T., 441
Snyder, George W., 72–5, 93, 112–14,
    164, 173, 262, 267
  Beadle fan installed by, 47
  bought out by Philadelphia and Reading
    Coal and Iron Company, 428
  steam engines manufactured by, 39, 64,
    71–2, 81
  strike against, 285

Snyder, Harry, 173
Snyder's Iron Works, 432
social control, 407–8
social Darwinism, 196
socialism, 194, 202, 398–9
social science, 195–6
Society of Friends, 56
Soldier's Monument, 386–8
songs, 167–71
   see also specific titles
Sons of Temperance, 156, 159, 168
Spencer, Herbert, 189
splitting the air, 43–5
Spohn, Eliza, 74
Spohn Tract, 80
spontaneous combustion, 52–3
squibs, 12, 50, 441
Stahl, George, 156
Standard Oil, 414
Stanton, Edwin M., 326
steamboat coal, 16
steamboat explosions, 272
steam engine, invention of, 229
steam jets, 42, 43
   at Hickory Colliery, 116–17
Stephenson, George, 229–31
Stephenson, John, 154
Stephenson, William, 153–4
Stephenson lamp, 48
Steuben Shaft, fire at, *see* Avondale disaster
Stockton disaster, 304
strikes, 147, 196, 269, 275, 276, 283–8, 291–2, 419–22
   Carey on, 194
   Siney and, 390, 395–7
   at Steuben Shaft, 297
   see also Long Strike
strip mining, 8, 39, 441, 443, 444
subsistence, 141–8
Sumner, William Graham, 196
sump, 10, 13
Supreme Court, U.S., 34
Sylvis, William H., 303, 399, 400
synclinal axes, 7
System of Mining Coal (Phillips), 52

Tamaqua cricket club, 173
tariffs, *see* protectionism
taverns, 159, 164–6
taxes, Carey's opposition to, 194
Taylor, John, 387

Taylor, Richard Cowling, 56
telegraph chute, 36
Temperance Society, 65
Tempest, Henry ("Harry"), 154, 169, 170
Tempest, Thomas, 153, 154, 289–90
Tempest family, 153–4, 290, 437
testimonial dinners, 237–43
Theory of Moral Sentiments (Smith), 228
Thomas, David, 89–90
Thomas, John J., 351
Thomas, William M. "Bully Bill," 351–3
Thomas case, 331
Thorne, Theodore, 156
Three Months' Campaign, 325, 326
timbering, 11, 51–2
Toward Safer Underground Coal Mines (National Academy of Sciences), 448
Tower, Charlemagne, 325, 326
trappers, 20
Trevaro and Other Occasional Poems (Daddow), 231
Trevellick, Richard, 390, 399
Trinity Church, 72, 73, 158
Tucker, John, 66, 97, 240, 262
tunnels, 8–10
   breakers of, 15
   drainage of, 10
   ventilation in, 13, 42
Tunnel Vein, 82, 83
Turkey Run Colliery, 359
Turner, Samuel G., 294–5, 297, 303–5
Tversky, Amos, 449, 451, 452
Twin Shafts, *see* Pottsville Twin Shafts Colliery

Underground (play), 170
unemployment, 194, 426
Union Cooperative Association, 392
unions:
   Carey's opposition to, 194
   in England, 162
   industrial versus craft, 137
   rise of, 275–93
   Siney and, 388–403
   strikes by, *see* strikes
   suppression of, 174
   see also Workingmen's Benevolent Association
United Brethren, 383
United Mine Workers, 403, 442

United Mine Workers Journal, 400
Unity of Law, The (Carey), 195
Uren, William, 345, 346
utopian socialism, 194, 202, 398–9

Valley of Fear, The (Conan Doyle), 343
Valley Furnace Tract, 62
Vanuxem, Lardner, 56
ventilation, 13–14, 39–53
    of Hickory Colliery, 116–18
    of Pine Forest Shaft, 114
    safety standards on, 306–10, 312
    of St. Clair Shaft and Slope, 109–10
    of Wadesville Shaft, 120
    of York Farm Colliery, 83
Ventilation of Mines, The (Moore), 31
Vethake, Henry, 197
vigilantes, 343–5
Virginia Geological Survey, 201, 205

Wadesville, 62, 139, 140
    cricket club of, 173
    destruction of, 444–5
    parades in, 168
Wadesville Shaft, 39, 44, 105, 118–21,
    154, 266, 328, 392, 440, 444, 445
    deaths and injuries in, 251, 252
    Eltringham's inspection of, 307–8
    fires and explosions in, 290, 312, 361–6,
        385–6
    under Philadelphia and Reading Coal
        and Iron Company, 418, 428, 430,
        435, 436, 438
    strikes at, 423
    visits by public figures to, 369
wages, 141–8
Walker, Judge, 351
Wallace and Rothermel Colliery, 121, 219,
    224, 226
Walls, Henry J., 303, 304
Walton, Thomas H., 44
War of 1812, 56, 57, 59, 199, 244, 246
Ward, Martin, 338, 342
Washburn, Reverend Mr. Daniel, 73, 74,
    158
Washington, George, 229, 408
Watt, James, 229
Watt engine, 37
Weaklin, Mrs., 339
Weber, John, 399
Weisbach, Julius, 259
Wells, David Ames, 197

Welsh, John, 339
Welsh immigrants, 130, 372
    in benevolent associations, 155
    churches of, 129, 160
    in Civil War, 325, 328, 388
    culture of, 171–4, 176, 179–82
    families of, 148, 152–4
    firing of, 420
    in mine patches, 139, 140
    murders of, 344
    music of, 168
    occupations of, 133–8, 374, 437
    politics and, 282, 287, 331
    property ownership by, 374, 375
West, Benjamin, 58
West Mount Laffee Colliery, 404
Westown School, 64
Westwood Tract, 65, 78–9
Wetherill, Anna Seitzinger, 61
Wetherill, Charles, 61
Wetherill, Charles Mayer, 61
Wetherill, Isabella, 63
Wetherill, John Macomb, 61, 63, 64, 68,
    72, 73, 173, 238, 243, 246
    in Civil War, 325
Wetherill, John Price, 61, 62, 240
Wetherill, John Price III, 61
Wetherill, Samuel, 60, 61
Wetherill, Samuel, Jr., 61
Wetherill, William, 61–3
Wetherill group, 54, 55, 60–5, 67, 69, 75,
    115, 118, 418, 427, 441
    and Coal Mining Association, 282
    and Eagle Colliery, 103
    and geological survey, 208
    and iron smelting, 86
Wetherill Rifles, 168, 246, 325, 327, 386
Wetherill Tract, 90
Wharton, Joseph, 195–7
Wharton School, 196
Whig Party, 198, 321, 324
White, Andrew, 158
White, John C., 88, 232
White, John R., 262
White, Josiah, 88–9
"White Slave of the Mine" (ballad), 170
*White Slaves of Monopolies, The; or, John
    Fitzpatrick, the Miner, Soldier and
    Workingman's Friend* (novel), 401–3
Wiggan's Patch massacre, 344–5
Wilcox, William, 351
Wildavsky, Aaron, 448

wildcat strikes, 421
Wilde, Robert, 290
Wilderness campaign, 327
Wildey, Thomas, 168
Williams, Christopher, 152
Williams, Daniel, 152
Williams, John, 152
Williams, John R., 128
Williams, Thomas M., 303, 312, 378
Winchester, The Spy of Shenandoah
 (play), 386
Wood, James, 165
Workingman's Advocate, 286, 391
Workingman's Party, 398
Workingmen's Benevolent Association
 (WBA), 153, 275–6, 280, 288, 291,
 293, 303, 309, 312, 330–4, 357, 390,
 394–5, 397, 403, 405, 416–17, 442
 collapse of, 346, 400
 and cooperative movement, 393

and labor violence, 343
and middle class, 376
and Molly Maguires, 332–4
Pinkerton investigation of, 334–8
strikes by, 395, 419–22; *see also* Long
 Strike
workmen's compensation laws, 272–3
Wright, Fanny, 398
Wyoming Valley, 70

Yale University, 196
Yearley, Clifton K., 30, 70, 258, 260,
 446
Yeo, William, 161
York Farm Colliery, 81–4, 209, 242
York Farm Tract, 65, 80, 85
Yost, Benjamin, 346, 347
Young family, 279

Zimmler, Conrad, 142

A NOTE ABOUT THE AUTHOR

ANTHONY F. C. WALLACE was born in Toronto and did both his undergraduate and graduate work at the University of Pennsylvania, where he has been Professor of Anthropology since 1961. He has also served as a medical research scientist at the Eastern Pennsylvania Psychiatric Institute. He has written six books, including *The Death and Rebirth of the Seneca* (1970), *Rockdale* (1978), and *The Social Context of Innovation* (1982).

A NOTE ON THE TYPE

This book was set in a digitized version of the type face called Primer, designed by Rudolph Ruzicka (1883–1978). Ruzicka was earlier responsible for the design of Fairfield and Fairfield Medium, faces whose virtues have for some time been accorded wide recognition.

The complete range of sizes of Primer was first made available in 1954, although the pilot of 12-point was ready as early as 1951. The design of the face makes general reference to Century—long a serviceable type, totally lacking in manner or frills of any kind—but brilliantly corrects its characterless quality.

Composition by
American–Stratford Graphics Services, Inc.
Brattleboro, Vermont.
Printing and binding by
The Maple-Vail Book Manufacturing Group,
Binghamton, New York

Design by Julie Duquet